Bryant Julstrom

Geometric Reasoning

Special Issues of *Artificial Intelligence: An International Journal*

The titles in this series are paperback, readily accessible editions of the Special Volumes of *Artificial Intelligence: An International Journal*, edited by Daniel G. Bobrow and produced by special agreement with Elsevier Science Publishers B.V.

Qualitative Reasoning about Physical Systems, edited by Daniel G. Bobrow, 1985

Geometric Reasoning, edited by Deepak Kapur and Joseph L. Mundy, 1989

Geometric Reasoning

edited by
Deepak Kapur and Joseph L. Mundy

A Bradford Book
The MIT Press
Cambridge, Massachusetts
London, England

First MIT Press edition, 1989

Reprinted from *Artificial Intelligence: An International
Journal*, Volume 37, Numbers 1–3 (1988). The MIT Press has
exclusive license to sell this English-language book edition
throughout the world.

This book was printed and bound in the United States of America.

Library of Congress Cataloging-in-Publication Data

Geometric reasoning / edited by Deepak Kapur and Joseph L. Mundy
        p. cm.
    Papers presented at an International Workshop on Geometric
Reasoning, held at Oxford University, June 30 to July 3, 1986.
    Reprinted from Artificial Intelligence, v, 37, no. 1–3 (1988).
    "A Bradford book."
    Includes index.
    ISBN 0-262-61058-2
    1. Artificial intelligence—Congresses. 2. Automatic theorem
proving—Congresses. 3. Computer vision—Congresses. 4. Robotics-
-Congresses. I. Kapur, Deepak. II. Mundy, Joseph L.
III. International Workshop on Geometric Reasoning (1986 : Oxford
University)
Q334G46 1989
006.3—dc20   89-32150
                                                      CIP

Contents

Preface

This book is a collection of papers presented at an international workshop on geometric reasoning held at Oxford University from June 30 to July 3, 1986. It includes papers which appeared in a special volume of the *Artificial Intelligence Journal* (Vol. 37, December 1988) on Geometric Reasoning and three additional papers by Buchberger, Durrant-Whyte and Woodwark. Since these three papers had already been published elsewhere, they could not be included in the special volume.

In order to expedite the production of this book, the three additional papers could not be included into appropriate sections of the book. Instead, they have been made into a separate section of the book. The first paper by Buchberger, "Applications of Gröbner bases in nonlinear computational geometry" appeared in the *Proceedings of a Workshop on Scientific Computation* (editor: John Rice) published by Springer Verlag; it belongs to the automated geometric reasoning and geometric representation section of the book. The second paper by Durrant-Whyte, "Uncertain geometry" appeared in *IEEE J. of Robotics Automation* Vol. 4, 1988; it belongs to the robotics and motion planning section. The third paper by Woodwark "Some speculations on feature recognition" appeared in *Computer Aided Design Journal*, 1988; it belongs to the solid modeling section. We thank the authors and publishers of these journals for giving us permission to include these three papers in this book.

This book and the special volume of the Artificial Intelligence journal would not have been possible without the encouragement and support provided by Danny Bobrow, Mike Brady, and John Hopcroft. We would also like to express our appreciation to Elma Kleikamp of Elsevier, Holland, for help in the production of the special volume, to Harry Stanton of the MIT Press and Bradford Books for interest in the book and Sally Goodall of State University of New York at Albany, for typesetting the last three papers and preparing an index for the book.

Deepak Kapur
Joseph Mundy

Geometric Reasoning and Artificial Intelligence: Introduction to the Special Volume*

Deepak Kapur

Department of Computer Science, State University of New York at Albany, Albany, NY 12222, U.S.A.

Joseph L. Mundy

Corporate Research and Development, GE Company, Schenectady, NY 12345, U.S.A.

1. Introduction

Geometry plays an important role in our understanding of the world. It is therefore important for Artificial Intelligence (AI) systems to be able to represent and reason about geometry. This special volume presents a formal approach to the representation of geometric concepts in selected AI applications and describes some recent developments in algebraic methods for reasoning about geometry.

Geometry is also the oldest subject in mathematics to be subjected to considerable rigor and formalism. The axiomatic treatment of geometry has been actively investigated for thousands of years, starting with Euclid. In the early 1950s and 1960s, when there was considerable excitement about theorem proving in AI, Gelernter and his associates [14, 15] initiated an effort in mechanical theorem proving in geometry. After some initial success, Gelernter's approach faced the stumbling block of combinatorial search space, even for relatively simple plane geometry theorems.

Gelernter's approach towards mechanical geometry theorem proving was *synthetic*, i.e., it used properties of points, lines, triangles, etc. He employed the properties and definitions of these key geometry concepts in plane geometry to prove theorems using diagram and geometric construction. Earlier in the

* We gratefully acknowledge the support of the National Science Foundation and the Science Research Council for funding the workshop at Keble College, Oxford University, on which this special volume is based.

1930s, Tarski had developed a decision procedure for elementary algebra and geometry using the *analytic* (or *algebraic*) approach [38]. Tarski's approach has not been widely used in AI applications; this could be due to the enormously high complexity of his decision procedure. A more likely factor is that algebraic manipulation is conceptually quite different from the approach humans take in solving geometric problems.

The situation seems to be changing somewhat now. Recent work of Collins and his students [1, 2, 11] substantially improved Tarski's decision procedure using the cylindrical algebraic decomposition method. This method has in fact been extensively used in theoretical research in robot path planning (see Schwartz and Sharir's paper in this volume as well as [35]). Furthermore, Collins' method has been implemented in a computer algebra system SAC2 and is being extensively investigated by the computer algebra community.

More recently, a new method for algebraic geometry has been proposed by a Chinese mathematician Wu Wen-tsun [39–41] and has been found to be extremely successful in proving many nontrivial theorems in plane geometry [9, 40, 41]. Inspired by Wu's work, researchers [10, 22, 25] have also begun investigations of other related algebraic techniques and methods for geometry reasoning such as the Gröbner basis computation; preliminary results have been quite encouraging.

Because of these important new developments in automated geometry reasoning, a need was felt to bring together researchers interested in auto-mated geometry theorem proving and researchers in disciplines relying exten-sively on geometric and topological concepts. As a result, a workshop was held at Keble College, Oxford from June 30 to July 3, 1986. The Workshop was planned and organized by J. Michael Brady of Oxford University, John Hopcroft of Cornell University and Joseph Mundy of General Electric Com-pany. The Workshop was sponsored by both the United States National Science Foundation and the Science Research Council of Great Britain. About 35 researchers working in automated geometry reasoning and related applica-tions were invited to participate in this workshop.

Three application areas in Artificial Intelligence were identified where geometric reasoning is extensively used:

– robotics and motion planning;
– machine vision;
– solid modeling.

This volume is a collection of some of the papers presented at the Workshop. Other papers not included in this volume either have already been published elsewhere or are expected to appear elsewhere.

In the rest of this introduction, we will discuss the importance of geometric reasoning in robotics, motion planning, machine vision, and solid modeling. We will give a brief overview of the papers on these applications which are included in this volume. Later, we discuss developments and issues related to geometric reasoning and representation which need to be addressed for geometry to play a useful role in these and other AI applications.

2. The Importance of Geometric Reasoning

Algorithms for machine vision, solid modeling, and robot planning are largely dominated by geometric concepts. The development of these algorithms requires extensive insight into the relationship between geometric concepts and corresponding computational structures. For example, the following is a sample of the range of geometric problems that arise in the applications mentioned above:

– Determine an effective representation for the degrees of freedom inherent in a robot workspace. Use this representation to plan a collision-free path for the robot motion.
– Plan an assembly task, which involves the ordering of insertion operations and grasp positions. Adapt the plan to accommodate unforseen part tolerance variations.
– Find a three-dimensional representation of a scene that is consistent with the constraints imposed by a two-dimensional projection of the scene.
– Find an efficient decomposition of an object into three-dimensional solid primitives such as spheres and ellipsoids.
– Use a solid object model to plan numerically controlled machining operations.

In all of these cases, it is necessary to develop an approach for representing geometric and topological properties and then implement geometric procedures that manipulate these representations. These representations and procedures are then tested in the actual problem environment.

In many application implementations, geometric relations and constraints are not explicit. Instead, they are distributed throughout the software and algorithmic design in the form of simplifying assumptions and restricted data structures. Another important issue for the implementation is the treatment of all of the special conditions and degeneracies that usually arise in geometric problems. For example, the design of a program for computing the convex hull of a polygon can easily overlook problems in the definition of cumulative external vertex angle for complex polygons.

Research in geometric reasoning can lead to progress in the application of geometric knowledge in several ways. First, a better conceptual framework for representing and manipulating geometric knowledge can lead to implementation designs that provide more adequate separation between generic geometric principles and specific constraints of the application. Secondly, the ability to carry out reasoning about geometric concepts and relationships can allow a more comprehensive evaluation of geometric algorithms than can be provided by test cases.

2.1. Robotics and motion planning

A primary task in robotics is to plan collision-free paths in cluttered environments. One of the earliest robot planning projects, SHAKEY [13], used resolution proof methods to plan paths and tasks. These early planning programs were not efficient enough to be practical. However, the philosophy of using logical deduction to plan robot tasks has recently received renewed theoretical interest with the emergence of more effective algebraic proof methods such as cylindrical algebraic decomposition [35].

The finding of collision-free paths has been identified in the more mathematical literature as the "piano movers" problem. Usually a high-dimensional space, called *configuration space*, is defined in terms of the degrees of freedom of the robot. Obstacles can then be represented as algebraic surfaces in configuration space. This approach has been studied extensively over the past few years [27].

It is now recognized that the problem difficulty rises rapidly with the number of degrees of freedom. In order to achieve more tractable computation limits, it is necessary to take advantage of specific geometric relationships in the environment. These relationships can plausibly be discovered by geometric reasoning methods. For example, the impossibility of a given proposed trajectory can often be demonstrated from a few constraints without considering the entire path in detail (e.g. square peg in round hole).

Three papers on this application in this volume focus on motion planning. The paper by Schwartz and Sharir surveys recent algorithmic developments in motion planning in theoretical robotics. As Schwartz and Sharir observed, "This area has shown itself to have significant mathematical content; tools drawn from classical geometry, topology, algebraic geometry, algebra and combinatorics have all been used in it." The paper by Mitchell discusses algorithms for optimal path planning problems based on concepts in Dijkstra's shortest path algorithm when a map of a region of terrain is given. The paper by John Canny is an attempt to understand the complexity of constructing a roadmap for path planning given the configuration of a moving robot and constraints on its motion due to obstacles.

The fourth paper by Donald addresses the problem of error detection and recovery in motion planning strategies in the context of errors and uncertainties in the geometric models of the environment and the robot. A related paper by Durrant-Whyte, which was presented at the Workshop and appeared elsewhere[1], discussed a methodology and uncertain geometries for

---

[1] Durrant-Whyte, H.F., Uncertain geometry in robotics, *IEEE J. Rob. Autom.* **4** (1) (1988) 23–31.

representing and manipulating uncertainties, especially in the context of task planning and kinematics. It is argued that uncertainty should be represented as an intrinsic part of all geometric descriptions.

2.2. Machine vision

The field of machine vision has experienced a number of philosophical cycles over the last two decades. The initial work by L.G. Roberts [33] set the tone for much of the early research in vision and image understanding. His basic approach was bottom-up scene segmentation, along with a polyhedral geometric model to provide the framework to integrate primitive descriptions such as line segments and vertices.

Since that time the emphasis has oscillated between efforts to develop more effective models of the three-dimensional world [4, 5] and more robust primitive representations [3, 28]. The experience to date suggests that the most successful vision systems are those that have powerful models for image data and geometric relations which can interact at all levels of the process [17, 32].

There is currently a great deal of interest in the application of machine vision techniques to navigation for an autonomous vehicle. This is a very difficult application, since the characteristics of roadways and natural terrain are difficult to model, and it presents a great deal of variability in appearance. It is clear that a robust solution to this problem must involve as much generic information as possible about space and the relationship between objects in space. A good example of the use of geometry within this application is the mapping of two-dimensional views of the roadway into a three-dimensional representation which can be used for navigation. It is well known [12] that the interpretation of multiple fields of view cannot be done completely by local feature matching. The disparity relationships at discontinuities in range can only be explained by a global three-dimensional model of the scene.

Ultimately it will be necessary to reason geometrically within the vision system itself in order to accommodate unexpected conditions. This application requires great efficiency in the reasoning process because of the large inherent complexity of visual scenes. In this regard, the development of a reasoning system which is specialized, for example, to the geometry of perspective viewing may allow the introduction of highly efficient heuristics.

There are three papers in the volume on the vision application. The paper by Walker and Herman gives an overview of the approach in the MOSAIC system towards model-based vision for extracting three-dimensional information from two-dimensional aerial views (both monocular and stereo). Their approach assumes the existence of only horizontal and vertical lines in three-dimensional objects and also exploits the fact that the images have a single vertical vanishing point. The paper by Barry, Cyrluk, Kapur, Mundy and Nguyen describes a system for model-based reasoning for vision in which geometry plays a major role. It is suggested that algebraic, geometric and other higher-level reasoning methods based on topological and geometric constraints, such as labeling of images can play complementary roles in deducing depth information as well as other three-dimensional features at all levels. The Gröbner basis method is used for solving equational algebraic constraints. The view consistency problem for convex polyhedral objects based on partially deriving a three-dimensional model from a two-dimensional image to match against another two-dimensional image using algebraic reasoning is discussed.

The paper by Horaud and Brady proposes a computational model for three-dimensional interpretation of two-dimensional views based on contour classification and contour interpretation. The paper analyzes the extent to which image contours constrain both the shape and orientation of a scene surface arising from generalized cylinders. A labeling scheme for image contours based in terms of surface contours is proposed.

2.3. Solid modeling

One of the major issues in the design of solid objects and related CAD systems is determining an adequate representation of solid objects which can be manipulated to study and evaluate different designs and which also approximates reality as closely as possible [34]. Feature recognition and extraction appear to play a crucial role in this as features relevant in a solid object differ from one application to another. Topological and geometric properties are extensively used for representation, manipulation and feature extraction.

Often models are described either in terms of Boolean operations on a set of primitive solids or by describing boundaries of objects using polynomials. In the former case, there are many representations possible; choosing one representation from many possibilities is a serious issue. Furthermore, because of limitations of manufacturability and approximations used in numerical and algebraic calculations, tolerances must be specified. The inclusion of tolerances makes representation and geometry issues even more complicated. The study of approximate geometries and approximate geometric calculations is thus extremely important in solid and geometric modeling.

The paper by Hoffman and Hopcroft discusses the geometry of blending surfaces which arise when two solid objects smoothly intersect in a CAD or solid modeling system. A method, called the *potential* method, is discussed for studying blending surfaces and their properties using quadratic base polynomials. The paper by Milenkovic proposes two methods for manipulating geometric properties when represented using finite precision arithmetic. It discusses geometric properties which are preserved by these methods even when there are difficulties due to approximation and round-off errors.

The paper by Fleming discusses a representation of parts in a solid object with geometric tolerances and the relationship between toleranced features. Three kinds of tolerance features of a part are discussed: position, size and form. Also discussed are constraints among different features due to tolerances which can be described as a network and later converted to algebraic inequalities. An extension of the approach to assemblies of parts is outlined. A related paper by Woodwark, which was presented at the Workshop and appeared elsewhere[2], is a review of techniques used in solid modeling for feature extraction with a particular emphasis on the approach of the set-theoretic representation of solid models; implications of imposing restrictions on set-theoretic representations for solid models are discussed. Relationship between models based on set-theoretic representations and boundary models is mentioned.

3. Automated Geometric Reasoning and Geometric Representation

Automatic theorem proving in geometry has a long history. The first extensive theorem proving program by Gelernter and his associates [14, 15] used the idea of a diagram to constrain the search for a proof. This program was able to prove some elementary theorems in plane geometry. The work was extended by Nevins [31] using a combination of forward and backward chaining. However, this experiment did not make much headway even in proving relatively simple theorems in plane geometry and was subsequently abandoned.

As we said above, Tarski's approach for geometry theorem proving went unnoticed by AI researchers primarily because of the complexity of Tarski's method and its algebraic nature. Improvements to Tarski's method using the cylindrical algebraic decomposition technique introduced by Collins and his students [11] have been quite encouraging. As a result, a number of researchers in robotics have used Collins' approach for developing algorithms for path planning [35]. Collins' method involves the formation of regions, or cells, where a set of polynomials have a constant sign or are zero. Since systems of inequalities only are affected when the corresponding polynomials change sign, the system needs only to be evaluated at generic points within each cell.

Wu's approach to automatic theorem proving in algebraic geometry became known to researchers in North America and Europe in 1984 through a volume on the progress made in automated theorem proving in the last 25 years (see [9, 40, 41]). It is based on Ritt's decomposition algorithm for algebraic varieties. The method checks whether a conjectured geometric relation follows from a given set of geometric hypotheses by deciding whether the conjecture vanishes on all the common zeros (in the algebraic closed field of complex numbers) of the hypotheses. Wu's method has been used successfully in proving a large number of theorems including fairly nontrivial geometry theorems [9, 23, 25, 40, 41]. Wu's method is restricted as it can only deal with a

---

[2] Woodwark, J., Some speculations on feature extraction, *Comput. Aided Des. J.* (1988).

proper subset of geometric properties handled by Tarski's and Collins' methods. Problems associated with containment and relative positions cannot be solved by Wu's method.

Interest in Wu's method has resulted in other algebraic methods [10, 22, 25] for geometry theorem proving based on the Gröbner basis method [6].

It seems evident that a serious attack on practical geometric problems in machine vision and robotics will require a combination of algebraic and logical deductive mechanisms. This combination may be possible especially due to the close relationship being observed in completion-procedure-based approaches in theorem proving based on rewriting techniques and computational methods in computer algebra. In particular, as shown in [21], theorem proving in first-order predicate calculus can also be viewed purely algebraically; logical formulae are considered as polynomials over atomic formulae in a Boolean ring. This method is closely related to the method for geometry theorem proving discussed in [22] based on Hilbert's Nullstellensatz.

Another area in computer algebra which is important in geometric reasoning is methods for solving systems of polynomial equations. Rapid progress has been made recently [8, 26] in this area.

In spite of the recent progress in methods for geometric and algebraic reasoning, several major problems must be solved before practical performance of these methods can be realized in the applications mentioned earlier. A number of major issues are:

   (i) reasoning about inequalities and their incorporation into Wu's and Gröbner basis methods;
   (ii) interpreting algebraic expressions geometrically;
   (iii) efficient algorithms for determining whether a multivariate polynomial has real solutions.

3.1. Representation of geometric concepts

In order to usefully exploit geometric and spatial knowledge, it is necessary to have a representation language for geometry that allows efficient manipulation; further, it should be possible to integrate reasoning methods with this representation. Knowledge about space and spatial relationships can be expressed in this language in the form of definitions and properties of geometric concepts. The axioms can be grouped into small partitions called *concepts*. The encoding of knowledge in this fashion can be referred to as *conceptual programming*. A formal concept is like a theory in logic and thus goes beyond the "object" or "type" in providing a theoretical framework for data structures and operations on structures. These ideas have evolved out of work in abstract data types as well as artificial intelligence languages. The modular nature of concepts is related to the notion of abstract data types in ADA as well as object-oriented programming languages such as SMALLTALK.

Several examples of formal conceptual languages are: CLEAR [7], OBJ [16], AFFIRM [30] and TECTON [19]. A good review of the literature on data structures and semantic networks for representing concepts is given by Sowa [36]. Also, the reader may wish to refer to the work on SCRATCHPAD II, a computer algebra system being designed at IBM, based on the idea of types and theories [18].

The type of formal conceptual structure developed in these languages is important in geometric reasoning in several ways:

(i) Geometry is developed in terms of a system of small modular concepts with a well-defined hierarchy of abstractions. A geometric reasoning system must support this intrinsic structure.

(ii) Even with powerful algebraic deductive methods, it is necessary to constrain the search for proofs. A conceptual framework can provide the necessary constraints.

(iii) The communication of geometric ideas between the user and the system is facilitated by allowing representation directly in terms of geometric concepts such as "convex", "parallel to", "intersection" and "occlusion". These terms can be represented directly as concept modules.

It is expected that the already well-defined system of geometric concepts will fit easily into a concept hierarchy. An important research issue is the integration of this type of system with algebraic deduction techniques and heuristic constraints provided by the geometric domain and application areas.

This volume has four papers related to deductive methods for geometry. The fifth paper by Goguen discusses a methodology for representing geometric knowledge which admits parameterization, multiple representation and hierarchical structuring.

The paper by Kapur and Mundy provides an informal introduction to Wu's method for theorem proving in algebraic geometry. It also discusses the application of Wu's method for deducing properties of perspective viewing relevant for image understanding. The paper by Arnon provides a summary of Collins' quantifier elimination method for elementary algebra and geometry, and discusses examples of its application to actual geometry problems. A paper by Buchberger, which was presented at the Workshop and appeared elsewhere[3], gives an overview of the Gröbner basis method and discusses how it can be applied to problems in nonlinear computational geometry.

The paper by Kapur discusses methods for solving two classes of geometric problems based on a refutational approach using Gröbner bases. The first method assumes a complete and precise formulation of a geometry formula being proved; the geometry formula under consideration is translated into an

---

[3] Buchberger, B., Applications of Gröbner bases in nonlinear computational geometry, in: J. Rice (Ed.), *Proceedings Workshop on Scientific Computation*, Minneapolis, MN (Springer, New York, 1987).

equivalent set of polynomial equations so that these equations have a solution if and only if the formula is a theorem. The second method is an extension of the first method to incomplete formulations in which some degenerate conditions may not be specified. The paper by Ko proposes a method for deciding a class of geometry theorems based on considering the difference of common zeros of two sets of polynomials; a geometry statement including its degenerate cases is expressed as an algebraic difference set. The method is based on decomposing an algebraic difference set into disjoint triangular algebraic difference sets using the Ritt–Wu principle.

REFERENCES

 1. Arnon, D.S., Collins, G.E. and McCallum, S., Cylindrical algebraic decomposition I: The basic algorithm, *SIAM J. Comput.* **13** (1984) 865–877.
 2. Arnon, D.S., Collins, G.E. and McCallum, S., Cylindrical algebraic decomposition II: An adjacency algorithm for the plane, *SIAM J. Comput.* **13** (1984) 878–889.
 3. Asada, H. and Brady, J.M., The curvature primal sketch, in: *Proceedings Workshop on Computer Vision: Representation and Control*, Bellaire, MI (1985) 8.
 4. Binford, T., Inferring surfaces from images, *Artificial Intelligence* **17** (1981) 205–244.
 5. Brooks, R.A., Symbolic reasoning among 3-D models and 2-D images, *Artificial Intelligence* **17** (1981) 285–348.
 6. Buchberger, B., Gröbner bases: An algorithmic method in polynomial ideal theory, in: N.K. Bose (Ed.), *Multidimensional Systems Theory* (Reidel, Dordrecht, The Netherlands, 1985) 184–232.
 7. Burstall, R.M. and Goguen, J.A., Putting theories together to make specifications, in: *Proceedings IJCAI-77*, Cambridge, MA (1977) 1045.
 8. Chistov, A.L. and Grigoryev, D.Y., Subexponential-time solving systems of algebraic equations—I, II, USSR Academy of Sciences, Steklov Mathematical Institute, Leningrad Department, Leningrad, U.S.S.R. (1983).
 9. Chou, S.-C., Proving elementary geometry theorems using Wu's algorithm, in: W.W. Bledsoe and D.W. Loveland (Eds.), *Theorem Proving: After 25 Years*, Contemporary Mathematics **29** (1984) 243–286.
10. Chou, S.-C. and Schelter, W.F., Proving geometry theorems with rewrite rules, *J. Autom. Reasoning* **2–3** (1986) 253–273.
11. Collins, G.E., Quantifier elimination for real closed fields by cylindrical algebraic decomposition, in: *Proceedings 2nd GI Conference on Automata Theory and Formal Languages*, Lecture Notes in Computer Science **33** (Springer, New York, 1975) 134–183.
12. Fischler, M. et al., Modeling and using physical constraints in scene analysis, in: *Proceedings AAAI-82*, Pittsburgh, PA (1982) 30.
13. Fikes, R.E., and Nilsson, N.J., STRIPS: A new approach to the application of theorem proving to problem solving, *Artificial Intelligence* **2** (1971) 189–208.
14. Gelernter, H. and Rochester, N., Intelligent behavior in problem solving machines, *IBM J.* (1958).
15. Gelernter, H., Realization of a geometry theorem proving machine, in: E.A. Feigenbaum and J. Feldman (Eds.), *Computers and Thought* (McGraw-Hill, New York, 1963) 134–152.
16. Goguen, J.A. and Tardo, J., OBJ-0 preliminary users manual, Semantics and Theory of Computation Report, UCLA, Los Angeles, CA (1977).
17. Grimson, W.E.L. and Lozano-Pérez, T., Search and sensing strategies for recognition and localization of two and three dimensional objects, in: *Proceedings Third International Symposium on Robotics Research* (1985).
18. Jenks, R.D., A primer: 11 keys to new Scratchpad, in: *Proceedings EUROSAM-84*, International Symposium on Symbolic and Algebraic Computation, Cambridge, England, Lecture

Notes in Computer Science **174** (Springer, New York, 1984) 123–147.

19. Kapur, D., Musser, D.R. and Stepanov, A.A., TECTON: A language for manipulating generic objects, in: *Proceedings Program Specification Workshop*, Lecture Notes in Computer Science **134** (Springer, New York, 1982).

20. Kapur, D., Musser, D.R., Mundy, J.L. and Narendran, P., Reasoning about three dimensional space, in: *Proceedings IEEE International Conference on Robotics and Automation*, St. Louis, MO (1985) 405–410.

21. Kapur, D. and Narendran, P., An equational approach to theorem proving in first-order predicate calculus, in: *Proceedings IJCAI-85*, Los Angeles, CA (1985).

22. Kapur, D., Using Gröbner bases to reason about geometry problems, *J. Symbolic Comput.* **2** (4) (1986) 399–408.

23. Ko, H.P. and Hussain, M.A., A study of Wu's method—a method to prove certain theorems in elementary geometry, in: *Congr. Numer.* **48** (1985) 225–242.

24. Ko, H. and Hussain, M.A., ALGE-prover: An algebraic geometry theorem proving software, Tech. Rept. 85CRD139, General Electric Company, Schenectady, NY (1985).

25. Kutzler, B. and Stifter, S., On the application of Buchberger's algorithm to automated geometry theorem proving, *J. Symbolic Comput.* **2** (4) (1986) 409–420.

26. Lazard, D., Systems of algebraic equations, in: *Proceedings Symbolic and Algebraic Computation*, Lecture Notes in Computer Science **72** (Springer, Berlin, 1979) 88–94.

27. Lozano-Pérez, T., Spatial planning: A configuration space approach, *IEEE Trans. Comput.* **32** (1983).

28. Marr, D., *Vision* (Freeman, New York, 1982).

29. Mundy, J.L., Image understanding research at General Electric, in: *Proceedings Image Understanding Workshop*, Miami Beach, FL (1985) 83–88.

30. Musser, D.R., Abstract data type specification in the AFFIRM system, *IEEE Trans. Softw. Eng.* **6** (1980).

31. Nevins, A.J., Plane geometry theorem proving using forward chaining, *Artificial Intelligence* **6** (1975) 1–23.

32. Porter, G.B. and Mundy, J.L., A model driven visual inspection system, in: J.M. Brady and R.P. Paul (Eds.), *Proceedings First International Symposium on Robotics Research* (MIT Press, Cambridge, MA, 1983).

33. Roberts, L.G., Machine perception of three-dimensional solids, Ph.D. Thesis, MIT, Cambridge, MA (1963).

34. Requicha, A.A.G., Representations of rigid solids: Theory, methods and systems, *Comput. Surv.* **12** (4) (1980) 437–464.

35. Schwartz, J.T. and Sharir, M., On the piano movers problem II. General techniques for computing topological properties of real algebraic manifolds, Courant Institute of Mathematics, Rept. No. 41, New York (1982).

36. Sowa, J., *Conceptual Structures* (Addison-Wesley, New York, 1984).

37. Swain, M.J. and Mundy, J.L., Experiments in using a geometry theorem prover to prove and develop theorems in computer vision, in: *Proceedings IEEE Conference on Robotics and Automation*, San Francisco, CA (1986) 280–285.

38. Tarski, A., *A Decision Method for Elementary Algebra and Geometry* (University of California Press, Berkeley, CA, 1948; 2nd ed., 1951).

39. Wu, W., On the decision problem and the mechanization of theorem proving in elementary geometry, *Sci. Sinica* **21** (1978) 150–172; also in: W.W. Bledsoe and D.W. Loveland (Eds.), *Theorem Proving: After 25 Years*, Contemporary Mathematics **29** (1984) 213–234.

40. Wu, W., Some recent advances in mechanical theorem proving of geometries, in: W.W. Bledsoe and D.W. Loveland (Eds.), *Theorem Proving: After 25 Years*, Contemporary Mathematics **29** (1984) 235–241.

41. Wu, W., Basic principles of mechanical theorem proving in geometries, *J. Syst. Sci. Math. Sci.* **4** (3) (1984) 207–235; also *J. Autom. Reasoning* **2** (1986) 221–252.

Received April 1987; revised version received April 1988

Automated Geometric Reasoning
and
Geometric Representation

Wu's Method and Its Application to Perspective Viewing

Deepak Kapur* and Joseph L. Mundy

General Electric Company, Corporate Research and Development, Schenectady, NY 12345, U.S.A.

ABSTRACT

An algebraic method for proving a class of geometry theorems recently proposed by Wu is informally discussed. Key concepts relevant to the method are explained. An application of this method to perspective viewing in image understanding is discussed. Finally, it is outlined how the method can be helpful to prove geometry theorems involving inequalities to capture the relation of a point being in between two given points. This is also illustrated using an example from image understanding.

1. Introduction

An extremely elegant method for automatically proving theorems in algebraic geometry was proposed by a Chinese mathematician Wu Wen-tsun in 1978 [18]. This method became known to researchers in North America and Europe in 1984 following the publication of the volume *Automated Theorem Proving: After 25 Years*. The method has been implemented by Wu [19, 20], Chou [2, 3], Ko and Hussain [11], and Kutzler and Stifter [13]. Chou's program [3], in particular, has automatically proved hundreds of theorems in plane geometry, including many nontrivial theorems, using this method. The experience with Wu's method as well as other algebraic methods for geometric reasoning [4, 8, 13] has been quite encouraging in comparison to synthetic geometric reasoning methods based on natural deduction, construction, resolution, etc. (see [5] for a summary of such approaches for geometry theorem proving). Many plane geometry theorems which humans find difficult to prove can be easily proven automatically by the algebraic methods (the Butterfly theorem is one such example).

---

* Current address: Department of Computer Science, State University of New York at Albany, Albany, NY 12222, U.S.A.

Our group at GE-CRD has also been successful in applying Wu's method for proving properties of perspective viewing relevant to image understanding (see [7, 14, 16]).

The success of Wu's method and its simplicity have sparked considerable interest in automatic geometry theorem proving using algebraic techniques (see *Proceedings SYMSAC-86*). In this paper, we provide an informal overview of Wu's method. We first illustrate Wu's method on an extremely simple example in plane geometry; Wu's method in the general case is then informally discussed. In the next section, we discuss its application to deducing properties of perspective viewing in image understanding. In the final section, we outline an approach using Wu's method for handling nonlinear inequalities; this approach is illustrated using an example from image understanding. For details, mathematical foundations of the method, as well as information about hundreds of theorems proved by this method, the reader should consult [3, 10, 18, 20].

2. Wu's Method

Most approaches to geometric reasoning are formulated in terms of synthetic geometry which is a logical system expressed using properties of points, lines, angles, etc., considered as primitive elements. In contrast, Wu's method is algebraic. Hypotheses and conclusions (conjectures) in a geometry problem are represented as polynomial equations with integer coefficients; variables or indeterminates in these polynomials are coordinates of points. The method considers the following class of universally quantified formulae:

Given a set $H = \{h_1, \ldots, h_i\}$ of hypotheses,
show whether a conjecture c follows from the hypotheses.

Note. We will abuse the notation somewhat. In the subsequent discussion, no distinction is made between a polynomial p and a polynomial equation $p = 0$.

The above formulation is equivalent to showing that the *common zeros* of $h_1, \ldots, h_i$ (values of coordinates for which the hypotheses are satisfied) are zeros of c also. Often, this is not the case; a number of degenerate cases needs to be ruled out. Thus, except for certain zeros of $h_1, \ldots, h_i$, ruled out by saying $d_1 \neq 0, d_2 \neq 0, \ldots, d_i \neq 0$, other zeros of $h_1, \ldots, h_i$ are the zeros of c also. See Fig. 1. The inequations $d_j \neq 0$, $j = 1, \ldots, i$, have been called *nondegenerate conditions* or *subsidiary conditions* in the literature. The common zeros of polynomials considered in Wu's method are complex numbers, the algebraically closed field including the rational numbers.

2.1. A simple example

Consider the following simple example in plane geometry: Given two lines AB and AC which are perpendicular to each other, and another line CD also perpendicular to AC, show that AB is parallel to CD. See Fig. 2.

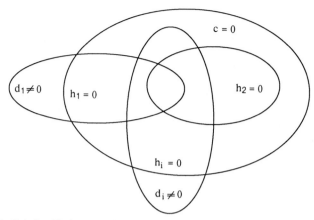

Fig. 1. Relationship between the zeros of conclusion and the zeros of hypotheses.

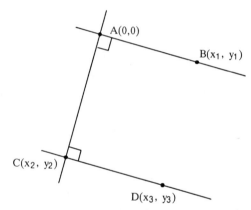

Fig. 2. A simple example.

An algebraic formulation of this problem can be obtained as follows: Without any loss of generality, A is assumed to be the origin $(0,0)$, $B = (x_1, y_1)$, $C = (x_2, y_2)$, $D = (x_3, y_3)$. The polynomial equation corresponding to the hypothesis that AB is perpendicular to AC is:

$$y_1 y_2 = -x_1 x_2 ,\tag{1}$$

and the polynomial equation corresponding to the second hypothesis that CD is perpendicular to AC is:

$$y_2(y_3 - y_2) = -(x_3 - x_2)x_2 .\tag{2}$$

The polynomial equation corresponding to the conjecture that AB and CD are parallel is:

$$y_1(x_3 - x_2) = x_1(y_3 - y_2) . \tag{3}$$

In Wu's method, to check whether the conjecture vanishes on the common zeros of the hypotheses, the conjecture is *pseudodivided* by the hypotheses. The operation of pseudodivision of a polynomial by another polynomial is a crucial primitive step in Wu's method. Multivariate polynomials are assumed to be represented in recursive form, i.e., they are considered as polynomials in a single variable whose coefficients are also polynomials. Given a polynomial p in x, say,

$$p = a_m x^m + \cdots + a_1 x + a_0 ,$$

where a_j, $j = 0, \ldots, m$ are themselves polynomials not having x; a_m, the coefficient of the leading monomial of p, is called the *initial* of p; m is called the *highest degree* of x in p. Pseudodivision is different from polynomial division in the sense that if need be, the polynomial being divided can be multiplied by a suitable power of the initial of the divisor and their result then is divided using polynomial division (see [9, p. 407] for details).

Before the conjecture is pseudodivided by the hypotheses, the hypothesis polynomials should be in a *triangular form*. Variables in the problem are classified into *independent* and *dependent* variables, and dependent variables are totally ordered. We will denote the independent variables as $u_1, \ldots, u_k$, and the dependent variables as $z_1 < \cdots < z_l$ with a total order. A variable z_j is called the *highest* (or *main*) variable of a polynomial p if and only if z_j appears in p and no variable greater than z_j in the ordering appears in p.

A set $G = \{ g_1, \ldots, g_l \}$ of polynomials is said to be in triangular form if and only if $g_1, g_2, \ldots, g_l$ are respectively, polynomials in $\{ u_1, \ldots, u_k, z_1 \}$, $\{ u_1, \ldots, u_k, z_1, z_2 \}, \ldots, \{ u_1, \ldots, u_k, z_1, \ldots, z_l \}$.[1]

In the above example, the polynomials in equations (1) and (2) are luckily already in triangular form if y_2 and y_3 are chosen as dependent variables and the rest of the variables are independent, and furthermore, $y_3 > y_2$. This choice can be considered to be dictated by the geometric construction:

---

[1] Wu [20] defined an *ascending set* of polynomials which is a set of polynomials in a triangular form with the additional property that each g_j is *reduced* (i.e., cannot be pseudodivided) with respect to every polynomial in the set $\{ g_1, \ldots, g_{j-1} \}$. A polynomial g_j is reduced with respect to another polynomial $g_{j'}$ if and only if the highest degree of the highest variable, say $z_{j'}$, of $g_{j'}$ is higher than the highest degree of $z_{j'}$ in g_j. For computational performance, Wu also defined an ascending set in the *loose sense* or in the *weak sense* in which each g_j is *reduced* with respect to every polynomial g_m, $1 \leq m < j$, where z_m appears in the initial of g_j.

(i) Choose point A arbitrarily.

(ii) Choose point B arbitrarily which determines the line AB.

(iii) Choose point C such that AC is perpendicular to AB. In this case, exactly one of the two coordinates x_2 or y_2 can be chosen arbitrarily; we have chosen x_2 as an independent variable. As a result, y_2 is dependent and is determined by the relation that AC is perpendicular to AB and the rest of the coordinates.

(iv) Finally, choose point D such that CD is perpendicular to AC. Again, exactly one of the two coordinates x_3 or y_3 can be chosen arbitrarily; we have chosen x_3 independently, thus y_3 is dependent and is determined by the relation that CD is perpendicular to AC and the rest of the coordinates.

The order in which the construction takes place also determines the ordering on dependent variables; in this case, $y_3 > y_2$. (In the next subsection, we discuss the effect of choosing a different ordering on dependent variables.)

In this example, to show whether the conjecture (3) follows from the hypotheses (1) and (2), (3) is first pseudodivided by (2) to eliminate the variable y_3. The second hypothesis when considered as a polynomial in the highest variable y_3 has y_2 as its initial. When the conjecture is multiplied by y_2 and the result divided by the second hypothesis, the remainder is:

$$y_1 y_2 (x_3 - x_2) + x_1 x_2 (x_3 - x_2) .$$

This remainder is now divided by the first hypothesis to eliminate y_2, and the final remainder is 0.

The conjecture thus indeed follows from the two hypotheses under the condition that $y_2 \neq 0$; y_2 is the polynomial the conjecture was multiplied with for pseudodivision. The polynomial $y_2 = 0$ is declared as a degenerate case of the above picture. The conjecture polynomial is related to the hypotheses as:

$$y_2 * \text{conjecture} = x_1 * \text{hypothesis}_1 + (x_3 - x_2) * \text{hypothesis}_2 .$$

It should be obvious that under the condition that $y_2 \neq 0$, the conjecture indeed vanishes on the common zeros of the two hypotheses.

We now discuss the method in general. As illustrated above, there are two key steps in the method: (i) obtaining a triangular form from the hypotheses given as input, and (ii) checking the conjecture. And, in both steps, pseudo-division is the basic operation.

2.2. Generating a triangular form

Computing a triangular form G from a given set H of hypotheses roughly corresponds to generating a new set of hypotheses. The new hypotheses are obtained by "recomputing" the dependency among the given hypotheses in H

according to the order chosen on dependent variables. Then there is exactly one hypothesis in G for every dependent variable. Before computing a triangular form, the variables in a geometry problem must be classified first into independent and dependent sets. As is to be expected, different classifications of variables into independent and dependent sets and different orderings on dependent variables result in different triangular forms.

2.2.1. *Classification of variables*

One way to understand this classification of variables into dependent and independent sets is to draw an analogy from solving an underconstrained (underspecified) system of linear equations. Variables in a system of equations can be partitioned into independent and dependent subsets. This partitioning appears to be somewhat arbitrary, except that the set of independent variables must be chosen so that for every value assigned to each independent variable, the system of equations has a solution. The values of the remaining variables are considered to depend on the values assigned to independent variables; that is why the remaining variables are called dependent. Certain classifications of variables lead to maximal sets of independent variables. The number of elements in these maximal sets is usually the dimension of the variety of the equation system.

There is an analogy between this algebraic concept of dependent and independent variables and geometric relations in a geometric problem. For example, if we define an equilateral triangle, we can consider that two vertices can be specified at independent locations and the coordinates of the third vertex depend on the locations of the first two. On the other hand, if the equilateral triangle is specified as the intersection of three lines, then only the first line can be placed independently. The equivalent dimension, i.e., number of degrees of freedom, for a geometric configuration thus depends on the way that it is specified. It appears that the concept of dimension is not an intrinsic property of the configuration itself.

There does not seem to be any natural choice for the partition of variables arising in a geometry problem into independent and dependent subsets. However, the efficiency of the algorithms for generating triangular forms is quite dependent on the choice for independent and dependent variables. This sensitivity appears to be a consequence of the algebraic syntactic structure of the equations, rather than the manifestation of any deep geometric semantic structure. Heuristics dictated by the syntactic formulation of a geometric problem can often be used to classify variables into independent and dependent sets [3]. Usually, if a geometric configuration is properly specified, the number of dependent variables is the same as the number of nonredundant hypotheses.

For the above example, there are many possibilities for picking independent and dependent variables: (i) x_2 and x_3 can be dependent variables and every other variable is independent, or (ii) x_1 and x_3 can be dependent variables and other variables are independent, or (iii) x_1 and y_3 can be dependent variables and other variables are independent, and so on.

A total order on dependent variables is assumed which specifies the order in which the constraints imposed on these variables are to be made dependent of each other. Typically, a total order that requires minimal computation in generating a triangular form is chosen. In many cases, this order is implicit in the way a geometry problem is specified; see, for instance, the example discussed in Section 2.1.

2.2.2. *An algorithm for computing a triangular form*

In [20], Wu discussed an algorithm to generate a *characteristic set*, which is a *minimal* ascending set G (also called a *basic set* by Wu) from a given set H of hypotheses (the algorithm is discussed on page 229 of the *Journal of Automated Reasoning* 2 (1986)). A characteristic set has interesting additional properties not satisfied by a triangular form (for instance, Theorem 2.1 in Section 2.4). However, Wu's algorithm is not computationally efficient on many examples (see Wu's comments on page 246 of the *Journal of Automated Reasoning* 2 (1986)). Chou [3] discussed different algorithms for generating triangular forms. Below, we give an algorithm similar to the one reported in [2] which has been found to be computationally more efficient in practice on many examples.

Let $H = h_1, \ldots, h_i$, where each h_j is a polynomial from $Q[u_1, \ldots, u_k, z_1, \ldots, z_l]$, $u_1, \ldots, u_k$ are independent variables, and $z_1, \ldots, z_l$ are dependent variables, with a total order $z_1 < \cdots < z_l$. In the following algorithm, G is a triangular form obtained from the input set H of hypotheses; T is a temporary set consisting of those polynomials that still have to be used to compute the remaining part of G.

```
1  T := H; G := ∅; j := ℓ;
2  g := a polynomial from T such that degree(g, z_j) is the lowest;
3  P := {q | q = pseudodivide(p, g, z_j),
           p ∈ T and is a polynomial in z_j, q ≠ 0};
4  If P does not have any polynomial in z_j Then
   Begin
5      G := G ∪ {g};
6      T := T − {p | p is a polynomial in z_j};
7      j := j − 1
   End;
8  T := T ∪ P;
9  If j > 0 Then Goto 2;
10 Return G
```

In the example of Fig. 2, if we choose a different ordering on dependent variables, say $y_2 > y_3$, then the given hypotheses (1) and (2) are not in a triangular form as both the hypotheses are polynomials in y_2. Since (1) is of lower degree, we pseudodivide (2) by (1), and obtain the remainder:

$$x_2 x_3 y_1^2 - x_1 x_2 y_1 y_3 - x_2^2 y_1^2 - x_1^2 x_2^2 . \tag{4}$$

The above polynomial does not involve y_2 anymore. Hypotheses (1) and (4) are in a triangular form. Whereas hypothesis (2) is expressed using point C, the remainder (4) above, on the other hand, corresponds to hypothesis (2) obtained after eliminating the dependence of (2) on the y-coordinate of point C. Remainder (4) specifies the geometric relation of hypothesis (2) directly in terms of the independent variables of the geometric construction; it is the hypothesis that CD is perpendicular to AC where C is the point on the line perpendicular to AB.

In the process of generating a triangular form T from a given set of hypotheses, if a rational number is generated, this implies that the given set of hypotheses is *inconsistent* meaning that the hypotheses do not have a common zero. Otherwise, the final result of this computation is a triangular form of hypotheses. Note that the above algorithm considers the variables in the descending order, whereas the algorithms given in [20] considered the variables in the ascending order. Because of this difference, the initial (the leading coefficient) of a polynomial in a triangular form obtained using the above algorithm may not be reduced with respect to other polynomials in the triangular form. It is also possible that requiring such initials to be nonzero may be inconsistent with the hypotheses.

Often, for a proper choice and ordering of dependent variables, hypoheses given in a geometry statement are either already in a triangular form or can be easily brought into a triangular form. For instance, this is the case in the above example as well as examples in the next section. The worst-case complexity of generating a triangular form, however, is likely to be quite high. The performance of Wu's method is extremely sensitive to different choices of dependent and independent variables as well as of a total ordering on dependent variables. The performance of the method can also vary significantly on different equivalent formulations of the same geometry problem.

It can be easily verified that (i) the common zeros of G, the hypotheses in a triangular form obtained from the original set H of hypotheses, include the common zeros of H, and furthermore (ii) the common zeros of G minus the zeros of the product of the initials of polynomials in G are the common zeros of H [20]. This is because of the following property of pseudodivision of a polynomial h by another polynomial g with initial I:

$$I^m h = qg + r .$$

The common zeros of h and g are also the zeros of the remainder r. Furthermore, if r is 0, then the common zeros of h and g are the same as the zeros of g insofar as they are not the zeros of the initial I of g.

2.3. Proving conjectures

In order to check whether a conjecture follows (under certain conditions) from a set of hypotheses in a triangular form, pseudodivide the conjucture starting with the hypothesis in the highest variable. As stated earlier, this may require multiplying the conjecture with the initials of the hypotheses. If the conjecture psudeodivides with a zero remainder, then the conjecture follows from the hypotheses under the conditions that none of the initials used to multiply the conjecture is zero.

In the example in Fig. 2, if we use the triangular form (i.e., (1) and (4)) of polynomials obtained in Section 2.2.2 to pseudodivide the conjecture (3), then we again get the remainder 0 under the conditions that the initials y_1 and $x_1 x_2 y_1$ are not zero. Notice that these conditions are different from the one obtained earlier.

The algebraic relation between the conjecture and the hypotheses in a triangular form can be expressed as:

$$I_1^{k_1} \cdots I_l^{k_l} c = q_1 g_1 + \cdots + q_l g_l \,,$$

where I_j is the initial of g_j, $j = 1, \ldots, l$. It follows from the above stated property of pseudodivision that the conjecture indeed vanishes on the common zeros of the original set H of hypotheses provided the initials used to multiply the conjecture are not zero.

2.4. Disproving conjectures: Completeness

If a conjecture polynomial pseudodivides to 0 using the hypotheses in a triangular form, then the conjecture is true. However, if it does not pseudo-divide to 0, it cannot always be said that the conjecture is false. Some additional assumptions need to be checked. We need to make sure that each of the hypothesis polynomials in the triangular form is *irreducible* in successive extension fields in the sense that it does not factor to a disjunction of two or more simpler hypotheses. This means that each g_j in G cannot be factored over the extension field

$$Q(u_1, \ldots, u_k)[z_1, \ldots, z_{j-1}] / \{g_1, \ldots, g_{j-1}\} \,.$$

The following theorem is the basis of correctness of Wu's method.

Theorem 2.1 [18, 20]. *If G is an irreducible ascending set of hypotheses, a conjecture c follows from G (in every extension field containing Q) under nondegenerate conditions of $I_1 \neq 0, \ldots, I_l \neq 0$ if and only if c pseudodivides to 0 using G.*

Only nondegenerate conditions corresponding to polynomials in G with whose initials c is multiplied in pseudodivision have to be considered. By consequence, we mean that the conclusion vanishes on all the common zeros of the hypotheses.

2.4.1. *Decomposition into irreducible components*

In the case that any of the hypotheses in a triangular form can be factored into irreducible factors there is a need to split the hypotheses then. There is a branch for each irreducible factor as the zeros of g_j are the union of the zeros of each of the irreducible factors. This corresponds to the case of a disjunction in a hypothesis as in the case of propositional logic. So, we need to check that the conjecture holds in each of the branches along which the split takes place due to the reducibility of the hypotheses.

Sometimes the reducibility of the hypotheses is inherent in a problem statement because of more than one case in a general geometrical configuration. Such cases have been discussed by Wu in a recent paper [21]. Uninteresting and irrelevant cases in a geometry problem can be ruled out by having negations of equations in the hypotheses as suggested by Kapur [8]. In other cases, reducibility may arise because of the peculiarities of a problem formulation, a choice of independent variables and a choice in total ordering on dependent variables. Problem statements in which hypotheses are irreducible, correspond to formulae in propositional logic which can be proved or disproved without splitting. This perhaps explains why Wu's method works well on problems which result in irreducible triangular forms.

For details about the mathematical foundations, the reader may consult [20]. For an algorithm to check irreducibility and factorization in the case of reducibility in problems in plane geometry, the reader may consult [3].

There is another mathematical detail the reader ought to be aware of. As stated by Wu [20], the above method works for all extension fields of Q (rationals) including the field of reals. Thus, the completeness theorem holds for an arbitrary extension field, i.e., if a conjecture cannot be proved, then the conjecture does not follow from the hypotheses because there is an extension field such that the conjecture does not vanish on all the common zeros of the hypotheses in that extension field. The conjecture however may vanish for all the common real zeros of the hypotheses. For example, consider the single hypothesis:

$$y^2 + x^2 = 0 ;$$ (5)

the conjecture is:

$$y = 0 .$$ (6)

Obviously, the hypothesis is already in triangular form assuming x as the independent variable and y as the dependent variable. The conjecture cannot be pseudodivided using the hypothesis. Although, the conjecture vanishes on the only real zero $(0, 0)$ of the hypothesis, yet it does not vanish on all the complex zeros of the hypothesis.

Wu's method is thus incomplete for deciding universally quantified formulae (without betweenness relation) in Tarski's geometry.

Ko [12] has recently proposed a way to deal with this inherent incompleteness in Wu's method for real closed fields. The main idea is to compare the real zeros of irreducible hypotheses in a triangular form with the real zeros of the subsidiary conditions as well as with the real zeros of the remainder obtained after pseudodividing the conjecture by the hypotheses. This could either be done by inspection or by using Collins' method [1].

3. Examples from Perspective Viewing

In the image understanding application, our goal is often either to deduce constraints on a scene imposed by a property in an image or to deduce constraints in an image because of an assumption made in a model (scene). Properties of perspective viewing, which is a good approximation to the process of taking a picture, can be used to make such deductions [6]. Wu's method can be modified for this purpose.

In contrast to the discussion in the previous section where the goal is to check whether a conjecture follows (under certain conditions) from a set of hypotheses, the objective here is to find the missing hypotheses so that a given conclusion follows from a given incomplete set of hypotheses.

3.1. Example of parallel lines

In our first attempt to apply Wu's method to image understanding, the goal was to deduce conditions under which two parallel lines in a scene remain parallel in its image [7]. This problem can be formulated as follows (for background and further details, the reader may consult [6, 7]). Without any loss of generality and for simplicity, we assume that the view plane is the plane $y = 0$, and the viewpoint is at $(0, -f, 0)$. For each point p'_i in the image, there is an equation using perspective transformation, relating this image point to the point p_i in the scene. Let (x_i, y_i, z_i) and $(x'_i, 0, z'_i)$ be the coordinates of p_i and p'_i respectively.

$$x'_i(f + y_i) = fx_i, \quad i = 1, 2, 3, 4,$$

$$z'_i(f + y_i) = fz_i, \quad i = 1, 2, 3, 4.$$

In addition, the line $p_1 p_2$ is parallel to the line $p_3 p_4$, which is expressed as:

$$(z_2 - z_1)(x_4 - x_3) = (x_2 - x_1)(z_4 - z_3) ,$$

$$(y_2 - y_1)(z_4 - z_3) = (z_2 - z_1)(y_4 - y_3) .$$

These constitute the hypotheses. See Fig. 3.

The conclusion, that the images of these lines are also parallel to each other, is expressed as:

$$(z_2' - z_1')(x_4' - x_3') = (x_2' - x_1')(z_4' - z_3') .$$

The hypotheses are already in triangular form assuming that

$$\{x_1, y_1, z_1, x_2, y_2, z_2, x_3, y_3, z_3, x_4\}$$

is the set of independent variables, and among the dependent variables,

$$z_4 < y_4 < x_1' < z_1' < x_2' < z_2' < x_3' < z_3' < x_4' < z_4' .$$

This choice of independent variables is dictated by the fact that points p_1 and p_2 can be arbitrarily chosen to define a line, and that point p_3 can be arbitrarily chosen, and exactly one coordinate of point p_4 can also be arbitrarily chosen to

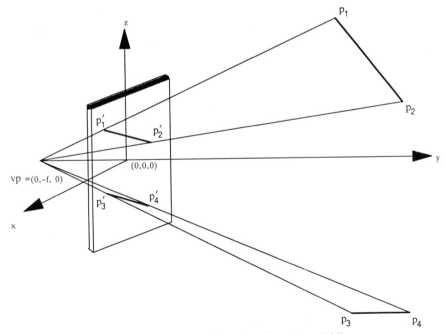

Fig. 3. Perspective image formation: Case of parallel lines.

have the line p_3p_4 parallel to the line p_1p_2. The above ordering on dependent variables is chosen so that the hypothesis polynomials are already in triangular form.

When the above conclusion is pseudodivided, there is a nonzero remainder which can be factored as:

$$f^2(y_2 - y_1)(x_4 - x_3)(x_2z_3f - x_1z_3f - x_3z_2f + x_3z_1f + x_1z_2f - x_2z_1f$$

$$- x_1y_2z_3 + x_2y_1z_3 + x_1y_3z_2 - x_2y_3z_1 - x_3y_1z_2 + x_3y_2z_1) .$$

In addition, the initials f, $z_2 - z_1$, and $x_2 - x_1$ are used to multiply the conclusion in pseudodivision. For the conclusion to follow from the hypotheses, these initials should be nonzero and some factor of the above remainder should be zero.

Each of the factors corresponds to either a degenerate condition or a geometric constraint:

(1) The condition $f = 0$ corresponds to the viewpoint being on the view plane and contradicts a nondegenerate condition. So it cannot hold.

(2) The condition $y_2 = y_1$ corresponds to the line p_1p_2 being parallel to the view plane, under which the conclusion indeed follows from the hypotheses.

(3) The condition $x_4 = x_3$, along with nondegenerate conditions and the hypotheses, correspond to a degenerate case of $p_3 = p_4$.

(4) The condition corresponding to the most complicated factor of the remainder being 0 is the constraint that lines in the scene lie in the same plane with each other and the viewpoint, so that their image on the view plane is the same line, i.e., $p_1'p_2' = p_3'p_4'$. This case is depicted in Fig. 4.

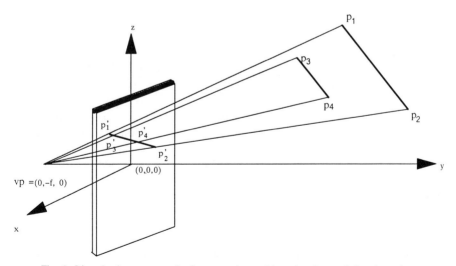

Fig. 4. Lines in the scene are in the same plane with each other and the viewpoint.

This example illustrates the power of Wu's method and the use of geometric reasoning in image understanding. Interestingly, we had failed to consider the fourth case, which was derived by the method. Such situations often arise in the design of image understanding algorithms when certain degenerate cases or special cases are not taken into account.

3.2. Vanishing points

In the above example, the conclusion was a property in the image and we were interested in finding conditions on the scene vis à vis the view plane. In the following example, the goal was to deduce constraints on the vanishing points of two lines in an image given that these lines are perpendicular to each other in a scene [14, 16].

As in the first example, it is assumed in this example that $y = 0$ is the view plane and the viewpoint is at $(0, -f, 0)$. For each point in the image, there is an equation using perspective transformation, relating the image point to the point in the scene. For a point P in a three-dimensional space, let P_x, P_y, and P_z stand for the x, y, and z coordinates of P, respectively. Since we are interested in relating the vanishing points V_1 and V_2 of vectors W_1 and W_2, respectively (given a viewpoint and the associated view plane, the vanishing point of a line l is the point of the intersection of the view plane and the line through the viewpoint parallel to l), we can assume that f is very small compared to the y-coordinates of W_1 and W_2. The images of vectors W_1 and W_2 in a scene can be related to the corresponding vanishing points as follows:

$$W_{1y}V_{1x} = fW_{1x} \,,$$

$$W_{1y}V_{1z} = fW_{1z} \,,$$

$$W_{2y}V_{2x} = fW_{2x} \,,$$

$$W_{2y}V_{2z} = fW_{2z} \,.$$

These hypotheses do not constrain the direction of the lines in the space, but merely the dependence of the vanishing point locations on the line directions (Fig. 5).

We wish to find conditions on the vanishing points in the image imposed by the fact that the lines are perpendicular to each other in the scene. The conclusion that W_1 is perpendicular to W_2 can be expressed as:

$$W_{1x}W_{2x} + W_{1y}W_{2y} + W_{1z}W_{2z} = 0 \,.$$

The set of dependent variables is $W_{1x} < W_{1z} < W_{2x} < W_{2z}$; this classification of

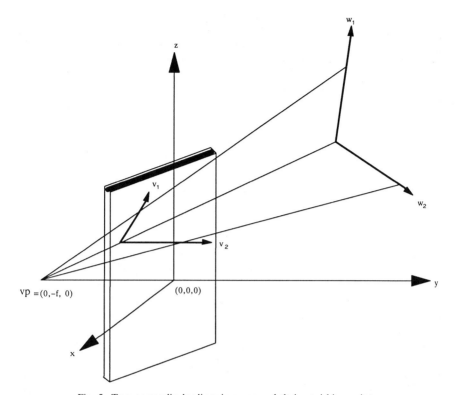

Fig. 5. Two perpendicular lines in space and their vanishing points.

independent and dependent variables is dictated by the fact that (i) we are interested in a relation between the coordinates of the vanishing points and (ii) using the camera position (i.e., the positions of the viewpoint and view plane) and the coordinates of the vanishing points, two coordinates of points on vectors W_1 and W_2 can be determined if the third coordinates of the points are given. Using the above total order on dependent variables, the hypotheses are already in triangular form. After pseudodividing the conclusion, we are left with a nonzero remainder which can be factored as:

$$W_{1y}W_{2y}(f^2 + V_{1x}V_{2x} + V_{1z}V_{2z}) .$$

The first two factors correspond to one or both of the lines being parallel to the view plane. In such a case, the vanishing point of the line will be at infinity in the view plane. This case should be ruled out as it violates the assumptions underlying the hypotheses. The third factor is the most interesting: It states the geometric relation that must be satisfied by their vanishing points for the two perpendicular lines in a scene. This relation depends upon the focal length of the camera and the directions of the lines in the image plane. Several pairs of lines which satisfy the constraint for $f = 1$ are shown in Fig. 6. This result was initially unknown to us. However, Kanade subsequently told us that it had been published elsewhere [15].

4. Handling Inequalities

Wu's method appears to handle universally quantified formulae involving the equality relation pretty well especially when interpreted over algebraically closed extension fields. However, often geometry formulae involve $\leq$ used to specify the betweenness relation and direction which lead to inequalities. As illustrated by [16, 20], Wu's method can also be used for handling some universally quantified formulae involving $\leq$. In this section, we consider such formulae.

Given a quantifier-free formula involving inequalities (expressed using $<$, $\leq$, $\geq$, $>$ relations), it can be converted to another formula involving only the equality relation using the trick of introducing new auxiliary variables proposed by Seidenberg. As discussed by Kapur [8], for an inequation of the form $p \neq 0$, a new variable w can be introduced such that $p \neq 0$ is equivalent to $(\exists w)\ pw = 1$ over any integral domain. Similarly, an inequality of the form $p \geq 0$ is equivalent to $(\exists w)\ p - w^2 = 0$ for real closed fields, i.e., w should be a real number; similarly, $p \leq 0$ is equivalent to $(\exists w)\ p + w^2 = 0$ for reals. Strict inequalities of the form $p < 0$ and $p > 0$ can also be transformed in a similar way: $p < 0$ is equivalent to $(\exists w)\ pw^2 + 1 = 0$ over the reals; $p > 0$ is equivalent to $(\exists w)\ pw^2 - 1 = 0$ for reals.

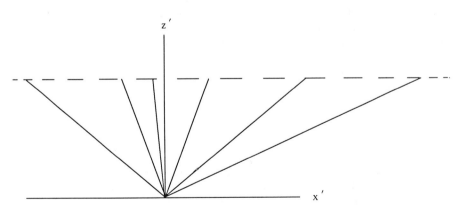

Fig. 6. Pairs of lines with vanishing points satisfying the constraint.

Consider a Horn formula:

$$[h_1 \wedge \cdots \wedge h_i] \Rightarrow c , \tag{7}$$

where each h_i as well as c is an equation, inequation or an inequality. Converting inequations and inequalities in the hypotheses (the h_j) into equations using new variables does not change the structure of the formula; an existential quantifier in the antecedent of an implication becomes a universal quantifier when pushed all the way out in front of the formula.

If c in (7) is an equation, in that case, (7) translates to an equivalent quantifier-free formula:

$$[h_1' \wedge \cdots \wedge h_i'] \Rightarrow c , \tag{8}$$

over the reals. Wu's method can be helpful in deciding this formula. If the polynomial in c pseudodivides to 0, then we need to check whether any common real zero of the hypotheses is also a zero of the product of the initials. If not, then the conclusion unconditionally follows from the hypotheses; otherwise, the conclusion follows from the hypotheses under the condition that the product of the initials is not equal to 0.

If the polynomial in c does not pseudodivide to 0, leaving a nonzero remainder r, then r must also be checked for real zeros. If r does not have a real zero or r vanishes on all common real zeros of the hypotheses, then c follows from the hypotheses either unconditionally or conditionally, depending upon the real zeros of the product of the initials vis à vis the common real zeros of the hypotheses as discussed above. For the example at the end of Section 2.4.1, the conclusion (6) cannot be pseudodivided by the hypothesis (5); so the remainder, which is (6), is nonzero. Polynomial (6) however vanishes on the only real zero $(0, 0)$ of (5).

For the case when all dependent variables from a remainder r have been eliminated, if r does not vanish on some common real zeros of the hypotheses, then the conjecture can be considered to be a consequence of the hypotheses with $r = 0$ being viewed as specifying an additional hypothesis (this situation is similar to the example discussed in Section 3.1).

After a conjecture polynomial has been pseudodivided using hypotheses, Collins' method [1] can be used to check whether a remainder polynomial vanishes on the common real zeros of a finite set of hypothesis polynomials. This check is likely to be easier computationally as compared to using Collins' method on the original geometry problem itself which admittedly has the same structure. Pseudodivision results in a remainder that is a polynomial in fewer variables as well as in lower degrees of variables. Sometimes, this check is quite easy as shown in the example given below.

Even in the case when a conjecture c is an inequality, Wu's method is useful in deciding a Horn formula (7) which translates to:

$$[h_1' \wedge \cdots \wedge h_i'] \Rightarrow (\exists w)\, c' . \tag{9}$$

The new variable introduced to transform c into an equation is existentially quantified. If c' pseudodivides to 0, then like the case above, this formula is a theorem if the product of the initials used to multiply c' in pseudodivision does not have a common real zero with the hypotheses; otherwise, it is a theorem under the condition that this product of the initials is not equal to 0.

If the polynomial in c' does not pseudodivide to 0, then the nonzero remainder r needs to be analyzed. If for any real value of every variable other than w, there is a real value of w which makes r vanish, then the formula is a theorem. This check needs to be done only for the real zeros of the hypotheses.

To illustrate this approach, let us first consider a simple example involving linear polynomials in which we derive the transitivity of $\geq$ over the reals:

$$[y \geq x \wedge z \geq y] \Rightarrow z \geq x .$$

Using the method discussed above, new variables are introduced giving an equivalent formula:

$$[y - x - w_1^2 = 0 \wedge z - y - w_2^2 = 0] \Rightarrow (\exists w_3)\, z - x - w_3^2 = 0 .$$

Pseudodividing the conclusion polynomial $z - x - w_3^2$ by the hypotheses which are already in triangular form gives the remainder:

$$w_1^2 + w_2^2 - w_3^2 .$$

Since for every real value of w_1 and w_2, there is a w_3 such that the above remainder is zero, the conclusion indeed follows from the hypotheses.

We have not yet experimented enough with this approach to comment on its efficiency. However, it does seem to be promising and a good way to combine Collins' method with Wu's method. Below, we give an example from two-dimensional shadowing illustrating the use of inequalities.

4.1. Shadowing

As illustrated in Fig. 7, consider a light source S above an opaque plane surface barrier floating in space and extending to infinity in the east direction. The goal is to find conditions under which an observer O can see the shadow of the northwest corner (I) of the barrier. Without any loss of generality, the barrier

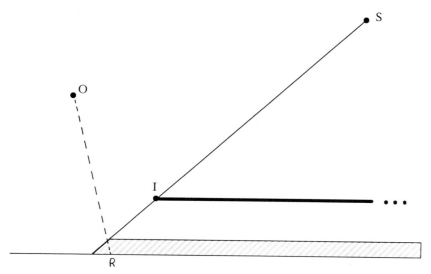

Fig. 7. Shadowing situation.

is assumed to be 1 unit above the floor; the origin is assumed to be situated on the floor with the y-axis passing through the northwest corner I of the barrier. The barrier thus is a ray starting at $(0, 1)$ and extending in the east direction.

The observer O is assumed to be above the floor and to the left of the line joining I and the source S. A point R in the shadow is on the floor and to the right of the line joining I and S. The observer O can see the shadow point R if and only if the line of sight OR is not obstructed by any point in the barrier. The following constraints specify the hypotheses for the problem.

(1) I is the northwest corner of the barrier.

$$I_x = 0, \qquad I_y = 1.$$

(2) The light source S is above the barrier.

$$S_y > 1: \quad (\exists w_1)(S_y - 1)w_1^2 - 1 = 0.$$

(3) The observer O is above the floor and to the left of the line joining I and S.

$$O_y > 0: \quad (\exists w_2)\, O_y w_2^2 - 1 = 0,$$

$$\frac{O_y - I_y}{O_x - I_x} > \frac{S_y - I_y}{S_x - I_x}: \quad (\exists w_3)\,[(O_y - 1)S_x - O_x(S_y - 1)]w_3^2 - 1 = 0.$$

(4) A point R is on the floor and in the shadow (i.e., to the right of the line joining I and S).

$$R_y = 0,$$

$$\frac{R_y - I_y}{R_x - I_x} < \frac{S_y - I_y}{S_x - I_x}: \quad (\exists w_4) \, [(R_y - 1)S_x - R_x(S_y - 1)]w_4^2 + 1 = 0.$$

(5) A point B is on the top of the barrier.

$$B_x > 0: \quad (\exists w_5) \, B_x w_5^2 - 1 = 0,$$

$$B_y = 1.$$

The goal is to find the conditions for the point R in the shadow to be visible (i.e., O, B, and R are not collinear), which is the inequation:

$$\frac{O_y - B_y}{O_x - B_x} \neq \frac{R_y - B_y}{R_x - B_x},$$

or equivalently

$$(\exists w_6) \, [(O_y - B_y)(R_x - B_x) - (O_x - B_x)(R_y - B_y)]w_6 = 1.$$

New variables introduced for transforming inequalities are considered independent along with S_x. The variables corresponding to the coordinates of points O, B, I, R and S are considered dependent since there are conditions constraining their values. The above hypotheses are already in triangular form if the total order

$$R_x > O_x > O_y > S_y > B_x > B_y > R_y > I_y > I_x$$

is used on dependent variables.

After pseudodividing the conclusion with the hypotheses, the following condition is obtained:

$$w_1^2 w_3^2 w_5^2 (1 - w_2^2) \neq w_4^2 (w_3^2 + w_1^2 w_2^2 w_5^2),$$

i.e.

$$w_4^2 \neq \frac{w_1^2 w_3^2 w_5^2 (1 - w_2^2)}{w_3^2 + w_1^2 w_2^2 w_5^2}.$$

The above inequation is to be interpreted as follows: A point R in the shadow is visible if the value of parameter w_4 for R in (4) above satisfies this inequality, i.e., for every value of w_1 (the variable corresponding to the inequality over S_y), w_2 and w_3 (the variables corresponding to the inequalities over the coordinates of O), as well as w_5 (the variable corresponding to the inequality over B_x), if an appropriate value of w_4 (the variable corresponding to the inequality over R_x) can be chosen to satisfy the above inequation, then the point R in the shadow can be seen.

As stated earlier, the use of Wu's method for reasoning about geometry statements involving inequalities needs further investigation and experimentation. An approach combining Wu's method with Collins' method appears to have considerable appeal.

ACKNOWLEDGMENT

The work on the use of geometric reasoning and Wu's method in deriving properties of perspective viewing in image understanding was done jointly with David Musser, Paliath Narendran, and Michael Swain. We also thank Hai-Ping Ko for help in the use of ALGE-prover and David Cyrluk and Shang-Ching Chou for their comments and suggestions on earlier drafts of this paper.

REFERENCES

1. Arnon, D.S., Collins, G.E. and McCallum, S., Cylindrical algebraic decomposition I: The basic algorithm; II: An adjacency algorithm for the plane, *SIAM J. Comput.* **13** (1984) 865–877; 878–889.
2. Chou, S.-C., Proving elementary geometry theorems using Wu's algorithm, in: W.W. Bledsoe and D.W. Loveland (Eds.), *Theorem Proving: After 25 Years*, Contemporary Mathematics **29** (1984) 243–286.
3. Chou, S.-C., Proving and discovering theorems in elementary geometry using Wu's method, Ph.D. Thesis, Department of Mathematics, University of Texas, Austin, TX (1985).
4. Chou, S.-C. and Schelter, W.F., Proving geometry theorems with rewrite rules, *J. Autom. Reasoning* **2** (3) (1986) 253–273.
5. Coelho, H. and Pereira, L.M., Automated reasoning in geometry theorem proving with PROLOG, *J. Autom. Reasoning* **2** (4) (1986) 329–390.
6. Duda, R.O. and Hart, P., *Pattern Classification and Scene Analysis* (Wiley, New York, 1973) Chapter 10, 379–404.
7. Kapur, D., Musser, D.R., Mundy, J.L. and Narendran, P., Reasoning about three dimensional space, in: *Proceedings IEEE International Conference on Robotics and Automation*, St. Louis, MO (1985) 405–410.
8. Kapur, D., Geometry theorem proving using Hilbert's Nullstellensatz, in: *Proceedings 1986 Symposium on Symbolic and Algebraic Computation* (*SYMSAC 86*), Waterloo, Ont. (1986) 202–208 (an expanded version is in this volume).
9. Knuth, D.E., *Seminumerical Algorithms: The Art of Computer Programming* **2** (Addison-Wesley, Reading, MA, 2nd ed., 1980) 407–408.
10. Ko, H.P. and Hussain, M.A., A study of Wu's method—A method to prove certain theorems in elementary geometry, *Congr. Numer.* **48** (1985) 225–242.
11. Ko, H.P. and Hussain, M.A., ALGE-prover: An algebraic geometry theorem proving software, Tech. Rept. 85CRD139, General Electric Corporate Research and Development, Schenectady, NY (1985).
12. Ko, H.P., Geometry theorem proving by decomposition of quasi-algebraic sets: An application of the Ritt–Wu principle, *Artificial Intelligence* **37** (1989) this volume.
13. Kutzler, B. and Stifter, S., Automated geometry theorem proving using Buchberger's algorithm, in: *Proceedings 1986 Symposium on Symbolic and Algebraic Computation* (*SYMSAC 86*), Waterloo, Ont. (1986) 209–214.

14. Mundy, J.L., Image understanding research at General Electric, in: *Proceedings Image Understanding Workshop*, Miami Beach, FL (1985) 83–88.
15. Shafer, S., Kanade, T. and Kender, J., Gradient space under orthography and perspective, *Comput. Vision Graph. Image Process.* **24** (1983).
16. Swain, M.J. and Mundy, J.L., Experiments in using a geometry theorem prover to prove and develop theorems in computer vision, in: *Proceedings IEEE Conference on Robotics and Automation*, San Francisco, CA (1986) 280–285.
17. Tarski, A., *A Decision Method for Elementary Algebra and Geometry* (University of California Press, Berkeley, CA, 1948; 2nd ed., 1951).
18. Wu, W., On the decision problem and the mechanization of theorem proving in elementary geometry, *Sci. Sinica* **21** (1978) 150–172; also in: W.W. Bledsoe and D.W. Loveland (Eds.), *Theorem Proving: After 25 Years*, Contemporary Mathematics **29** (1984) 213–234.
19. Wu, W., Some recent advances in mechanical theorem proving of geometries, in: W.W. Bledsoe and D.W. Loveland (Eds.), *Theorem Proving: After 25 Years*, Contemporary Mathematics **29** (1984) 235–241.
20. Wu, W., Basic principles of mechanical theorem proving in geometries, *J. Syst. Sci. Math. Sci.* **4** (3) (1984) 207–235; also: *J. Autom. Reasoning* **2** (1986) 221–252.
21. Wu, W., On reducibility problem in mechanical theorem proving of elementary geometries, Unpublished Manuscript, Institute of Systems Science, Academia Sinica, China (1986).

Received May 1987; revised version received February 1988

Geometric Reasoning with Logic and Algebra*

Dennis S. Arnon

Xerox PARC, 3333 Coyote Hill Road, Palo Alto, CA 94304, U.S.A.

ABSTRACT

Geometric reasoning is concerned with (geometric) objects that often are definable by formulae of the language of the first-order theory of the real numbers. Certain problems that arise in geometric reasoning can be cast into one of the following forms: query problem—*does a certain collection of objects possess a certain (first-order) property;* constraint problem—*given a quantified formula defining an object, find an equivalent definition by a quantifier-free formula;* display problem—*describe an object, e.g. determine its dimension or specify its topology. In the last fifteen years, feasible algorithms for the exact solution of these problems have been discovered, implemented, and used to solve nontrivial problems. We give examples of problems that fall within the scope of these methods, provide a tutorial introduction to the principal algorithms currently in use, and describe the solution of the sample problems using those algorithms.*

1. Introduction

Geometric reasoning is concerned with (geometric) objects that often are "first-order", in a sense we will soon make precise, such as planes, spheres, cylinders, and Bezier patches. Certain problems that arise in geometric reasoning can be cast into one of the following forms: *query* problem—does a certain collection of objects possess a certain (first-order) property; *constraint* problem—given a parameterized family of objects, and a property, write down the conditions on the parameters that characterize the objects in the family that have that property; *display* problem—describe or show an object. In the last fifteen years, feasible algorithms for the exact solution of these problems have been discovered, implemented, and used to solve nontrivial problems. In this introduction we give some examples of such problems and state the main theoretical results that underlie the algorithms we discuss. The remainder of

---

*This work is supported by the Xerox Corporation. This paper was typeset at Xerox PARC using TeX in the Cedar environment.

the paper will provide a tutorial overview of these algorithms, show how various sample problems can be solved using them, and assess their present status and future prospects. A more detailed outline of the paper is given at the end of the introduction.

First some formalities. We assume that the reader is familiar with first-order logic; see [7] for a review of the subject. A typical set L of primitive nonlogical symbols (i.e. symbols for functions, relations, and constants) for a first-order language appropriate for the theory of the real numbers is $L = \{+, *, <, 0, 1\}$. We will find it convenient to use a larger set $L' = \{+, -, *, <, \leq, >, \geq, \neq, 0, 1\}$; obviously any formula involving these symbols can be rewritten in terms only of the symbols in L. We recall that the terms of the language L are multivariate polynomials with integer coefficients. We may nonetheless write polynomials with rational number coefficients; clearing denominators brings us back to syntactical correctness.

The first-order theory of the real numbers, written $\mathrm{Th}(\mathbb{R})$, is the collection of all sentences of the language L which are true for the real numbers. For example,

$$(\exists x)\, x^3 + x - 1 = 0$$

belongs to $\mathrm{Th}(\mathbb{R})$, whereas

$$(\exists x)\, x^2 + 1 = 0$$

does not. It is known that for any sentence ϕ of L, either $\phi \in \mathrm{Th}(\mathbb{R})$ or $\neg \phi \in \mathrm{Th}(\mathbb{R})$.

We follow the convention that $\Psi(x_1, \ldots, x_k)$ denotes a formula in which all occurrences of $x_1, \ldots, x_k$ are free, each x_i may or may not actually occur, and there are no free variables other than $x_1, \ldots, x_k$. For any $k \geq 0$, let E^k denote k-dimensional Euclidean space, i.e. $\mathbb{R}^k$ with the usual topology (E^0 consists of a single point). A subset X of E^n is $definable$ if for some formula $\phi(x_1, \ldots, x_n)$ of L, X is the set of points in E^n that satisfy ϕ. We say that X is defined by ϕ, and that ϕ is a $defining$ $formula$ for X. Given formula $\phi(x_i, \ldots, x_n)$, we write $\mathrm{Set}(\phi)$ to denote the set defined by ϕ.

Example 1.1. *Surface intersections.* Suppose given polynomials

$$\delta(p, q, r) = 256r^3 - 128p^2r^2 + 144pq^2r + 16p^4r - 27q^4 - 4p^3q^2$$

and

$$L(p, q, r) = 8pr - 9q^2 - 2p^3;$$

then the formulae

$$\phi_1(p, q, r) := [\delta(p, q, r) = 0] \quad \text{and} \quad \phi_2(p, q, r) := [L(p, q, r) = 0]$$

each define a surface in E^3. Let

$$\phi(p, q, r) := [\phi_1(p, q, r) \text{ AND } \phi_2(p, q, r)].$$

The query "do the two surfaces surfaces intersect?" can be answered by deciding the sentence:

$$(\exists p)(\exists q)(\exists r)\phi(p, q, r).$$

If we wish to know what the intersection curve looks like, we have the task of displaying the set defined by ϕ.

We say that formulae $\phi(x_1, \ldots, x_n)$ and $\psi(x_1, \ldots, x_n)$ are *equivalent* if for all real numbers $a_1, \ldots, a_n$, $\phi(a_1, \ldots, a_n)$ is true if and only if $\psi(a_1, \ldots, a_n)$ is true, i.e. if the sentence

$$(\forall x_1)(\forall x_2) \ldots (\forall x_n)[\phi(x_1, \ldots, x_n) \Leftrightarrow \psi(x_1, \ldots, x_n)]$$

belongs to Th($\mathbb{R}$). A *quantifier elimination* (*qe*) problem is the task, given some formula $\phi(x_1, \ldots, x_n)$ of L, of giving an equivalent formula $\psi(x_1, \ldots, x_n)$ which is free of quantifiers.

Example 1.2. *Ellipse problem.* Consider the equation:

$$\frac{(x - c)^2}{a^2} + \frac{(y - d)^2}{b^2} - 1 = 0.$$

For any particular assignment of values to a, b, c, d, the set of points (x, y) that satisfy the equation constitute an ellipse with width $2a$, height $2b$, and center (c, d). Suppose we wish to find the conditions on a, b, c, and d so that the corresponding ellipse is inside the unit circle $y^2 + x^2 - 1 = 0$ (here "inside the circle" means either "strictly inside", i.e. no contact, or "inside and touching", i.e. the ellipse contacts the circle but has no points outside it, or "coincident", i.e. the ellipse is identical with the circle). Assume $ab \neq 0$, since otherwise the ellipse is degenerate. The desired constraints can be found by eliminating the quantifiers from the following formula, which asserts that "for all points (x, y) in the plane, if (x, y) is on the ellipse, then (x, y) is on or inside the unit circle":

$$ab \neq 0 \text{ AND } (\forall x)(\forall y)[b^2(x - c)^2 + a^2(y - d)^2 - a^2b^2 = 0$$
$$\Rightarrow y^2 + x^2 - 1 \leq 0].$$

Thus we have a constraint problem: we are interested in an object which is a certain subset of (a, b, c, d) space, we are given one definition of it by a formula involving quantifiers, and we wish to find a definition of it that does not involve quantifiers. The problem was proposed by Kahan [19]; Lauer [23] and Lazard [24] have given mathematical derivations of solutions to it. In Section 3 we present a solution to the special case of this problem in which the center of the ellipse is constrained to lie on the x-axis (i.e. $d = 0$), obtained by the algorithms we describe in this paper.

At the risk of belaboring the obvious, note that given a solution to this constraint problem, we can substitute any particular 4-tuple (a, b, c, d) of real numbers into the equivalent quantifier-free formula (qff) and determine whether or not it corresponds to an ellipse which is inside the circle. Obviously, a solution of any constraint problem is useful in this way.

From the above two examples, the reader may already see that "query problem" and "constraint problem" are just different names for the familiar decision and quantifier elimination problems of mathematical logic. Formally, a *decision problem* is the task of determining whether a particular sentence of L belongs to $Th(\mathbb{R})$. For $Th(\mathbb{R})$, decision problems can be treated as qe problems. Suppose, for example, that ϕ is a sentence of L; then an equivalent qff will contain no variables whatsoever, hence we can determine its truth or falsity by inspection, and thereby determine the truth or falsity of ϕ. For example, $0 = 0$ is a qff equivalent to $(\exists x) \, x^3 + x - 1 = 0$, and $0 = 1$ is equivalent to $(\exists x) \, x^2 + 1 = 0$. Thus, for $Th(\mathbb{R})$, a qe algorithm gives us a decision algorithm, and so we will henceforth treat query and constraint problems as instances of qe problems.

The fundamental, positive, result for quantifier elimination for $Th(\mathbb{R})$ was first proved by Tarski:

Quantifier Elimination Theorem [28]. *For any formula $\phi(x_1, \ldots, x_n)$ of L, there is an algorithm that constructs an equivalent qff $\psi(x_1, \ldots, x_n)$.*

Tarski's result was the starting point and impetus for much of the work we discuss in this paper.

Note that for Example 1.2, the Quantifier Elimination Theorem tells us not only that there is an algorithm to construct the constraints we seek, but also that those constraints can be expressed in terms of polynomial equations and inequalities, i.e. without radicals, logarithms, exponentials, etc. The following is also worth noting: the QE Theorem tells us that we can answer decision questions such as that posed in Example 1.1 when the coordinates of points are allowed to take on real number values; if, however, we ask about the existence of intersection points all of whose coordinates are integers, by the unsolvability of Hilbert's 10th problem [16], there is no general decision algorithm for such questions.

Tarski did not consider display problems; in fact, the roots of the display algorithms discussed in this paper are in algebraic geometry and topology rather than logic. We need some more definitions (cf. [4]) in order to state the main theorem for display. We use the term *region* to mean a non-empty connected subset of E^r. Given $X \subseteq E^r$, a *decomposition* of X is a finite collection of disjoint regions whose union is X. For $0 \leq i \leq r$, an *i-dimensional cell* in E^r is a subset of E^r which is homeomorphic to E^i. Given $X \subseteq E^r$, a decomposition of X is *cellular* if each of its regions is a cell. Figure 1 shows a cellular decomposition (cd) of a closed annulus into two 0-cells, three 1-cells, and one 2-cell.

A subset X of E^r is *semi-algebraic* if it has a quantifier-free defining formula. By the QE Theorem, a set is definable if and only if it is semi-algebraic. A decomposition is *algebraic* if each of its regions is a semi-algebraic set.

A point $p = (p_1, \ldots, p_r)$ in E^r is *algebraic* if each p_i is a real algebraic number. For concreteness, let us review one method for exact representation of algebraic points in finite terms (cf. [25, Section 1]). A real algebraic number γ is represented by its minimal polynomial $M(x)$ and an isolating interval for a particular root of $M(x)$. This is an exact representation of γ, for we can repeatedly halve the isolating interval (by comparing the sign of the minimal polynomial at the midpoint with its signs at the endpoints) until it is of any desired smallness. If degree$(M) = m$, then the real algebraic numbers that comprise the field $Q(\gamma)$ are in one-one correspondence with the elements of $Q[x]$ of degree $\leq m - 1$. For any algebraic point p in E^i, there exists a (real algebraic number) γ such that each coordinate of p is an element of $Q(\gamma)$; we say that γ is a *primitive element* for p. A representation for p is: the minimal polynomial and isolating interval representation for γ, plus an i-tuple of representations of the coordinates of p as elements of $Q(\gamma)$. For example, let $M(x)$ be the irreducible polynomial $x^4 - 15x^2 - 10x + 14$, let α be the unique root of M in the interval $(-4, -3]$, and let $\beta = -\frac{1}{3}\alpha^2$. Then the algebraic point (α, β) in E^2 is exactly represented by the triple:

$$[M(x), (-4, 3], (x, -\tfrac{1}{3}x^3)] .$$

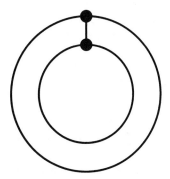

Fig. 1. Cellular decomposition of an annulus.

As for γ, a decimal approximation to (α, β) of any desired accuracy can be constructed.

Here now is the main theorem for display, due to Collins:

Cellular Decomposition Theorem [11]. *Given a formula $\phi(x_1, \ldots, x_n)$ of L, there is an algorithm that finds an algebraic cellular decomposition D of Set(ϕ), and constructs a description of D in the following sense: for each cell of D, its dimension, an algebraic sample point belonging to it (represented as specified above), and a quantifier-free defining formula for it, are constructed.*

Thus our basic semantics for "displaying an object" is: give a cd of it, of the kind specified in the CD Theorem. Note that for any constraint problem which yields an equivalent qff ϕ, we can display Set(ϕ) and obtain an understanding of the locus of solutions as a subset of the appropriate E^k. This might be called "strong solution" of the constraint problem.

Note that the formula ϕ in the hypotheses of the CD Theorem is not required to be quantifier-free; hence if ϕ has quantifiers, then by forming the disjunction of the defining formulae of the individual cells comprising a cd of Set(ϕ), we obtain a quantifier-free formula equivalent to ϕ. This is no coincidence: Collins' result yields, and was intended to yield, exactly this qe method, as well as a display method.

Here is one more example of a geometric reasoning problem that falls within our scope:

Example 1.3. *Implicitization of a parametric curve.* Given the parametric cubic curve:

$$x = f(t) = -505t^3 + 864t^2 - 570t + 343 ,$$

$$y = g(t) = 211t^3 - 276t^2 - 90t + 345 ,$$

find an "implicit description" of the curve, i.e. a qff $\phi(x, y)$, such that any pair (a, b) of real numbers satisfies ϕ if and only if (a, b) is on the curve. We might be tempted to think that there is a polynomial $F(x, y)$ such that the single atomic formula $[F(x, y) = 0]$ is the desired ϕ, but we shall see below that, for this example, such is not the case. In any event, ϕ is obtained by eliminating the quantifiers from the formula:

$$(\exists t) [x = f(t) \text{ AND } y = g(t)] .$$

So far we have described a constraint problem. We might in addition wish to display the curve.

Clearly this method of implicitization by quantifier elimination extends to parametric surfaces, and indeed to parametric hypersurfaces of any dimension.

The contents of the rest of the paper is as follows. In Section 2, we sketch proofs of the QE and CD Theorems, and in so doing, give a tutorial introduction to the qe and display algorithms currently in use. In Section 3 we present the solutions of the three sample problems above using these algorithms. Sections 4 and 5 present two additional kinds of geometric reasoning problems that can be attacked with these algorithms: finding the conditions on the coefficients of a polynomial that characterize each qualitatively different behavior of its real roots, and proving theorems of Euclidean geometry. Section 6 assesses the present and future outlook for the techniques we have presented.

2. Cylindrical Algebraic Decompositions

The actual qe software whose use we describe later in this paper uses a modified form of Collins' method. Hence, we don't describe all parts of Collins' method in detail here, only what we need. Other descriptions of the algorithms we discuss in this section can be found in references [1, 4, 9, 11, 15, 27].

Cohen [10] has given a simple proof of the QE Theorem that is summarized by Rabin [26].

To start on the proof of the CD Theorem, we need some definitions (most of which are from [4] or [11]). Let X and Y be any sets, and let $T : X \rightarrow Y$ be a function. T is *invariant* on X, and X is *T-invariant*, if T is constant on X. Now let X be a subset of E^k, and let $\Psi(x_1, \ldots, x_k)$ be a formula. We say that Ψ is invariant on X (and that X is *truth-invariant* (*with respect to* Ψ), and Ψ-invariant), if the function truthValue(Ψ) is invariant on X.

Let $\phi(x_1, \ldots, x_r)$ be a quantifier-free formula. As we know, ϕ consists of a (finite) collection of atomic formulae, combined using the propositional connectives. Each atomic formula can be written in the form $[F(x_1, \ldots, x_r) \sim 0]$, where $F \in I_r$ (we write I_r to denote $\mathbb{Z}[x_1, \ldots, x_r]$), and $\sim$ is one of $<, \leqslant, >, \geqslant, =, \neq$. When its atomic formulae are written in this form, we say that ϕ is a *standard* formula, and refer to the set of all F which occur in at least one of its atomic formulae as its (*set of*) *polynomials*.

Let X be a subset of E^r, and let F be an element of I_r. We say that F is invariant on X (and that X is *sign-invariant* (*with respect to* F), and *F-invariant*), if the function signum(F) is invariant on X. Let $A = \{A_1, \ldots, A_n\}$, be a (finite) subset of I_r. We say that A is invariant on X (and that X is *sign-invariant* (*with respect to* A), and *A-invariant*) if each A_i is invariant on X. A collection C of subsets of E^r is *A-invariant* if each element of the collection is. We say that C is sign-invariant if there exists some $A \subset I_r$ such that C is *A-invariant*.

The reader will note that our definition of "F-invariant" (and "A-invariant" as well) constitutes an abuse of language. Its most natural meaning would be "the *value* of the function $F(\alpha_1, \ldots, \alpha_r)$ is invariant as $\alpha = (\alpha_1, \ldots, \alpha_r)$ ranges over X", but instead, we define it to mean that the *sign* of $F(\alpha_1, \ldots, \alpha_r)$ is invariant on X. This is deliberate: it is the sign of $F(\alpha_1, \ldots, \alpha_r)$, and not its value, which is crucial for the theory we are presenting.

The following lemma is rather obvious, but should be carefully considered, for it opens the way to bringing algebra and topology to bear on logic.

Lemma 2.1. *Let $\phi(x_1, \ldots, x_r)$, $r \geq 0$, be a quantifier-free formula in standard form, and let $A \subset I_r$ be the polynomials of ϕ. An A-invariant decomposition of E^r is ϕ-invariant.*

Hence, given quantifier-free ϕ, if we construct an A-invariant cd D of E^r, then each cell of D is ϕ-invariant, and if we have a sample point for each cell, then we can determine the cells comprising $\text{Set}(\phi)$ by evaluating ϕ at these sample points. This is exactly the strategy of Collins' method; the particular sort of sign-invariant cellular decompositions he constructs are called *cylindrical algebraic decompositions*, which we now take up.

For a region R, the cylinder over R, written $Z(R)$, is $R \times E$. A *section* of $Z(R)$ is a locus s of points $(a, f(a))$, where a ranges over R, and $f : R \to E$ is continuous. In other words, s is the graph of f. A *sector* of $Z(R)$ is a locus of points (a, b), where a ranges over R, and for certain continuous functions $f_1, f_2 : R \to E$ such that $f_1 < f_2$, b ranges over the (open) interval $(f_1(a), f_2(a))$. The constant functions $f_1 = -\infty$, and $f_2 = +\infty$, are allowed. Clearly sections and sectors of cylinders are regions. Note that if $R = E^0$, then $Z(R) = E^1$, any point of E^1 is a section of $Z(R)$, and any open interval of E^1 is a sector of $Z(R)$.

Continuous, real-valued functions $f_1 < f_2 < \cdots < f_k$, $k \geq 0$, defined on R, naturally determine a decomposition of $Z(R)$ into sections and sectors, consisting of the k graphs of the f_i as sections, and the $k + 1$ sectors obtained by subtracting the graphs of the f_i from $Z(R)$. We call such a decomposition of $Z(R)$ a *stack* over R.

A decomposition D of E^r is *cylindrical* if either (1) $r = 1$ and D is a stack over E^0, or (2) $r > 1$, and there is a cylindrical decomposition D' of E^{r-1} such that for each region R of D', some subset of D is a stack over R. It is clear that D' is unique for D, and thus associated with any cylindrical decomposition of E^r are unique *induced* cylindrical decompositions of E^i for $i = r - 1$, $r - 2$, $\ldots, 1$.

It is not difficult to see that if c is an i-cell, then any section of $Z(c)$ is an i-cell, and any sector of $Z(c)$ is an $(i + 1)$-cell. It follows by induction that every element of a cylindrical decomposition is an i-cell for some i. Hence any cylindrical decomposition is cellular.

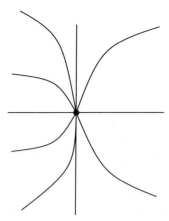

Fig. 2. Sample cylindrical algebraic decomposition.

Let's look at an example of a sign-invariant cylindrical algebraic decomposition (cad), i.e. a cd which is sign-invariant, cylindrical, and algebraic. Consider the following set A of polynomials in $\mathbb{Z}[p, q]$: $\{9q^2 + 2p^3, 27q^2 - p^3, 27q^2 + 8p^3, q\}$. Figure 2 shows an A-invariant cad of the plane, consisting of one 0-cell, ten 1-cells, and ten 2-cells:

For $F \in I_r$, $r \geqslant 1$, let $V(F)$ denote the real variety of F, i.e. $V(F) = \text{Set}(F = 0)$. Let R be a region in E^{r-1}. F is *delineable* on R if the portion of $V(F)$ lying in $Z(R)$ consists of k disjoint sections of $Z(R)$, for some $k \geqslant 0$. Clearly when F is delineable on R, it gives rise to a stack over R, namely the stack determined by the continuous functions whose graphs make up $V(F) \cap Z(R)$. We write $\text{Stack}(F, R)$ to denote this stack, and speak of the F-sections of $Z(R)$. One easily sees that $\text{Stack}(F, R)$ is F-invariant.

Lemma 2.2. *If R is semi-algebraic, then $\text{Stack}(F, R)$ is algebraic.*

Proof. It will be convenient to use an extension to our language L called *numerical existential quantifiers*. If n is a nonnegative integer, and $\phi(x)$ a formula with one free variable x, then the formula $(\exists_n x)\phi(x)$ is true if and only if there are exactly n (distinct) values of x which satisfy ϕ. It is easy to provide a translation of any formula of the form $(\exists_n x)\phi(x)$ into a syntactically legal formula (see [28, p. 21]).

Now let $\phi(x)$ be a defining formula for R. For any $j \geqslant 1$, the jth section of $Z(R)$ is the set of all points (x, y) satisfying the formula:

$$\psi_j(x, y) := \phi(x) \text{ AND } F(x, y) = 0$$

$$\text{AND } (\exists_{j-1} z)\,[z < y \text{ AND } F(x, z) = 0]\,.$$

The sector lying between the jth and $(j + 1)$st sections of $Z(R)$ is the set of all points (x, y) satisfying:

$$(\exists u)(\exists v)\,[\psi_j(x, u) \text{ AND } \psi_{j+1}(x, v) \text{ AND } u < y < v]\,.$$

Definitions of the bottommost and topmost sectors of $Z(R)$ are similar. $\square$

Note that by the QE Theorem, defining formulae of the kind given in the above proof can be converted to quantifier-free formulae. Collins gave a different and quite feasible algorithm for constructing quantifier-free defining formulae for the elements of Stack(F, R), given a qff that defines R. Although this elegant algorithm was crucial for his qe method as originally given, alternative methods of constructing quantifier-free defining formulae have recently been devised that are often more efficient in practice, and can yield simpler formulae (see [6]). It is these more recent methods that are used in the actual solutions of Examples 1.1–1.3 discussed in Section 3. Since we don't actually use Collins' formula construction algorithm we will not describe it here. The interested reader may consult [1] or [11].

We say $F \in I_r$ is *nullified* on $X \subset E^{r-1}$ if $F(a, x_r)$ is the zero polynomial for every $a \in X$. Let $A = \{A_1, \ldots, A_n\}$ be a finite subset of I_r, let R be a region in E^{r-1}. A is *delineable* on R if every element of A is either delineable or nullified on R, and if for every A_i, $A_j \in A$, every A_i-section s_i of $Z(R)$, and every A_j-section s_j of $Z(R)$, s_i and s_j are either disjoint or identical. Clearly when A is delineable on R, it gives rise to an A-invariant stack over R, namely the stack whose sections are all the distinct A_i-sections of $Z(R)$. We write this stack as Stack(A, R). If R is semi-algebraic, then by an easy generalization of Lemma 2.2, Stack(A, R) is algebraic.

We now come to a key theorem for Collins' method. It involves a map PROJ which, for any $r \ge 1$, takes a finite subset of I_r to a finite subset of I_{r-1}. The definition of PROJ, although straightforward, is somewhat long, so we refer the interested reader to [4]. Suffice it to say here: given some $A \subset I_r$, if the elements of A are viewed as polynomials in x_r whose coefficients are elements of I_{r-1}, then the computation of PROJ(A) involves only addition, subtraction, and multiplication of those coefficients. A proof of this next theorem may be found in [4] or [11]:

Theorem 2.3. *For any $A \subset I_r$, $r \ge 1$, A is delineable on any* PROJ(A)-*invariant region in E^{r-1}.*

The following corollary of Theorem 2.3 points the way to the first phase of Collins' algorithm.

Corollary 2.4. *Given $A \subset I_r$, $r \ge 1$, any* PROJ(A)-*invariant cad of E^{r-1} is induced by some A-invariant cad of E^r.*

Proof. Let D' be a PROJ(A)-invariant cad of E^{r-1}. For any $c \in D'$, A is delineable on c by Theorem 2.3, and since c is semi-algebraic, by the generalization of Lemma 2.2, Stack(A, c) is algebraic. Hence

$$\bigcup_{c \in D'} \text{Stack}(A, c)$$

is an A-invariant cad of E^r that induces D'.   □

Thus, given $a \subset I_r$, the first phase of Collins' algorithm is the successive computation of PROJ(A), PROJ$^2(A) = \text{PROJ}(\text{PROJ}(A)), \ldots, \text{PROJ}^{r-1}(A) = P_1$. P_1 is a set of univariate polynomials. It is not hard to see that any set of univariate polynomials is delineable on E^0, hence Stack(P_1, E^0) is a cad of E^1. The second phase of Collins' algorithm applies standard root isolation algorithms to P_1 and constructs sample points for the cad of E^1 (see [4]). Collins [11] gave an algorithm for constructing quantifier-free defining formulae for the cells of the cad of E^1 which, following our remark above, we will not examine explicitly. Determining cell dimensions in E^1 is trivial.

The third phase of Collins' algorithm consists of successive extensions of the cad of E^1 to a cad of E^2, the cad of E^2 to a cad of $E^3, \ldots,$ until finally a cad of E^r is obtained. At the start of each such extension step, we have a cad D' of E^{i-1}, including a sample point and defining formula for each cell, and a set $P_i \subset I_i$ that is delineable on each cell of D'. Suppose that a cell c of such a D' has a sample point $\alpha = (\alpha_1, \ldots, \alpha_{i-1})$, where for some real algebraic number γ, each $\alpha_j \in Q(\gamma)$. We form the set

$$\bar{P}_i = \{ F(\alpha_1, \ldots, \alpha_{i-1}, x_i) \mid F \in P_i \} \subset Q(\gamma)[x_i] \,,$$

and apply (just as we did for E^1) standard root isolation techniques to determine the cells of Stack($\bar{P}_i, c$), followed by application of standard algebraic number algorithms to construct a sample point for each cell (see [4]). We have noted Collins' algorithm [11] for constructing quantifier-free defining formulae for the cells of Stack($\bar{P}_i, c$). Given that we know the dimension of c, we immediately know the dimensions of the cells of Stack($\bar{P}_i, c$). This completes our description of Collins' algorithm to construct an A-invariant, cylindrical, algebraic decomposition of E^r, given $A \subset I_r$, and proves the CD Theorem for the case of quantifier-free ϕ.

Now let us prove the CD Theorem for the case that ϕ has quantifiers. First some definitions and a theorem. A *prenex* formula of L is a formula $\Psi(x_1, \ldots, x_k)$ of the form:

$$(Q_{k+1} x_{k+1})(Q_{k+2} x_{k+2}) \cdots (Q_r x_r) M(x_1, \ldots, x_r), \quad 0 \leq k \leq r \,,$$

where each Q_i is an existential or universal quantifier, and $M(x_1, \ldots, x_r)$ is a quantifier-free formula, the *matrix* of Ψ. Any formula of L is easily converted to an equivalent prenex formula. We say that a prenex formula is standard if its matrix is standard. The following theorem is implicit in [11]:

Theorem 2.5. *Let* $\Phi(x_1, \ldots, x_k)$, $k \geq 0$, *be a standard prenex formula whose matrix M involves* $r \geq k$ *variables. If* D^r *is an M-invariant cad of* E^r, *then the induced cad* D^k *of* E^k *is* Φ-*invariant.*

Proof. By induction on $q = r - k$, i.e. the number of quantifiers. If $q = 0$, then the theorem is trivial. Suppose $q = 1$. Then D^r consists of stacks over the cells of D^k. Let c be any cell of D^k. If the single quantifier Q_r of Φ is existential, then clearly Φ is true on c if and only if M is true on at least one element of the stack over c. If Q_r is universal, then Φ is true on c if and only if M is true on every element of the stack over c. This proves the theorem for $q = 1$. Now suppose the assertion has been proved for $q' \geq 1$, and let $q = q' + 1$. Let Φ' denote Φ with its outermost quantifier $(Q_{k+1}x_{k+1})$ removed. By the inductive hypothesis, the cad D^{k+1} of E^{k+1} induced by D^r is Φ'-invariant. By the QE Theorem, there is a quantifier-free formula $\Psi(x_1, \ldots, x_{k+1})$ equivalent to Φ'; then D^{k+1} is Ψ-invariant. The cad of E^k induced by D^{k+1} is just D^k, hence by the inductive hypothesis, D^k is $[(Q_{k+1}x_{k+1})\Psi]$-invariant. Since $(Q_{k+1}x_{k+1})\Psi$ is equivalent to Φ, D^k is Φ-invariant. $\square$

Proof of the CD Theorem. Assume given a standard prenex formula $\phi(x_1, \ldots, x_k)$, $k \geq 0$. We have proved the theorem for the case ϕ is quantifier-free, so suppose that ϕ has bound variables, let $M(x_1, \ldots, x_r)$ denote ϕ's matrix, and let A be the set of polynomials of M. Construct an A-invariant cad of E^r by the algorithm we have described. Determine which cells in E^r belong to $\text{Set}(M)$ by evaluating M at cell sample points, then by the method of the proof of Theorem 2.5, identify the cells of the induced cad of E^k that comprise $\text{Set}(\phi)$ (Theorem 2.5 tells us that $\text{Set}(\phi)$ is the union of certain of the cells in E^k). The collection of such cells constitutes the required cd of $\text{Set}(\phi)$. $\square$

The method we described above for determining which cells in E^k belong to $\text{Set}(\phi)$ is essentially Collins' original method. Recently, a variation of Collins' approach, in which we only construct a P-invariant cad D of E^k (where $P \subset I_k$ is $\text{PROJ}^{r-k}(A)$), and give some alternative way of determining which cells of this cad belong to $\text{Set}(\phi)$, has been used successfully. This variation can be more efficient in practice, and has been used in the solution of Example 1.2 that we report in Section 3; see [6] for more information on it.

3. Solutions to Examples

3.1. Surface intersection

We have $A = \{\delta, L\}$, where δ and L are as in Section 1. $\text{PROJ}(A)$ is the set of polynomials we saw in the sample cad in Section 2, i.e. $\{9q^2 + 2p^3, 27q^2 - p^3, 27q^3 + 8p^3, q\}$. $\text{PROJ}^2(A)$ is $\{p\}$.

Our implementation of the cad algorithm (in the SAC2 computer algebra system [12] on a VAX 11/785) took 22 minutes to construct an A-invariant cad of E^3. The cad has 123 cells. By evaluating $\phi(p, q, \tau)$ at the sample points of the E^3 cells, we learn that Set(ϕ) is non-empty, and indeed consists of four 1-cells and a 0-cell. Hence the answer to the question "do the surfaces intersect?" is affirmative. We also get display information from the cad algorithm. Since the intersection curve contains a 1-cell, we may say that it is "one-dimensional", i.e. it does not consist only of isolated points. The cad algorithm also tells us that the union of the five cells is connected, and thus that the intersection curve has just one connected component.

3.2. Ellipse problem

Currently we are only able to solve the special case of the problem in which the center of the ellipse is constrained to lie on the x-axis (i.e. $d = 0$), defined by a formula

$$\phi(a, b, c) := (\forall x)(\forall y)[(ab \neq 0 \ \text{AND} \ b^2(x - c)^2 + a^2y^2 - a^2b^2 = 0)$$
$$\Rightarrow y^2 + x^2 - 1 \leq 0].$$

The polynomials of ϕ are:

$$A \equiv \{ab, \ b^2x^2 - 2b^2cx + b^2c^2 + a^2y^2 - a^2b^2, \ y^2 + x^2 - 1\},$$

Before going further, let us make some basic observations. Clearly we must have $a \neq 0$ and $b \neq 0$. It is also clear that the semi-axes of the ellipse must each be less than or equal to the radius of the circle, and that the center of the ellipse must be (strictly) inside the circle. Whether to allow negative a and b seems to us to be a matter of choice; we choose not to. Hence we know that Set(ϕ) satisfies the following contraints:

$$0 < a \leq 1, \tag{R1}$$

$$0 < b \leq 1, \tag{R2}$$

$$c^2 < 1. \tag{R3}$$

Let us next observe that whenever $a = 1$, for any point (a, b, c) of Set(ϕ) it must necessarily be the case that $c = 0$ and $b \leq 1$. A similar argument applies whenever $b = 1$. Finally, whenever $c = 0$, then any choice of a and b in the range $(0, 1]$ gives us a point of Set(ϕ). Here we have a complete description of all points of Set(ϕ) for which $a = 1$, $b = 1$, or $c = 0$, and so need only be concerned about the points of Set(ϕ) for which $0 < a < 1$, $0 < b < 1$, and $0 < c^2 < 1$.

By applying these observations, and some additional simplifications discussed in [6], we obtain PROJ(A) consisting of:

$$\{x^2 - 1, \, ab(x - c + a)(x - c - a) ,$$
$$b^2x^2 - a^2x^2 - 2b^2cx + b^2c^2 - a^2b^2 + a^2\} ,$$

and $P = \text{PROJ}^2(A)$ consisting of:

$$\{a, \, a - 1, \, b, \, b - 1, \, b - a, \, c, \, c - 1, \, c + 1, c + a + 1, \, c + a - 1,$$
$$c - a + 1, \, c - a - 1, \, b^2c^2 + b^4 - a^2b^2 - b^2 + a^2\} .$$

The time required to construct a P-invariant cad D of E^3 was 75 minutes. D has 2291 cells. As per our remarks in Section 2, we use a special technique to determine which cells in the cad of E^3 belong to Set(ϕ), and an "alternative" method of constructing defining formulas. As detailed in [6], we obtain a solution to the case $d = 0$ of the ellipse problem of:

$$[c = 0 \text{ AND } 0 < a \leq 1 \text{ AND } 0 < b \leq 1] \text{ OR}$$
$$[0 < a < 1 \text{ AND } 0 < b < 1 \text{ AND } c^2 < 1 \text{ AND } (c + a - 1)(c - a + 1) \leq 0$$
$$\text{AND } [b^2 - a \leq 0 \text{ OR } b^2c^2 + b^4 - a^2b^2 - b^2 + a^2 \leq 0]] .$$

3.3. Implicitization problem

For this example we used essentially Collins' original qe method as described in Section 2. Construction of the cad of E^3 took 89 minutes, and there were 855 cells. From the data produced by the cad algorithm we learn that an "implicit equation" for the parametric curve is:

$$F(x, y) = 128787625y^3 + 161430825xy^2 - 123690261954y^2$$
$$+ 67449315x^2y - 118396536972xy + 43730624273196y$$
$$+ 9393931x^3 - 28185530898x^2 + 20125457356836x$$
$$- 4937175920971288 = 0 ,$$

in the sense that every point which is on the parametric curve satisfies this equation. However, we also learn that the following zero of $F(x, y)$:

$$\left(a = \frac{4842167022180059}{45767461033} , \, b = \frac{-2166473912400475}{45767461033} \right)$$

does not satisfy the input formula, i.e. $F(a, b) = 0$, but there is no real t such that $a = f(t)$, $b = g(t)$. The explanation for this is that there is a nonreal complex number s such that $a = f(s)$, $b = g(s)$, and $F(a, b) = 0$. Hence the "implicit equation" defines more (real) points than the parametric equations do. Thus a correct "implicit description" for the parametric curve is the formula:

$$F(x, y) = 0 \text{ AND } (x \neq a \text{ OR } y \neq b).$$

We also learn from the cad algorithm that the curve $F(x, y) = 0$ has two connected components, one one-dimensional, and the other an isolated point. Indeed, it turns out that the isolated point is just the point (a, b) above. Thus the parametric curve has a single one-dimensional component.

4. Root Classification

Suppose given this quadratic polynomial with undetermined coefficients:

$$f_2(x) = x^2 + px + q.$$

Consider the following family of problems: we wish to find the conditions on the (real) coefficients p and q so that $f_2(x)$ has k distinct real roots, for each k, $0 \leq k \leq 2$. For f_2, we can probably write down these conditions upon a moment's reflection: where $\delta(p, q) = \text{discriminant}(f_2) = p^2 - 4q$, f_2 has no real roots if and only if $\delta < 0$, one (distinct) real root if and only if $\delta = 0$, and two real roots if and only if $\delta > 0$.

The case $\delta = 0$ above points out the issue of root multiplicity: when $\delta = 0$, f_2 has one distinct real root, but it is a root of multiplicity two, whereas when $\delta > 0$, f_2 has two distinct real roots, each of multiplicity one. In order to handle the multiplicity issue precisely, and to make the data we accumulate more useful, we proceed as follows. For any polynomial $f(x)$ with real coefficients, the *real root multiplicity multiset* of f, written RRMM(f), is the multiset $\{e_1, \ldots, e_k\}$, $k \geq 0$, of positive integers such that $f(x)$ has k distinct real roots $\alpha_1, \ldots, \alpha_k$, and α_i is a root of f of multiplicity e_i.

A polynomial of degree n has at most n distinct roots, and any particular root of f has multiplicity at most n. Hence let us now precisely formulate the families of problems we are interested in. Given the monic polynomial:

$$f_n(x) = x^n + p_1 x^{n-1} + p_2 x^{n-2} + \cdots + p_n$$

with undetermined coefficients $p_1, \ldots, p_n$, identify which of the n^n length-n multisets of the integers $[1, \ldots, n]$ are RRMMs of $f_n(x)$ for at least one particular assignment of values to $p_1, \ldots, p_n$, and for each such RRMM, find the conditions on $p_1, \ldots, p_n$ so that $f_n(x)$ have that RRMM. For each $f_n(x)$, the data we collect can be arranged into a *root classification table*, e.g. for $f_2(x)$:

Root classification table for $f_2(x) = x^2 + px + q$

RRMM	Conditions
{ }	$p^2 - 4q < 0$
{2}	$p^2 - 4q = 0$
{1, 1}	$p^2 - 4q > 0$

Such a table is useful in at least two ways. First, given any particular quadratic polynomial, e.g. $h(x) = x^2 - \frac{33}{12}x + 2$, we can determine the RRMM of h by evaluating at $p = -\frac{33}{12}$, $q = 2$ the condition for each RRMM in the table, by which we will identify the unique condition in the table which is satisfied by this particular p and q. For this $h(x)$, we find that $p^2 - 4q < 0$, and so its RRMM is { }. Of course, we have to employ a rootfinding or root isolation algorithm if we want approximations to the values of h's roots.

A second use of root classification tables is in solving qe problems by "intelligent table lookup". Suppose, for example, we are given the qe problem:

$$(\forall x)[x^2 + px + q \geq 0] .$$

This is a constraint problem; we are asked to find the conditions on p and q so that the real-valued function $x^2 + px + q$ of a real number x be everywhere nonnegative. We may now observe that $x^2 + px + q \geq 0$ for all x if and only if it only has RRMMs of either { } or {2}. Hence, forming the disjunction of the two appropriate conditions in the above table, an equivalent qff is $\delta(p, q) = p^2 - 4q \geq 0$.

The example leads to the following observation: each condition in a root classification table is in fact the solution of a certain qe problem. This is because, as was observed in [2], the assertion that $f_n(x)$ has a particular RRMM can be expressed as a formula of our first-order language L. To show this, we define a predicate $M^j_{f_n}(x)$, for $j \geq 0$, which is true for particular j, f_n, and x if and only if x is a root of f_n of multiplicity j. We use the notation $f^1_n(x)$ for $\partial f_n / \partial x$ and inductively define $f^i_n(x)$ for any $i \geq 2$. Then

$$M^j_{f_n}(x) := [f_n(x) = 0 \text{ AND } f^1_n(x) = 0$$

$$\text{AND } \ldots \text{ AND } f_n^{(j-1)}(x) = 0 \text{ AND } f_n^{(j)}(x) \neq 0] .$$

Let us now write the assertion that $f_n(x)$ has RRMM {1, 2} (recall that the notation $\exists_j$ was defined in the proof of Lemma 2.2):

$$(\exists_2 x)[f_n(x) = 0] \text{ AND } (\exists x_1)(\exists x_2)[x_1 \neq x_2 \text{ AND } M^1_{f_n}(x_1) \text{ AND } M^2_{f_n}(x_2)] .$$

From this example it should be clear how to handle any other RRMM. Hence, in principle, we could build a root classification table for each f_n by individually solving such a qe problem for each a priori possible RRMM. However there is a much easier way.

Let us first make use of the following classical technique: if we "translate" $f_n(x)$ to $g_n(x) = f_n(x - p_1/n)$, then we "kill" the x^{n-1} term, i.e.

$$g_n(x) = x^n + v_2 x^{n-2} + v_3 x^{n-3} + \cdots + v_n .$$

Clearly g_n and f_n have the same RRMM and since g_n has one less coefficient, it is easier to work with. Thus we will build our table for $g_n(x)$; from a table for g_n, we can easily recover a table for f_n by substitution.

The following theorem, implicit in [11], is the basis for a convenient method of building root classification tables:

Theorem 4.1. *Let* $F(x_1, \ldots, x_r)$ *be an element of* I_r, *and let* R *be a region in* E^{r-1}. *If* R *is* PROJ(F)-*invariant, then* RRMM $(F(\alpha_1, \ldots, \alpha_{r-1}, x_r))$ *is invariant on* R, *i.e. invariant over all* $\alpha = (\alpha_1, \ldots, \alpha_{r-1}) \in R$.

For each n, Theorem 4.1 tells us that if we build a PROJ(g_n)-invariant cad of $(v_2, v_3, \ldots, v_n)$-space (i.e. E^{n-1}), then RRMM(g_n) is invariant on each cell of this c.a.d. Since the cad algorithm will construct a sample point α for each cell, we can then use a multiplicity reporting root isolation algorithm (see e.g. [13]) to discover what is the RRMM of g_n^α, where $\alpha = (\alpha_2, \ldots, \alpha_n)$, and

$$g_n^\alpha(x) = x^n + \alpha_2 x^{n-2} + \alpha_3 x^{n-3} + \cdots + \alpha_n .$$

Then, for each RRMM which actually occurs, we construct a defining formula for (the semi-algebraic set that is) the union of all cells which give rise to that RRMM.

Here are the root classification tables for g_3 and g_4:

Root classification table for $g_3(x) = x^3 + px + q$

RRMM	Conditions
$\{1, 1, 1\}$	$-4p^3 - 27q^2 > 0$
$\{1, 2\}$	$-4p^3 - 27q^2 = 0$
$\{1\}$	$-4p^3 - 27q^2 < 0$

Let $\delta(p, q, r)$ and $L(p, q, r)$ be the polynomials defined in Example 1.1.

Root classification table for $g_4(x) = x^4 + px^2 + qx + r$

RRMM	Conditions
$\{1, 1, 1, 1\}$	$\delta > 0$ AND $L > 0$ AND $p < 0$.
$\{1, 1, 2\}$	$\delta = 0$ AND $L > 0$ AND $p < 0$.
$\{1, 3\}$	$\delta = 0$ AND $L = 0$ AND $p < 0$ AND $q \neq 0$.
$\{2, 2\}$	$\delta = 0$ AND $L = 0$ AND $p < 0$ AND $q = 0$.
$\{1, 1\}$	$\delta < 0$.
$\{4\}$	$\delta = 0$ AND $L = 0$ AND $p = 0$.
$\{2\}$	$\delta = 0$ AND $L < 0$.
$\{\}$	$[\delta > 0$ AND $(L \leq 0$ OR $p > 0)]$ OR $[\delta = 0$ AND $L = 0$ AND $p > 0]$.

The table for g_4 is obtained from the same cad used for Example 1.1. Thus the cad itself took 22 minutes to generate; the formulae in the table were obtained in another 30 minutes of human-computer interaction.

Let us now consider a qe problem similar to the one above.

$$(\forall x)\ x^4 + px^2 + qx + r \geq 0 .$$

This is a nontrivial problem; its solution was sought by Delzell [17] in connection with finding a solution of a certain kind to Hilbert's 17th problem for a form of degree four. As above, it is not hard to see that $x^4 + px^2 + qx + r \geq 0$ for all x if and only if it has only RRMMs of either { }, {2}, {4}, or {2, 2}. By forming the disjunction of the appropriate table entries and simplifying, we obtain an equivalent qff of:

$$\delta \geq 0 \ \text{AND} \ [\,p \geq 0 \ \text{OR} \ L < 0 \ \text{OR} \ (L = 0 \ \text{AND} \ q = 0)\,] .$$

This solution to the problem was first reported in [5], and is discussed in more detail in [6].

Note that the cad of $E^n - 1$ that we construct in building the table for each g_n is of interest in its own right. If $\phi(v_2, \ldots, v_n)$ denotes the table entry for one of the RRMMs of g_n, then we can use the cad to display Set(ϕ), and thus gain an understanding of the set of all g_n that have that RRMM. This is just the "strong solution" of constraint problems that we discussed earlier.

Although the data we propose to collect in root classification tables is of classical interest in algebra (see e.g. [29] or [8]), such tables seem never to have been compiled in a systematic fashion for $n \geq 4$. We hope to have indicated the potential benefits of doing so.

5. Geometry Theorem Proving

We now consider a class of sentences of our language L which has been of considerable recent interest: propositions of Euclidean geometry. Let us consider a proposition suggested by Fig. 3.

Proposition 5.1. *ABCD is a square. CG is parallel to the diagonal BD. Point E is on CG such that $BE \equiv BD$. F is the intersection of BE and DC. Then $DF \equiv DE$.*

Here is a choice of coordinates which we will use to encode the proposition as a formula of L:

$$A = (0,0), \qquad B = (u_1, 0), \qquad C = (u_1, u_1) ,$$
$$D = (0, u_1), \qquad E = (x_1, x_2), \qquad F = (x_3, u_1) .$$

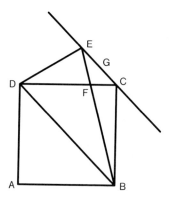

Fig. 3. Illustration of Proposition 5.1.

This coordinate choice already captures the hypotheses that $ABCD$ is a square, and that F is on DC. We can encode the remaining hypotheses, and the conclusion, as certain polynomial equations:

$BE \equiv BD$: $\quad (x_1 - u_1)^2 + x_2^2 = 2u_1^2$.

$CE \parallel BD$: $\quad \dfrac{u_1 - x_2}{u_1 - x_1} = -1$.

F on BE: $\quad$ slope(EF) = slope(FB), i.e.

$$\frac{(x_2 - u_1)}{(x_1 - x_3)} = \frac{u_1}{(x_3 - u_1)} .$$

$DF \equiv DE$: $\quad x_3^2 = x_1^2 + (x_2 - u_1)^2$

Simplifying, we have hypotheses and conclusion:

$BE \equiv BD$:

$h_1(u_1, x_1, x_2, x_3) = x_2^2 + x_1^2 - 2u_1 x_1 - u_1^2 = 0$;

$CE \parallel BD$:

$h_2(u_1, x_1, x_2, x_3) = x_2 + x_1 - 2u_1 = 0$;

F on EB:

$h_3(u_1, x_1, x_2, x_3) = x_2 x_3 - u_1 x_2 - u_1 x_1 + u_1^2 = 0$;

$DF \equiv DE$:

$g(u_1, x_1, x_2, x_3) = x_3^2 - x_2^2 + 2u_1 x_2 - x_1^2 - u_1^2$.

This proposition is now captured by sentence:

$$(\forall u_1)(\forall x_1)(\forall x_2)(\forall x_3)$$
$$[h_1(u_1, x_1, x_2, x_3) = 0$$
$$\text{AND } h_2(u_1, x_1, x_2, x_3) = 0$$
$$\text{AND } h_3(u_1, x_1, x_2, x_3) = 0 \Rightarrow g(u_1, x_1, x_2, x_3) = 0].$$

Before attempting to determine the truth or falsity of this sentence, i.e. whether or not it belongs to Th($\mathbb{R}$), we must consider an issue which we have already encountered in the ellipse problem (Example 1.2): the question of degenerate and unwanted instances of hypotheses. Recall in the ellipse problem that each point of (a, b, c, d)-space (i.e. E^4) corresponds to a particular ellipse, and that this ellipse is degenerate when $a = 0$ or $b = 0$, and so excluded. Also, the cases a negative or b negative can be either allowed or disallowed; we chose to disallow them. This indicates what we mean by "degenerate and unwanted instances of hypotheses".

In our current example, $u_1 = 0$ is a degenerate case of the hypotheses; presumably we want to exclude it. The case of negative u_1 is illustrated by Fig. 4; we may arbitrarily decide to allow or disallow this case; let us disallow it.

Thus, for $u_1 \leqslant 0$, we don't care whether $g(u_1, x_1, x_2, x_3) = 0$ when $h_i(u_1, x_1, x_2, x_3) = 0$ for $1 \leqslant i \leqslant 3$. Hence, where

$$\psi(u_1, x_1, x_2, x_3) := [u_1 > 0 \text{ AND } h_1(u_1, x_1, x_2, x_3) = 0$$
$$\text{AND } h_2(u_1, x_1, x_2, x_3) = 0$$
$$\text{AND } h_3(u_1, x_1, x_2, x_3) = 0],$$

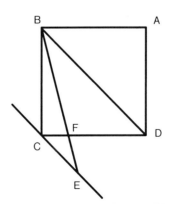

Fig. 4. Case of negative u_1 in Proposition 5.1.

the sentence we really want to test for membership in $\mathrm{Th}(\mathbb{R})$ is:

$$\phi := (\forall u_1)(\forall x_1)(\forall x_2)(\forall x_3)$$

$$[\psi(u_1, x_1, x_2, x_3) \Rightarrow g(u_1, x_1, x_2, x_3) = 0].$$

When we apply the cad-based decision procedure we have described in Section 2, we find that it requires eleven minutes to construct the induced cad of E^3, and this cad has 579 cells. By the improved techniques mentioned in Section 2, this is as far as we need construct the cad. An additional 15 minutes of human-computer interaction with this cad establishes that ϕ is true, i.e. that $\mathrm{Set}(\psi) \subset \mathrm{Set}(g = 0)$. In point of fact, we find that $\mathrm{Set}(\psi)$ corresponds to two 1-cells in E^4, each of which is the portion of some line in E^4 for which $u_1 > 0$. The first 1-cell gives the family of hypotheses instances that we saw in Fig. 3. The second 1-cell gives the family of hypotheses instances shown in Fig. 5. Since $\mathrm{Set}(\psi) \subset \mathrm{Set}(g = 0)$, the proposition is true for both instances.

In general, if we neglect to explicitly write down the degenerate and unwanted instances of hypotheses that we do in fact wish to exclude, the cad algorithm will construct them for us. In general, the proposition we give as input has the form:

$$\ldots (\forall u_i) \ldots (\forall x_j) \ldots$$

$$[\psi(\ldots, u_i, \ldots, x_j, \ldots) \Rightarrow g(\ldots, u_i, \ldots, x_j, \ldots) = 0],$$

for some particular ψ and g. The cad algorithm gives us a cd of the set:

$$S' := \mathrm{Set}(\psi) - \mathrm{Set}(g = 0),$$

and a defining formula Ψ' for S'. Then we know that the revised proposition

$$\ldots (\forall u_i) \ldots (\forall x_j) \ldots$$

$$[\neg \Psi'(\ldots, u_i, \ldots, x_j, \ldots) \text{ AND } \psi(\ldots, u_i, \ldots, x_j, \ldots)$$

$$\Rightarrow g(\ldots, u_i, \ldots, x_j, \ldots) = 0]$$

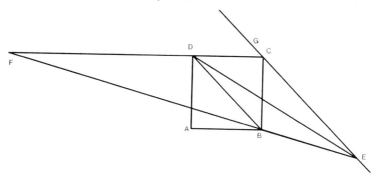

Fig. 5. Case of second kind of positive u_1 in Proposition 5.1.

belongs to Th($\mathbb{R}$), i.e. $\neg\Psi'$ is the required "nondegeneracy condition" that makes the proposition true, and we can study Set($\neg\Psi'$) to see if it is what we want or expect. Of course, the cad algorithm will also tell us if $S' = \text{Set}(\psi)$, i.e. if the revised proposition is vacuous.

The papers by Kapur and Mundy [21], Kapur [20], and Ko [22] in this volume describe other methods currently in use for proving theorems of Euclidean geometry. The cad-based method we have described may be said to belong to the algebraic geometry of real closed fields; in contrast, these other methods may be said to belong to the classical algebraic geometry of algebraically closed fields. For Euclidean geometry, they are not decision methods, but proof methods: they return an answer of either "true" or "don't know" for a given proposition, rather than "true" or "false". On the other hand, they have so far proved to be significantly more efficient than the cad-based approach.

6. Conclusions

We hope that this paper has established two points: (1) quantifier elimination, and algebraic cell decompositions, provide a rigorous semantics for query, constraint, and display problems that arise in geometric reasoning, (2) if a geometric reasoning problem can be cast into one of these three forms, then there is an deterministic algorithm for its exact solution. Thus, for example, there was no need for the conjecture in [18] that no algorithm exists for the implicitization of a bicubic patch.

Although the currently implemented versions of the algorithms discussed in this paper can already solve certain geometric reasoning problems faster or more concisely than humans or other algorithms are likely to, one cannot at the present time have confidence that these algorithms will run to completion in reasonable time or space in any particular application of them. In other words, we can only do small problems at present. We expect, however, that this state of affairs can and will be considerably improved. Thus, for example, we hope to soon be able to solve the general ellipse problem with these algorithms, rather than only the special case $d = 0$ that we presented in this paper.

Although we did not so use it in this paper, the information computed by the cad algorithm is sufficient to enable drawing actual pictures of the objects that occur in a particular problem to which it is applied (provided that three or fewer variables are present). For example, the cad algorithm provides the necessary data for rendering the intersection curve of the two surfaces considered in Example 1.1. Preliminary display facilities of this kind for the plane were described in [3].

ACKNOWLEDGMENT

I am grateful to B. Buchberger, S. Chou, D. Kapur, and H.P. Ko for helpful discussions on geometry theorem proving.

REFERENCES

1. Arnon, D.S., A cellular decomposition algorithm for semi-algebraic sets, Tech. Rept. No. 353, Computer Sciences Department, University of Wisconsin, Madison, WI (1979).
2. Arnon, D.S. and McCallum, S., Cylindrical algebraic decomposition by quantifier elimination, in: *Proceedings European Computer Algebra Conference (EUROCAL-82)*, Lecture Notes in Computer Science **144** (Springer, Berlin, 1982) 215–222.
3. Arnon, D.S., Topologically reliable display of algebraic curves, *Comput. Graph.* **17** (1983) 219–227.
4. Arnon, D.S., Collins, G.E. and McCallum, S., Cylindrical algebraic decomposition, I: The basic algorithm, *SIAM J. Comput.* **13** (1984) 865–877.
5. Arnon, D.S., On mechanical quantifier elimination for elementary algebra and geometry: Automatic solution of a nontrivial problem, in: *Proceedings EUROCAL-85*, Lecture Notes in Computer Science **204** (Springer, Berlin, 1985) 270–271.
6. Arnon, D.S. and Mignotte, M., On mechanical quantifier elimination for elementary algebra and geometry, *J. Symbolic Comput.* **5** (1988) 237–259.
7. Barwise, J., An introduction to first-order logic, in: J. Barwise (Ed.), *Handbook of Mathematical Logic* (North-Holland, Amsterdam, 1977) 5–46.
8. Burnside, W.S. and Panton, A.W., *The Theory of Equations* (Longman's Green, London, 4th ed., 1899).
9. Chazelle, B., Fast searching in a real algebraic manifold with applications to geometric complexity, in: *Proceedings CAAP-85*, Lecture Notes in Computer Science (Springer, Berlin, 1985).
10. Cohen, P.J., Decision procedures for real and *p*-adic fields, *Comm. Pure Appl. Math.* **22** (1969) 131–151.
11. Collins, G.E., Quantifier elimination for real closed fields by cylindrical algebraic decomposition, in: *Proceedings Second GI Conference on Automata Theory and Formal Languages*, Lecture Notes in Computer Science **33** (Springer, Berlin, 1975) 134–183.
12. Collins, G.E., SAC-2 and ALDES now available, *SIGSAM Bull. ACM* **14** (1980) 19.
13. Collins, G.E. and Loos, R.G.K., Real zeros of polynomials, in: *Computing, Supplementum* **4**: *Computer Algebra—Symbolic and Algebraic Computation* (Springer, New York, 1982) 83–94.
14. Collins, G.E., Quantifier elimination for real closed fields: A guide to the literature, in: *Computing, Supplementum* **4**: *Computer Algebra—Symbolic and Algebraic Computation* (Springer, New York, 1982) 79–81.
15. Davenport, J., Computer algebra for cylindrical algebraic decomposition, Tech. Rept. TRITA-NA-8511, Royal Institute of Technology, Department of Numerical Analysis and Computer Science, Stockholm, Sweden (1985).
16. Davis, M., Unsolvable problems, in: J. Barwise (Ed.), *Handbook of Mathematical Logic* (North-Holland, Amsterdam, 1977) 567–594.
17. Delzell, C., A continuous, constructive solution to Hilbert's 17th problem, *Invent. Math.* **76** (1984) 365–384.
18. Faux, I.D. and Pratt, M.J., *Computational Geometry for Design and Manufacture* (Ellis Horwood, Chichester, England, 1981).
19. Kahan, W. Problem no. 9: An ellipse problem, *SIGSAM Bull. ACM* (35) (1975) 11.
20. Kapur, D., A refutational approach to geometry theorem proving, *Artificial Intelligence* **37** (1988) 61–93 (this volume).
21. Kapur, D. and Mundy, J.L., Wu's method and its application to perspective viewing, *Artificial Intelligence* **37** (1988) 15–36 (this volume).
22. Ko, H.P., Geometry theorem proving by decomposition of quasi-algebraic sets: An application of the Ritt–Wu principle, *Artificial Intelligence* **37** (1988) 95–122 (this volume).
23. Lauer, M., A solution to Kahan's problem (SIGSAM problem no. 9), *SIGSAM Bull. ACM* **11** (1977) 16–28.

24. Lazard, D., Quantifier elimination: Optimal solution for 2 classical examples, *J. Symbolic Comput.* **5** (1988) 260–266.
25. Loos, R.G.K., Computing in algebraic extensions, in: *Computing, Supplementum* **4**: *Computer Algebra—Symbolic and Algebraic Computation* (Springer, New York, 1982) 173–187.
26. Rabin, M., Decidable theories, in: J. Barwise (Ed.), *Handbook of Mathematical Logic* (North-Holland, Amsterdam, 1977) 595–630.
27. Schwartz, J. and Sharir, M., On the piano movers' problem, II: General techniques for computing topological properties of real algebraic manifolds, *Adv. Appl. Math.* **4** (1983) 298–351.
28. Tarski, A., *A Decision Method for Elementary Algebra and Geometry* (University of California Press, Berkeley, CA, 1948; 2nd revised ed., 1951).
29. Weber, H., *Lehrbuch der Algebra* (2nd ed. 1898); (reprinted by Chelsea, New York).

Received April 1987; revised version received February 1988

A Refutational Approach to Geometry Theorem Proving*

Deepak Kapur**

General Electric Company, Corporate Research and Development, Schenectady, NY 12345, U.S.A.

ABSTRACT

A refutational method for proving universally quantified formulae in algebraic geometry is proposed. A geometry statement to be proved is usually stated as a finite set of hypotheses implying a conclusion. A hypothesis is either a polynomial equation expressing a geometric relation or a polynomial inequation (the negation of a polynomial equation) expressing a subsidiary condition that rules out degenerate cases and perhaps some general cases. A conclusion is a polynomial equation expressing a geometry relation to be derived. Instead of showing that the conclusion directly follows from the hypothesis equations and inequations, the proof-by-contradiction technique is employed. It is checked whether the negation of the conclusion is inconsistent with the hypotheses. This can be done by converting the hypotheses and the negation of the conclusion into a finite set of polynomial equations and checking that they do not have a common solution. There exist many methods for this check, thus giving a complete decision procedure for such geometry statements. This approach has been recently employed to automatically prove a number of interesting theorems in plane Euclidean geometry. A Gröbner basis algorithm is used to check whether a finite set of polynomial equations does not have a solution. Two other formulations of geometry problems are also discussed and complete methods for solving them using the Gröbner basis computations are given.

1. Introduction

In the early days of Artificial Intelligence research, there was considerable interest in developing computer programs for automatically proving geometry theorems. Gelernter and his colleagues [17] investigated automating geometric reasoning using a synthetic approach to geometry. Mimicking techniques in

*A preliminary version of this paper appeared in *Proceedings ACM Symbolic and Algebraic Computation (SYMSAC) Conference* held in July 1986 at Waterloo, Canada. Some of the results reported in this paper appeared without proofs as an application letter in the *Journal of Symbolic Computation*.

**Current address: Department of Computer Science, State University of New York at Albany, Albany, NY 12222, U.S.A.

high school geometry books, Gelernter characterized various geometric concepts including parallel line, vertical angle, collinear, congruence, equilateral triangle, etc., by axioms and rules of inference. These axioms and rules of inference along with geometric construction techniques and examples were used to prove some simple plane geometry theorems; see also [18]. This work was subsequently extended by Nevins using a combination of forward and backward chaining methods. Coelho and Pereira [15] recently surveyed this approach toward geometry theorem proving and discussed its limitations.

Much before Gelernter's efforts, there was a major breakthrough in algebra, geometry and logic when Tarski [39] showed in the 1930s that the theory of elementary algebra and elementary geometry is decidable. Subsequently, Tarski's decision algorithm, which used an ingenious quantifier elimination technique, was improved by others—notably among them Seidenberg [37], Monk [34], and Collins [16], and recently by Ben-Or et al. [4]. In contrast to Gelernter's synthetic method, these methods are algebraic and are based on translating geometry statements into first-order formulae using the operations $0, 1, -1, +, *, \geq, =$ of an ordered field with variables ranging over the real numbers. Among these decision procedures, Collins' method based on the cylindrical algebraic decomposition technique is, to our knowledge, the only decision procedure implemented so far; see [2, 3] for details. Unfortunately, Collins' method has been found too general and slow to be useful in proving plane geometry theorems.

Recently, Wu Wen-tsun [42, 43] has revived interest in automated geometry theorem proving by showing how a subclass of geometry theorems (expressed using the concepts of parallelism, incidence and congruence) can be proved using a fairly simple and elegant algebraic method. A geometry statement of the form—a finite set of hypotheses implying a conclusion—is considered. Hypotheses are polynomial equations expressing geometric relations and the conclusion is also a polynomial equation stating a geometric relation to be derived; a subset of variables corresponding to coordinates of points that can be arbitrarily chosen in a geometry statement are viewed as parameters. Unlike the methods of Tarski, Seidenberg, Monk, Collins and Ben-Or et al., variables in Wu's method range over an algebraically closed field.

This method has been implemented by Wu in China and Chou at the University of Texas independently. Both Wu [42, 43] and Chou [10, 11] have extensively experimented with the method, and have been successful in proving many nontrivial theorems in geometry. Chou's program [10], in particular, has proved over 200 theorems in Euclidean and non-Euclidean geometries. Further, Wu's method has also been used for proving some interesting results about perspective projections in the application area of image understanding [25, 35, 38].

In this paper, an alternative approach for proving similar algebraic geometry theorems is proposed. Two types of geometry problems are considered and complete decision methods are discussed for these problems. The first type consists of deciding whether a given universally quantified formula is a theorem or not. The second type of geometry problems (suggested by Wu's approach) includes the first type and consists of three parts:

(i) decide whether a given universally quantified formula is a theorem or not,

(ii) if it is not a theorem, check whether there is an additional hypothesis possibly ruling out degenerate cases and perhaps some general cases (called nondegenerate conditions or subsidiary conditions) such that the original formula subject to this additional hypothesis becomes a theorem, and

(iii) in case such a hypothesis exists, find it.

The proposed approach is based on Hilbert's Nullstellensatz and is complete in Wu's geometry but is incomplete in Tarski's geometry, that is, geometry statements are not restricted to hold over the real numbers only. Both Wu's approach and the proposed approach are sound in the sense that a geometry statement declared a theorem by these approaches is indeed a theorem even when interpreted over the real numbers only; however, the converse is not true. These approaches are thus good heuristics for deciding geometry statements over the reals.

Unlike Wu's approach, the proposed approach does not use factorization of polynomials over successive extension fields of a base field, which is generally considered a difficult problem (cf. [10, pp. 278–279; 46, p. 3]). Further, degenerate cases, which should be an integral part of a complete geometry statement, are handled in a natural way in this approach. It was suggested in a preliminary version of this paper [28] that degenerate cases can be stated a priori in Wu's approach also; recently, Wu [45] has suggested a method which can be used for handling degenerate cases, and Ko [30] has investigated its use in geometry theorem proving over the reals.

In the proposed approach, a geometry statement is translated to checking whether a finite set of polynomials does not have a common zero in an algebraically closed field. Since it follows from Hilbert's Nullstellensatz that a set of polynomials has a common zero if and only if their ideal is not the unit ideal, to prove a geometry statement it is sufficient to check whether an equivalent finite set of polynomials generates the unit ideal. There exist many methods for checking whether a given set of polynomials generates the unit ideal [6, 8, 9, 33, 36, 40, 41, 45]. In this paper, the use of the Gröbner basis method [5–8, 22] is investigated for this check. Kutzler and Stifter [31, 32] and Chou and Schelter [12] have also independently investigated the use of the Gröbner basis method for proving geometry theorems. Their approaches are somewhat different; their works are discussed later in the paper.

1.1. Organization of the paper

The paper is organized as follows. In the next section, we briefly discuss Wu's method; we introduce the language of geometry statements under consideration and call it Wu's geometry. In Section 3, two types of geometry problems are precisely defined. The fourth section relates theorem proving in algebraic geometry to Hilbert's Nullstellensatz. It is shown that deciding universally quantified geometry statements is equivalent to checking whether a finite set of polynomials corresponding to the geometry statement does not have a common zero. From this observation, one obtains a complete method for deciding universally quantified geometry statements discussed in Section 2. The incompleteness of the method as well as of Wu's method in Tarski's geometry of reals are shown even for this restricted class of geometry statements. Section 5 lists methods which could be used for checking whether a finite set of polynomial equations has no solution.

Section 6 discusses the use of Gröbner bases for geometry theorem proving. This method is illustrated on simple examples. A table of geometry statements proved by this method and the time taken on a Symbolics 3640 LISP machine for proving these theorems is given. Related work on using the Gröbner basis computation for proving geometry theorems is also discussed. In Section 7, it is shown how the proposed approach can also be used for deriving subsidiary conditions if a given geometry statement is not a theorem. The method is shown to be complete for deriving such conditions when interpreted over an algebraically closed field. Conditions deduced by this method are usually simpler and weaker than those reported in [10, 11] as well as in [12, 32, 33]. Tables giving the time taken on a Symbolics 3640 LISP machine to deduce subsidiary conditions for a number of geometry statements are given. Section 8 outlines how additional information given about certain points in a geometry statement being general can be used in deciding geometry statements. Some empirical observations made while using the proposed approach in proving a large class of geometry theorems are reported in Section 9. Section 10 discusses some differences between the methods based on Gröbner basis computations and Wu's method based on Ritt's characteristic sets.

2. Wu's Geometry

As stated above, Wu's method as well as the proposed method are algebraic. A coordinate system is associated with a geometry problem with points in a geometry problem having coordinates taken from an algebraically closed field. Further, geometry problems under consideration can only be stated using the concepts of parallelism, incidence and congruence.

Consider a field k of characteristic zero intrinsic to geometry under consideration, for example, the field of rationals; let K be an algebraically closed field containing k [41]. Let $+$, $*$, 0, 1, -1 be the operations of K. Assume a denumerable set of variables ranging over K. Consider the set of all quantifier-free formulae constructed using these operations, the equality predicate and Boolean connectives, in which the variables range over K. Let this language be

W, after Wu, and such a geometry *Wu's geometry*. It is worthwhile noting again that unlike Tarski's language of elementary geometry, (i) there is no order relation on polynomials in this language; thus, geometry problems expressed using the betweenness relation cannot be stated in this language, (ii) alternation of quantifiers is not allowed, and (iii) variables do not range over the real closed field, instead they range over the algebraically closed field. Such geometries are called metric geometries in [13]. Thus, the language W is a highly restricted subset of Tarski's language of elementary geometry.

2.1. Wu's method

A geometry statement considered by Wu [42, 44, 46] is of the following type:

> Given a finite set of hypotheses, say $\{h_1, \ldots, h_i\}$, expressed as polynomials over k, involving variables $x_1, \ldots, x_n$, decide whether a given conclusion polynomial c is *generically true* or not.

Variables above are coordinates of points in a geometry statement. Variables corresponding to coordinates of points that can be "arbitrarily chosen" in a geometry statement are called *parameters* (or *independent variables*) by Wu whereas the remaining indeterminates are called *dependent variables*. Polynomials $h_1, \ldots, h_i$ specify geometry relations, such as points being collinear, lines being parallel or perpendicular, etc., in a geometry statement; polynomial c expresses a geometry relation being derived such as two line segments being of the same length.

Wu's method for deciding the above class of geometry statements is based on (i) generating from the hypothesis polynomials, a set of polynomials in a triangular form with certain additional properties, called a *characteristic set*, a concept due to Ritt (also called a *basic set* by Wu), (ii) checking whether the conclusion polynomial c *pseudodivides* to 0 using the polynomials in the characteristic set. Characteristic sets are computed using pseudodivision by introducing a total ordering on dependent variables. For any given finite set of polynomials, its characteristic set exists and can be effectively computed. Wu also gave an algorithm for computing a characteristic set from a given finite set of polynomials.

Let $\mathrm{Zeros}(\{f_1, \ldots, f_i\})$ be the set of all common zeros in K of $f_1, \ldots, f_i$; this set is also called the *algebraic variety* or *algebraic manifold* defined by $\{f_1, \ldots, f_i\}$. Wu [44, Theorem (Ritt), p. 230] showed that

$$\mathrm{Zeros}(CHS/J) \subseteq \mathrm{Zeros}(Hyp) \subseteq \mathrm{Zeros}(CHS) ,$$

$$\mathrm{Zeros}(Hyp) = \mathrm{Zeros}(CHS/J) \cup \bigcup_j \mathrm{Zeros}(Hyp_j) ,$$

where CHS is a characteristic set of $Hyp = \{h_1, \ldots, h_i\}$, J is the product of initials[1] of polynomials in *CHS*, and CHS_j is the enlarged set of polynomials obtained by adjoining I_j, the initial of the *j*th polynomial in *CHS*, to *Hyp*. The set Zeros(*CHS*/*J*) is the set of zeros of *CHS* that are not zeros of the polynomial *J*, i.e.,

$$\text{Zeros}(CHS/J) = \text{Zeros}(CHS) - \text{Zero}(J) .$$

In case the conclusion *c* does not pseudodivide to 0 with respect to *CHS*, the geometry statement can be said to be not generically true only if the characteristic set *CHS* is irreducible [44, Theorem 2, p. 242]. Otherwise, in case a characteristic set is reducible, then the characteristic set must be decomposed using factorization over extension fields by successively adjoining the factors of polynomials in the characteristic set. Wu defined that a geometry statement is *generically true* if and only if the conclusion *c* pseudodivides to 0 on each of the irreducible basic sets obtained after decomposition.

A by-product of Wu's method is the generation of a set of polynomials, $\{s_1, \ldots, s_j\}$ representing *degenerate cases* such that the conclusion polynomial *c* vanishes at the zeros in *K* of $\{h_1, \ldots, h_i\}$ that are not zeros of $\{s_1, \ldots, s_j\}$. These polynomials are the initials of polynomials from irreducible basic sets used to pseudodivide *c* to 0. Negations of these polynomial equations, i.e., $s_1 \neq 0, \ldots, s_j \neq 0$, or equivalently $s_1 * \cdots * s_j \neq 0$, are called *nondegenerate* or *subsidiary conditions*. This is an important advantage of Wu's approach to geometry theorem proving. One does not need to worry about ruling out degenerate cases, such as points not being distinct, circles being of zero radius, etc., in geometry problems, such degenerate cases are often tedious to precisely enumerate. An interested reader may consult [10, 42, 44, 46] for further details.

Chou [10, 11] experimented with Wu's method and, based on his extensive implementation experience with Wu's method, Chou developed a way to interpret the subsidiary conditions geometrically. An interested reader may consult [10, 42, 44, 46].

Wu [44] showed that his method is complete for deciding geometry theorems in a generic sense over an algebraically closed field. However, the major stumbling block in his method is the need to factor polynomials over successive extension fields of a base field in obtaining irreducible basic set(s) of hypothesis polynomials. Chou developed an algorithm for factoring polynomials in which indeterminates have at most degree two [10, 11]; he has found his factoring algorithm to be quite adequate and efficient for proving plane geometry theorems. However, factoring arbitrary polynomials over successive extension fields is generally considered a difficult problem (cf. [10, pp. 278–279; 46, p.

---

[1]The initial of a polynomial is its leading coefficient when the polynomial is expressed in recursive form as a polynomial in its leading variable; see [44]. The leading variable of a polynomial is the highest dependent variable (with respect to a chosen ordering) appearing in the polynomial.

3]). As a result, theorems which need factorization of arbitrary polynomials over successive extension fields in Wu's method are likely to be not easily handled.

3. Geometry Problems in Wu's Geometry

Two different problems in Wu's geometry are considered. The first problem is the decision problem of universally quantified formulae, which is, given a universally quantified formula in Wu's geometry, decide whether the formula is a theorem or not. Usually, one is interested in deciding universally quantified formulae having the following structure:

$$\forall x_1, \ldots, x_n \in K,$$

$$[[h_1 = 0 \text{ AND} \ldots \text{AND } h_i = 0 \text{ AND } s_1 \neq 0 \text{ AND} \ldots s_j \neq 0] \Rightarrow [c = 0]].$$

Each of the h, s and c are in $k[x_1, \ldots, x_n]$. As in the case of Wu's method, polynomials $h_1, \ldots, h_i$ specify geometry relations, such as two lines being parallel, a line intersecting a circle, etc.; c expresses a geometry relation being derived, such as two line segments being of equal length.

Polynomials $s_1, \ldots, s_j$ correspond to (i) degenerate cases such as points being distinct, line segments being of nonzero length, etc., (ii) complex zeros of the hypotheses, and (iii) general subcases of the hypotheses on which the conclusion may not hold. Case (iii) often arises in the form of the reducibility condition in Wu's method in which, as stated above, the characteristic set obtained from the hypotheses is not irreducible and, further, the conclusion does not hold on all irreducible components obtained after factorization but only on some components. Wu [46] and Chou and Yang [13] have recently discussed such geometry problems. Wu's method as discussed in [42, 44, 46] did not allow polynomial inequations as hypotheses. However, the structure theorem presented by Wu in [45] allowed polynomial inequations in the hypotheses also.

It is easy to see that the above decision problem is the same as checking whether the zeros in K of c include all the zeros of $\{h_1, \ldots, h_i\}$, on which $s_1, \ldots,$ and s_j do not vanish, i.e., whether

$$\text{Zeros}(\{h_1, \ldots, h_i\}/s_1 \cdots s_j) \subseteq \text{Zeros}(\{c\}).$$

The second problem is more general than the first problem and is suggested by Wu's approach for handling geometry statements; this author is not aware of any other literature in the field of theorem proving in which this problem has appeared in such form. Its formulation is:

> Given a universally quantified formula, decide whether it is a theorem or not, and if it is not a theorem, change the formula "slightly" so that the modified formula is a theorem.

This formulation can be made precise in case of Horn formulae:

> Given a finite set of hypotheses and a conclusion, decide whether
> the conclusion follows from the hypotheses and if not, find an
> additional hypothesis, if any, that is consistent with the original set
> of hypotheses such that the conclusion follows from the original set
> of hypotheses and this additional hypothesis.

Thus, we have:

> Given a set of hypotheses $\{h_1 = 0, \ldots, h_i = 0\}$, and a conclusion
> $c = 0$, if the hypotheses are consistent and $c \not\in k$, and $m \leqslant n$, decide
> whether $c = 0$ holds and if not, find s_i, if any, expressed in
> $\{x_1, \ldots, x_m\}$ such that
> (i) $\forall x_1, \ldots, x_n \in K$, $[[h_1 = 0 \text{ AND} \ldots \text{AND } h_i = 0] \Rightarrow [s_1 = 0 \text{ OR}$
> $\ldots \text{OR } s_j = 0]]$, is not a theorem, and
> (ii) $\forall x_1, \ldots, x_n \in K$, $[[h_1 = 0 \text{ AND} \ldots \text{AND } h_i = 0 \text{ AND } s_1 \neq 0$
> $\text{AND} \ldots \text{AND } s_j \neq 0] \Rightarrow [c = 0]]$, is a theorem .

The condition (i) ensures that the deduced hypothesis is consistent with the
original set of hypotheses in a geometry statement. In the above, $s_1, \ldots, s_j$ can
be combined into a single polynomial $s_1 * \cdots * s_j$ also. It is possible to consider
a more flexible formulation in which the set of hypotheses could also include
some subsidiary conditions expressed as polynomial inequations.

It will of course be nice to put some additional restrictions on the s_i above so
that they have a geometric meaning but it is not clear how that can be done.
One possible way is to identify a subset of variables as parameters, as is done
in Wu's method, and require that the s_i be polynomials in these parameters.
Later in the paper, it is discussed how such information can be used for solving
the above two geometry problems.

The first geometry problem is considered next in Sections 4, 5, and 6. In
Section 7, the second geometry problem is considered. Complete decision
methods are given for both problems.

4. Hilbert's Nullstellensatz and Algebraic Geometry

It is shown how a geometry statement involving Boolean connectives including
negations can be reduced with the help of new variables to a conjunction of
polynomial equations.

Definitions. A polynomial equation $p = 0$, where $p \in k[x_1, \ldots, x_n]$, is *satisfiable* (or *consistent*, $p = 0$ *has a solution*, or equivalently, p has a *zero* in K) if
and only if there exist $v_1, \ldots, v_n$ in K such that $p(x_1 \leftarrow v_1, \ldots, x_n \leftarrow v_n)$, the
result of substituting $v_1, \ldots, v_n$ for $x_1, \ldots, x_n$, respectively, in p, also written

as $p(v_1, \ldots, v_n)$, evaluates to 0. Then, $(v_1, \ldots, v_n)$ is a zero of p in K^n. An equation $p = 0$ is *unsatisfiable* (or *inconsistent*) otherwise. Similarly, a polynomial inequation $p \neq 0$ is *satisfiable* if and only if there exist $v_1, \ldots, v_n$ in K such that $p(v_1, \ldots, v_n)$ does not evaluate to 0; $p \neq 0$ is *unsatisfiable* otherwise. Given a set S of polynomial equations and inequations in $k[x_1, \ldots, x_n]$, S is *satisfiable* (or *consistent* or equivalently, *S has a common solution*) if and only if there exist $v_1, \ldots, v_n$ in K such that for every polynomial equation $p = 0$ in S, $p(v_1, \ldots, v_n)$ evaluates to 0, and for every polynomial inequation $p \neq 0$, $p(v_1, \ldots, v_n)$ does not evaluate to 0. The set S is *unsatisfiable* (or *inconsistent*) otherwise.

For deciding geometry statements, the proof-by-contradiction technique is employed in this paper, much like the refutational approach used in resolution-based theorem proving and equational approaches to theorem proving in predicate calculus [20, 26]. It is checked whether the hypotheses including the subsidiary conditions, and the negation of the conclusion together are unsatisfiable. Note that unlike Wu's formulation, there is no need to classify variables appearing in a geometry statement into independent variables and dependent variables.

In general, the problem is to decide whether a universally quantified formula in language W is a theorem or equivalently, whether an existentially quantified formula in W is unsatisfiable. It is shown below how the satisfiability problem of any arbitrary quantifier-free formula in Wu's geometry is equivalent to the problem of finding whether an equivalent finite set of polynomial equations is satisfiable. This is done by showing how to simulate various Boolean connectives by introducing new variables [37].

Lemma 4.1. *The satisfiability of $p \neq 0$ is equivalent to the satisfiability of $pz - 1 = 0$, where z is a new variable.*

This construction is similar to the one used in the proof of Hilbert's Nullstellensatz [41].

Proof. ($\Rightarrow$) There is an assignment of variables in p at which p does not vanish; then that assignment extended with $z = 1/v$, where v is the value of p for that assignment, is a zero of $pz - 1$.

($\Leftarrow$) There is an assignment of variables at which $pz - 1$ vanishes. Then p cannot vanish at that assignment. $\square$

Similarly, we have:

Lemma 4.2. *The satisfiability of $(p_1 = 0$ OR $p_2 = 0)$ is equivalent to the satisfiability of $p_1 p_2 = 0$, and the satisfiability of $(p_1 = 0$ AND $p_2 = 0)$ is equivalent to the satisfiability of $\{ p_1 = 0, p_2 = 0 \}$.*

If there is more than one conclusion in a geometry statement, they can also be handled easily using the above transformations. From these transformations, it is obvious that the satisfiability of any quantifier-free formula involving Boolean connectives is equivalent to the satisfiability of an equivalent finite set of polynomial equations as constructed above. (For instance, convert an arbitrary quantifier-free formula into a conjunctive normal form, and then use the above transformations to obtain a set of polynomial equations.)

Theorem 4.3. *The satisfiability of any quantifier-free formula in the language W is equivalent to the satisfiability of an equivalent finite set of polynomial equations obtained as discussed above.*

4.1. A decision procedure for universally quantified formulae of W

Using the above theorem, the problem of deciding the satisfiability of a quantifier-free formula in W is equivalent to finding whether there exists a solution in K of a finite set of equations. This is a special case of the problem addressed by Hilbert's Nullstellensatz over K [41, Vol. II, p. 157].

Hilbert's Nullstellensatz. *If f is a polynomial of $k[x_1, \ldots, x_n]$ which vanishes at all the common zeros of $f_1, \ldots, f_i$ in the n-dimensional affine space of K, then*

$$f^q = h_1 f_1 + h_2 f_2 + \cdots + h_i f_i$$

for some natural number q and polynomials $h_1, h_2, \ldots, h_i \in k[x_1, \ldots, x_n]$.

A special case of the above theorem is the following corollary:

Corollary 4.4. *If $f_1, \ldots, f_i$ have no common zero in the n-dimensional affine space of K, then 1 is in the ideal generated by $f_1, \ldots, f_i$, written as $1 \in (f_1, \ldots, f_i)$* [41, Vol. II, p. 157].

Theorem 4.5. *The validity of a universally quantified formula in W is equivalent to (i) finding whether an equivalent set of polynomial equations has no solution, and (ii) whether the ideal generated by the equivalent set of polynomials is the unit ideal.*

As a corollary of the above theorem, we have:

Corollary 4.6. *The validity of a geometry statement of the form*:

$$\forall x_1, \ldots, x_n \in K,$$
$$[[h_1 = 0 \text{ AND} \ldots \text{ AND } h_i = 0 \text{ AND } s_1 \neq 0 \text{ AND} \ldots \text{ AND } s_j \neq 0]$$
$$\Rightarrow [c = 0]]$$

is equivalent to deciding whether the ideal $(h_1, \ldots, h_i, s_1 z_1 - 1, \ldots, s_j z_j - 1,$ *c zz* $- 1)$ *is the unit ideal, where* $h_1, \ldots, h_i, s_1, \ldots, s_j, c \in k[x_1, \ldots, x_n]$, *and* $z_1, \ldots, z_j$, *zz are distinct variables different from* $x_1, \ldots, x_n$.

The problem of checking whether an ideal generated by a finite set of polynomials is the unit ideal or equivalently whether a finite set of polynomials has a common zero in an algebraically closed field is known to be decidable. This gives us a complete decision procedure for universally quantified formulae in Wu's geometry. Section 5 addresses the problem of checking whether a given finite set of polynomials generates the unit ideal.

4.2. Incompleteness of Wu's method and proposed method in Tarski's geometry

As the following example provided by Singer[2] illustrates, both Wu's method and the proposed approach based on Hilbert's Nullstellensatz are incomplete in Tarski's geometry even for the decision problem of universally quantified geometry statements. Both methods consider complex zeros in contrast to Tarski's method which considers real zeros (see also [29]).

$$(\forall x)(\forall y) x^2 + y^2 = 0 \Rightarrow [x = 0 \text{ AND } y = 0].$$

The above formula is a theorem if x and y are assumed to range over the real numbers. However, the above is not a theorem if x and y are assumed to range over K. If Wu's method is used, the hypothesis polynomial is already in triangular form (assuming $x > y$), and the conclusion polynomials cannot be pseudodivided. The above formula is not a theorem by the approach proposed in this paper either, as the polynomial equations

$$x^2 + y^2 = 0,$$

$$(xz_1 - 1)(yz_2 - 1) = 0,$$

do have a complex solution; for example take $y^2 = -c^2$ for any nonzero rational c; then $x = c$ and $y = ci$, $z_1 = 1/c$, $z_2 = d$ is a zero. However, these polynomial equations do not have a real solution.

5. Checking the Existence of a Solution of a System of Equations

There are many methods for deciding whether a finite set of polynomials generates the unit ideal or equivalently whether a finite set of polynomial equations has a solution; this is called the *triviality problem of polynomial*

---

[2]Personal communication, 1984.

ideals in [1]. In this paper, the use of the Gröbner basis method [5–8, 22] is investigated for this problem because of the author's familiarity with the method. Other methods worth investigating are

   (i) Hermann's method [19],
   (ii) a method based on combining elimination, resultants and S-polynomials of the Gröbner basis computation [36],
   (iii) Wu's method based on triangulation [45], and
   (iv) a recent method proposed by Chistov and Grigoryev [9] which extends Lazard's method [33] and has a complexity of subexponential time.

Below some observations regarding Wu's method for this problem are discussed. In the next section, the use of the Gröbner basis method is illustrated.

5.1. Factoring is essential in Wu's method

If Wu's method is to be used for deciding whether an ideal generated by a set of polynomials is the unit ideal, factorization of polynomials over successive extension fields of a base field is essential in the triangulation procedure. The need for factorization in Wu's method is illustrated by the following simple example due to Narendran.[3]

$$p_1 = x^2 + 2x + 1 , \qquad p_2 = (x + 1)y^2 + x .$$

It is easy to see that the ideal generated by p_1 and p_2 is the unit ideal; this can be tested also using the Gröbner basis method. However, the two polynomials are in triangular form under the ordering $x < y$. This shows that it is not just sufficient to bring the polynomials in triangular form to check whether a set of polynomials generates the unit ideal. The polynomial p_1 can be factored, i.e., $p_1 = (x + 1)^2$. So, if the problem is decomposed considering each of the factors (in this case, the two factors are identical), one gets $p_1' = (x + 1)$. The polynomial p_1' simplifies p_2, giving 1 as the triangular form.

6. A Gröbner Basis Method for Geometry Theorem Proving

The concept of a Gröbner basis was introduced by Buchberger [5, 6] for deciding the ideal membership problem for polynomial ideals over a field, and other related problems. Since then, this concept has been extensively studied and extended to other algebraic structures; see [8, 22] for details. In a Gröbner basis algorithm, a polynomial is viewed as a rule for simplifying other polynomials. Informally, a Gröbner basis of an ideal is defined as a special basis such that every polynomial in the ideal simplifies to 0 using this basis. In particular,

---

[3] Personal communication, 1985.

Theorem (Buchberger). *A Gröbner basis of the unit ideal must include* 1.

So, the decision problem for universally quantified formulae in Wu's geometry can be done using the Gröbner basis computation. We now give a method used for deciding geometry theorems of the following kind:

$$\forall x_1, \ldots, x_n \in K,$$
$$[[h_1 = 0 \text{ AND} \ldots \text{AND } h_i = 0 \text{ AND } s_1 \neq 0 \text{ AND} \ldots \text{AND } s_j \neq 0]$$
$$\Rightarrow [c = 0]].$$

Method I. Given hypotheses $h_1, \ldots, h_i$, degenerate cases $s_1, \ldots, s_j$, and a conclusion c, each a polynomial in $Q[x_1, \ldots, x_n]$:

$$1 \in \text{Gröbner}(\{h_1, \ldots, h_i, s_1 z_1 - 1, \ldots, s_j z_j - 1, c\, zz - 1\},$$
$$Q[x_1, \ldots, x_n, z_1, \ldots, z_j, zz])?$$

     yes: return THEOREM
     no: return FALSIFIABLE

end.

The function Gröbner above takes a finite set of polynomials and a polynomial ring from which these polynomials are taken as arguments, and computes a Gröbner basis of the ideal specified by the input basis. The reader may wish to consult [7, 8, 22] for an algorithm for computing a Gröbner basis as well as for testing membership of a polynomial in an ideal using its Gröbner basis.

The above method is illustrated on three simple examples which can be done by hand. The first example is due to Mundy; the second example is taken from [10]; the third example is from [11].

Example 6.1. Given three lines such that AB is perpendicular to AC and CD is perpendicular to AC, prove that AB is parallel to CD; see Fig. 1. Set

$$A = (0,0), \qquad B = (x_1, y_1), \qquad C = (x_3, y_3), \qquad D = (x_2, y_2).$$

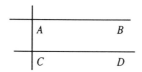

Fig. 1. A simple example.

The hypothesis polynomial equations are:

$$y_1 y_3 = -x_1 x_3 \qquad\qquad ;AB \text{ is perpendicular to } AC, \qquad (1)$$

$$y_3(y_2 - y_3) = -(x_2 - x_3)x_3 \quad ;CD \text{ is perpendicular to } AC. \qquad (2)$$

The subsidiary condition is that points A and C be distinct, i.e.,

$$x_3 \neq 0 \text{ OR } y_3 \neq 0.$$

By introducing new variables z_1 and z_2, the above transforms to

$$(x_3 z_1 - 1)(y_3 z_2 - 1) = 0. \qquad (3)$$

Polynomial equation for the conclusion is

$$y_1(x_2 - x_3) = x_1(y_2 - y_3) \quad ;AB \text{ and } CD \text{ are parallel}. \qquad (4)$$

And, its negation translates, after introducing a new variable zz_1, to

$$(y_1(x_2 - x_3) - x_1(y_2 - y_3))zz_1 - 1 = 0. \qquad (5)$$

The Gröbner basis of the set $\{1, 2, 3, 5\}$ of polynomials includes 1, which implies that under the condition that A and C are distinct points, the theorem holds. Some of the steps in the derivation of the Gröbner basis are given below; for details, the reader can consult [8]. The ordering on variables is

$$x_3 < y_3 < x_1 < y_1 < x_2 < y_2 < z_1 < z_2 < zz_1 ;$$

the *head-monomial* of a polynomial is picked using the *degree ordering* (comparing terms by degree first and terms of equal degree by lexicographic (dictionary) ordering). The rules corresponding to the above polynomials are:

$$y_3 y_1 \rightarrow -x_3 x_1, \qquad (1)$$

$$y_3 y_2 \rightarrow -x_3 x_2 + x_3 x_3 + y_3 y_3, \qquad (2)$$

$$x_3 y_3 z_1 z_2 \rightarrow y_3 z_2 + x_3 z_1 - 1, \qquad (3)$$

$$x_1 y_2 zz_1 \rightarrow y_1 x_2 zz_1 - x_3 y_1 zz_1 + y_3 x_1 zz_1 - 1. \qquad (4)$$

The *overlapping* of rules (2) and (4) gives a *superposition* $x_1 y_2 y_3 zz_1$ obtained by the least common multiple of the headterms on which both the rules can be applied as shown in Fig. 2; this gives a *critical pair* possibly resulting in a new rule.

$$x_1 \, y_2 \, y_3 \, zz_1$$

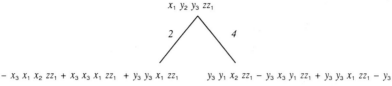

$$- x_3 \, x_1 \, x_2 \, zz_1 + x_3 \, x_3 \, x_1 \, zz_1 \; + y_3 \, y_3 \, x_1 \, zz_1 \qquad y_3 \, y_1 \, x_2 \, zz_1 - y_3 \, x_3 \, y_1 \, zz_1 + y_3 \, y_3 \, x_1 \, zz_1 - y_3$$

Fig. 2. Superposition and critical pairs.

After these polynomials are further simplified and their difference is taken, the polynomial y_3 is generated. The rule corresponding to this polynomial is:

$$y_3 \to 0 \,, \tag{5}$$

which simplifies all the above rules to:

$$x_3 x_1 \to 0 \,, \tag{1'}$$

$$x_3 x_2 \to x_3 x_3 \,, \tag{2'}$$

$$x_3 z_1 \to 1 \,, \tag{3'}$$

$$x_1 y_2 zz_1 \to y_1 x_2 zz_1 - x_3 y_1 zz_1 - 1 \,. \tag{4'}$$

Polynomial $(1')$ now corresponds to x_3 being 0 or x_1 being 0. Since polynomial $(3')$ corresponds to x_3 being not 0, rules $(1')$ and $(3')$ superpose to generate a new rule, $x_1 \to 0$. This new rule simplifies rule $(4')$ to give

$$y_1 x_2 zz_1 \to x_3 y_1 zz_1 + 1 \,. \tag{4''}$$

This rule with rule $(2')$ has a superposition $x_3 y_1 x_2 zz_1$, on which $(2')$ and $(4'')$ are applied and the resulting polynomials are further simplified. The difference of the resulting polynomials gives a new rule, $x_3 \to 0$, which with the rule $(3')$ gives a rule $1 \to 0$, a contradiction. Hence the proof.

Example 6.2. Let $ABCD$ be a parallelogram as shown in Fig. 3; prove that $|AO| = |OC|$.

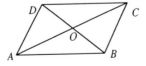

Fig. 3. Parallelogram example.

The coordinate system chosen is

$$A = (0,0), \qquad B = (u_1, 0),$$
$$C = (u_2, u_3), \qquad D = (x_2, x_1), \qquad O = (x_3, x_4).$$

Polynomial equations of the hypotheses are:

$$u_3 - x_1 = 0 \qquad\qquad ; AB \text{ is parallel to } CD, \qquad (6)$$

$$x_1(u_2 - u_1) - x_2 u_3 = 0 \qquad ; BC \text{ is parallel to } AD, \qquad (7)$$

$$x_4(x_2 - u_1) - x_1(x_3 - u_1) = 0 \quad ; B, O, \text{ and } D \text{ are collinear}, \qquad (8)$$

$$x_3 u_3 - x_4 u_2 = 0 \qquad\qquad ; A, O, \text{ and } C \text{ are collinear}. \qquad (9)$$

The subsidiary conditions are: $u_1 \neq 0$ AND $u_3 \neq 0$, which means that A, B, and C are distinct points which are not collinear. This condition translates to:

$$u_1 u_3 z_1 - 1 = 0. \qquad (10)$$

The polynomial equation for the conclusion is:

$$(x_3^2 + x_4^2) = (u_2 - x_3)^2 + (u_3 - x_4)^2.$$

The polynomial equation corresponding to its negation is:

$$z z_1 ((x_3^2 + x_4^2) - ((u^2 - x_3)^2 + (u_3 - x_4)^2)) - 1 = 0. \qquad (11)$$

The Gröbner basis of the above polynomials is 1, implying that the above statement is a theorem.

Example 6.3 (Theorem of orthocenter taken from [11]). Let ABC be a triangle, H be the point of intersection of altitudes BE and CF. Show that AH is perpendicular to BC. Let

$$A = (0,0), \qquad B = (u_1, 0),$$
$$C = (x_1, x_2), \qquad E = (u_2, u_3), \qquad H = (x_1, x_3).$$

Polynomial equations for the hypotheses are:

$$x_2 u_3 + (u_2 - u_1) x_1 = 0 \qquad ; BE \text{ is perpendicular to } AC, \qquad (12)$$

$$-u_2 x_2 + u_3 x_1 = 0 \qquad\qquad ; A, E, \text{ and } C \text{ are collinear}, \qquad (13)$$

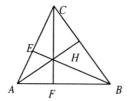

Fig. 4. Theorem of orthocenter.

$$(u_1 - u_2)x_3 + u_3x_1 - u_1u_3 = 0 \quad ; B, E, \text{ and } H \text{ are collinear}. \quad (14)$$

The subsidiary condition is $(x_2 \neq 0 \text{ AND } u_1 \neq 0)$ OR $u_3 \neq 0$, which translates to

$$(z_1x_2u_1 - 1)(z_2u_3 - 1) = 0. \quad (15)$$

Polynomial equation for the conclusion is

$$x_2x_3 = -x_1(x_1 - u_1),$$

stating that AH is perpendicular to BC. The negation of the conclusion is:

$$zz_1(x_2x_3 + x_1(x_1 - u_1)) - 1 = 0. \quad (16)$$

The Gröbner basis of these polynomials is 1 thus proving the original theorem.

In the above examples, subsidiary conditions are in the form of points being distinct or points being not collinear. Subsidiary conditions are also used to rule out certain general subcases of the hypotheses for which the conclusion does not hold, such as in the case of the secants theorem discussed in [32, 46] and [13, Example 3.3.4] discussed by Chou and Yang.

Method I above was used to prove a number of geometry theorems including Simson's theorem, Pascal's theorem, Pappus' theorem, Desargues' theorem, the nine-point circle theorem, the butterfly theorem, and Gauss' theorem. An implementation of the Gröbner basis algorithm for the polynomial rings over the integers and rationals developed by Rick Harris at General Electric Corporate Research and Development, was used for this purpose. This implementation incorporates optimizations for not considering certain critical pairs proposed by Buchberger [7] and Kapur et al. [24], and it supports lexicographic, degree, as well as mixed (see definition later) orderings on terms. The implementation runs on a Symbolics 3640 LISP machine. Table 1 gives computation times on some representative geometry theorems taken from [10–12, 31, 32]. The Gröbner basis computation for these theorems was performed using the degree ordering as that was found to be generally much

Table 1
Time needed to prove theorems

Theorem	Time (seconds)
Centroid	0.7
Ceva	20.9
Secants	9.6
Equidistant	0.2
Simson	13.7
Pappus	3.0
Square	0.3
Tangent circle	1.5
Peripheral angle	6.5
Altitudes	0.4
Desargues	1.2
Nine-point circle	12
Isosceles midpoint	6.4
Pentagon	0.05
Tetrahedron	5.2
Pappus' dual	6.9
Quadrangle in $\mathbb{R}^2$	0.45
Quadrangle in $\mathbb{R}^3$	0.7
Gauss	0.2
Pascal	640
Brahmagupta	1.1
Wang	19.6
Butterfly	25.1

faster than the pure lexicographic ordering; see [8] for similar observations about the performance of the Gröbner basis algorithm using degree and lexicographic orderings on terms. As one can see from the table, most of the theorems can be automatically proved in less than a minute of computer time. These include fairly nontrivial theorems such as the butterfly theorem, the nine-point circle theorem, Simson's theorem, Ceva's theorem and Wang's theorem, some of which humans find difficult to prove. To our knowledge, such theorems have not been proven using an automatic or semi-automatic theorem prover based on the synthetic approach initiated by Gelernter [15]. This shows the power of the algebraic methods. One serious drawback of algebraic methods though is that the proofs obtained cannot be translated back into a form that uses high-level geometry concepts so that they are understandable by humans.

6.1. Related work on the use of the Gröbner bases for geometry theorem proving

Kutzler and Stifter [31, 32] have independently investigated the use of the Gröbner basis method for geometry theorem proving. Their method assumes that in a geometry statement, a subset of variables is identified to be parameters. This method is based on checking whether the conclusion polynomial is in the ideal generated by the hypothesis polynomials; they compute the Gröbner basis of polynomials over the field $Q(u_1, \ldots, u_d)$, where $u_1, \ldots, u_d$ are parameters in Wu's sense. Polynomials in $u_1, \ldots, u_d$, that are needed to be nonzero in checking whether the conclusion polynomial is in the ideal of hypothesis polynomials are produced as the subsidiary conditions by their method.

Chou and Schelter [12] have also been using a Gröbner basis of polynomial ideals over $Q(u_1, \ldots, u_d)$ for checking whether the conclusion polynomial is in the ideal of hypothesis polynomials under certain conditions. Further, instead of first generating a Gröbner basis and then checking whether the conclusion polynomial belongs to the ideal generated by the hypothesis polynomials, they make the check every time new polynomials are added to the basis. Their method also produces subsidiary conditions which are polynomials required to be nonzero in generating a Gröbner basis and simplifying the conclusion polynomial. They compared the Gröbner basis approach with Wu's method on 80 examples and found Wu's method to be faster than the Gröbner basis approach.

The approaches pursued by Kutzler and Stifter as well as Chou and Schelter are based on checking whether a conclusion polynomial is in the ideal generated by the hypothesis polynomials under subsidiary conditions. This is a first approximation to checking whether the conclusion polynomial is in the radical of the ideal generated by the hypothesis polynomials; however, as shown by their results, even this first approximation works on many examples. These approaches are incomplete. For completeness, if the conclusion polynomial is not in the ideal generated by the hypothesis polynomials, one needs to successively examine powers of the conclusion polynomial for membership. Chou and Schelter have also reported results based on an approach very similar to ours for geometry statements in which a subset of variables are identified as parameters, but they have not investigated it in detail.

Since the check for triviality of an ideal is a special case of the check for the ideal membership problem, the theoretical complexity of the ideal membership problem is obviously at least as much as the theoretical complexity of the triviality problem. In fact, we conjecture that the membership problem for the radical of a polynomial ideal is easier than the polynomial ideal membership problem. Further, if a polynomial p simplifies to 0 using a basis, then using the same basis and using at most one more reduction, the polynomial $pz - 1$, where z does not appear in p, reduces to -1. Thus, a suitable implementation of the triviality check should be at least as fast as the membership check for ideals. This along with the fact that the method based on Hilbert's Nullstellensatz is complete for Wu's geometry are our reasons for investigating the proposed approach.

7. Deducing Subsidiary Conditions

In this section, the second geometry problem stated in Section 3 is discussed. Recall that the second geometry problem is:

> Given a Horn formula, i.e., a finite set of hypotheses implying a conclusion, decide whether it is a theorem or not. If it is not a theorem, then find an additional hypothesis, if any, that is consistent with the original set of hypotheses such that with the additional hypothesis, the Horn formula is a theorem.

This problem is more general than the geometry problem considered by Wu and Chou as hypotheses could include polynomial inequations expressing subsidiary conditions to rule out some degenerate cases or general subcases. We show below how this problem can be solved using the Gröbner basis method. Although the proposed approach is inefficient as compared to Wu's approach, subsidiary conditions found using it are often simpler and weaker than the ones reported using Wu's method [10] or those reported in [12] and [31, 32] using the Gröbner basis approach. Before discussing the technical details, the method is illustrated using examples.

Example 6.1 Revisited. For instance, for Example 6.1 (Fig. 1), if a Gröbner basis of the hypothesis polynomials (1) and (2), and the polynomial (5), corresponding to the negation of the conclusion is computed without the subsidiary condition that points A and C be distinct, the result does not include 1. (In fact, the statement of Example 6.1 translates to polynomial equations (1), (2), and (5), as it does not mention that points A and C be distinct.) Instead, there appear x_3, y_3, and other polynomials in the Gröbner basis. This implies that the hypothesis polynomials indeed have common zeros which are not zeros of the conclusion polynomial; these zeros are $x_3 = 0$, $y_3 = 0$, and suitably chosen values of the remaining variables. Further, these zeros are real zeros, suggesting that the statement is a theorem only when such zeros are ruled out, i.e., when $x_3 \neq 0$ OR $y_3 \neq 0$, which is the condition that A and C are distinct points thus making AC indeed determine a line.

In contrast, if Wu's method is used for this example, we obtain stronger conditions. If we partition the variables such that y_1 and y_2 are dependent variables, then the hypothesis polynomials are already in triangular form. The conclusion polynomial can be pseudodivided to 0 under the condition that $y_3 \neq 0$. This condition is sufficient as imposing this condition would make points A and C distinct. However it is too strong. If instead, we choose x_1 and x_2 as dependent variables, then again, the hypothesis polynomials are still in triangular form with respect to this choice of variables. The conclusion polynomial can be pseudodivided to 0 under the condition that $x_3 \neq 0$, which is still too strong.

If any of the approaches in [12, 31, 32] based on computing a Gröbner basis of polynomial ideals over $Q(u_1, \ldots, u_d)$ is used, the conditions obtained are too strong then also. For instance, the two hypothesis polynomials of Example 6.1 above constitute a Gröbner basis over $Q(x_3, y_3, x_1, x_2)$. The conclusion polynomial (4) simplifies to 0 under the condition that $y_3 \neq 0$, which is stronger than the condition that points A and C be distinct. Similarly, the two hypothesis polynomials of Example 6.1 constitute a Gröbner basis over $Q(x_3, y_3, y_1, y_2)$; the conclusion (4) simplifies to 0 with the condition that $x_3 \neq 0$.

Example 6.2 Revisited. Similarly, for Example 6.2 (Fig. 3), if a Gröbner basis is computed of the hypothesis polynomials (6), (7), (8) and (9), along with the polynomial (11) corresponding to the negation of the conclusion, and without the subsidiary condition that A, B, and C are distinct points which are not collinear, the result again does not include 1. Instead, the result has among other polynomials, $u_1 u_3$. From this, we get the subsidiary condition that $u_1 u_3 \neq 0$, which implies that A and B are distinct points and C is not collinear with AB. However, if the hypotheses also include the subsidiary condition that A, B, and C are distinct points, computing the Gröbner basis still does not result in 1 in the basis; instead, the basis includes u_3, which implies that the theorem still does not hold in case $u_3 = 0$, i.e., when A, B, and C are distinct but collinear points.

Example 6.3 Revisited. For Example 6.3 (Fig. 4) also, the Gröbner basis of the hypothesis polynomials (12), (13) and (14), along with the polynomial (16) corresponding to the negation of the conclusion does not include 1; instead it has among other polynomials, $x_2 u_1$ and u_3 in the basis. This gives us the subsidiary condition that $(x_2 \neq 0$ AND $u_1 \neq 0)$ OR $u_3 \neq 0$, which states that A, B, C are distinct and are not collinear.

For Pappus' theorem [10, Example 3], when a Gröbner basis is computed of the hypothesis polynomials along with the polynomial corresponding to the negation of the conclusion without the subsidiary conditions, the result includes

$$x_1 x_4, \quad x_2 x_5, \quad x_3 x_6, \quad x_1 x_2 x_3, \quad x_4 x_5 x_6$$

as polynomials, among others. The subsidiary condition under which the theorem holds is a disjunction of the following conditions: (i) $x_1 x_4 \neq 0$, i.e., points A_1 and B_1 are distinct, (ii) $x_2 x_5 \neq 0$, i.e., A_2 and B_2 are distinct, (iii) $x_3 x_6 \neq 0$, i.e., A_3 and B_3 are distinct, (iv) $x_1 x_2 x_3 \neq 0$, i.e., neither of A_1, A_2, and A_3 is the point of intersection of lines $A_1 A_2 A_3$ and $B_1 B_2 B_3$, (v) $x_4 x_5 x_6 \neq 0$, i.e., neither of B_1, B_2 and B_3 is the point of intersection of lines $A_1 A_2 A_3$ and $B_1 B_2 B_3$. For the square example, [10, Example 4], the condition found by our method is simply that the square have a nonzero side. For the triangle altitudes theorem [10, Example 5], the subsidiary condition found using the Gröbner basis method is $u_3 \neq 0$.

Let us now precisely state the second problem as discussed in Section 3:

> Given a consistent set of hypotheses $\{h_1 = 0, \ldots, h_i = 0\}$, a conclusion $c = 0$ such that $c \not\in k$, and $m \leq n$, find s_i, if any, expressed in $\{x_1, \ldots, x_m\}$ such that
> (i) $\forall x_1, \ldots, x_n \in K$, $[[h_1 = 0 \text{ AND} \ldots \text{AND } h_i = 0] \Rightarrow [s_1 = 0 \text{ OR} \ldots \text{OR } s_j = 0]]$, is not a theorem, and
> (ii) $\forall x_1, \ldots, x_n \in K$, $[[h_1 = 0 \text{ AND} \ldots \text{AND } h_i = 0 \text{ AND } s_1 \neq 0 \text{ AND} \ldots \text{AND } s_j \neq 0] \Rightarrow [c = 0]]$ is a theorem.

It should be noted that there is no requirement above that the s_i should have a geometric meaning. It is not clear how such a requirement can be algebraically stated. Chou and Yang [13] have argued that if independent variables among the variables of a geometry problem are identified as a part of the problem statement and geometry statements are proved in a generic sense, then it is possible to impose a geometric requirement on the s_i. Independent variables can be viewed as degrees of freedom in a geometry problem. In our opinion, classification of variables into independent and dependent variables is also purely syntactic and may not necessarily have any geometric meaning. Further, there is no guarantee that the s_i expressed as polynomials in independent variables will necessarily have any geometric meaning. At best, one can hope for an algebraic meaning. The above formulation indeed has a precise algebraic meaning.

If for a given geometry problem, a Gröbner basis of the ideal $(h_1, \ldots, h_i, c\,zz - 1)$ does not include 1, which implies that $c \not\in$ Radical$(h_1, \ldots, h_i)$, the radical ideal of $(h_1, \ldots, h_i)$, then any polynomial $p \in k[x_1, \ldots, x_m]$ from the Gröbner basis such that p is not a consequence of the hypotheses (i.e., $p \not\in$ Radical$(h_1, \ldots, h_i)$), is a candidate to be used for stating an additional hypothesis. One can examine the Gröbner basis for this purpose and pick a desired "simplest" such candidate (in fact, a set of polynomials).

The following theorem serves as the basis of this approach (Method II below):

Theorem 7.1. Let $\{h_1 = 0, \ldots, h_i = 0\}$ be a consistent set of hypotheses, and $c = 0$, where $c \not\in k$, be a conclusion, such that there is a polynomial $p \in k[x_1, \ldots, x_m]$, $m \leq n$, and $p \not\in$ Radical$(h_1, \ldots, h_i)$ but $pc \in$ Radical$(h_1, \ldots, h_i)$. Let GB be a Gröbner basis of $(h_1, \ldots, h_i, c\,zz - 1)$ under a lexicographic ordering on terms induced by the ordering $x_1 < \cdots <$

$x_n < zz$, where zz is an indeterminate different from $x_1, \ldots, x_n$. Then there exists a polynomial $q \in GB$ such that

(i) $q \in k[x_1, \ldots, x_m]$ and $q \not\in \text{Radical}(h_1, \ldots, h_i)$,
(ii) $s_1, \ldots, s_j$ are the irreducible factors of q, and
(iii) $qc \in \text{Radical}(h_1, \ldots, h_i)$, thus implying

$$\forall x_1, \ldots, x_n \in K,$$
$$[[h_1 = 0 \text{ AND} \ldots \text{ AND } h_i = 0 \text{ AND } s_1 \neq 0 \text{ AND} \ldots \text{ AND } s_j \neq 0]$$
$$\Rightarrow [c = 0]].$$

Proof. Let $J = (h_1, \ldots, h_i, c\,zz - 1)$ and $J' = J \cap k[x_1, \ldots, x_n]$. Since there is a polynomial $p \in k[x_1, \ldots, x_m]$ such that $pc \in \text{Radical}(h_1, \ldots, h_i)$, for some m, there is an r such that $(pc)^r \in (h_1, \ldots, h_i)$. It is easy to see that $p^r \in J'$ since

$$p^r = (p\,c\,zz)^r - p^r((c\,zz)^r - 1).$$

So, p^r reduces to 0 using polynomials in $x_1, \ldots, x_m$ from GB. There is at least one polynomial among them which is not in $\text{Radical}(h_1, \ldots, h_i)$, as otherwise $p \in \text{Radical}(h_1, \ldots, h_i)$ leading to a contradiction. Call that q. The rest of the proof follows. $\square$

The following method is a complete decision method for deriving subsidiary conditions. It is often better to identify independent variables and pick polynomials from GB expressed in independent variables only to state subsidiary conditions. Examples reported in Tables 2 and 3 were computed in this manner.

Method II. Given hypotheses $h_1, \ldots, h_i$, and a conclusion c, each a polynomial in $Q[x_1, \ldots, x_n]$, and $m \leq n$:

$\{g_1, \ldots, g_r\} := \text{Gröbner}(\{h_1, \ldots, h_i, c\,zz - 1\}, Q[x_1, \ldots, x_n, zz]);$
    if $g_1 = 1$
        then return THEOREM: NO CONDITION NEEDED
        else repeat from $v = 1$ to r
            if $g_v \in Q[x_1, \ldots, x_m]$ and $g_v \not\in \{h_1, \ldots, h_i\}$
            then
                if $1 \not\in \text{Gröbner}(\{h_1, \ldots, h_i, g_v zz - 1\}, Q[x_1, \ldots, x_n, zz])$
                    then return THEOREM UNDER CONDITION $g_v \neq 0$;
        end repeat;
        return THEOREM NOT CONFIRMED
    end;

The function Gröbner above is assumed to return polynomials in a Gröbner basis in ascending order using the lexicographic ordering on terms. Notice that in the above method, the function Gröbner may be called several times. For geometry statements in which additional subsidiary conditions are required, two calls to the function Gröbner are often sufficient—the first for computing the Gröbner basis of $(h_1, \ldots, h_i, c\, zz - 1)$ and the second to ensure that the subsidiary condition deduced is consistent with the hypotheses. Picking an appropriate polynomial expressing the subsidiary conditions from the Gröbner basis of $(h_1, \ldots, h_i, c\, zz - 1)$ such that it has a geometric meaning is found to be quite a challenge. Method II returns THEOREM NOT CONFIRMED only in case the hypotheses and conclusion do not satisfy the conditions of Theorem 7.1. Because of a lack of any geometric justification of this method, a potential disadvantage is that this method may produce an additional hypothesis even if the conclusion c cannot be derived from the original set of hypotheses in the geometric sense.

Table 2 gives timings for deducing subsidiary conditions for some representa-

Table 2
Statistics for deducing subsidiary conditions (lexicographic ordering)

Problem	Time (seconds)		Conditions
	First call	Second call	
Centroid	1.2	0.4	Three corners of the triangle are not collinear
Ceva	312	5.3	Three corners of the triangle are not collinear
Secants	~3200	24.6	Well-defined secants
Equidistant secants	0.25		No condition needed
Simson	~13100	1.2	Well-defined triangle, stated as sides being of nonzero length
Pappus	138	6.4	Two lines do not intersect at any of the given points
Square	0.9	0.2	Square is of nonzero size
Tangent circle	7.1	10.3	Secant is not a tangent
Peripheral angle	6.6		No condition needed
Altitudes	8.2	4	Two corners of the triangle are distinct
Desargues	13.4	3.4	Two lines do not coincide
Nine-point circle	309	7.1	Triangle is not right-angled and has a side of nonzero length
Isosceles midpoint	738	7.0	Well-defined triangle with D distinct from A (cf. [12, Example 8])
Pentagon	0.08		No condition needed
Tetrahedron	6.8	2.2	Tetrahedron is well-defined
Dual of Pappus	~21100	1750	Three points are distinct
Quadrangle in $\mathbb{R}^2$	0.35		No condition needed
Quadrangle in $\mathbb{R}^3$	0.15		No condition needed
Gauss	0.17		No condition needed
Pascal	?		
Brahmagupta	446	41.3	Circle of nonzero radius and 4 points are distinct
Wang	2456	990	$(u_5 - u_6)(u_5(u_2 - u_1) - u_3(u_4 - u_1)) \neq 0$ (cf. [12, Example 10])
Butterfly	?		

tive geometry problems along with an English description of the subsidiary condition. The first column gives timings for the first call to the function Gröbner; the second column gives timings for the second call to Gröbner for checking that the deduced subsidiary condition is indeed consistent with the hypotheses.

From empirical observations, it is known that computing a Gröbner basis is often much more time consuming using a lexicographic ordering on terms than the degree ordering. The following refinement of Theorem 7.1 above is perhaps the best we can hope for in which degree and lexicographic orderings are combined; we will call such an ordering on terms a *mixed* ordering.

Given a total ordering on variables, say $x_1 < \cdots < x_n$, another total term ordering mixing the degree ordering and lexicographic ordering with x_i as the *separating variable* is defined as:

$$t_1 = x_1^{d_1} \cdots x_n^{d_n} <_m t_2 = x_1^{g_1} \cdots x_n^{g_n}$$

if and only if

$$x_i^{d_i} \cdots x_n^{d_n} <_d x_i^{g_i} \cdots x_n^{g_n}$$

$$\text{OR } (x_i^{d_i} \cdots x_n^{d_n} = x_i^{g_i} \cdots x_n^{g_n} \text{ AND } x_1^{d_1} \cdots x_{i-1}^{d_{i-1}} <_d x_1^{g_1} \cdots x_{i-1}^{g_{i-1}}),$$

where $<_d$ is the degree ordering on terms.

Note that if the separating variable is chosen to be x_1, then the mixed ordering is the same as the degree ordering. The above total ordering on terms induces a total ordering on polynomials in a natural way as is done in [8]. Trinks [40] considered such a class of orderings also. The following theorem is a generalization of Theorem 7.1.

Theorem 7.2. *Let* $\{h_1 = 0, \ldots, h_i = 0\}$ *be a consistent set of hypotheses, and* $c = 0$, *where* $c \not\in k$, *be a conclusion, such that there is a polynomial* $p \in k[x_1, \ldots, x_m]$, $m \leq n$, *and* $p \not\in \text{Radical}(h_1, \ldots, h_i)$ *but* $pc \in \text{Radical}(h_1, \ldots, h_i)$. *Let GB be a Gröbner basis of* $(h_1, \ldots, h_i, c\, zz - 1)$ *under a mixed ordering on terms induced by the ordering* $x_1 < \cdots < x_{n+1} = zz$, *where* x_{m+1} *is the separating variable and zz is an indeterminate different from* $x_1, \ldots, x_n$. *Then there exists a polynomial* $q \in GB$ *such that*

(i) $q \in k[x_1, \ldots, x_m]$ *and* $q \not\in \text{Radical}(h_1, \ldots, h_i)$,
(ii) $s_1, \ldots, s_j$ *are the irreducible factors of* q, *and*
(iii) $qc \in \text{Radical}(h_1, \ldots, h_i)$, *thus implying*

$$\forall x_1, \ldots, x_n \in K,$$

$$[[h_1 = 0 \text{ AND} \ldots \text{ AND } h_i = 0 \text{ AND } s_1 \neq 0 \text{ AND} \ldots \text{ AND } s_j \neq 0]$$
$$\Rightarrow [c = 0]].$$

Table 3
Statistics for deducing subsidiary conditions

	Time (seconds)		
Problem	Mixed ordering	Degree ordering	Checking consistency
Centroid	1.5	1.1	0.3
Ceva	172	150	10.3
Secants	289	215	96
Equidistant secants	0.3	0.2	
Simson	723	492	336
Pappus	28.5	11.3	21
Square	1.2	0.75	0.2
Tangent circle	6.6	3.4	5.1
Peripheral angle	9.3	6.8	
Altitudes	2.6	2.0	2.7
Desargues	6.6	4.7	3.2
None-point circle	225	164	48.6
Isosceles midpoint	192	124	107.6
Pentagon	0.08	0.05	
Tetrahedron	9.3	5.6	2.2
Dual of Pappus	516	106	1169
Quadrangle in $\mathbb{R}^2$	0.15	0.15	
Quadrangle in $\mathbb{R}^3$	0.2	0.2	
Gauss	0.2	0.17	
Pascal	?	?	
Brahmagupta	68	55	29.7
Wang	868	628	320
Butterfly	?	?	

The proof of Theorem 7.2 is the same as that of Theorem 7.1. Table 3 gives the timings using the mixed ordering for computing Gröbner bases with zz, the variable introduced to obtain a polynomial equivalent to the negation of the conclusion, as the separating variable. For the second call computation to check whether the deduced subsidiary condition is indeed consistent with the hypotheses, timings in Table 3 are given when the computation was done using the degree ordering. For each example, the condition deduced in this case is the same as the one reported in Table 2; so they are omitted from this table. Timings using the degree ordering for computing the Gröbner bases are also included in Table 3 for comparison. In the case of the degree ordering, we have not been able to prove a result analogous to Theorems 7.1 and 7.2; we conjecture that in this case, the result does not hold. However, for all examples discussed above, a suitable polynomial in *GB* computed using the degree ordering to state subsidiary conditions was found.

7.1. Picking subsidiary conditions

If a single polynomial is selected from a Gröbner basis for stating a subsidiary condition, then a subsidiary condition is a conjunction of polynomial inequations, each corresponding to an irreducible factor of the polynomial g_v above. Method II can be easily modified to select in general a set of polynomials from a Gröbner basis instead of a single polynomial. In that case, a subsidiary condition is a disjunction of conjunctions of polynomial inequations. A subsidiary condition, in general, rules out three types of cases: (i) geometrically degenerate cases, (ii) common complex zeros of the hypotheses which are not zeros of the conclusion, and (iii) general cases for which the conclusion does not follow from the hypotheses. Developing a good method to distinguish between these three types is an interesting open research problem.

It was observed in practice that computing a Gröbner basis without a subsidiary condition can be quite time consuming on big examples. For all examples, deducing subsidiary conditions took more time than proving a geometry theorem when subsidiary conditions were stated as part of the input. For examples such as the butterfly theorem and Pascal's theorem, their Gröbner bases could not be computed without subsidiary conditions in a reasonable amount of time. In many cases, it is possible to derive subsidiary conditions without having to fully compute a Gröbner basis. It is possible to preempt the computation after it has "sufficiently progressed" (meaning that all the hypothesis polynomials have interacted with the negation of the conclusion), and examine the basis to pick polynomials for deriving subsidiary conditions.

8. Using Information That Some Variables Are Parameters

Wu and Chou have argued that an integral part of a geometry statement is the specification of general points in a geometry statement. As Chou has shown, this information can be used to identify parameters (independent variables) among the variables appearing in a geometry statement. As discussed in Section 6.1, following this approach, Chou and Schelter as well as Kutzler and Stifter [31, 32] have investigated the use of Gröbner bases for geometry theorem proving by computing Gröbner bases of polynomial ideals over rational functions expressed in terms of these parameters. However, their approaches crucially depend upon precisely identifying these parameters among variables. Kutzler and Stifter have given a way of testing whether a subset of variables is correctly identified as parameters in a geometry statement using the concept of independence of variables.

Below, we outline how our approach can be used to exploit such information about a subset of variables to decide the two geometry problems discussed in Sections 6 and 7. It is not necessary to assume that all the parameters are identified in a geometry statement.

Let $u_1, \ldots, u_d$ be a subset of parameters among the variables $x_1, \ldots, x_n$ appearing in a geometry statement; let $\{y_1, \ldots, y_{n-d}\}$ be the remaining set of variables. Unlike in Section 3, where each variable ranges over K, in this case, every variable in $\{y_1, \ldots, y_{n-d}\}$ ranges over $K(u_1, \ldots, u_d)$.

For the decision problem of universally quantified formulae, compute a Gröbner basis of the hypotheses polynomials with the negation of the conclusion polynomial and see whether 1 is generated during the computation. The Gröbner basis algorithm now computes over $k(u_1, \ldots, u_d) [y_1, \ldots, y_{n-d}]$. If yes, then the conclusion follows from the hypotheses under the condition obtained by multiplying out the coefficients of all the polynomials that were used to reduce the polynomial corresponding to the negation of a conclusion. If 1 is not generated during the computation, then the conclusion does not follow from the hypotheses under the conditions which can be expressed as negations of polynomials in $k[u_1, \ldots, u_d]$. Either the choice of parameters is incomplete or wrong, or the conclusion does not follow from the hypotheses.

For the second geometry problem, the method is the same as discussed in Section 7 except that the Gröbner basis algorithm now computes over $k(u_1, \ldots, u_d)[y_1, \ldots, y_{n-d}]$. If 1 is not in a Gröbner basis, pick a polynomial(s) in $u_1, \ldots, u_d, y_1, \ldots, y_i$ from the Gröbner basis that can be used to express an additional hypothesis. Another alternative is to modify the set of parameters.

9. Empirical Observations

We list below some observations that we made while trying to prove geometry theorems using the methods discussed in this paper. Some of these observations are similar to the ones made for generating canonical systems for equational theories using the rewriting approach as well as for computing Gröbner bases of polynomial ideals. However, some are quite specific to the use of the Gröbner basis approach for geometry theorem proving. Some of these observations are also similar to the ones made by Chou about Wu's method [10].

(1) The choice of an ordering on variables significantly affects the performance of this method. The dependence of the method on this choice is, however, not as sensitive as in Wu's method where one ordering may lead to an irreducible characteristic set, while another may lead to a reducible characteristic set thus requiring decomposition of the problem into many subproblems. (Chou claimed to have solved this problem of choosing an appropriate ordering for Wu's method.) Further, in contrast to Wu's method and Chou's method as well as the approaches discussed in [12, 31, 32], there is no need to classify variables into independent variables and dependent variables. It is not always clear how to make this selection. In cases where such a choice can be made (even partially), it may be computationally better to view a geometry problem as involving polynomials whose coefficients are rational functions over independent variables as discussed in Section 8. It may be easier to derive subsidiary conditions and missing hypotheses using this mixed approach.

(2) The order in which critical pairs are generated in the Gröbner basis

computation also considerably affects the performance. The incorporation of the optimizations suggested in [7, 24], which significantly reduces the number of critical pairs that must be considered, made significant improvements in the performance of the Gröbner basis algorithm.

(3) The time taken to decide a geometry statement using this method depends on the kind of subsidiary conditions in the statement. Including additional subsidiary conditions in a statement does not necessarily reduce the time taken to decide the statement.

(4) Different equivalent formulations of the same geometry problem (based on choosing the origin and the axes, etc.) also significantly affect the timings. Examples are the butterfly theorem and Simson's theorem.

(5) In checking whether a Gröbner basis of an ideal includes 1 (i.e., deciding whether a geometry statement is a theorem), keeping the right-hand sides of rules in bases in normal form does not affect the performance much; for some examples it helps, while for other examples it slows the computation a little. However, for deducing subsidiary conditions for geometry statements for solving the second geometry problem, keeping the right-hand sides of these rules in normal form considerably helps the performance while computing Gröbner bases.

10. Comparison with Wu's Method

Chou and Schelter [12] have experimentally compared Wu's method with their approach based on the Gröbner basis computation, and their results indicate that Wu's method takes less time than the approaches based on the Gröbner basis computation. Comparison of timings given in Table 1 with the timings for Wu's method available from Chou for these examples also suggests that Wu's method is faster than the proposed approach. Below, we give plausible reasons why Wu's method takes less computational time than the approaches based on the Gröbner basis computation; see also [14].

We feel that the pseudodivision and triangulation are strongly related to the critical pair computation among polynomials which is central to the Gröbner basis method. For instance, consider the four hypothesis polynomials in Example 6.2. They are not in triangular form with respect to the ordering $x_4 > x_3 > x_2 > x_1 > u_3 > u_2 > u_1$. In particular, polynomial (8) has to be pseudodivided using polynomial (9) to get a triangular form. The result is:

$$(u_3 x_2 - u_2 x_1 - u_1 u_3)x_3 + u_1 u_2 x_1 = 0 . \tag{8'}$$

If a critical pair is computed between polynomials (8) and (9), then one obtains polynomial (8') above.

Critical pair computation is, however, significantly reduced in obtaining a triangular form as compared to computing a Gröbner basis. In triangulation, critical pairs are computed only among certain subset of polynomials; one of the polynomials in a critical pair computation is the smallest polynomial among all polynomials with the same highest variable.

There is however a price to be paid, which is the need to ensure that every polynomial p introducing a new variable is irreducible over the extension field defined by the polynomials lower in the ordering than p. As discussed in Section 5.1, this requirement is essential and a triangular form not satisfying this condition cannot be used to check for ideal membership.

Kandri-Rody, in his dissertation [21] (see also [23]), gave an algorithm for computing a different triangular form for a basis of an ideal which was used to develop a primality test of an ideal as well as to compute the dimension of an ideal. His triangular form, called an *extracted characteristic set* following Ritt, is obtained from a Gröbner basis using pure lexicographic ordering and thus does not have the limitation of triangular forms used by Wu and Chou. Kandri-Rody proved that every polynomial in an ideal pseudodivides to 0 using this triangular form ([21, Theorem 4.2.1, p. 68]).

Since for geometry theorem proving as well as for theorem proving in predicate calculus, we are interested only in the triviality problem, namely whether an ideal generated by a set of polynomials is the unit ideal, it will be worthwhile exploring a basis similar to a Gröbner basis, such that for the unit ideal, the basis includes 1 but for ideals that are not unit, it does not necessarily have the properties of a Gröbner basis. This is also related to the problem of generating term rewriting systems which compute canonical forms for certain equivalence classes of interest, and not necessarily canonical forms for all equivalence classes induced by a congruence relation.

11. Conclusion

We have discussed two complete decision methods for a subclass of geometry problems using a Gröbner basis approach. As shown above, these methods as well as Wu's method, which are algebraic, have been successful in proving many nontrivial plane geometry theorems. As far as we can tell, most of these theorems have not been proven using geometry theorem provers based on the synthetic approach [15]. Some of these theorems have been found extremely difficult to prove by humans including computer scientists. This seems to suggest that these algebraic methods have a lot of promise. Wu's method has also been used to prove nontrivial properties of perspective viewing in image understanding applications [25, 35, 38]; the reader may also see a paper by Kapur and Mundy in this volume.

One of the serious drawbacks of the algebraic methods is that the reasoning employed in these methods is significantly different from the reasoning used by humans while proving such theorems. Human reasoning in developing proofs of geometry problems is more along using synthetic properties and some trigonometric properties. An interesting area of research is to develop methods and heuristics which translate algebraic manipulations used in Gröbner basis approaches as well as Wu's approach in geometry theorem proving to synthetic concepts so that an understandable proof can also be generated from these algebraic manipulations. This research will also be helpful in integrating algebraic methods with synthetics methods. Such integration of the two approaches will especially be useful in proving difficult theorems that may need human guidance. This is also likely to be helpful in the application of the algebraic methods in practical applications such as image understanding and solid modeling.

Note Added in Proof

The complexity of checking whether a finite set of polynomial equations has a solution has been shown to have an upper bound of single exponential time by Brownawell [47]. Further, it has been recently announced that such a bound can be achieved using a Gröbner basis algorithm (quoted in [48]). The worst-case complexity for computing a Gröbner basis is, however, double exponential time.

ACKNOWLEDGMENT

Rick Harris implemented the Gröbner basis algorithm on Symbolics LISP machine. David Cyrluk provided his lively company during my experiments and subsequently implemented a more tolerable interface to the Gröbner basis algorithm for geometry theorem proving. Shang-Ching Chou persuaded me during his visit to GE R&D Center in 1985 to experiment once again with the Gröbner basis approach. Hai-Ping Ko provided many geometry statements in polynomial forms so that I could quickly test them using my approach. Paliath Narendran provided a lot of ideas for the improvement of the method; many ideas in this paper originated during discussions with him. David Musser and Joe Mundy provided encouragement and support; thanks are especially to Joe who posed a challenge in the early summer of 1984 whether the Gröbner basis method and rewrite rules could be used for geometry theorem proving.

REFERENCES

1. Agnarsson, S., Kandri-Rody, A., Kapur, D., Narendran, P. and Saunders, B.D., Complexity of testing whether a polynomial ideal is non-trivial, in: *Proceedings MACSYMA Users' Conference*, Schenectady, NY (1984) 452–458.
2. Arnon, D.S., Collins, G.E. and McCallum, S., Cylindrical algebraic decomposition, I: The basic algorithm, *SIAM J. Comput.* 13 (1984) 865–877.
3. Arnon, D.S., Collins, G.E. and McCallum, S., Cylindrical algebraic decomposition, II: An adjacency algorithm for the plane, *SIAM J. Comput.* 13 (1984) 878–889.
4. Ben-Or, M., Kozen, D. and Reif, J., The complexity of elementary algebra and geometry, in: *Proceedings 16th ACM Symposium on Theory of Computing* (1984) 457–464.
5. Buchberger, B., An algorithm for finding a basis for the residue class ring of a zero-

dimensional polynomial ideal (in German), Ph.D. Thesis, University of Innsbruck, Austria (1965).

6. Buchberger, B., An algorithmic criterion for the solvability of an algebraic system of equations, *Aequations Math.* **4** (3) (1970) 374–383.

7. Buchberger, B., A criterion for detecting unnecessary reductions in the construction of Gröbner bases, in: *Proceedings EUROSAM-79*, Marseille, France, (1979), Lecture Notes in Computer Science **72** (Springer, New York, 1979) 3–21.

8. Buchberger, B., Gröbner bases: An algorithmic method in polynomial ideal theory, in: N.K. Bose (Ed.), *Multidimensional Systems Theory* (Reidel, Dordrecht, The Netherlands, 1985) 184–232.

9. Chistov, A.L. and Grigoryev, D.Y., Subexponential-time solving systems of algebraic equations—I, II, USSR Academy of Sciences, Steklov Mathematical Institute, Leningrad Department, Leningrad, U.S.S.R. (1983).

10. Chou, S.-C., Proving elementary geometry theorems using Wu's algorithm, in: W.W. Bledsoe and D.W. Loveland (Eds.), *Theorem Proving: After 25 Years*, Contemporary Mathematics **29** (1984) 243–286.

11. Chou, S.-C., Proving and discovering theorems in elementary geometry using Wu's method, Ph.D. Thesis, Department of Mathematics, University of Texas, Austin, TX (1985).

12. Chou, S.C. and Schelter, W.F., Proving geometry theorems with rewrite rules, *J. Autom. Reasoning* **2** (3) (1986) 253–273.

13. Chou, S.-C. and Yang, J.-G., On the algebraic formulation of geometry theorems, Presented at *International Workshop on Geometry Reasoning*, Oxford, England (1986).

14. Chou, S.-C., Schelter, W.F. and Yang, J.-G., Characteristic sets and Gröbner bases in geometry theorem proving, Unpublished Manuscript, Department of Mathematics, University of Texas, Austin, TX (1986).

15. Coelho, H. and Pereira, L.M., Automated reasoning in geometry theorem proving with PROLOG, *J. Autom. Reasoning* **2** (4) (1986) 329–390.

16. Collins, G.E., Quantifier elimination for real closed fields by cylindrical algebraic decomposition, in: *Proceedings 2nd GI Conference on Automata Theory and Formal Languages*, Lecture Notes in Computer Science **33** (Springer, New York, 1975) 134–183.

17. Gelernter, H., Realization of a geometry theorem proving machine, in: E.A. Feigenbaum and J.E. Feldman (Eds.), *Computers and Thought* (McGraw-Hill, New York, 1963) 134–152.

18. Gilmore, P.C., An examination of the geometry theorem proving machine, *Artificial Intelligence* **1** (1970) 171–187.

19. Hermann, G., Die Frage der endlich vielen Schritte in der Theorie der Polynomideale, *Math. Ann.* **95** (1926) 736–788.

20. Hsiang, J., Refutational theorem proving using term-rewriting systems, *Artificial Intelligence* **25** (3) (1985) 255–300.

21. Kandri-Rody, A., Effective methods in the theory of polynomial ideals, Ph.D. Thesis, Department of Mathematics, Rensselaer Polytechnic Institute, Troy, NY (1984).

22. Kandri-Rody, A. and Kapur, D., Algorithms for computing the Gröbner bases of polynomial ideals over various Euclidean rings, in: *Proceedings EUROSAM-84*, Cambridge, England, Lecture Notes in Computer Science **174** (Springer, New York, 1984).

23. Kandri-Rody, A. and Saunders, B.D., Primality of ideals in polynomial rings, in: *Proceedings MACSYMA Users' Conference*, Schenectady, NY (1984).

24. Kapur, D., Musser, D.R. and Narendran, P., Only prime superpositions need be considered for the Knuth–Bendix completion procedure, Unpublished Manuscript, General Electric R&D Center, Schenactady, NY (1984); also: *Symbolic Comput.* (to appear).

25. Kapur, D., Musser, D.R., Mundy, J.L. and Narendran, P., Reasoning about three dimensional space, in: *Proceedings IEEE International Conference on Robotics and Automation*, St. Louis, MO (1985) 405–410.

26. Kapur, D. and Narendran, P., An equational approach to theorem proving in first-order

predicate calculus, in: *Proceedings IJCAI-85*, Los Angeles, CA (1985).

27. Kapur, D., Using Gröbner bases to reason about geometry problems, *J. Symbolic Comput.* **2** (4) (1986) 399–408.

28. Kapur, D., Geometry theorem proving using Hilbert's Nullstellensatz, in: *Proceedings SYMSAC-86*, Waterloo, Ont. (1986) 202–208.

29. Ko, H.P. and Hussain, M.A., A Study of Wu's method—A method to prove certain theorems in elementary geometry, in: *Congr. Numer.* **48** (1985) 225–242.

30. Ko, H.-P., Geometry theorem proving by decomposition of semi-algebraic sets—an application of Wu's structure theorem, Presented at *International Workshop on Geometry Reasoning*, Oxford, England (1986).

31. Kutzler, B. and Stifter, S., On the application of Buchberger's algorithm to automated geometry theorem proving, *J. Symbolic Comput.* **2** (4) (1986) 409–420.

32. Kutzler, B. and Stifter, S., Automated geometry theorem proving using Buchberger's algorithm, in: *Proceedings SYMSAC-86*, Waterloo, Ont. (1986) 209–214.

33. Lazard, D., Systems of algebraic equations, in: *Proceedings Symbolic and Algebraic Computation*, Lecture Notes in Computer Science **72** (Springer, Berlin, 1979) 88–94.

34. Monk, L.G., Elementary-recursive decision procedures, Ph.D. Thesis, Department of Mathematics, University of California, Berkeley, CA (1975).

35. Mundy, J.L., Image understanding research at General Electric, in: *Proceedings Image Understanding Workshop*, Miami Beach, FL (1985) 83–88.

36. Pohst, M.E. and Yun, D.Y.Y., On solving systems of algebraic equations via ideal bases and elimination theory, in: *Proceedings ACM Symposium on Symbolic and Algebraic Computation* (1981) 206–211.

37. Seidenberg, A., A new decision method for elementary algebra, *Ann. Math.* **60** (2) (1954) 365–374.

38. Swain, M.J. and Mundy, J.L., Experiments in using a geometry theorem prover to prove and develop theorems in computer vision, in: *Proceedings IEEE Conference on Robotics and Automation*, San Francisco, CA (1986) 280–285.

39. Tarski, A., *A Decision Method for Elementary Algebra and Geometry* (University of California Press, Berkeley, CA, 1948; 2nd ed., 1951).

40. Trinks, W., Uber, B. Buchbergers Verfahren, Systeme algebraischer Gleichungen zu losen, *J. Number Theory* **10** (1978) 475–488.

41. van der Waerden, B.L., *Modern Algebra* **I**, **II** (Fredrick Ungar, New York, 1966).

42. Wu, W., On the decision problem and the mechanization of theorem proving in elementary geometry, *Sci. Sinica* **21** (1978) 150–172; also in: W.W. Bledsoe and D.W. Loveland (Eds.), *Theorem Proving: After 25 Years*, Contemporary Mathematics **29** (1984) 213–234.

43. Wu, W., Some recent advances in mechanical theorem proving of geometries, in: W.W. Bledsoe and D.W. Loveland (Eds.), *Theorem Proving: After 25 Years*, Contemporary Mathematics **29** (1984) 235–241.

44. Wu, W., Basic principles of mechanical theorem proving in geometries, *J. Syst. Sci. Math. Sci.* **4** (3) (1984) 207–235; also appeared in *J. Autom. Reasoning* **2** (1986) 221–252.

45. Wu, W., On zeros of algebraic equations—An application of Ritt principle, *Kexue Tongbao* **31** (1) (1986) 1–5.

46. Wu., W., On reducibility problem in mechanical theorem proving of elementary geometries, Unpublished Manuscript, Institute of Systems Science, Academia Sinica, China (1986).

47. Brownawell, D., Bounds for the degrees in the Nullstellensatz, *Ann. Math. (2)* **126** (3) (1987) 577–591.

48. Ericson, L.W. and Yap, C.-K., The design of LINETOOL, a geometric editor, in: *Proceedings Fourth ACM Symposium on Computational Geometry*, Urbana, IL (1988) 83–92.

Received September 1986; revised version received January 1988

Geometry Theorem Proving by Decomposition of Quasi-Algebraic Sets: An Application of the Ritt–Wu Principle

Hai-Ping Ko*

The MITRE Corporation, Burlington Road, Bedford, MA 01730, U.S.A.

ABSTRACT

We use differences of two algebraic sets, called quasi-algebraic sets, to represent various geometrical properties. To determine the truth value of a geometry statement, we use the Ritt–Wu Principle to decompose the corresponding algebraic difference set into disjoint triangular quasi-algebraic sets, and then examine properties of elements of these triangular quasi-algebraic sets.

1. Introduction

Wu Wen-tsün introduced a notion of "generically true" for many geometrical statements and discovered an algorithmic method to determine whether or not such geometrical statements were generically true [13]. Since then, the notion of generically true has been further studied and partially, or completely, adopted by many people, notably by Chou (see [1–3]). It is known that if a geometric statement is generically true then it is true subject to some algebraic conditions, called subsidiary conditions. It is noted that (1) most geometrical statements do not include any precise statement about their degenerate cases, and thus make it difficult to evaluate their truth value in a formal manner, and (2) the notion of generically true requires a specification of independent variables and uses dimension to give a definition for degenerate cases (e.g., see examples best presented by Chou et al. [3, 5]), but one can still argue or feel discontent about the settlement. It becomes apparent to us that (1) we should use our successful experience with generically true to revisit problems of geometry theorem proving without being too much constrained by the notion

* This work was conducted during the year of 1986 at Corporate Research and Development, General Electric Company, Schenectady, NY 12345, U.S.A.

of generically true or by the related notion of independent variables. In this way, we expect to understand better all possibly different interpretations of the truth value of some geometry statements. And (2) if we view "subsidiary conditions" simply as conditions under which a given formulation of a given geometrical statement has truth value "true", then it seems sensible to invite human interaction in the process to find subsidiary conditions. Our work here is motivated by the above thought.

By decomposing a quasi-algebraic set, we mean to express the quasi-algebraic set as a union of a finite number of other quasi-algebraic sets, hopefully forming a certain type of canonical basis. An algebraic set can be considered as a quasi-algebraic set. Wu Wen-tsün's Zero Structure Theorem [17] gives an algorithmic method to decompose an algebraic set into a finite number of triangular quasi-algebraic sets. The decomposition results from an extensive application of the Ritt–Wu principle. The decomposition method given in the Zero Structure Theorem requires computation of polynomial pseudodivision and polynomial factorization over successive extended fields of a base field. We use only part of the Zero Structure Theorem to develop a decomposition. The main reason for taking such a detour is to avoid the possible computation difficulty of doing polynomial factorization over an extended field.

This work has similarities and differences with many other existing work such as [1–5, 7, 9, 12]. For instance, a study of geometry theorem proving without using the notion of generically true has been already conducted by Chou, Kapur, and Schelter [5, 7] by using the Gröbner basis method. Their method gives a decision procedure for a large range of geometrical statements with an algebraically closed field as the associated field. Also, the cylindrical algebraic decomposition method [6] gives a decision procedure for a large range of geometrical statements in Euclidean geometry.

Our method will similarly give an answer as either true or false but requires a certain amount of human effort to examine solutions of a system of polynomials of triangular form. So the method is a decision method but not totally mechanical. We consider that, in proving geometrical theorems algebraically, one has to deal with the problems of solving a system of equations or inequations anyway and, thus, the above type of demand of human interaction is reasonable.

This work is an exploration of using a computer to evaluate the truth value of certain geometry statements. We develop a method which can be used to analyze various aspects of the truth value of these geometry statements. We feel contented with the framework but consider that many aspects of the method can be further polished and improved. In this paper, we shall show our methods and examples of proving geometry theorems. We shall show that Simson's Theorem gives a surprising subsidiary condition when the associated field is the field of complex numbers. The reader is expected to learn the algorithmic method and the proof of the Ritt–Wu Principle from [16].

2. Algebraic Characteristics

For any geometric statement (S), (S) is said to have algebraic characteristics (C) if there exist a field K, an extended field $\bar{K}$ of K, variables $y_1, y_2, \ldots, y_n$ $(n \geq 1)$, and polynomials g and $h_1, h_2, \ldots, h_s$ $(s \geq 1)$, in the polynomial ring $KK = K[y_1, y_2, \ldots, y_n]$ such that (S) is true iff

for all common zeros, say z, of $\{h_1, h_2, \ldots, h_s\}$ for $(y_1, y_2, \ldots, y_n)$ in $\bar{K}^n$, z is a zero of g. (A1)

Fields K and $\bar{K}$ will be called the base field and associated field of (S), respectively. It is easy to show that for (S) to have algebraic characteristics (C), a necessary and sufficient condition is that there exist a field K, an extended field $\bar{K}$ of K, variables $y_1, y_2, \ldots, y_n$ $(n \geq 1)$, and polynomials $D, g, h_1, h_2, \ldots, h_s$ $(s \geq 1)$, in the polynomial ring $KK = K[y_1, y_2, \ldots, y_n]$ such that (S) is true iff

for all common zeros, say z, of $\{h_1, h_2, \ldots, h_s\}$ for $(y_1, y_2, \ldots, y_n)$ in $\bar{K}^n$, if z is not a zero of D then z is a zero of g. (A2)

The above two specifications for algebraic characteristics (C) are equivalent, but (A2) seems to correspond to practical geometrical cases better.

Throughout this paper, let K be a field and $\bar{K}$ be an extended field of K. Let $y_1, y_2, \ldots, y_n$ $(n \geq 1)$, be variables, and g and $h_1, h_2, \ldots, h_s$ $(s \geq 1)$, be polynomials in the polynomial ring $KK = K[y_1, y_2, \ldots, y_n]$.

Definition 2.1. $V(h_1, h_2, \ldots, h_s)$, called the *algebraic set* determined by polynomials $h_1, h_2, \ldots, h_s$, is defined as the set of all those common zeros of $\{h_1, h_2, \ldots, h_s\}$ for $(y_1, y_2, \ldots, y_n)$ in $\bar{K}^n$. $V(h_1, h_2, \ldots, h_s/g)$, called a *quasi-algebraic set*, is defined as $V(h_1, h_2, \ldots, h_s) - V(g)$. $\{h_1, h_2, \ldots, h_s\}$, and g will be called the numerator and denominator of the quasi-algebraic set $V(h_1, h_2, \ldots, h_s/g)$, respectively.

It is easy to see that $V(h_1, h_2, \ldots, h_s)$ is always a disjoint union of $V(h_1, h_2, \ldots, h_s/g)$ and $V(h_1, h_2, \ldots, h_s, g)$.

Let $H = \{h_1, h_2, \ldots, h_s\}$, and D be a polynomial in KK. For convenience, let

$$V(H) = V(h_1, h_2, \ldots, h_s) \,,$$

$$V(H/g) = V(h_1, h_2, \ldots, h_s/g) \,,$$

$$V(H, g) = V(h_1, h_2, \ldots, h_s, g) \,,$$

$$V(H, g/D) = V(h_1, h_2, \ldots, h_s, g/D) \,.$$

Then property (A1) is equivalent to say that

$$V(H/g) \text{ is empty,}$$

and property (A2) is equivalent to say that

$$V(H/D \cdot g) \text{ is empty.}$$

We show in Appendix A characterizations of some elementary geometric properties by using quasi-algebraic sets. We shall also show examples of geometric statements which have algebraic characteristics (C).

Suppose H_1, H_2 are subsets of KK, and D, g_1, g_2 are also polynomials in KK. Let $V(H_1, H_2/g) = V(H_1 \cup H_2/g)$. It is easy to prove the following properties for quasi-algebraic sets of form $V(H/g)$:

Combination of two $V(H/g)$:

$$V(H_1/g_1) \cap V(H_2/g_2) = V(H_1, H_2/g_1 \cdot g_2) \,. \tag{B0}$$

Disjoint decomposition by factorization:

$$V(h_1 \cdot h_2, h_3/g) = V(h_1, h_3/g) \cup V(h_2, h_3/h_1 \cdot g) \,. \tag{B1}$$

Square-free simplification:

> if h_1, h_2 have the same collection of prime factors, and g_1, g_2 have the same collection of prime factors, then $V(h_1/g_1) = V(h_2/g_2)$. (B2)

Common factor elimination:

> if D is nonzero then $V(D \cdot h_1, D \cdot h_2, \ldots, D \cdot h_s/d \cdot g) = V(h_1, h_2, \ldots, h_s/D \cdot g)$; for instance, $V(x^3 \cdot y^7 \cdot z, u^3 \cdot v/x^2 \cdot w^5) = V(y \cdot z, u \cdot v/x \cdot w)$. (B3)

Simplification by numerator:

> if any element of H is a nonzero element of K, or the ideal generated by H is KK, then $V(H/g)$ is empty . (B4)

Simplification by denominator:

if g is an element of the radical ideal generated by H, then
$V(H/g)$ is empty .   (B5)

Inclusion of no-harm polynomials:

if $V(H/g) = V(H_1/g_1) \cup V(H_2/g_2)$ and $V(D/g)$ is empty, then
$V(H/g) = V(H/D \cdot g) = V(H_1/D \cdot g_1) \cup V(H_2/D \cdot g_2)$.   (B6)

Dynamic decomposition:

if $V(H/g) = V(H_1/g_1) \cup V(H_2/g_2)$ then $V(H, h/D \cdot g) = V(H_1,$
$h/D \cdot g_1) \cup V(H_2, h/D \cdot g_2)$.   (B7)

We give below examples of geometric statements in Euclidean plane geometry that have algebraic characteristics (C).

Example 2.2 (Theorem of Centroid [5]). The three medians AD, BE and CF of a triangle ABC are concurrent (Fig. 1).

If "points A, B, and C are collinear" is considered as the only degenerate case, then we prove, in Appendix B, that points A and D are distinct, points B and E are distinct, points C and F are distinct, and lines AD and BE are neither the same nor parallel.

The rest of the statement we will prove is the following:

Example 2.2R. Suppose points A, B, C are noncollinear. If AD, BE, and CF are three medians of a triangle ABC, and lines AD and BE intersect at a point

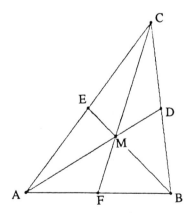

Fig. 1. Theorem of Centroid.

M, then line CF passes point M. Then, we can use the similar polynomial equations as given in [5] to investigate the truth value of the given statement. The above statement is true iff (A2) is true for

$$K = \mathbb{Q}, \qquad \bar{K} = \mathbb{R}, \qquad n = 10, \qquad s = 7,$$

$$\{y_1, y_2, \ldots, y_{10}\} = \{u_1, u_2, u_3, x_1, x_2, x_3, x_4, x_5, x_6, x_7\},$$

$$H = \{h_1, h_2, \ldots, h_7\}$$
$$= \{2x_1 - u_2 - u_1, 2x_2 - u_3 \quad (D \text{ is the midpoint of } BC),$$
$$\quad 2x_3 - u_2, 2x_4 - u_3 \quad (E \text{ is the midpoint of } CA),$$
$$\quad 2x_5 - u_1 \quad (F \text{ is the midpoint of } AB)$$
$$\quad x_3x_7 - u_1x_7 - x_4x_6 + u_1x_4 \quad (M, B, E, \text{collinear}),$$
$$\quad x_1x_7 - x_2x_6 \quad (M, A, D \text{ collinear})\},$$

$$D = u_1u_3 \quad (A, B, C \text{ collinear}),$$

$$g = x_5x_7 - u_2x_7 + u_3x_6 - u_3x_5 \quad (M, C, F \text{ collinear}),$$

where

$$A = (0, 0), \qquad B = (u_1, 0), \qquad C = (u_2, u_3), \qquad D = (x_1, x_2),$$
$$E = (x_3, x_4), \qquad F = (x_5, 0), \qquad M = (x_6, x_7).$$

Example 2.3 (Pascal's Theorem [5]). Let A, B, C, D, E, and F be six points on a circle (O). Let

$$P = AB \cap DF, \qquad Q = BC \cap FE, \qquad S = CD \cap EA.$$

Then P, Q and S are collinear (Fig. 2).

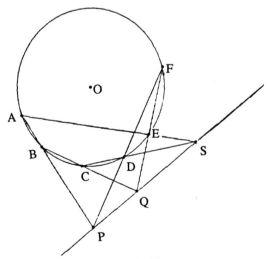

Fig. 2. Pascal's Theorem.

If the only degenerate cases to be considered include

$$"A = B, \quad D = F, \quad B = C, \quad F = E, \quad C = D, \quad E = A,$$

one of the following pairs of lines represents either identical or parallel lines:

$$(A, B), \quad (D, F), \quad (B, C), \quad (F, E), \quad (C, D), \quad (E, A)",$$

then we can use the similar polynomial equations as given in [5] to investigate the truth value of the given statement. Therefore the given geometry statement is true iff (A2) is true for

$$K = \mathbb{Q}, \qquad \bar{K} = \mathbb{R}, \qquad n = 16, \qquad s = 10,$$

$$\{y_1, y_2, \ldots, y_{16}\}$$
$$= \{u_1, u_2, u_3, u_4, u_5, u_6, x_1, x_2, x_3, x_4, x_5, x_6, x_7, x_8, x_9, x_{10}\},$$

$$H = \{h_1, h_2, \ldots, h_{10}\}$$
$$= \{x_2^2 - (u_2 - x_2)^2 + x_1^2 - (u_3 - x_1)^2 \quad (OA = OC),$$
$$x_2^2 - (u_1 - x_2)^2 \quad (OA = OB),$$
$$-(x_3 - x_2)^2 + x_2^2 + x_1^2 - (u_4 - x_1)^2 \quad (OA = OD),$$
$$-(x_5 - x_2)^2 + x_2^2 + x_1^2 - (u_6 - x_1)^2 \quad (OA = OE),$$
$$-(x_4 - x_2)^2 + x_2^2 + x_1^2 - (u_5 - x_1)^2 \quad (OA = OF),$$
$$-u_5 x_6 + u_4 x_6 - u_4 x_4 + u_5 x_3 \quad (P, D, F \text{ collinear}),$$
$$-u_3 x_8 + u_2 x_7 - u_1 x_7 + u_1 u_3 \quad (Q, B, C \text{ collinear}),$$
$$u_6 x_8 - u_5 x_8 - x_5 x_7 + x_4 x_7 + u_5 x_5 - u_6 x_4 \quad (Q, F, E \text{ collinear}),$$
$$x_3 x_9 - u_2 x_9 - u_3 x_3 - u_4 x_{10} + u_3 x_{10} + u_2 u_4 \quad (S, C, D \text{ collinear}),$$
$$x_5 x_9 - u_6 x_{10} \quad (S, A, E \text{ collinear})\},$$

$$D = u_1(u_4 - u_5)(u_3(x_4 - x_5) + (u_2 - u_1)(u_6 - u_5))$$
$$\times (u_6(x_3 - u_2) - (u_4 - u_3)x_5),$$

$$g = x_8 x_9 - x_6 x_9 + x_6 x_7 - x_{10} x_7 \quad (P, Q, S \text{ collinear}),$$

where

$$A = (0, 0), \qquad B = (u_1, 0), \qquad C = (u_2, u_3),$$
$$O = (x_2, x_1), \qquad D = (x_3, u_4), \qquad F = (x_4, x_5),$$
$$E = (x_5, u_6), \qquad P = (x_6, 0), \qquad Q = (x_8, x_7), \qquad S = (x_{10}, x_9).$$

The above two algebraic formulations fit (A2) and have the following property:

$h_1 = 0, h_2 = 0, \ldots, h_s = 0$ are polynomial equations mainly characterizing the geometrical conditions in the hypothesis, $D = 0$ is a polynomial equation mainly characterizing all degenerate cases, and $g = 0$ is a polynomial equation mainly characterizing the conclusion. (B)

However, geometry theorems of algebraic characteristics (C) may also include formulations not satisfying the above property (B). For instance, in the following example, some of the $h_i = 0$ are polynomial equations corresponding to some nondegenerate conditions and the whole formulation fits form (A1).

Example 2.4 (Mundy, 1985). If A, B, C, D are four points, and both lines AB and CD are perpendicular to line BC, then lines AB and CD are parallel (Fig. 3).

Suppose the only degenerate cases to be considered include

$$\text{``} A = B \quad \text{or} \quad C = D \quad \text{or} \quad B = C \text{''}.$$

Then the given geometry statement is true iff (A1) is true for

$$K = \mathbb{Q}, \qquad \bar{K} = \mathbb{R}, \qquad n = 11, \qquad s = 5,$$

$$\{y_1, y_2, \ldots, y_{11}\} = \{x_1, x_2, x_3, x_4, x_5, z_1, z_2, z_3, z_4, z_5, z_6\},$$

$$H = \{h_1, h_2, \ldots, h_5\}$$
$$= \{h_1 = x_1 x_2 \quad (h_1, h_3, h_4: AB, BC \text{ perpendicular}),$$
$$h_2 = x_1(x_4 - x_1) \quad (h_2, h_4, h_5: CD, BC \text{ perpendicular}),$$
$$h_3 = (x_2 z_1 + 1)(x_3 z_2 + 1) \quad (A \neq B),$$
$$h_4 = 1 - x_1 z_3 \quad (B \neq C),$$
$$h_5 = ((x_1 - x_4)z_5 + 1)(1 - x_5 z_6) \quad (C \neq D)\},$$

$$g = x_2 x_5 - x_3(x_4 - x_1) \quad (g, h_3, h_4: AB, CD \text{ parallel}).$$

Here, we let

$$A = (x_2, x_3), \qquad B = (0, 0), \qquad C = (x_1, 0), \qquad D = (x_4, x_5).$$

For all the above geometric statements which have algebraic characteristics (C), it is easy to see that the given algebraic formulation is not uniquely determined.

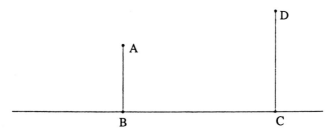

Fig. 3. Mundy's example.

3. WDT Zero Basis

To simplify our presentation, we assume, throughout this paper, that prem, abbreviated from pseudoremainder, is the remainder of pseudodivision defined in [8]. Therefore, in a polynomial ring, say KK, over a field, if y is a variable, and

$$f = a_0 + a_1 \cdot y + \cdots + a_s \cdot y^s ,$$

$$g = b_0 + b_1 \cdot y + \cdots + b_t \cdot y^t ,$$

with a_i and b_j as polynomials in KK containing no variable y and $a_s \neq 0$ and $b_t \neq 0$, then $\text{prem}(g, f, y)$ is g if $t < s$; otherwise, $\text{prem}(g, f, y)$ is the polynomial, say R, such that $\deg(R, y) < s$ and there exists a polynomial Q in KK such that

$$a_s^{t-s+1} \cdot g = Q \cdot f + R .$$

Let $\deg(0, y) = -1$, $\text{prem}(g, 0, y)$ be undefined, and $\text{prem}(0, f, y) = 0$ if $f \neq 0$. Note that prem is computable in the case $K = \mathbb{Q}$ or a finite field. We extend the above definition of prem to a pseudoremainder of multiple divisors so that for all g in KK, $f_1, f_2, \ldots, f_m$ in $KK - \{0\}$ $(1 \leq m \leq n)$, and $z_1, z_2, \ldots, z_m$ in $\{y_1, y_2, \ldots, y_n\}$,

$$\text{prem}(g, (f_1, f_2, \ldots, f_m), (z_1, z_2, \ldots, z_m))$$

$$= \begin{cases} \text{prem}(g, f_1, z_1) , & \text{if } m = 1 , \\ \text{prem}(\text{prem}(g, (f_2, \ldots, f_m), (z_2, \ldots, z_m)), f_1, z_1) , & \text{if } m > 1 . \end{cases}$$

Theorem 3.1 (Ritt–Wu Principle [16]). *Suppose* $h_1, h_2, \ldots, h_s$ *are nonzero polynomials of* KK. *Then for any linear ordering on* $\{y_1, y_2, \ldots, y_n\}$, *say* $y_1 < y_2 < \cdots < y_n$, *there exists an algorithmic method to find nonzero polynomials* $f_1, f_2, \ldots, f_r$ $(r \geq 1)$, *in the ideal generated by* $h_1, h_2, \ldots, h_s$ *in* KK, *and variables* $x_1, x_2, \ldots, x_r$ *in* $\{y_1, y_2, \ldots, y_n\}$ *such that either* $r = 1$ *and* f_1 *is an element of* K, *or all of the following conditions are satisfied:*

(1) $x_1 < x_2 < \cdots < x_r$,
(2) $(f_1, f_2, \ldots, f_r)$ *is strictly triangular w.r.t.* $(x_1, x_2, \ldots, x_r)$ *with initials* $(I_1, I_2, \ldots, I_r)$, *i.e., for each* $i < j$, $\deg(f_i, x_j) = 0$, $\deg(f_i, x_i) > 0$, *and* I_i *is the leading coefficient of* f_i *w.r.t.* x_i,
(3) *for each* $i > 1$, $\text{prem}(I_i, (f_1, f_2, \ldots, f_{i-1}), (x_1, x_2, \ldots, x_{i-1})) \neq 0$,
(4) *for each* i, $\text{prem}(h_i, (f_1, f_2, \ldots, f_r), (x_1, x_2, \ldots, x_r)) = 0$.

The algorithmic method is elegant, and the proof needs the following type of notion of ordering on "chains" of KK. From now on, we assume $y_1 < y_2 < \cdots < y_n$.

For any polynomial, say g, of KK, define class$(g) = 0$ if g is an element of K, and class$(g) = p$ if p is the largest integer such that deg$(g, y_p) > 0$. A chain is defined as a sequence of polynomials, say $(f_1, f_2, \ldots, f_r)$ $(r \geq 1)$, such that

$$\text{class}(f_1) < \text{class}(f_2) < \cdots < \text{class}(f_r).$$

For any chain, say $F = (f_1, f_2, \ldots, f_r)$, if $p_i = \text{class}(f_i)$ for all i, then let rank$(F) = (d_1, d_2, \ldots, d_n)$ such that for all j, if $j = p_i$ for some i, then $d_j = \deg(f_i, y_i)$, otherwise $d_j = 0$. For chains F and G, if rank$(F) = (c_1, c_2, \ldots, c_n)$ and rank$(G) = (d_1, d_2, \ldots, d_n)$, then define rank$(F) <$ rank(G) iff there exists i, $1 \leq i \leq n$, such that $c_i < d_i$, and for all j with $i < j \leq n$, $c_j = d_j$.

Corollary 3.2. *In Theorem* 3.1, *in case* f_1 *is an element of* K, *let* $I = f_1$, *otherwise, let* $I = I_1 \cdot I_2 \cdots \cdot I_r$. *Then for any polynomial* g *in* KK, *the given conditions in Theorem* 3.1 *imply the following properties*:

   (1) $V(h_1, h_2, \ldots, h_s/g)$ *is a disjoint union of* $V(f_1, f_2, \ldots, f_r/I \cdot g)$ *and* $V(h_1, h_2, \ldots, h_s, I/g)$,
   (2) $V(h_1, h_2, \ldots, h_s, I/g) = V(h_1, h_2, \ldots, h_s, f_1, f_2, \ldots, f_r, I/g)$,
   (3) $V(h_1, h_2, \ldots, h_s/I \cdot g) = V(f_1, f_2, \ldots, f_r/I \cdot g)$,
   (4) $V(h_1, h_2, \ldots, h_s/g) = V(f_1, f_2, \ldots, f_r/I \cdot g)$ *iff* $V(h_1, h_2, \ldots, h_s, I/g)$ *is empty*,
   (5) *if* $V(f_1, f_2, \ldots, f_r, I/g)$ *is empty then* $V(h_1, h_2, \ldots, h_s/g) = V(f_1, f_2, \ldots, f_r/I \cdot g)$.

Definition 3.3. $((f_1, f_2, \ldots, f_r), g, (x_1, x_2, \ldots, x_r))$ *is called a Wu's triangular polynomial set*, *or simply a WT polynomial set if, for some polynomials* $I_1, I_2, \ldots, I_r$ *in* KK, $(f_1, f_2, \ldots, f_r)$ *is strictly triangular w.r.t.* $(x_1, x_2, \ldots, x_r)$ *with initials* $(I_1, I_2, \ldots, I_r)$, *and every nontrivial prime factor of any* I_i *is also a prime factor of* g. *In this case,* $V(f_1, f_2, \ldots, f_r/I \cdot g)$ *is called the WT quasi-algebraic set determined by* $((f_1, f_2, \ldots, f_r), g, (x_1, x_2, \ldots, x_r))$. $((f_1, f_2, \ldots, f_r), g, (x_1, x_2, \ldots, x_r))$ *is called the polynomial set of* $V(f_1, f_2, \ldots, f_r/g)$.

Note that if $f_1, f_2, \ldots, f_r$ are nonzero polynomials in KK, and $(f_1, f_2, \ldots, f_r)$ is strictly triangular w.r.t. $(x_1, x_2, \ldots, x_r)$ with initials $(I_1, I_2, \ldots, I_r)$ then for some nonnegative integers i_j and polynomials Q_j in KK, we have

$$I_1^{i_1} \cdot I_2^{i_2} \cdots \cdot I_r^{i_r} \cdot g$$
$$= Q_1 \cdot f_1 + Q_2 \cdot f_2 + \cdots + Q_r \cdot f_r$$
$$+ \text{prem}(g, (f_1, f_2, \ldots, f_r), (x_1, x_2, \ldots, x_r)).$$

Therefore, if furthermore, $((f_1, f_2, \ldots, f_r), g, (x_1, x_2, \ldots, x_r))$ is a WT polynomial set and

$$\text{prem}(g, (f_1, f_2, \ldots, f_r), (x_1, x_2, \ldots, x_r)) = 0 ,$$

then $V(f_1, f_2, \ldots, f_r/g)$ is empty. We also have related properties as stated in Theorems 3.8 and 3.9.

Definition 3.4. $\{(T_i, g_i, V_i): i = 1, 2, \ldots, c\}$ is called a *Wu's disjoint triangular zero basis*, or simply *WDT zero basis*, of $V(h_1, h_2, \ldots, h_s/g)$ if each (T_i, g_i, V_i) is a WT polynomial set and $V(h_1, h_2, \ldots, h_s/g)$ is a disjoint union of the $V(T_i/g_i)$ for $i = 1, 2, \ldots, c$.

Without detailed explanation, we claim that the following theorems can be proved.

Theorem 3.5. *If there exists an algorithm to find all the prime factors of any nonzero polynomial in* KK, *then Theorem 3.1 is also true if we require* $f_1, f_2, \ldots, f_r$ *as square-free polynomials in the radical ideal generated by* $h_1, h_2, \ldots, h_s$.

Theorem 3.6. *There exists an algorithmic method to find a WDT zero basis of* $V(h_1, h_2, \ldots, h_s/g)$ *for any nonzero polynomials* $g, h_1, h_2, \ldots, h_s$ $(s \geqslant 1)$ *in* KK. *Suppose* $\{(T_i, g_i, V_i): i = 1, 2, \ldots, c\}$ $(c \geqslant 1)$ *is a WDT zero basis of* $V(h_1, h_2, \ldots, h_s/g)$. *Then*

(1) $V(h_1, h_2, \ldots, h_s/g)$ *is empty iff* $V(T_i/g_i)$ *is empty for all* i, *and*
(2) $V(h_1, h_2, \ldots, h_s/g)$ *is empty if* $\text{prem}(g_i, T_i, V_i) = 0$ *for all* i.

The algorithmic method is as follows:

> begin with empty WDT zero basis,
> initialize R as any $(d_1, d_2, \ldots, d_n)$ with $d_1 = d_2 = \cdots = d_n > \deg(h_i, y_j)$ for all i and j,
> initialize H_1 as $\{h_1, h_2, \ldots, h_s\}$ and g_1 as g,
> and add WT polynomial sets to the WDT zero basis by doing (E1), (E2), and (E3) defined below;
>
> (E1) Use the Ritt–Wu Principle to find a WT polynomial set $(T, I \cdot g_1, V)$ such that $\text{rank}(T) < R$, and $V(H_1/g_1)$ is a disjoint union of $V(T/I \cdot g_1)$ and $V(H_1, T, I/g_1)$, where I is the product of all the initials of T w.r.t. V. If $\text{prem}(g_1, T, V) \neq 0$ then add $(T, I \cdot g_1, V)$ to the WDT zero basis.
> (E2) Suppose $I_1, I_2, \ldots, I_r$ are leading coefficients of T w.r.t. V. Then $V(H_1, T, I/g_1)$ is a disjoint union of the following quasi-

algebraic sets:

$$V(H_1, T, I_1/g_1),$$
$$V(H_1, T, I_2/I_1 \cdot g_1),$$
$$\vdots$$
$$V(H_1, T, I_r/I_1 \cdot I_2 \cdots I_{r-1} \cdot g_1).$$

(E3) For each of the above r quasi-algebraic sets, say Q, do (E1), (E2), and (E3) with R being re-assigned as rank(T), H_1 being re-assigned as the numerator of Q, and g_1 being re-assigned as the denominator of Q.

Theorem 3.7. *If there exists an algorithm to find all prime factors of any nonzero polynomial in KK, then in Theorem 3.6 we may require that if the WDT zero basis is nonempty then for every element, say (T, g, V) of the WDT zero basis, every polynomial in T is either 1 or a prime polynomial.*

Theorem 3.8. *Suppose $T = (f_1, f_2, \ldots, f_r)$ is strictly triangular w.r.t. $(x_1, x_2, \ldots, x_r)$ with initials $(I_1, I_2, \ldots, I_r)$. Let $I = I_1 \cdot I_2 \cdots I_r$, then for any polynomial g in KK, if $\bar{g} = \text{prem}(g, T, (x_1, x_2, \ldots, x_r))$ then $V(T/I \cdot g) = V(T/I \cdot \bar{g})$. In particular, if $\bar{g} = 0$ then $V(T/I \cdot g)$ is empty.*

Theorem 3.9. *In Theorem 3.8 if $g = g_1 \cdot g_2 \cdots g_c$ and for each i, $\bar{g}_i = \text{prem}(g_i, T, (x_1, x_2, \ldots, x_r))$ in KK, then $V(T/I \cdot g) = V(T/I \cdot \bar{g}_1 \cdot \bar{g}_2 \cdots \bar{g}_c)$. In particular, if $\bar{g}_i = 0$ for some i then $V(T/I \cdot g)$ is empty.*

4. Problems and the Methods

If a geometric statement (S) has algebraic characteristics (C) with format (A2), then (S) is true iff $V(h_1, h_2, \ldots, h_s/D \cdot g)$ is empty and the problem of determining the truth value of (S) is equivalent to the following algebraic problems:

$$\text{determine whether or not } V(h_1, h_2, \ldots, h_s/D \cdot g) \text{ is empty.} \quad \text{(P1)}$$

If a geometric statement (S) has algebraic characteristics (C) subject to some not yet specified degenerate cases of (S) with format (A2), then (S) is true iff every element of $V(h_1, h_2, \ldots, h_s/D \cdot g)$ corresponds to degenerate cases of (S) and the problem of determining the truth value of (S) is equivalent to the following algebraic and geometric problem:

$$\text{determine whether or not every element of } V(h_1, h_2, \ldots, h_s/D \cdot g) \text{ corresponds to a degenerate case of } (S). \quad \text{(P2)}$$

Suppose (S) is a geometric statement satisfying one of the above characteristics and there is an algorithm to find all prime factors of any nonzero polynomial of KK. We use Theorem 3.6 as the basic structure to develop decision methods for (P1) and (P2), and thus for the truth value of statements (S) of the above type. According to our experiments, a straightforward implementation of Theorem 3.6 does not give tolerable computing time for the purpose of proving geometry theorems. The computing time was significantly improved after we adopted other properties of quasi-algebraic sets as stated in (B1)–(B7), and Theorems 3.7 and 3.9. All the methods here have been implemented and considered as an extension of our algebraic geometry theorem prover called ALGE-prover [10, 11].

We first modify the previous method for finding the WDT zero basis as follows.

Find WDT zero basis:
Input: nonzero polynomials $h_1, h_2, \ldots, h_s$, and g in KK ($s \geq 1$);
Output: a WDT zero basis of $V(h_1, h_2, \ldots, h_s/g)$;
Procedure (X):

> begin with empty WDT zero basis,
> and add WT polynomial sets to the WDT zero basis by doing (X1), (X2), (X3) (X4), and (X5) as defined below;
> throughout, let the rank of the produced WT polynomial sets decrease in the same fashion as before.
>
> (X1) Simplify the given quasi-algebraic set by (B2), (B3) and (B4) such that (1) all polynomials in the numerator and denominator are square-free, (2) no polynomial in the numerator consists of a nontrivial prime factor of the denominator, and (3) no polynomial in the numerator is a nonzero element of K.
>
> (X2) (Optional) Decompose the resulting quasi-algebraic set into disjoint quasi-algebraic sets by (B1) such that for each component, all the polynomials in the numerator are prime polynomials.
>
> (X3) For each of the above components, use Theorem 3.5 to decompose it into two quasi-algebraic sets: the first, called type-1 component, is a WT quasi-algebraic set, and the second, called type-2 component, is not necessarily triangular. Use Theorem 3.9 to see if the first is empty; if it cannot be decided this way, then simplify this WT polynomial set by (B2) and add the resulting WT polynomial set to the WDT zero basis. Suppose I is the product of all the initials of the triangular quasi-algebraic set, then do the following:
>
> > *Ask1.* Show to the user all the irreducible factors of I and g and ask the user to input any factor of I, say q, which would make

$V(q/g)$ empty. If the user gives a value for q other than a nonzero constant in K, then q is multiplied to all the denominators of all the remaining components of the decomposition procedure.

This factor q will be called no-harm factor because its inclusion does not change the content of the original quasi-algebraic set, as formulated in (B6).

(X4) Further decompose each of the above type-2 components by (X1)–(X4).

(X5) The whole procedure stops when there is no more type-2 component to be further decomposed. In this case, the resulting WDT zero basis is returned as the answer to this procedure.

Ask1 provides an opportunity for the user to help simplifying the whole decomposition process, by using properties of $\bar{K}$. A trivial answer to Ask1 is 1. Ask1 suggests, but does not require, the user to identify all possible polynomials that can be used to eliminate useless factors from all the numerators of all the remaining quasi-algebraic sets.

Decision Method for (P1)

Input: nonzero polynomials $h_1, h_2, \ldots, h_s$, and g in KK ($s \geqslant 1$) for a quasi-algebraic set $V(h_1, h_2, \ldots, h_s/g)$;

Output: YES if $V(h_1, h_2, \ldots, h_s/g)$ is empty; NO otherwise;

Method:

WDT zero basis (containing Ask1): Find a WDT zero basis, say W, of $V(h_1, h_2, \ldots, h_s/g)$ by the previous method. If W is empty then return YES as the answer and stop the process. Otherwise, proceed to Ask2.

Ask2. For each WT polynomial set, say (T, D, V), in W, ask the user to decide the emptiness of the corresponding quasi-algebraic set. If any of the above is determined to be nonempty, then return NO as the answer, and any element found in the nonempty WT-quasi algebraic set is an element of $V(h_1, h_2, \ldots, h_s/g)$. Otherwise, return YES as the answer.

Decision Method for (P2)

Input: a geometric statement (S) with some unspecified degenerate cases, and nonzero polynomials $h_1, h_2, \ldots, h_s$, and g in KK ($s \geqslant 1$), such that (S) is true iff every element of $V(h_1, h_2, \ldots, h_s/g)$ corresponds to a degenerate case of (S);

Output: YES if every element of $V(h_1, h_2, \ldots, h_s/g)$ corresponds to a degenerate case of (S); NO otherwise;

Method:

Do (X1), (X2), and (X3-P2), (X4-P2), (X5-P2) as defined below;

(X3-P2) For each of the above components, use Theorem 3.5 to decompose it into two quasi-algebraic sets: the first is triangular and the second is not necessarily triangular. Use Theorem 3.9 to see if the first is empty; if it cannot be decided this way, then do Ask2, that is, to ask the user to decide whether any element of the triangular quasi-algebraic set corresponds to a degenerate case of (S). If such an element is found, then the answer to (P2) is NO and this element gives a disproof example for (P2); in this case, return NO and stop the procedure. Otherwise, suppose I is the product of all the initials of the triangular quasi-algebraic set, then do Ask1, i.e., show to the user all the irreducible factors of I and g and ask the user to input any factor of I, say q, that would either make $V(q/g)$ empty or make every element of $V(q/g)$ correspond to a degenerate case of (S). If the user gives q other than a nonzero constant in K, then q is multiplied to all the denominators of all the remaining components of the decomposition procedure.

(X4-P2) Decompose each of the above components, if there is any, by (X1), (X2), (X3-P2), and (X4-P2).

(X5-P2) When there is no more component to be further decomposed, return YES as the answer and stop the procedure.

In case (S) is not true, the above methods can be used to identify those subsidiary conditions, in the form of triangular quasi-algebraic sets, for (S) to become true.

All the methods presented here decompose the given quasi-algebraic set into triangular quasi-algebraic sets with user's assistance (Ask1), and then they leave almost all the rest of the responsibility to the user (Ask2). According to our experience with these methods in our geometry theorem proving problems in Euclidean plane geometry, if the user can respond to problems of the following type:

determine whether or not "$x^2 + y^2 = 0$ implies $g(x, y, z) = 0$" is true,

then Ask2 is either never activated or easy to answer. In fact, for those geometry statements that do not involve order, Ask2 has never been activated.

Another natural way of determining whether $V(H/D \cdot g)$ is empty is to find a WDT zero basis of $V(H/D)$, say $\{(T_1, D_1, V_1), (T_2, D_2, V_2), \ldots\}$ and then determining whether or not each $V(T_i/D_i \cdot g)$ is empty by trying Theorem 3.9 and then Ask2 if necessary. This approach may take longer time to terminate than the earlier approach. But in case g corresponds to the conclusion, and H and D correspond to hypothesis and degenerate cases, this approach has the advantage of developing a WDT zero basis of the quasi-algebraic set determined by the hypothesis and degenerate conditions only. The WDT zero basis can thus be used to verify the validity of possibly different conclusions.

For Example 2.2R the WDT zero basis found for $V(H/D)$ consists of two WT polynomial sets:

T_1: $[1] = 2x_1 - u_2 - u_1$
$[2] = 2x_2 - u_3$
$[3] = 2x_3 .- u_2$
$[4] = 2x_4 - u_3$
$[5] = 2x_5 - u_1$
$[6] = 3x_6 - u_2 - u_1$
$[7] = 3x_7 - u_3$

D_1: $u_1(u_2 - 2u_1)u_3$

V_1: $(x_1, x_2, x_3, x_4, x_5, x_6, x_7)$

T_2: $[1] = u_2 - 2u_1$
$[2] = 2x_1 - 3u_1$
$[3] = 2x_2 - u_3$
$[4] = x_3 - u_1$
$[5] = 2x_4 - u_3$
$[6] = 2x_5 - u_1$
$[7] = x_6 - u_1$
$[8] = 3x_7 - u_3$

D_2: $u_1 u_3$

V_2: $(u_2, x_1, x_2, x_3, x_4, x_5, x_6, x_7)$.

Here, under each T_i, $[j]$ means the jth element of T_i. The pseudoremainder of g w.r.t. each of the above WT polynomial sets is zero and thus the given geometry statement is true with the given consideration of degenerate cases. In fact, the above two WT polynomial sets can be easily combined as one WT polynomial set. For Example 2.2, the WDT zero basis found for $V(H/D)$ consists of four WT polynomial sets:

T_1: $[1] = 2u_3 x_1 - u_3^2 - u_2^2 + u_1 u_2$
$[2] = 2x_2 - u_1$
$[3] = u_3 x_3^2 - u_1 u_3 x_3 + u_3 u_4^2 - u_3^2 u_4 - u_2^2 u_4 + u_1 u_2 u_4$
$[4] = u_3 x_4^2 - u_1 u_3 x_4 + u_3 u_5^2 - u_3^2 u_5 - u_2^2 u_5 + u_1 u_2 u_5$
$[5] = u_3 x_5^2 - u_1 u_3 x_5 + u_3 u_6^2 - u_3^2 u_6 - u_2^2 u_6 + u_1 u_2 u_6$
$[6] = u_5 x_6 - u_4 x_6 + u_4 x_4 - u_5 x_3$
$[7] = u_3 x_5 x_7 - u_3 x_4 x_7 - u_2 u_6 x_7 + u_1 u_6 x_7 + u_2 u_5 x_7 - u_1 u_5 x_7 - u_3 u_5 x_5$
$\quad + u_3 u_6 x_4 - u_1 u_3 u_6 + u_1 u_3 u_5$

$$[8] = u_3x_5x_8 - u_3x_4x_8 - u_2u_6x_8 + u_1u_6x_8 + u_2u_5x_8 - u_1u_5x_8 - u_2u_5x_5$$
$$+ u_1u_5x_5 - u_1u_3x_5 + u_2u_6x_4 - u_1u_6x_4 + u_1u_3x_4$$
$$[9] = u_4x_5x_9 - u_3x_5x_9 - u_6x_3x_9 + u_2u_6x_9 + u_3u_6x_3 - u_2u_4u_6$$
$$[10] = u_3x_3x_5 + u_4x_{10}x_5 - u_3x_{10}x_5 - u_2u_4x_5 - u_6x_{10}x_3 + u_2u_6x_{10}$$

$D_1:$ $\quad u_1u_3(u_5 - u_4)u_6(u_3x_5 - u_3x_4 - u_2u_6 + u_1u_6 + u_2u_5 - u_1u_5)(u_4x_5$
$\qquad - u_3x_5 - u_6x_3 + u_2u_6)(u_3u_4x_4x_5 - u_3^2x_4x_5 + u_3u_6x_3x_5 + u_2u_4u_6x_5$
$\qquad - u_1u_4u_6x_5 - 2u_2u_3u_6x_5 + u_1u_3u_6x_5 - u_2u_4u_5x_5 + u_1u_4u_5x_5$
$\qquad + u_2u_3u_5x_5 - u_1u_3u_5x_5 - u_1u_3u_4x_5 + u_1u_3^2x_5 - u_3u_6x_3x_4 + u_2u_3u_6x_4$
$\qquad - u_2u_6^2x_3 + u_1u_6^2x_3 + u_2u_5u_6x_3 - u_1u_5u_6x_3 + u_3u_4u_6^2 - u_3^2u_6^2 + u_2^2u_6^2$
$\qquad - u_1u_2u_6^2 - u_2^2u_5u_6 + u_1u_2u_5u_6 - u_3^2u_4u_6 - u_2^2u_4u_6 + u_1u_2u_4u_6$
$\qquad + u_3^3u_6 - u_2^2u_3u_6 - u_1u_2u_3u_6)$

$V_1:$ $\quad (x_1, x_2, x_3, x_4, x_5, x_6, x_7, x_8, x_9, x_{10})$

$T_2:$ $\quad [1] = u_6$
$\qquad [2] = 2u_3x_1 - u_3^2 - u_2^2 + u_1u_2$
$\qquad [3] = 2x_2 - u_1$
$\qquad [4] = u_3x_3^2 - u_1u_3x_3 + u_3u_4^2 - u_3^2u_4 - u_2^2u_4 + u_1u_2u_4$
$\qquad [5] = u_3x_4^2 - u_1u_3x_4 + u_3u_5^2 - u_3^2u_5 - u_2^2u_5 + u_1u_2u_5$
$\qquad [6] = x_5 - u_1$
$\qquad [7] = u_5x_6 - u_4x_6 + u_4x_4 - u_5x_3$
$\qquad [8] = u_3x_5x_7 - u_3x_4x_7 + u_2u_5x_7 - u_1u_5x_7 - u_3u_5x_5 + u_1u_3u_5$
$\qquad [9] = u_3x_5x_8 - u_3x_4x_8 + u_2u_5x_8 - u_1u_5x_8 - u_2u_5x_5 + u_1u_5x_5$
$\qquad\qquad - u_1u_3x_5 + u_1u_3x_4$
$\qquad [10] = x_9$
$\qquad [11] = u_3x_3 + u_4x_{10} - u_3x_{10} - u_2u_4$

$D_2:$ $\quad u_1u_3(u_4 - u_3)(u_5 - u_4)(u_3x_4 - u_2u_5 + u_1u_5 - u_1u_3)x_5(u_3x_5 - u_3x_4$
$\qquad + u_2u_5 - u_1u_5)$

$V_2:$ $\quad (u_6, x_1, x_2, x_3, x_4, x_5, x_6, x_7, x_8, x_9, x_{10})$

$T_3:$ $\quad [1] = u_2$
$\qquad [2] = u_3$
$\qquad [3] = 2x_2 - u_1$
$\qquad [4] = x_3^2 - u_1x_3 - 2u_4x_1 + u_4^2$
$\qquad [5] = x_4^2 - u_1x_4 - 2u_5x_1 + u_5^2$
$\qquad [6] = x_5^2 - u_1x_5 - 2u_6x_1 + u_6^2$
$\qquad [7] = u_5x_6 - u_4x_6 + u_4x_4 - u_5x_3$
$\qquad [8] = x_7$

$$[9] = u_6 x_8 - u_5 x_8 + u_5 x_5 - u_6 x_4$$
$$[10] = u_4 x_5 x_9 - u_6 x_3 x_9 + u_2 u_6 x_9 - u_2 u_4 u_6$$
$$[11] = u_4 x_{10} x_5 - u_2 u_4 x_5 - u_6 x_{10} x_3 + u_2 u_6 x_{10}$$

D_3: $u_1(u_2 - u_1)u_4(u_5 - u_4)(u_6 - u_5)(u_4 x_5 - u_6 x_3)(u_4 x_5 - u_6 x_3 + u_2 u_6)$

V_3: $(u_2, u_3, x_2, x_3, x_4, x_5, x_6, x_7, x_8, x_9, x_{10})$

T_4: $[1] = u_2$
$[2] = u_3$
$[3] = u_4$
$[4] = 2x_2 - u_1$
$[5] = x_3 - u_1$
$[6] = x_4^2 - u_1 x_4 - 2u_5 x_1 + u_5^2$
$[7] = x_5^2 - u_1 x_5 - 2u_6 x_1 + u_6^2$
$[8] = x_6 - x_3$
$[9] = x_7$
$[10] = u_6 x_8 - u_5 x_8 + u_5 x_5 - u_6 x_4$
$[11] = x_9$
$[12] = x_{10}$

D_4: $u_1(u_2 - u_1)u_5 u_6(u_6 - u_5)x_3(x_3 - u_2)$

V_4: $(u_2, u_3, u_4, x_2, x_3, x_4, x_5, x_6, x_7, x_8, x_9, x_{10})$.

Similarly, the pseudoremainder of g w.r.t. each of the above WT polynomial sets is zero and thus the given geometry statement is true with the given consideration of degenerate cases. For Example 2.4, the WDT zero basis found for $V(H/D)$ consists of one WT polynomial set:

T_1: $[1] = x_2$
$[2] = x_4 - x_1$
$[3] = x_3 z_2 + 1$
$[4] = x_1 z_3 - 1$
$[5] = x_5 z_6 - 1$

D_1: $x_1 x_3 x_5$

V_1: $(x_2, x_4, z_2, z_3, z_6)$.

The pseudoremainder of g w.r.t. the above WT polynomial set is zero and thus the given geometry statement is true with the given consideration of degenerate cases.

5. Other Examples

The methods mentioned for problems (P1) and (P2) have been used to prove at least 25 existing geometric theorems in Euclidean plane geometry with understandable degenerate cases. We give two other representative examples for such successful experiments. Here again, $K = \mathbb{Q}$ and $\bar{K} = \mathbb{R}$.

Example 5.1 (Desargues' Theorem in Euclidean plane geometry [15]). If the corresponding sides of two triangles $A_1 A_3 A_5$ and $A_2 A_4 A_6$ are parallel, then the lines joining corresponding vertices will be either concurrent or all parallel to each other (Fig. 4). (Suppose parallel lines are lines which do not intersect.)

We observe that each of the following should be considered as a degenerate case:

$$\text{points } A_1, A_3, A_5 \text{ are collinear},$$
$$\text{points } A_2, A_4, A_6 \text{ are collinear},$$
$$A_1 = A_2, \tag{D1}$$
$$A_3 = A_4,$$
$$A_5 = A_6.$$

We shall prove that the given statement is true under the following non-degenerate conditions:

$$\text{points } A_1, A_3, A_5 \text{ are not collinear},$$
$$\text{points } A_2, A_4, A_6 \text{ are not collinear},$$
$$A_1, A_2, \text{ and } A_3 \text{ are not collinear}, \tag{D2}$$
$$A_1, A_2, \text{ and } A_4 \text{ are not collinear},$$
$$A_3, A_4, \text{ and } A_5 \text{ are not collinear}.$$

It is not hard to see if the given geometry statement is true under the nondegenerate conditions (D2) then it is true with (D1) being considered as

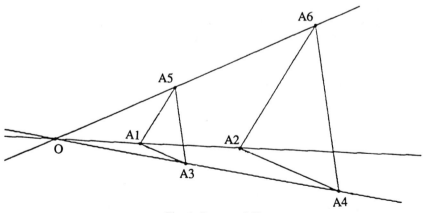

Fig. 4. Desargues' Theorem.

the only degenerate condition. We use (D2) rather than (D1) because the algebraic formula for (D2) is much more simple than that for condition (D1). We prove the theorem in two cases:

Case 1: *Lines* A_1A_2 *and* A_3A_4 *are parallel.* Then it suffices to prove that line A_5A_6 is parallel to line A_1A_2.

Case 2: *Lines* A_1A_2 *and* A_3A_4 *intersect at a point, say* O. Then it suffices to prove that line A_5A_6 passes point O with the point coordinates set up the same as in [15].

We used our decision method to confirm all the above cases. No question is asked from Ask2 and the resulting no-harm factor is 1 and thus the given theorem is proved with the above (D1) as the only necessary consideration on degenerate cases. For Case 1, point coordinates are assigned as

$$A_1 = (0,0), \qquad A_2 = (X_2, 0), \qquad A_3 = (X_3, X_4),$$
$$A_4 = (X_5, X_6), \qquad A_5 = (X_7, X_8), \qquad A_6 = (X_9, X_{10});$$

H is the list of the following polynomials:

$$[1] = X_4(X_5 - X_2) - X_3X_6 \quad (A_1A_3, A_2A_4 \text{ parallel})$$
$$[2] = X_8(X_9 - X_2) - X_{10}X_7 \quad (A_1A_5, A_2A_6 \text{ parallel})$$
$$[3] = (X_8 - X_4)(X_9 - X_5) + (X_6 - X_{10})(X_7 - X_3)$$
$$\quad (A_3A_5, A_4A_6 \text{ parallel})$$
$$[4] = X_2(X_4 - X_6) \quad (A_1A_2, A_3A_4 \text{ parallel});$$

D is the following polynomial

$$X_2^2 X_4 X_8 (X_3X_8 - X_4X_7)(X_5X_8 - X_3X_8 - X_6X_7 + X_4X_7$$
$$+ X_3X_6 - X_4X_5)(-X_6X_9 + X_2X_6 + X_{10}X_5 - X_{10}X_2)$$
$(A_1, A_2, A_3$ collinear, or A_1, A_2, A_5 collinear, or A_3, A_4, A_5 collinear, or A_1, A_3, A_5 collinear, or A_2, A_4, A_6 collinear);

and g is the following polynomial:

$$X_2(X_{10} - X_8) \quad (A_5A_6, A_1A_2 \text{ are parallel under condition } D \neq 0).$$

In this case the WDT zero basis of $V(H/D)$ consists of one WT polynomial set:

$$((X_5 - X_3 - X_2, X_6 - X_4, X_9 - X_7 - X_2, X_8 - X_{10}),$$
$$X_2X_4X_8(X_8 - X_4)(X_3X_8 - X_4X_7), (X_5, X_6, X_9, X_{10})).$$

For Case 2, point coordinates are given as:

$$O = (0, 0),$$
$$A_1 = (X_1, 0), \quad A_2 = (X_2, 0), \quad A_3 = (0, X_4),$$
$$A_4 = (0, X_6), \quad A_5 = (X_7, X_8), \quad A_6 = (X_9, X_{10});$$

and H is the list of the following polynomials:

$$[1] = X_1 X_6 - X_2 X_4 \quad (A_1 A_3, A_2 A_4 \text{ parallel})$$
$$[2] = X_8(X_9 - X_2) - X_{10}(X_7 - X_1) \quad (A_1 A_5, A_2 A_6 \text{ parallel})$$
$$[3] = (X_8 - X_4)X_9 + (X_6 - X_{10})X_7 \quad (A_3 A_5, A_4 A_6 \text{ parallel});$$

D is the following polynomial:

$$(X_2 X_4 - X_1 X_4)(-X_1 X_8 - X_4 X_7 + X_1 X_4)(X_2 X_8 - X_1 X_8)(-X_6 X_9$$
$$+ X_2 X_6 - X_{10} X_2)$$

$(A_1, A_2, A_3$ collinear, or A_1, A_2, A_5 collinear, or A_1, A_3, A_5 collinear, or A_2, A_4, A_6 collinear);

and g is the following polynomial:

$$X_{10} X_7 - X_8 X_9 \quad (O, A_5, A_6 \text{ collinear}).$$

In this case, WDT zero basis of $V(H/D)$ consists of two WT polynomial sets:

$$[1] = ((X_1 X_6 - X_2 X_4, X_1 X_9 - X_2 X_7, X_2 X_8 - X_1 X_{10}),$$
$$X_1 X_2(X_2 - X_1)X_4 X_7 X_8(X_1 X_8 + X_4 X_7 - X_1 X_4), (X_6, X_9, X_{10})),$$
$$[2] = ((X_1 X_6 - X_2 X_4, X_7, X_9, X_2 X_8 - X_1 X_{10}),$$
$$X_1 X_2(X_2 - X_1)X_4 X_8(X_8 - X_4), (X_6, X_7, X_9, X_{10})).$$

Example 5.2 (Simpson's Theorem [1, Example 2]). Let D be a point on the circumscribed circle of triangle ABC. From D, perpendiculars are drawn to the sides of the triangle. Prove that the feet of the perpendiculars are collinear (Fig. 5). (Fig. 5).

For the above statement, an obvious degenerate case is the case when points A, B, C are collinear. To confirm the given theorem, it suffices to prove the theorem with point coordinates of the form given in [1, Example 2, Choice 2], i.e.,

$$A = (0, 0), \quad B = (X_1, 0), \quad C = (X_2, X_3), \quad D = (X_4, X_7),$$
$$E = (X_8, X_9), \quad F = (X_{10}, X_{11}), \quad G = (X_4, 0), \quad O = (X_5, X_6).$$

We use our decision method to prove that $V(H/D \cdot g)$ is empty, where H is the list of the following polynomials:

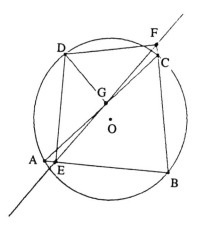

Fig. 5. Simson's Theorem.

$[1] = X_5^2 - (X_1 - X_5)^2 \quad (AO = OB)$

$[2] = X_6^2 - (X_3 - X_6)^2 + X_5^2 - (X_2 - X_5)^2 \quad (AO = OC)$,

$[3] = -(X_7 - X_6)^2 + X_6^2 + X_5^2 - (X_4 - X_5)^2 \quad (AO = OD)$,

$[4] = X_2 X_9 - X_1 X_9 - X_3 X_8 + X_1 X_3 \quad (B, C, E \text{ collinear})$

$[5] = X_3(X_9 - X_7) + (X_2 - X_1)(X_8 - X_4)$
       $(DE$ is perpendicular to $BC)$

$[6] = X_{11} X_2 - X_{10} X_3 \quad (A, C, F \text{ collinear})$

$[7] = X_3(X_{11} - X_7) + X_2(X_{10} - X_4) \quad (DF \text{ is perpendicular to } AC)$;

$D = X_1 X_3 \quad (A, B, C \text{ collinear})$;

and g is the following polynomial:

$$X_4 X_9 - X_{10} X_9 + X_{11} X_8 - X_{11} X_4 \quad (E, F, G \text{ collinear}).$$

No question from Ask2 is asked, and the identified no-harm factors from Ask1 include

$$(X_3^2 + X_2^2), \quad (X_3^2 + X_1^2), \quad (X_3^2 + X_2^2 - 2X_1 X_2 + X_1^2).$$

Therefore, the given theorem is proved under the observed nondegenerate condition "A, B, C are not collinear".

Note that in the above, we used the following property in $\mathbb{R}$: if $x^2 + y^2 = 0$ then $x = 0$ and $y = 0$; but not all fields possess the above property. If for a certain geometry, the polynomials for the corresponding geometric relationships remain the same, then the above result shows that in this geometry, the given geometry statement is true under the following subsidiary conditions:

A, B, C are not collinear,

$X_3^2 + X_2^2 \neq 0$,

$X_3^2 + X_1^2 \neq 0$,

$X_3^2 + X_2^2 - 2X_1X_2 + X_1^2 \neq 0$.

This is true regardless what associated field is considered. In case the associated field is the field of the complex numbers, it can be proved that for Simson's Theorem to be true under the condition "A, B, C not collinear", it is necessary to include the following subsidiary conditions:

$$X_3^2 + X_2^2 \neq 0, \qquad X_3^2 + X_1^2 \neq 0, \qquad X_3^2 + X_2^2 - 2X_1X_2 + X_1^2 \neq 0.$$

See Appendix C for the WDT zero basis for $V(H/D)$ when $\bar{K} = \mathbb{C}$ is the associated field. In that case, $V(H/D)$ is nonempty if any one of the above subsidiary conditions is not satisfied.

6. Conclusions

We presented methods and examples of examining different interpretations of the truth value of certain geometric statements. The methods require certain amount of human interaction but can be considered as decision methods. For all the examples that we tried in Euclidean plane geometry, all the input obtained from human interaction is based on the following simple type of knowledge in the field of real numbers:

if $x^2 + y^2 = 0$ then $x = 0$ and $y = 0$.

We have not found any surprising subsidiary condition for known geometrical theorems to be true in Euclidean geometry. We consider the required additional inclusion of subsidiary conditions, namely,

$$X_3^2 + X_2^2 \neq 0, \qquad X_3^2 + X_1^2 \neq 0, \qquad X_3^2 + X_2^2 - 2X_1X_2 + X_1^2 \neq 0,$$

for Simson's Theorem to be true over the field of complex numbers to be surprising and worth noting.

Appendix A. Use Quasi-Algebraic Sets for Elementary Geometrical Properties

In Euclidean plane geometry, let points A, B, C, D, E have coordinates of form

$$A = (x_1, y_1), \qquad B = (x_2, y_2), \qquad C = (x_3, y_3),$$
$$D = (x_4, y_4), \qquad E = (x_5, y_5)$$

in a coordinate system. Then

(1) "A, B, C collinear" can be characterized by $V(f_1/1)$, with

$$f_1 = (y_2 - y_1)(x_3 - x_1) - (y_3 - y_1)(x_2 - x_1),$$

to mean that all the solutions to $x_1, y_1, x_2, y_2, x_3, y_3$ for the given geometric relation are exactly those in $V(f_1/1)$; similarly,

(2) "A, B, C form a triangle" can be characterized by $V(0/f_1)$;

(3) "points A, B are distinct" can be characterized by $V(f_2/1)$, with

$$f_2 = (z_1(x_1 - x_2) - 1)(z_2(y_1 - y_2) - 1),$$

for some z_1, z_2;

(4) "lines AB and CD are parallel to each other" can be characterized by $V(f_3, f_2, f_4/f_1)$, with

$$f_3 = (y_2 - y_1)(x_4 - x_3) - (x_2 - x_1)(y_4 - y_3),$$
$$f_4 = (z_3(x_3 - x_4) - 1)(z_4(y_3 - y_4) - 1),$$

for some z_1, z_2, z_3, and z_4; and

(5) "distinct lines AB, CD intersect at point E" can be characterized by

$$V((y_2 - y_1)(x_5 - x_1) - (x_2 - x_1)(y_5 - y_1),$$
$$(y_4 - y_3)(x_5 - x_3) - (x_4 - x_3)(y_5 - y_3)/f_3).$$

The above algebraic representations and interpretations are not uniquely determined, but the notion of quasi-algebraic set seems to be useful when certain geometrical meanings need to be fully grasped by algebra.

Appendix B. Supplementary Proof to the Theorem of Centroid

We prove that for a triangle ABC, suppose points A, B, C are noncollinear, AD, BE, CF are three medians of the triangle, then

(1) points A and D are distinct, and thus similarly, points B and E are distinct, points C and F are distinct, and

(2) lines AD and BE are neither the same nor parallel.

Let

$$A = (X_1, X_2), \qquad B = (X_3, X_4), \qquad C = (X_5, X_6),$$
$$D = (X_7, X_8), \qquad E = (X_9, X_{10}).$$

Let

$h_1 = 2X_7 - X_5 - X_3 \quad (h_1, h_2: D \text{ is the midpoint of } BC),$
$h_2 = 2X_8 - X_6 - X_4,$
$h_3 = 2X_9 - X_5 - X_1 \quad (h_3, h_4: E \text{ is the midpoint of } AC),$
$h_4 = -X_6 - X_2 + 2X_{10},$
$h_5 = -X_3 + 2X_{11} - X_1 \quad (h_5, h_6: F \text{ is the midpoint of } AB),$
$h_6 = -X_4 - X_2 + 2X_{12},$

$D = X_3 X_6 - X_1 X_6 - X_4 X_5 + X_2 X_5 + X_1 X_4 - X_2 X_3$
    $(A, B, C \text{ are collinear}),$

$f_1 = X_1 - X_7 \quad (f_1, f_2: A = D),$
$f_2 = X_2 - X_8,$
$f_3 = (X_8 - X_2)(X_9 - X_3) + (X_4 - X_{10})(X_7 - X_1)$
    $(AD, BC \text{ are either identical or parallel}).$

Then the WDT zero bases for $V(h_1, h_2, h_3, h_4, h_5, h_6, f_1, f_2/D)$ and $V(h_1, h_2, h_3, h_4, h_5, h_6, f_3/D)$ are all empty; and thus the above conclusions are true.

Appendix C. WDT Zero Basis of Simson's Theorem

When $\bar{K}$ is the field of complex numbers, the WDT zero basis of $V(H/D)$ in Example 5.2 (Simson's Theorem) consists of the following six WT polynomial sets:

$T_1:$ $[1] = 2X_5 - X_1$
        $[2] = 2X_3 X_6 - X_3^2 - X_2^2 + X_1 X_2$
        $[3] = X_3 X_7^2 - X_3^2 X_7 - X_2^2 X_7 + X_1 X_2 X_7 + X_3 X_4^2 - X_1 X_3 X_4$
        $[4] = X_3^2 X_8 + X_2^2 X_8 - 2X_1 X_2 X_8 + X_1^2 X_8 - X_2 X_3 X_7 + X_1 X_3 X_7 - X_2^2 X_4$
           $+ 2X_1 X_2 X_4 - X_1^2 X_4 - X_1 X_3^2$
        $[5] = X_3^2 X_9 + X_2^2 X_9 - 2X_1 X_2 X_9 + X_1^2 X_9 - X_3^2 X_7$
           $- X_2 X_3 X_4 + X_1 X_3 X_4 + X_1 X_2 X_3 - X_1^2 X_3$
        $[6] = X_2 X_3 X_7 + X_2^2 X_4 - X_{10} X_3^2 - X_{10} X_2^2$
        $[7] = X_3^2 X_7 + X_2 X_3 X_4 - X_{11} - X_3^2 X_{11} X_2^2$

$D_1:$ $X_1 X_2 X_3 (X_3^2 + X_2^2)(X_3^2 + X_2^2 - 2X_1 X_2 + X_1^2)$

$V_1:$ $(X_5, X_6, X_7, X_8, X_9, X_{10}, X_{11})$

T_2: $[1] = X_3^2 + X_2^2 - 2X_1X_2 + X_1^2$
          $[2] = 2X_5 - X_1$
          $[3] = 2X_3X_6 - X_1X_2 + X_1^2$
          $[4] = X_3X_7 + X_2X_4 - X_1X_4 - X_1X_2 + X_1^2$
          $[5] = X_2X_9 - X_1X_9 - X_3X_8 + X_1X_3$
          $[6] = X_2X_4 + X_2^2 - 2X_{10}X_2 - X_1X_2 + X_1X_{10}$
          $[7] = X_2^2X_4 - 2X_1X_2X_4 + X_1^2X_4 + 2X_{11}X_2X_3 - X_1X_{11}X_3 + X_2^3$
          $\qquad - 3X_1X_2^2 + 3X_1^2X_2 - X_1^3$

D_2: $X_1X_2(X_2 - X_1)(2X_2 - X_1)X_3$

V_2: $(X_3, X_5, X_6, X_7, X_9, X_{10}, X_{11})$

T_3: $[1] = X_3^2 + X_2^2$
          $[2] = 2X_5 - X_1$
          $[3] = 2X_3X_6 + X_1X_2$
          $[4] = X_3X_7 + X_2X_4$
          $[5] = 2X_2X_8 - X_1X_8 - X_2X_4 + X_1X_4 - X_2^2$
          $[6] = 2X_2X_3X_9 - X_1X_3X_9 + X_2^2X_4 + X_2^3 - X_1X_2^2$
          $[7] = X_{10}X_3 - X_{11}X_2$

D_3: $X_1X_2(2X_2 - X_1)X_3$

V_3: $(X_3, X_5, X_6, X_7, X_8, X_9, X_{11})$

T_4: $[1] = X_2$
          $[2] = 2X_5 - X_1$
          $[3] = 2X_6 - X_3$
          $[4] = X_7^2 - X_3X_7 + X_4^2 - X_1X_4$
          $[5] = X_3^2X_8 + X_1^2X_8 + X_1X_3X_7 - X_1^2X_4 - X_1X_3^2$
          $[6] = X_3^2X_9 + X_1^2X_9 - X_3^2X_7 + X_1X_3X_4 - X_1^2X_3$
          $[7] = X_{10}$
          $[8] = X_7 - X_{11}$

D_4: $X_1X_3(X_3^2 + X_1^2)$

V_4: $(X_2, X_5, X_6, X_7, X_8, X_9, X_{10}, X_{11})$

T_5: $[1] = 2X_2 - X_1$
          $[2] = 4X_3^2 + X_1^2$
          $[3] = 2X_4 - X_1$
          $[4] = 2X_5 - X_1$
          $[5] = 4X_3X_6 + X_1^2$
          $[6] = X_7 - X_3$
          $[7] = X_1X_9 + 2X_3X_8 - 2X_1X_3$
          $[8] = 2X_{10}X_3 - X_1X_{11}$

D_5: $X_1 X_3$

V_5: $(X_2, X_3, X_4, X_5, X_6, X_7, X_9, X_{11})$

T_6: $[1] = X_2$
$[2] = X_3^2 + X_1^2$
$[3] = 2X_5 - X_1$
$[4] = 2X_3 X_6 + X_1^2$
$[5] = X_3 X_7 - X_1 X_4 + X_1^2$
$[6] = X_1 X_9 + X_3 X_8 - X_1 X_3$
$[7] = X_{10}$
$[8] = X_1 X_4 - X_{11} X_3 - X_1^2$

D_6: $X_1 X_3$

V_6: $(X_2, X_3, X_5, X_6, X_7, X_9, X_{10}, X_{11})$.

ACKNOWLEDGMENT

The author is deeply indebted to Dr. Shang-ching Chou, University of Texas at Austin, for his valuable comments and suggestions.

REFERENCES

1. Chou, S.-C., Proving elementary geometry theorems using Wu's algorithm, in: W.W. Bledsoe and D.W. Loveland (Eds.), *Automated Theorem Proving: After 25 Years*, Contemporary Mathematics **29** (1984) 243–286.
2. Chou, S.-C., Proving and discovering theorems in elementary geometries using Wu's method, Ph.D. Thesis, Department of Mathematics, University of Texas, Austin, TX (1985).
3. Chou, S.-C., Proving geometry theorems using Wu's method: A collection of geometry theorems proved mechanically, Tech. Rept. 50, Institute for Computing Science, The University of Texas at Austin, Austin, TX (1986).
4. Chou, S.-C. and Ko, H.-P., On mechanical theorem proving in Minkowskian plane geometry, in: *Proceedings LICS Conference* (1986) 187–191.
5. Chou, S.-C. and Schelter, W.F., Proving geometry theorems with rewrite rules, *J. Autom. Reasoning* **2-3** (1986) 253–273.
6. Collins, G.E., Quantifier elimination for real closed fields by cylindrical algebraic decomposition, in: *Proceedings 2nd GI Conference on Automata Theory and Formal Languages*, Lecture Notes in Computer Science **33** (Springer, New York, 1975) 134–183.
7. Kapur, D., Geometry theorem proving using Hilbert's Nullstellensatz, in: *Proceedings 1986 Symposium on Symbolic and Algebraic Computation (SYMSAC 86)*, Waterloo, Ont. (1986) 202–208.
8. Knuth, D.E., *The Art of Computer Programming* **2** (Addison-Wesley, Reading, MA 1981).
9. Ko, H.-P. and Hussain, M.A., A study of Wu's method—A method to prove certain theorems in elementary geometry, *Congr. Numer.* **48** (1985) 225–242.
10. Ko, H.-P. and Hussain, M.A., ALGE-prover: An algebraic geometry theorem proving software, Tech. Rept. 85CRD139, General Electric Company, Schenectady, NY (1985).
11. Ko, H.-P., ALGE-prover II: A new edition of ALGE-prover, Tech. Rept. 86CRD081, General Electric Company, Schenectady, NY (1986).

12. Kutzler, B. and Stifter, S., Automated geometry theorem proving using Buchberger's algorithm, in: *Proceedings 1986 Symposium on Symbolic and Algebraic Computation (SYMSAC 86)*, Waterloo, Ont. (1986) 209–214.
13. Wu, W.-T., On the decision problem and the mechanization of theorem proving in elementary geometry, *Sci. Sinica* **21** (1978) 159–172.
14. Wu, W.-T., Toward mechanization of geometry—Some comments on Hilbert's Grundlagen der Geometrie, *Acta Math. Sci.* **2** (2) (1982) 125–138.
15. Wu, W.-T., Some remarks on mechanical theorem proving in elementary geometry, *Acta Math. Sci.* **3** (1983) 357–360.
16. Wu, W.-T., Basic principles of mechanical theorem proving in elementary geometries, *J. Syst. Sci. Math. Sci.* **4** (3) (1984) 207–235.
17. Wu, W.-T., On zeros of algebraic equations—an application of Ritt principle, *Kexue Tongbao* **31** (1) (1986).

Received May 1987; revised version received December 1987

Modular Algebraic Specification of Some Basic Geometrical Constructions*

Joseph A. Goguen**

SRI International, Menlo Park, CA 94025, U.S.A.;
and Center for the Study of Language and Information,
Stanford, CA 94305, U.S.A.

ABSTRACT

This paper applies some recent advances in algebraic specification technology to plane geometry. The two most important specification techniques are parameterized modules and order-sorted algebra; the latter provides a systematic treatment of subtypes. This exercise also indicates how a rigorous semantic foundation in equational logic can be given for many techniques in knowledge representation, including is-a hierarchies (with multiple inheritance), multiple representations, implicit (one-way) coercion of representation and parameterized modular structuring. Degenerate cases (which can be a particular nuisance in computational geometry), exception handling, information hiding, block structure, and pattern-driven rules are also treated, and again have rigorous semantic foundations. The geometric constructions which illustrate all this are specified over any ordered field having square roots of nonnegative elements; thus, we also specify some algebra, including rings, fields, and determinants. All specifications are written in a variant of the OBJ language.

1. Introduction

There are several reasons why one might be interested in the algebraic specification of geometrical constructions:

(1) This is an interesting exercise in specification (i.e., in knowledge representation) because of the way that it challenges current technology, including modularity, error handling, parameterization, and multiple representation.

(2) Algebraic specifications provide a compact (and even executable) description of the entities and constructions involved, and of how they inter-

* Supported in part by Office of Naval Research contracts N00014-82-C-0333, N00014-85-C-0417, and N00014-86-C-0450, NSF grant CCR-8707155, and a gift from the System Development Foundation.
** Present address: Oxford University Computing Laboratory, Programming Research Group, 8–11 Keble Road, Oxford OX1 3QD, England, U.K.

relate. In particular, they give a precise understanding of the degenerate cases that arise, and also some insight into the general nature of degenerate cases in geometry.

(3) These specifications are logically rigorous and provide a standard of correctness for other representations, implementations and algorithms.

(4) In addition, a suitable algebraic manipulation system, like EQLOG [15] could solve systems of the formulae given here, thus giving solutions to many particular problems.

The basic geometrical constructions that are treated here include the line through two points, the intersection of two lines, the circle through three points, and the tangent to a circle through a point. These are all completely specified in a version of the OBJ language [6, 7, 22]. Although this paper does not attempt a formal explanation of the semantics of the specification features used, pointers to the relevant technical literature are given. The specification uses standard representations from analytic geometry[1] and encodes what amounts to a small textbook (e.g., much of the first 160 pages of [30] plus some algebra) in a language that is more rigorous than that usually found in textbooks.

The following issues seem particularly interesting in regard to algebraic specification techniques:

(1) Since there are many different sorts of data, including points, lines and circles, it seems very desirable to have a many-sorted logic, to prevent these very different entities from interacting in unintended ways (e.g., we do not even want to consider "the line through two circles" as a well-formed construction). Also, some sorts of data have interesting subsorts; for example, the nonnegative real numbers are a subsort of all the reals.

(2) Under certain conditions, some of these constructions fail. For example, two lines fail to meet if they are parallel. This means that we must consider exceptions or errors.

(3) Alternative representations are sometimes required for "degenerate" cases. For example, if we choose to represent lines in "slope-intercept form", i.e., as pairs (m, b) that determine the set of all points (x, y) such that $y = mx + b$, then we need a separate representation for vertical lines, such as their x-intercept, (a), determining the points (x, y) such that $x = a$. A related issue is the use of *multiple* representations, for example, the use of *both* Cartesian *and* polar coordinates. (See Section 6.1.)

(4) Since this is a fairly complex problem, we should break it into parts, much as a textbook on analytic geometry is broken into chapters, sections, and subsections. We should also try to use standard specifications from a library as much as possible. The library should be *hierarchically* organized into books,

---

[1] One could also consider using the axioms for plane geometry given by Euclid, or by Hilbert.

chapters, etc., and all these should be as *parameterized* as possible, so that they can be "fine tuned" to as many different applications as possible, thus enhancing reusability.

(5) Giving explicit formulae for constructions has the great advantage that the specifications can be executed. However, it has the disadvantage that the specification seems to depend on particular representations, such as Cartesian coordinates,[2] and this seems to conflict with the principles of "information hiding" of Parnas [31] and others. Section 6.1 argues that this is not really a problem.

(6) Analytic geometry is usually thought to be based upon the real numbers. How can we specify this particular structure, or avoid having to specify it?

Points (4) and (5) concern the structuring of complex specification, which is also desirable to enhance their readability, writability, modifiability, and verifiability. To do all this while providing a rigorous semantics for all the constructions involved seems a significant challenge.

The specification given here is based on one originally written during 1981 in a language that we called ORDINARY [11], in response to a problem posed by Staunstrup [34]. The current specification is written in a version of OBJ [6, 7, 22] making heavy use of specification technology developed in the last few years by the OBJ group at SRI, in collaboration with Kokichi Futatsugi, Jean-Pierre Jouannaud, Claude and Helene Kirchner, David Plaisted, and especially Rod Burstall, José Meseguer, and Timothy Winkler. I particularly thank Dr. Meseguer, whose comments and suggestions caught many bugs, and also helped to complete the treatment of multiple representation. The main features that are used here but not found in our current implementation of OBJ are:

– specification blocks, which may even be parameterized;
– implicit variable declarations;
– a relational notation for Boolean-valued operations;
– implicit error supersorts;
– a more powerful way to combine modules (denoted combining_and_over_);
– multiple representations for data types, including implicit selectors; and
– coercions between related or unrelated sorts.

There are also some minor syntactic variations.

The geometrical constructions are specified using standard analytic geometry, with explicit representations for all operations and exceptions. Although this is very convenient for an algebraic specification, it is in some ways simpler to use an implicit set-theoretic approach, as in [34]; such an approach would be well-supported by a language like Z [1]. A difficulty for set-theoretic ap-

---

[2] For example, Staunstrup [34] argues that the construction for a tangent to a circle through a point requires access to previously defined representations.

proaches is that one should still prove, for example, that the intersection of two lines is exactly one point, unless the lines are either parallel or identical; however, such proofs will be most convenient using the algebraic representations of analytic geometry, which will require a specification like the one given here anyway. An advantage of the algebraic approach is that it is directly executable.

The use of multiple representations in functional programming has been discussed by Wadler [35], who has given some interesting examples, but not a formal semantics; here we give some further examples, as well as a more general approach that has an initial algebra semantics. An algebraic semantics for coercions has been given by Reynolds [33]; here we extended this to user-definable coercions and integrate it with our notion of retract. Both discussions make strong use of order-sorted algebra.

2. Theories and Objects

This section marks the beginning of a gradual development of the geometrical constructions specification. Much of the work is necessarily devoted to describing the specification (i.e., knowledge representation) technology that is used. The description given here is informal, but hopefully it is sufficiently clear and precise so that the specification can be understood; in fact, it is a completely precise mathematical theory with a well-understood proof theory, and references to the specification literature are given for technical details. The specification itself is relatively short, and is entirely self-contained, in the sense that every concept used is defined; much of it consists of highly reusable subspecifications, including some basic set theory and basic abstract algebra (e.g., rings, fields and vectors); many of these specifications are parameterized. It is fortunate that the simplest concepts that underlie the geometric specification correspond to the simplest features of our specification language, so that we can develop both the specification and its language in parallel.

The basic unit for specification and encapsulation is the *module*. We use two kinds of module:

(1) *Theories*, which define a *class* of structures, namely all those structures that satisfy the given axioms. The axioms in theories are first-order combinations of atomic equalities.

(2) *Objects*, which specify a particular structure (up to isomorphism), including its sorts of data and its operations (including constants), by using initial algebra semantics (see Section 2.1 for more on this topic). The axioms are just (universally quantified conditional) equations.[3]

OBJ is a "wide spectrum" language, in the sense that it integrates program-

---

[3] The machinery for using two different kinds of sentence, equational and first-order, is described in [13] and [3], under the heading of "duplex institutions".

ming, specification, and rapid prototyping. More specifically, the code in objects constitutes an executable program, while that in theories can be used for specification. Depending on what features appear, the efficiency of the code in objects can vary greatly. For example, associative-commutative operations can be rather expensive; however, they may be regarded as a mere convenience for rapid prototyping, to be replaced by more efficient code at a later stage of program development.

The basic syntax for modules can be illustrated with the "trivial" theory, TRIV, which is satisfied by any set of elements:

```
theory TRIV is
    sorts Elt.
endth
```

A theory module begins with the keyword theory or th, and ends with endth, while an object module begins with object or obj and ends with endo. The opening keyword is followed by the module name, by convention all caps, here TRIV. Then, following is comes the *signature*, consisting of declarations for any new sorts and operations. The signature of TRIV consists of just one sort declaration, for Elt. Then comes the body, which is a collection of axioms; in this case, there are none, but the BOOL object below illustrates this feature. Our notational conventions call for sort names to begin with a capital letter, for operation and relation names to begin either with a special character or a small letter, and for variable names to begin with a capital letter. There may also be some declarations indicating what other modules are imported, as discussed further in Section 3; these should come before the signature.

Just as TRIV is perhaps the most basic theory, BOOL is perhaps the most basic object. The following specification (which is executable) introduces some further specification features:

```
obj BOOL is
    sorts Bool.
    ok-ops
      _and_ : Bool Bool→ Bool [assoc comm id: true].
      _or_ : Bool Bool→ Bool [assoc comm id: false].
      not_ : Bool→ Bool.
      _implies_ : Bool Bool→ Bool.
    ok-eqns
      false and B = false.
      true or B = true.
      not true = false.
      not false = true.
      B implies B' = (not B) or B'.
endo
```

An operation ∗ can be declared binary infix of sort S just by writing

_∗_: S S→ S.

Here the underbar characters, _ , in "_∗_", indicate that ∗ takes one argument before and one argument after the ∗. In general, "mixfix" syntax for operations among several sorts is indicated by the distribution of underbars and keywords, and the number of underbars should equal the number of sorts in the list between the " : " and the "→". In this case, there are two, both of sort S. Similarly, not_ is prefix of sort Bool.

The "attribute" assoc for an operation ∗ indicates that associative syntax (such as 1∗2∗3) can be used in expressions, and also that an associative equation is asserted for ∗; moreover, the print form of expressions using ∗ will have associative syntax. Similarly, operations can be declared commutative with the attribute comm, and can be given an identity nil with the attribute id: nil. All these conventions follow OBJ [6, 7, 22].

The prefixes "ok-" that occur here will be explained in Section 4, as will the notion of well-formed expression. First-order combinations of equalities use the keyword axioms, while plain equations use eqns.

A gesture in the direction of "logic" programming (in the sense of pure PROLOG, although this might better be called "relational" programming) is to allow a relational syntax for Bool-valued operations; this results in a notation rather like that of EQLOG [15], but neither unification nor backtracking are supported. Here is a simple example, the theory of partially ordered sets:

```
theory POSET is
  sorts Elt.
  ok-relns (_ > _)( _ >= _) : Elt Elt.
  ok-eqs
    X > Y and Y > Z implies X > Z.
    not X > X.
    X >= Y = X > Y or X == Y.
endth
```

Here the variables X, Y, Z all have sort Elt, and the relation declarations are just syntactic sugar for

_ > _ : Elt Elt→ Bool.
_ >= _ : Elt Elt→ Bool.

When an "equation" is really just an expression of sort Bool, as in the first equation in POSET above, it is to be taken as an abbreviation for the equation obtained by adding "= true." Thus, the first equation in POSET really means

X > Y and Y > Z implies X > Z = true.

The built-in equality operation == is discussed in Section 2.1 just below. Since any module involving relations *must* use the object BOOL, we adopt the convention that *every* module imports BOOL without having to say so explicitly.

Here is another theory, the theory of Abelian groups, using some of the features introduced above.

```
theory ABGP is
   sorts Elt.
   ok-ops
      _ + _ : Elt Elt→ Elt [assoc comm id: 0].
      − _ : Elt→ Elt.
      _ − _ : Elt Elt→ Elt.
   ok-eqns
      X + (−X) = 0.
      X − Y = X + (−Y).
endth
```

The denotation of a theory is just the class of all algebras that satisfy it. Thus, ABGP denotes the class of all Abelian groups, TRIV denotes the class of all sets, and POSET denotes the class of all partially ordered sets (modeled as algebras with Bool-valued operations). This "loose" semantics is in contrast to the semantics of objects, to which we turn in the next subsection.

2.1. Operational and denotational semantics of objects

The specification of geometric constructions only involves unchanging "Platonic" entities (such as points, lines and circles), and does not require "mutable" entities having a state that may change. Therefore we may regard these "immutable" entities as belonging to *abstract data types*, and use initial algebra semantics [21] to describe them. However, an extension of the techniques used here can handle entities with state [20],[4] and this would be needed for many other problems.

Objects actually have two different semantics, one denotational and one operational; it is a pleasant fact that these two agree under certain simple and common conditions. The denotational semantics is "initial algebra semantics" and the operational semantics is term rewriting.

---

[4] Final algebra semantics, as advocated for example by Wand [36] and (seemingly) Guttag [23], does not seem to me appropriate for either mutable or immutable entities, although it does have conceptual value for certain "fully abstract" models.

Let us first discuss the operational semantics, using BOOL as an example. The basic idea is to apply the given equations to *ground terms* (which are terms without variables), as left-to-right *rewrite rules*, progressively transforming them until a *reduced* or *normal form* is reached, where no further rules are applicable. For example, using $\Rightarrow$ for "rewrites to", in the BOOL object above we have

(true implies (true or false)) and (not false) $\Rightarrow$
(true implies true) and (not false) $\Rightarrow$
((not true) or true) and (not false) $\Rightarrow$
(false or true) and (not false) $\Rightarrow$
true and (not false) $\Rightarrow$
true and true $\Rightarrow$
true

A set of rewrite rules is said to be *terminating* if every sequence of rewrites on ground terms eventually reaches a normal form. It is said to be *Church–Rosser* if and two rewrite sequences starting from the same term (two such sequences are shown as solid arrows in Fig. 1) can always be further rewritten in such a way that they reach equal values (two further rewrite sequences that accomplish this are shown as dashed lines in Fig. 1; the stars on arrows indicate that they represent a sequence of 0, 1 or more individual rewriting steps). It is a basic result of term rewriting theory that if a system of rewrite rules is Church–Rosser and terminating, then every term has a *unique* normal form. (Huet and Oppen [26] give a nice survey of rewrite rule theory.)

Let us now consider the denotational semantics. The basic idea of *initial algebra semantics* is to take an initial algebra (it turns out nicely that any two are isomorphic) as the denotation of a set of equations [21]. Given a *signature* Σ, i.e., a collection of sort and operation symbols, and given a set E of Σ-equations, then the class of all Σ-algebras that satisfy E has *initial algebras*, which in a sense are the "most prototypical" models of E, and which can be characterized in various ways. Perhaps the most intuitive characterization (from [5]) is that the following two conditions should be satisfied:

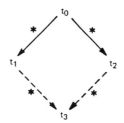

Fig. 1. The Church–Rosser property.

- *No junk*: every element of an initial algebra is denoted by some Σ-term.
- *No confusion*: two Σ-terms denote the same element of an initial algebra iff they are *provably equal*, using the equations in E as axioms. (Rules of deduction for many-sorted algebra are given in [29], and for order-sorted algebra in [18].)

The other characterization is more technical: an algebra is *initial* in a class $\mathscr{C}$ of algebras iff it is in $\mathscr{C}$ and there is a *unique* homomorphism from it to every member of $\mathscr{C}$.

Goguen [10] proves that if a set E of equations is terminating and Church–Rosser when regarded as a set of rewrite rules, then the set of all normal forms constitute an algebra that is initial among all the algebras satisfying E. This theorem says that term rewriting is a *correct* implementation of initial algebra semantics. (This result extends to the order-sorted case.)

Two built-in operations, $\_ == \_$ and $\_ =/= \_$, use a decision procedure for ground term equality for Church–Rosser and terminating rewrite rule sets: given ground terms t and t', reduce them to normal form and then see if the normal forms are equal. If they are, then $(t == t')$ is true and $(t =/= t')$ is false; if they are not, then $(t == t')$ is false and $(t =/= t')$ is true. These operations are *polymorphic*, in the sense that they can take arguments of any two sorts that are compatible.

We allow two kinds of conditional. The first is the usual polymorphic mixfix operation if_then_else_fi, defined by the equations

> if true then X else Y = X.
> if false then X else Y = Y.

whenever X and Y can be matched to subterms of the same sort (and the first argument has sort Bool). The second kind of conditional is the *conditional equation*; its denotational semantics says that the equality holds if the condition is true, while its operational semantics says that the rule is applied only if its condition—which follows the keyword if and must be of sort Bool—evaluates to true. For example, we will later see equations like

> X/X = 1 if X =/= 0.

For associative operations, pattern matching modulo associativity is used to determine whether a rule applies; the same applies to associative-commutative matching, etc. For example, with associative-commutative matching for and, the rule

> false and B = false

from BOOL reduces the term

   true and false and f(3)
to
   false.

3. Specification Structuring

There are many reasons for wanting to structure specifications. Perhaps the most important reason is that structured specifications can be much easier to read, write, and debug. Another major reason is that structured specifications are much easier to reuse, so that we can set up and draw upon a library of predefined specifications. Parameterized (i.e., generic) specifications can greatly improve the reusability of specifications, and multi-level hierarchies, in which modules are grouped together in module blocks, which may import other such blocks, are another useful structuring technique. Many specification languages fail to provide any way to structure specifications beyond the purely syntactic, such as allowing comments at certain places, supporting conventions for indentation, allowing lines to be drawn at certain places, or providing various facilities for copying and editing code (LARCH [24] provides an unusually rich collection of such facilities). In my view, the challenge is to provide structuring techniques that have both a well-defined semantic basis and an intuitively suggestive syntax.

This section discusses: (i) how modules import other modules, including block structuring for modules; and (ii) how parameterized modules work, giving the power of higher-order specifications while retaining a first-order logic. The related issues of information hiding and multiple representation are discussed in Section 6.1.

3.1. Importing modules

Modules can import other modules in three different ways, which are indicated by three different keywords:

(1) protecting indicates that nothing defined within the imported module is affected by the signature or equations of the importing module, or more precisely:
  – *no junk*: no new data items of old sorts are introduced by the signature of new module; and
  – *no confusion*: no data items of old sorts are identified by the equations in the new module.
(2) extending only guarantees that there is no confusion.
(3) using makes no guarantees at all.

A simple example with theories is rings, which build upon the theory of Abelian groups:

```
theory RING is
   using ABGP.
   ok-op _ * _ : Elt Elt→ Elt [assoc id: 1].
   ok-eqns
      X * (Y + Z) = (X * Y) + (X * Z).
      X * 0 = 0.
endth
```

Theories can also import objects in any of the three ways; for example, POSET (implicitly) protects BOOL.

3.1.1. *Module blocks*

Blocks are just as useful in specification languages as they are in ALGOL-like languages. The basic purposes of block structuring are:

– to group together code that is closly related conceptually; and
– to control the scope of names and representations.

Of course, these two purposes are intertwined, since modules that are closely related conceptually may need to share information that should be hidden elsewhere. The first issue is discussed here, while the second is deferred to Section 6.1.

There are some natural blocks in our geometrical constructions specification. For example, it is natural to block together the "most basic" theories and objects, such as TRIV, BOOL, NAT, INT and POSET. Another natural block would include the various theories from abstract algebra, including GROUP, ABGP, RING and FIELD.

Although it is not needed in this paper, it is also convenient to be able to nest blocks within other blocks, since this provides a natural way to hierarchically structure libraries. Blocks should also be allowed to have parameters, and then they will have requirement theories.

The syntax for blocks is straightforward: after the keyword block comes the name of the block, followed by its formal parameters and requirement theories (if any) followed by the keyword is, followed by (optional) import and export declarations (these are discussed in Section 6). The body consists of a sequence of modules, which may be theories or objects, and other (embedded) blocks. All parameters which occur in the block head may be used freely in the body. The block ends with the keyword endblock or endbl, which may be followed by the name of the block once again. This syntax can be seen in the geometrical constructions block GEOM given in Section 7, and would have been used elsewhere, except that it would have undermined the expository continuity of the paper. When a block is imported, one gets the sum of everything in the body, except for things that are hidden. When a parameterized block is instantiated, all instances of the parameters are instantiated.

3.2. Parameterized modules

Parameterized programming [12] is a powerful form of programming-in-the-large that involves putting together parameterized modules to form larger program units, with the interfaces between previously written program units described by theories. We will see how this substantially generalizes the functional composition that is the basis of functional programming.

Parameterized programming is based on the systematic use of parameterized (generic) modules. Encapsulating related code makes it more reusable, and parameterized modules can be even more reusable, since they can be "tuned" for a variety of applications by choosing different parameter values; moreover, debugging, maintenance, readability and portability are all enhanced. The interface declarations of our parameterized modules are *not* purely syntactic, like ADA's; instead, they are given by *semantic* theories that actual modules must satisfy before they can be meaningfully substituted. This can prevent many subtle bugs.

Parameterized modules have *requirement theories* which describe "interface" conditions that must be satisfied in order for a module to be meaningful as an actual parameter. For example, the module R3[R :: RING] below specifies three-dimensional vectors and determinants over an arbitrary ring R, and has the requirement theory RING; the notation [R :: RING] says that any R that is used as an actual parameter must be a ring.

Similarly, STACK[X :: TRIV] might be a parameterized object for specifying stacks of Xs, where the only requirement on X is that some particular sort, i.e., some set of data items, is designated. If a formal parameter is named X, and its requirement theory has a principal sort, then the principal sort of X is also denoted X; this is better than trying to use the principal sort of the requirement theory as a name, because there may be more than one instance of any given requirement theory in the module interface, as in 3TUPLE below. However, if there is more than one sort in the requirement theory, another convention is needed. Suppose that the parameter part of some generic is [X Y :: TH], where TH has sorts A and B. Then in the body of this module, we can refer to the four sorts that are involved as A.X, B.X, A.Y and B.Y. If one of the sorts of TH is a principal sort, say A, then we can more simply write the sorts involved as X, B.X, Y and B.Y.

In order to apply R3, or STACK, to INT, the integers, we must say *how* INT is viewed as a ring, or as a set. In general, there may be more than one way of doing this. For example, there are many views of INT as a POSET, depending on what ordering relation we choose for integers; $<=, >=$, and "divides" are all possibilities. As in CLEAR [4, 5],[5] this is done by giving a "binding" of the sorts and operations in the requirement theory to those in the actual parameter. We call such bindings *views*. It is often convenient to let the system infer *default views*, which formalize the idea of *the obvious binding*; see [12] for details. This allows us to write just R3[INT] or STACK[INT]. Assuming the sorts of RING and TRIV are Ring and Elt, respectively, then these two views in more detail are (Ring to Int) and (Elt to Int), respectively; we do not need to write "+ to +" or "0 to 0" because the default convention allows omitting components of the binding that are syntactically the same in the two modules. The reason that we do not even need to write (Ring to Int) is that default views try to map principal sorts to principal sorts. (Every module has a *principal sort*, which is either the first new sort that it introduces, or else the principal sort of the first module that is imports. For example, FIELD is defined using RING; therefore, every field is a ring, and the principal sort of FIELD is the same as that of RING, namely Elt.)

In a more technical language, views are *theory morphisms*, and they define *forgetful functors* on the corresponding categories of algebras. A view as TRIV (which just designates a sort) always determines a forgetful functor to the category of sets, i.e., it determines an underlying set functor. See [13] for more detail on these issues.

A novel feature is that commands are provided to modify and combine modules; thus, (a form of) program transformation is provided within the language itself. These commands appear in *module expressions*, which describe (and when executed, create) complex combinations of modules. This capability goes beyond that provided by the Module Interconnection Languages (MILs) that are sometimes available as a separate tool in a programming environment, since MILs are purely descriptive, and do not actually construct programs.

TUPLE is a "polymorphic" parameterized object, in that it can take any number of actual parameters, each having the requirement theory TRIV, and it then constructs tuples of values of the arguments that it is supplied. For example, TUPLE[NAT,NAT] gives pairs of natural numbers. Similarly, if TUPLE is applied to n arguments, it constructs n-tuples; moreover, n selectors are automatically supplied, with the notation 1, 2, 3, etc. Here is some code that defines 3-tuples, which are used in the module R3 below:

---

[5] Actually, we are developing a whole family of languages with similar features. In particular, OBJ [6], EQLOG [15] and FOOPS [16] are languages offering functional, combined functional and logic, and combined functional and object-oriented programming, respectively. FOOPLOG [16] even combines all three paradigms.

```
obj 3TUPLE[X,Y,Z :: TRIV] is
  sort Tuple.
  ok-ops
    ⟨_,_,_⟩ : X Y Z → Tuple.
    1_ : Tuple → X.
    2_ : Tuple → Y.
    3_ : Tuple → Z.
  ok-eqns
    1⟨X,Y,Z⟩ = X.
    2⟨X,Y,Z⟩ = Y.
    3⟨X,Y,Z⟩ = Z.
endo
```

The comma is special as a mixfix operator keyword in that it does not require extra spaces around it for parsing. Although the default selector notation, $1, 2, 3$, may not be appropriate for some applications of 3TUPLE, we can easily change it, e.g., to first-name, middle-initial, last-name, by *renaming*, with syntax like the following

TUPLE[ID,ID,ID] * (1 to first-name, 2 to middle-initial, 3 to last-name).

Similarly, we can rename the Tuple sort; for example,

TUPLE[R,R,R] * (Tuple to R3)

constructs three-dimensional vectors. We can go a little further, by defining a parameterized module to enrich any ring R with the concepts of three-dimensional vectors and determinants, including vector addition, scalar multiplication, and a special constant that is used in our geometrical constructions:

```
obj R3[R :: RING] is
  protecting TUPLE[R,R,R] * (Tuple to R3).
  ok-ops
    _ + _ : R3 R3 → R3.
    _ * _ : R R3 → R3.
    det3 : R3 R3 R3 → Elt.
    one : → R3.
  ok-eqns
    P1 + P2 = ⟨1(P1) + 1(P2),2(P1) + 2(P2),3(P1) + 3(P2)⟩.
    R * P = ⟨R * 1(P),R * 2(P),R * 3(P)⟩.
    det3(P1,P2,P3) = (1(P1) * 2(P2) * 3(P3)) − (2(P1) * 1(P2) * 3(P3))
                   + (2(P1) * 3(P2) * 1(P3)) − (3(P1) * 2(P2) * 1(P3))
                   + (1(P1) * 3(P2) * 2(P3)) − (3(P1) * 1(P2) * 2(P3)).
    one = ⟨1,1,1⟩.
endo
```

A final operation that can appear in module expressions is the *sum* of two module expressions, written A + B. This represents a new module in which the information in both A and B is available (except for things that are hidden). An interesting issue here is what happens to modules that are imported by both A and B; for example, both A and B will import BOOL in any case, and they may also import NAT or INT. The correct semantics is that such modules should be *shared* rather than just copied. For more detail, see [12].

To conclude, the kind of module interconnection supported by module expressions has a number of advantages:

(1) Module composition is much more powerful than the purely functional composition that is usual in functional programming, since a single module instantiation can perform many different function compositions at once. For example, a complex arithmetic module CPXA that takes real arithmetic modules as actual parameters could be instantiated with
– single-precision reals, CPXA[SP-REAL],
– double-precision reals, CPXA[DP-REAL], or
– multiple-precision reals, CPXA[MP-REAL],
each involving the substitution of dozens of functions into dozens of other functions; this would be *much* more effort using only functional composition.

(2) The logic remains first-order, so that understanding and verifying code is much simpler than with higher-order logic [9].

(3) Semantic declarations are allowed at module interfaces (given by requirement theories).

(4) Strong type checking will catch many errors.

(5) Besides instantiation, module expressions also allow renaming of module parts and "addition" of modules.

4. Subsorts and Exceptions

To handle cases where things of one sort are also of another sort—for example, all natural numbers are also rational numbers—and cases where something may have several different sorts, we shall use "order-sorted algebra" [18]. In this approach, a partial ordering relation is given on the set of sorts, e.g. Nat < Rat. Although I hope that the specifications given here can be understood without technical knowledge of this theory, a fully rigorous foundation is in fact available; see [17–19].

A term over an order-sorted signature is considered to be *well-formed* iff it has a *unique* parse of lowest sort. (Goguen and Meseguer [18, 19] show that, under certain very mild and natural assumptions, order-sorted terms do in fact always have well-defined least sorts.)

Sometimes subexpressions are not of the expected sort, and must be "coerced". This is trivial from a subsort to a supersort; for example, if an operation + is only defined for rationals, then (2 + 2) is fine, where 2 is a natural number, because Nat < Rat. It is less trivial the other way; for example, consider $(-4/-2)!$, where ! is only defined for natural numbers. At parse time, we cannot know that the subexpression $(-4/-2)$ will turn out to be a natural number—in fact, the expression does not parse in the conventional sense—but we can "give it the benefit of the doubt" by having the parser insert a *retract*, which is removed at run time if the subexpression really does become a natural, and otherwise remains behind as an informative error message. Thus, the parser turns the expression $(-4/-2)!$ into $(r.rat.nat(-4/-2))!$, which becomes $(r.rat.nat(2))!$ and then $2!$ at run time, using the key equation

$$r.rat.nat(X) = X$$

where X is a variable of sort Nat. [14] and [18] give details of the operational semantics of retracts based on order-sorted rewriting, and Section 6.1 significantly extends the practical utility of this mechanism.

4.1. Exceptions

Most specification techniques do not provide an adequate treatment of exceptions. One common approach is to use partial operations, which are simply undefined under the exceptional conditions. Although this can be developed rigorously, as in [28], it is not entirely satisfactory for practical applications, because it does not allow for giving error messages, or for recovering from errors. The treatment of exceptions in this paper is to translate aspects of "error algebra" notation (introduced in [8]) into order-sorted algebra; this permits explicit and informative error messages to be given in exceptional conditions.

In this approach, every sort S automatically has an *error supersort*, denoted S?, with S < S?; data elements of sort S are said to be *ok*, while data elements of sort S? but not of sort S are said to be *erroneous*. Operations declared as ok-ops are *safe*, in the sense that if all their arguments are ok, then so is their result; but they *may* have erroneous values in other cases; safety is expressed formally by overloading the operation. Operations declared as ops are *unsafe*, in the sense that they may have erroneous values even if all their arguments are ok. Operations may also be declared err-ops; the translation to order-sorted algebra treats these exactly the same as ops, but this declaration should be used when the user believes that all values are definitely erroneous. (If such declarations were given formal meaning, we would not be able to guarantee their consistency, or even the existence of initial algebras, so they are treated purely as annotations.)

There is a convention that variables are assumed to have the highest ok-sorted parse that makes sense. If necessary to circumvent the convention, variables may be qualified with their sort, as in X.Sort, and they can also be declared explicitly in front of an axiom, in the form (X : Sort). Just as there are three kinds of operation, we also distinguish three kinds of equation (or axiom): an ok-eqn (or ok-axiom) only applies if its right-hand side has an ok sort after the values of the variables produced by the match are substituted into it; for an err-eqn (or err-axiom) to apply, the instantiated right-hand side must have an error sort; there are no special conventions for an eqn (or axiom), but the general convention about the sorts of variables still applies. (There are actually only equations in the specifications in this paper.)

For example, the intersection of two lines can be empty, or one point, or else a line. Our specification treats the meet operation on lines as an unsafe operation that normally returns the (single) point in common, regarding the cases where the lines are parallel or coincide as exceptions, where error messages are returned.

4.2. Fields and reals

Fields are an important example that cannot be specified without somehow either handling or avoiding exceptions, since division is only meaningful when the denominator is nonzero. Here is one way to specify this theory:

```
theory FIELD is
  using RING.
  sort NonZero < Elt iff X =/= 0.
  ok-ops
    _**−1 : NonZero→ Elt.
    _/_ : Elt NonZero→ Elt.
  ok-eqns
    X * Y = Y * X.
    X/Y = X * (Y**−1).
    X * (X**−1) = 1.
endth
```

The new sort NonZero is a subsort of the old sort Elt of FIELD, restricted to be the nonzero elements by a *sort constraint*; see [18] for a precise definition and some relevant theory of sort constraints. The models of FIELD are just fields, as usually defined in algebra.

Now, the real numbers are an *uncountable* structure, which therefore *cannot* be specified with standard inital algebra semantics. Perhaps the reals could be specified with *continous* initial algebra semantics, but all the geometrical constructions given here only need a field having square roots of nonnegative elements, and therefore our specification can be *parameterized* over all such fields. Although the real numbers are the model used in ordinary Cartesian geometry, there are some others, such as that formed by closing the rational numbers under square roots of nonnegative numbers; this field seems particularly attractive because it is computable in the sense of [32]. The p-adic numbers are another possibility. (Of course, any implementation of these geometrical constructions on a computer will have to use a set of approximations to the reals that is not only not uncountable, but is actually finite.)

Specifying ordered fields in which all nonnegative elements have square roots, requires key excerpts from a few chapters of a modern algebra textbook, which is just what we have been doing. Before defining this structure, we need the theory of ordered fields, in which being nonnegative makes sense:

```
theory OFIELD is
   combining FIELD and POSET over TRIV.
   sort Noneg < Elt iff X > = 0.
   ok-eqns
      X == 0 or X > 0 or -X > 0.
      X > 0 and Y > 0 implies X + Y > 0.
      X > 0 and Y > 0 implies X * Y > 0.
endth
```

The new sort Noneg of the sort Elt from FIELD is again defined by a sort constraint.

The combining_and_over_ construction assumes that the first two modules mentioned (this can be generalized to n) are viewed as the last mentioned module, in this case TRIV; if this does not work out automatically with default views, then explicit views must be given in place of module names. The semantics is given by the pushout of all these views, taking account of any shared subtheories, as in CLEAR [5]. Now we can specify fields that have square roots of their nonnegative elements:

```
theory SQTFIELD is
   extending OFIELD.
   ok-ops
      _ **2 : Elt → Elt.
      sqrt_ : Noneg → Noneg.
   ok-eqns
      X**2 = X * X.
      (sqrt X) **2 = X.
endth
```

5. Set Constructions

This section gives some standard constructions from set theory, following [15]. Although these are not needed for our geometrical constructions specification, they would be needed for some more complex constructions, and are of independent interest. We begin with a parameterized module that defines the most basic set-theoretic constructions, using some ideas of Hsiang [25]. These constructions include the empty set (denoted {}), the singleton set constructor {_}, disjoint union (denoted +), and intersection (denoted &). This module is later enriched with further set-theoretic concepts, including union, difference, some standard predicates (i.e., implicitly Bool-valued operations), and cardinality.

```
obj BSET[X :: TRIV] is
   sort Set.
   ok-ops
      {_} : Elt→ Set.
      _ + _ : Set Set→ Set [assoc comm id: {}].
      _ & _ : Set Set→ Set [assoc comm id: omega].
   ok-eqs
      S & S = S.
      S + S = {}.
      {E} & {E'} = {} if not E = = E'.
      S & {} = {}.
      S & (S' + S") = (S & S') + (S & S").
endo
```

Here, omega represents the "universal" set, i.e., the set of all things of sort Elt. Now the enrichment:

```
obj SET[X :: TRIV] is
   protecting BSET[X].
   extending INT.
   ok-ops
      _ U _ : Set Set→ Set [assoc comm id: {}].
      _ − _ : Set Set→ Set.
      #_ : Set → Int.
   ok-relns
      _in_ : Elt Set.
      _in_ : Set Set.
      empty?_ : Set.
   ok-eqns
      S U S' = (S & S') + S + S'.
      S − S' = S + (S & S').
      empty? S = S = = {}.
      X in S = not {X} + S = = S.
      S in S' = S U S' = = S'.
      # {} = 0.
      # ({X} + S) = 1 + # S if not X in S.
endo
```

```
obj INTSET is
   protecting SET[INT] * (omega to ints).
endo
```

Notice that the specification allows not only all finite subsets of omega, but also all *cofinite* subsets, which are the complements of finite sets. INT is extended, rather than protected, because we may be adding the value # omega when X is instantiated with a nonfinite set, such as INT.

Although # does not yield the answer ∞ for infinite sets, it does behave reasonably. For example, in INSET, (# ints) is just (# ints) again, a reduced term rather than a nonterminating computation. If omega is a finite set, one should add an equation saying explicitly what it is, e.g.,

omega = {1}U{2}U{3}.

and in case omega is infinite, one may want to add other equations like

succ(# ints) = # ints.

in order to get the expected behavior.

6. Information Hiding and Alternative Representations

The definition of abstract interfaces—i.e., the designation of which sorts and operations that have already been defined can be exported and which are for internal use only (i.e., are "hidden")—arises naturally in our geometrical constructions specification. The simplest linguistic convention is that a module exports all sorts and operations except those that are labeled hidden; for example, the operation _[_] in the object CIRCLE below has attribute hidden. A dual convention allows hiding all sorts and operations except those explicitly labeled visible (this convention is not needed for our geometrical constructions).

Similar issues arise in hierarchically structuring a specification by blocks. This permits a finer control of import and export declarations. For example, we may write imports A B C after a block declaration to indicate that modules (or other blocks) named A, B and C are imported into a given module block. A, B and C must have been declared earlier in the specification text than the block in question; only sorts and operations from imported modules (or blocks) can be used within a given block.

We also allow hidden declarations in blocks, to prohibit the use of designated sorts and/or operations outside of the block, even when the whole block is imported. Or we can invoke an opposite convention, in which everything is hidden, except certain things which are declared visible. This permits local definitions, i.e., definitions that are given and only used inside of a block.

6.1. Degenerate cases, multiple representations and coercions

Novel features of the specification language used here include its ability to deal with degenerate cases, multiple representations, and coercions.

Let us first consider *degenerate cases*, which seem to be a particular nuisance in computational geometry. For example, the object LINE given below involves two cases for the sort Line, the General case and the Vertical case, the latter of which is degenerate, in the sense that its representation has lower dimension, i.e., involves fewer parameters. Perhaps surprisingly, this phenomenon is already understood in the order-sorted theory of abstract data types, where it amounts to having more than one constructor for a given sort, some of which involve fewer arguments than others, and produce values that may lie in subsorts. Let us consider the following specification for lists of integers, using a syntax similar to Pascal's "variant records" [27]:

```
obj LIST-INT is
  protecting INT.
  rep List by case(Empty) is: {}
     or by case(NonEmpty) is: _._ with head : Int and tail : List.
endo
```

The order-sorted algebraic semantics for the above is just

```
obj LIST-INT is
  protecting INT.
  sorts Empty NonEmpty < List.
  ok-ops
     {} : → Empty.
     _._ : Int List → NonEmpty.
     head : NonEmpty → Int.
     tail : NonEmpty → List.
  ok-eqns
     head(l.L) = l.
     tail(l.L) = L.
endo
```

Thus, we see that Empty and NonEmpty are *subsorts* of List (they could more clearly be designated EmptyList and NonEmptyList, but these seem rather long). Here {} and _._ are *constructors*, and the additional operations declared following the keyword with are *selectors* for the corresponding constructor; in this case, {} has no selectors since it has no arguments, while _._ has head and tail. (Order-sorted algebra is actually *necessary* here, since many-sorted algebra is *not strong enough* to define selectors, as shown in [19].)

This translation is very convenient, since it allows us to use the full machinery of order-sorted algebra, and in particular, *sort predicates*, which are Bool-valued operations that are true iff their argument has the appropriate sort. Thus,

    Empty({ }) = true
while
    NonEmpty({ }) = false.

A "case analysis" for rep statements is also useful in the right-hand sides of equations. For example, given

    rep S by case(A) is: . . .
        or by case(B) is: . . .

we may translate an equation of the form

    t = t′(case(A X) is: t1 or case(B X) is: t2).

where t, t′(_), t1 and t2 are expressions, and where X occurs in t, into the following two conditional equations using sort predicates:

    t = t′(t1) if A(X).
    t = t′(t2) if B(X).

Here, t1 can use the selectors associated with the constructor for case A, while t2 can use the selectors associated with B and t2 cannot use those associated with B, but t1 cannot use those associated with A.

Case analyses may also involve more than one variable, with syntax like

    case(A X,Y ; B Z) is: . . .

which will generate the condition

    . . . if A(X) and A(Y) and B(Z).

The rep construction is useful even when there are no degenerate cases, as illustrated in the specification of points with Cartesian coordinates in the object POINT below.

Let us now consider *multiple representations*. Interestingly, and perhaps surprisingly, using a selector does not *require* the corresponding representation, since its value could be computed from any underlying representation where it is defined. Let us consider an example, points represented *either* by Cartesian *or* by polar coordinates. The following module declares both representations, together with *coercions* (i.e., implicit conversions or translations) between them, and a distance function. We name each representation to help distinguish between the two coercions that are given. Rather than parameterize the module illustrating this point, we just use a module REAL that already defined the auxiliary operations that are needed, including some trigonometric functions and the constant pi. Two new subsorts of the sort Real are needed, and these are defined by sort constraints, namely, Pos and Angle, for positive elements and for angles.

```
obj POINT is
  protecting REAL.
  sort Pos < Real if P > 0.
  sort Angle < Real if 0 <= A < 2 * pi.
  rep(Cart) Point by 〈 _,_ 〉 with x : Real and y : Real.
  rep(Polar) Point by case(General) is: [ _,_] with theta : Angle and rho : Pos
    or by case(Origin) is: *.
  coerce(Cart to Polar) by
    if x =/= 0 then [arctan(y/x), sqrt((x**2) + (y**2))]
      else if Y == 0 then * else if y > 0
      then [pi/2, y] else [3 * pi/2, -y] fi fi fi.
  coerce(Polar to Cart) by
    case(General) is: 〈 rho * cos(theta), rho*sin(theta) 〉
    or case(Origin) is: 〈0,0〉.
  ok-op d : Point Point → Real.
  ok-eqn d(P,Q) = sqrt(((x(P) - x(Q))**2) + ((y(P) - y(Q))**2)).
endo
```

There is no need for variables in the coercion definitions, since there is only one item involved that has the indicated representation, and the selectors implicitly take it as their argument. An interesting point about this example is that one representation has a degenerate case, while the other does not; however, the two representations are completely intertranslatable.

Given this POINT object, any of the four selectors can be used anywhere in a program, without having to worry about what the underlying representation might actually be. Semantically, each representation of a given sort defines a new subsort of it, and each case of a given representation defines a new subsubsort. Thus, Point has subsorts Cart and Polar, and Polar has subsorts General and Origin. Figure 2 shows all the subsorts involved here. Operations on points should use the sort Point, rather than one of the representations, in order to obtain the full benefits of this facility. (If one wants to use the same name for cases that belong to different representations, a qualification notation can be used to distinguish them; for example, if we had a General case of Cart,

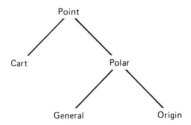

Fig. 2. Subsorts involved in the two representations of points.

the two different General cases would be named General.Cart and General.Polar, respectively.)

Although this example has just two representations and one coercion from each representation to the other, the construction also allows any number of representations, and also *one-way* coercions, whereby some representations can carry more information than others; however, the construction syntactically enforces that there is *at most* one coercion from any given representation to another. In addition, we require that the coercions *compose correctly*, in the sense that if there is a coercion c from representation R_1 to representation R_2, and another c' from R_2 to R_3, and a third c'' from R_1 to R_3, then the composition cc' must equal c''. In particular, if c goes from R_1 and R_2 and c' goes from R_2 to R_1, then cc' must be the identity, and in fact, R_1 and R_2 must be isomorphic representations; this special case corresponds to what Wadler [35] calls *views*. In fact, and seemingly by chance, our coercions resemble OBJ-style default views, in that they form a category with at most one morphism from any given object to another. This imposes a preorder structure on the sort set, and ensures that each item has at most one translation, i.e., that the implicit conversions are consistent.

It might seem that this construction assumes that the representations are "free" (or one might say, "anarchic"), i.e., that they do not satisfy any nontrivial equations. However, the only disadvantage to adding equations for constructors is that it may be harder to ensure the consistency of operations defined over them, including coercions; it might require some theorem proving, whereas it is automatic in the anarchic case.

Let us now consider the semantics of this feature more carefully. In order to obtain an initial algebra semantics, it is convenient to regard the coercion definitions as equations.[6] This ensures, model theoretically, that the sorts Cart, Polar and Point have identical carriers in the initial model, thus achieving *representation independence*, since the different representations are identified, and appear in the same equivalence class. Under this view, it is necessary to use different constructors for each representation, and non-injective one-way

―――――――――

[6] I thank Dr. José Meseguer for the remarks in this paragraph.

coercions cannot be handled (however, a more general semantics given below is not subject to these restrictions). Thus, the intended semantics is the initial algebra of an object involving the following ok-equations, the first three of which have sort Point and arise from the coercions:

$\langle X,Y \rangle$ = if X =/= 0 then [arctan(Y/X), sqrt((X**2) + (Y**2))]
               else if Y == 0 then * else if Y > 0 then [pi/2, Y]
               else [3 * pi/2, −Y] fi fi fi.
[Rho, Theta] = $\langle$ Rho * cos(Theta), Rho * sin(Theta) $\rangle$.
* = $\langle 0,0 \rangle$.
d($\langle X,Y \rangle, \langle X',Y' \rangle$) = sqrt(((X − X')**2) + ((Y − Y')**2)).

Operationally, the coercion equations should not be treated as rewrite rules, but rather, the remaining equations should be matched *modulo* the coercion equations. For example, the last equation above matches the expression d($\langle 7,0 \rangle$, [pi, −6]) modulo the second equation above, and then rewrites to

sqrt(((7 − ((−6) * cos(pi)))**2) + ((0 − ((−6) * sin(pi)))**2)) .

which eventually simplifies to 1.

Let us now consider a more complex example, the ASCII coercion from natural numbers to characters. Here, neither sort Nat nor Char is a subsort of the other, and the coercion operation, let us denote it ascii, is defined only on a subset of the naturals, those between 0 and 127, inclusive; let us denote this subsort Nat[0 .. 127] and assume that it is already defined in a module NATS. Then the code involved here looks like the following:

```
obj CHAR is
    protecting NATS.
    sort Char.
    sort Nat[0 .. 127] < Char.
    rep Char by null, . . . . . . . .
    coerce(Nat[0 .. 127] to Char) by
        0 is: nul
        . . . . . . . . .
endo
```

Thus, the sort Char is defined by a large list of cases, and the coercion is, in effect, defined by a large table.

Coercions are also meaningful in more general cases than multiple representation, but here the simple approach of regarding the coercion definitions as equations may break down. For example, suppose that Int < Rat and that we want to define a coercion from rationals to integers that takes the integer part of a rational; since this operation (let's denote it int-part : Rat→Int) is not injective, dividing by the congruence relation generated by the equation R = int-part(R) would simply destroy the rationals! What we really want here, is to apply int-part iff some operation needs an integer but has been supplied a rational. This kind of behavior is familiar from the retracts that we have already considered: the parser inserts a special operation symbol r.rat.int when it gets a subexpression of sort Rat but needs one of sort Rat. All we have to do then, is provide the conditional equation

r.rat.int(R) = int-part(R) if not Int(R).

in addition to the equation that we already have for retracts,

r.rat.int(I) = I.

where I has sort Int; actually, in this case, we don't need the second equation at all, or the condition in the first equation, since int-part(I) = I. Thus, in the most general case, we may regard coercions as operation symbols having empty syntax that are invoked iff run time type checking fails to yield an argument of the right sort; they are defined by conditional equation whose left-hand side is a retract and whose right-hand side is a coercion definition. In fact, this gives a fully general way to handle coercions, since retracts will only arise inside of expressions that do not, properly speaking, parse anyway. This guarantees correctness, since the coercion equations only affect expressions outside the initial algebra of well-sorted terms. It also provides a more efficient operational semantics. However, it is less satisfying when applied to the multiple representation case, since the corresponding representations are not actually identified. Nevertheless, we can just add the relevant equations in such cases, and get the advantages of both approaches.

I believe that this discussion satisfies the concerns about the visibility of representations raised in [34], for example, that the construction for a tangent to a circle through a point requires access to previously defined representations, in conflict with principles of information hiding. The solution is simply that the use of some particular selectors, such as x and y coordinates, does not imply a commitment to the corresponding representation, since we can convert from any underlying representation that points may happen to have.

Let us conclude with a discussion of related work. Our coercions resemble Wadler's "views" [35], except that our coercions can be one-way, i.e., mutual inter-translatability is not required; also, we use order-sorted algebra to get selectors, we allow any number of representations, and we do not restrict to anarchic representations. The work of John Reynolds [33] on "category-sorted algebra" is also closely related; however, Reynolds does not support user-defined coercions (although Wadler does), does not use order-sorted algebra to get selectors, and his category-sorted algebra may be too general, since it allows any number of coercions between a given pair of representations.[7] Our work on coercions is also related to some work of Kim Bruce and Peter Wegner [2]. All three of these works have influenced the approach reported here.

7. Geometrical Constructions

This section contains the "meat" of our specification, consisting of about fifty lines, many of which are declarations. A new feature here is the _where_ = _ construction, which introduces names for subexpressions that are local to a given equation; a similar effect could be achieved with hidden operations. A variation of this is the given_let_ = _ construction, which defines subexpressions that can be used in any equation whose lefthand side involves the variables mentioned in the given part of the declaration. Both of these constructions extend to multiple subexpressions definitions, using the word and. ALGEBRA denotes the block containing RING, FIELD, SQTFIELD, etc. Note the use of nonconstant err-ops, to produce more informative error messages.

Recall that representing lines in "slope-intercept form," i.e., as pairs (m, b) that determine the set of all points (x, y) such that $y = mx + b$, requires a separate representation for vertical lines, here we use their x-intercept, (a), determining the points (x, y) such that $x = a$.

```
·    block GEOM[F :: SQTFIELD] is
         import ALGEBRA.

     obj POINT is
         rep Point by ⟨_,_⟩ with x : F and y : F.
         ok-op d : Point Point→ Noneg.  -- distance
         ok-eqn d(P,Q) = sqrt((x(P) − x(Q))**2 + (y(P) − y(Q))**2).
     endo

     obj LINE is
         protecting POINT.
         rep Line by case(General) ⟨_,_⟩ with m : NonZero.F and b : F
         or by case(Vertical) ⟨_⟩ with a : F.
     ops
         line : Point Point→ Line.
         meet : Line Line→ Point.
```

---

[7] It may be worth remarking that Reynolds' category-sorted algebra is a special case of ordinary many-sorted algebra, in the sense that there is a simple translation which preserves the models, and that no special rules of deduction are required. The case of order-sorted algebra is quite different, since new rules of deduction really are needed to account for the requirement that some carriers *must* be contained in others.

err-ops
   same-point : Point $\rightarrow$ Line.
   no-point : $\rightarrow$ Point.
   same-line : Line $\rightarrow$ Point.
ok-eqns
   given P1,P2 let x1 = x(P1) and y1 = y(P1) and
                x2 = x(P2) and y2 = y(P2).
   line(P1,P2) = $\langle$x1$\rangle$ if x1 = = x2.
   line(P1,P2) = $\langle$(y1 − y2)/(x1 − x2),((y2 ∗ x1) − (y1 ∗ x2))/(x1 − x2)$\rangle$
      if x1 =/= x2.
   meet(L1,L2) = case(General L1,L2) is
      $\langle$(b2 − b1)/(m1 − m2),((m1 ∗ b2) − (m2 ∗ b1))/(m1 − m2)$\rangle$
        if m1 =/= m2
     or case(General L1 : Vertical L2) is: $\langle$a(L2),(a(L2) − b2)/m2$\rangle$
     or case(Vertical L1 : General L2) is: $\langle$a(L1),(a(L1) − b1)/m1$\rangle$
        where m1 = m(L1) and b1 = b(L1) and m2 = m(L2) and
          b2 = b(L2).
err-eqns
   line(P1,P2) = same-point(P1) if P1 = = P2.
   meet(L1,L2) = if L1 = = L2 then same-line(L2) else
      case(General L1,L2) is: no-point if m(L1) = = m(L2)
     or case(Vertical L1,L2) is: no-point.
endo

obj D3 is protecting R3[F].
endo

obj CIRCLE is
   protecting POINT LINE D3.
   rep Circle by $\langle$_,_$\rangle$ with center : Point and radius : Noneg.
   ops
      circle : Point Point Point $\rightarrow$ Circle.
      _[_] : Circle Point $\rightarrow$ F [hidden].
      tangent : Point Circle $\rightarrow$ Line.
   ok-reln concentric : Circle Circle.
   err-ops
      no-circle : $\rightarrow$ Circle.
      no-tangent : $\rightarrow$ Line.
   ok-eqns
      circle(P1,P2,P3) = $\langle\langle$d,e$\rangle$,(d ∗∗ 2) + (e ∗∗ 2) + f$\rangle$ if det =/= 0
        where
          d = det3(c,y,one)/det and e = det3(x,c,one)/det and
          f = det3(x,y,one)/det and det = det3(x,y,one) and
          x = $\langle$x(P1),x(P2),x(P3)$\rangle$ and y = $\langle$y(P1),y(P2),y(P3)$\rangle$ and

$c = \langle x(P1)**2 + y(P1)**2, x(P2)**2 + y(P2)**2,$
$\quad x(P3)**2 + y(P3)**2 \rangle.$
$C[P] = d(P,center(C))**2 - radius(C)**2.$
$concentric(C1,C2) = (center(C1) == center(C2)).$
given P,C let $x = x(P)$ and $y = y(P)$ and $a = x(center(C))$ and
$\quad b = y(center(C))$ and $r = radius(C)$ and $d = (a - x)**2 - r**2$ and
$\quad m = (((a - x) * (b - y)) + (r * sqrt(C[P]))) / d.$
$tangent(P,C) = \langle m, b - (m * x) \rangle$ if $C[P] > 0$ or
$\quad (C[P] == 0$ and $d =/= 0).$
$tangent(P,C) = \langle a - x \rangle$ if $C[P] == 0$ and $d == 0.$
err-eqns
$\quad circle(P1,P2,P3) = no\text{-}circle$ if $det3(x,y,one) == 0$
$\quad$ where $x = \langle x(P1),x(P2),x(P3) \rangle$ and $y = \langle y(P1),y(P2),y(P3) \rangle.$
$\quad tangent(P,C) = no\text{-}tangent$ if $C[P] < 0.$
endo

endblock GEOM

Justification for the determinant formula for circle(P1,P2,P3) can be found, for example, in [30]. The other formulae are more straightforward.

8. Conclusions

We have given a specification of some basic constructions in plane geometry, illustrating certain recent advances in algebraic specification technology, and illuminating some issues in knowledge representation and computational geometry, including modularity, parameterization, hierarchical structuring, degenerate cases, exceptions, coercions, and multiple representations. It is pleasing that order-sorted algebra provides a rigorous unified foundation for the last four of these features, while parameterized modules provides for the first three. The specification is written in a variant of the OBJ language, and is both abstract and executable.

REFERENCES

1. Abrial, J.-R., Schuman, S.A. and Meyer, B., *Specification Language Z* (Massachusetts Computer Associates, 1979).
2. Bruce, K. and Wegner, P., An algebraic model of subtypes in object-oriented languages, *SIGPLAN Notices* **21** (10) (1986) 163–172.
3. Burstall, R. and Goguen, J., Algebras, theories and freeness: An introduction for computer scientists, in: M. Wirsing and G. Schmidt (Eds.), *Theoretical Foundations of Programming Methodology, Proceedings, 1981 Marktoberdorf NATO Summer School*, NATO Advanced Study Institute Series **C91** (Reidel, Dordrecht, The Netherlands, 1982) 329–350.
4. Burstall, R. and Goguen, J., Putting theories together to make specifications, in: *Proceedings IJCAI-77*, Cambridge, MA (1977) 1045–1058.
5. Burstall, R. and Goguen, J., The semantics of Clear, a specification language, in: *Proceedings*

1979 Copenhagen Winter School on Abstract Software Specification, Lecture Notes in Computer Science **86** (Springer, Berlin, 1980) 292–332.

6. Futatsugi, K., Goguen, J., Jouannaud, J.-P. and Meseguer, J., Principles of OBJ2, in: *Proceedings 12th ACM Symposium on Principles of Programming Languages* (1985) 52–66.

7. Futatsugi, K., Goguen, J., Meseguer, J. and Okada, K., Parameterized programming in OBJ2, in: *Proceedings Ninth International Conference on Software Engineering* (1987) 51–60.

8. Goguen, J., Abstract errors for abstract data types, in: *Proceedings First IFIP Working Conference on Formal Description of Programming Concepts* (1977) 21.1–21.32; also in: P. Neuhold (Ed.), *Formal Description of Programming Concepts* (North-Holland, Amsterdam, 1979) 491–522.

9. Goguen, J., Higher-order functions considered unnecessary for higher-order programming, in: *Proceedings, University of Texas Year of Programming, Institute on Declarative Programming* (1988).

10. Goguen, J., How to prove algebraic inductive hypotheses without induction: With applications to the correctness of data type representations, in: *Proceedings Fifth Conference on Automated Deduction*, Lecture Notes in Computer Science **87** (Springer, Berlin, 1980) 356–373.

11. Goguen, J., Ordinary specification of some construction in plane geometry, in: *Proceedings Workshop on Program Specification*, Lecture Notes in Computer Science **134** (Springer, Berlin, 1982) 31–46.

12. Goguen, J., Parameterized programming, *IEEE Trans. Softw. Eng.* **10** (5) (1984) 528–543.

13. Goguen, J. and Burstall, R., Institutions: Abstract model theory for computer science, Tech. Rept. CSLI-85-30, Center for the Study of Language and Information, Stanford University, Stanford, CA (1985); also in: *Proceedings, Logics of Programming Workshop*, Lecture Notes in Computer Science **164** (Springer, Berlin, 1984) 221–256.

14. Goguen, J., Jouannaud, J.-P. and Meseguer, J., Operational semantics of order-sorted algebra, in: *Proceedings, 1985 International Conference on Automata, Languages and Programming*, Lecture Notes in Computer Science **194** (Springer, Berlin, 1985).

15. Goguen, J. and Meseguer, J., EQLOG: Equality, types, and generic modules for logic programming, in: D. DeGroot and G. Lindstrom (Ed.), *Functional and Logic Programming* (Prentice-Hall, Englewood Cliffs, NJ, 1986) 295–363; also: *Logic Program.* **1** (2) (1984) 179–210.

16. Goguen, J. and Meseguer, J., Extensions and foundations for object-oriented programming, in: B. Shriver and P. Wegner (eds.), *Research Directions in Object-Oriented Programming* (MIT Press, Cambridge, MA, 1987) 417–477; also: *SIGPLAN Notices* **21** (10) (1986) 153–162; also: Tech. Rept. CSLI-87-93, Center for the Study of Language and Information, Stanford University, Stanford, CA (1987).

17. Goguen, J. and Meseguer, J., Models and equality for logical programming, in: *Proceedings 1987 TAPSOFT*, Lecture Notes in Computer Science **250** (Springer, Berlin, 1987) 1–22; also: Tech. Rept., Center for the Study of Language and Information, Stanford University, Stanford, CA (1987).

18. Goguen, J. and Meseguer, J., Order sorted algebra I: Partial and overloaded operations, errors and inheritance, Tech. Rept., SRI International, Computer Science Lab, Menlo Park, CA (1988).

19. Goguen, J. and Meseguer, J., Order-sorted algebra solves the constructor-selector, multiple representation and coercion problems, in: *Proceedings Second Symposium on Logic in Computer Science* (1987) 18–29; also: Tech. Rept. CSLI-87-92, Center for the Study of Language and Information, Stanford University, Stanford, CA (1987).

20. Goguen, J. and Meseguer, J., Universal realization, persistent interconnection and implementation of abstract modules, in: *Proceedings 9th International Conference on Automata, Languages and Programming*, Lecture Notes in Computer Science **140** (Springer, Berlin, 1982).

21. Goguen, J., Thatcher, J. and Wagner, E., An initial algebra approach to the specification, correctness and implementation of abstract data types, Tech. Rept. RC 6487, IBM T.J. Watson Research Center, Yorktown Heights, NY (1976); also in: R. Yeh (Ed.), *Current Trends in Programming Methodology* **IV** (Prentice-Hall, Englewood Cliffs, NJ, 1978) 80–149.
22. Goguen, J.A., Principles of parameterized programming, in: T. Biggerstaff and A. Perlis (Eds.), *Software Reusability* (Addison-Wesley, Reading, MA, 1988).
23. Guttag, J., Abstract data types and the development of data structures, *Comm. ACM* **20** (1977) 297–404.
24. Guttag, J., Horning, J. and Wing, J., Larch in five easy pieces, Tech. Rept. 5, Digital Equipment Corporation, Systems Research Center (1985).
25. Hsiang, J., Refutational theorem proving using term rewriting systems, *Artificial Intelligence* **25** (1985) 255–300.
26. Huet, G. and Oppen, D., Equations and rewrite rules: A survey, in: R. Book (Ed.), *Formal Language Theory: Perspectives and Open Problems* (Academic Press, New York, 1980).
27. Jensen, K. and Wirth, N., *Pascal User Manual and Report* (Springer, Berlin, 2nd ed., 1978).
28. Kaphengst, H. and Reichel, H., Initial algebraic semantics for non-context-free languages, in: M. Karpinski (Ed.), *Fundamentals of Computation Theory*, Lecture Notes in Computer Science **56** (Springer, Berlin, 1977) 120–126.
29. Meseguer, J. and Goguen, J., Initiality, induction and computability, in: M. Nivat and J. Reynolds (Eds.), *Algebraic Methods in Semantics* (Cambridge University Press, Cambridge, England, 1985) 459–541.
30. Morrill, W.K., Selby, S.M. and Johnson, W.G., *Modern Analytic Geometry* (Intext, Scranton, PA, 3rd ed., 1972).
31. Parnas, D., On the criteria to be used in decomposing systems into modules, *Comm. ACM* **15** (1972) 1053–1058.
32. Rabin, M., Computable algebra: General theory and theory of computable fields, *Trans. Am. Math. Soc.* **95** (1960) 341–360.
33. Reynolds, J., Using category theory to design implicit conversions and generic operators, in: N.D. Jones (Ed.), *Semantics Directed Compiler Generation*, Lecture Notes in Computer Science **94** (Springer, Berlin, 1980) 211–258.
34. Staunstrup, J., Geometrical constructions, in: *Proceedings Aarhus Workshop on Specification*, Lecture Notes in Computer Science **134** (Springer, Berlin, 1982) 25–30.
35. Wadler, P., Views: A way for pattern matching to cohabit with data abstraction, in: *Proceedings 14th ACM Symposium on Principles of Programming Languages* (1987) 307–312.
36. Wand, M., Final algebra semantics and data type extension, *J. Comput. Syst. Sci.* **19** (1979) 27–44.

Received April 1987; revised version received March 1988

Robotics
and
Motion Planning

A Survey of Motion Planning and Related Geometric Algorithms

J.T. Schwartz and M. Sharir

*Courant Institute of Mathematical Sciences,
New York University, New York, NY 10003, U.S.A.; and
School of Mathematical Sciences, Tel-Aviv University,
Ramat-Aviv, Tel-Aviv 69978, Israel*

1. Introduction

This paper surveys recent developments in motion planning and related geometric algorithms, a theoretical research area that has grown rapidly in response to increasing industrial demand for automatic manufacturing systems which use robotic manipulators and sensory feedback devices, and, more significantly, in anticipation of a future generation of substantially more autonomous and intelligent robots. These future robots are expected to possess advanced capabilities of sensing, planning, and control, enabling them to gather knowledge about their environment, construct a symbolic world model of the environment, and use this model in planning and carrying out tasks set to them in high-level style by an application programmer.

Current research in theoretical robotics therefore aims to identify these basic capabilities that an autonomous intelligent robot system will need to advance understanding of the mathematical and algorithmic principles fundamental to these capabilities.

Among these capabilities, planning involves the use of an environment model to carry out significant parts of a robot's activities automatically. The aim is to allow the robot's user to specify a desired activity in very high-level general terms, and then have the system fill in the missing low-level details. For example, the user might specify the end product of some assembly process, and ask the system to construct a sequence of assembly substeps; or, at a less demanding level, to plan collision-free motions which pick up individual subparts of an object to be assembled, transport them to their assembly position, and insert them into their proper places.

Techniques for the automatic planning of robot motions have advanced substantially during the last several years. This area has shown itself to have significant mathematical content; tools drawn from classical geometry, topology, algebraic geometry, algebra, and combinatorics have all been used in it. This work relates closely to work in computational geometry, an area which has also progressed very rapidly during the last few years.

This survey concentrates on exact algorithmic solutions to the motion planning problem, and does not address other heuristic or approximating approaches which have also been recently developed, some of which may have significant practical advantages. These include works by Lozano-Pérez, Brooks, Mason and Taylor (cf. [4–6, 30, 31]) of the MIT school, to which researchers at many other places are beginning to contribute.

2. Statement of the Problem

In its simplest form, the motion planning problem can be defined as follows. Let B be a robot system consisting of a collection of rigid subparts (some of which may be attached to each other at certain joints while others may move independently) having a total of k degrees of freedom, and suppose that B is free to move in a two- or three-dimensional space V amidst a collection of obstacles whose geometry is known to the robot system. The *motion planning problem* for B is: Given an initial position Z_1 and a desired final position Z_2 of B, determine whether there exists a continuous obstacle-avoiding motion of B from Z_1 to Z_2, and if so plan such a motion.

This problem has been studied in many recent papers (cf. [4–6, 14, 15, 17, 19, 21–24, 26–28, 30–32, 37, 39–41, 45, 49–52, 60, 63, 68, 70]). It is equivalent to the problem of calculating the path-connected components of the (k-dimensional) space FP of all *free positions* of B (i.e. the set of positions of B in which B does not contact any obstacle), and is therefore a problem in "computational topology". In general FP is a high-dimensional space with irregular boundaries, and is thus hard to calculate efficiently.

This standard motion planning problem can be extended and generalized in many possible ways. For example, if the geometry of the environment is not fully known to the robot system, one must employ "exploratory" approach in which plan generation is tightly updated to gathering of data on the environment and to dynamic updating of a world model. Another interesting extension of the motion planning problem is to the case in which the environment contains objects moving in some known and predictable manner. Although this problem has been little studied, the few results obtained so far seem to indicate that it is inherently harder than the static problem.

All the problem variants mentioned so far aim to determine whether a collision-free path exists between two specified system positions, and, if so, to produce such a path. A further issue is to produce a path which satisfies some criterion of optimality. For example, if a mobile robot is approximated as a single moving point, one might want to find the shortest Euclidean path between the initial and final system positions. In more complex situations the notion of optimal motion is less clearly defined, and has as yet been little studied.

Studies of the motion planning problem tend to make heavy use of many algorithmic techniques in computational geometry. Various motion-planning-related problems in computational geometry will also be reviewed.

3. Motion Planning in Static and Known Environments

As above, let B be a moving robot system, k be its number of degrees of freedom, V denote the two- or three-dimensional space in which B is free to move, and FP denote the space of free positions of B, as defined above. The space FP is determined by the collection of algebraic inequalities which express the fact that at position Z the system B avoids collision with any of the obstacles present in its workspace. We will denote by n the number of inequalities needed to define FP, and call it the "geometric (or combinatorial) complexity" of the given instance of the motion planning problem. As noted, we make the reasonable assumption that the parameters describing the degrees of freedom of B can be chosen in such a way that each of these inequalities is algebraic. Indeed, the group of motions (involving various combinations of translations and rotations) available to a given robot can ordinarily be given algebraic representation, and the system B and its environment V can typically be modeled as objects bounded by a collection of algebraic surfaces (e.g., polyhedral, quadratic, or spline-based).

3.1. The general motion planning problem

Assuming then that FP is an algebraic or semi-algebraic set in E^k, Schwartz and Sharir [50] show that the motion planning problem can be solved in time polynomial in the number n of algebraic constraints defining FP and in their maximal degree, but double exponential in k. The general procedure described uses a decomposition technique due to Collins [9] and originally applied to Tarski's theory of real closed fields. Though hopelessly inefficient in practical terms, this result nevertheless serves to calibrate the computational complexity of the motion planning problem.

3.2. Lower bounds

The result just cited suggests that motion planning becomes harder rapidly as the number k of degrees of freedom increases; this conjecture has in fact been proved for various model "robot" systems. Specifically, Reif [45] proved that motion planning is PSPACE-hard for a certain 3-D system involving arbitrarily many links and moving through a complex system of narrow tunnels. Since then PSPACE-hardness has been established for simpler moving systems, including 2-D systems of mechanical linkages (Hopcroft, Joseph, and Whitesides [15]), a system of 2-D independent rectangular blocks sliding inside a rectangular box (Hopcroft, Schwartz and Sharir [17]), and a single 2-D arm with many links moving through a 2-D polygonal space (Joseph and Plantinga [21]). Several weaker results establishing NP-hardness for still simpler systems have also been obtained.

3.3. The "projection method"

In spite of these negative worst-case results, algorithms of varying levels of efficiency for planning the motions of various single robot systems have been developed. These involve several general approaches to the design of motion planning algorithms. The first such approach, known as the *projection method*, uses ideas similar to those appearing in the Collins decomposition procedure described above. One fixes some of the problem's degrees of freedom (for the sake of exposition, suppose just one parameter y is fixed, and let $\bar{x}$ be the remaining parameters); then one solves the resulting restricted $(k-1)$-dimensional motion planning problem. This subproblem solution must be such as to yield a discrete combinatorial representation of the restricted free configuration space (essentially, a cross-section of the entire space FP) that changes only at a finite collection of "critical" values of the final parameter y. These critical values of y are then calculated; they partition the entire space FP into connected cells, and by calculating relationships of adjacency between these cells one can describe the connectivity of FP by a discrete *connectivity graph* CG. This graph has the aforesaid cells as vertices, and has edges which represent relationships of cell adjacency in FP. The connected components of FP correspond in a one-to-one manner to the connected components of CG, reducing the problem to a discrete path searching problem in CG.

This relatively straightforward technique was applied in a series of papers by Schwartz and Sharir on the "piano movers" problem, to yield polynomial-time motion planning algorithms for various specific systems, including a rigid polygonal object moving in 2-D polygonal space [49], two or three independent discs moving in coordinated fashion in 2-D polygonal space [51], certain types of multi-arm linkages moving in 2-D polygonal space [60], and a rod moving in 3-D polyhedral space [52]. These initial solutions were coarse and not very efficient; subsequent refinements have improved substantially their efficiency. For example, Leven and Sharir [26] obtained an $O(n^2 \log n)$ algorithm for the case of a line segment (a "rod") moving in 2-D polygonal space (improving the $O(n^5)$ algorithm of [49]); the Leven–Sharir result was later shown to be nearly optimal.

3.4. The "retraction method" and other approaches to the motion planning problem

Several other important algorithmic motion planning techniques were developed subsequent to the series of papers just reported. The so-called *retraction method* proceeds by retracting the configuration space FP onto a lower-dimensional (usually a one-dimensional) subspace N, so that two system positions in FP lie in the same connected component of FP if and only if their retractions to N lie in the same connected component of N. This reduces the dimension of the problem, and if N is one-dimensional the problem becomes one of searching a graph.

O'Dunlaing and Yap [39] introduced this retraction technique in the simple case of a disc moving in 2-D polygonal space. Here the subspace N can be taken to be the Voronoi diagram associated with the set of given polygonal obstacles. Their technique yields an $O(n \log n)$ motion planning algorithm. After this first paper, O'Dunlaing, Sharir and Yap [40, 41] generalized the retraction approach to the case of a rod moving in 2-D polygonal space by defining a variant Voronoi diagram in the 3-D configuration space FP of the rod, and by retracting onto this diagram. This achieves $O(n^2 \log n \log^* n)$ performance in this case (a substantial improvement on the naive projection technique first applied to this case, but nevertheless a result shortly afterward superceded by Leven and Sharir [26]).

A similar retraction approach was used by Leven and Sharir [27] to obtain an $O(n \log n)$ algorithm for planning the purely translational motion of a simple convex object amidst polygonal barriers. This last result uses another generalized variant of Voronoi diagram. (A somewhat simpler $O(n \log^2 n)$ algorithm, based on a general technique introduced by Lozano-Pérez and Wesley [32], was previously obtained by Kedem and Sharir [23] (cf. also [22]); this last result exploits an interesting topological property of intersecting planar Jordan curves.)

Recently Sifrony and Sharir [63] devised another retraction-based algorithm for the motion of a rod in 2-D polygonal space. The retraction used maps the rod's free configuration space FP onto a network containing all edges of the boundary of FP, plus some additional arcs which connect particular vertices of FP. They obtain an $O(n^2 \log n)$ algorithm which has the advantage that it runs much faster than that of Leven and Sharir [26] if the obstacles do not lie close to one another.

Hybrid techniques are also appropriate for certain cases of motion planning. For example, in an analysis of the motion planning problem for a convex polygonal object moving in 2-D polygonal space, Kedem and Sharir [24] obtained an $O(n^2 \beta(n) \log n)$ motion planning algorithm (where $\beta(n)$ is a very slowly growing function of n), using a hybrid approach which involves projection of FP onto a 2-D space in which the orientation θ of the object is fixed, followed by retraction of the 2-D space roughly onto its boundary. This result makes use of a combinatorial result of Leven and Sharir [28].

4. Variants of the Motion Planning Problem

4.1. Optimal motion planning

The only optimal motion planning which has been studied extensively thus far is that in which the moving system is represented as a single point, in which case one aims to calculate the shortest Euclidean path connecting initial and final system positions, given that specified obstacles must be avoided. Most existing work on this problem assumes that the obstacles are either polygonal (in 2-space) or polyhedral (in 3-space).

The 2-D case is considerably simpler than the 3-D case. When the free space V in 2-D is bounded by n straight edges, it is easy to calculate the desired shortest path in time $O(n^2 \log n)$. This is done by constructing a *visibility graph* VG whose edges connect all pairs of boundary corners of V which are visible from each other through V, and then by searching for a shortest path through VG (see [60] for a sketch of this idea). This procedure was improved to $O(n^2)$ by Asano et al. [1], by Welzl [69], and by Reif and Storer [47], using a cleverer method for constructing VG. Their quadratic-time bound has been improved in certain special cases. However, it is not known whether shortest paths for a general polygonal space V can be calculated in subquadratic time. Among the special cases allowing more efficient treatment the most important is that of calculating shortest paths inside a simple polygon P. Lee and Preparata [25] gave a linear-time algorithm for this case, assuming that a triangulation of P is given in advance. (As a matter of fact, a recent algorithm of Tarjan and van Wyk shows that triangulation in $O(n \log \log n)$ time is possible.) The Preparata–Lee result was recently extended by Guibas et al. [12], who gave a linear-time algorithm which calculates all shortest paths from a fixed source point to all vertices of P.

Other results on 2-D shortest paths include an $O(n \log n)$ algorithm for *rectilinear* shortest paths avoiding n rectilinear disjoint rectangles [48]; an $O(n^2 \log n)$ algorithm for Euclidean shortest motion of a circular disc in 2-D polygonal space [7]; algorithms for cases in which the obstacles consist of a small number of disjoint convex regions [47]; algorithms for the "weighted region" case (in which the plane is partitioned into polygonal regions and the path has a different multiplicative cost weight when it passes through each of these regions) [35]; and some other special cases.

The 3-D polyhedral case is substantially more difficult. To date, only exponential-time algorithms for the general polyhedral case have been developed [47, 62], and it is not yet known whether the problem is really intractable. However, more efficient algorithms exist in certain special cases. The simplest case is that in which we must calculate the shortest path between two points lying on the surface of a convex polyhedron; it was shown that this can be done in $O(n^2 \log n)$ time (see [30, 62]). Generalizations of this result include algorithms for shortest paths along a (not necessarily convex) polyhedral surface [36], algorithms for shortest paths in 3-space which must avoid a fixed number of convex polyhedra [3, 57], and an approximating pseudo-polynomial scheme for the general case [43].

4.2. Adaptive and exploratory motion planning

If the environment is not known to the robot system a priori, but the system is equipped with sensory devices, motion planning assumes a more "exploratory" character. If only tactile (or proximity) sensing is available, then a plausible strategy might be to move along a straight line (in physical or configuration space) directly to the target position, and when an obstacle is reached, to follow its boundary until the original straight line of motion is reached again [33]. If vision is also available, then other possibilities need to be considered, e.g. the system could obtain partial information about its environment by viewing it from the present position, and then "explore" it to gain progressively more information until the desired motion can be fully planned. However, problems of this sort have hardly begun to be investigated.

Even when the environment is fully known to the system, other interesting issues arise if the environment is changing. For example, when some of the objects in the robot's environment are picked up by the robot and moved to a different position, one wants fast techniques for incremental updating of the environment model and the data structures used for motion planning. Moreover, whenever the robot grasps an object to move it, robot plus grasped object become a new moving system and may require a different motion planning algorithm, but one whose relationship to motions of the robot alone needs to be investigated. Adaptive motion planning problems of this kind have hardly been studied as yet.

4.3. Motion planning in the presence of moving obstacles

Interesting generalizations of the motion planning problem arise when some of the obstacles in the robot's environment are assumed to be moving along known trajectories. In this case the robot's goal will be to "dodge" the moving obstacles while moving to its target position. In this "dynamic" motion planning problem, it is reasonable to assume some limit on the robot's velocity and/or acceleration. Two initial studies of this problem by Reif and Sharir [46] and by Sutner and Maass [65] indicate that the problem of avoiding moving obstacles is substantially harder than the corresponding static problem. By using time-related configuration changes to encode Turing machine states, they show that the problem is PSPACE-hard even for systems with a small and fixed number of degrees of freedom. However, polynomial-time algorithms are available in a few particularly simply special cases.

5. Results in Computational Geometry Relevant to Motion Planning

The various studies of motion planning described above make extensive use of efficient algorithms for the geometric subproblems which they involve, for which reason motion planning has encouraged research in computational geometry. Problems in computational geometry whose solutions apply to robotic motion planning are described in the following subsections.

5.1. Intersection detection

The problem here is to detect intersections and to compute shortest distances, e.g. between moving subparts of a robot system and stationary or moving obstacles. Simplifications which have been studied include that in which all objects involved are circular discs (in the 2-D case) or spheres (in the 3-D case). In a study of the 2-D case of this problem, Sharir [55] developed a generalization of Voronoi diagrams for a set of (possibly intersecting) circles, and used this diagram to detect intersections and computing shortest distances between discs in time $O(n \log^2 n)$ (an alternative approach to this appears in [20]). Hopcroft, Schwartz and Sharir [16] present an algorithm for detecting intersections among n 3-D spheres which also runs in time $O(n \log^2 n)$. However, this algorithm does not adapt in any obvious way to allow proximity calculation or other significant problem variants.

Other intersection detection algorithms appearing in the computational geometry literature involve rectilinear objects and use multi-dimensional searching techniques for achieving high efficiency (see [34] for a survey of these techniques).

5.2. Generalized Voronoi diagrams

The notion of Voronoi diagram has proven to be a useful tool in the solution of many motion planning problems. We have also mentioned the use of various variants of Voronoi diagram in the retraction-based algorithms for planning the motion of a disc [39], or of a rod [40, 41], or the translational motion of a convex object [27], and in the intersection detection algorithm for discs mentioned above [55]. The papers just cited, and some related works [29, 71] describe the analysis of these diagrams and the design of efficient algorithms for their calculations.

5.3. Davenport–Schinzel sequences

Davenport–Schinzel sequences are combinatorial sequences of n symbols which do not contain certain forbidden subsequences of alternating symbols. Sequences of this sort appear in studies of efficient techniques for calculating the lower envelope of a set of n continuous functions, if it is assumed that the graphs of any two functions in the set can intersect in some fixed number of points at most. These sequences, whose study was initiated in [10, 11], have proved to be powerful tools for analysis (and design) of a variety of geometric algorithms, many of which are useful for motion planning.

More specifically, an (n, s) Davenport–Schinzel sequence is defined to be a sequence U composed of n symbols, such that (i) nor two adjacent elements of U are equal, and (ii) there do not exist $s + 2$ indices $i_1 < i_2 < \cdots < i_{s+2}$ such that $u_{i_1} = u_{i_3} = u_{i_5} = \cdots = a$, $u_{i_2} = u_{i_4} = u_{i_6} = \cdots = b$, with $a \neq b$. Let $\lambda_s(n)$ denote the maximal length of an (n, s) Davenport–Schinzel sequence. Early study by Szemeredi [66] of the maximum possible length of such sequences shows that $\lambda_s(n) \leq C_s n \log^* n$, where C_s is a constant depending on s. Improving on this result, Hart and Sharir [13] proved that $\lambda_3(n) = \Theta(n\alpha(n))$ where $\alpha(n)$ is the very slowly growing inverse of the Ackermann function. In [56, 59] Sharir established the bounds

$$\lambda_s(n) = O(n\alpha(n)^{O(\alpha(n)^{s-3})})$$

and

$$\lambda_s(n) = \Omega(n\alpha^{\lfloor (s-1)/2 \rfloor}(n))$$

for $s > 3$. These results show that, in practical terms, $\lambda_s(n)$ is an almost linear function of n (for any fixed s).

Recently, numerous applications of these sequences to motion planning have been found. These include:

(i) an upper bound of $O(kn\lambda_6(kn))$ on the number of simultaneous triple contacts of a convex k-gon translating and rotating in 2-D polygonal space bounded by n edges [28]; an extension of this result was used to produce an $O(kn\lambda_6(kn)\log kn)$ motion planning algorithm for a moving convex k-gon in such a 2-D space [24];

(ii) an $O(mn\alpha(mn)\log m \log n)$ algorithm for separating two interlocking simple polygons by a sequence of translations [44], where it assumed that the polygons have m and n sides respectively;

(iii) an $O(n^2\lambda_{10}(n)\log n)$ algorithm for finding the shortest Euclidean path between two points in 3-space avoiding the interior of two disjoint convex polyhedra having n faces altogether [3].

Other applications are found in [2, 8, 13, 41, 61].

5.4. Topological results related to motion planning

Motion planning is equivalent to the topological problem of calculating the connected components of semi-algebraic varieties in E^k (namely free configuration spaces of robot systems). It is therefore of interest to study topological properties of such varieties which have close relationships to motion planning. A result of this kind by Hopcroft and Wilfong [19], which applies techniques drawn from homology theory, shows that when an object A moves in the presence of just a single (connected) planar obstacle B, then if collision-free motion of A is possible between two positions in which it makes contact with B, then A can move between these two positions so that it always stays in contact with B.

REFERENCES

1. Asano, T., Asano, T., Guibas, L., Hershberger, J. and Imai, H., Visibility polygon search and Euclidean shortest paths, in: *Proceedings 26th Symposium on Foundations of Computer Science* (1985) 155–164.
2. Atallah, M., Dynamic computational geometry, in: *Proceedings 24th Symposium on Foundations of Computer Science* (1983) 92–99.
3. Baltsan, A. and Sharir, M., On shortest paths between two convex polyhedra, *J. ACM* **35** (1988) 267–287.
4. Brooks, R.A., Solving the find-path problem by good representation of free space, *IEEE Trans. Syst. Man Cybern.* **13** (1983) 190–197.
5. Brooks, R.A., Planning collision-free motions for pick-and-place operations, *Int. J. Rob. Res.* **2** (4) (1983) 19–40.
6. Brooks, R.A. and Lozano-Pérez, T., A subdivision algorithm in configuration space for findpath with rotation, AI Memo 684, MIT, Cambridge, MA (1982).
7. Chew, L.P., Planning the shortest path for a disc in $O(n^2 \log n)$ time, in: *Proceedings ACM Symposium on Computational Geometry* (1985) 214–223.
8. Cole, R. and Sharir, M., Visibility problems for polyhedral terrains, *J. Symbolic Comput.* (to appear).
9. Collins, G.E., Quantifier elimination for real closed fields by cylindrical algebraic decomposition, in: *Proceedings Second GI Conference on Automata Theory and Formal Languages*, Lecture Notes in Computer Science **33** (Springer, New York, 1975) 134–183.
10. Davenport, H., A combinatorial problem connected with differential equations, II, *Acta Arithmetica* **17** (1971) 363–372.
11. Davenport, H. and Schinzel, A., A combinatorial problem connected with differential equations, *Am. J. Math.* **87** (1965) 684–694.
12. Guibas, L., Hershberger, J., Leven, D., Sharir, M. and Tarjan, R.E., Linear time algorithms for shortest path and visibility problems inside triangulated simple polygons, *Algorithmica* **2** (1987) 209–233.
13. Hart, S. and Sharir, M., Nonlinearity of Davenport–Schinzel sequences and of generalized path compression schemes, *Combinatorica* **6** (1986) 151–177.
14. Hopcroft, J.E., Joseph, D.A. and Whitesides, S.H., On the movement of robot arms in 2-dimensional bounded regions, *SIAM J. Comput.* **14** (1985) 315–333.
15. Hopcroft, J.E., Joseph, D.A. and Whitesides, S.H., Movement problems for 2-dimensional linkages, *SIAM J. Comput.* **13** (1984) 610–629.
16. Hopcroft, J.E., Schwartz, J.T. and Sharir, M., On the complexity of motion planning for multiple independent objects; PSPACE hardness of the 'warehouseman's problem', *Int. J. Rob. Res.* **3** (4) (1984) 76–88.
17. Hopcroft, J.E., Schwartz, J.T. and Sharir, M., Efficient detection of intersections among spheres, *Rob. Res.* **2** (4) (1983) 77–80.
18. Hopcroft, J.E., Schwartz, J.T. and Sharir, M. (Eds.), *Planning, Geometry and Complexity of Robot Motion* (Ablex, Norwood, NJ, 1987).
19. Hopcroft, J.E. and Wilfong, G., On the motion of objects in contact, Tech. Rept. 84-602, Computer Science Department, Cornell University, Ithaca, NY (1984).

20. Imai, H., Iri, M. and Murota, K., Voronoi diagram in the Laguerre geometry and its applications, Tech. Rept. RMI 83-02, Department of Mathematical Engineering and Instrumentation Physics, University of Tokyo (1983).

21. Joseph, D.A. and Plantinga, W.H., On the complexity of reachability and motion planning questions, in: *Proceedings ACM Symposium on Computational Geometry* (1985) 62–66.

22. Kedem, K., Livne, R., Pach, J. and Sharir, M., On the union of Jordan regions and collision-free translational motion amidst polygonal obstacles, *Discrete Comput. Geometry* **1** (1986) 59–71.

23. Kedem, K. and Sharir, M., An efficient algorithm for planning collision-free translational motion of a convex polygonal object in 2-dimensional space amidst polygonal obstacles, in: *Proceedings ACM Symposium on Computational Geometry* (1985) 75–80.

24. Kedem, K. and Sharir, M., An efficient motion-planning algorithm for a convex polygonal object in two-dimensional polygonal space, *Discrete Comput. Geometry* (to appear).

25. Lee, D.T. and Preparata, F.P., Euclidean shortest paths in the presence of rectilinear barriers, *Networks* **14** (1984) 393–410.

26. Leven, D. and Sharir, M., An efficient and simple motion planning algorithm for a ladder moving in two-dimensional space amidst polygonal barriers, *J. Algorithms* **8** (1987) 192–215.

27. Leven, D. and Sharir, M., Planning a purely translational motion for a convex object in two-dimensional space using generalized Voronoi diagrams, *Discrete Comput. Geometry* **2** (1987) 9–31.

28. Leven, D. and Sharir, M., On the number of critical free contacts of a convex polygonal object moving in 2-D polygonal space, *Discrete Comput. Geometry* **2** (1987) 255–270.

29. Leven, D. and Sharir, M., Intersection and proximity problems and Voronoi diagrams, in: Schwartz, J. and Yap, C. (Eds.), *Advances in Robotics* **I** (Erlbaum, Hillsdale, NJ, 1987) 187–228.

30. Lozano-Pérez, T., Spatial planning: A configuration space approach, *IEEE Trans. Comput.* **32** (2) (1983) 108–119.

31. Lozano-Pérez, T., A simple motion planning algorithm for general robot manipulators, Tech. Rept., AI Lab, MIT, Cambridge, MA (1986).

32. Lozano-Pérez, T. and Wesley, M., An algorithm for planning collision-free paths among polyhedral obstacles, *Comm. ACM* **22** (1979) 560–570.

33. Lumelsky, V.J. and Stepanov, A., Path planning strategies for a traveling automaton in an environment with uncertainty, Tech. Rept. 8504, Center for Systems Science, Yale University, New Haven, CT (1985).

34. Mehlhorn, K., *Data Structures and Algorithms, III: Multidimensional Searching and Computational Geometry* (Springer, New York, 1984).

35. Mitchell, J., Mount, D. and Papadimitriou, C., The discrete geodesic problem, Tech. Rept., Department of Operations Research, Stanford University, Stanford, CA (1985).

36. Mitchell, J. and Papadimitriou, C., The weighted region problem, Tech. Rept., Department of Operations Research, Stanford University, Stanford, CA (1985).

37. Moravec, H.P., Robot rover visual navigation, Ph.D. Dissertation, Stanford University, Stanford, CA (1981).

38. Mount, D.M., On finding shortest paths on convex polyhedra, Tech. Rept., Computer Science Department, University of Maryland, College Park, MD (1984).

39. O'Dunlaing, C. and Yap, C., A 'retraction' method for planning the motion of a disc, *J. Algorithms* **6** (1985) 104–111.

40. O'Dunlaing, C., Sharir, M. and Yap, C., Generalized Voronoi diagrams for a ladder, I: Topological analysis, *Comm. Pure Appl. Math.* **39** (1986) 423–483.

41. O'Dunlaing, C., Sharir, M. and Yap, C., Generalized Voronoi diagrams for a ladder, II: Efficient construction of the diagram, *Algorithmica* **2** (1987) 27–59.

42. O'Rourke, J., Lower bounds on moving a ladder, Tech. Rept. 85/20, Department of EECS, Johns Hopkins University, Baltimore, MD (1985).

43. Papadimitriou, C., An algorithm for shortest path motion in three dimensions, *Inf. Proc. Lett.* **20** (1985) 259–263.
44. Pollack, R., Sharir, M. and Sifrony, S., Separating two simple polygons by a sequence of translations, *Discrete Comput. Geometry* **3** (1988) 123–136.
45. Reif, J.H., Complexity of the mover's problem and generalizations, in: *Proceedings 20th IEEE Symposium on Foundations of Computer Science* (1979) 421–427.
46. Reif, J.H. and Sharir, M., Motion planning in the presence of moving obstacles, Tech. Rept. 39/85, The Eskenasy Institute of Computer Science, Tel-Aviv University (1985).
47. Reif, J.H. and Storer, J.A., Shortest paths in Eucidean space with polyhedral obstacles, Tech. Rept. CS-85-121, Computer Science Department, Brandeis University, Waltham, MA (1985).
48. de Rezende, P.J., Lee, D.T. and Wu, Y.F., Rectilinear shortest paths with retangular barriers, in: *Proceedings ACM Symposium on Computational Geomedtry* (1985) 204–213.
49. Schwartz, J.T. and Sharir, M., On the piano movers' problem, I: The case of a two-dimensional rigid polygonal body moving amidst polygonal barriers, *Comm. Pure Appl. Math.* **36** (1983) 345–398.
50. Schwartz, J.T. and Sharir, M., On the piano movers' problem, II: General techniques for computing topological properties of real algebraic manifolds, *Adv. Appl. Math.* **4** (1983) 298–351.
51. Schwartz, J.T. and Sharir, M., On the piano movers' problem, III: Coordinating the motion of several independent bodies: The special case of circular bodies moving amidst polygonal barriers, *Rob. Res.* **2** (3) (1983) 46–75.
52. Schwartz, J.T. and Sharir, M., On the piano movers' problem, V: The case of a rod moving in three-dimensional space amidst polyhedral obstacles, *Comm. Pure Appl. Math.* **37** (1984) 815–848.
53. Schwartz, J.T. and Sharir, M., Efficient motion planning algorithms in environments of bounded local complexity, Tech. Rept. 164, Computer Science Department, Courant Institute, New York (1985).
54. Schwartz, J.T. and Sharir, M., Mathematical problems and training in robotics, *Notices Am. Math. Soc.* **30** (1983) 478–481.
55. Sharir, M., Intersection and closest-pair problems for a set of planar discs, *SIAM J. Comput.* **14** (1985) 448–468.
56. Sharir, M., Almost linear upper bounds on the length of general Davenport–Schinzel sequences, *Combinatorica* **7** (1987) 131–143.
57. Sharir, M., On shortest paths amidst convex polyhedra, *SIAM J. Comput.* **16** (1987) 561–572.
58. Sharir, M., On the two-dimensional Davenport Schinzel problem, Tech. Rept. 193, Computer Science Department, Courant Institute, New York (1985).
59. Sharir, M., Improved lower bounds on the length of Davenport Schinzel sequences, *Combinatorica* **8** (1988) 117–124.
60. Sharir, M. and Ariel-Sheffi, E., On the piano movers' problem, IV: Various decomposable two-dimensional motion planning problems, *Comm. Pure Appl. Math.* **37** (1984) 479–493.
61. Sharir, M. and Livne, R., On minima of functions, intersection patterns of curves, and Davenport–Schinzel sequences, in: *Proceedings 26th Symposium Foundations of Computer Science* (1985) 312–320.
62. Sharir, M. and Schorr, A., On shortest paths in polyhedral spaces, *SIAM J. Comput.* **15** (1986) 193–215.
63. Sifrony, S. and Sharir, M., An efficient motion planning algorithm for a rod moving in two-dimensional polygonal space, *Algorithmica* **2** (1987) 367–402.
64. Spirakis, P. and Yap, C.K., Strong NP-hardness of moving many discs, *Inf. Proc. Lett.* **19** (1984) 55–59.
65. Sutner, K. and Maass, W., Motion planning among time dependent obstacles, Manuscript (1985).

66. Szemeredi, E., On a problem by Davenport and Schinzel, *Acta Arithmetica* **25** (1974) 213–224.
67. Tarjan, R.E. and van Wyk, C., An $O(n \log \log n)$ time algorithm for triangulating simple polygons, *SIAM J. Comput.* **17** (1988).
68. Udupa, S., Collision detection and avoidance in computer controlled manipulators, Ph.D. Dissertation, California Institute of Technology, Pasadena, CA (1977).
69. Welzl, E., Constructing the visibility graph for n line segments in $O(n^2)$ time, *Inf. Proc. Lett.* **20** (1985) 167–172.
70. Yap, C.K., Coordinating the motion of several discs, Tech. Rept. 105, Computer Science Department, Courant Institute, New York (1984).
71. Yap, C.K., An $O(n \log n)$ algorithm for the Voronoi diagram of a set of simple curve segments, Tech. Rept. 161, Computer Science Department, Courant Institute, New York (1985).

Received September 1986

An Algorithmic Approach to Some Problems in Terrain Navigation

Joseph S.B. Mitchell

*School of Operations Research and Industrial Engineering,
Cornell University, Ithaca, NY 14853, U.S.A.*

ABSTRACT

Recent advances in the field of computational geometry have provided efficient algorithms for a variety of shortest path problems. Many problems in the field of terrain navigation can be cast as optimal path problems in a precise geometric model. With such a model one can develop and analyze algorithms for the solution of the original problem and can gain insights into how to design more efficient heuristics to deal with more complex problems. We examine the path planning problem in which we are given a "map" of a region of terrain and we are expected to find optimal paths from one point to another. This, for example, is a task which must be done repeatedly for the guidance of an autonomous vehicle. We examine how to formulate some path planning problems precisely, and we report algorithms to solve certain special cases.

1. Introduction

One of the basic tasks required of an autonomous vehicle is to move from one location to another. Usually, the robot has some knowledge (which we refer to as a *map*) of the terrain on which it is navigating, although it may initially have none. It should try to exploit as much of this knowledge as possible in order to make the best decisions about its path. Two types of navigation problems immediately arise: How does the robot *locate* its position in the map, and how does one use the map and the current location of the robot to *plan* a route to the goal? In this paper, we concentrate on the latter type of problem. We use the word "terrain" to refer to both indoor and outdoor environments for a vehicle.

The problem of location involves using sensory data to compute the coordinates of the robot. This can be done only to within some error bounds; however, we will assume that the errors involved are small enough in comparison with the scale of the planning problem that we can assume the exact position of the robot is known at each point in time and that the robot can be controlled exactly to follow a specified trajectory. The issue of location uncertainty is very important, and it is an area of continuing research.

In planning paths through the map, we typically wish to minimize some objective function which specifies the *cost* of motion along the path (the *path length*). Depending on how the terrain is modeled and what the optimization criteria are, this results in various versions of the *shortest path problem*. The shortest path problem for a mobile robot was one of the early problems addressed by researchers in artificial intelligence (see Nilsson [59] and Moravec [58]).

In this paper we discuss some of the issues that go into selecting a representation of a map, and we report some of the recent results from the field of *computational geometry* which are of use in solving terrain navigation problems. Computational geometry and algorithmic motion planning have recently erupted as important areas of research in computer science. We certainly cannot do justice here to the field of motion planning, so we refer the interested reader to the superb new books of Schwartz and Yap [78] and Schwartz et al. [77], which collect together many of the landmark papers of this exciting field. We also refer the reader to the award-winning thesis of Canny [9]. Much of our discussion uses concepts from the field of computational geometry. We refer the interested reader to three recent books on the subject: Edelsbrunner [19], Mehlhorn [44], and Preparata and Shamos [65].

While many of the problems of terrain navigation have been addressed before from a heuristic or approximation point of view, we feel that it is important to formalize some of the models and to discuss the computational complexity of exact algorithms. We have found that an understanding of the underlying geometry can lead to new heuristics and faster algorithms for a variety of problems.

How do we go about representing varied terrain? What representations yield particularly natural or efficient algorithms for path planning? What do shortest paths "look like"; that is, can we understand enough about the local optimality criteria to cut down the search for optimal paths?

We begin addressing some of these issues in the following sections, where we describe the *obstacle avoidance problem*, the *discrete geodesic problem*, the *weighted region problem*, and some special cases of these problems that arise naturally in finding shortest paths through terrain. Throughout our discussions, we concentrate on the fundamental algorithmic issues of computing paths, and we are interested in worst-case asymptotic running times. Where appropriate, we will allude to the practicality of the algorithms and approaches we suggest.

2. Obstacle Avoidance in the Plane

The simplest surface to model is a plane, and the simplest nontrivial terrain map on a plane is a binary partitioning of the plane into regions that are obstacles and regions that are traversable by the vehicle. Usually, the robot can be modeled as a point, which is a reasonable assumption if it is small in comparison with the dimensions of the terrain map. Also, by *configuration space* techniques, many problems of moving a nonpoint robot among obstacles can be reduced to the case of moving a point (possibly in higher dimensions), by "growing" the obstacles in an appropriate way, as in [41]. The problem of planning a shortest Euclidean path from one point to another is then the usual *obstacle avoidance shortest path problem*. This problem has been studied by many researchers over the last twenty years. A survey of many algorithms is given in [49, 55].

Some recent work of Papadimitriou and Silverberg [64] and O'Rourke [61] has started to address the tough problem of *shortest* paths for a nonpoint noncircular body in the plane. While this can be mapped into a shortest path problem in three-dimensional configuration space, calculating shortest paths in three dimensions has been shown to be quite difficult, as we will mention later.

There are two standard approaches to modeling the terrain for the obstacle avoidance problem. The first subdivides the plane into small regular pieces ("pixels") and labels each piece as obstacle or nonobstacle. If all of the pieces are squares of exactly the same size, then we get the standard grid tesselation, and we can represent the map as a binary array. A measure of the size of the problem instance is given by n, the total number of pixels. Of course, n depends on the resolution of the grid used to approximate the set of obstacles. Picking a very small pixel (very high resolution) allows a better model of the obstacle space, but it costs us significantly in problem size. If using a regular grid, we may be forced to have pixels smaller than a certain size in order to assure that skinny passage ways between obstacles or tiny little obstacles appear in the map. Other subdivision representations exist which are hierarchical in nature, such as the *quadtree* (see Samet and Webber [76] or Kambhampati and Davis [31]). These schemes have the advantage that they conglomerate groups of contiguous small squares into single larger squares.

Another standard approach to modeling terrain which is obstacle or nonobstacle is to give a description of a polygonal space in terms of its boundary representation. Obstacles are given as a list of k simple polygons, each represented by a doubly linked list of vertices (each vertex just being a pair of coordinates, either integer or real). Usually, the obstacles are assumed to be disjoint. Let n be the total number of vertices of all polygonal obstacles. We refer to n as the "complexity of the scene", as it is proportional to the number of bytes of storage needed to represent the map. To be more precise, though, the complexity of the scene should be the pair (n, k), since some of the complexities of algorithms depend not only on n, but also on k. (Of course, k is always less than or equal to n, but it may be significantly less than n, in which case it is important to know precisely how the running times depend on k). The objective of the algorithmic study of the shortest path problem is to determine an algorithm whose worst-case running time is a low-degree polynomial in n and k. Most work in computational geometry focuses on *worst-case* running times; however, it is an important issue (not addressed here) to consider the *average-case* running times of shortest path algorithms.

An example of a set of obstacles is given in Fig. 1. In Fig. 1(a), we show the representation of the obstacles as a set of $k = 2$ polygons with $n = 8$ vertices and the shortest path from start to goal. Then, in Fig. 1(b) we show the digitized representation on a grid of 16×16 pixels ($n = 256$). In Fig. 1(c) we show the same set of obstacles represented as a quadtree, where the free space is also subdivided into a quadtree representation. The total size of the representation in this case is $n = 124$.

There are other methods of modeling the terrain in the obstacle avoidance problem. The obstacles may be given as a list of circles, ellipses, or other nonpolygonal objects. The shortest path problem among circular or elliptical obstacles has been addressed by Baker [5], Chew [11], and Mitchell [49]. Souvaine [81] introduced the notion of *splinegons* as a means of describing simple closed *curved* figures, and she describes many generalizations of standard computational geometry algorithms to the case of splinegons. A different approach to modeling obstacle maps is given by Brooks [7] and Brooks and Lozano-Pérez [8], who give a decomposition of the free space into generalized cylinders. Their (heuristic) method is similar to the retraction method of motion planning (see Schwartz and Yap [78]).

Shortest paths according to the Euclidean metric will be "taut string" paths: imagine threading a string from START to GOAL among the obstacles, then pulling the string until it is taut. The question really comes down to how the string should be threaded. One cannot afford to try all of the exponentially many possible threadings.

The algorithm one uses to find shortest paths among obstacles depends on the representation used in the map. For the case of a binary grid representation, the search for shortest paths is easy and straightforward. Shortest paths are found by restricting the robot's motion to connect centers of adjacent free squares. Then, we can consider the graph (so-called *grid graph*) whose nodes are the free space squares and the edges connect adjacent free squares. The degree of a node is thus at most 8, so the graph has at most n nodes and no more than $8n$ edges. Lengths are assigned to edges in the obvious way: diagonal edges are of length $\sqrt{2}$ times the size of a square, and horizontal and vertical edges are of length equal to the size of a square. We can then search the graph for shortest paths by applying the A* algorithm (Nilsson [59]) or the Dijkstra [18] algorithm (which is "uniformed" A*). The worst-case running time of Dijkstra's algorithm (and hence of A*) is $O(|E| + |V|\log|V|)$ for a graph with $|E|$ edges and $|V|$ nodes (Fredman and Tarjan [21]); thus, the worst-case running time of the shortest path algorithm is $O(n \log n)$ for a grid with n pixels. Note that for A* there is an obvious admissible heuristic

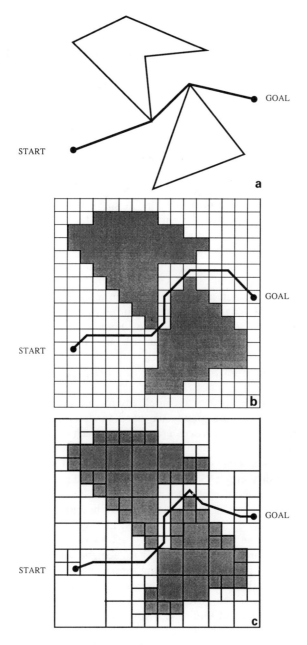

Fig. 1(a) Polygonal obstacles and a shortest path. (b) Digitized representation. (c) Quadtree representation.

function, $h(v)$, for node v, namely, the straight line Euclidean distance from v to the goal.

Figure 1(b) shows the path from START to GOAL which results from finding the shortest path through the grid graph. Note that the path is not shortest according to the Euclidean metric. This is a common problem with the grid graph approach—it introduces a "digitization bias", a product of requiring paths to stay on the grid graph. Within the same time bounds ($O(n \log n)$), an algorithm of Keirsey and Mitchell [33] can be run which attempts to correct for this digitization bias imposed by requiring paths to stay on the grid graph. See also [57, 85, 86]. These grid-based planners do not, however, solve the exact Euclidean shortest path problem.

For maps given in the form of a list of polygonal obstacles, there are two basic approaches to finding shortest paths. A survey of these methods is given by Mitchell and Papadimitriou [55] or Mitchell [49].

The first approach is to build a *visibility graph* of the obstacle space, whose nodes are the vertices of the obstacles and whose edges connect pairs of vertices for which the segment between them does not cross the interior of any obstacle. The resulting graph can be searched using Dijkstra's algorithm or A*, where the heuristic function may again be taken to be the straight line distance from a point to the goal. The time required for searching the graph is $O(K + n \log n)$, where K is the number of edges in the visibility graph. The result of the search is actually more than just the shortest path from START to GOAL; we actually get a *shortest path tree* on the set of obstacle vertices which gives a shortest path from the START (or the GOAL) to every other obstacle vertex.

The bottleneck in the worst-case complexity for the visibility graph approach is in the construction of the graph. We need to determine for every pair of vertices whether or not the vertices are visible to each other. There are $O(n^2)$ such pairs. A trivial $O(n^3)$ algorithm simply checks every pair of vertices against every obstacle edge. With a little more care, $O(n^2 \log n)$ suffices to compute the visibility graph [38, 49, 79]. The basic idea is to sort (angularly) the set of all vertices about each vertex and then to do an angular sweep about each vertex, keeping track of the closest obstacle boundary. Using a trick from duality theory that maps the vertices to lines, Lee and Ching [39] showed that the n sorts can be done in total time $O(n^2)$ rather than $O(n^2 \log n)$. This fact allowed Welzl [87] and Asano et al. [3] to achieve an $O(n^2)$ algorithm for constructing visibility graphs. This running time is not likely to be improved for the worst case since there are visibility graphs of quadratic size.

However, the most recent development in the analysis of visibility graphs is the algorithm of Ghosh and Mount [23] which computes the visibility graph of a set of n disjoint line segments in time $O(K + n \log n)$, where K is the number of edges in the visibility graph. This *output-sensitive* algorithm takes advantage of the fact that K is not always of size $\Theta(n^2)$, but rather can be as small as

$\Theta(n)$. So, when the visibility graph is sparse (say, $O(n \log n)$ edges), the algorithm is very fast, building the visibility graph in time $O(n \log n)$. Thus, when $K = O(n \log n)$, Dijkstra's algorithm (or A^*) requires worst-case complexity $O(K + n \log n) = O(n \log n)$, so the shortest path can be found in time $O(n \log n)$.

A second technique for finding shortest paths is that of building a *shortest path map*. A shortest path map is a subdivision of the plane into regions each of which is the locus of all goal points whose shortest paths from the START have the same topology (i.e., pass through the same sequence of obstacle vertices.) With such a subdivision, the shortest path from START to GOAL is obtained simply by locating the GOAL point in the subdivision (which takes time $O(\log n)$) and then backtracking an optimal path. See Lee and Preparata [40] or Mitchell [49] for precise definitions and examples. Reif and Storer [69] have given an algorithm to compute the shortest path map in time $O(kn + n \log n)$, where k is the number of obstacles. Note that this is an improvement over $O(n^2)$ when the number of obstacles is small in comparison with the number of obstacle vertices. Their algorithm simulates the propagation of a "wavefront" from the START, in much the same way that expansion operates in the Dijkstra or A^* algorithms. Because of its similarity to the discrete Dijkstra algorithm, this technique has come to be called the "continuous Dijkstra" paradigm.

The continuous Dijkstra paradigm, in the form of a plane sweep algorithm, has lead to $O(n \log n)$ algorithms in a few special cases [40, 49, 79]. Basically, if the obstacles are known to have disjoint projections onto some line (e.g., if the obstacles are vertical line segments), then the shortest path will always be monotone with respect to that line (except, perhaps, at the ends of the path). This monotonicity allows one to use plane sweep algorithms for the iterative construction of the shortest path map.

In the simple case of finding shortest paths required to stay inside a single simple polygonal room with n sides (without other obstacles), the shortest path can be found in linear ($O(n)$) time once a triangulation of the polygon is known [25, 40]. (Triangulation of a simple polygon is now known to require $o(n \log n)$ time, as Tarjan and van Wyk [84] have provided an $O(n \log \log n)$ algorithm. It is suspected that triangulation can be done in linear time, but this is another outstanding open problem in computational geometry.) Furthermore, a triangulated simple polygon can be processed in linear time so that in time $O(\log n)$ one can find the length of the shortest path from any given START to any given GOAL [26]. Furthermore, in time proportional to the number of bends in the optimal path, one can output the actual path from START to GOAL.

Lower bounds are known for the shortest obstacle-free path problem. In the worst case, computing the shortest path among k obstacles with a total of n vertices requires $\Omega(n + k \log k)$ time. One can use a shortest path algorithm to find convex hulls, which in turn can be used to sort integers, for which the lower bound is well known (see [65]).

The big open problem in this field is to determine whether or not the shortest path among n disjoint line segments can be computed in optimal time $\Theta(n \log n)$, and more generally if shortest paths among k simple polygons can be found in time $\Theta(n + k \log k)$. We should note that for some metrics other than Euclidean, such as the L_1 ("Manhattan") metric and "fixed orientation" metrics [88], optimal or near-optimal shortest path algorithms are known (see [15, 17, 50]).

3. Shortest Paths on a Surface

A natural generalization of the obstacle avoidance problem in the plane is to consider the case of finding shortest paths for a point which is constrained to move on a nonplanar (possibly nonconvex) surface. To see that this is a generalization of the above problem, consider the surface which results from making each obstacle into a very tall cylinder whose base is in the plane of motion. Then, one can show that the shortest path on such a (nonconvex) surface will stay in the plane and follow the shortest obstacle avoidance path. Note that the problem we wish to solve is a calculus of variations problem: Find the shortest *geodesic* path between two points on a surface. Since the surface is modeled in a discrete manner, we refer to this problem as the *discrete geodesic problem*.

Here, we assume that our vehicle is not able to fly, but is able to travel over all types of terrain with uniform efficiency. We can go up hills, down hills, and even perhaps on the underside of an overhang. (Our tires are "magnetic" and the ground has a very high iron content.) Such is the problem faced by the crawling insect in Fig. 2. He desires to get to the cheese in the shortest possible path, but he does not have wings to be able to fly there. Along what route should he crawl?

First, let us mention something about the representation of the problem. What is the map in this case? It is simply some representation of a surface in three dimensions. Formally, the surface might be represented as a polyhedral surface, giving faces, edges, and vertices, along with all of the usual adjacency relationships that allow one to give the faces on each side of any edge and to "walk around" a vertex while enumerating adjacent faces. (The winged-edge data structure of Baumgart [6] or the similar quad-edge data structure of Guibas and Stolfi [27] would work nicely here.) Another possible surface representation that is often used in practice is that of contour lines. We might be given a set of iso-elevation curves, as is usually the case with geological maps of terrain. A third common representation is that of an *elevation array*. In this case, we are simply given a two-dimensional array of numbers which represent the altitude at each grid point. Digital terrain data bases of the form compiled by the Defense Mapping Agency fall into this category. (Typically, pixels are of size 5, 12.5, or 100 meters.) These are just some of the methods of specifying a discrete approximation of a surface. Note that the last two representations require that the surface be the image of a single-valued function of the plane (i.e., there are no "overhangs"), an assumption that generally holds for most outdoor terrain.

The case of a surface represented with an elevation array can be solved easily if one makes the approximation that paths are constrained to follow the corresponding grid graph. We just connect each pixel to each of its eight neighbors, assigning a length measured by the three-dimensional Euclidean distance, and then search the graph for a shortest path using Dijkstra or an A* algorithm. This requires $O(n \log n)$ time in the worst case, where n is the number of array elements (pixels).

Research in the field of algorithmic motion planning has favored the representation of a surface in terms of a polyhedron. The general problem of finding shortest paths for a point in three dimensions amidst polyhedral obstacles has been of interest for some time [1, 2, 14, 20, 63, 69, 79]. The general problem seems very hard to solve, as Canny and Reif [10] have shown the problem to be NP-hard, and the best known exact algorithm is the singly exponential algorithm of Reif and Storer [69]. Papadimitriou [63] and Clarkson [14] have solved the problem approximately with fully polynomial approximation schemes (meaning that the running time is polynomial in n, K, and $1/\varepsilon$,

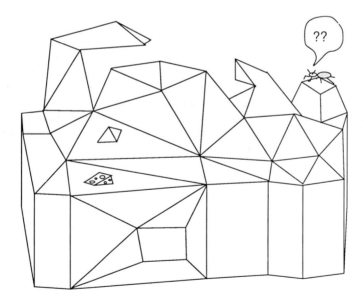

Fig. 2. The problem of navigating on a surface.

where K is the number of bits to represent the problem instance). The complexity of their algorithms is $O(n^3 K^2/\varepsilon)$. The special case, though, of our bug crawling on the surface of a single polyhedron is interesting because it admits a polynomial-time algorithm which is exact.

Franklin and Akman [20] and Akman [1, 2] have given exponential (worst-case) algorithms for the shortest path problem on a surface, and have shown that their algorithms perform reasonably well in practice. The first polynomial-time algorithm was an $O(n^3 \log n)$ algorithm of Sharir and Schorr [79] which worked only for the case of convex polyhedra (where n is the number of edges of the polyhedron). Most interesting terrain is not convex, though, since it will usually have many mountains and valleys. An algorithm which works for nonconvex surfaces was devised by O'Rourke et al. [62], and its complexity is $O(n^5)$. Both of these running times were improved by the algorithm of Mitchell et al. [54], which runs in time $O(n^2 \log n)$. The algorithm actually constructs, for a fixed start point, a subdivision (a *shortest path map*) of the surface such that after the $O(n^2 \log n)$ preprocessing required to build the subdivision, the distance to any particular destination can be found by locating the goal in the subdivision (a task which is well known to take $O(\log n)$ time; see, for example, [34]). Listing of a path can be done in time proportional to the number of turns in the optimal path.

Let us make a few simple observations that were cricital to all of the algorithms mentioned above. We can state a few known facts about how optimal paths must behave:

(1) Optimal paths are simple (not self-intersecting), and they can pass through any one face at most once.

(2) Optimal paths "unfold" into straight lines. This is an observation that any high school geometry student has made if he has tried to solve the problem of finding the shortest path between two points on the surface of a box: Simply "cut open" the box and flatten it in such a way that the start and goal can be connected by a straight line segment that stays on the flattened cardboard. One such unfolding is guaranteed to produce a shortest path. An optimal path which passes through an edge of the polyhedron must obey the *local optimality criterion* that it unfolds to give a straight line. More generally, for any type of surface there is a similar statement of the principle of optimality, and this produces a characterization of the *geodesics* of that type of surface. (Recall that the geodesics of a sphere are arcs of great circles; the geodesics of a polyhedral surface are characterized by the above unfolding property.) Of course, the question that must be answered by an algorithm is which of the (possibly exponentially many) unfoldings yields a shortest path?

(3) On a convex surface, optimal paths will not go through vertices (except perhaps at their endpoints), while on a nonconvex surface, an optimal path may pass through a vertex only if the angle it makes in so doing is greater than π (see [54] for a more precise statement).

Obviously, any algorithm which attempts to solve a shortest path problem should exploit as much of the structure of the paths as possible. It is also sometimes possible to exploit special structure when designing good heuristics. For example, to solve a shortest path problem on a given surface, we could use the simple heuristic which connects the start with the goal along the path "as the crow flies" (that is, the intersection of the surface with the vertical plane through the start and goal), and then iteratively improves the path by applying the local optimality criterion of (1) above. This will result in a *locally* optimal path which will frequently be very good in practice (while it is certainly not guaranteed to be *globally* optimal). Perhaps a planner which combines some "intelligence" with this heuristic would produce reasonably good paths. For example, one might have knowledge that there is only one feasible way through a mountain range, say through a specific gorge, and we would then want to route our initial guess through this passage, so that the locally optimal path produced will be reasonable. Further experimental and theoretical research is needed on these problems.

4. Weighted Regions

We now consider a more general terrain navigation problem. Assume that our map represents a set of *regions* in the plane, each of which has an associated *weight*, or cost, α. The weight of a region specifies the "cost per unit distance" of a vehicle (considered to be a point) traveling in that region. Our objective is then to find a path from START to GOAL in the plane which minimizes total cost according to this weighted Euclidean metric. For example, the weights may represent the reciprocal of the maximum speed in each region, in which case minimizing the weighted Euclidean length of a path is simply minimizing the length of time it takes the vehicle to execute the path.

This problem has been termed the *weighted region problem*. Note that it is a generalization of the obstacle avoidance problem in the plane, for the obstacle avoidance problem is simply the weighted region problem in which the weights are either 1 or $+\infty$ depending on whether a region is "free space" or obstacle, respectively. Thus, an important theoretical reason for considering the weighted region problem is that it is a natural generalization of the well-studied obstacle avoidance problem.

An example of a typical map is illustrated in Fig. 3. Basically, the ground surface is subdivided into uniform regions, with a label (or some traversability index) attached to each region which gives information about how fast one can move in that region (or how costly it is to do so). Presumably, the robot can move through different types of terrain at different speeds. Speeds may also depend on other factors such as time of day, precipitation, or the location of other vehicles; however, we assume that a given problem instance has fixed weights. In military applications, there may be regions which correspond to high threat risk, perhaps because the enemy has good visibility of you when

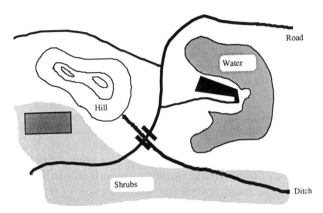

Fig. 3. Map for terrain navigation.

you are in these regions. Costs can be assigned to traveling in these risky regions as well.

We will discuss two basic types of map representations: regular tesselations (e.g., grids of pixels, or quadtrees), and straight line planar subdivisions.

Representing terrain in the form of a regular grid of pixels is natural and simple. Figure 4 shows the map of Fig. 3 in digitized form, on a grid of size 26 × 40 (1040 pixels). Frequently, terrain data is given in the form of a set of arrays, with each array giving information about some aspect of the terrain (e.g., ground cover, land usage, hydrography data, man-made features, and traversability indices). This, for example, is the form in which the Defense

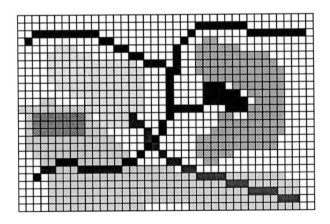

Fig. 4. Digitized terrain map.

Mapping Agency terrain data is supplied. Pixels are usually squares 5, 12.5, or 100 meters on a side. From this type of data, we can specify the map by taking the superposition of all the data arrays to form one composite map (a "terrain array"), whose regions of equal attributes will have descriptions such as "brush-covered, drainage plain", or "forested land, sandy soil, small boulders". Each composite region may be assigned a weight representing the cost of motion in that type of terrain. Certain types of terrain features have priority over others. For example, if the "roads array" tells us there is a road surface occupying pixel (i, j) while the ground cover array describes the pixel as "grassland", then the composite region attribute at (i, j) should say that there is a road there.

If the terrain map is given as a grid of weighted pixels, then a straightforward solution to the weighted region problem is to search the corresponding grid graph for shortest paths [29, 33, 66]. This is simply a generalization of the approach described earlier for the case of digitized obstacle maps. The grid graph will have either 4- or 8-connectivity depending on whether or not we consider diagonal neighbors of pixels. Costs may be assigned in the natural way to arcs connecting adjacent pixels of the grid, taking into account the weights of the two pixels by, say, taking the cost of the arc between them to be their average weight. Then, Dijkstra's algorithm or A* may be used to compute minimum-cost paths in the grid graph. For a grid with n pixels, this results in an algorithm that runs in worst-case time $O(n \log n)$. This approach is particularly appealing in cases in which the data is given to us in the form of feature arrays.

One problem with the grid graph approach is that it may require extremely fine grids to capture the content of a relatively simple piece of terrain. Frequently, there may be just a couple of large uniform regions, perhaps with a road running through them, and the pixel representation of the map requires, say, a 512×512 array. The shortest path may indeed be obvious (such as a simple straight line segment), but the algorithm must still search and expand thousands of pixels during its execution (although hierarchical algorithms can avoid much of the expansion). Another problem with the grid graph approach is that it creates a *digitization bias* because of the metrication error imposed by confining movements to 4 or 8 orientations. See Keirsey and Mitchell [33] for a more detailed discussion of digitization bias and the various possible remedies for it. See Quek et al. [66] for a technique that uses grid graphs of multiple resolutions to design a hierarchical algorithm.

If, instead of being a regular tesselation, the map is modeled as a straight line planar subdivision then the regions are just simple polygons. Figure 5 shows the map of Fig. 3 drawn as a straight line planar subdivision with 85 edges. An appropriate data structure would be either a winged-edge [6] or a quad-edge [27] data structure. Roads and other linear features (such as ditches, fences, streams, etc.) can be modeled as very skinny polygonal regions or

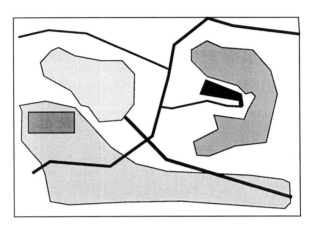

Fig. 5. Polygonal subdivision map.

approximated as sets of line segments. In the planar subdivision, then, we allow edges to be assigned a weight which may be different from the weights of the faces on either side of it. If an edge is a line segment of a road, then, presumably, its weight will be less than the weights on either side of it (assuming that it is cheaper to travel on roads than off roads). If an edge is a line segment of a ditch or a fence, then it may be assigned a fixed cost of crossing it. The fixed cost would be $+\infty$ if the edge cannot be crossed.

The representation of regions as polygonal patches and of roads as linear features has been used in the work on the DARPA Autonomous Land Vehicle project. One advantage of encoding the map information originally in the form of polygonal patches is that it can save greatly on the storage costs, while increasing the resolution of the data. The centerline of a road need not be specified only to the resolution of a pixel (say 12.5 meters), but can be specified to any desired degree of accuracy and can be specified to a higher resolution than other less critical features of the terrain.

In order to put the terrain array into the representation of a polygonal subdivision, we must fit polygonal boundaries about the sets of pixels with uniform attributes. At the highest resolution, each pixel can be considered to be a polygonal patch, namely, a square; however, this extreme will usually result in many more regions than desired, and it does not reflect the fact that the original data was only approximate in the first place. Usually, we will also want to represent roads, fences, and power lines as linear features by fitting a piecewise-linear path to them.

Assume now that we are given a planar subdivision with weights. One approach to solving the weighted region problem is to build a "region graph" in which nodes correspond to regions and arcs correspond to boundaries between adjacent regions. Assume that the subdivision is fine enough that all regions are convex. (We could, for example, make the subdivision a triangulation each of the simple polygonal regions; however, we may want to subdivide in such a way that each convex region is as close to being circular as possible.) Then we can think of placing a node at the "center" (e.g., center of mass) of each region. Two nodes are joined by an edge if the corresponding regions are adjacent. We then assign costs to arcs according to the weighted distance between adjacent nodes. (An alternative graph can be constructed by placing nodes at the midpoints of region edges and linking two nodes if the corresponding edges share a common region.) Note that a grid graph is a special case of a region graph in which all the regions are equal-sized squares. Searching this graph for shortest paths yields a "region path" from the START to the GOAL, giving a sequence of regions through which a "good" path should pass. We could then do some postprocessing (e.g., using Snell's Law of Refraction from optics, a local optimality criterion that we will mention below) to make the path locally optimal at region boundaries. The problem with this approach is that it can produce paths that are far from being optimal, for the optimal path need not have any relationship to the shortest region-path. In practice, however, it promises to be a very useful technique, particularly in cases in which the data is not very accurate or the assignment of weights is somewhat subjective. (Can one really say that grassland deserves a weight of 5 while brushland deserves a weight of 15? It seems likely that weights will be highly subjective.)

Thus, the region graph approach does not guarantee that the resulting path is close to being optimal. Another approach given by Mitchell and Papadimitriou [56] yields a polynomial-time algorithm for computing ε-optimal paths. The length of the produced path is guaranteed to be within a factor of $1 + \varepsilon$ of the length of an optimal path. The complexity of the algorithm is $O(n^7 L)$, where L is the number of bits needed to represent the problem data and ε. The algorithm is a generalization of the algorithm for the discrete geodesic problem given by Mitchell et al. [54], and it too uses the continuous Dijkstra paradigm.

Let us be more precise about the problem solved in [56]. We are given a (straight line) planar subdivision, $\mathscr{S}$, specified by a set of faces (regions), edges, and vertices, with each edge occurring in two faces and two faces intersecting either at a common edge, a vertex, or not at all. We consider faces to be *closed* polygons (they include their boundaries) and edges to be *closed* line segments (they include their endpoints, which are vertices). We are also given an initial point, START. Without loss of generality, we assume that all faces are triangles and that s and t are vertices of the triangulation. Assume that $\mathscr{S}$ has n edges (and hence $O(n)$ triangular faces and $O(n)$ vertices). Our complexity measures will be written in terms of n.

Each face f has associated with it a weight $\alpha_f \in [0, +\infty]$ which specifies the cost per unit distance of traveling on face f. Similarly, each edge e has associated with it a weight $\alpha_e \in [0, +\infty]$. The weighted distance between any two points x and y on edge e is simply the product $\alpha_e |xy|$, where $|xy|$ is the usual Euclidean distance between x and y. Likewise, the weighted distance between any two points x and y on face f (but not both on the same edge of f) is the product $\alpha_f |xy|$. The weighted length of a path through the subdivision is then the sum of the weighted lengths of its subpaths through each face.

We are asked to find the minimal length (in the weighted sense) path from START to some goal point. The algorithm of [56] actually solves the *query* form of the weighted region problem: Build a structure which allows one to compute a shortest path (in the weighted Euclidean metric) from START to *any* query point t. It turns out that this single-source version of the problem is no harder (in worst-case asymptotic time) than the problem with a given fixed goal point.

As with the discrete geodesic problem, the algorithm for the weighted region problem exploits certain facts about the local behavior of optimal paths:

(1) Shortest paths are piecewise-linear, bending only at points where they cross an edge or pass through a vertex. This follows from the fact that each region is assumed to have a *uniform* weight. (The case of *non*uniform weighted regions gives rise to other types of curves and is an interesting area for further research.)

(2) When an optimal path passes through an edge between regions, it does so while obeying Snell's Law of Refraction at that edge. This is the local optimality criterion which is analogous to the fact that shortest paths on the surface of a polyhedron unfold to be straight lines. It is a simple property of locally optimal paths through weighted regions which has been observed by many researchers (Lyusternik [43], Mitchell and Papadimitriou [55, 56], Richbourg [70], Richbourg et al. [71, 72], Rowe and Richbourg [74], Smith [80]).

Snell's Law of Refraction. *The path of a light ray passing through a boundary e between regions f and f' with indices of refraction α and β obeys the relationship that $\alpha \sin \theta = \beta \sin \phi$, where θ and ϕ are the angles of incidence and refraction (respectively).*

The *angle of incidence*, θ, is defined to be the counterclockwise angle between the incoming ray and the normal to the region boundary. The *angle of refraction*, ϕ, is defined as the angle between the outgoing ray and the normal. Refer to Fig. 6.

The fact that light obeys Snell's Law comes from the fact that light seeks the path of minimum time (this is *Fermat's Principle*). The index of refraction for a region is proportional to the speed at which light can travel through that region. Hence, the shortest paths in our weighted region problem must also obey Snell's Law. This can be shown formally [49, 56].

(3) The angle of incidence of an optimal path at a boundary that it crosses

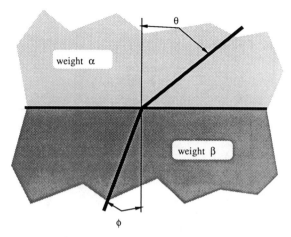

Fig. 6. Light ray crossing a boundary.

will not be greater (in absolute value) than the *critical angle* defined at that boundary. This fact comes from examining the relationship specified in Snell's Law and making sure it is well-defined. Without loss of generality, assume that $\alpha_f > \alpha_{f'} > 0$. Then, we must assure that

$$-1 \leq \sin \theta_{f'} = \frac{\alpha_f}{\alpha_{f'}} \sin \theta_f \leq 1 .$$

The angle, $\theta_c(e) = \theta_c(f, f')$, at which

$$\frac{\alpha_f}{\alpha_{f'}} \sin[\theta_c(f, f')] = 1$$

is called the *critical angle* defined by edge e. If $\alpha_f > 0$ and $\alpha_{f'} \geq 0$, then the critical angle is defined and is given by $\theta_c(f, f') = \sin^{-1}(\alpha_{f'}/\alpha_f)$, *provided* that $\alpha_f \geq \alpha_{f'}$. A ray of light which strikes e at the critical angle will (theoretically) travel along e rather than enter into the interior of f'. We can think of it as if the light ray wishes to be "just inside" the "cheap" region on the other side of e.

(4) Optimal paths will not reflect from a boundary, except when they are "critically reflected" as shown in Fig. 7: A path is incident (from a face f of weight β) on edge e (of weight $\gamma < \min\{\alpha, \beta\}$) at the critical angle $\phi = \theta_c$ at some point $y \in \text{int}(e)$, it then travels along edge e for some positive distance, and then exits edge e *back into face f* at some point $y' \in \text{int}(e)$, leaving the edge at an angle $\phi = \theta_c$. We then say that the path is *critically reflected* by edge e and that segment $\overline{yy'}$ is a *critical segment* of p along e. The phenomenon of critical

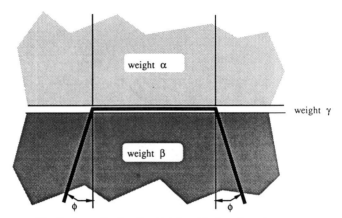

Fig. 7. An optimal path which is critically reflected.

reflection is not just an unlikely event of degeneracy. It is commonly the case that the shortest path between two points consists of a single critical reflection along an edge.

(5) If $\alpha_e > \min\{\alpha_f, \alpha_{f'}\}$, then an optimal path will never travel along edge e, since it would be better to travel "just inside" either region f or region f' (whichever is cheaper).

(6) An optimal path can cross a "road" (that is, an edge whose cost is less than that of the regions on either side of it) in one of two ways: either by obeying Snell's Law while passing through the boundary, or by "hitching a ride" along the edge, as illustrated in Fig. 8. The path hits edge e at the *incoming* critical angle $\phi = \theta_c(f, e) = \sin^{-1}(\alpha_e/\alpha_f)$, then travels along edge e (of

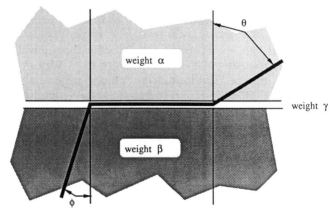

Fig. 8. Shortest path "hitching a ride" on a road.

weight α_e) for some distance, then leaves edge e into f' at the *outgoing* critical angle $\theta = \theta_c(f', e) = \sin^{-1}(\alpha_e/\alpha_{f'})$.

(7) On an optimal path, between any critical point of exit and the next critical point of entry, there must be a vertex of $\mathcal{S}$. This fact turns out to be very important in the proofs of the complexity of the algorithm of Mitchell and Papadimitriou [56].

The local optimality criteria outlined above are sufficiently strong that they uniquely specify a locally optimal path which passes through a given sequence of edges. (This follows from the global convexity of the objective function when written in terms of the coordinates at which the path crosses each edge.) The problem remains, however, of how to select the proper sequence of edges for the optimal path.

The continuous Dijkstra algorithm of Mitchell and Papadimitriou [56] simulates propagation of a wavefront from START. Each time the wavefront first hits a region boundary, passes through a vertex, or otherwise changes its description (that is, the list of regions through which it passes), we record the effect of the event in an appropriate data structure. When the wave has propagated throughout the surface, we have completed the construction of a shortest path map. For the application to the weighted region problem, it can be shown that the worst-case number of *event* points is $O(n^3)$, thereby establishing a polynomial-time bound.

Processing each event involves calling certain functions. One such function locates a point in an "access channel" between representative optimal paths that have already been established. This is easy and can be done by binary search in $O(\log n)$ time. However, we must also do $O(n^3)$ operations of the form "Find the refraction path from a given point r that passes through a given sequence of edges (while obeying Snell's Law) to hit a given point x". This is not an easy problem to solve exactly. It is handled by a numerical routine that does binary search to find a path whose length is at most $(1 + \varepsilon)$ times the length of the optimal path, where $\varepsilon > 0$ is an arbitrary error tolerance value that is given in the problem specification. The search requires time which is polynomial in n and L, the number of bits necessary to represent the problem instance (namely, $\log(nNW/\varepsilon w)$, where N is the largest integer value of any vertex coordinate, W is the largest finite weight, and w is the smallest nonzero weight). A crude calculation shows that the time to run the numerical search is bounded by $O(n^4 L)$.

It would be great if we could calculate exactly the refraction path from point r to point x, but this problem seems to be hard. The complication is that when we write down the equations that represent the local optimality criterion (Snell's Law) at each edge, and then try to solve for the points where the path crosses edges we get k quartic equations in k unknowns (where k is the length of the edge sequence through which the refraction path is known to pass).

Elimination among these equations yields a very high-degree polynomial (of degree exponential in k). Alternatively, we could apply the cylindrical decomposition technique of Collins [16] to arrive at a doubly exponential-time procedure to determine whether or not a given rational path length is achievable. This would also provide us with a technique of comparing the lengths of paths through two different edge sequences, and thus would solve the entire problem precisely in doubly exponential time (outputting the sequence of edges and vertices along the optimal path). The same technique led Sharir and Schorr [79] to a doubly exponential-time solution to the three-dimensional shortest path problem.

In practice, a very straightforward numerical approach to solving the search problem can be used. For example, one technique begins with a path from r to x that connects the edges in the sequence along their midpoints. We then iteratively shorten the path by applying the local optimality criterion to adjacent segments of the path. We simply pick an edge at which Snell's Law is violated, and then let the crossing point "slide" along the edge until Snell's Law is obeyed. (This is a coordinate descent method for searching for the minimum of the convex function which describes the path length.) Each iteration can be computed in constant time and results in a strict decrease in the weighted path length. Hence, this procedure will converge to the locally optimal path from r to x, which is also the retraction path from r to x. The problem with this approach is that we do not have good bounds on the rate of convergence or on the number of iterations necessary to guarantee that the solution is close (say, within $\varepsilon\%$) to optimal.

In practice, however, the convergence rate has been observed to be "very fast". In particular, in some recent implementation work of Karel Zikan [89], he has observed that a version of the abovementioned coordinate descent method tends to take only about 5–10 iterations to get within 1 percent of optimality for problems with up to about 20 edges. By employing certain "overrelaxation" methods, he is able to improve the convergence rate, cutting approximately in half the number of iterations needed.

5. Special Cases of the Weighted Region Problem

There are a few special cases of the weighted region problem which admit alternative polynomial-time algorithms and are of interest in terrain navigation. We have already mentioned the special case in which all weights are 1 or $+\infty$. This leads to the usual obstacle avoidance problem in the plane.

Consider now the special case in which all the weights on faces and edges are 0, 1, or $+\infty$. Infinite-cost regions are obstacles, cost-one regions are simply "free space" (through which we can move at some fixed speed), and cost-zero regions are "freebies" (through which motion costs nothing; we can move at infinite speed). If there are no zero-cost regions, then the problem is simply the usual obstacle avoidance shortest path problem in the plane. When there are zero-cost regions, they behave like "islands" between which one may want to "hop" to get from the source to the destination.

As a motivation for this special case, let us first note that it may be a reasonable approximation to the case in which the terrain is divided into three categories: obstacles (or very costly regions), very low-cost regions, and regions whose costs are in between, but similar. Such would be the case for a runner (who is not a very good swimmer) trying to find a route from one point (say, on a flat island) to another point (say, in the water). There are many islands around. Some are flat and can be crossed easily on foot. Others have huge cliffs surrounding them which make them impassable. Swimming through the water is possible, but the runner would much prefer to be running across a flat island. So how can he get from one point to another in the shortest time? His path will "hop" from one flat island to another, swimming in between, and avoiding the mountainous islands.

An application of this problem which has arisen in practice is the *maximum concealment* problem. There are regions of the plane which are "visible" to an enemy threat, and these are hopefully to be avoided. There are also obstacles, which *must* be avoided. Then there are regions (e.g., between mountain ranges, or behind rocks) which are hidden from the enemy's view, and are hence extremely cheap in comparison with the visible regions. See Fig. 9 for an example in which there is a single enemy observer whose view is obstructed by tall obstacles, but who can see over the bodies of water. The tall obstacles cast "shadows", which are regions of essentially free travel. The problem is to find an obstacle-avoiding path between two points which maximizes the conceal-ment (minimizing the length of time in the exposed regions). In the context of the weighted region problem, the model is that water and mountain ranges are infinite-weight regions, shadowed regions behind mountains are zero-cost regions (for purposes of concealment), and all other terrain has weight 1. (It makes sense that the cost of being seen by a threat should depend on the distance from the threat. Models that make this assumption are discussed by Mitchell [53], where polynomial-time algorithms are given for some special cases.)

Other applications also use the $\{0, 1, +\infty\}$ special case of the weighted region problem. It can be used to find the shortest path from one *region* to another *region* in the presence of obstacles (by letting the source and destina-tion regions be zero-weight regions), as was independently considered by Asano et al. [4]. It can also be used to find lexicographically shortest paths through weighted regions: minimize the length of path in the most expensive region, then, subject to this being minimal, minimize the length in the next most costly region, etc. Lexicographically shortest paths may be good initial

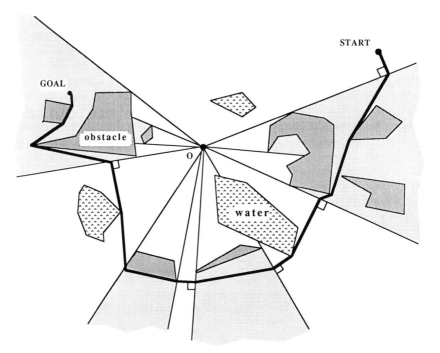

Fig. 9. Maximum concealment from a single enemy observer.

guesses for heuristic algorithms that try to find shortest paths through weighted regions. Also, there is an intimate connection between shortest path problems and *maximum flow* problems, and the algorithms for maximum flow need to find shortest paths through $\{0, 1, +\infty\}$ weighted regions. These and other applications are discussed in Mitchell [51, 52].

An interesting application discussed by Gewali et al. [22] is that of the "least-risk watchman route problem". The watchman problem asks one to find the shortest path that a watchman would have to make from his current location in order to be able to "see" all of a given space (e.g., a polygonal room, or a polygonal room with "holes"). Chin and Ntafos [12, 13] have shown that the optimum watchman route problem is NP-complete in a polygonal room with holes, but that there is a polynomial-time algorithm for polygonal rooms without holes. The *least-risk watchman route problem* asks one to find the path of minimum exposure to threats which sees the entire space. Then, for rectilinear polygons with n sides, Gewali et al. [22] give an $O(k^2 n^3)$ algorithm for the case of k threats.

The algorithm described by Mitchell and Papadimitriou [56] for the weighted region problem does in fact solve the $\{0, 1, +\infty\}$ special case in polynomial time. But the special case has structure which allows an alternative approach which is faster and easier to implement. The approach by Mitchell [51] and Gewali et al. [22] to this case is to build a special kind of "extended visibility graph", VG^*, after shrinking the zero-cost regions to single nodes. The graph VG^* can be constructed in polynomial time (in fact, quadratic time), and it can then be searched for shortest paths in the usual way using Dijkstra or A*. The result is an exact polynomial-time algorithm. The basic idea is to exploit the local optimality criteria, which allow the problem to be discretized by limiting our search to the graph VG^*.

(1) The behavior of optimal paths with respect to the obstacles is the same as it was in the obstacle avoidance problem (see [49]). Namely, the path behaves around obstacles as if it were a "taut string", being locally tangent to obstacles and forming a convex angle when it comes in contact with an obstacle vertex.

(2) An optimal path will either enter a zero-cost region at a vertex or at a normal to the interior of an edge bounding the region. If it enters at a vertex, then it must make an angle greater than $\frac{1}{2}\pi$ with the edges incident to the vertex.

Thus, the extended visibility graph has edges of two types: those that join two vertices (of obstacles or zero-cost regions), and those that join a vertex (of either an obstacle or a zero-cost region) to an edge of a zero-cost region (in such a way as to be perpendicular to the edge). This immediately implies a quadratic bound on the size of the graph. The exact details of the construction are given in either of the abovementioned papers [22, 51]. The result is an $O(n^2)$ algorithm for shortest paths.

Another special case of interest in terrain navigation is that in which all of the terrain has the same (finite) weight, but there exists a (piecewise-linear) network of roads or other linear features (of possibly different sizes, which admit different speeds of traversal). This is the case illustrated in Fig. 10, and is simply the weighted region problem in which all face weights, α_f, are identical, and edge weights, α_e, are arbitrary. Then, we apply the following local optimality criterion:

(3) Shortest paths will enter a road segment either at one of its endpoints, or by hitting at the critical angle of incidence defined by the ratio of the edge's weight to that of the surrounding terrain.

This observation again leads to a discrete graph (a *critical graph*) which can be searched for shortest paths. Mitchell [51] and Gewali et al. [22] show how to construct this critical graph and search it in time $O(n^2)$, where n is the number of road edges. See also [73].

A generalization of this technique is possible by putting together all of the

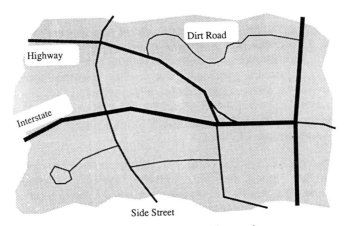

Fig. 10. A map consisting of just roads.

abovementioned local optimality criteria. Assume now that we have a weighted region problem in which the weights on faces are in the set $\{0, 1, +\infty\}$, and the weights on edges are arbitrary ($\in [0, +\infty]$). Additionally, there can be a fixed cost, ξ_e, associated with crossing an edge e. The model is that there are obstacles, zero-cost regions, and background regions (all of the same weight). Additionally, there are roads, fences, etc. of arbitrary weights. Then, the algorithm given by Mitchell [51] or Gewali et al. [22] finds shortest paths in time $O(n^2)$, again by building a critical graph.

6. Generalizations and Extensions

Several generalizations to the discrete geodesic and weighted region problems are possible. Some are solved by minor changes to the algorithms of Mitchell et al. [54] and Mitchell and Papadimitriou [56], while others are open research problems.

(1) First, one can generalize to the case of *multiple-source points*. This means that instead of building a shortest path map for one point, START, we consider several given point sites (called "source points"), and we compute a subdivision of the plane or the surface which tells us for each point t which source point is closest to it and how to backtrace a shortest path to the closest source point. The resulting structure is then a classic *Voronoi diagram* according to the metric of interest (either shortest Euclidean paths on a surface or weighted Euclidean lengths through a weighted map).

As a further generalization along these lines, we could allow the source and goal to be *regions* rather than single points. This generality is actually already incorporated in the model of Mitchell and Papadimitriou [56] by allowing there to be zero-cost regions. One simply makes the starting region have zero weight, and places the starting point anywhere inside; a similar accommodation is made for the goal region. The applicability of this problem is apparent: Goals are frequently specified in the form "Get me to the town square", or "Get me to Highway 95". Any point within the square or on the highway will suffice as a goal.

(2) We can generalize the cost structure from being that of a *uniform* cost per distance in a region to that of allowing a cost function (such as a linear function) in each region. The function should be specified by some fixed number of parameters, and should allow computation of geodesics. In the uniform-cost case, the geodesics within a given region are simply straight lines. In more general cases, geodesics would have to be computed by techniques of calculus of variations [43]. The algorithm must then be modified to apply the local optimality criterion (Snell's Law) to curved arcs at the boundaries of regions. If an optimal path passes through the point y interior to edge e, then the tangent lines at y to the geodesic curves in f and in f' must meet at y such that they obey Snell's Law. Using this local optimality criterion, then, it should be possible to run an analogous algorithm to that of Mitchell and Papadimitriou [56], this time piecing together curves from region to region. The details of this generalization need to be examined further.

(3) We could allow boundaries between regions to be curved (e.g., splinegons; see [81]). Then, for the weighted region problem, Snell's Law at a point y interior to a boundary curve must be applied as if the boundary at y is the straight line tangent to the boundary at y. Again, more research is needed on this problem.

(4) The weighted region problem can be generalized to the case of a weighted polyhedral surface. Then the local optimality criterion becomes Snell's Law applied to the "unfolded problem" at each boundary. That is, for an edge $e = f \cap f'$, we must "unfold" f' about e so that f and f' are made coplanar, and then we can apply Snell's Law to points interior to e in this rotated coordinate frame.

(5) We could allow the traversal of a region to be directionally dependent. This comment applies both to the (unweighted) discrete geodesic problem and to the weighted region problem. For example, it makes sense that it should be more costly to go "up" a hill than to go down it. We are currently investigating this case.

(6) An important open problem is that of incorporating other types of vehicle constraints into the shortest path problem. For example, we may want a minimum time path for a vehicle which has a bounded amount of power (implying bounded acceleration). Or it may be that the vehicle will tip over if it is on too steep of a slope. Or the vehicle may have fuel consumption constraints. Solving the exact shortest path problem in the presence of other such constraints is an important area for continuing research.

7. Conclusion

We have examined some of the models of shortest path problems which are relevant to route planning for an autonomous vehicle. We have discussed problems which admit exact solutions, and have discussed the currently best known algorithms. Many important issues remain to be addressed.

Obviously, there remains the question of reducing the worst-case running times of the algorithms discussed. In particular, it may be possible to improve the $O(n^7 L)$ bound on the weighted region problem. It is a challenging problem to determine the *expected* running times of shortest path algorithms.

Problems involving the design of a good terrain map need to be studied more. We have discussed regular tesselations and polygonal subdivisions as representations for map data, and we have mentioned some of the benefits of each. What is probably needed is some kind of hybrid representation which can take advantage of the strengths of each, while also providing a hierarchical representation of the terrain.

If we were to compose a "wish list" of features for a map representation, we would most certainly want to include the ability to handle the following.

(1) *Discovery of new information.* Ideally, as the vehicle moves about through terrain, it will update its map with new information it "learns". It may, for example, discover that road construction is causing congestion along some stretch of highway or that a certain bridge it thought was there has been closed. It is therefore important to have a representation of a map which allows updating and annotations.

This also brings up the issue of interfacing the map-based path planner with some *sensor*-based planner that accumulates local information during the execution of a plan and must then modify the path accordingly. We have not addressed here the issue of planning routes in unknown or uncertain terrains, but we can refer the reader to a few of the myriad of papers on the subject: Goldstein et al. [24], Iyengar et al. [28], Jorgensen et al. [30], Kauffman [32], Kuan [35], Kuan et al. [36], Kuan et al. [37], Lumelsky and Stepanov [42], Meng [45, 46], Metea and Tsai [47], Mitchell [48], Mitchell et al. [57], Moravec [58], Oommen et al. [60], Rao et al. [67, 68], Rueb and Wong [75], Stern [82], Sutherland [83], and Thorpe [86].

(2) *Temporal nature of information.* Annotations might carry with them some estimated *duration* which bounds the interval of time for which the information is valid. For example, road construction is usually known to affect traffic flow only during certain times of the day, and it remains in effect only until it achieves completion.

Of course, uncertainty assures that the planner will never be able to guarantee that the routes it selects in advance are optimal. All types of map information are subject to some uncertainty. For example, roads can be closed or become impassable, open terrain can become flooded or reforested, boundaries of lakes and rivers certainly change with the seasons and with the rainfall pattern. A truly "intelligent" planner should have information about the kinds of circumstances which potentially affect different types of terrain and be able to reason about it. If it has knowledge, for example, that there was recently a greater than average rainfall, it should adjust the probabilities it places on the traversability of a low-water bridge.

Many open questions remain. How can these issues be addressed within the framework of exact or approximate algorithms? What are the appropriate mathematical models of the path planning process? How can our knowledge of algorithmic path planners be translated into useful heuristics for complex terrain problems?

ACKNOWLEDGMENT

This research was partially supported by a generous grant from the Hughes Aircraft Company. Part of this research was conducted while J. Mitchell was supported by a Howard Hughes Doctoral Fellowship at Stanford University and affiliated with the Hughes Artificial Intelligence Center in Calabasas, California. This research was also partially supported by a grant from the National Science Foundation (IRI-8710858).

REFERENCES

1. Akman, V., Shortest paths avoiding polyhedral obstacles in 3-dimensional Euclidean space, Ph.D. Thesis, Computer and Systems Engineering, Rensselaer Polytechnic Institute, Troy, NY (1985).
2. Akman, V., Unobstructed shortest paths in polyhedral environments, in: G. Goos and J. Hartmanis, (Eds.), Lecture Notes in Computer Science **251** (Springer, New York, 1987).
3. Asano, T., Asano, T., Guibas, L., Hershberger, J. and Imai, H., Visibility of disjoint polygons, *Algorithmica* **1** (1986) 49–63.
4. Asano, T., Asano, T. and Imai, H., Shortest paths between two simple polygons, *Inf. Process. Lett.* **24** (1987) 285–288.
5. Baker, B., Shortest paths with unit clearance among polygonal obstacles, in: *Proceedings SIAM Conference on Geometric Modeling and Robotics*, Albany, NY (1985).
6. Baumgart, B.G., A polyhedron representation for computer vision, in: *AFIPS Conference Proceedings* **44**, *National Computer Conference* (1975) 589–596.
7. Brooks, R.A., Solving the find-path problem by good representation of free space, *IEEE Trans. Syst. Man Cybern.* **13** (3) (1983) 190–197.
8. Brooks, R.A. and Lozano-Pérez, T., A subdivision algorithm in the configuration space for find path with rotation, *IEEE Trans. Syst. Man Cybern.* **15** (2) (1985) 224–233.
9. Canny, J.F., The complexity of robot motion planning, Ph.D. Thesis, Department of Electrical Engineering and Computer Science, MIT, Cambridge, MA (1987).
10. Canny, J. and Reif, J., New lower bound techniques for robot motion planning problems, in: *Proceedings 28th Annual IEEE Symposium on Foundations of Computer Science*, Los Angeles, CA (1987) 49–60.
11. Chew, L.P., Planning the shortest path for a disk in $O(n^2 \log n)$ time, in: *Proceedings First Annual ACM Conference on Computational Geometry*, Baltimore, MD (1985) 214–220.
12. Chin W.P. and Ntafos, S., Optimum watchman routes, in: *Proceedings 2nd ACM Symposium on Computational Geometry*, Yorktown Heights, NY (1986) 24–33.

13. Chin, W.P. and Ntafos, S., Watchman routes in simple polygons, Tech. Rept., Computer Science Department, University of Texas at Dallas, TX (1987).

14. Clarkson, K., Approximation algorithms for shortest path motion planning, in: *Proceedings 19th Annual ACM Symposium on Theory of Computing*, New York (1987) 56–65.

15. Clarkson, K., Kapoor, S. and Vaidya, P., Rectilinear shortest paths through polygonal obstacles in $O(n \log^2 n)$ time, in: *Proceedings Third Annual ACM Conference on Computational Geometry*, Waterloo, Ont. (1987) 251–257.

16. Collins, G.E., Quantifier elimination for real closed fields by cylindric algebraic decomposition, in: *Proceedings Second GI Conference on Automata Theory and Formal Languages*, Lecture Notes in Computer Science **33** (Springer, New York, 1975) 134–183.

17. de Rezende, P.J., Lee, D.T. and Wu, Y.F., Rectilinear shortest paths with rectangular barriers, in: *Proceedings First ACM Conference on Computational Geometry*, Baltimore, MD (1985) 204–213.

18. Dijkstra, E.W., A note on two problems in connection with graphs, *Numer. Math.* **1** (1959) 269–271.

19. H. Edelsbrunner, *Algorithms in Combinatorial Geometry* (Springer, Heidelberg, F.R.G., 1987).

20. Franklin, W.R. and Akman, V., Shortest paths between source and goal points located on/around a convex polyhedron, in: *Proceedings 22nd Allerton Conference on Communication, Control and Computing* (1984) 103–112.

21. Fredman, M. and Tarjan, R., Fibonacci heaps and their uses in improved network optimization algorithms, in: *Proceedings 25th Annual IEEE Symposium on Foundations of Computer Science* (1984) 338–346.

22. Gewali, L., Meng, A., Mitchell, J.S.B. and Ntafos, S., Path planning in 0/1/∞ weighted regions with applications, Extended Abstract, in: *Proceedings Fourth Annual ACM Conference on Computational Geometry*, Urbana-Champaign, IL (1988) 266–278.

23. Ghosh, S.K. and Mount, D.M., An output sensitive algorithm for computing visibility graphs, in: *Proceedings 28th Annual IEEE Symposium on Foundations of Computer Science*, Los Angeles, CA (1987) 11–19.

24. Goldstein, M., Pin, F.G., de Saussure, G. and Weisbin, C.R., 3-D world modeling with updating capability based on combinatorial geometry, Tech. Rept. CESAR-87/02, Oak Ridge National Laboratory, Oak Ridge, TN (1987).

25. Guibas, L., Hershberger, J., Leven, D., Sharir, M. and Tarjan, R., Linear time algorithms for visibility and shortest path problems inside simple polygons, *Algorithmica* **2** (1987) 309–233.

26. Guibas, L.J. and Hershberger, J., Optimal shortest path queries in a simple polygon, in: *Proceedings Third Annual ACM Conference on Computational Geometry*, Waterloo, Ont. (1987) 50–63.

27. Guibas, L. and Stolfi, J., Primitives for the manipulation of general subdivisions and the computation of Voronoi diagrams, *ACM Trans. Graph.* **4** (1985) 74–123.

28. Iyengar, S.S., Jorgensen, C.C., Rao, S.V.N. and Weisbin, C., Robot navigation algorithms using learned spatial graphs, *Robotica* **4** (1986) 93–100.

29. Jones, S.T., Solving problems involving variable terrain, Part 1: A general algorithm, *BYTE* **5** (2) (1980).

30. Jorgensen, C., Hamel, W. and Weisbin, C., Autonomous robot navigation, *BYTE* **11** (1) (1986) 223–235.

31. Kambhampati, S. and Davis, L.S., Multiresolution path planning for mobile robots, *IEEE J. Rob. Autom.* **2** (3) (1986) 135–145.

32. Kauffman, S., An algorithmic approach to intelligent robot mobility, *Rob. Age* **5** (3) (1983) 38–47.

33. Keirsey, D.M. and Mitchell, J.S.B., Planning strategic paths through variable terrain data, *Proc. SPIE Appl. Artif. Intell.* **485** (1984).

34. Kirkpatrick, D.G., Optimal search in planar subdivisions, *SIAM J. Comput.* **12** (1983) 28–35.
35. Kuan, D.T., Terrain map knowledge representation for spatial planning, in: *Proceedings First IEEE Conference of Artificial Intelligence Applications*, Denver, CO (1984) 578–584.
36. Kuan, D.T., Brooks, R.A., Zamiska, J.C. and Das, M., Automatic path planning for a mobile robot using a mixed representation of free space, in: *Proceedings First IEEE Conference of Artificial Intelligence Applications*, Denver, CO (1984) 70–74.
37. Kuan, D.T., Zamiska, J.C. and Brooks, R.A., Natural decomposition of free space for path planning, in: *Proceedings IEEE International Conference on Robotics and Automation*, St. Louis, MO (1985) 168–173.
38. Lee, D.T., Proximity and reachability in the plane, Ph.D. Thesis, Tech. Rept. ACT-12, Coordinated Science Laboratory, University of Illinois, Urbana, IL (1978).
39. Lee, D.T. and Ching, Y.T., The power of geometric duality revisited, *Inf. Process. Lett.* **21** (1985) 117–122.
40. Lee, D.T. and Preparata, F.P., Euclidean shortest paths in the presence of rectilinear boundaries, *Networks* **14** (1984) 393–410.
41. Lozano-Pérez, T. and Wesley, M.A., An algorithm for planning collision-free paths among polyhedral obstacles, *Comm. ACM* **22** (10) (1979) 560–570.
42. Lumelsky, V.J. and Stepanov, A.A., Path-planning strategies for a point mobile automaton moving amidst unknown obstacles of arbitrary shape, *Algorithmica* **2** (1987) 403–430.
43. Lyusternik, L.A., *Shortest Paths: Variational Problems* (Macmillan, New York, 1964).
44. Mehlhorn, K., *Multi-dimensional Searching and Computational Geometry*, EATCS Monographs on Theoretical Computer Science (Springer, New York, 1984).
45. Meng, A., Free-space modeling and geometric motion planning under unexpected obstacles, Tech. Rept., Texas Instruments Artificial Intelligence Lab (1987).
46. Meng, A., Free-space modeling and path planning under uncertainty for autonomous air robots, Tech. Rept., Texas Instruments Artificial Intelligence Lab (1987).
47. Metea, M.B. and Tsai, J.J.-P., Route planning for intelligent autonomous land vehicles using hierarchical terrain representation, in: *Proceedings IEEE International Conference on Robotics and Automation*, Raleigh, NC (1987).
48. Mitchell, J.S.B., An autonomous vehicle navigation algorithm, *Proc. SPIE Appl. Artif. Intell.* **485** (1984) 153–158.
49. Mitchell, J.S.B., Planning shortest paths, Ph.D. Thesis, Department of Operations Research, Stanford University, Stanford, CA (1986); also: Research Rept. 561, Artificial Intelligence Series, No. 1, Hughes Research Laboratories, Malibu, CA (1986).
50. Mitchell, J.S.B., Shortest rectilinear paths among obstacles, Tech. Rept. No. 739, School of Operations Research and Industrial Engineering, Cornell University, Ithaca, NY (1987).
51. Mitchell, J.S.B., Shortest paths among obstacles, zero-cost regions, and roads, Tech. Rept. 764, Department of Operations Research, Cornell University, Ithaca, NY (1987).
52. Mitchell, J.S.B., On maximum flows in polyhedral domains, Extended Abstract, in: *Proceedings Fourth Annual ACM Conference on Computational Geometry*, Urbana-Champaign, IL (1988) 341–351.
53. Mitchell, J.S.B., On the maximum concealment problem, Tech. Rept., Department of Operations Research, Cornell University, Ithaca, NY (1988).
54. Mitchell, J.S.B., Mount, D.M. and Papadimitriou, C.H., The discrete geodesic problem, *SIAM J. Comput.* **16** (4) (1987) 647–668.
55. Mitchell, J.S.B. and Papadimitriou, C.H., Planning shortest paths, in: *Proceedings SIAM Conference on Geometric Modeling and Robotics*, Albany, NY (1985).
56. Mitchell, J.S.B. and Papadimitriou, C.H., The weighted region problem, Tech. Rept., Department of Operations Research, Stanford University, Stanford, CA (1986); Extended Abstract, in: *Proceedings Third Annual ACM Conference on Computational Geometry*, Waterloo, Ont. (1987); also: *J. ACM* (to appear).

57. Mitchell, J.S.B., Payton, D.W. and Keirsey, D.M., Planning and reasoning for autonomous vehicle control, *Int. J. Intell. Syst.* **2** (1987) 129–198.
58. Moravec, H.P., Obstacle avoidance and navigation in the real world by a seeing robot rover, Tech. Rept. CMU-RI-TR-3, Carnegie-Mellon Robotics Institute, Pittsburgh, PA (1980).
59. Nilsson, N.J., *Principles of Artificial Intelligence* (Tioga, Palo Alto, CA, 1980).
60. Oommen, B.J., Iyenger, S.S., Rao, S.V. and Kashyap, R.L., Robot navigation in unknown terrains using learned visibility graphs, Part I: The disjoint convex obstacle case, Tech. Rept. SCS-TR-86, School of Computer Science, Carleton University, Ottawa, Ont. (1986).
61. O'Rourke, J., Finding a shortest ladder path: A special case, Tech. Rept., Institute for Mathematics and its Applications, Preprint Series No. 353, University of Minnesota, Minneapolis, MN (1987).
62. O'Rourke, J., Suri, S. and Booth, H., Shortest paths on polyhedral surfaces, Manuscript, Johns Hopkins University, Baltimore, MD (1984).
63. Papadimitriou, C.H., An algorithm for shortest-path motion in three dimensions, *Inf. Process. Lett* **20** (1985) 259–263.
64. Papadimitriou, C.H., and Silverberg, E.B., Optimal piecewise linear motion of an object among obstacles, *Algorithmica* **2** (1987) 523–539.
65. Preparata, F.P. and Shamos, M.I., *Computational Geometry* (Springer, New York, 1985).
66. Quek, F.K.H., Franklin, R.F. and Pont, F., A decision system for autonomous robot navigation over rough terrain, in: *Proceedings SPIE Applications of Artificial Intelligence*, Boston, MA (1985)
67. Rao, N.S.V., Iyengar, S.S., Jorgensen, C.C. and Weisbin, C.R., Robot navigation in an unexplored terrain, *J. Rob. Syst.* **3** (4) (1986) 389–407.
68. Rao, N.S.V., Iyengar, S.S., Jorgensen, C.C. and Weisbin, C.R., On terrain acquisition by a finite-sized mobile robot in plane, in: *Proceedings IEEE International Conference on Robotics and Automation*, Raleigh, NC (1987) 1314–1319.
69. Reif, J.H. and Storer, J.A., Shortest paths in Euclidean space with polyhedral obstacles, Tech. Rept. CS-85-121, Computer Science Department, Brandeis University, Waltham, MA (1985).
70. Richbourg, R.F., Solving a class of spatial reasoning problems: Minimal-cost path planning in the Cartesian plane, Ph.D. Thesis, Naval Postgraduate School, Monterey, CA (1987).
71. Richbourg, R.F., Rowe, N.C. and Zyda, M.J., Exploiting capability constraints to solve global, two-dimensional path planning problems, Tech. Rept. NPS-86-006, Department of Computer Science, Naval Postgraduate School, Monterey, CA (1986).
72. Richbourg, R.F., Rowe, N.C., Zyda, M.J. and McGhee, R., Solving global two-dimensional routing problems using Snell's law and A* search, in: *Proceedings IEEE International Conference on Robotics and Automation*, Raleigh, NC (1987) 1631–1636.
73. Rowe, N.C., Roads, rivers, and rocks: Optimal two-dimensional route planning around linear features for a mobile robot, Tech. Rept. NPS52-87-027, Computer Science Department, Naval Postgraduate School, Monterey, CA (1987).
74. Rowe, N.C. and Richbourg, R.F., A new method for optimal path planning through nonhomogeneous free space, Tech. Rept. NPS52-87-003, Computer Science Department, Naval Postgraduate School, Monterey, CA (1987).
75. Rueb, K.D. and Wong, A.K.C., Structuring free space as a hypergraph for roving robot path planning and navigation, *IEEE Trans. Pattern Anal. Mach. Intell.* **9** (2) (1987) 263–273.
76. Samet, H. and Webber, R.E., Storing a collection of polygons using quadtrees, *ACM Trans. Graph.* **4** (3) (1985) 182–222.
77. Schwartz, J.T., Sharir, M. and Hopcroft, J. (Eds.), *Planning, Geometry, and Complexity of Robot Motion*, Ablex Series in Artificial Intelligence (Ablex, Norwood, NJ, 1987).
78. Schwartz, J.T. and Yap, C., (Ed.), *Algorithmic and Geometric Aspects of Robotics* **1** (Erlbaum, Hillsdale, NJ, 1987).
79. Sharir, M. and Schorr, A., On shortest paths in polyhedral spaces, *SIAM J. Comput.* **15** (1) (1986) 193–215.

80. Smith, T., Private communication, Department of Computer Science, University of California, Santa Barbara, CA (1986).
81. Souvaine, D., Computational geometry in a curved world, Ph.D. Thesis, Tech. Rept. CS-TR-094-87, Department of Computer Science, Princeton University, Princeton, NJ (1986).
82. Stern, H.I., A routing algorithm for a mobile search robot, in: S.I. Gass, H.J. Greenburg, K.L. Hoffman, and R.W. Langley (Eds.), *Impacts of Microcomputers on Operations Research* (North-Holland, Amsterdam, 1986) 73–87.
83. Sutherland, I.E., A method for solving arbitrary wall mazes by computer, *IEEE Trans. Comput.* **18** (12) (1969) 1092–1097.
84. Tarjan, R.E. and van Wyk, J., An $O(n \log \log n)$ algorithm for triangulating simple polygons, Tech. Rept., Bell Labs, Murray Hill, NJ (1986); also: *SIAM J. Comput.* (to appear).
85. Thorpe, C.E., Path relaxation: Path planning for a mobile robot, in: *Proceedings AAAI-84*, Austin, TX (1984) 318–321.
86. Thorpe, C.E., FIDO: Vision and navigation for a robot rover, Ph.D. Thesis, Tech. Rept. CMU-CS-84-168, Department of Computer Science, Carnegie-Mellon University, Pittsburgh, PA (1984).
87. Welzl, E., Constructing the visibility graph for n line segments in $O(n^2)$ time, *Inf. Process. Lett.* **20** (1985) 167–171.
88. Widmayer, P., Wu, Y.F. and Wong, C.K., Distance problems in computational geometry with fixed orientations, in: *Proceedings First Annual ACM Conference on Computational Geometry*, Baltimore, MD (1985).
89. Zikan, K., Private communication, Department of Operations Research, Stanford University, Stanford, CA (1986).

Received October 1986; revised version received January 1988

Constructing Roadmaps of Semi-Algebraic Sets I: Completeness

John Canny

Artificial Intelligence Laboratory,
Massachusetts Institute of Technology,
Cambridge, MA 02139, U.S.A.

ABSTRACT

This paper describes preliminary work on an algorithm for planning collision-free motions for a robot manipulator in the presence of obstacles. The physical obstacles lead to forbidden regions in the robots configuration space, and for collision-free motion we need paths through configuration space which avoid these regions. Our method is to construct a certain one-dimensional subset or "roadmap" of the space of allowable configurations. If S denotes the set of allowable configurations, the roadmap has the property that any connected component of S contains a single connected component of the roadmap. It is also possible, starting from an arbitrary point p ∈ S to rapidly construct a path from p to a point on the roadmap. Thus given any two points in S we can rapidly determine whether they lie in the same connected component of S, and if they do, we can return a candidate path between them. We do not give a complete description of the algorithm here, but we define the roadmap geometrically, and verify that it has the necessary connectivity.

1. Introduction

This work is motivated by the path planning problem in robotics. The path planning problem is actually a broad class of problems, and includes planning for a polyhedral object with no constraints on its motion, also known as the "piano movers' problem", as well as planning for almost all types of robot arm. A free object has six degrees of motion freedom, three translational and three rotational. A robot arm on the other hand, has several links which can move, but their motion is highly constrained by the joints. The joint between two links normally allows the links only one degree of relative motion freedom. This makes the free polyhedron and the robot arm seem like very different systems, but from a certain perspective, they are identical. This perspective is *configuration space*.

In order to describe the configuration of the polyhedron, we attach a reference frame (a set of local coordinate axes) to it. Then we can represent the configuration of the free polyhedron with six numbers, say the x, y, and z

coordinates of the origin of the object's reference frame, and three angles which specify the orientation of the frame. All these numbers are measured with respect to some other reference frame fixed in the environment. These six numbers also define a point in a six-dimensional space called the configuration space of the polyhedron. Points in configuration space represent configurations of the polyhedron, and a path in configuration space represents a continuous motion of the object.

In contrast, we cannot freely place the links of the robot arm anywhere in space because of the constraints imposed by the links. However, if the links are not connected in a loop, we can freely choose all of the angles (or lengths for sliding joints) of the joints. Each choice of joint parameters completely determines the position and orientation of all of the links in the arm. Instead of the true coordinates of all the links, the configuration space now has generalized coordinates, which are the joint angles. If the robot has n variable parameters, then the configuration space is n-dimensional. Once again, a continuous motion of the robot corresponds to a path through configuration space.

If there are obstacles near the robot (or free object), then these impose additional constraints on motion. In configuration space they define forbidden regions, which are the configurations where some part of the robot overlaps an obstacle. The set of configurations where the robot is clear of obstacles is often called its *free space*. To plan an obstacle-avoiding motion in physical space, we must find a path through configuration space which lies wholly within free space. Once the obstacles are mapped to forbidden regions in configuration space, then motion planning for both the free object and for the robot arm are the same process. The explicit use of configuration space for planning collision-free motions was first proposed by Lozano-Pérez [6].

In many cases the motion constraints arising from obstacles have an algebraic description, and the free space can be defined as a *semi-algebraic set* (Schwartz and Sharir [8], Canny [2]). A semi-algebraic set is a subset of some real space $\mathbb{R}^n$ formed by intersection and union of algebraic half-spaces. An algebraic half-space is the set of points in $\mathbb{R}^n$ that satisfy a polynomial inequality.

In principle, algorithms based on cellular algebraic decomposition (Collins [4]) can then be used to decompose a semi-algebraic set into simple connected pieces or cells, and the existence of a path demonstrated by computing cell adjacency (Schwartz and Sharir [8]). However, these algorithms are also capable of deciding the theory of reals with addition, which is hard for exponential time with a polynomial number of alterations (Berman [1]). The average-case performance of cell decomposition algorithms is not much better than worst-case and they basically run in double-exponential time. Thus cell decomposition seems completely impractical for even simple problems. Reif [7] first showed that the general robot motion planning problem is PSPACE-hard (if the number of degrees of freedom is allowed to grow), which suggests that exponential time may be required in the worst case.

On the other hand, there do exist many efficient algorithms for restricted classes of motion planning problems (Schwartz and Yap [9]). In particular, if the number of degrees of freedom is fixed, then motion planning is doable in polynomial time (Schwartz and Sharir [8]). Our objective here is to produce an algorithm for the problem with a running time exponent roughly equal to the number of degrees of freedom. This is quite useful in practice, where the number of degrees of freedom is best thought of as a small constant rather than an input parameter. Here we present a first step in that direction, a definition of an exponential-size skeleton or roadmap of a semi-algebraic set. It is thought that with suitable algebraic techniques, it will be possible to compute the roadmap in exponential time, with exponent equal to the number of degrees of freedom.

In this paper we define the roadmap, and establish its most important topological property, namely that it is connected within each connected component of S. The roadmap C is itself a semi-algebraic set, and it is described here in sufficient detail that a formula for C could be readily computed from a formula for S. The details of construction of the connectivity graph of C and analysis of complexity of the roadmap algorithm are forthcoming, although an outline of the former is given by Canny [3].

The paper is organized as follows: Section 2 gives definitions of basic terms and concepts for semi-algebraic sets. In Section 3 we borrow some tools from differential topology and specialize them to manifolds which are defined as preimages. In Section 3 we also give two general position lemmas. Using these lemmas it is possible to systematically eliminate singularities in constraint intersections or in the roadmap itself. Section 4 gives a brief overview of Morse theory, with a generalization to semi-algebraic sets. The theory is used to establish the key result about connectivity of slices through the set S. Finally in Section 5 we describe the algorithm, and show that it has the desired properties.

2. Preliminaries

Let Q_r be the ring of polynomials in r variables with rational coefficients, $Q_r = Q[x_1, \ldots, x_r]$.

Definition 2.1. We define an *atomic formula* as one of the 6 forms $A = 0$, $A \geq 0$, $A \leq 0$, $A \neq 0$, $A > 0$, $A < 0$ with $A \in Q_r$.

Definition 2.2. A *standard formula* is a formula constructed from atomic formulae using logical connectives and quantifiers. A standard formula which contains no quantifiers is said to be *quantifier-free*. Thus a quantifier-free formula F can be defined recursively as

$$F = F_0 \quad \text{or} \quad F = F_1 \vee F_2 \quad \text{or} \quad F = F_1 \wedge F_2, \tag{1}$$

where F_0 is an atomic formula, and F_1 and F_2 are quantifier-free formulae.

Definition 2.3. A *semi-algebraic set* $S \subseteq \mathbb{R}^r$ is the set of points in $\mathbb{R}^r$ which satisfy some quantifier-free formula in r variables. By virtue of Tarski's quantifier elimination procedure, any set defined by a standard formula also has a quantifier-free defining formula, and is therefore semi-algebraic.

Definition 2.4. A non-empty semi-algebraic set S is a (topological) *manifold* of dimension m (an m-manifold) if every point in S has a neighborhood which is homeomorphic to an open subset of $\mathbb{R}^m$. By convention, the empty set has dimension -1. More generally, if S can be expressed as a finite union of subsets which are manifolds, then we define the dimension of S as the maximum of the dimensions of these subsets. Later we will need the fact that a relatively open subset of a manifold is also a manifold.

Definition 2.5. For a sequence of n polynomials $[f_1, \ldots, f_n]$, a *sign sequence* $\sigma \in \{-, 0, +\}^n$ is an n-tuple specifying the signs of all the polynomials. Suppose F is a formula defining the semi-algebraic set S and containing n polynomials. Then we define the sign-invariant set S_σ as $\{x \in \mathbb{R}^r \mid \forall i \; \text{sgn}(f_i) = \sigma_i\}$. The S_σ are disjoint for distinct values of σ, and their union is $\mathbb{R}^r$. Each S_σ is entirely contained in or is entirely outside of S, depending only on σ. Therefore S can be written as the union of all the S_σ that it contains. Finally we note that each S_σ is a (relatively) open subset of the algebraic variety defined by the polynomials which are zero in σ.

Definition 2.6. A real *algebraic variety* is the set of points in $\mathbb{R}^r$ which are the zeros of some set of polynomials. The variety associated with an ideal I, written $V(I)$, is the set of common zeros of all the polynomials in I. Dually, the ideal associated with a variety V is the set of polynomials which are zero on all of V, it is written $I(V)$.

3. Eliminating Singularities

The purpose of the roadmap algorithm is to compute one-dimensional "silhouettes" of the set S. These are defined as the critical points of a certain projection map. Before we can proceed, we need to eliminate possible singularities in the set S, so that we can represent it as a union of manifolds. Then we must choose the projection map so that its critical points do lie on a one-dimensional manifold.

Let f be a smooth map of manifolds $f : M \to N$, where M and N have dimension r and n respectively. We define the differential of f at $x \in M$ (denoted df_x) as the induced map of tangent spaces $df_x : T_x M \to T_{f(x)} N$. At each point the tangent spaces $T_x M$ and $T_{f(x)} N$ are isomorphic to the Euclidean spaces $\mathbb{R}^r$ and $\mathbb{R}^n$ respectively. By choosing suitable local coordinates for $T_x M$

and $T_{f(x)}N$, the differential can be represented as the Jacobian

$$
\mathrm{d}f_x = \begin{pmatrix} \dfrac{\partial f_1}{\partial x_1}(x) & \cdots & \dfrac{\partial f_1}{\partial x_r}(x) \\ \vdots & & \vdots \\ \dfrac{\partial f_n}{\partial x_1}(x) & \cdots & \dfrac{\partial f_n}{\partial x_r}(x) \end{pmatrix}. \tag{2}
$$

Definition 3.1. A point x in M is a *critical point* of f if the differential $\mathrm{d}f_x$ is not surjective at x, i.e. if the Jacobian has rank less than n at x. Points where the Jacobian has rank n are called *regular points*. We will call the set of all critical points of f its *critical set*.

The image of a critical point $x \in M$ is a critical *value* of f. Values $v \in \mathbb{R}^n$ which are not critical values are called *regular* values. So a value v is regular if and only if all the points in $f^{-1}(v)$ are regular.

We have the following theorem:

Preimage Theorem. *If v is a regular value of the smooth map $f : M \to N$ then the preimage $L = f^{-1}(v)$ is a submanifold of M of dimension $\dim(M) - \dim(N)$. Furthermore, we have a simple representation of $T_x L$,*

$$
T_x L = \ker(\mathrm{d}f_x) , \tag{3}
$$

since locally the tangent space to L is the set of differential displacements which do not change the value of f.

A major theorem from calculus tells us that almost all values in the range of a smooth function are regular values. It will give us the first two "general position" lemmas which we will use to avoid unpleasant singularities.

Theorem 3.2 (Sard). *Let $f : M \to N$ be a smooth map of manifolds, and let C be the set of critical points of f in M, then $f(C)$ has measure zero in N. In particular, let $f : \mathbb{R}^r \to \mathbb{R}^n$ be a smooth map with $r \geqslant n$, then for almost all $v \in \mathbb{R}^n$ the set $f^{-1}(v)$ is either empty or a manifold of dimension $r - n$.*

Sard's theorem gives us a way of placing the polynomials that define a semi-algebraic set in "general position". That is, we can take an arbitrary semi-algebraic set S and add a small constant term to each polynomial and obtain a new set of polynomials whose kernels always intersect as manifolds. Almost any choice of these constants will work, and we can make them arbitrarily small. So as long as the set is robust with respect to small perturbations, i.e. as long as there is some ε such that the addition of constants of magnitude less than ε does not change the path connectivity of S, we will still be able to construct a roadmap of S.

General Position Lemma 1. *Let $f_1, \ldots, f_n$ be smooth maps from $\mathbb{R}^r$ to $\mathbb{R}$. Define a new set of maps $f_i^\varepsilon = f_i - \varepsilon_i$, where each ε_i is a real constant, and let $\varepsilon = (\varepsilon_1, \ldots, \varepsilon_n)$. Then for almost all $\varepsilon \in \mathbb{R}^n$ the kernels of all the f_i^ε and their intersections are manifolds.*

Proof. First note that $f_i^{-1}(\varepsilon_i) = \ker(f_i^\varepsilon)$. Let f be any tuple of functions $(f_{i_1}, \ldots, f_{i_k}) : \mathbb{R}^r \to \mathbb{R}^k$, and let f^ε be the corresponding tuple of perturbed functions. Then the set E of values $v \in \mathbb{R}^k$ for which $f^{-1}(v)$ fails to be a manifold is a measure zero set in $\mathbb{R}^k$, being just the set of critical values of f. The set of $\varepsilon \in \mathbb{R}^n$ such that $\ker(f^\varepsilon)$ fails to be a manifold is of the form $E \times \mathbb{R}^{n-k}$ and has measure zero in $\mathbb{R}^n$. For n functions there are only finitely many (2^n) tuples f, and finitely many measure zero sets in $\mathbb{R}^n$ where some $\ker(f^\varepsilon)$ fails to be a manifold. Since the union of finitely many measure zero sets has measure zero, for almost all ε the kernels of all the f_i^ε and their intersections are manifolds. $\square$

Corollary 3.3. *Once we have the polynomials in general position, every sign-invariant set in S is a manifold, since each is an open subset of the kernel of some function $f = (f_1, \ldots, f_n) : \mathbb{R}^r \to \mathbb{R}^n$, and all these kernels are manifolds.*

Later we will want to compute the critical points of a globally defined map $g : \mathbb{R}^r \to \mathbb{R}^m$ when restricted to M, where M is itself the preimage of a regular value of some map $f : \mathbb{R}^r \to \mathbb{R}^n$. Some care must be taken not to confuse the two maps. Furthermore the critical points of g and its restriction to M, $g|_M$ do not coincide in general. $d(g|_M)_x$ may not be surjective even if dg_x is. The examples later in this section all have this property. In order to clarify the roles of the maps f and g, we next derive a simple condition for a point $x \in M$ to be a critical point of $g|_M$.

Lemma 3.4. *Suppose that M is the preimage of a regular value of some map $f : \mathbb{R}^r \to \mathbb{R}^n$, and let $g|_M$ denote the restriction of the map $g : \mathbb{R}^r \to \mathbb{R}^m$ to M, where $n + m \leqslant r$. Then $x \in M$ is a critical point of $g|_M$ iff the matrix*

$$
d(f, g)_x = \begin{pmatrix}
\dfrac{\partial f_1}{\partial x_1}(x) & \cdots & \dfrac{\partial f_1}{\partial x_r}(x) \\
\vdots & & \vdots \\
\dfrac{\partial f_n}{\partial x_1}(x) & \cdots & \dfrac{\partial f_n}{\partial x_r}(x) \\
\dfrac{\partial g_1}{\partial x_1}(x) & \cdots & \dfrac{\partial g_1}{\partial x_r}(x) \\
\vdots & & \vdots \\
\dfrac{\partial g_m}{\partial x_1}(x) & \cdots & \dfrac{\partial g_m}{\partial x_r}(x)
\end{pmatrix} \tag{4}
$$

is singular at x.

Proof. We note that the first n rows of $d(f, g)_x$ are the rows of df_x, while the second m rows are the rows of dg_x. The point x is a critical point of $g|_M$ iff $d(g|_M)_x$ is not surjective, i.e. iff $\dim(dg_x(T_xM)) < m$. This will be true iff there is a nonzero vector $u \in T_xM$ such that $dg_x(u) = 0$. But T_xM is just $\ker(df_x)$ so u must be orthogonal to all the rows of df_x and all the rows of dg_x. Such a u exists iff $d(f, g)_x$ is singular. $\square$

Corollary 3.5. *If f and g are polynomials, then the set of critical points of $g|_M$ is an algebraic set. The matrix $d(f, g)_x$ is singular iff all its $(n + m) \times (n + m)$ subdeterminants are zero. All these subdeterminants are polynomials, and let J denote the ideal generated by them. Then the critical set of $g|_M$ is the intersection of the algebraic sets $V(J)$ and $\ker(f)$, and so is an algebraic set.*

Example 3.6. Let f be the polynomial $f(x, y, z) = x^2 + y^2 + z^2 - 1$. Then $M = \ker(f)$ is the unit 2-sphere in $\mathbb{R}^3$. Suppose $g(x, y, z) = x$ is the function of interest. Then the critical points of $g|_M$ are the points on M where the matrix

$$d(f, g) = \begin{pmatrix} 2x & 2y & 2z \\ 1 & 0 & 0 \end{pmatrix} \tag{5}$$

is singular. The matrix has rank less than 2 iff $y = z = 0$ and the only points on the manifold satisfying this condition are $(-1, 0, 0)$ and $(1, 0, 0)$. These are the points where the function $g|_M$ attains its extremal values of -1 and 1. Notice that the function g defined on all of $\mathbb{R}^r$ has no critical points.

Example 3.7. Let f be the same polynomial as in the previous example, and let $g : \mathbb{R}^3 \to \mathbb{R}^2$ be the projection on the x-, y-coordinates, $g(x, y, z) = (x, y)$. Then matrix (4) has the form

$$d(f, g) = \begin{pmatrix} 2x & 2y & 2z \\ 1 & 0 & 0 \\ 0 & 1 & 0 \end{pmatrix} \tag{6}$$

and this matrix is singular iff $z = 0$. The solution set is the set of points on the equator of the sphere, which is a unit circle in the x-y plane.

If the matrix $d(f, g)_x$ is nonsingular at x then we say the functions f and g are *independent* at x. Let $M = f^{-1}(u)$ and $N = g^{-1}(v)$ be preimages of regular values of f and g. If f and g are independent everywhere on $M \cap N$, then we say that M and N intersect *transversally*, written $M \pitchfork N$. If $M \pitchfork N$, then $M \cap N$ is a manifold of codimension $\mathrm{codim}(M) + \mathrm{codim}(N)$. Equivalently, $M \pitchfork N$ iff (u, v) is a regular value of the map $(f, g) : \mathbb{R}^r \to \mathbb{R}^{n+m}$.

Later we will need to be able to choose a projection function g such that the critical set of $g|_M$ is a 1-manifold for any $M \subseteq S$. In the course of showing that we can always do this, we give a simple expression for the critical set which will be used later in an algorithm.

Let M be the preimage of a regular value of $f : \mathbb{R}^r \to \mathbb{R}^n$. Let $g : \mathbb{R}^r \to \mathbb{R}^m$ be any smooth map where $r \geq n + m$, and let g^a be a perturbation of g by a linear map $a : \mathbb{R}^r \to \mathbb{R}^m$ so that $g^a = g + a$. The map a can be viewed as an element of $\mathbb{R}^{rm}$ since it is determined by rm values a_{ij} viz:

$$a_i(x) = \sum_{j=1}^{r} a_{ij} x_j \quad \text{for } i \in \{1, \dots, m\} \, . \tag{7}$$

We denote by C_p the set of critical points of $g^a|_M$ where the differential $d(g^a|_M)$ has corank p, i.e. the critical points where the rank of $d(g^a|_M)$ drops to $m - p$. We can also define the set $C_{\geq p}$ as the set of critical points where $d(g^a|_M)$ has corank *greater than or equal to* p. For each p, the set $C_{\geq p}$ is a closed set. It is precisely the set of points where the matrix $d(f, g^a)_x$ has corank greater than or equal to p. Thus it is the intersection of M and the vanishing set of all the subdeterminants of $d(f, g^a)_x$ of size $(n + m - p + 1) \times (n + m - p + 1)$, and so is a closed set.

We now define a function F_a whose kernel is diffeomorphic to C_1, but lies in a higher-dimensional space. Specifically, we use the fact that $x \in \mathbb{R}^r$ is a critical point of $d(g^a|_M)$ iff there exists a vector $(s, t) \in \mathbb{R}^{n+m}$ in the kernel of $d(f, g)_x$. We form a parameter space consisting of the values of x, s, t where $d(g^a|_M)_x$ has corank not greater than 1, and then find the critical points of $d(g^a|_M)_x$ within this set.

Let N be the subset of parameter space where $d(g^a|_M)_x$ has corank not greater than 1. Then $N = (\mathbb{R}^r - C_{\geq p}) \times \mathbb{R}^{(n+m)}$, and N an open set in parameter space, hence a manifold.

Lemma 3.8. *Let F_a be the function*

$$F_a : N \to \mathbb{R}^{(n+r+1)} \, ,$$

$$(x, s, t) \mapsto (f(x), (s * df_x + t * dg_x^a), (s \cdot s + t \cdot t - 1)) \, , \tag{8}$$

where the products $*$ are matrix products with s and t considered as row vectors. Then for almost every $a \in \mathbb{R}^{rm}$, $\ker(F_a)$ is an $(m - 1)$-manifold.

Proof. Firstly, it should be clear from the definition of F_a that $(x, s, t) \in \ker(F_a)$ iff $d(f, g^a)_x$ is singular at x, i.e. iff x is a critical point of $g^a|_M$. Next we consider the sets $\ker(F_a)$ for all possible a. We define a function $F : N \times \mathbb{R}^{rm} \to \mathbb{R}^{(n+m+1)}$ as

$$F(x, s, t, a) \overset{\text{def}}{=} F_a(x, s, t) \, ,$$

then $\ker(F)$ is a manifold. Let p be the point (x, s, t, a). $\ker(F)$ is a manifold because dF_p is surjective at every point $p \in \ker(F)$. dF_p is given by:

$$
dF_p = \begin{array}{c}
\overbrace{}^{r \text{ cols.}} \quad \overbrace{}^{n \text{ cols.}} \quad \overbrace{}^{m \text{ cols.}} \quad \overbrace{}^{rm \text{ cols.}} \\
\left(\begin{array}{cccc}
df_x & 0 & 0 & 0 \\
R & (df_x)^{\mathrm{T}} & (dg_x^a)^{\mathrm{T}} & T \\
0 & 2s & 2t & 0
\end{array} \right)
\begin{array}{l}
n \text{ rows} \\
r \text{ rows} \\
1 \text{ row}
\end{array}
\end{array}
\tag{9}
$$

where R is some $r \times r$ matrix, and T is the $r \times rm$ matrix

$$
T = \begin{pmatrix}
t & 0 & \cdots & 0 \\
0 & t & \cdots & 0 \\
\vdots & \vdots & & \vdots \\
0 & 0 & \cdots & t
\end{pmatrix}.
\tag{10}
$$

Now if p is a point in $\ker(F)$ we know that $x \in M$ and therefore df_x is surjective, so that the first n rows of dF_p are independent. Since s and t satisfy $s * df_x + t * dg_x^a = 0$, we must have t nonzero, or df_x would be singular. Therefore the matrix T has r independent rows, and the last row of dF_p is independent of all previous rows. We conclude that dF_p is surjective for all $p \in \ker(F)$ so that $\ker(F)$ is a manifold of dimension $rm + m - 1$.

Let $\pi_A : \ker(F) \to \mathbb{R}^{rm}$ be projection on the a-coordinates of $\ker(F)$. π_A is a smooth map of manifolds, and we make use of Theorem 3.2 here to infer that almost any a is a regular value of π_A, so that $\pi_A^{-1}(a)$ is a manifold of dimension $m - 1$. We observe that $\pi_A^{-1}(a) = \ker(F_a)$ and we are done. $\square$

This is the manifold we are after, but it currently inhabits parameter space rather than the position space $\mathbb{R}^r$. Showing that it can be embedded in position space gives us the second general position result.

General Position Lemma 2. *If* $g : M \to \mathbb{R}^m$ *is a smooth map, then for almost any linear perturbation* g^a *of* g, *the set* C_1 *of critical points of* $g^a|_M$ *which have corank 1, is an* $(m - 1)$*-manifold.*

Proof. Using Lemma 3.8 we know that for almost all a, the set $L = \ker(F_a)$ is an $(m - 1)$-manifold. We show that projection on the x-coordinates $\pi_X : L \to \mathbb{R}^r$ is an embedding of L. First we note that π_X is one-one, since $d(f, g)_x$ has corank 1 at any point in $\ker(F_a)$, so that given x there is exactly one tuple (s, t) such that $(x, s, t) \in \ker(F_a)$. Strictly speaking the tuple $(x, -s, -t)$ is also a solution, but we can identify these two points and treat them as a single point in projective $(n + m - 1)$-space $P^{(n+m-1)}$. This makes sense because of the condition $s \cdot s + t \cdot t = 1$, and the fact that $P^{(n+m-1)}$ can be obtained by identifying opposite points on the $(n + m - 1)$-sphere.

Let q denote the point (x, s, t). We show next that the induced map $d(\pi_X)_q : T_q L \to T_{\pi_X(q)} \mathbb{R}^r$ is injective, by showing that $\ker(d(\pi_X)_q)$ is $\{0\}$.

Suppose there was a nonzero $u \in \ker(d(\pi_X)_q)$, then u must be of the form $(0, s, t)$. Now u lies in $T_q L$ and hence in $\ker(d(F_a)_q)$. Thus u must be orthogonal to all the rows of $d(F_a)_q$. Now $d(F_a)_q$ is just the first $r + n + m$ columns of the matrix dF_p where $p = (q, a)$. Referring back to (9) we see that there is precisely one vector of the form $(0, s, t)$ which is orthogonal to the rows containing $(df_x)^T$ and $(dg_x^a)^T$ but this vector is parallel to the last row of dF_p, a contradiction, so there can be no nonzero $u \in \ker(d\pi_X)$.

Finally, we must show that π_X is proper, i.e. that the preimage of any compact set $X \subset \mathbb{R}^r$ is compact. X is a compact subset of a Hausdorff space and is closed. Its preimage is a closed subset of $X \times P$, where P is the set of (s, t) such that $s \cdot s + t \cdot t = 1$ which is a unit sphere in $\mathbb{R}^{(n+m)}$. P is compact, and $\pi_X^{-1}(X)$ being a closed subset of the compact space $X \times P$, is compact. Thus $\pi_X : L \to \mathbb{R}^r$ is an embedding, and $C_1 = \pi_X(L)$ is an $(m - 1)$-manifold. $\square$

In particular, if $m = 2$, the set C_1 is a 1-manifold for almost all a. By an argument very similar to the one given above, we could show that the set C_2 is a manifold of *negative* dimension for almost all a, which implies that it is empty. Thus, if $m = 2$, the entire critical set of $g^a|_M$, which is the union of C_1 and C_2, is a 1-manifold for almost all a.

Notice the symmetry of the matrix condition (4). The critical points of the function g restricted to some manifold $f^{-1}(v)$ will also be critical points of f restricted to some manifold $g^{-1}(w)$. In fact we can even change the role of a single row of the matrix to obtain a different characterization of a set of critical points. g can be thought of as a tuple of functions, each of which may be used either to *define* the manifold M, or to act on it. This alternative view will prove useful later on in showing that slices through M always contain a point on the roadmap of M. For now we have

Slice Lemma. *Let M be an embedded manifold which is the kernel of some map $f : \mathbb{R}^r \to \mathbb{R}^n$, and let $g_1 : M \to \mathbb{R}^l$ and $g_2 : M \to \mathbb{R}^m$ be the restrictions to M of two maps defined on $\mathbb{R}^r$. Also, let $g : M \to \mathbb{R}^{l+m}$ be the map (g_1, g_2), and let C be the critical set of g. Assume that g is in general position, so that its critical set is a manifold. Then the critical set C is the union of the critical set Γ of g_1 and the critical sets of all slices $g_2|_N$ where $N = g_1^{-1}(v) - \Gamma$ for some $v \in \mathbb{R}^l$. More prosaically, the critical set of a slice through M is a slice through the critical set of M.*

Proof. First we form a matrix of the form (4) whose rows are the rows of the Jacobian of f followed by g_1, followed by g_2. Then C is the set of points where the matrix is singular. The set C can be broken into two subsets corresponding to two ways that the matrix can be singular:

(i) the first $n + l$ rows are dependent, which is true iff x is a critical point of $g_1|_M$.

(ii) the last m rows, once orthogonalized to the first $n + l$, are dependent, which is true iff x is a critical point of $g_2|_N$ for some slice $N = g_1^{-1}(v) - \Gamma$ of M. $\square$

Example 3.9. Suppose that M is again the sphere defined by $f(x, y, z) = x^2 + y^2 + z^2 - 1$ and that g_1 and g_2 are projection on the x and y coordinate respectively, with their domains restricted to M. Then C is once again the unit circle in the x-y plane. The critical points of g_1 are the two points $(-1, 0, 0)$ and $(1, 0, 0)$. Each set $g_1^{-1}(v)$ is a circle which is a slice through M at $x = v$. The critical points of $g_2|_N$ on each slice $N = g_1^{-1}(v)$ are the extremal points in y of the slice, and satisfy the constraint $z = 0$. The union of the critical points of all such slices together with the critical points of g_1 gives the curve C.

4. Morse Theory

It turns out that a great deal of global topological information about a manifold can be inferred from its local behavior in the neighborhood of critical points of certain functions. These functions are called Morse functions, and it can be shown that a manifold can be classified up to homotopy type through the analysis of the critical points of a Morse function defined on it.

Morse theory makes use of a Morse function g to define a smoothly varying vector field on the manifold which vanishes only at critical points. This vector field can be used to smoothly deform subsets of the manifold onto smaller subsets, and eventually down to the neighborhoods of critical points. Since homotopy type is unchanged by such a deformation, analysis of these neighborhoods gives global information about homotopy type.

We are interested here in the connectivity of semi-algebraic sets, which can be represented as a union of manifolds. We define the critical points of a semi-algebraic set S w.r.t. some function g as the union of the critical points of all the manifolds that comprise S w.r.t. g. We will show that, by analogy to Morse theory, given a suitable function g it is possible to construct a smooth vector field on S which vanishes only at critical points. This will allow us to smoothly deform subsets of S onto *lower-dimensional* subsets without affecting homotopy type (and therefore connectivity).

Let $f : \mathbb{R}^r \to \mathbb{R}^n$ be a smooth map having 0 as a regular value. Then $M = \ker(f)$ is a manifold. Let $g : \mathbb{R}^r \to \mathbb{R}$ be a real-valued function, and $g|_M$ its restriction to M. We will need some inner product $\langle , \rangle$ on $\mathbb{R}^r$ and the usual Euclidean inner product will do. We define a (non-associative) operator $\perp$ on vectors $\perp : \mathbb{R}^r \times \mathbb{R}^r \to \mathbb{R}^r$ such that

$$u \perp v \stackrel{\text{def}}{=} u\langle v, v \rangle - v\langle u, v \rangle \tag{11}$$

then $u \perp v$ is a vector orthogonal to v, and is zero iff u or v are zero or u and v

are parallel. We can use $\perp$ to produce a set of orthogonal vectors $(u_1, \ldots, u_m)$ from an arbitrary set of vectors $(v_1, \ldots, v_m)$ by setting $u_1 = v_1$ and inductively defining

$$u_i = v_i \perp u_1 \perp u_2 \perp \cdots \perp u_{i-1} , \qquad (12)$$

where the operation $\perp$ associates to the left. Then we find that u_i is orthogonal to v_j for every $j < i$ and $u_i = 0$ iff $v_1, \ldots, v_i$ are dependent. By repeated application of the Schwarz inequality we find that $\langle v_i, u_i \rangle \geqslant 0$, with identity iff $u_i = 0$. We use the suggestive notation $u_i = v_i \perp (v_1, \ldots, v_{i-1})$ for the vector u_i obtained from $v_1, \ldots, v_i$ by the above process.

Let ∇g_x be the vector dual to dg_x under $\langle \, , \, \rangle$ i.e.

$$\langle \nabla g_x, u \rangle = dg_x(u) \quad \forall u \in \mathbb{R}^r . \qquad (13)$$

Since the inner product is Euclidean, the components of ∇g_x are exactly the components of the linear functional dg_x. Similarly for the n-valued function f, ∇f_x is an n-tuple of vectors s.t.

$$\langle (\nabla f_x)_i, u \rangle = d(f_i)_x(u) \quad \forall u \in \mathbb{R}^r \qquad (14)$$

for $i \in \{1, \ldots, n\}$. The vectors in ∇f_x span a space called the normal space to M at x. This space is orthogonal to the tangent space $T_x M$. Now let V_x be the vector field

$$V_x = \nabla g_x \perp \nabla f_x , \qquad (15)$$

then V_x varies smoothly throughout $\mathbb{R}^r$. Furthermore if $x \in M$ then $V_x \in T_x M$ since V_x is orthogonal to all the vectors in ∇f_x, which are just the rows of df_x. V_x vanishes iff the vectors ∇g_x and $(\nabla f_x)_i$ are dependent, i.e. iff the rows of df_x and dg_x are dependent. If $x \in M$, this is exactly the condition for x to be a critical point of $g|_M$, so V_x is a smooth vector field on M which vanishes only at the critical points of $g|_M$.

We assume that the semi-algebraic set S is given as a union of sign-invariant sets S_σ, where each S_σ is an open subset of the kernel of some tuple of n polynomials. We define the critical points of $g|_S$ to be the union of the critical points of all the maps $g|_{S_\sigma}$. Then it is possible to define a smoothly varying vector field on all of S which vanishes only at the critical points of $g|_S$. Consider the vector field

$$V_x = \sum_{j=1}^{r} \sum_{i_1 < i_2 \cdots < i_j \in \{1, \ldots, n\}} V_x^{i_1 \cdots i_j} \prod_{k \notin \{i_1, i_2, \ldots, i_j\}} f_k^2(x) , \qquad (16)$$

where $V_x^{i_1 \cdots i_j} = \nabla g_x \perp \nabla(f_{i_1}, \ldots, f_{i_j})$. This field has the following properties:

(1) If $x \in S_\sigma$ then $V_x \in T_x S_\sigma$.
(2) $dg_x(V_x) \geq 0$.
(3) V_x vanishes only at critical points of $g|_S$.

Proof. (1) If $x \in S_\sigma$ then $V_x \in T_x S_\sigma$. Let $f = (f_{i_1}, \ldots, f_{i_j})$ be the tuple of functions which are zero at x. Then the product of f_k^2 in (16) is nonzero and positive, so the vector $V_x^{i_1, \cdots, i_j} \in T_x \ker(f)$ makes a positive contribution to V_x. In fact the only vectors which contribute to V_x are of the form $V_x^{i_1, \cdots, i_m}$ where $\{i_1, \ldots, i_j\} \subseteq \{i_1, \ldots, i_m\}$, since for all other vectors, the product of f_k^2 vanishes. These vectors lie in the tangent spaces of submanifolds of $\ker(f)$, and therefore in $T_x \ker(f)$. Hence $V_x \in T_x \ker(f) = T_x S_\sigma$ where S_σ is the sign-invariant set containing x.

(2) $dg_x(V_x) \geq 0$. V_x is a linear combination with positive coefficients of vectors $V_x^{i_1, \cdots, i_j}$ such that $dg_x(V_x^{i_1, \cdots, i_j}) \geq 0$.

(3) V_x vanishes only at critical points of $g|_S$. Recall that the vector field we defined in (15) for manifolds vanishes only at critical points. If $x \in S_\sigma$ is a critical point of $g|_{S_\sigma}$ then it is also a critical point of $g|_M$ for any submanifold $M \subset S_\sigma$ which contains x. Thus the only vectors with nonzero scalar coefficients in (16) are themselves at x, so $V_x = 0$ at critical points.

Conversely, if $V_x = 0$ then all the vectors with nonzero coefficients in (16) vanish. This is true because $dg_x(V_x^{i_1, \cdots, i_j}) \geq 0$ for any $V_x^{i_1, \cdots, i_j}$, and V_x is a sum with positive coefficients of the $V_x^{i_1, \cdots, i_j}$. Therefore $dg_x(V_x) = 0$ iff $dg_x(V_x^{i_1, \cdots, i_j}) = 0$ for all the $dg_x(V_x^{i_1, \cdots, i_j})$ with nonzero coefficients in (16). So if $V_x = 0$ we must have $dg_x(V_x^{i_1, \cdots, i_j}) = 0$ where $f_{i_1}, \ldots, f_{i_j}$ are the functions which vanish at x, and so x must be a critical point of $g|_{S_\sigma}$. $\square$

We now define a normalized vector field $\hat{V}_x$ in terms of V_x so that $dg_x(\hat{V}_x) = 1$ at regular points. i.e. we set

$$\hat{V}_x = V_x / dg_x(V_x) \tag{17}$$

and we denote by S' the set S minus the critical points of $g|_S$, and similarly let S'_σ denote the set S_σ minus the critical points of $g|_{S_\sigma}$. Then $\hat{V}_x$ is a smoothly varying vector field on S', and on all the sets S'_σ.

Theorem 4.1. *Let $\hat{V}_x \in T_x M$ be a smooth nonvanishing vector field on some manifold M. For each point $x \in M$, there is a unique smooth curve $\phi_x : (a_x, b_x) \to M$ where (a_x, b_x) is an open interval in $\mathbb{R}$ which contains 0, and where $\phi_x(t)$ satisfies the equation*

$$d\phi_x / dt = \hat{V}_{\phi_x(t)} \tag{18}$$

with $\phi_x(0) = x$.

The functions ϕ_x are called integral curves. Note that the domain of definition depends on how far the curve extends within the manifold M. It can be shown that there exists a maximal open interval $(a_x, b_x) \subseteq \mathbb{R}$ such that all curves satisfying (18) on some open interval (c, d) have $(c, d) \subseteq (a_x, b_x)$ and that they agree with ϕ_x on (c, d). Let Ω denote the set of (x, t) such that $\phi_x(t)$ is defined:

$$\Omega = \{(x, t) \in M \times \mathbb{R} \mid t \in (a_x, b_x)\} , \tag{19}$$

then Ω is an open set in $M \times \mathbb{R}$. The flow $\phi : \Omega \to M$ defined as $\phi(x, t) = \phi_x(t)$ is a continuous function.

In particular, if we take the manifold M to be $\mathbb{R}^r$ minus the critical points of $g|_S$, and if $\hat{V}_x$ is the vector field defined by (17), we obtain the following useful corollary to the uniqueness of ϕ_x:

Corollary 4.2. *If* $x \in S'_\sigma$ *is an integral curve of the global vector field* $\hat{V}$, *then* $\phi_x(t) \in S'_\sigma$ *for all* $t \in (a_x, b_x)$. *That is, if we start from a point* x *in some sign-invariant set* S_σ *and move in the direction of the global vector field* $\hat{V}_x$, *we remain in* S'_σ *until we leave* M, *i.e. until we reach a critical point of* $g|_S$. *We can think of the integral curves as field lines each of which is contained in some sign-invariant set and each of which begins and ends at a critical point.*

Proof. Since if $x \in \ker(f)$, then $\hat{V}_x \in T_x \ker(f)$, so $\phi_x(t) \in \ker(f)$ for all $t \in (a_x, b_x)$. It is clear then, that the polynomials which are zero at x will be zero at all points on ϕ_x. On the other hand, suppose there were some t such that $f_i(\phi_x(t)) = 0$ but $f_i(x) \neq 0$. Then ϕ_x is an integral curve through the point $y = \phi_x(t) \in \ker(f_i)$. But there is a single unique integral curve through y, and it lies entirely in $\ker(f_i)$, so we cannot have $f_i(x) \neq 0$ if x is some other point on the curve.

Thus polynomials which are zero at some point on the curve must be zero everywhere, and polynomials which are nonzero must be nonzero everywhere. Since no polynomial can change sign on ϕ_x, we must have ϕ_x entirely in $S'_\sigma \ni x$. $\square$

In order to relate changes in t to changes in the value of $g(\phi_x(t))$, we define a height function $h_x(t) = g(\phi_x(t))$. Then the vertical velocity of a point on any integral curve is:

$$\frac{dh_x}{dt} = dg_x\left(\frac{d\phi_x}{dt}\right) = dg_x(\hat{V}_x) = 1 . \tag{20}$$

We have the initial condition $\phi_x(0) = x$, and by integrating along the curve, we find that

$$h_x(t) = g(\phi_x(t)) = t + g(x) . \tag{21}$$

From this relation we see that the inverse of ϕ_x is given by $\phi_x^{-1}(y) = g(y) - g(x)$. Since ϕ_x is one-one and onto its image, and since its inverse is smooth, each curve $\phi_x(a_x, b_x)$ is diffeomorphic to the interval (a_x, b_x).

Let (c, d) be an interval in $\mathbb{R}$ containing no critical points of $g|_S$. Let $S|_{(c, d)}$ denote the set $S \cap g^{-1}(c, d)$, and let $S|_v$ denote the set $S \cap g^{-1}(v)$ for some $v \in (c, d)$. Then the flow $\phi(x, t)$ is defined on all of $S|_v \times (c - v, d - v)$. Let $r : S|_v \times (c, d) \to S|_{(c, d)}$ be the map

$$r(x, t) = \phi(x, t - v) . \tag{22}$$

Then from (21) we find that $g(r(x, t)) = t$. Now r is a diffeomorphism of $S|_v \times (c, d)$ and $S|_{(c, d)}$, because r is a smooth map, it is one-one and onto, and its inverse $r^{-1}(x) = (\phi(x, v - g(x)), g(x))$ is smooth, being a composition of smooth maps.

If (c, d) contains no critical values of $g|_S$, then we can extend r to a map $\bar{r} : S|_v \times [c, d] \to S|_{[c, d]}$ which is continuous, but not necessarily a diffeomorphism. We define $\bar{r}$ by adjoining limit points of the curves ϕ_x. If we look at the image of a monotonically decreasing sequence $(c_n) \subset (c, d)$ such that $(c_n) \to c$, under $r_x(t) = r(x, t)$, then that image must have a convergent subsequence, since it lies in the compact set S. Suppose the subsequence converges to x_c, then by (22) and continuity of g, we must have $g(x_c) = c$. By uniqueness of the integral curves, and the fact that the vector field vanishes only at isolated points, there can be only one x_c for each curve $r_x(c, d)$. If $\phi_x(c - v)$ is defined, then we must have $x_c = \phi_x(c - v)$, otherwise, x_c must be a critical point of $g|_S$. We can also define a point x_d as the limit of the image of an increasing sequence which converges to d. For each x, we define

$$\bar{r}(x, t) = \begin{cases} \phi(x, t - v) , & \text{if } t - v \in (a_x, b_x) , \\ x_c , & \text{if } t = c , \\ x_d , & \text{if } t = d . \end{cases} \tag{23}$$

Then $\bar{r}$ is continuous. $\bar{r}$ is continuous at noncritical points since the flow ϕ is continuous there. At a critical point x, we look at the preimage of an open set $U \ni x$. The preimage is the union of the open set $\bar{r}^{-1}(U - \{x\})$ and the set $\bar{r}^{-1}(x)$ which lies on the boundary of $S|_v \times [c, d]$. Now $\bar{r}^{-1}(x)$ is a closed set, but it is separated from the rest of $S|_v \times [c, d]$ by $\bar{r}^{-1}(U - \{x\})$. Thus the union $\bar{r}^{-1}(U - \{x\}) \cup \bar{r}^{-1}(x)$ is open, and $\bar{r}$ is continuous.

The diffeomorphism r, and the function $\bar{r}$ give us a simple way to join together components of $S|_{(c, d)}$ and components of $S|_c$ and $S|_d$. First we need some terminology. We say two subsets of S are *adjacent* if a point in one set lies in the closure of the other. Two connected, adjacent sets have a connected union.

Adjacency Lemma. *Let $S \subseteq \mathbb{R}^r$ be a compact semi-algebraic set, and let (c, d) be an open interval in $\mathbb{R}$ not containing any critical points of $g|_S$. Then every component of $S|_{(c, d)}$ is adjacent to exactly one component of $S|_c$ and one component of $S|_d$.*

Proof. Since $S|_{(c, d)}$ is diffeomorphic to $S|_v \times (c, d)$, any component D_α of $S|_{(c, d)}$ is diffeomorphic to $D_\alpha|_v \times (c, d)$, where $D_\alpha|_v$ is connected. Now the set $\bar{r}(D_\alpha|_v, c)$ lies in the closure of D_α since it consists of limit points of D_α. Since S is closed, $\bar{r}(D_\alpha|_v, c) \subset S|_c$, and since $\bar{r}$ is continuous, $\bar{r}(D_\alpha|_v, c)$ is connected. Therefore $\hat{r}(D_\alpha|_v, c)$ lies in a single component of $S|_c$. Similarly, the set $\bar{r}(D_\alpha|_v, d)$ lies in a single component of $S|_d$. $\square$

5. The Roadmap Algorithm

We now have the hardware necessary to describe the algorithm for construction of roadmaps. The objective is to take a compact semi-algebraic set S in $\mathbb{R}^r$ and a set P of points $x_1 \ldots x_p \in S$ and to produce a 1-dimensional subset C of S containing P and such that every (connected) component of S contains a single component of C. We asume that S is represented as a disjoint union of manifolds. If the polynomials defining S are in general position, then the sign-invariant sets S_σ are a suitable disjoint set of manifolds.

Throughout this section we will use the following notation for slices through subsets of $\mathbb{R}^r$. Let $S \subset \mathbb{R}^r$, and let U be any subset of $\mathbb{R}$, then $S|_U$ denotes the set $S \cap g_1^{-1}(U)$. Thus $S|_c$ denotes the set $S \cap g_1^{-1}(c)$, and $S|_{(c, d)}$ denotes the set $S \cap g_1^{-1}(c, d)$, etc.

5.1. Roadmap algorithm, version 0

First we describe a simple recursive algorithm for the construction of roadmaps in $\mathbb{R}^r$. The algorithm works by constructing 1-dimensional curves which are the critical sets of a projection function g. These curves may not be connected within a component of S, but by calling the algorithm recursively on certain slices through S we can guarantee that they are.

Step 1. The base case occurs when S is 1-dimensional. Then we simply set $C = S$ and return.

Step 2. Otherwise we choose a linear map $g = (g_1, g_2) : \mathbb{R}^r \to \mathbb{R}^2$ in general position. We compute the *silhouette* of S, denoted Σ, which is the critical set of $g|_S$. Σ is a compact semi-algebraic set.

Step 3. We compute the set of critical *points* Γ of $g_1|_\Sigma$. For every $x_i \in P \cup \Gamma$, let $v_i = g_1(x_i)$. We call the algorithm recursively on the *lower-dimensional* semi-algebraic set C_i containing all these points.

Step 4. The roadmap C of S is the union of Σ and all the C_i.

Claim 5.0. *C is a compact semi-algebraic set.*

Claim 5.1. *C contains P,*

Claim 5.2. *Every connected component of S contains a single connected component of C.*

Proof of Claim 5.0. The set C is semi-algebraic because it is the union of silhouette curves and slices through the set S. The silhouette of a set S_σ is semi-algebraic because it is the intersection of S_σ and the critical set of $g|_M$ where $M = \ker(f)$, and f is the tuple of polynomials which are zero on S_σ.

C is closed because each silhouette and slice is closed. To show that the silhouette Σ is closed, we must ensure that Σ contains all the limit points of the curves $S_\sigma \cap \Sigma$. If x is a limit point of $S_\sigma \cap \Sigma$, then it must be in the (closed) critical set of $g|_{\ker(f)}$, where f is the tuple of polynomials which are zero on S_σ. Thus the matrix $d(f, g)_x$ is singular at x. If x is not in S_σ, then some polynomials must be zero at x which are not zero in S_σ. Let h be the tuple of these polynomials. Now x lies in some sign-invariant set which is a subset of $\ker(f, h)$. Furthermore, x lies in the silhouette of this set, because $d(f, h, g)_x$ cannot have independent rows if the rows of $d(f, g)_x$ are dependent. Therefore $d(f, h, g)_x$ is singular at x and so x lies on the silhouette of some sign-invariant set. Since C contains all its limit points and is a subset of the compact set S, C must be compact. $\square$

Proof of Claim 5.1. The proof is by induction on dimension of S. Clearly the assertion is true if $\dim(S) = 1$. Otherwise we assume the assertion is true if S is $(n-1)$-dimensional.

If S has dimension $n > 0$, then the slice $S|_{v_i}$ is at most $(n-1)$-dimensional. This is because for each n-manifold $M \subseteq \ker(f)$, the functions f and g_1 are independent on $M - \Gamma_M$, where Γ_M is the finite critical set of $g_1|_M$. Therefore the slice $(M - \Gamma_M)|_v$ is a manifold of dimension at most $n - 1$ for any v (it may be empty). The slice $M|_v$ is the union of $(M - \Gamma_M)|_v$ and the finite set $\Gamma_M|_v$, and therefore has dimension at most $n - 1$. Thus the slice $S|_{v_i}$ has dimension at most $n - 1$.

Now $P \subset C$ is easy, since every point $x_i \in P$ lies in some slice $P|_{v_i}$, and by the induction hypothesis $P|_{v_i} \subset C_i \subset C$. $\square$

Before we can prove Claim 5.2 about connectivity of C, we must establish some local results about connectivity of the roadmap. We start by defining a local property of a decomposition of S which suffices to prove the global property.

Linking Property. A collection of connected subsets $\{S_\alpha\}$ of S is said to have the *linking property* if every S_α has non-empty roadmap $S_\alpha \cap C$, and whenever

S_α and S_β are adjacent, their roadmaps $S_\alpha \cap C$ and $S_\beta \cap C$ have a connected union.

Linking Lemma. *If there exists a finite collection of sets $\{S_\alpha\}$ whose union is S which has the linking property, and if every component of S contains at least one $S|_\alpha$ s.t. $S|_\alpha$ is connected, then every component of S contains a single component of C.*

Proof. Let D be any component of S. We can "build" D by choosing elements from the collection $\{S_\alpha\}$ which are contained in D, starting with an element having a connected roadmap. Let D_i be the partially built set at the ith step. We pick a new element of $\{S_\alpha\}$ which is adjacent to one of the elements we have already chosen. Thus every D_i is connected. Every roadmap $D_i \cap C$ is connected, because when a new set D_α is added which is adjacent to some D_β already in the collection, the roadmap $(D_\alpha \cup D_\beta) \cap C$ is connected, and shares a point in common with the connected set $D_i \cap C$, since $D_\beta \cap C$ is non-empty. After picking all the (say n) elements of $\{S_\alpha\}$ which are contained in D, we have $D = D_n$ and $D \cap C$ connected. $\square$

Lemma 5.3. *Let (c, d) be an open interval containing no critical values of $g_1|_\Sigma$. Let D_α be a connected component of $S|_{(c, d)}$, and let D_β be a connected component of $S|_c$ (or $S|_d$) which is adjacent to D_α. Then every component of $D_\alpha \cap C$ is adjacent to a component of $D_\beta \cap C$.*

Proof. Every critical point of $g_1|_S$ is also a critical point of $g_1|_\Sigma$, so the interval (c, d) contains no critical values of $g_1|_S$. Therefore, by the adjacency lemma, D_β is the only component of $S|_c$ which is adjacent to D_α. Any component E_α of $D_\alpha \cap C$ will be adjacent to some component E_β of $C|_c$ since C is compact semi-algebraic. We must have $E_\beta \subset D_\beta$, for if E_β were in some other component D_γ of $S|_c$, then D_γ would be a second component of $S|_c$ which is adjacent to D_α, a contradiction. $\square$

Lemma 5.4. *Suppose Claim 5.2 holds for $(n-1)$-dimensionless slices $S|_c$ through critical values of $g_1|_S$. Then every component of S contains a single component of C.*

Proof. Consider the collection of sets $\{D_\alpha\}$ where each D_α is a connected component of either (a) a slice through a critical value $S|_c$, or (b) a slice $S|_{(c, d)}$ where c and d are consecutive critical values of $g_1|_S$. The union of this collection is S, and we claim that the collection has the linking property. First we must show that every D_α has non-empty roadmap.

If D_α lies in some $S|_c$ it has non-empty roadmap by hypothesis of the lemma. Otherwise, if $D_\alpha \subset S|_{(c, d)}$ recall that C contains Σ, which is the critical set of

$g|_S$. By the slice lemma, Σ includes the critical points of all slices $g_2|_N$ where $N = S|_v$, for some $v \in \mathbb{R}$. Choose any $v \in (c, d)$ so that $D_\alpha|_v$ is non-empty. $D_\alpha|_v$ is compact, so g_2 attains an extremal value at some point $x \in D_\alpha|_v$. Now x lies in some manifold in $S|_v$, and is a critical point of g_2 restricted to this manifold, since any tangent vector in the manifold must lie in the kernel of $d(g_2)_x$ or x would not be a stationary point. Thus x is a critical point of $g_2|_N$ and so $D_\alpha \cap C$ is non-empty.

Suppose two sets D_α and D_β are adjacent. Then they must lie in adjacent slices say $S|_{(c, d)}$ and $S|_d$ respectively. They cannot lie in the same slice, since they are each components of that slice by definition, and therefore could not be adjacent. By Lemma 5.3, every component of $D_\alpha \cap C$ is adjacent to some component of $D_\beta \cap C$, but by hypothesis of the present lemma, $D_\beta \cap C$ has only one component, since D_β is a component of a slice through a critical value. Thus the union of $D_\alpha \cap C$ and $D_\beta \cap C$ is connected. The proof for $D_\beta \subset S|_c$ is similar, and we conclude that the set $\{D_\alpha\}$ has the Linking Property.

The Linking Lemma can be applied because every component of S is closed and therefore contains some D_α in a slice $S|_c$ which has a connected roadmap. Thus every component of S contains a single component of C. $\square$

Proof of Claim 5.2. Lemma 5.4 shows that if Claim 5.2 holds for all slices through critical values of S, then it holds also for S. From the proof of Claim 5.1, we know that a slice through an n-dimensional set S has dimension at most $(n - 1)$. We know also that the algorithm works on 1-dimensional slices. Finally, we know that the original set S has dimension at most r, the number of variables. So, by induction on dimension, we conclude that Claim 5.2 holds for S. $\square$

6. Conclusions

In this paper we defined for a semi-algebraic set S, a 1-dimensional set R which we called the roadmap of S. We demonstrated that the roadmap has exactly one connected component within each component of S, which is the key property for motion planning in configuration space. If the set S is not already in general position, this can be readily achieved by randomly perturbing the constant terms of all the polynomials.

In a future paper, we plan to present the algorithm in more detail and examine its complexity. We intend to show the roadmap can be computed in time which is single-exponential in the dimension of the space, and that in fact paths can be found in exponential time.

REFERENCES

1. Berman, L., Precise bounds for Presburger arithmetic and the reals with addition, in: *Proceedings 18th IEEE Symposium on Foundations of Computer Science* (1977).

2. Canny, J.F., Collision detection for moving polyhedra, *IEEE Trans. Pattern Anal. Mach. Intell.* **8** (2) (1986).

3. Canny, J.F., A Voronoi method for the piano-movers problem, in: *Proceedings IEEE International Conference on Robotics and Automation*, St. Louis, MO (1985).

4. Collins, G.E., Quantifier elimination for real closed fields by cylindrical algebraic decomposition, in: *Proceedings Second GI Conference on Automata Theory and Formal Languages*, Lecture Notes in Computer Science **33** (Springer, New York, 1975).

5. Hopcroft, J. and Wilfong, G., Motion of objects in contact, *Int. J. Rob. Res.* **4** (4) (1986).

6. Lozano-Pérez, T., Spatial planning: A configuration space approach, *IEEE Trans. Comput.* **32** (2) (1983) 108–120.

7. Reif, J., Complexity of the mover's problem and generalizations, in: *Proceedings 20th IEEE Symposium on Foundations on Computer Science* (1979).

8. Schwartz, J. and Sharir, M., On the piano movers' problem, II: General techniques for computing topological properties of real algebraic manifolds, *Adv. Appl. Math.* **4** (1983) 298–351.

9. Schwartz, J. and Yap, C.K., *Advances in Robotics* (Erlbaum, Hillsdale, NJ, 1986).

Received October 1986; revised version received January 1988

A Geometric Approach to Error Detection and Recovery for Robot Motion Planning with Uncertainty*

Bruce R. Donald

Computer Science Department, Cornell University, Ithaca, NY 14853, U.S.A.

ABSTRACT

Robots must plan and execute tasks in the presence of uncertainty. Uncertainty arises from sensing errors, control errors, and uncertainty in the geometric models of the environment and of the robot. The last, which we will call model uncertainty, has received little previous attention. In this paper we present a formal framework for computing motion strategies which are guaranteed to succeed in the presence of all three kinds of uncertainty. We show that it is effectively computable for some simple cases. The motion strategies we consider include sensor-based gross motions, compliant motions, and simple pushing motions.

We show that model uncertainty can be represented by position uncertainty in a generalized configuration space. We describe the structure of this space, and how motion strategies may be planned in it.

It is not always possible to find plans that are guaranteed to succeed. In the presence of model error, such plans may not even exist. For this reason we investigate error detection and recovery (EDR) strategies. We characterize what such strategies are, and propose a formal framework for constructing them. Our theory represents what is perhaps the first systematic attack on the problem of error detection and recovery based on geometric and physical reasoning.

PART I. INFORMAL DEVELOPMENT

1. Introduction

Robots must plan and execute tasks in the presence of uncertainty. Uncertainty arises from sensing errors, control errors, and uncertainty in the geometric

* This report describes research done at the Artificial Intelligence Laboratory of the Massachusetts Institute of Technology. Support for the Laboratory's Artificial Intelligence research is provided in part by the Office of Naval Research under Office of Naval Research contract N00014-81-K-0494 and in part by the Advanced Research Projects Agency under Office of Naval Research contracts N00014-80-C-0505 and N00014-82-K-0334. The author was funded in part by a NASA fellowship administered by the Jet Propulsion Laboratory.

models of the environment and of the robot. The last, which we will call *model uncertainty*, has received little previous attention. In this paper we present a formal framework for computing motion strategies which are guaranteed to succeed in the presence of all three kinds of uncertainty. We show that it is effectively computable for some simple cases. The motion strategies we consider include sensor-based gross motions, compliant motions, and simple pushing motions.

We show that model uncertainty can be represented by position uncertainty in a generalized configuration space. We describe the structure of this space, and how motion strategies may be planned in it.

It is not always possible to find plans that are guaranteed to succeed. In the presence of model error, such plans may not even exist. For this reason we investigate *error detection and recovery (EDR) strategies*. We characterize what such strategies are, and propose a formal framework for constructing them.

This paper offers two contributions to the theory of manipulation. The first is a framework for planning motion strategies with model error. Model error is a fundamental problem in robotics, and we have tried to provide a principled, theoretical approach. Our framework can be described very compactly, although many algorithmic and implementational questions remain.

The second contribution is a formal, geometric approach to EDR. While EDR is largely motivated by the problems of uncertainty and model error, its applicability may be quite broad. EDR has been a persistent but ill-defined theme in both AI and robotics research. Typically, it is viewed as a kind of source-to-source transformation on robot programs: for example, as a method for robustifying them by introducing sensing steps and conditionals. We have taken the view that if one can actually plan to sense an anomalous event, and to recover from it, then it is not an error at all. When such plans can be guaranteed, they fall out of a strategy such as LMT [21]. In our view of EDR, an "error" occurs when the goal cannot be recognizably achieved given the resources of the executive and the state of the world. The EDR framework fills a gap when guaranteed plans cannot be found or do not exist: it provides a technology for constructing plans that might work, but fail in a "reasonable" way when they cannot. Our theory represents what is perhaps the first systematic attack on the problem of error detection and recovery based on geometric and physical reasoning.

The first part of this paper develops the framework informally. A more detailed development may be found in Part II. At the end of Part I, we describe an implementation in a restricted domain.

1.1. Application and motivation

1.1.1. *A simple example*

Consider Fig. 1, which depicts a peg-in-hole insertion task. One could imagine a manipulation strategy derived as follows: The initial plan is to move the peg

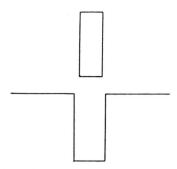

Fig. 1. The goal is to insert the peg in the hole. No rotation of the peg is allowed. One can imagine a strategy which attempts to move straight down, but detects contact on the top surfaces of the hole if they occur. If the peg sticks on the top surfaces, the manipulator tries to move to the left or right to achieve the hole. Are these contact conditions "errors"? We maintain that they are not, since they can be planned for and verified.

straight down towards the bottom of the hole. However, due to uncertainty in the initial position of the peg, the insertion may fail because the peg contacts to the left or right of the hole. Either event might be regarded as an "error". The "recovery" action is to move to the right (if the peg contacted to the left) and to move to the left (if the peg contacted to the right). Thus a plan can be obtained by introducing sensing steps and conditional branches.

Suppose that this conditional plan can be guaranteed—that is, it is a complete manipulation strategy for this simple task. In this case, it seems strange to view the contact conditions as "errors". We do not regard these events as "errors". Our reasoning is that if they can be detected and planned for, then they are simply events in a guaranteed plan.

We are interested in a different class of "errors". Now suppose that there is uncertainty in the width of the hole. If the hole is too small, we will consider this an error, since it causes all plans to fail. Similarly, if some object blocks the hole, and cannot be pushed aside, this is also an error, since it makes the goal unreachable. If either error is possible, there exists no guaranteed plan, for there is no assurance that the task can be accomplished. Since no guaranteed plan can be found, we are left with the choice of giving up, or of considering a broader class of manipulation strategies: plans that might work, but fail in an "reasonable" way when they cannot. Specifically, we propose that EDR strategies should achieve the goal when it exists and is recognizably reachable, and should signal failure when it is not.

1.1.2. *Application*

The theory developed here is quite general. However, it may help to keep in mind a particular application task. We will later return to this task in describing an implementation and experiments.

An interesting application domain for EDR is gear meshing. Let us consider a simplified instance of this problem. In Fig. 2 there are two planar gear-like objects, A and B. The task is to plan a manipulation strategy which will mesh the gears. The state in which the gears are meshed is called the *goal*.

We will consider two variants of this problem. In the first, we assume that the manipulator has grasped A, and that neither A nor B can rotate. However, A can slide along the surfaces of B. In the second, B is free to rotate about its center, but this rotation can only be effected by pushing it with A. In both cases, the initial orientation of B is unknown. We regard A as the moving object and B as the environment; hence the uncertainty in B's orientation is a form of model uncertainty. In the first case, the system has only two degrees of motion freedom. In the second, there are three degrees of motion freedom, one of which is rotational, since B can be pushed.

In both variations, there is uncertainty in control, so when a motion direction is commanded, the actual trajectory followed is only approximately in that direction. There is also uncertainty in position sensing and force sensing, so that the true position and reaction forces are only known approximately. The magnitude of these uncertainties are represented by error balls.

In general, a commanded motion of A may cause A to move through free space, and contact B, possibly causing B to rotate. Our EDR theory is a technique for analyzing these outcomes geometrically to generate strategies that achieve the goal when it is recognizably reachable, and signal failure when it is not. After developing the EDR theory in general, we will return and apply it to the gear example.

1.2. Examples of model error

We will begin developing the EDR theory by examining some very simple planning problems with model error.

Fig. 2. Geometric models of two gear-like planar objects A and B. A is grasped and can translate but not rotate. B can rotate about its center if pushed. The orientation of B is unknown. The task is to generate a motion strategy to mesh the gears.

Example 1.1. Consider Fig. 3. There is position-sensing uncertainty, so that the start position of the robot is only known to lie within some ball in the plane. The goal is to bring the robot in contact with the right vertical surface of A.

We will simplify the problem so that the computational task is in configuration space [2, 7, 9, 10, 19, 20]. This transformation reduces the planning task for a complicated moving object to navigating a point in configuration space. Consider Fig. 4. The configuration point starts out in the region R, which is the position-sensing uncertainty ball about some initial sensed position. To model sliding behavior, we will assume Coulomb friction and generalized damper dynamics, which allows an identification of forces and velocities. Thus the actual commanded velocity v_0 is related to the effective velocity v by $f = B(v - v_0)$ where f is the reaction force and B is a scalar. Given a nominal commanded velocity v_0^*, the control uncertainty is represented by a cone of

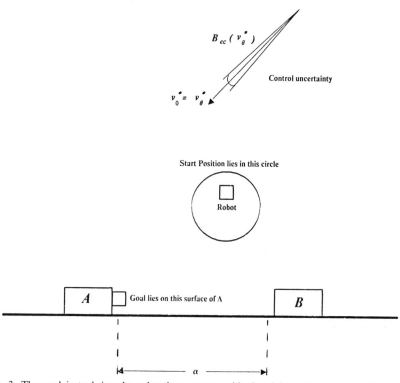

Fig. 3. The goal is to bring the robot into contact with the right vertical surface of A. (For example, the "robot" could be a gripper finger.) There is position-sensing uncertainty, so in the start position the robot is only known to lie within some uncertainty ball. There is also control uncertainty in the commanded velocity to the robot. It is represe 'ed as a cone, as shown.

velocities (B_{ec} in the figure). The actual commanded velocity v_0 must lie within this cone.

The goal in Fig. 4 is to move to the region G. Now, with Coloumb friction, sticking occurs on a surface iff the (actual) commanded velocity points into the friction cone. We assume the friction cones are such that sliding occurs (for all possible commanded velocities in B_{ec}) on all surfaces save G, where all velocities stick. We will assume that the planner can monitor position and velocity sensors to determine whether a motion has reached the goal. Velocity sensing is also subject to uncertainty: for an actual velocity v, the sensed velocity lies in some cone B_{ev} of velocities about v.

Now we introduce simple model error. The shape of A and B are known precisely, and the position of A is fixed. However, the position of B, relative to A is not known. B's position is characterized by the distance α. If $\alpha > 0$ the goal is reachable. But if $\alpha = 0$, then the goal vanishes. No plan can be guaranteed to succeed if $\alpha = 0$ is possible. Suppose we allow α to be negative.

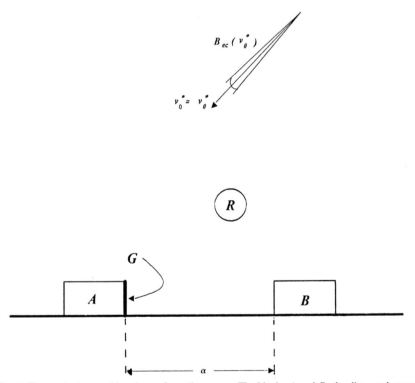

Fig. 4. The equivalent problem in configuration space. The blocks A and B, the distance between the blocks α, and the commanded velocity $v_\theta = v_0^*$ with control error cone $B_{ec}(v_0^*)$. The position of A is fixed.

In this case the blocks meet and fuse. Eventually, for sufficiently small α, B will emerge on the other side of A. In this case, the goal "reappears", and may be reachable again. Let us assume that α is bounded, and lies in the interval $[-d_0, d_0]$.

Our task is to find a plan that can attain G in the cases where it is recognizably reachable. Such a plan is called a *guaranteed strategy in the presence of model error*. But the plan cannot be guaranteed for the α where the goal vanishes. In these cases we want the plan to signal failure. Loosely speaking, a motion strategy which achieves the goal when it is recognizably reachable and signals failure when it is not is called an *error detection and recovery (EDR) strategy*. Such strategies are more general than guaranteed strategies, in that they allow plans to fail.

Example 1.2. Before we attack the problem of constructing guaranteed strategies and EDR strategies (both in the presence of model error), let us look at a second example. Figure 5 illustrates the peg-in-hole (or more precisely, point-in-hole) problem with model error. Here, there are five, interacting types of model error. Our framework will also cover this case. Although in these examples model error has been represented by a kind of "tolerancing", the framework can represent arbitrary model error. For example, we could represent CAD surfaces with real coefficients, and allow the coefficients to vary. Discrete and discontinuous model error may also be represented. Finally, note that we permit gross topological changes in the environment—for example, the goal can vanish.

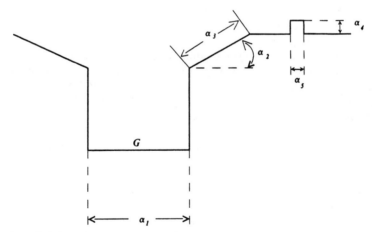

Fig. 5. A peg-in-hole environment with model error. The width of the hole (α_1), angle of chamfer (α_2), length of chamfer (α_3), and height and width of bump (α_4 and α_5) are the model parameters. The hole is allowed to close up.

1.3. Review of previous work

For previous work on configuration space, see [1, 2, 7, 9, 10, 19–22, 29]. For previous work on motion planning with uncertainty, see [4–6, 13, 14, 21, 32]. We will exploit the LMT notion of *preimages* [13, 14, 21] to construct guaranteed strategies. There is little previous work on planning with model uncertainty. However, see [3, 6, 28, 30]. There has been almost no formal analysis of the EDR problem. In [4, 16–18, 26, 31, 33, 34] the problem is considered, and the classical planning literature [8] is also relevant. This paper is an expansion of [11], based on [12].

1.4. Representing model error

To represent model error, we will choose a parameterization of the possible variation in the environment. The degrees of freedom of this parameterization are considered as additional degrees of freedom in the system. For example, in Fig. 4, we have the x- and y-degrees of freedom of the configuration space. In addition, we have the model error parameter α. A coordinate in this space has the form (x, y, α). The space itself is the Cartesian product $\mathbb{R}^2 \times [-d_0, d_0]$. Each α-*slice* of the space for a particular α is a configuration space with the obstacles A and B instantiated at distance α apart. Figure 4 is such a slice.

More generally, suppose we have a configuration space C for the degrees of freedom of the moving object. Let J be an arbitrary index set which parameterizes the model error. (Above, J was $[-d_0, d_0]$.) Then the *generalized configuration space* with model error is $C \times J$. One way to think of this construction is to imagine a collection of possible "universes", $\{C_\alpha\}$ for α in J. Each C_α is a configuration space, containing configuration space obstacles. The ambient space for each C_α is some canonical C. $C \times J$ is simply the natural product representing the ambient space of their disjoint union. There is no constraint that J be finite or even countable. In Fig. 5, C is again the Cartesian plane, and J is a five-dimensional product space. One of the J-dimensions is circular, to parameterize the angular variation represented by α_2.

In Fig. 6 we show the generalized configuration space for Example 1.1. Note that the goal in generalized configuration space becomes a two-dimensional surface, and the obstacles are three-dimensional polyhedra.

Given a configuration space corresponding to a physical situation, it is well known how to represent motions, forces, velocities, and so forth in it (e.g., see [2]). The representations for classical mechanics exploit the geometry of differentiable manifolds. We must develop a similar representation to plan motions, forces, and velocities in generalized configuration space. Henceforth, we will denote the generalized configuration space $C \times J$ by $\mathcal{G}$. We develop the following "axioms" for "physics" in $\mathcal{G}$.

(1) At execution time, the robot finds itself in a particular slice of $\mathcal{G}$ (although it may not know which). Thus we say there is only one "real"

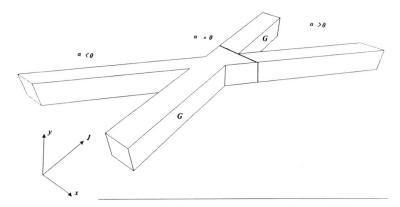

Fig. 6. The generalized configuration space obstacles for Example 1.1. The generalized configuration space is three-dimensional, having x- and y-degrees of motion freedom, and an α-degree of model error freedom. Legal motions are parallel to the x-y plane, and orthogonal to the J-axis.

universe, α_0 in J.[1] This α_0 is fixed. However, α_0 is not known a priori. Thus all motions are confined to a particular (unknown) α_0-slice, such as Fig. 4. This is because motions cannot move between universes. In Fig. 6, any legal motion in $\mathcal{G}$ is everywhere orthogonal to the J-axis and parallel to the x-y plane.

(2) Suppose in any α-slice the position-sensing uncertainty ball about a given sensed position is some set B_{ep}. The set R in Fig. 4 is such a ball. We cannot sense across J: position-sensing uncertainty is infinite in the J-dimensions.[2] Thus the position-sensing uncertainty in $\mathcal{G}$ is the cylinder $B_{ep} \times J$. In Figs. 4 and 6, this simply says that x and y are known to some precision, while α is unknown. The initial position in Fig. 4 is given by $R \times [-d_0, d_0]$. This cylinder is a three-dimensional solid, orthogonal to the x-y plane and parallel to the J-axis in Fig. 6.

(3) Suppose in the configuration space C, the velocity control uncertainty about a given nominal commanded velocity is a cone of velocities B_{ec}. Such a cone is shown in Fig. 4. This cone lies in the *phase space* for C, denoted TC. (Phase space is simply position-space $\times$ velocity-space. A point in phase space has the form (x, v), and denotes an instantaneous velocity of v at configuration x.) Phase space represents all possible velocities at all points in C. The phase space for $\mathcal{G}$ is obtained by indexing TC by J to obtain $TC \times J$. All velocities in generalized configuration space lie in $TC \times J$. For Example 1.1, $TC \times J$ is $\mathbb{R}^4 \times [-d_0, d_0]$. The generalized velocity uncertainty cones are two-dimensional, parallel to the x-y plane, and orthogonal to the J-axis.

(4) Generalized damper dynamics extend straightforwardly to $\mathcal{G}$, so motions

---

[1] α_0 is a multi-dimensional point of J.
[2] One generalization of the framework would permit and plan for sensing in J. In this case one would employ a bounded sensing uncertainty ball in the J-dimensions.

satisfy $f = B(v - v_0)$ where f, v, and v_0 lie in $TC \times J$. Thus friction cones from configuration space (see [13, 14]) naturally embed like generalized velocity cones in $TC \times J$.

These axioms give an intuitive description of the physics of $\mathscr{G}$. A formal axiomatization is given in [12]. We have captured the physics of $\mathscr{G}$ using a set of *generalized uncertainties*, friction, and control characteristics (1)–(4). These axioms completely characterize the behavior of motions in $\mathscr{G}$.

1.5. Representing pushing operations in generalized configuration space

By relaxing axiom (1), above, we can consider a generalization of the model error framework, in which pushing motions are permitted, as well as compliant and gross motions. We relax the assumption that motion between universes is impossible, and permit certain motions across J. Consider Example 1.1. Observe that a displacement in J corresponds to a displacement in the position of the block B. Thus a motion in J should correspond to a motion of B. Suppose the robot can change the position of B by pushing on it, that is, by exerting a force on the surface of B. The key point is that pushing operations may be modeled by observing that commanded forces to the robot may result in changes in the environment. That is, a commanded force to the robot can result in motion in C (sliding) as well as motion in J (pushing the block). Let us develop this notion further.

Our previous discussion assumed that motion across J was impossible. That is, all motion is confined to one α-slice of generalized configuration space. In Example 1.1, this is equivalent to the axiom that B does not move or deform under an applied force. Such an axiom makes sense for applications where B is indeed immovable, for example, if A and B are machined tabs of a connected metal part. However, suppose that B is a block that can slide on the table. See Fig. 7. Then an applied force on the surface of the block can cause the block to slide. This corresponds to motion in J. In general, the effect of an applied force will be a motion which slides or sticks on the surface of B, and which causes B to slide or stick on the table. This corresponds to a coupled motion in both C and J. When the motion maintains contact, it is tangent to a surface S in generalized configuration space.

Our goal is to generalize the description of the physics of $\mathscr{G}$ to permit a rigorous account of such motions. This model can then be employed by an automated planner. *Such a planner could construct motion strategies whose primitives are gross motions, compliant motions, and pushing motions.*[3]

The description of the physics should embrace the following observations: The phase space for C corresponds to forces exerted at the center of mass of

---

[3] Our model of pushing is less general than [24], since it requires knowledge of the center of friction. See [12] for details.

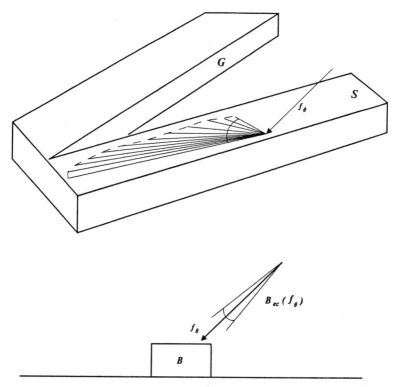

Fig. 7. A force f_θ applied to the top surface of B can cause sliding (or sticking) on the top of B, coupled with motion of B on the table. This corresponds to a pushing motion in $\mathcal{G}$. By giving the right geometric structure to the surface S, we can predict the resulting cone of motions in $\mathcal{G}$, given a commanded velocity f_θ subject to control uncertainty. A planner could generate a motion along S in order to plan pushing operations.

the robot. The phase space for J corresponds to forces acting at the center of mass of B. When pushing is allowed, the phase space for generalized configuration space is not $TC \times J$ but $TC \times TJ$. In the pushing application, all forces are exerted in C, but may be "transferred" to J via the contact. In other words, the applied forces we consider will have zero component along J. However, they may result in a motion in J, via the transferred pushing force.

In free space, or on surfaces generated by immovable objects, all differential motions lie within one α-slice. This is because objects can only be pushed when the robot is in contact with them.

Along surfaces generated by objects that can be pushed, the differential motions are tangent to the surface in $\mathcal{G}$, and may move along J as well as C. See Fig. 7.

A motion in free space corresponds to a gross motion. A motion on a surface staying within one α-slice corresponds to a compliant motion. A motion on a surface which moves across J corresponds to a pushing motion.

Configuration space surfaces share many properties with real space surfaces. When pushed on, they push back. In particular, they have a normal. In the absence of friction, they can exert reaction forces only along this normal direction. We must define what the normals to generalized configuration space surfaces are. For example, see Fig. 8. The normal is transverse to J, so that even when the applied force lies exclusively in C, the surface exerts a reaction force with a J-component. Thus the resultant force can cause a motion across J, tangent to S. In Fig. 8 this implies that pushing on the side of B results in a transferred force to J, causing B to slide. In generalized configuration space, this is simply viewed as applying a force to a surface S, which exerts a reaction force across J. Since the resultant force is across J, the motion in $\mathscr{G}$ will be in that direction.

The physics is complicated by the introduction of friction. Given an applied force, one of four qualitative outcomes are possible.

(1) The motion may slide in C and J. This corresponds to pushing while sliding[4] at the point of contact.

(2) The motion may stick in C and slide in J. This corresponds to pushing with no relative motion.

(3) The motion may slide in C and stick in J. This corresponds to compliant motion in one α-slice.

(4) The motion may break contact. This corresponds to the initiation of gross motion in one α-slice.

In order to generalize physical reasoning to generalized configuration space, we must provide a generalization of the Erdmannian configuration space friction cone [13, 14] for generalized configuration space. The friction cone represents the range of reaction forces that a surface in generalized configuration space can exert. A picture of this generalized cone is shown in Fig. 8. Using the friction cone, it is possible to specify a geometrical computation of reaction forces. Such an algorithm is necessary for a planner to predict the possible resulting motions from an uncertainty cone of commanded applied forces. For example, see Fig. 7.

By characterizing the physics of pushing and sliding via geometrical constraints in generalized configuration space, it appears that a unified planning framework for gross, compliant, and pushing motions emerges. However, certain aspects of the physics require elaboration and simplification before a practical planner for pushing operations can be implemented; see [12] for details.

---

[4] Or rotating.

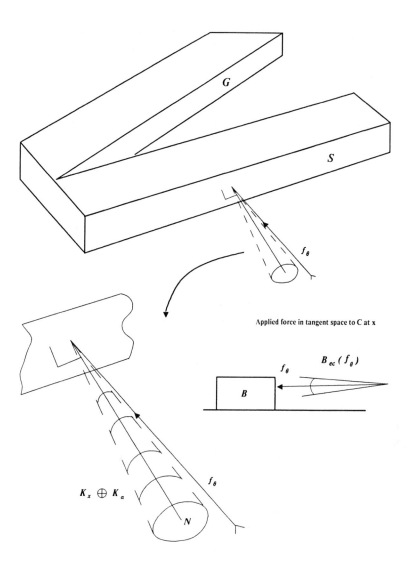

Fig. 8. Pushing on the side of B can cause B to slide, even in the absence of friction. This behavior can be modeled by giving the surface S a normal which points across J. The surface can exert reaction forces along this normal. Thus, applying a force in C results in a reaction force with a J-component. The resulting motion moves across J, tangent to S. That is, it pushes the block. Friction can also be introduced on S. A picture of the friction cone developed in [12] is shown. It represents the range of reaction forces the surface S can exert.

1.6. Guaranteed plans in generalized configuration space

A motion strategy [21] is a commanded velocity (such as v_θ^* in Fig. 4) together with a *termination predicate* which monitors the sensors and decides when the motion has achieved the goal. Given a goal G in configuration space, we can form its *preimage* [21]. The preimage of G is the region in configuration space from which all motions are guaranteed to move into G in such a way that the entry is recognizable. That is, the preimage is the set of all positions from which all possible trajectories consistent with the control uncertainty are guaranteed to reach G recognizably. For example, see Fig. 9. The entry is recognized by monitoring the position and velocity sensors until the goal is attained. Figure 9 is a *directional* preimage: only one commanded velocity v_θ^* is considered. Here all preimage points reach the goal recognizably under this particular v_θ^*. The *nondirectional* preimage is the union of all directional preimages.

We envision a backchaining planner which recursively computes preimages of a goal region. Successive subgoals are attained by motion strategies. Each motion terminates when all sensor interpretations indicate that the robot must be within the subgoal. In [13, 14, 21] a formal framework (LMT) for computing preimages is provided where there is sensing and control uncertainty, but no model error. In particular, Erdmann [13, 14] shows how *backprojections* may be used to approximate preimages. The backprojection of a goal G (with respect to a commanded velocity v_θ^*) consists of those positions guaranteed to

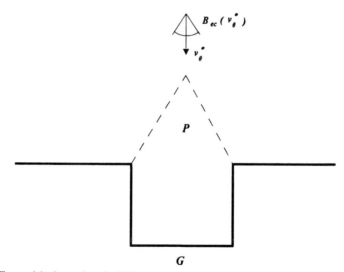

Fig. 9. The goal is the region G. Sliding occurs on vertical surfaces, and sticking on horizontal ones. The commanded velocity is v_θ^*, and the control uncertainty is $B_{ec}(v_\theta^*)$. The *preimage* of the G with respect to θ is the region P.

enter the goal (under v_θ^*). Recognizability of the entry plays no role. Figure 10 illustrates the difference between backprojections and preimages. Here the radius of position-sensing uncertainty is greater than twice the diameter of the hole. Sliding occurs on all surfaces. The backprojection $B_\theta(G)$ strictly contains the preimage $P_\theta(G)$: while all points in the backprojection are guaranteed to reach G, the sensing inaccuracy is so large that the termination predicate cannot tell whether the goal or the left horizontal surface has been reached. Only from the preimage can entry into G be recognized.

Preimages provide a way to construct guaranteed plans for the situation with no model error. Can preimages and backprojections be generalized to situations with model error? The answer is yes. Consider Figs. 4 and 6. The goal in generalized configuration space is the surface G (which has two components). The start region is the cylinder $R \times J$ (where J is $[-d_0, d_0]$). The generalized control and sensing uncertainties in $\mathcal{G}$ are given by the physics axioms above. These uncertainties completely determine how motions in generalized configuration space must behave. We form the backprojection of G under these uncertainties. The backprojection has two components, shown in Figs. 11 and 12. It is a three-dimensional region in $\mathcal{G}$ of triples (x, y, α) that are guaranteed to reach G under the control uncertainty shown in Fig. 4. Equivalently, we can view it as all points in $\mathcal{G}$ guaranteed to reach G under the generalized

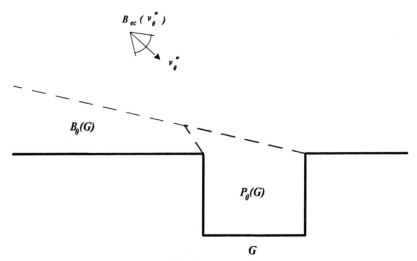

Fig. 10. Here, the radius of the position-sensing uncertainty ball is twice the width of the hole. Sliding occurs on all surfaces under the control velocities shown. The preimage of the goal under commanded velocity v_θ^* is $P_\theta(G)$. The backprojection $B_\theta(G)$ strictly contains this preimage: while all points in the backprojection are guaranteed to reach G, the sensing inaccuracy is so large that the termination predicate cannot tell whether the goal or the left horizontal surface has been reached. Only from the preimage can entry into G be recognized.

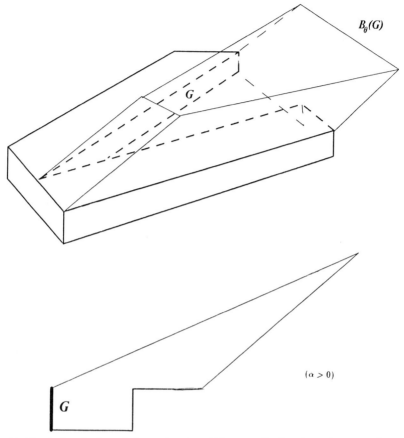

Fig. 11. The backprojection of the goal surface G in generalized configuration space for commanded velocity v_θ^* is denoted $B_\theta(G)$. Here is the backprojection for α positive. A typical α-slice of the backprojection is shown below.

uncertainties that specify $\mathcal{G}$'s physics. Note that backprojections do not "converge to a point" along the J-axis (compare Fig. 9). This is because there is perfect control along J, and the commanded velocity along J is zero. This is why in this particular $\mathcal{G}$ there are two disjoint backprojection regions, one from each component of G. Furthermore, recursively computed backprojections can *never* cover any slice of $\mathcal{G}$ in which the goal vanishes.

The trick here was to view the motion-planning problem with n degrees of motion freedom and k degrees of model error freedom as a planning problem in an $(n + k)$-dimensional generalized configuration space, endowed with the

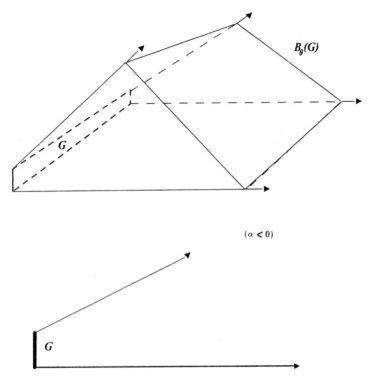

$(\alpha < 0)$

Fig. 12. The backprojection of the other component of G. A typical α-slice for α negative is shown below. The backprojection in $\mathscr{G}$ of the entire goal surface is the union of the backprojections shown in Figs. 11 and 12.

special physics described above. The physics is characterized precisely by axioms defining certain special sensing and control uncertainties in $\mathscr{G}$. The definitions and results for preimages and backprojections [13, 14, 21] in configuration space generalize mutatis mutandis to $\mathscr{G}$ endowed with this physics; this is proved in [12]. Thus our framework reduces the problem of constructing guaranteed motion strategies with model error to computing preimages in a somewhat more complicated, and higher-dimensional configuration space.

In this example, because the position of B varies linearly with α, the surfaces in $\mathscr{G}$ are planar and the generalized configuration space obstacles are polyhedral. This means that three-dimensional backprojections of G in $\mathscr{G}$ may be computed in polynomial time [12, 35]. While they have been computed by hand here, note that this reduction gives us an efficient planning algorithm for an important special case.

2. Error Detection and Recovery

If we were exclusively interested in constructing guaranteed motion strategies in the presence of model error, we would be done: having reduced the problem to computing preimages in $\mathcal{G}$, we could now turn to the important and difficult problems of computing and constructing $\mathcal{G}$, and further extend the work of [13, 14, 21] on computing preimages in general configuration spaces (see [12]).

However, guaranteed strategies do not always exist. In Example 1.1, there is no guaranteed strategy for achieving the goal, since the goal may vanish for some values of α. Because tolerances may cause gross topological changes in configuration space, this problem is particularly prevalent in the presence of model error. In Example 1.2, the goal may also vanish (the hole may close up) for certain regions in J. More generally, there may be values of α for which the goal may still exist, but it may not be reachable. For example, in Fig. 5, if we have $\alpha_2 = 180°$ and α_1 positive, then G is non-empty, but also not reachable. Finally, and most generally, there may be values of α for which the goal is reachable but not *recognizably* reachable. In this case we still cannot guarantee plans, since a planner cannot know when they have succeeded.

These problems may occur even in the absence of model error. However, without model error a guaranteed plan is often obtainable by backchaining and adding more steps to the plan. In the presence of model error this technique frequently fails: in Example 1.1, no chain of recursively computed preimages can ever cover the start region $R \times J$. The failure is due to the peculiar sensing and control characteristics (1)–(4) in generalized configuration space.

In response, we will develop error detection and recovery (EDR) strategies.

– An EDR strategy should attain the goal when it is recognizably reachable, and signal failure when it is not.
– It should also permit serendipitous achievement of the goal.
– Furthermore, no motion guaranteed to terminate recognizably in the goal should ever be prematurely terminated as a failure.
– Finally, no motion should be terminated as a failure while there is any chance that it might serendipitously achieve the goal due to fortuitous sensing and control events.

These are called the "EDR axioms", they will be our guiding principles. Can we construct such strategies? The answer is, basically, yes. Let us construct one for a variant of Example 1.1. We first restrict our attention to the environments where α lies in the interval $[d_1, d_0]$ where d_1 is small and negative.

Call the start region $U = R \times J$. The strategy of Example 1.1 commands velocity v_0^* (Fig. 4). It tries to terminate the motion in G by detecting sticking. Call this strategy θ. We will use θ as a starting point, and try to build an EDR strategy from it. Now, U is divided into a "good" region, from which θ is guaranteed, and a "bad" region, from which it is not. The goal vanishes for the bad region. We wish to *extend* θ to an EDR strategy from all of U.

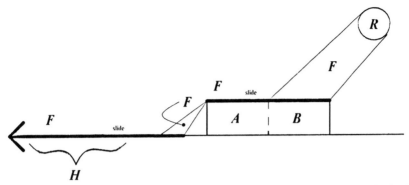

Fig. 13. A typical α-slice of the forward projection of the "bad" region. The forward projection is the region F. α is negative and almost zero. H is an EDR region in the forward projection.

Let us investigate the result of executing θ from the "bad" region. We employ the forward projection [14]. The *forward projection* of a set V under θ is all configurations[5] which are possibly reachable from V under v_0^* (subject to control uncertainty). It is denoted $F_\theta(V)$. Forward projections only address reachability: the termination predicate is ignored and only the commanded velocity v_0^* is needed to specify the forward projection.

Figure 13 shows a typical α-slice of the forward projection of the "bad" region. We can now define an EDR strategy as follows. Consider the region H in Fig. 13. The termination predicate can distinguish between G and H based on position sensing, velocity sensing, or elapsed time.[6] (Consider H as a two-dimensional region in $\mathcal{G}$; just a slice of it is shown in Fig. 13.) Thus the motion is guaranteed to terminate recognizably in G iff the motion originated in the "good" region of U. Otherwise the motion terminates recognizably in H. In the first case, the termination predicate signals success, in the latter, failure.

Clearly this EDR strategy satisfies the "EDR axioms" above. The problem of constructing EDR strategies may be attacked as follows: We take a strategy θ as data. Next, an *EDR region* H is found. H is introduced as a "bad goal", and a strategy is found which achieves either G or H (subject to the EDR axioms). Finally, we must not only recognize that G or H has been attained, but also know *which* goal has been reached.

Now, think of θ as indexing the "angular direction" of the commanded velocity. By quantifying over all θ, we can in principle define "nondirectional" EDR strategies. This problem is similar to constructing nondirectional preimages. For now, we restrict our attention to one-step plans. Later, we consider n-step plans.

---

[5] Actually, forward projections are in phase space, so this is the position component of the forward projection.

[6] Given the sensing uncertainties of Example 1.1.

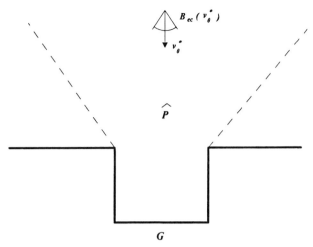

Fig. 14. The *weak* preimage of the goal G under v_θ^*. Compare Fig. 9.

2.1. Generalizing the construction

We now present an informal account of how the construction of EDR regions and strategies may be generalized. Don't be alarmed if some of our examples are without model error. Since we've reduced the planning problem with model error to planning in a (different) configuration space, it suffices to consider general configuration spaces in this discussion.

So far the preimages we have considered are *strong* preimages, in that *all* possible motions are guaranteed to terminate recognizably in the goal. The *weak* preimage [21] (with respect to a commanded velocity) is the set of points which could *possibly* enter the goal recognizably, given fortuitous sensing and control events. See Fig. 14.

Now consider Fig. 15. Sliding occurs on the vertical edges, and sticking on the horizontal ones. The (strong) preimage of the goal G is denoted P. A motion strategy θ with commanded velocity v_θ^* is guaranteed for the region R', but the starting region is the larger[7] R. The weak preimage of G is denoted $\hat{P}$. The forward projection of the "bad" region $R - R'$ is also shown: it is $F_\theta(R - R')$. Using θ as data, how can we construct an EDR strategy that is applicable for all of R? Let us first try taking the EDR region $H = H_0$, where H_0 is the set difference of the forward projection of the "bad" region and the weak preimage:

$$H_0 = F_\theta(R - R') - \hat{P}. \tag{1}$$

[7] Note that in general, R and R' need not be cylinders, but can be arbitrary subsets of $\mathcal{G}$.

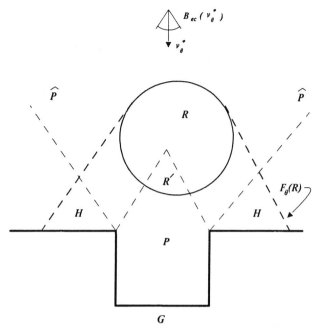

Fig. 15. R is the start region. P is the strong preimage of G. R' is the region in R from which the strategy is guaranteed to reach G recognizably. $\tilde{P}$ is the weak preimage. H is the forward projection of R outside of weak preimage. It is the EDR region.

If we can distinguish between G and H, then H is a good EDR region, and we have constructed an EDR strategy.

Taking $H = H_0$ as above is not sufficiently general. Consider Fig. 16. It is possible for a motion from R to stick forever in the region H_s, which is within the weak preimage. However, a motion through H_s is not guaranteed to stick in H_s: it may eventually slide into the goal. We want sliding motions to pass through H_s unmolested, while the termination predicate should halt sticking motions in H_s.

The EDR region H region should include H_0. But it should also include H_s, when sticking occurs. In other words, H should include H_0 for *all* velocities, but should only include H_s for *sticking* velocities (that is, zero velocities). To handle this idea we introduce simple velocity goals, as well as position goals. The position and velocity goals are regions in phase space.

A goal in phase space is a region in position-space $\times$ velocity-space. A phase space goal is attained when the actual position and velocity can be guaranteed to lie in the region. Let us construct the phase space EDR region $\tilde{H}$. If x is in H_0, then for any velocity v over x, (x, v) must be in $\tilde{H}$. Let $\pi^{-1}(H_0)$ denote all such (x, v) in phase space.

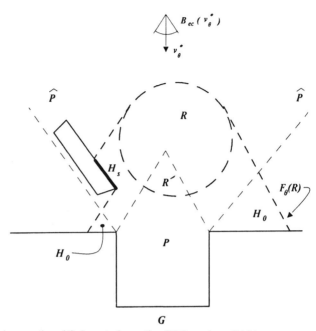

G

Fig. 16. H_0 in equation (1) is not the entire EDR region. Sticking may occur within the weak preimage in H_s. The EDR region must include H_0 for all possible velocities, and H_s for "sticking velocities".

Now, H_s is the set of all points x in the weak but not strong preimage, such that sticking can occur at x.[8] We wish to distinguish the sticking velocities in H_s. Under generalized damper dynamics, these are essentially the zero velocities. Let $Z(H_s)$ denote the zero velocities over H_s, that is, the set of pairs $(x, 0)$ for x in H_s. This set is in phase space. Then we see that $Z(H_s)$ is also in the phase space EDR region $\tilde{H}$. Thus $\tilde{H}$ is the union of the sticking velocities over H_s, and all velocities over the forward projection outside the weak preimage:

$$\tilde{H} = Z(H_s) \cup \pi^{-1}(H_0) . \tag{2}$$

To use $\tilde{H}$ as an EDR region, we must now ensure that $\tilde{H}$ and the cylinder over G are distinguishable goals. In [12], we show that if the strong preimage is known, the definition of (phase space) EDR regions is *constructive up to reachability*. By this we mean that when backprojections, set intersections and differences, and friction cones can be computed, then so can $\tilde{H}$. With $\tilde{H}$ in hand, we add the recognizability constraint to obtain an EDR strategy.

---

[8] Erdmann [14] shows how to compute H_s using configuration space friction cones.

The structure of the "weak but not strong preimage", $\hat{P} - P$ suggests a number of implementation issues. Consider Figs. 16 and 17 once more. Suppose we have a trajectory originating in R, subject to the control uncertainty shown. We do not wish to terminate the motion while it remains in the weak preimage, since fortuitous sensing and control events could still force recognizable termination in G. However, we can terminate the motion as soon as we recognize egress from the weak preimage. This is why the forward projection outside the weak preimage is contained in the EDR region.

As we have seen, however, it is possible for a trajectory to remain within the weak but not strong preimage forever. For example, it can stick in H_s forever. To handle this case, we introduced phase space EDR goals.

There are other conditions under which a trajectory could stay in $\hat{P} - P$ forever: (a) if the environment is infinite, or $\hat{P} - P$ is unbounded; (b) the trajectory "loops" in $\hat{P} - P$ forever. (a) and (b) are qualitatively different from the case of sticking forever in H_s, because they require motion for infinitely long. In practice this may be handled by terminating the motion in $\hat{P} - P$ after a certain elapsed time. This is called "constructing termination predicates which time-out". In fact, this "solution" works for sticking in H_s also.

An alternative is to extend our earlier zero velocity analysis to all of $\hat{P} - P$. That is, we terminate the motion in the weak but not strong preimage when the actual velocity is (close to) zero. It seems that time-out termination predicates and/or velocity thresholding must be used to solve the looping problem. The issue is subtle and is addressed further in Part II.

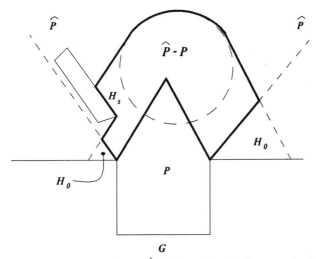

Fig. 17. The weak but not strong preimage $\hat{P} - P$, from Fig. 16. Can a motion from R remain in $\hat{P} - P$ forever? One way this may happen is by sticking in H_s. In general, however, there are other ways.

3. Generalization to n-Step EDR Strategies

3.1. An example

Example 3.1. So far we have only considered one-step EDR strategies. We now generalize the construction to n-step strategies. Consider Fig. 18. Here there are two possible universes, both in the plane, so J is the two-element discrete set, $\{1, 2\}$. The start region is the union of R_1 in universe 1, and R_2 in universe 2. The goal exists in universe 1 but not in universe 2. There is no one-step EDR strategy which, from the start region, can guarantee to achieve G or recognize that we are in universe 2. In particular, there is no one-step EDR strategy which can be derived from the motion v_θ^*.

There is an 8-step plan in universe 1 which recognizably achieves G from start region R_1. It is obtained by backchaining preimages in universe 1. The plan moves from R_1 to the region S_1 under v_θ^*. Then it slides along the top surface to vertex f, and then to the successive vertex subgoals e through a, and

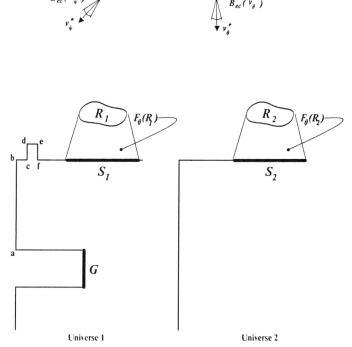

Fig. 18. There are two possible universes; the goal G exists in the first but not the second. The start region is $R_1 \cup R_2$. Motion θ is guaranteed to move from R_1 into S_1. Motion ψ is guaranteed to move from S_1 into f. There is an 8-step plan achieving G from R_1. The forward projections of R_1 and R_2 are indistinguishable. There exists no one-step EDR strategy from the motion θ.

finally into G. We can construct a 2-step EDR strategy, from this plan. First, we execute motion θ from the union of R_1 and R_2. This achieves a motion into S_1 in universe 1, or into S_2 in universe 2. The termination predicate cannot distinguish which has been attained. Suppose the second motion in the 8-step plan is v_ψ^* (see Fig. 18), and is guaranteed to achieve the vertex subgoal f from start region S_1. We'll try to construct an EDR strategy out of this second motion. Take as data: the subgoal f, the start region $S_1 \cup S_2$, the horizontal motion ψ, and the preimage of f under ψ. The EDR region for these data is the forward projection of S_2 under ψ (see Fig. 19). Presumably this EDR region is distinguishable from f, and so we have constructed an EDR strategy at the second step. After executing the second step, we either terminate the plan as a failure, or proceed to vertex e, and eventually to the goal.

There is a subtle issue of where to terminate the motion within the forward projection of $R_1 \cup R_2$; this "where" is $S_1 \cup S_2$ here, and is called the *push-forward*. Since they address termination, push-forwards are to forward projections as preimages are to backprojections. In Part II, they are defined more formally and the n-step EDR construction is given in detail.

4. What Is "Recovery"?

So far, we have taken a "radical" view with respect to "recovery". We assume that in planning for error and recovery, one essentially specifies the maximum

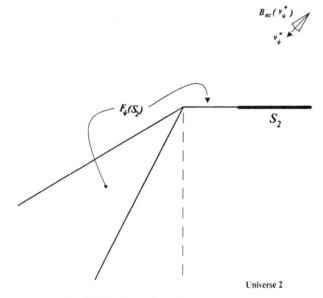

Fig. 19. The forward projection under ψ of S_2.

length plan one is willing to contemplate. The EDR planner considers the class of n-step strategies and tries to formulate a plan which will achieve the goal given the sensing, control, and model uncertainty.[9] Perhaps such a plan can be guaranteed. If not, then termination in an EDR region would signal failure. This means that there was no guaranteed n-step plan. The recovery action might then be "give up", or "try again, using up the remaining number of steps in the plan", if we are serious in refusing to contemplate plans longer than n steps. As a corollary, the only "error", then, is "being in the wrong universe", or more accurately, "being in the wrong start region" This viewpoint is a consequence of trying to address EDR and completeness simultaneously. More concretely, suppose we consider some sensory-control-geometric event to be an "error", make a plan to detect it, and a recovery plan in case it is detected. If the plan can be guaranteed, then it can be found using [21]. In this case the "error" is no longer an error, but simply an "event" which triggers a conditional branch of the plan. If the plan cannot be guaranteed, then we have proposed the EDR framework, which allows us to try it anyway. If it fails, however, the only obvious recovery action entails the recursive construction of EDR subplans (see below). It is not clear what other kinds of recovery could be attempted without exploiting additional knowledge: the recovery branches have already been tried. As usual the issue is subtle, and deserves further attention.

We give one example which highlights the complexity of the recovery problem. Suppose that we consider the class of 4-step plans. Given a 4-step plan as data, suppose we construct a multi-step EDR strategy which pushes forward on the first motion, and executes an EDR strategy on the second. After executing the second motion, we have recognizably either achieved the second subgoal, or some EDR region H. If H is achieved, what is the correct recovery action? We could do nothing, and signal failure. Alternatively, we could try to construct a plan (of length less than or equal to two) to achieve the goal. Now, if such a plan exists and can be guaranteed, then the entire EDR analysis was unnecessary, since the LMT framework [21] can (formally) find such plans. However, there might exist a 2-step EDR strategy to (try to) achieve the goal from H. While such a plan could not be guaranteed, it might be worth a try. This suggests that the failure recovery action in an n-step EDR strategy should be to recursively construct *another* EDR strategy to achieve the goal from the EDR region, using no more than the remaining number of steps. If n is 1, the planner should simply signal failure and stop.

5. Implementation and Experiments

In this section we describe experiments with an implemented EDR planner, called LIMITED. We approximate preimages using backprojections (see [13]).

---

[9] Of course, one could in principle search for strategies of increasing length by quantifying over n. At any one time, however, one would reduce to the case described here and iterate.

LIMITED can compute slice approximations to EDR regions for one-step plans where the generalized configuration space is three-dimensional. The particular generalized configuration space we consider is that of the gear example described in Section 1.1. (See Fig. 2.) In this case, C is the Cartesian plane, representing translations of gear A, and J is the 2D rotation group (i.e., a circle), representing orientations of the gear B. The implementation uses slices: by a *slice* we mean an α-slice of generalized configuration space for some α in J. α is the model error parameter, and represents the orientation of B. We have implemented an algorithm which computes slices of the three-dimensional EDR regions for both variants of the gear example. In the first, B cannot rotate, so no motion across J is possible. In the second, B can rotate when pushed, so motion across J is possible. In the latter case, backprojections and forward projections must be computed across J, since it is possible to achieve the goal by moving across J (rotating B by pushing and possibly sliding on its surface).

Given a 2D slice of generalized configuration space, LIMITED employs a plane-sweep algorithm for computing unions, intersections, and projections. (By *projections* we mean forward projections, backprojections, and weak backprojections in that slice.) The algorithm uses exact (rational) arithmetic, and computes unions in $O((n + c) \log n)$ time, and projections in $O(n \log n)$ time.[10] The design and implementation of the 2D plane-sweep module is joint work with John Canny; the algorithm is related to [27] (which gives a union algorithm) and [13] (which describes an $O(n \log n)$ backprojection algorithm).

To compute projections in the 3D generalized configuration space, LIMITED propagates projections across slices. For example, given a forward projection in a slice, the algorithm finds all obstacle edges and vertices from which it is possible to exert a positive torque on the obstacle (which is gear B in the figures). See Fig. 28. Thus by pushing on these edges it is possible to move across slices in the $+\alpha$-direction. Each such edge is a slice of an algebraic ruled surface in generalized configuration space. The vertices are slices of algebraic helicoids. Sliding along the surface of B while causing B to rotate corresponds to following the surface (or helicoid). The surface is traced into the next α-slice, and taken as a start region from which to forward-project in that slice. For example, see Figs. 29–30. The propagated forward projection must then be unioned with propagated forward projections from other slices, and with the forward projection of any start regions in that slice. See Fig. 33. Weak backprojections are computed analogously.

In order to compute weak backprojections and forward projections, we assume that there can be stiction at the rotation center of B. Thus the ratio of sliding to turning is indeterminate. In general, the computation of strong backprojections under rotation due to pushing will be a second-order problem, since it depends on the derivatives of this ratio. We employ a conservative

---

[10] Where n is the number of vertices in the slice, and c is the number of intersections.

approximation to the strong backprojection (namely, the backprojection in free space alone) to construct the EDR regions. This suffices, since EDR strategies require only the weak backprojection and forward projection (which depend only on the possibility, and not the velocity, of sliding and turning). Thus there is a deep sense in which EDR strategies with model error seem easier to compute than guaranteed strategies, because EDR strategies are "first-order". This jibes with the intuition that weak backprojections should be easier to compute than strong backprojections.

Figures 20–27 show the EDR regions for the gear example when no rotation of B is permitted. Only one slice of $\mathcal{G}$ is shown. In all the figures, the commanded velocity is "towards the center of B", up and to the right.

Next, we allow B to rotate. Figures 31–35 show the EDR regions at four α-slices of the 3D generalized configuration space. In this case motion across J is possible by pushing B, when B rotates. The projections have been propagated across slices and unioned. The results are slices of the 3D EDR regions across J.

The computation of the EDR regions is at the heart of EDR planning. For example, a one-step EDR planner can be implemented as follows. First, we require a module which determines when two regions are distinguishable using sensors and history. This module will be applied to the goal and the EDR regions H to verify the EDR strategy. Such a module could be implemented naively, by "shrinking" the goals and H based on the sensing uncertainties. One can also envision a more complicated algorithm which employs the history

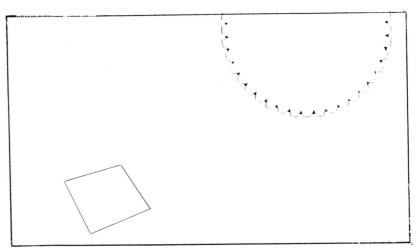

Fig. 20. The configuration space for the gear example (Fig. 2) at one α-slice ($\alpha = 0$) of $\mathcal{G}$. The goal region is the "valleys" of the configuration space obstacle. The start region is the diamond to the lower left. For Figs. 20–27, B is not allowed to rotate, so no motion across J is possible.

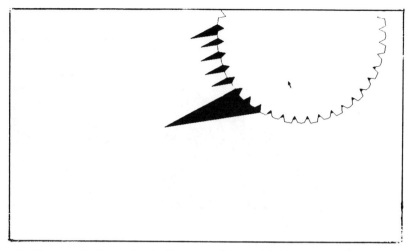

Fig. 21. The strong backprojection in slice $\alpha = 0$ of the goals in Fig. 20, assuming that B cannot rotate. In all these experiments, the coefficient of friction is taken to be 0.25.

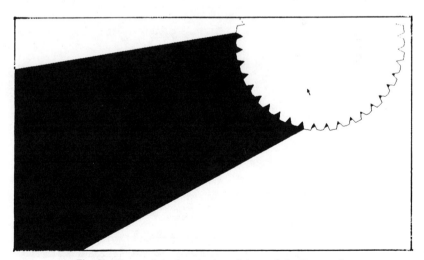

Fig. 22. The weak backprojection of the goals in slice $\alpha = 0$.

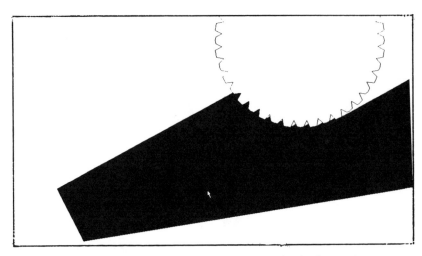

Fig. 23. The forward projection of the start region in slice $\alpha = 0$.

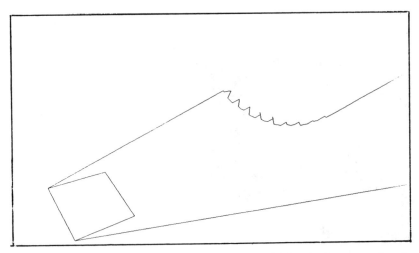

Fig. 24. The forward projection of the start region in slice $\alpha = 0$. Note the degenerate edges due to sliding.

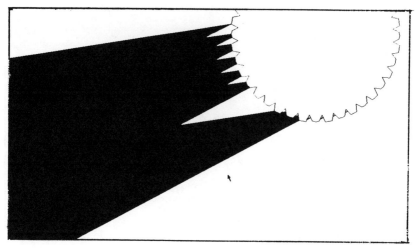

Fig. 25. The weak minus the strong backprojection.

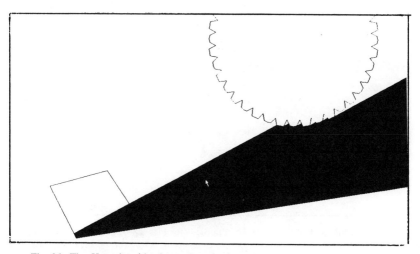

Fig. 26. The H_0 region (the forward projection minus the weak backprojection).

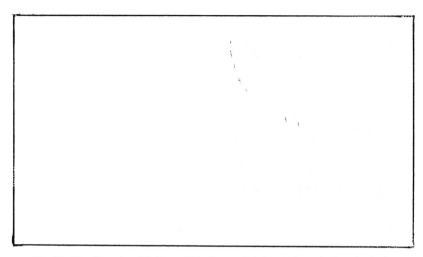

Fig. 27. The H_s region (sticking within the weak but not strong backprojection).

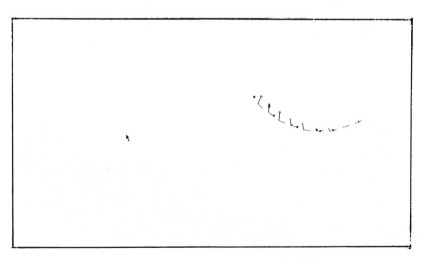

Fig. 28. Now assume that B can rotate when pushed (for Figs. 28–35). Here we show the region within the forward projection (Fig. 23) from which it is possible to exert positive torque on B. This region is called the *differential forward projection across J in the +α-direction*.

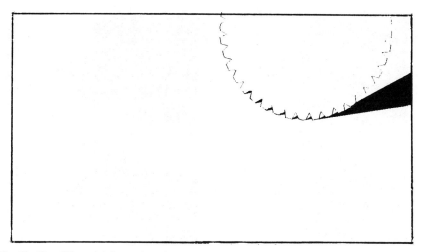

Fig. 29. The differential forward projection is propagated to the next slice in the $+\alpha$-direction. Here we take its forward projection in the next slice.

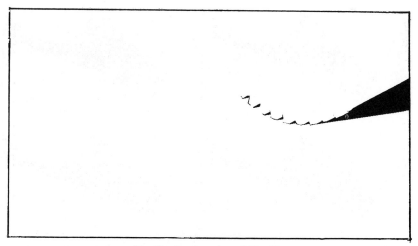

Fig. 30. Another view of Fig. 29.

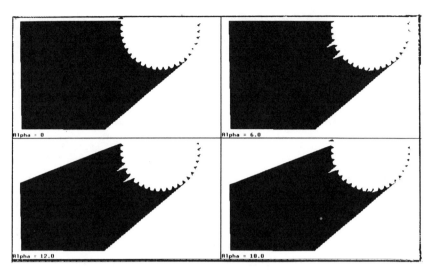

Fig. 31. In the next figures, *B* is permitted to rotate when pushed. The projection regions are computed across *J* by the propagation and union algorithm. We show four slices of generalized configuration space, at $\alpha = 0°$, $6°$, $12°$, and $18°$. The projections take into account possible rotation of *B* under pushing. Here the weak backprojections across slices are shown. The "spikes" represent regions from which jamming of the gears must occur.

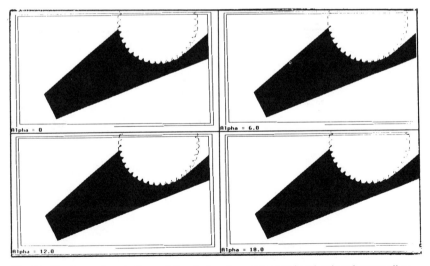

Fig. 32. The forward projections of the start region, propagated and unioned across slices.

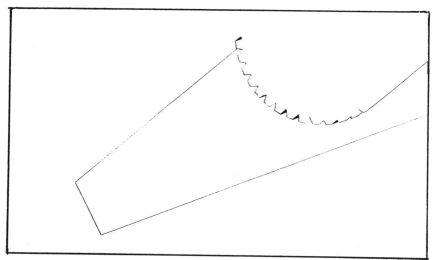

Fig. 33. Detail of the forward projection for $\alpha = 12°$. Note the effect of propagation in the clockwise-most region of the forward projection. This region can only be reached when rotated to from neighboring slice. The shaded region shows the portion of the forward projection which has been propagated by pushing from slice $\alpha = 18°$.

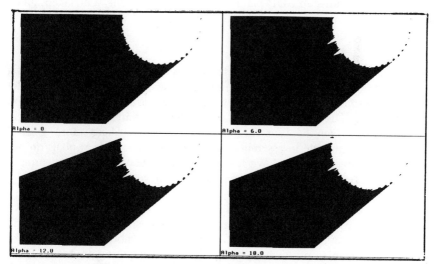

Fig. 34. The weak minus strong backprojections, propagated and unioned across slices.

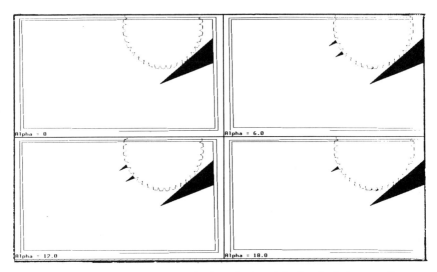

Fig. 35. The H_0 region (forward projection minus weak backprojection) across slices.

available in the forward projection; see [12]. Next, a control structure must be implemented which searches for a commanded velocity yielding an EDR strategy. For example, a generate-and-test technique could compute and verify EDR regions for different commanded velocities. A gross motion planner can be used to generate commanded velocities to try. We have implemented both a one-step and a multi-step EDR planner; see [12]. This is only a first step; much work remains to be done in developing the theory and practice of EDR.

6. Conclusions

This paper offers two contributions to the theory of manipulation. The first is a technique for planning compliant motion strategies in the presence of model error. The second is a precise, geometrical characterization of error detection and recovery (EDR). These led to a constructive definition of EDR plans in the presence of sensing, control, and model error. These more general strategies are applicable in assembly planning where guaranteed plans do not exist, or are difficult to find. We tested the EDR theory by implementing a planner, LIMITED, and running experiments to have LIMITED automatically synthesize EDR strategies.

A number of mathematical tools were developed for the EDR theory. First, we considered compliant motion planning problems with n degrees of motion freedom, and k dimensions of variational geometric model uncertainty. We reduced this planning problem to the problem of computing preimages in an $(n + k)$-dimensional generalized configuration space, which encompasses both the motion and the model degrees of freedom, and encodes the control uncertainty as a kind of nonholonomic constraint. We also showed how pushing motions could be planned using generalized configuration space.

Next, we characterized EDR strategies geometrically via the EDR region H. Determining whether a strategy satisfied the EDR axioms was reduced to a decision problem about forward projections and preimages in generalized configuration space. Making this process formal and algorithmic required a detailed investigation of the geometric and preimage structure of the EDR regions. See the weak EDR theory of [12] for new mathematical tools for studying multi-step strategies.

In [12, 35], we explored the complexity of EDR planning. We derived bounds both for the implemented planner LIMITED, and for theoretical extensions. While in general it is known that compliant motion planning with uncertainty is intractable, we were able to demonstrate a number of special cases where there exist efficient theoretical algorithms. In particular, we show a case where $n = 2$, $k = 1$ and containment in the backprojection could be computed in polynomial time (note for $n = 3$, $k = 0$, this is false[11]). We also investigated the structure of the nondirectional backprojection in the plane. It led to a polynomial-time algorithm for computing one-step (guaranteed) strategies, and a singly exponential algorithm for multi-step strategies.

Our theory represents what is perhaps the first systematic attack on the problem of error detection and recovery based on geometric and physical reasoning. For more on the structure of constraints in $\mathcal{G}$, a formal description of the EDR construction, push-forwards, and n-step strategies, see Part II.

PART II

We now undertake a more detailed analysis of the ideas and results described above.

7. On the Recognizability of EDR Regions

In Section 2.1 it was observed that if the termination predicate can distinguish between the goal G and the EDR region H, then H is a good EDR region and an EDR strategy was in hand. Formally, we write this recognizability constraint as[12]

$$P_{R,\theta}(\{G, H\}) = R . \tag{3}$$

This says that the (strong) preimage of the set of goals $\{G, H\}$, with respect

---

[11] Canny and Reif, Personal communication.

[12] We view $P_{R,\theta}$ as a map. In the informal development we denoted the image of this preimage map by P.

to commanded velocity v_θ^*, is all of R. When we have a *set* of goals, the termination predicate must return *which* goal (G or H) has been achieved. This is different from $P_{R,\theta}(G \cup H)$, which means the termination predicate will halt saying "we've terminated in G or H, but I don't know which." The region R appears on both sides of (3) because the preimage depends on knowing where the motion started. This is a subtle point, see [13, 14, 21]. Thus solving preimage equations like (3) for R is like finding the fixed point of a recursive equation. Here, however, we know R, H, and G, so (3) is a constraint which must be true, rather than an equation to solve. Presumably (3) is easier to check than to solve[13]; see [12–14, 21].

With this understood, we can now characterize P and R' precisely. This requires specifying the start regions:

$$R' = P_{R',\theta}(G),\tag{4}$$

$$P = P_{F_\theta(R),\theta}(G).\tag{5}$$

$\hat{P}$ is analogously defined by adding "hats" to the P in (5).

8. The Structure of Goals in Phase Space

In this section, we examine the structure of phase space goals in some detail.

A goal in phase space is a region in position-space × velocity-space. A phase space goal is attained when the actual position and velocity can be guaranteed to lie in the region. We have actually been using phase space goals all along, since the velocity sensors are used to recognize goals. The introduction of arbitrary phase space goals is problematic, see [14]. Here the goals are sufficiently simple that these dangers are avoided.

We'll begin with the simpler example. In Fig. 15 we propose a partition of the forward projection F of R into three regions:

strong preimage, P,
weak but not strong preimage, $\hat{P} - P$,
forward projection outside the weak preimage, $F - \hat{P}$.

Here, the partition was "good" for the purposes of EDR for all velocities, and we could let H be the forward projection outside the weak preimage. We can extend this partition into phase space as shown in Fig. 36. There is a natural projection π of position-space × velocity-space onto position space which sends a pair (x, velocity-at-x) to its position x. Given a region U in position space, we can lift it to phase space to obtain $\pi^{-1}(U)$, the *cylinder* of all velocities over U. A point in $\pi^{-1}(U)$ is (x, v) where x is in U, and v is any velocity at x.[14]

---

[13] I.e., than to solve for R.
[14] The cylinders may then be intersected with the forward projection of R (in phase space) to obtain more constraints. This may be done by first restricting the domain of π to the forward projection.

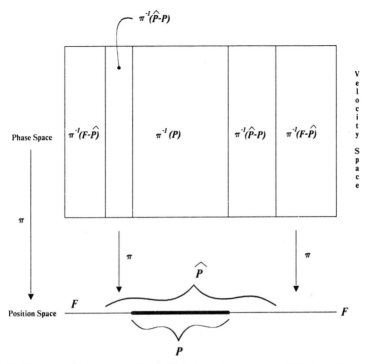

Fig. 36. Position space is one-dimensional. Therefore phase space, which is position-space $\times$ velocity-space, is two-dimensional. The velocity "axis" is shown vertically. π projects a position and velocity to the position. We lift the strong preimage P to a cylinder $\pi^{-1}(P)$. We also obtain the cylinders over the weak but not strong preimage $\hat{P} - P$, and over the forward projection outside the weak preimage, $F - \hat{P}$.

We lift the partition by applying the inverse projection map to obtain a partition of phase space:

> cylinder over strong preimage, $\pi^{-1}(P)$,
> cylinder over weak but not strong preimage, $\pi^{-1}(\hat{P} - P)$,
> cylinder over forward projection outside the weak preimage, $\pi^{-1}(F - \hat{P})$.

See Fig. 36. Now, the cylinder over G and the cylinder over $F - \hat{P}$ are the new goals in phase space. The latter cylinder is the *phase space EDR region* for Fig. 15. Both are simply cylinders: all velocities are legal.[15]

Now we must deal with the tricky sticking region H_s in Fig. 16. We begin by

---

[15] The weak and strong preimage, and the forward projection are drawn Venn diagrammatically in 1D.

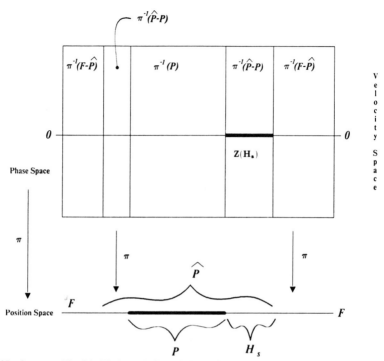

Fig. 37. Compare Fig. 36. We have indicated the sticking region H_s in the weak preimage. The zero velocities $Z(H_s)$ over H_s are in the cylinder over H_s. The EDR region $\tilde{H}$ is the union of $Z(H_s)$ and the shaded cylinders over the forward projection outside the weak preimage $F - \hat{P}$.

lifting the partition to phase space again (see Fig. 37). Next, we "mark off" regions in the lifted partition to form a phase space EDR region, which we denote $\tilde{H}$. The entire cylinder over $F - \hat{P}$ is clearly in $\tilde{H}$, since its projection (under π) is outside the weak preimage. But the cylinder over H_s is not entirely within $\tilde{H}$: only sticking velocities over H_s are.

Formally, H_s is the set of all points x in the weak but not strong preimage, such that sticking can occur at x. We wish to distinguish the sticking velocities in H_s. Under generalized damper dynamics, these are essentially the zero velocities. Let $Z(H_s)$ denote the zero velocities over H_s, that is, the set of pairs $(x, 0)$ for x in H_s. This set is in phase space.[16] Then we see that $Z(H_s)$ is also in the phase space EDR region $\tilde{H}$. Thus $\tilde{H}$ is the union of the sticking velocities over H_s, and all velocities over the forward projection outside the weak preimage:

$$\tilde{H} = Z(H_s) \cup \pi^{-1}(F - \hat{P}) .\tag{6}$$

---

[16] We could also let $Z(H_s)$ be the set of velocities over H_s which are smaller than some threshold.

To use $\tilde{H}$ as an EDR region, we must now ensure that $\tilde{H}$ and the cylinder over G are distinguishable goals. This amounts to allowing goals in phase space—that is, allowing the preimage operator to take simple phase space goals as arguments, and rewriting (3) as

$$P_{R,\theta}(\{\pi^{-1}(G), \tilde{H}\}) = R .$$ (3')

The impact of (3') is discussed in more detail in [12]. One point is worthy of comment. If the strong preimage is known, the definition of (phase space) EDR regions is *constructive up to reachability*. By this we mean that when backprojections, set intersections and differences, and friction cones can be computed, then so can $\tilde{H}$. With $\tilde{H}$ in hand, we add the recognizability constraint (3') to obtain an EDR strategy.

9. More on Weak Preimages

We now examine the structure of the "weak but not strong preimage," $\hat{P} - P$ in more detail. It suggests a number of implementation issues. Consider Figs. 16 and 17 once more. Suppose we have a trajectory originating in R, subject to the control uncertainty shown. We do not wish to terminate the motion while it remains in the weak preimage, since fortuitous sensing and control events could still force recognizable termination in G. However, we can terminate the motion as soon as we recognize egress from the weak preimage. This is why the forward projection outside the weak preimage is contained in the EDR region.

As we have seen, however, it is possible for a trajectory to remain within the weak but not strong preimage forever. For example, it can stick in H_s forever. To handle this case, we introduced phase space EDR goals.

These are other conditions under which a trajectory could stay in $\hat{P} - P$ forever: (a) if the environment is infinite, or $\hat{P} - P$ is unbounded; (b) the trajectory "loops" in $\hat{P} - P$ forever. (a) and (b) are qualitatively different from the case of sticking forever in H_s, because they require motion for infinitely long. In practice this may be handled by terminating the motion in $\hat{P} - P$ after a certain elapsed time. This is called "constructing termination predicates which time-out." In fact, this "solution" works for sticking in H_s also.

An alternative is to extend our earlier zero velocity analysis to all of $\hat{P} - P$. That is, we terminate the motion in the weak but not strong preimage when the actual velocity is (close to) zero. Formally this rewrites (6) as

$$\tilde{H} = Z(\hat{P} - P) \cup \pi^{-1}(F - \hat{P}) .$$ (6')

Both this and our formal handling of phase space goals for H_s (6) are subject to the "Rolle's theorem bug". That is, a trajectory which "reverses direction" will have zero velocity at some point. Hence by (6) and (6') it will be judged to have stuck. This is undesirable. In practice this can be fixed by again requiring the trajectory to stick for some elapsed time. Time-out termination predicates have the following practical justification. We imagine some low-level control mechanism which detects sticking, and after a certain time interval freezes the robot at that configuration and signals termination. Presumably such a mechanism is designed to avoid damage to the robot by detecting excessive torques. It also avoids plans with long delays while the planner waits for the motion to slide again.

The role of time in constructing EDR regions can be formalized by explicitly introducing time into the goal specification. Thus, goals become regions in phase space-time; points in goals have the form (x, v, t), where x is a position, v a velocity, and t a time. Suppose given a goal G in generalized configuration space, we form a phase space-time goal which is the product of $\pi^{-1}(G)$ with a compact time interval. It seems hopeful that the EDR axioms are satisfiable by EDR regions which have the form of a product of (6) with a compact time interval. More study is required.

One also can conceive of alternative models for sticking behavior. H_s is all points in the weak but not strong preimage such that sticking *might* occur there. Note that we cannot guarantee that sticking will occur, since then the point would not be in the weak preimage. We could assume a probabilistic distribution of control velocities in B_{ec}. In this case we could infer that eventually, given an unbounded amount of time, a motion will be commanded which will cause sliding away from any point in H_s at which a trajectory originating in R sticks. In this case, the trajectory cannot stick forever in H_s. I don't think robot controllers reliably enforce probabilistic distributions of commanded velocities, even if "dithering" control strategies are employed. Even if they could, this model of sticking makes life easier, since it essentially eliminates the possibility of sticking forever in $\hat{P} - P$. We will not make this assumption here. It does not address with the problem of "looping forever" within $\hat{P} - P$ in finite environments. It seems that time-out termination predicates and/or velocity thresholding must be used to solve the looping problem. Both solutions seem inelegant; the issue is subtle and is addressed further in [12].

10. Generalization to *n*-Step EDR Strategies

This section discusses the construction of n-step EDR strategies in more detail.

We first review Example 3.1 (Figs. 18 and 19), highlighting a subtle recognizability issue not emphasized in the prelude. However, this review may be skipped at first reading if you already have Example 3.1 firmly in mind.

10.1. A Review of Example 3.1

Consider Fig. 18. Here there are two possible universes, both in the plane, so J is the two-element discrete set, $\{1, 2\}$. The start region is the union of R_1 in universe 1, and R_2 in universe 2. The goal exists in universe 1 but not in universe 2. There is no one-step EDR strategy which, from the start region, can guarantee to achieve G or recognize that we are in universe 2. In particular, there is no one-step EDR strategy which can be derived from the motion v_θ^*.

However, there clearly exist multi-step EDR strategies. We will construct one as follows. Recall that to construct one-step EDR strategies, we took as data a goal, a start region R, a commanded motion θ, and the preimage of the goal under θ. Given these data we constructed an EDR region. From the EDR region, we attempted to construct an EDR strategy that achieved the distinguishable union of the goal *or* the EDR region. Now, why does this fail in Fig. 18? To answer this question, let us consider what the motion θ was supposed to achieve in universe 1. There is an eight-step plan in universe 1 which recognizably achieves G from start region R_1. It is obtained by backchaining preimages in universe 1. The plan moves from R_1 to the region S_1 under v_θ^*. Then it slides along the top surface to vertex f. Next it slides to vertex e. It slides to the successive vertex subgoals d through a, and then a horizontal sliding motion achieves the goal G.

The strategy θ is guaranteed to achieve the surface S_1 from start region R_1. Suppose we try to extend it to an EDR strategy with start region the union of R_1 and R_2. The EDR region (6) is then simply the (cylinder over the) forward projection of the "bad" region, $F_\theta(R_2)$. (See Fig. 18.) There is no way that the termination predicate can distinguish between the forward projection of R_1 and the forward projection of R_2, hence no EDR strategy from θ exists.

We can easily construct a two-step EDR strategy, however. First, we execute motion θ from the union of R_1 and R_2. This achieves a motion into S_1 in universe 1, or into S_2 in universe 2. The termination predicate cannot distinguish which has been attained. Suppose the second motion in the eight-step plan is v_ψ^* (see Fig. 18), and is guaranteed to achieve the vertex subgoal f from start region S_1. We'll try to construct an EDR strategy out of this second motion. Take as data: the subgoal f, the start region $S_1 \cup S_2$, the horizontal motion ψ, and the preimage of f under ψ.[17] The EDR region for these data is the forward projection of S_2 under ψ (see Fig. 19). Presumably this EDR region is distinguishable from f, and so we have constructed an EDR strategy at the second step. After executing the second step, we either terminate the motion as a failure, or proceed to vertex e, and eventually to the goal.

10.2. Generalization: Push-forwards

Now, let us attempt to capture the salient aspects of the n-step EDR strategy construction. We take as data an n-step plan, with start region R_1. The actual

---

[17] While S_1 is the preimage under ψ with respect to start region S_1, the preimage with respect to the entire forward projection of $S_1 \cup S_2$ includes the top edge between S_1 and f. (See (5).)

start region is some larger region, say, R. Above, we had R as the union of R_1 and R_2. The first motion in the plan is guaranteed to achieve some subgoal S_1 from R_1. Using this first motion from start region R, we try to construct an EDR region H_1, and a one-step EDR strategy that either achieves S_1 or signals failure by achieving H_1. If this succeeds, we are, of course, done.

Suppose we cannot distinguish between H_1 and S_1. In this case, we want to execute the first motion "anyway", and terminate "somewhere" in the union of S_1 and H_1. The termination predicate cannot be guaranteed to distinguish which goal has been entered.

This "somewhere" is called the *push-forward* of the first motion from R. The push-forward is a function of the commanded motion θ, the actual start region R, the region R_1 from which θ is guaranteed, and the subgoal S_1.[18] A particular example of push-forward is defined formally in [12]. In Example 3.1, the push-forward (under θ) of R_2 is S_2. The push-forward of $R_1 \cup R_2$ is $S_1 \cup S_2$. The push-forward is similar to a forward projection, except that it addresses the issue of termination. In Example 3.1, informally speaking, the push-forward from the region R (under some commanded motion θ) is the result of executing θ from R and seeing what happens. It is defined even when the strategy θ is only guaranteed from some subset (R_1) of R.

Having terminated in the push-forward of R (the union of S_1 and S_2 above), we next try to construct a one-step EDR strategy at the second motion of the n-step plan. The data are: the next subgoal T_1 after S_1 in the plan, the actual start region $S_1 \cup S_2$, the second commanded motion in the plan, and the preimage of T_1 under this motion.[19] This defines a formal procedure for constructing n-step EDR strategies. At each stage we attempt to construct a one-step EDR strategy; if this fails, we push forward and try again.

Actually, this description of the procedure contains a taradiddle. At each step we construct the EDR region as described. However, the one-step strategy we seek must achieve the distinguishable union of the EDR region and *all unattained subgoals* in the plan. That is, the EDR motion must distinguishably terminate in the EDR region, or the next subgoal, or *any* subsequent subgoal. This allows serendipitous skipping of steps in the plan.

By considering different data, that is, quantifying over all motions at each branch point of the n-step strategy, we can in principle consider all n-step strategies and define nondirectional EDR strategies. This is at least as difficult as computing n-step nondirectional preimages. If we wish to consider plans of different lengths, we must also quantify over all n. Needless to say, the branching factor in the backchaining search would be quite large.

---

[18] Of course, it also depends on the termination predicate, sensing and control characteristics, etc.

[19] The preimage is with respect to the forward projection of the actual start region $S_1 \cup S_2$.

10.3. More on the push-forward

The problem of defining the push-forward may be stated informally as follows: "Where should the motion be terminated so that later, after some additional number of push-forwards, a one-step EDR strategy may be executed."

Many different push-forwards can be defined. Using the notation above, note the motion is not even guaranteed to terminate when executed from R: it is only guaranteed from R_1. This means that velocity thresholding and time may be necessary in the termination predicate. There are other difficulties: for example, a priori it is not even necessary that entry into the union of the subgoal S_1 and the EDR region H_1 be recognizable. Thus defining the push-forward is equivalent to defining where in $S_1 \cup H_1$ the motion can and should be terminated.

Depending on which push-forward is employed, we may or may not obtain an n-step EDR strategy. It is possible to define constraints on the push-forward that must be satisfied to ensure that a strategy will be found if one exists. These constraints are given in [12]. While we can give equations that the push-forward must satisfy, at this time a constructive definition is not known. This situation is similar to, and possibly harder than the problem of solving the general preimage equation.

10.4. An approximation to the push-forward

We may have to approximate the desired push-forward. We give such an approximation here. In general, it does not satisfy the constraints given in [12]. We provide it to show what the push-forwards alluded to above are like. Such approximate push-forwards may prove useful in approximating the desired push-forward. The issue deserves more study; see [12]. Since this approximate push-forward is incomplete, the reader should consider its description here as illustrative of the research problem, and not as an endorsement.

The push-forward employed in Example 3.1 was formed by "executing the strategy anyway, and seeing where it terminated". How do we formalize this idea? Consider the termination predicate as a function of the starting region, the initial sensed position, the commanded velocity, the goal(s), and the sensor values. The sensor values are changing; the predicate monitors them to determine when the goal has been reached.[20] Now, if the termination predicate "knew" that in Example 3.1 the start region was the union of R_1 and R_2, then the first motion strategy θ could never be terminated: the predicate could never ensure that the subgoal S_1 had been reached. This is simply because S_1 and S_2 are indistinguishable. But if we "lie" to the termination predicate and tell it that the motion really started in R_1, then the predicate will happily terminate

---

[20] See [13, 14, 21] for a thorough discussion of termination predicates.

the motion in $S_1 \cup S_2$, thinking that S_1 has been achieved. Viewing the termination predicate as a function, this reduces to calling it with the "wrong" arguments, that is, applying it to R_1 instead of $R_1 \cup R_2$. The push-forward we obtain is "where the termination predicate will halt the motion from all of $R_1 \cup R_2$, thinking that the motion originated in R_1."

Even formalizing the construction of this simple push-forward is subtle; details are given in [12]. While this approximate push-forward is incomplete, it does suffice for a wide variety of EDR tasks. The approximate push-forward captures the intuitive notion of "trying the strategy anyway, even if we're not guaranteed to be in the right initial region." It is incomplete because it fails to exploit sufficiently the geometry of the forward projection of the "bad" region. Better push-forwards must be found; this one is merely illustrative of the problems.

11. Geometric Reasoning about Pushing in Generalized Configuration Space

11.1. Example: The sticking cone

As an example of how a planner could reason about friction in generalized configuration space, see Fig. 38. Here we take the configuration spaces of the robot and of B to be Cartesian planes. Assume that we can apply a two-dimensional force f_c on the robot, and a two-dimensional force f_j at the center of mass of B. (This assumption is for the sake of discussion; in pushing applications, f_j would be zero.) The friction cone in generalized configuration space will then be four-dimensional. This is hard to draw; we have selected a fixed, negative normal component for f_j. The 3D force space at the point of contact $\bar{x}$ represents the product of the 2D forces that can be exerted by the robot on the surface of B, with the 1D tangential forces that can be applied at the center of mass of B. An applied force (f_c, f_j) in the cone in Fig. 38 represents a combination of forces that causes no motion in $\mathcal{G}$, that is, neither sliding on the surface of B, nor of B on the table. Note that the cone in $\mathcal{G}$ is skewed out of the embedded tangent space to C at x. This is because when a force f_c is applied in the friction cone on the top surface of B, the block B can slide unless an opposing force is exerted tangentially at the center of mass of B.

Let us call the cone in Fig. 38 the *sticking cone* $\mathcal{H}$. Using the sticking cone, we can now specify a geometrical computation to determine when sticking occurs at $\bar{x}$, assuming generalized damper dynamics: Simply intersect the negative velocity control uncertainty cone $-B_{ec}(v_\theta^*)$ with $\mathcal{H}$. If the intersection is trivial, then sticking cannot occur. If the intersection is nontrivial, then sticking can occur. If the negative velocity cone lies inside $\mathcal{H}$, then sticking must occur.

This shows that the computation to determine whether sticking is possible at a point reduces to simple geometric cone intersection.

Now we return to the pushing application, by restricting the applied force f_j

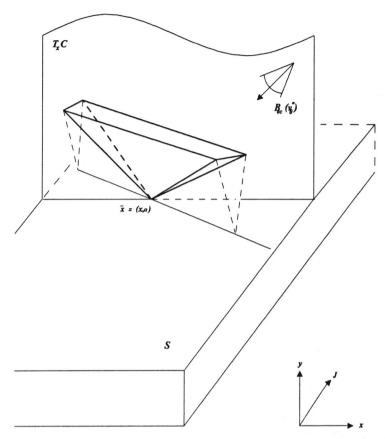

Fig. 38. Assume a fixed, negative normal force at the center of mass of B. The 3D force space at $\bar{x}$ represents the product of the 2D forces f_c that can be exerted by the robot on the surface of B, with the 1D tangential forces f_j that can be exerted at the center of mass of B. An applied force (f_c, f_j) in the cone represents a combination of forces that causes no motion in $\mathcal{G}$, that is, neither sliding on the surface of B, nor of B on the table. Note that the cone in $\mathcal{G}$ is skewed out of the embedded tangent space to C at x. This is because when a force f_c is applied in the friction cone on the top surface of B, the block B can slide unless an opposing force is exerted tangentially at the center of mass of B. By intersecting the sticking cone with the negative velocity cone, we can determine whether sticking is possible on S.

in J to be zero. See Fig. 38. Assume it is impossible to apply force at the center of mass of B. Therefore, the velocity cone is two-dimensional and lies entirely in the tangent space to C at x; it has no J component. This two-dimensional cone is intersected with the 3D cone $\mathcal{H}$ to determine whether sticking is possible at $\bar{x}$.

Let us emphasize that by insisting that the force f_j applied in J be zero, we obtain a two-dimensional control uncertainty cone, even though generalized configuration space has four degrees of freedom. Thus, in the model error framework, the generalized control uncertainty can be viewed as a *nonholonomic constraint*.[21] Holonomic constraints are constraints on the degrees of freedom of the moving object(s); nonholonomic constraints are constraints on their differential motions. Holonomic constraints can be captured by surfaces in (generalized) configuration space. To capture nonholonomic constraints geometrically, we must introduce constraints in the phase space. This viewpoint is developed in [12], where we provide a more rigorous account of the construction of normals, friction cones, sticking cones, and the computation of reaction forces in generalized configuration space.

ACKNOWLEDGMENT

I would like to thank Tomas Lozano-Pérez, Michael Erdmann, Rod Brooks, Steve Buckley, John Canny, Eric Grimson, and Margaret Fleck for comments on an earlier draft of this paper, and for valuable discussions on motion planning and uncertainty. I am very grateful to John Canny for all the time he spent hacking on our 2D plane-sweep module used in the implementation described here.

REFERENCES

1. Abraham, R. and Marsden, J., *Foundations of Mechanics* (Benjamin/Cummings, London, 1978).
2. Arnold, V.I., *Mathematical Methods of Classical Mechanics* (Springer, New York, 1978).
3. Brooks, R.A., Symbolic error analysis and robot planning, *Int. J. Rob. Res.* **1** (4) (1982) 29–68.
4. Brooks, R.A., A robust layered control system for a mobile robot, AI Lab Memo 864, MIT, Cambridge, MA (1985).
5. Brost, R.C., Planning robot grasping motions in the presence of uncertainty, CMU-RI-TR-85-12, Computer Science Department and the Robotics Institute, Carnegie-Mellon University, Pittsburgh, PA (1985).
6. Buckley, S.J., Planning and teaching compliant motion strategies, Ph.D. Thesis, AI-TR-936, Department of EECS, MIT, Cambridge, MA (1987).
7. Canny, J.F., Collision detection for moving polyhedra, *IEEE Trans. Pattern Anal. Mach. Intell.* **8** (1986).
8. Chapman, D., Planning for conjunctive goals, AI-TR-802, MIT, Cambridge, MA (1985).
9. Donald, B.R., Motion planning with six degrees of freedom, AI-TR-791, Artificial Intelligence Lab., MIT, Cambridge, MA (1984).
10. Donald, B.R., A search algorithm for motion planning with six degrees of freedom, *Artificial Intelligence* **31** (1987) 295–353.
11. Donald, B.R., Robot motion planning with uncertainty in the geometric models of the robot and environment: A formal framework for error detection and recovery, in: *Proceedings IEEE International Conference on Robotics and Automation*, San Francisco, CA (1986).
12. Donald, B.R., Error detection and recovery for robot motion planning with uncertainty, Ph.D. Thesis, AI-TR-982, Department EECS, Artificial Intelligence Laboratory, MIT, Cambridge, MA (1987).

---

[21] Michael Erdmann [15] pointed out the relationship between nonholonomic constraints and the physics of $\mathscr{G}$ under pushing.

13. Erdmann, M., Using backprojections for fine motion planning with uncertainty, *Int. J. Rob. Res.* **5** (1986).
14. Erdmann, M., On motion planning with uncertainty, AI-TR-810, AI Lab., MIT, Cambridge, MA (1984).
15. Erdmann, M., Personal communication (1986).
16. Fikes, R.E. and Nilsson, N.J., STRIPS: A new approach to the application of theorem proving to problem solving, *Artificial Intelligence* **2** (1971) 189–208.
17. Gini, M. and Gini, G., Towards automatic error recovery in robot programs, in: *Proceedings IJCAI-83*, Karlsruhe, F.R.G. (1983).
18. Hayes, P., A representation for robot plans, in: *Proceedings IJCAI-75*, Tblisi, U.S.S.R. (1975).
19. Lozano-Pérez, T., Automatic planning of manipulator transfer movements, *IEEE Trans. Syst. Man Cybern.* **11** (1981) 681–698.
20. Lozano-Pérez, T., Spatial planning: A configuration space approach, *IEEE Trans. Comput.* **32** (1983) 108–120.
21. Lozano-Pérez, T., Mason, M.T. and Taylor, R.H., Automatic synthesis of fine-motion strategies for robots, *Int. J. Rob. Res.* **3** (1984).
22. Lozano-Pérez, T. and Wesley, M.A., An algorithm for planning collision-free paths among polyhedral obstacles, *Comm. ACM* **22** (1979) 560–570.
23. Mason, M.T., Compliance and force control for computer controlled manipulators, *IEEE Trans. Syst. Man Cybern.* **11** (1981) 418–432.
24. Mason, M.T., Manipulator grasping and pushing operations, AI-TR-690, AI Lab., MIT, Cambridge, MA (1982).
25. Mason, M.T., Automatic planning of fine motions: Correctness and completeness, in: *Proceedings IEEE International Conference on Robotics*, Atlanta, GA (1984).
26. McDermott, D., A temporal logic for reasoning about processes and plans, *Cognitive Sci.* **6** (1982) 101–155.
27. Nievergelt, J. and Preparata, F.P., Plane-sweep algorithms for intersecting geometric figures, *Comm. ACM* **25** (10) (1982).
28. Requicha, A.A., Representation of tolerances in solid modeling: Issues and alternative approaches, in: *Solid Modeling by Computers: From Theory to Applications* (Plenum, New York, 1984).
29. Schwartz, J.T. and Sharir, M., On the piano movers' problem, II: General techniques for computing topological properties of real algebraic manifolds, *Adv. Appl. Math.* **4** (1983) 298–351.
30. Shapiro, V., Parametric modeling and analysis of tolerances, Rept. CS-460, GM Research Lab., Schenectady, NY (1985).
31. Srinivas, S., Error recovery in robot systems, Ph.D. Thesis, Computer Science Department, CalTech (1977).
32. Taylor, R.H., The synthesis of manipulator control programs from task-level specifications, AIM-82, Artificial Intelligence Laboratory, Stanford University, Stanford, CA (1976).
33. Ward, B. and McCalla, G., Error detection and recovery in a dynamic planning environment, in: *Proceedings AAAI-83*, Washington, DC (1983).
34. Wilkins, D.E., Domain-independent planning: Representation and plan generation, *Artificial Intelligence* **22** (1984) 269–301.
35. Donald, B.R., The complexity of planar compliant motion planning under uncertainty, in: *Proceedings Fourth Annual ACM Symposium on Computational Geometry*, Urbana, IL (1988).

Received October 1986; revised version received December 1987

Machine Vision

Geometric Reasoning for Constructing 3D Scene Descriptions from Images*

Ellen Lowenfeld Walker
Computer Science Department, Carnegie-Mellon University, Pittsburgh, PA 15213, U.S.A.

Martin Herman
Robot Systems Division, National Bureau of Standards, Gaithersburg, MD 20899, U.S.A.

ABSTRACT

There are many applications for a vision system which derives a three-dimensional model of a scene from one or more images and stores the model for easy retrieval and matching. The derivation of a 3D model of a scene involves transformations between four levels of representation: images, 2D features, 3D structures, and 3D geometric models. Geometric reasoning is used to perform these transformations, as well as for the eventual model matching. Since the image formation process is many-to-one, the problem of deriving 3D features from 2D features is ill-constrained. Additional constraints may be derived from knowledge of the domain from which the images were taken. The 3D MOSAIC system has successfully used domain specific knowledge to drive the geometric reasoning necessary to acquire 3D models for complex real-world urban scenes. To generalize this approach, a framework for the representation and use of domain knowledge for geometric reasoning for vision is proposed.

1. Generating 3D Descriptions from Images

The goal of a computer vision system is to derive a meaningful symbolic interpretation of a scene, given one or more images of that scene. A particularly useful interpretation is a three-dimensional geometric model of the scene. Such a model can be used for path planning for a robot, generation of alternate views, or change detection, as well as model-guided interpretation of additional images.

* This research was sponsored in part by AT&T Bell Laboratories' Graduate Research Program for Women, and in part by the Air Force Office of Scientific Research under contract F49620-83-C-0100. The views and conclusions contained in this document are those of the authors and should not be interpreted as representing the official policies, either expressed or implied, of the Air Force Office of Scientific Research, or the US Government.

In the process of image interpretation, the information is transformed through four levels of representation. These are:

(1) *Image(s)*. The original input image may be a single black and white image, a color image, a stereo pair, or a set of related views.

(2) *2D features*. Two-dimensional features extracted from the original images include vertices, lines, and regions of uniform intensity.

(3) *3D structures corresponding to 2D features*. Three-dimensional structures include 3D vertices, edges, and surface patches.

(4) *3D geometric models*. Three-dimensional geometric models may be edge-based, surface-based, or volume-based.

The system must be able to move between these levels, both extracting higher-level features from lower-level ones, and predicting lower-level features to match, using a higher-level model. Additionally, the current image-derived hypotheses may be matched to an internal model. Geometric reasoning is used both to move between levels, and to match representations at a given level.

2D feature extraction is exemplified by choosing a set of lines to fit edge points extracted from the image, or determining the best polygonal approximation of a region according to some criteria. When deriving 3D structures from 2D features, knowledge of the camera projection is combined with domain knowledge and the image data to derive the most reasonable explanation for each 2D feature. In the case of stereo or motion, additional constraints are derived from matching features from more than one image. When completing a model from a set of 3D structures, geometric reasoning is used to determine the type, position, and orientation of the structures necessary to complete each object, and to hypothesize additional structures or objects necessary for the model to conform to domain constraints. In the real world, for example, objects may not float in the air without support. In the domain of airplanes, all airplanes must have two symmetric wings.

Within this context, vision systems can be compared by asking the following questions:

– Which levels of representation are used?
– How is domain knowledge represented at each level?
– At which level is matching done?

Many early vision systems represented only 2D features, and their final model was a labeling of the regions in the image. For example, Ohta's system [8] divided a color image into regions, and labeled the regions as HOUSE, SKY, GRASS, or ROAD using region properties such as color, shape, position in the image, and adjacency. The domain knowledge was represented as a set of condition-action rules, and the matching was done at the 2D feature level. The ACRONYM system [2], in contrast, used all four levels of representation, represented its domain knowledge explicitly as graphs, and matched 2D features extracted from the image to 2D features predicted from the models.

The examples of geometric reasoning presented in this paper have been chosen from the 3D MOSAIC system, which is completely described in [4]. The 3D MOSAIC system also uses all four levels of representation. Its domain knowledge is represented implicitly within procedures, and matching is done at the 3D structure level.

The 3D MOSAIC system deals with complex real-world urban scenes, (e.g. Fig. 3(a)). These scenes contain many objects with a variety of shapes, surface textures and reflectances, as well as artifacts of the natural outdoor lighting conditions such as shadows and highlights. To deal with this complexity, multiple images obtained from multiple viewpoints are used. Objects extracted from each image are matched and the models are combined to derive a more complete model of the overall scene.

Figure 1 shows the levels of representation in the 3D MOSAIC system, and the processes which transfer between them. The input to the 3D MOSAIC system is a view of the scene, either a monocular image or a stereo pair. Processing occurs through the four levels of representation, from top to bottom in Fig. 1. First, 2D lines and junctions are extracted from the images. From these, 3D structures such as edges and vertices are derived, resulting in a

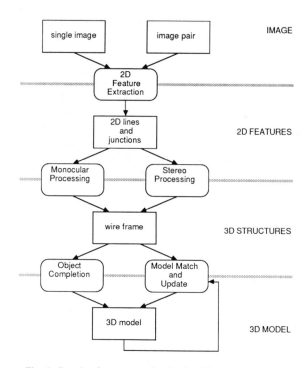

Fig. 1. Levels of representation in the 3D MOSAIC system.

sparse 3D wire frame description of the scene. The current scene model is represented as a graph of planar faces, edges, and vertices, and their topology and geometry. As each input image (or pair) is processed, the resulting wire frames are matched with the current scene model, and the model is modified to reflect them. Portions of the model for which there is no wire frame information are hypothesized using domain knowledge, in this case, knowledge about urban buildings.

The remainder of this paper discusses the use of geometric reasoning in the 3D MOSAIC system for the processes of monocular analysis and object completion. Some of the problems with the system are presented along with ideas for alleviating these problems in the next generation of the system.

2. Geometric Reasoning for Monocular Analysis

One method for determining 3D structures corresponding to 2D features extracted from a single image is to exploit strong geometric constraints from the domain along with the constraints of the projection to derive a unique interpretation for each 2D feature. This method is exemplified by the monocular analysis component of the 3D MOSAIC system [3–5], which generates a *wire frame* (see Fig. 3(c)) consisting of 3D descriptions of the edges and vertices corresponding to 2D lines and junctions that were extracted from the image.

In the 3D MOSAIC system under monocular analysis, all surfaces and edges are constrained to be either horizontal (parallel to the ground plane) or vertical (perpendicular to the ground plane). Therefore, the first step in generating the three-dimensional wire frame is to label each line as horizontal or vertical. The lines are labeled by exploiting a feature of the perspective projection: all vertical lines point at the vertical vanishing point [6]. Therefore, lines that point at the vertical vanishing point (a point specified by the user in the current implementation) are labeled vertical, and all others are labeled horizontal. In addition, since the views are known to be aerial, the end of each vertical line nearest the vertical vanishing point is labeled "bottom" and the other end is labeled "top".

Once the lines have been labeled, the 3D location of any endpoint of a line can be found given the 3D location of its other endpoint. There are two cases: horizontal lines and vertical lines. In Fig. 2, the 3D position of the vertex v_1 is known, line $p_1 p_2$ is the image of a horizontal line in space, line $p_1 p_3$ is the image of a vertical line in space, and u is a 3D vector in the vertical direction, found by calculating the vector from the focal point to the vertical vanishing point in the image plane [1]. The position of v_2, the far endpoint of the horizontal line, is found at the intersection of the ray from the focal point through p_2 and a plane parallel to the ground through v_1. The position of v_3, the far endpoint of the vertical line, is found at the intersection of the ray from the focal point through p_3 and a line parallel to u through v_1. Using these techniques, the position of any point can be derived, provided that a labeled

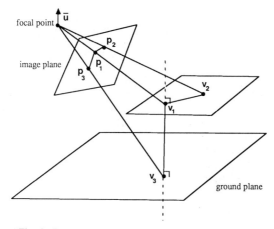

Fig. 2. Propagating 3D locations for monocular analysis.

line exists between it and a known point. Two techniques have been used to derive starting points.

The first technique uses points on the ground plane as starting points. The equation of the ground plane is $u \cdot p = -d$, where u is the vertical unit vector, p is a point on the plane, and d is the distance from the focal point to the ground plane. If d is not provided by the user, it remains a free variable in the plane equation, and only relative positions of vertices are obtained. The location of a point on the ground plane, such as v_3 in Fig. 2 is at the intersection of the ground plane and the ray through the point's image (in this case p_3). The points labeled "bottom" of vertical lines are considered to be on the ground for this analysis.

Not all junctions found in the image are connected to vertices on the ground. Some of these may be positioned using the second technique: if the 2D images of two lines are aligned, assume the 3D lines are aligned in the scene. This technique was also used in other systems [7]. When an unknown line aligns with a known one, the location of each endpoint on the unknown line may be found by intersecting the known line with the ray through the focal point and the endpoint's image.

This process of extracting wire frames from 2D lines and junctions depends on the following domain constraints:

- All surfaces and edges are either vertical or horizontal.
- An edge is vertical if and only if it points at the (known) vertical vanishing point.
- The bottom of a vertical edge lies on the (known) ground plane.
- Lines aligned in the image correspond to edges aligned in space.

The first two constraints allow each line to be labeled horizontal or vertical, ensuring that 3D locations may be propagated across each line. The remaining

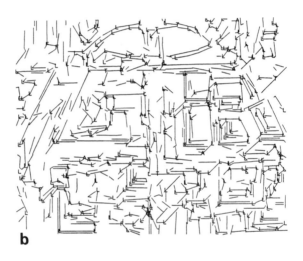

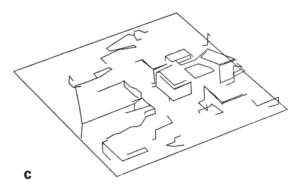

Fig. 3. Wire frame generation. (a) Initial image; (b) 2D lines and junctions; (c) wire frame.

two constraints allow for the two methods of determining initial starting points for the propagation.

Figures 3 and 4 are two examples of generating wire frames from monocular images using the techniques described in this section. Each figure contains (a) the grey scale image, (b) the extracted lines and junctions, and (c) a perspective view of the generated wire frame. Only junctions containing vertical lines and junctions whose 3D position could be obtained using the collinearity

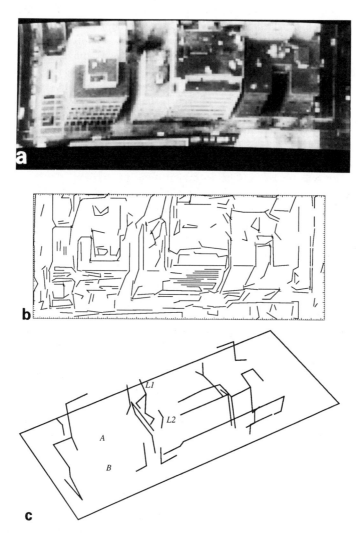

Fig. 4. Wire frame generation illustrating problems with monocular analysis. (a) Initial image; (b) 2D lines and junctions; (c) wire frame.

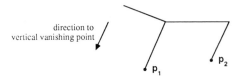

Fig. 5. The wire frame depends on the processing order.

constraint become vertices of the wire frame. The wire frame in Fig. 3 is a reasonable representation of the input image. Figure 4 illustrates several problems which can hamper the wire frame extraction.

One problem with monocular analysis is loss of information in the 2D feature extraction. For example, vertical lines in aerial images appear relatively short, so they are often ignored in the 2D feature extraction. In Fig. 4(c), the short vertical lines connecting the upper and lower roofs of the leftmost building were missed (area *A*). Therefore, no 3D structures were derived for the roof of that building. In addition, no 3D information is obtained for areas where there are no junctions, such as most of the front wall of the leftmost building in Fig. 4(c) (area *B*).

If short vertical lines are extracted, but their direction is off by only a few pixels, they will be labeled horizontal instead of vertical. An example is the line labeled *L*1 in Fig. 4(c). Occasionally a horizontal line (such as *L*2 in Fig. 4(c)) accidentally aligns with the vertical vanishing point and is labeled vertical. When lines are mislabeled, the errors in the wire frame propagate throughout the model, sometimes creating objects that should never occur in the domain. The current 3D MOSAIC system has no way to recover from these errors. Another problem is the possibility of generating inconsistent structures using this monocular extraction process. For example, in Fig. 5, if p_1 is processed first, then p_2 will lie above the ground. However, if p_2 is processed first, then p_1 will lie below the ground.

One goal of the 3D MOSAIC system was to use multiple views to recover reasonable three-dimensional models in spite of these problems. One possible area of research is to assign confidences to the 3D structures depending on their method of acquisition. Currently, hypotheses from higher-level processing are distinguished from structures found in the image, but structures from the image are not distinguished as to how they were derived. Another way to deal with the ambiguities in monocular images is to use more specific models of buildings: not just horizontal and vertical faces, but edge lengths, heights, etc., up to and possibly including complete CAD models of the buildings themselves.

3. Geometric Reasoning for Object Completion

To complete the generation of a 3D description from an image, the 3D structures extracted from the input views must be incorporated into a scene model. The completed scene model is the final result of the vision system. Therefore, the representation of the scene model is dependent on the use of the vision system. For some applications, for example, a space-filling representation might be most useful, while a surface-based representation would be best for other applications.

In the case of the 3D MOSAIC system, the model is designed to efficiently describe partially complete polyhedral objects, and to be easy to use in matching. The scene is represented as a graph of topological structures: vertices, edges, edge groups (rings of edges), faces, and objects, as well as the underlying geometric structures: points, lines, and planes. The topological features are linked to each other by part-of (topological) links, and to the geometric structures by geometric constraint links. This *structure graph* may be modified by adding or deleting nodes or links, or by changing the equations of geometric nodes. The effects of modifications are propagated to other parts of the graph. A complete description of the algorithms for updating the structure graph may be found in [4] or [5].

The wire frames are also represented by structure graphs, although the structure graphs of the wire frames contain only edge, vertex, line, and point nodes. The wire frame extracted from the first view of a particular scene forms the initial scene model. All vertices, edges, and points of the wire frame are tagged as confirmed. The initial scene model is augmented with additional vertices and edges, as well as edge rings, faces, and objects to derive a surface-based model of the scene, using knowledge of the domain. The elements of the final scene model that were not present in its initial state are tagged as unconfirmed. As an example, Fig. 6 shows the representations of an initial wire frame and a final model for a cube. In the initial wire frame, both topological and geometric nodes are shown, with the arrows representing part-of links and the thick lines representing geometric constraint links. The final model is simplified, showing only the topological nodes with confirmed nodes shaded.

To incorporate a wire frame extracted from a new view, the wire frame's structures are tagged as confirmed and matched to the current scene model. The wire frame is then merged into the model, "averaging" confirmed elements in the model with confirmed elements in the wire frame, and replacing unconfirmed elements in the model with their confirmed counterparts from the wire frame. The structures necessary to complete the model are then generated using domain knowledge, as for the first wire frame.

The steps taken by the 3D MOSAIC system for object completion are shown by an example in Fig. 7. The object to be completed (Fig. 7(a)) has one vertical edge and four coplanar horizontal edges. First, a face is hypothesized for each pair of edges that share a vertex. In Fig. 7(b) these faces are shown by "webs" between each face's edges. Then all pairs of faces that lie in the same plane and satisfy additional constraints are merged. One constraint is that faces that share

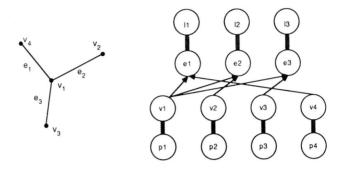

Initial wire frame

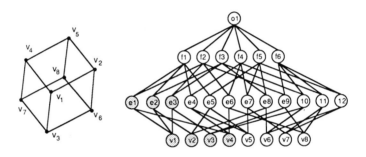

Final structure graph

Fig. 6. Completion of a cube.

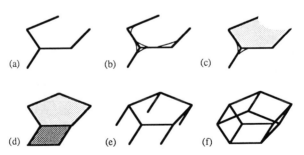

Fig. 7. Steps in object completion.

a single edge are merged (Fig. 8(a)), unless the shared edge separates the faces, as in Fig. 8(b). Another constraint is that if the confirmed edges of the faces do not touch, they must be within a threshold distance of one another. The result of this step is a set of partial faces. Only the "roof" face is represented in Fig. 7(c). Each partial face is then completed by adding one or two edges. If the partial face has two edges, two more are added, forming a parallelogram. If the face has more than two edges, then a single edge is added to complete the polygon formed by the edges of the face. These possibilities are exemplified by the roof and the front wall of the building in Fig. 7(d). Next, vertical edges are hypothesized to support all horizontal faces that lie more than a given distance above the ground (Fig. 7(e)). These edges are dropped from each vertex of the floating face to the next lower horizontal face, or to the ground. New faces are hypothesized for each pair of edges sharing a newly created vertex, and the process is repeated until no new faces can be hypothesized. Figure 7(f) shows the final building.

The knowledge used in completing wire frames is embedded in the procedures for hypothesizing, merging, and completing faces. Each wire is constrained to represent a boundary between two faces, and each vertex the intersection of three faces. Thus, a partial face is hypothesized for each pair of edges that meet at a vertex. This constraint is also used to derive the constraints on merging partial faces. For example, if two partial faces sharing an edge that separates them, as in Fig. 8(b), were merged, then the shared edge would not be the boundary between two faces. The distance threshold for merging nontouching edges is related to a constraint on the size of buildings in aerial images.

The domain constraint that buildings often have parallelogram faces is used to derive the strategy for completing faces. Finally, the real-world constraint that faces do not float in midair forces supporting edges to be hypothesized for floating faces.

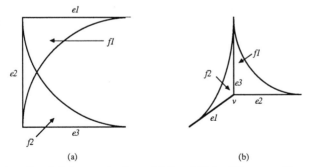

Fig. 8. Examples of heuristic for merging faces: (a) $f1$ and $f2$ should be merged because they share edge $e2$. (b) $f1$ and $f2$ should not be merged because $e3$ partitions them, rather than serving as a boundary. (This figure is adapted from [5].)

Errors in face completion are often caused by incorrectly assuming that a face with more than three edges should be completed by adding a single edge. Figure 9 shows two butterfly-shaped buildings that violate all the domain constraints. The dotted edge in each building was hypothesized by the system. In Fig. 9(a), the short spur S on one of the horizontal edges was connected to the opposite vertex with a single edge. In Fig. 9(b), vertical edge L was mislabeled as horizontal and connected to the other edges of the roof.

Even if all wires are correct, the true shape of the building can be lost if enough edges are not detected in early processing. For example, if only parts of the edges of a building were detected, the hypothesized edges would run through the middle of the building. Both types of errors could be prevented by accurately verifying hypothesized edges in the image.

Some experiments in verification have been run using an interactive version of the 3D MOSAIC system that allows the user to verify each edge and face hypothesis as it is made, by responding "yes", "no", or "change" the hypothesis. As an example, Fig. 10 shows a portion of the interactive completion of one building in Fig. 3(a). In the first two images, the web faces composing the roof are merged, with the user accepting each successive edge into the face. In the third image, the system proposes an incorrect completion of the face, and the user changes it to a more appropriate edge, in this case an extension of the previous edge. In the current version of the system, vertices are not deleted, so the vertex remains. The system then acceptably completes the face. The final two images show edges being dropped from the roof to the ground. The first is accepted by the user. The second edge, dropped from the vertex that should have been deleted, is rejected by the user.

In addition to providing hypothesis verification, the user may interactively create and modify the wire frames, and control the system's focus of attention. The interactive system is helpful in designing and debugging object completion algorithms, by observing real cases and generating relevant test cases. Watch-

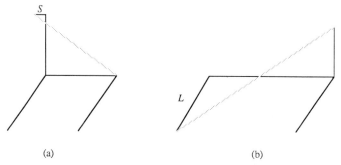

(a)   (b)

Fig. 9. Illegal "butterfly" buildings: (a) caused by "spur" (S) on horizontal edge; (b) caused by vertical line (L) mislabeled as horizontal.

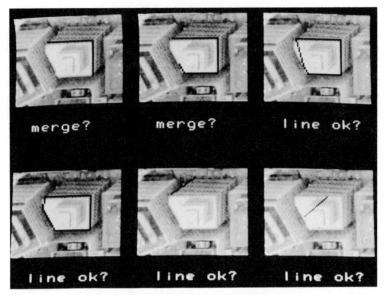

Fig. 10. Interactive object completion.

ing the system operate gives insight on domain assumptions which should be added to the system. These experiments have also shown the power of hypothesis verification, and a need for error correction when domain constraints are violated (such as the butterfly buildings in Fig. 9). The results of experiments with the interactive system are being used in designing the next generation of the 3D MOSAIC system.

4. Enhancing the System with Explicit Domain Knowledge

Much of the success of the 3D MOSAIC system can be attributed to its use of specific domain knowledge throughout its processing. For example, in monocular analysis, the knowledge that buildings have primarily horizontal and vertical faces is used, and during face completion, the information that many faces of buildings are parallelograms is used. Much of the geometric reasoning in the system exploits geometric constraints derived from the domain knowledge. However, all domain knowledge in the 3D MOSAIC system is represented implicitly in its interpretation and reasoning procedures.

The domain knowledge can be exploited more fully by combining an explicit representation of the domain constraints with geometric and symbolic reasoning. One system that has had success with such an approach is ACRONYM [2]. For example, consider the knowledge that walls are vertical rectangular faces. In the 3D MOSAIC system, this knowledge is used to derive a default method of completing faces, and contributes to the decision to label all edges as horizontal or vertical when generating wire frames. If the system had an explicit model of a generic wall that would match any vertical rectangular face, this knowledge could also be used to alleviate the error caused by vertical edges of unequal length in Fig. 5. Although the initial wire frame in this example would have one leg either above or below the ground, after fitting the wire frame to the model, both legs would be on the ground. The butterfly buildings in Fig. 9 would not match a generic building model, causing some recovery action to take place.

Using explicit models, it would be easy to add new constraints to the system, such as a maximum height for buildings, or a minimum distance between them. Other relationships between buildings could be added, for example, buildings are generally aligned with each other and with roads. The relationships would be represented so that they might be used both for prediction and for verification. For example, the parallel relationship would take four arguments: two lines, the angle between them, and the distance. Any subset of the arguments could be specified, and the parallel relationship would fill in the rest. To verify that two lines are indeed parallel, the two lines would be specified, and the angle between them would be restricted. The parallel relationship would then determine whether this restriction is satisfied. To find a line parallel to a given one, only one line would be specified, but both the angle and distance would be restricted. The parallel relationship would provide a second line parallel to the first, satisfying the angle and distance restrictions.

In addition to knowledge about objects in the domain and relationships between them, the camera model and projection could also be explicitly represented. Explicitly representing both camera and object knowledge would facilitate the verification of object hypotheses in the image. For a hypothesized structure, the camera and object knowledge could be combined to derive a prediction of the structure's appearance, which could then be verified in the image. The predictions would be improved by including surface appearance information with the geometric information in the model. Appearance information would propagate through the structure graph in a similar manner to geometric information. Knowledge about the 3D structure and appearance of an object in a similar manner to geometric information. Knowledge about the 3D structure and appearance of an object could also be used to choose an appropriate image operator, such as a specific edge detector, to extract the low-level features for verifying that object. Scene knowledge might even be used to determine an initial strategy to extract useful 2D features from the image.

The next generation of the 3D MOSAIC system will explicitly represent and use domain knowledge including the camera model and projection, the shape and surface properties of scene objects, and multi-way relationships between scene objects. This system will be built on top of the 3D FORM system [9], which uses frames to represent geometric objects and the relationships between them. By evaluating the relationships, the 3D FORM system does object completion in a more general way than the heuristics implemented in 3D MOSAIC allow. This allows a vision system using 3D FORM to be more flexible, organizing its reasoning to take advantage of the available information, while the 3D MOSAIC system must always operate according to its built-in heuristics. In addition, the frame representation is extensible to allow representations of surface properties of scene objects, camera models, and transformations between image and scene features. Finally, the frame representation allows easy extension to different building shapes, while this is difficult in the 3D MOSAIC system since knowledge of new building shapes would have to be embedded within the current procedures. Using 3D FORM, the processing in the current 3D MOSAIC system will be augmented with hypothesis verification and model-based predictions. The domain knowledge will be strengthened by adding appearance information, more objects, and more relationships between objects. The result should be a more robust, flexible, and extensible vision system.

5. Conclusion

This paper has described a method of generating 3D descriptions of a scene from images, using domain knowledge and geometric reasoning. Examples have been chosen from the 3D MOSAIC system that illustrate both the strengths and weaknesses of the current procedures. Finally, we have argued that the robustness, flexibility, and extensibility of the system can be improved by representing the domain knowledge explicitly, using the knowledge for prediction and verification, and incorporating geometric reasoning. We are developing a frame-based system to achieve this goal.

ACKNOWLEDGMENT

Takeo Kanade has provided excellent guidance and encouragement. The authors are also indebted to former members of the 3D MOSAIC project: Fumi Komura, Shigeru Kuroe, and Duane Williams.

REFERENCES

1. Barnard, S.T., Interpreting perspective images, *Artificial Intelligence* 21 (4) (1983) 435–462.
2. Brooks, R.A., Symbolic reasoning among 3-D models and 2-D images, *Artificial Intelligence* 17 (1981) 285–348; Special volume on computer vision.
3. Herman, M., Monocular reconstruction of a complex urban scene in the 3D MOSAIC system, in: *Proceedings ARPA Image Understanding Workshop* (1983) 318–326.
4. Herman, M. and Kanade, T., Incremental reconstruction of 3-D scenes from multiple, complex images, *Artificial Intelligence* 30 (1986) 289–341.
5. Herman, M., Representation and incremental construction of a three-dimensional scene model, in: A. Rosenfeld (Ed.), *Techniques for 3-D Machine Perception* (Elsevier Science Publishers, Amsterdam, 1986) 149–183, also: Carnegie-Mellon University Tech. Rept. CMU-CS-85-103, Pittsburgh, PA (1985).

6. Kender, J.R., Environmental labelings in low-level image understanding, in: *Proceedings IJCAI-83*, Karlsruhe, F.R.G. (1983) 1104–1107.
7. Lowe, D.G. and Binford, T., The interpretation of three-dimensional structure from image curves, in: *Proceedings IJCAI-81*, Vancouver, BC (1981).
8. Ohta, Y., *Knowledge-Based Interpretation of Outdoor Color Scenes* (Morgan Kaufmann, Palo Alto, CA, 1985).
9. Walker, E.L., Herman, M. and Kanade, T., A framework for representing and reasoning about three-dimensional objects for vision, *AI Mag.* **9** (2) (1988) 47–58.

Received October 1986; revised version received December 1987

A Multi-Level Geometric Reasoning System for Vision*

Michele Barry, David Cyrluk, Deepak Kapur**,
Joseph Mundy, and Van-Duc Nguyen
*General Electric Company, Corporate Research and
Development, Schenectady, NY 12345, U.S.A.*

ABSTRACT

Geometry is known to play an important role in image understanding and machine vision. Geometric reasoning is employed in different forms in model formation and model matching problems in model-based vision research. Geometric representations and reasoning methods are often used implicitly in the design of vision systems and algorithms used there. An approach towards model-based vision in which geometric and algebraic reasoning is explicit is discussed. A multi-level reasoning system for machine vision based on this approach is being designed and developed at General Electric Corporate Research and Development. Three key components of this system—a hierarchical organization of geometric knowledge for its systematic and efficient use as well as to control the search space, labeling algorithms and algebraic reasoning algorithms—are presented. The use of such a system for deriving a three-dimensional model from two-dimensional images as well as for using a two-dimensional image for matching against another two-dimensional image (called view consistency problems) is discussed.

1. Introduction

1.1. Model-based vision

There are many philosophical themes in the current practice of machine vision research. One important school of thought is model-based vision, where geometric models of objects are used to guide the recognition process. This point of view was initiated by Roberts [29] in his Ph.D. Thesis 25 years ago. Since that time the concept has been significantly refined and is widely accepted as the most promising approach to object recognition.

One primary basis for the recognition process in model-based vision is the

*The work reported here was partially supported by the DARPA Strategic Computing Program under the Army Engineer Topographic Laboratories, Contract No. DACA76-86-C-0007.
**Current address: Department of Computer Science, State University of New York at Albany, Albany, NY 12222, U.S.A.

concept of *viewpoint consistency* [26]. Under viewpoint consistency, all points of a three-dimensional object surface will project onto an image plane with the same perspective mapping transformation. The image projection is defined by a number of parameters such as the rotation and translation of the object coordinate frame relative to the camera reference frame, as well as the lens focal length. Each point on an object will map onto the image plane with identical values for these parameters, given a particular viewpoint for the camera.

Viewpoint consistency can be used to determine a correct set of assignments between elements of a three-dimensional object model and the corresponding two-dimensional image features. For example, if vertices are extracted from the image intensity data, then five or six correspondences between image vertices and three-dimensional model vertices will determine the perspective transformation between the object and the image reference frames. If a number of such groups of correct correspondences are defined, they all will determine the same viewpoint transformation. Incorrect assignments are detected by their inconsistency with respect to the majority of viewpoint parameter results [3]. Recognition can thus be considered as a voting process, with the most popular viewpoint transformation defining the correct match between an object model and geometric image features.

1.2. Recognition as geometric reasoning

The idea of viewpoint consistency can be extended to the more general idea of *view consistency* where recognition is a formal process of determining the logical consistency of geometric evidence. Within this more general perspective, the evidence derives from a number of sources:

- general properties of the object representation,
- general geometric properties of the viewing transformation,
- specific object properties and specific viewing constraints,
- geometry and topology derived from image data, in general from multiple viewpoints.

The main process of view consistency is to determine if a hypothesis, such as a particular object to image mapping, is consistent with the general assumptions as well as specific geometric constraints obtained from other views of the same scene. The determination of the consistency of these geometric and topological relationships can be approached exactly as the problem of formal logical deduction, i.e. geometric reasoning.

1.2.1. ACRONYM

Perhaps the most extensive previous work in view consistency is the ACRONYM system [6], which determines the consistency of a proposed object model and viewpoint using a system for reasoning about inequalities. The ability to handle inequalities is necessary due to the error associated with object model assumptions as well as the error encountered in extracting image geometry. The inequalities are used to express tolerances in these properties.

In ACRONYM, the objects are represented as generalized cylinders. A generalized cylinder is a solid volume formed by a varying cross-sectional area which is swept along a space curve. The image geometry is characterized by ribbons which are the projection of the boundaries of generalized cylinders. Thus a ribbon is characterized by a two-dimensional curve in the image plane, with the ribbon width defined as a parametric function of arc length along the curve.

The recognition of objects in ACRONYM is defined as the problem of determining if an object model, defined by generalized cylinders, is consistent with a set of image ribbons, within a set of predefined tolerances. A modified form of the SUP-INF method for reasoning about inequalities [5, 31] is used.

1.2.2. MOSAIC

Another aspect of view consistency is illustrated by the MOSAIC system [38]. In MOSAIC, the goal is to generate a geometric model of three-dimensional objects from a set of views of the objects. The general assumptions of perspective viewing and polyhedral objects are used to derive rules for inferring the specific object structures in the scene. The three topological elements: faces, edges and vertices, mutually constrain each other in forming a global interpretation of the polyhedral objects in the scene.

In the MOSAIC experiments, it is further assumed that the objects are rectangular prisms which provides a rich set of geometric constraints. This restriction is applicable to scenes of buildings and other man-made structures. For example, consider the drawing in Fig. 1. There are numerous constraining relationships between the image perspective vanishing points, the face normal directions, the edge directions and the vertex positions. These relationships are used in MOSAIC to build up a consistent model for the objects.

Another way of looking at the MOSAIC results is that one has recognized a generic model in the set of images by establishing a consistent set of viewing and model constraints. The specific object models which are derived are a by-product of this recognition process—a form of view consistency.

1.2.3. Ideal polyhedral projections

Another theme which is important to our current formulation of view consistency is the determination of the correctness of a polyhedral scene. An important subproblem in vision which has been extensively studied is the following:

> Given a line drawing which consists of edges and vertices, determine if this drawing is exactly a projection of some set of polyhedral objects.

Fig. 1. Man-made structures provide an extensive set of constraints on object construction and viewing perspective.

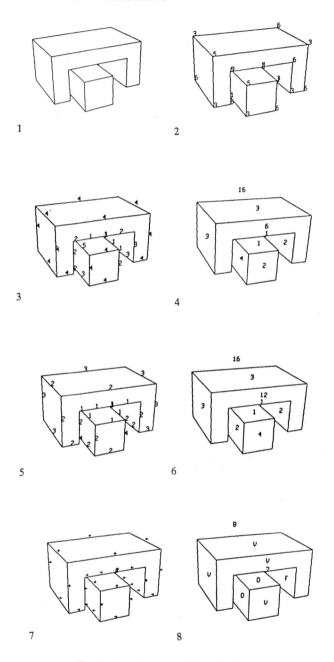

Fig. 2. Labeling of a polyhedral object.

This problem was initially solved by the use of surface edge labels which define the local three-dimensional geometry of adjacent faces and occlusion properties of the object [11, 20, 28, 30, 39]. Rules for the consistency of the edge labels which are adjacent at junctions define the possible face intersections at the junctions. The rules are derived by exhaustively enumerating the possible image projections of local junctions for any possible viewpoint. If all the edges in a drawing can be labeled in a globally consistent manner, then the drawing is a projection of a set of polyhedral objects. An example of a correctly labeled object is shown in Fig. 2. The consistency in this case can be considered mainly as a syntactic correctness, since the specific geometry of the figure does not enter directly into the labeling process.

The introduction of more explicit geometric constraints into the polyhedral consistency problem was made by Sugihara [35]. He showed that the correctness of a drawing is equivalent to the consistency of a set of linear algebraic equations and inequalities which are derived from the image projection. In addition, if these equations can be solved, then the solution will provide a set of feasible three-dimensional polyhedral surfaces corresponding to the drawing. If the equations and inequalities are inconsistent, i.e. that they have no common solution, then the drawing cannot be the projection of a well-formed set of polyhedra. Sugihara's formulation embodies occlusion and convexity face constraints as well as constraints on vertex location imposed by coplanarity. Sugihara also considers some aspects of error tolerance by allowing selected vertices to be moved to bring the drawing into a correct geometric configuration.

1.3. Multi-level geometric reasoning

We propose an approach to the view consistency problem which combines image labeling and geometric analysis with a symbolic method for determining the consistency of sets of nonlinear algebraic equations and inequalities. The approach supports the integration of empirical geometric constraints, such as image vertex locations, with general object class properties, such as the class of rectangular prisms. The consistency analysis is carried out at multiple levels of abstraction with reasoning mechanisms appropriate for each level.

In this approach, the concept of an object model is broadened to denote the collection of constraints that are associated with the general geometric class of the object, as well as the specific constraints derived from instances of image projections of the object. The process of recognition is that of determining the consistency among these specific and generic constraints. A primary focus of our initial experiments is to determine if one projection of an object is consistent with another projection of the same object. In effect, a particular projection forms an initial model for the object and constraints from additional consistent projections are used to refine the detail of the object description.

In the approach described below, the constraints are expressed as a system of algebraic equations and inequalities. A unique aspect of the system is the use of the Gröbner basis, which provides an effective mechanism for determining the consistency of equational constraints.

2. The View Consistency Problem

An important problem in image understanding which has many applications is to derive a partial model from a single two-dimensional perspective view of an object. This partial model can be used to match against another image from another viewpoint. The *view consistency* problem is defined as given a two-dimensional image of a scene, determine whether another two-dimensional image could possibly be of the same scene or not.

It is not possible to derive a complete, three-dimensional model from a single view without assuming a great deal about the relationships between object surfaces and edges. For example, a common assumption is that the object is a polyhedron with adjacent faces and edges perpendicular. With this assumption, it is possible to establish the three-dimensional structure of the visible surfaces from a single view [19]; the reader is also referred to the article [38] on MOSAIC in this volume where it is discussed how additional views of a scene can be merged with the partially solved single view.

Our investigations have centered on the case where the only assumption made about the object is that it is a polyhedron. The least restrictive constraint that can be derived from the projection is simply that the image vertices are related to the corresponding object vertices by projection equations. Once a set of projection constraints is established from a given view of the object, they can be used as a model for recognition.

Projection constraints and specific data from multiple images cannot usefully define the three-dimensional structure of the object in general. It is often necessary to introduce a grouping of vertices and edges into faces of the projection. This can be done through labeling, another higher-level geometric reasoning technique. The image is viewed as a line drawing and is partitioned using labeling techniques developed in [11, 20, 27, 28]. A labeled image provides information about the vertices that are coplanar as well as whether a face is nearer to the camera as compared to another face, and other visibility constraints. This information structurally partitions the vertices so that instead of matching one vertex in an image against a vertex in another image, we match a group of vertices on the same face in the first image to another group of vertices sharing a face in the second image.

The projection constraints are expressed as a set of algebraic equations in terms of unknown three-dimensional coordinates including depths of object vertices and transformation parameters. If we consider another two-dimensional projection, which is hypothesized to be another view of the object, then the equations derived from each projection should be algebraically consistent; of course, the correct assignment has to be made between the corresponding vertices of each view. The merging process in our approach can be thought of in terms of deciding the consistency of algebraic constraints imposed by different images.

The key steps in our method are:

Step 1. Segment images identifying vertices and edges.

Step 2. Identify faces using labeling and derive visibility constraints among faces.

Step 3. Match a face in the first image to a face in the second image, i.e., assign vertices on the face in the first image to vertices on the face in the second image. This is done using projection constraints.

Step 4. Check for consistency:

(a) If the match is way off, an inconsistency will usually be detected in the first match itself. If all vertex assignments between the two faces are inconsistent, then backtrack and try to match the first face against some other face in the second image. If no such face is left in the second image, then the two images are not of the same object.

(b) Otherwise, use the three-dimensional information already derived in the form of algebraic relations to match a second face in the first image against another face in the second image.

(c) Keep matching faces in one image against the corresponding faces in the other image until the desired three-dimensional information is derived.

In addition, other structural information such as the adjacency of vertices identified through the presence of edges could also be used in matching vertices thus further pruning the search space. In our experiments, we have not used this information.

We now describe the components of the multi-level geometric reasoning system.

3. A Multi-Level Geometric Reasoning System

The main component in the geometric reasoning system is a collection of algebraic reasoning methods to process algebraic constraints arising in machine vision problems. In this paper, we focus on the use of a Gröbner basis algorithm for reasoning about nonlinear algebraic equational constraints. The reader may also refer to [14] for the application of Brooks' extension of Bledsoe–Shostak's SUP-INF method for reasoning about nonlinear algebraic inequality constraints.

The blind use of algebraic reasoning is, however, not practical. On large problems the algebraic manipulation systems can take prohibitively long. A possible approach to address this problem is to reason at different levels of abstraction. One example of a higher-level geometric reasoning algorithm is the labeling of vertices, edges, and faces of images of polyhedral objects which can be used to partition vertices and edges into faces. Further, there seems to be a need to organize geometric knowledge and representations in a hierarchical manner so that we can access only the relevant information in a given context. A *concept hierarchy* can be useful for such a need which could be used to guide the deduction methods in a limited context using topological and geometric constraints.

So far, we have identified and used three major components in a geometry reasoning system:

– Hierarchical structuring of knowledge about geometry and object representations in the form of constraints. This knowledge can be used to control the search space while looking for key features in images.

– High-level geometric reasoning algorithms such as labeling exploiting topological and structural information of object representations.

– Low-level algebraic and geometric reasoning algorithms for solving constraints. At this level, specific information about the geometry of the objects and images are used to derive three-dimensional information. Uncertainty and imprecision in image data is also handled at this level.

In the prototype implementation being developed at General Electric Corporate Research and Development (GECRD), we have not yet fully integrated these components. In our experiments, each component was used separately and the information derived from each component was manually integrated into the input of the other components. The reader may also wish to refer to [24] where it is discussed how certain general geometric properties of perspective viewing can be derived using geometric reasoning methods and perhaps used later as indexing mechanisms for identifying features in images.

3.1. Hierarchical structuring of concepts

We will consider only polyhedral objects. A polyhedron is a collection of three elements: the vertex, the edge, and the face. A vertex is a three-dimensional point and represents the intersection of two or more edges or three or more faces. An edge is bounded by two vertices and is the intersection of at least two faces. A face is a planar region bounded by a sequence of edges and vertices.

It is possible to further restrict polyhedral objects to be rectilinear in which case adjacent faces and edges are perpendicular to each other. This assumption restricts the world enough so that it is possible to establish the three-dimensional structure of the visible surfaces from a single view. The MOSAIC system exploits such properties of rectilinear objects in constructing three-dimensional structure from two-dimensional scenes [19]. A concept hierarchy can be used for describing this relationship between polyhedral objects and rectilinear polyhedral objects.

It is often necessary and useful to have multiple representations of objects as a single representation cannot usually serve many diverse purposes. A polygon is a polyhedral object in a plane, and it can also be considered as the intersection of the half-spaces associated with the lines bounding the polygon. The polygon is simultaneously described by the sequence of line segments which form the boundary of the polygon. These might be thought of as multiple descriptions of the same polygon concept. For example, in computer graphics shading algorithms, the connected interior of the polygon is a key notion. On the other hand, convex hull algorithms are entirely dependent on the properties of the polygonal boundary sequence. The two views can also interact. The concept of a polygonal face, for instance, embodies both views. The face is defined as a closed cycle (sequence) of edges which bound a connected planar region. See Fig. 3.

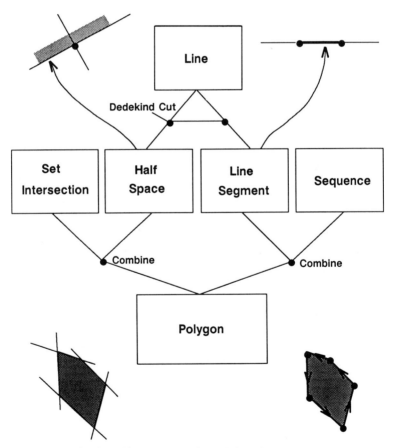

Fig. 3. Multiple representations of the polygon concept.

Let us now relate a polyhedron to its two-dimensional image. The least restrictive constraint that can be derived from the projection is simply that the image vertices are related to the corresponding object vertices by the transformation equations. An image of a point in 3D space can be expressed as a function

$$2D\text{-}p = \text{transform}(3D\text{-}p)\,.$$

Depending upon the nature of the transformation, this function can be refined and defined more precisely. This is illustrated in a fragment of a concept hierarchy for projections given in Appendix A. The above relation assumes no obstruction between the camera and the 3D point. In the case of perspective transformation, given the coordinates of the viewpoint, the equation of the view plane, the coordinates of a point in 3D space, its image in the image plane can be expressed as an algebraic relation.

If we consider a line segment as a set of points between its endpoints, it can be shown that its image under perspective viewing (in fact, any projection) is the line segment between the images of the endpoints of the original line segment. Using this property, we can derive a relation between a line segment in 3D and its image in the image plane as

$$2D\text{-line-segment} = \text{transform}(3D\text{-line-segment})\,.$$

In the derivation of this property, we will also find the degenerate case when the viewpoint lies on the line segment itself; in that case, every point on the line segment has the same point as its image. Such a view is not an example of a general view. In this case, we are also assuming no obstruction between the camera and the line segment. In general, we have to take into account the visibility constraints, which makes the analysis more complex and interesting.

These are some of the examples of the use of geometric concepts where structure can be of help. A major component in a multi-level system is a body of axioms that embody the properties of space and spatial relationships. These axioms would represent definitions of geometric concepts. The axioms are grouped into small partitions which we call *concepts*. In simplest terms, a concept is a partition of a logical theory with some desirable features.

– The theory is partitioned by a concept which corresponds to a "natural" set of events or relations in human experience or thought. An example of this would be the idea of a line (see Appendix B where a fragment of a concept hierarchy is given for specifying an automatic theorem prover for Euclidean plane geometry, called GEOMETER, developed at GECRD).

– The theory partition is efficient in the sense that a small number of concepts can account for a wide variety of behavior in the world. The basic concepts of geometry are an illustration of this requirement.

– The concept is an idealization of a complex set of phenomena. The concept segregates the essential properties which are invariant over a wide ensemble of similar events. For example, the perspective transformation approximates a wide range of image formation processes.

The ideas of a conceptual framework for geometry described here are similar to a number of other languages designed to represent formal knowledge [10, 23, 33]. A key idea is a system of concept formation operators that relate and generate concepts. Relationship among concepts can be expressed as a hierarchy as shown in Figs. 3 and 4. The following discussion is based on the work on the TECTON language for specifying software and algorithmic construction [23]; it should be read along with the examples in the appendices and Figs. 3 and 4. A detailed example is also presented in [23].

There are two types of concepts: *concept schema* and *instantiated concepts*. Concept schema is declared with parameter(s) that can later be instantiated. The parameters of a concept are themselves other concepts. Constraints on instantiations are inherited from the parameters.

3.1.1. Concept

A new concept is *created* by giving (i) syntax and type information of new functions and relations, (ii) parameters, if any, (iii) reference to related concepts and (iv) axioms and inference rules. The axioms describe the constraints and operations associated with a concept. For example, the concept of a line presents axioms that relate the line to its defining points (Appendix B). It is expected that in some cases it will be useful to use special rules of inference or proof techniques that are efficient for specific theory domains. Each concept can introduce such special methods. In most cases, the rules of inference and proof strategies are inherited from more generic concepts.

3.1.2. Define

This operation does not actually introduce a new concept. It is a syntactic mechanism for introducing abbreviations by defining a new relation or function symbol. The language is syntactically altered by the introduction of a new symbol, but the new theory (set of theorems) is only a conservative extension of the old theory. In that sense, the theory does not really change as no new axioms or rules of inference are introduced for the new symbol. The main purpose for defining a new symbol is to make the representations more compact and to simplify proofs. For example we can define the predicate Between(x, y, z) in terms of the predicate $\geq$ as follows:

$$Between(x, y, z) \Leftrightarrow (x \geq y \geq z) \vee (z \geq y \geq x)$$

where $\geq$ denotes the ordering of points on a line which can be introduced as a general ordering relation on set elements.

3.1.3. *Enrich*

The enrich operation also introduces a new symbol along with new axioms and rules of inference for the new symbol. A new concept is thus formed which contains the axioms needed to define the new symbol. For example, the algebraic concept *ring* is an enrichment of the concept *Abelian group* by the introduction of the multiplication function symbol *; see Fig. 4. Additional axioms are added to the Abelian group axioms to define the properties of * such as the associative and distributive laws.

3.1.4. *Restrict*

The restrict operation adds new axioms to an existing concept. The theory associated with the new concept becomes more specialized, i.e. more theorems can be proved than with the parent theory not containing the new axioms. The key distinction between the restrict and enrich operators is that the restrict

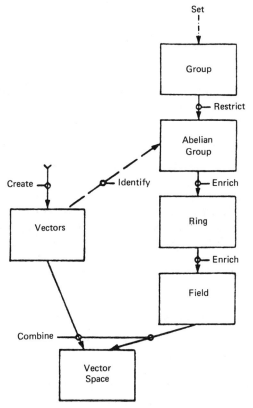

Fig. 4. A fragment of a concept hierarchy to define a vector space.

operator is used when no new function symbol is introduced. For example, the concept of polygon can be restricted to that of triangle by constraining the number of sides to three. Many more geometric relationships hold for a triangle than for a general polygon. Appendices A and B have many examples of the use of the restrict operator.

3.1.5. Combine

It is often the case that a new concept is formed by combining two or more existing concepts. The union of both concepts, with suitable integration of symbols, forms a new theory. A combined theory can often be interpreted as modeling distinct sets of elements each set corresponding to and structured by, one of the parent theories. The combined theory inherits the axioms of the parent theories. In addition, new axioms are added which define the behavior of operations acting on universes of discourses of the theories taken together.

An example of this operation is a vector space V which can be defined by combining a set of elements, called *vectors*, which obey the Abelian group laws, and the elements of a field F, called *scalars*. The combined theory introduces a new operation, $*$, which maps field elements and vectors into vectors. That is for $x \in F$ and $v \in V$, $x * v \in V$ (see Fig. 4).

3.1.6. Identification

The concept operator *identification* defines a mapping between theories associated with different concept families. The mapping consists of a translation between the function and predicate symbols in each theory. The identification operator can be used to relate multiple descriptions of concepts, for instance, relating analytic definitions of primitive geometric concepts with their synthetic properties. The use of the identification operator is illustrated in Fig. 4, Appendix A, as well as in [23].

A fairly extensive concept hierarchy starting from basic set theory concepts has been developed in which different kinds of geometries can be specified and related. The initial set of concepts give a complete development of concepts in Euclidean geometry. The hierarchy shows the development of general geometry and its relationship to affine and projective geometry. This hierarchy is supplemented with algebraic concepts leading to the definition of real closed field and vectors.

3.2. Visibility, volume and topological constraints: Labeling

This component is concerned with the relationship between the topology of the three-dimensional polyhedral surface and the topology of the corresponding projection. Information about the visibility of faces as well as how they appear to the viewer can also be derived. This information is qualitative and not quantitative; see Figs. 2 and 5. The following is based on Nguyen's work; for more details, see [28].

A polyhedral image is a segmentation of the image plane into regions joined by vertices and edges. These regions are called faces of the image, and define a vertex-edge-face topology in the image space similar to the one for three-dimensional polyhedral objects. In addition to the notion of a face, we also use the notion of a *cycle* which is a closed chain of vertices and edges. A cycle C is an out-cycle (respectively in-cycle) of a face F, if and only if the direction of the cycle C is clockwise (respectively counterclockwise), as one walks along C with the face F on the right side.

The segmentation of the image plane can be represented by a planar network of nodes. The nodes are not only the vertices as in [11, 20, 39], but also the edges and faces of the image. The polyhedral image is represented more explicitly by a planar network of nodes linked between themselves by adjacency links. The edges in an image can be labeled in terms of occlusion and convexity [20]. This planar network leads to a parallel implementation of image labeling; as a result, it is possible to label fairly complex objects, for example a model of a jeep with 122 vertices, 167 edges, and 47 faces, which would otherwise be almost impossible to label [28].

Our polyhedral world excludes Origami objects that have folds of planar surfaces. So, the junctions in the image come either from occlusion, or from projection of three-dimensional polyhedral vertices. We use Huffman–Clowes junctions for occlusion and trihedral vertices [11, 20], and Malik's junction equation for multihedral vertices [27]. However, junctions at vertices are not the only possible local constraints in labeling. We introduce two other labeling constraints around edges and face boundaries of the image, described respectively by *junction-pairs* and *junction-loops*. These extensions of the labeling system provide a unified body of constraints over the vertex, edge, and face components of a projection.

A face with holes has disjoint boundaries. We can label these boundaries independently of each other. The labeling constraints of these boundaries are represented by n-tuples of junctions, called junction-loops. A junction-loop is a consistent labeling of the chain or cycle of vertices and edges. The labeling consistency over arbitrary open chains of vertices and edges is captured by Waltz's filtering process [39]. Waltz and others are forced to do depth-first search for global labelings to capture the labeling consistency over boundary cycles. We also must do a depth-first search to enumerate all the junction-loops for a face boundary, however our depth-first search is local to a face, rather than global to the whole image. It is because of this property that complex objects such as a jeep can be labeled using our approach [28].

Similarly, a junction-pair is a consistent local labeling of an edge. The junction-pair is a more complete description of the edge than the edge label. Junctions, junction-pairs, and junction-loops are local labelings of a node consistent with itself and all its adjacent neighbors. Just as faces joined by vertices and edges completely represent the image segmentation, the junctions, junction-pairs, and junction-loops completely describe the local labeling constraints between the nodes in the image.

Nodes also have labels. For example, vertices are labeled V, Y, A, T, or M, respectively, for L, fork, arrow, T, or multihedral junctions. Edges are labeled +, −, or >, respectively, for convex, concave, or occluding. Faces are labeled B, V, or O, respectively, for background, visible, or partially occluded face. Labels and local labelings describe all the labeling constraints at a node, and are organized into hierarchies. A set of rules can be established which represent the possible labels that can occur in views of polyhedral solids. These rules are in effect theorems which are derived by enumerating all vertex configurations and all distinct viewing positions.

Labels and labelings at a node are related by the subset relation between hierarchical classes. The hierarchies and the subset relation lead to formal definitions of *constraint satisfaction* between two adjacent nodes. The image topology leads to a uniform constraint propagation over all vertex-edge, edge-face, and face-vertex links. Labeling of a polyhedral image is equivalent to *constraint satisfaction and propagation* (CSP) over all nodes in the image. Each node has local constraints described by labels and labelings. Each node only interacts with its adjacent neighbors. The result of CSP is local consistencies or inconsistencies at all the nodes in the network. The output is a network of nodes, with labels and local labelings attached to each node. This represents all locally/globally consistent labelings of the polyhedral image.

3.2.1. *Using labeling to identify vertex groups*

Labeling identifies groups of vertices lying on the same face as well as the relative distance of various faces relative to the camera position. Below, we discuss two simple examples to illustrate this.

Example 3.1 (*Two blocks*). Figure 2 depicts the labeling of two blocks, one on top of the other. The labeling method starts with the input image, and default labels (?) for all the nodes (i.e. vertices, edges, and faces) in the image (frame 1 in Fig. 2). Then, it finds all local labeling constraints at all vertices, face boundaries, and edges of the image, described respectively by junctions, junction-loops, and junction-pairs (frames 2–4). Constraint satisfaction and propagation is done uniformly at all the nodes in the image, from every node to its neighbors, through vertex-edge, edge-face, and face-vertex links. Frames 5 and 6 describe the result of CSP. Attached to each node is the number of local labelings.

The face surrounding the two blocks has 16 local labelings, corresponding to the blocks floating in air, or resting against some imaginary surface at some of its bounding edges (frame 6). The two interpretations correspond to the face labeled as image background (B) or as polyhedral face (F). Labeling identifies significant groups of vertices which can be used to derive algebraic constraints. For example, all the vertices in a visible face (labeled V) are related by coplanarity equations (frame 8). Locally, vertices connected by convex or concave edges (labeled respectively $+$, $-$) are on the planes of the adjacent faces. A vertex at a T occlusion only belongs to the occluding face. Occlusion gives an inequality relating the depths of the vertices on the same line of sight, but lying on different faces of the three-dimensional scene [35].

Example 3.2 (*Rectilinear block*). Consider a labeled rectilinear polyhedral block in Fig. 5. Using labeling it is clear that vertex c is *behind* points a and b. Constraints from the other vertices and faces rule out the case where c in front of points a and b. This additional information from labeling which relates depth variables by inequalities is thus useful to reduce the space of solutions.

A similar use of the labels is illustrated by the cycles shown in Fig. 6. The property discussed earlier of the image of a line segment being another line segment defined by the images of its two endpoints can be generalized to planar faces. By formalizing the concept of visibility in perspective viewing, it can be shown that if all the edges enclosing a planar face are visible, then the images of the boundary edges will form a closed minimum cycle in the view plane. However, the converse of this property is not valid. Unfortunately not all minimum cycles lie in the plane of the face they bound in the view plane. An example of this case is given by the cycle drawn as a bold curve in Fig. 6. Note that the direction of the occluding edges are opposite to each other and

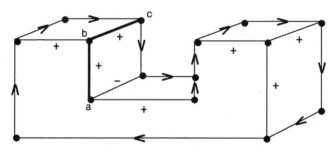

Fig. 5. A rectilinear polyhedral block with labels.

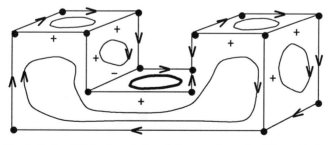

Fig. 6. Cycles defining boundaries of planar regions of rectilinear block.

cannot be oriented along a cycle. The labeling thus detects valid face images. If we assume that the T junction corresponds to a vertex in three-dimensional space and these high-level constraints are translated to equivalent algebraic constraints, then the equations corresponding to this bold cycle are inconsistent. Using high-level reasoning such as labeling, we can determine the inconsistency without having to solve any algebraic constraints.

3.2.2. *Orientation of faces*

Once the valid face cycles are determined, the algebraic conditions of viewing and coplanarity can be used to derive the orientation of the plane using techniques suggested in [16]. At least four edges, pairwise parallel, are needed to derive the orientation. Often these are not available due to occlusion and only a partially solved algebraic expression can be obtained; see the shaded face in Fig. 7. For the rectilinear block in Figs. 5 and 6, the depth of the object can be determined from labels and algebraic constraints using the assumption that edges and faces are perpendicular. In this case, multiple views are not required to complete the solutions for most faces; no special constraints on the viewpoint are required. A full solid can be obtained by making some simple assumptions about the closure of unseen faces [19].

3.2.3. *Constraints from coplanar vertex groups*

Vertices belonging to the same face result in additional constraints. The equation describing coplanarity is: $ax + by + cz + d = 0$, where a, b, c and d

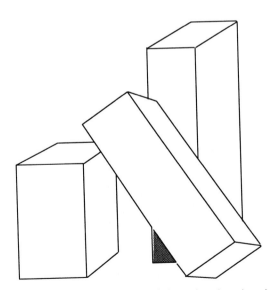

Fig. 7. Shaded face provides only partial information about its orientation.

are new variables which determine a plane, and (x, y, z) is a vertex in the object. For each point in the vertex group there will be one plane equation. In addition, from the labelings, we also get inequality constraints, which relate relative distances of faces from the camera.

A similar analysis can be found in [35], who also represented constraints as sets of equations. Our approach differs from Sugihara's approach in the manner in which underconstrained equations are handled. Sugihara dealt with the problem by introducing cost functions for intensity and texture properties, and then used a minimization procedure to select from the set of underconstrained solutions a "best" solution. In our approach we try to infer as much as possible from the available constraints by solving the set of equations symbolically. A main advantage of our approach is that a set of algebraic equations can naturally represent a set of multiple solutions to an underconstrained problem; i.e., we are not forced to select a specific solution.

3.3. Algebraic reasoning methods

Constraints derived using assumptions about models and projections using the concept hierarchy as well as from the labeling component are translated into an algebraic form. These algebraic constraints are typically nonlinear equations and inequalities. The consistency of the two views can be established by deciding whether algebraic constraints corresponding to the two views are consistent. In [13], we assumed that these constraints are nonlinear equations, which is the case for ideal images in which image coordinates are exactly known. The experiments were able to demonstrate the feasibility of this approach in such cases. A key result is that relatively few groups of constraints are sufficient to prove the inconsistency between two views. In the case that the views are consistent, it is then possible to determine the transformation between views and extend the model to include explicit three-dimensional constraints. More recently, we have also been using nonlinear inequality constraints to deal with imprecise data, tolerances as well as for parameterized model matching.

A Gröbner basis algorithm [9] is used to check whether the algebraic equations are consistent or not. In case the system of equations is consistent, their Gröbner basis embodies all the information about the model which can be extracted from images. In this sense, computing a Gröbner basis serves the role of incremental compilation of available knowledge. This information is stored for subsequent manipulation when equations corresponding to additional constraints are introduced.

There exist many complete methods for reasoning about nonlinear inequalities including Collins' cylindrical algebraic decomposition algorithm [1]. The algorithm however appears to be too complex in practice to solve nonlinear inequalities in model-based vision. Since Brooks [6] had reported considerable success in using an extension of Bledsoe–Shostak's SUP-INF method in solving nonlinear inequalities arising in ACRONYM, we experimented with Brooks' extended SUP-INF method. Many improvements were made to Brooks' procedure for enhancing its computational performance. Our experience with the use of the extended SUP-INF method has not been positive. More recently, we have developed a new approach for solving nonlinear inequalities which will be the subject of a forthcoming paper [15].

In this paper, the main focus is on the use of the Gröbner basis algorithm in the view consistency problem. We will briefly discuss the use of the extended SUP-INF method; an interested reader may consult [6, 14] for more details.

3.3.1. *Testing consistency of equational constraints by the Gröbner basis approach*

The concept of a Gröbner basis of a finite set of polynomials (or equations) was introduced by Buchberger [7, 8] in which he also gave an algorithm for computing such bases. Gröbner basis computation can be used to determine solutions of a system of nonlinear polynomial equations. In particular it can determine the consistency of a system of polynomial equations. For details of this application of a Gröbner basis algorithm, the reader may consult [9, 22]. Below, we give the key results used and an overview of the approach.

Let Q be the field of rationals. Let $Q[x_1, \ldots, x_n]$ be the set of all polynomials with indeterminates $x_1, \ldots, x_n$. Let $p_1 = 0, \ldots, p_j = 0$ be a finite system of nonlinear equations in which $p_1, \ldots, p_j$ are polynomials in $Q[x_1, \ldots, x_n]$.

Proposition 3.3. $p_1 = 0, \ldots, p_j = 0$ *are not consistent, i.e. do not have a solution in complex numbers if and only if a Gröbner basis of* $p_1, \ldots, p_j$ *includes* 1.

The above proposition does not hold completely if one is interested in solutions over the reals. The following holds but its converse is not true.

Corollary 3.4. $p_1 = 0, \ldots, p_j = 0$ *do not have a solution over the reals if a Gröbner basis of* $p_1, \ldots, p_j$ *includes* 1.

Proposition 3.5. *The set of all solutions in complex numbers of* $p_1 = 0, \ldots, p_j = 0$ *are also the common zeros of all polynomials of a Gröbner basis of* $p_1, \ldots, p_j$, *and vice versa.*

The main advantage of computing a Gröbner basis of the set of polynomials $p_1, \ldots, p_j$ corresponding to a consistent set of equations $p_1 = 0, \ldots, p_j = 0$ is that using the Gröbner basis, all solutions (even if one is interested only in solutions over the reals) of the equations can be systematically examined.

3.3.1.1. *Polynomials as rewrite rules and generation of S-polynomials*

Polynomials in this approach are viewed as rewrite (simplification) rules which can be used to generate normal forms for polynomials with respect to equational constraints. For rewriting the headterm of a polynomial (chosen depending upon an ordering used for terms) is replaced by the negative of the rest of the polynomial. A Gröbner basis algorithm is similar to the Knuth–Bendix completion procedure [25]; additional polynomials are generated from a given set of polynomials by overlapping the headterms of polynomials until it is possible to generate canonical forms (unique normal forms) for polynomials with respect to equational constraints.

The key inference step (apart from rewriting) is to generate a *critical pair* from two polynomials as illustrated by the following example:

Given two polynomials $x^2y - 3$ and $xy^2 - 1$, the least common multiple of their headterms can be computed, which is called the *superposition* or *overlap*. In this case, the superposition is x^2y^2. Now, either of the above two polynomials can be used to rewrite the superposition. Rewriting with the first one gives $3y$ as the result, whereas rewriting with the second one produces x. The pair $\langle 3y, x \rangle$ is called the *critical pair* of the above polynomials. The equation $3y - x = 0$ ($3y - x$ is called an *S-polynomial*) follows from the equations $x^2y - 3 = 0$ and $xy^2 - 1 = 0$. An S-polynomial is further rewritten until no more rewriting is possible. If its normal form is not 0, the normal form is augmented to the original set.

This process of generating new polynomials is continued until no new polynomials can be generated. This process is guaranteed to terminate because of Hilbert's Basis Condition, a combinatorial property of ideals over Noetherian rings [37]. If the polynomial 1 (in fact, any rational number) is generated in this process, this indicates the original set of equations is inconsistent; otherwise, the final set of polynomials is a Gröbner basis of the input set of polynomials. An algorithm for computing a Gröbner basis is discussed in [9] where many applications of the algorithm are also given.

We discuss below simple examples which can be done by hand and which illustrate key ideas in a Gröbner basis computation.

Example 3.6. Consider two polynomial equations $x^2y - y^2 = 0$ and $xy^2 = 3$. To compute the solutions of these equations, we will use the pure lexicographic (dictionary) ordering on terms induced by the variable ordering $y > x$. First the two equations are converted into rewrite rules in which the headterm in each equation is made the left side of the rule and the remaining monomials moved to the right. This gives us

$$y^2 \to x^2y \,, \tag{1}$$

$$xy^2 \to 3 \,. \tag{2}$$

Rule (1) can be used to simplify rule (2) to give a new equation $x^3y = 3$, which gives a simplified rule:

$$x^3y \rightarrow 3. \tag{2'}$$

Superposing rules (1) and (2′) gives the term x^3y^2 which can be simplified in two different ways using rules (1) and (2′) as follows:

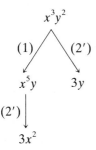

So a new rule is generated:

$$y \rightarrow x^2, \tag{3}$$

which makes rule (1) redundant and simplifies rule (2′) to:

$$x^5 \rightarrow 3. \tag{2''}$$

Rules (2″) and (3) constitute a Gröbner basis of the original polynomials. From these rules, the real solution of the original equations is: $x = 3^{1/5}$ and $y = 3^{2/5}$.

In general, computing a Gröbner basis using the lexicographic ordering generates a triangular form of equations like the one in the above example. From such a Gröbner basis, it is possibly to systematically enumerate all solutions of the original equations.

Example 3.7. It can be easily shown that the following equations are inconsistent, i.e., there is no common solution: $x^2 - x + 12 = 0$, $y^2 = 5$ and $xy = 12$. Solving the first equation for x and the second equation for y, we find that none of these solutions satisfies the third equation. A Gröbner basis computation detects the inconsistency as follows.

Without any loss of generality, the degree ordering on terms induced by the variable ordering $y > x$ is used; in the degree ordering, terms are compared by degree first and terms of the same degree are compared lexicographically. Rules corresponding to these equations are:

$$x^2 \to x - 12 , \tag{4}$$

$$y^2 \to 5 , \tag{5}$$

$$xy \to 12 . \tag{6}$$

Rules (4) and (5) do not overlap as they do not have a common subterm. Rules (4) and (6) overlap to generate a new rule

$$y \to 1 - x . \tag{7}$$

Similarly rules (5) and (6) overlap to generate a new rule

$$x \to 12/17 . \tag{8}$$

When this rule is used to simplify rule (4), the inconsistency (a nonzero rational becoming equal to 0) is detected, which generates a rule

$$1 \to 0 . \tag{9}$$

Rule (9) deletes every other rule. The Gröbner basis containing 1 implies that the equations do not have a common solution (real or complex).

Example 3.8. Consider three simple polynomial equations $xy = 6$, $yz = 15$ and $xz = -10$. One can easily check that these equations do not have any real solutions because to satisfy the first two equations, x, y and z must have the same sign (i.e., they all should be either positive or negative). In either of the two cases, the third equation cannot be satisfied. However the equations do have a complex solution.

Using the total degree ordering on terms induced by the variable ordering $z > y > x$, the following rules are obtained:

$$xy \to 6 , \tag{10}$$

$$yz \to 15 , \tag{11}$$

$$xz \to -10 . \tag{12}$$

Rules (10) and (11) overlap to give xyz as the superposition and the S-polynomial pair $6z - 15x$, from which the rule:

$$z \to (5/2)x \tag{13}$$

is generated. This rule deletes rule (11) which becomes redundant. Rule (12) gets simplified to:

$$x^2 \rightarrow -4 .$$ (12')

Rule (12') and rule (10) generate a new rule

$$y \rightarrow -(3/2)x .$$ (14)

Rules (12'), (13) and (14) constitute a Gröbner basis. Clearly this equation set has no real zeros but it does have complex zeros.

3.3.2. *Brooks' extension to the* SUP-INF *method for nonlinear inequalities*

Bledsoe [5] introduced the SUP-INF method to prove universally quantified linear inequalities over the integers; this method was subsequently extended by Shostak [31]. The goal is to decide whether these inequalities can be satisfied. If yes, the method produces lower and upper bounds for each variable appearing in the set of inequalities. The method is based on transforming inequalities such that for each variable x, they can be expressed as $x \leq ub_i$ or $x \geq lb_i$, where ub_i and lb_i are, in general, linear expressions in terms of the rest of the variables. An upper bound for x, SUP(x), is then the minimum over the ub_i, where as a lower bound for x, INF(x), is the maximum over lb_i. To compute SUP(ub_i), say, the algorithm is called recursively on each ub_i in an attempt to compute the lower and upper bounds on ub_i in terms of the variable x. Finally, linear equations in terms of x are obtained for these bounds, which can be solved. A dual technique is used for computing the lower bounds. In this way, the algorithm computes rational upper and lower bounds for each variable.

Brooks [6] extended Bledsoe–Shostak's SUP-INF method to be applicable to nonlinear inequalities including trigonometric functions. Brooks' extensions can at best be considered heuristics since the subclass of inequalities on which his extension works is not understood. For nonlinear inequalities also, the method works in the same way as in the linear case. The bounds for each variable x are computed in terms of other variables and possibly x itself, but unlike in the linear case, ub_i and lb_i may be rational functions in which terms involving x appear. Before dividing an expression by a variable or a term, the extended algorithm attempts to determine the parity (whether the value is always positive, zero or negative) of variables. Parity constraints from non-linear terms are propagated to generate parity constraints on variables, which in turn, constrain the parity of other nonlinear terms involving these variables. The method is limited, however, since for computing lower and upper bounds of nonlinear expressions, it deals with each nonlinear term separately without constraining other terms in which common variables appear. For lack of space, we omit more details and examples; an interested reader may refer to [6] and [14] for further details.

4. View Consistency Experiments

We have used the multi-level geometric reasoning system for the view consistency problem. Two types of constraints are generated using the concept hierarchy and labeling algorithm:

(1) equations describing the projections relating object points in terms of image points and projection parameters,

(2) topological constraints describing relationships in each vertex group; these equational constraints restrict vertices in each vertex group to be coplanar.

In addition, if the relation between two projections (images) is known such as in the case of stereo matching, then there are additional equational constraints relating them also. There may also be auxiliary relations arising from trigonometric identities relating trigonometric functions of rotation angles.

We are given two-dimensional projections of the object in each image plane. The goal is to determine if the two projections actually correspond to the same polyhedron, or equivalently, if one projection can match against another projection. The three-dimensional geometry and topological structure of the object is not known.

4.1. Algebraic formulation: Recognition as constraint satisfaction

The matching process is to first form assignments between vertex groups in each projection and then to test the algebraic consistency of the resulting equations. If the equations are consistent, then the two views may correspond to the same three-dimensional object; or at least they share some solutions for the possible objects that are consistent with both projections. The consistency also allows a more specific determination of the three-dimensional configuration of the object. For example, if the transformation between the views is given in advance, then the correspondence between equations is similar to the feature matching done in classical stereo analysis. The matching between vertices provides the relative depth value for each vertex match.

If the transformation between views is unknown, then the depths cannot be determined, but only constrained. It is reasonable to refer to this case as *algebraic stereo*. The object surface depth is not explicitly determined but the solutions of the equations represent a space of possible object surfaces. The introduction of new constraints, either from hypotheses about geometric constraints on groups of projection elements, or from new views of the object, will reduce the number of unknown coordinate values. In this sense, the approach is incremental. The method terminates if the desired three-dimensional information such as the depth of vertices and transformation parameters can be derived.

If an inconsistency is detected, then other assignments of vertex groups have to be tried. Various heuristics such as the number of vertices in a vertex group and adjacency information about vertices in a vertex group can be used to reduce the search space of possible assignments between the vertex groups of the two images.

The consistency of the two views can be established by deciding whether algebraic constraints corresponding to the two views are consistent. It turns out that relatively few groups of constraints are sufficient to prove the inconsistency between two views. In the case that the views are consistent, it is then possible to determine the transformation between views and extend the model to include explicit three-dimensional constraints. Some of the problems to consider are:

(1) Is a given assignment of vertex groups in two projections consistent?

(2) Given a consistent assignment, what can we conclude about the transformation parameters and depth of the object surfaces?

(3) Given two vertex groups with consistent assignments, can they be merged in a consistent manner?

We use constraints to form *maximally consistent assignment sets*. A maximally consistent assignment set is a consistent set of vertex assignments such that the addition of any additional vertex assignment would cause inconsistency. The set of equations associated with a maximally consistent assignment set forms a model for the object.

A set of constraints may be consistent simply because there are too many degrees of freedom. Such a set of constraints is of little use in further refining a model. Thus, when we use a vertex group to constrain a set of assignments, we want to make sure that its constraints are sufficiently strong to either cause inconsistency, or, in case of a consistent assignment, to allow us to significantly refine the model.

4.1.1. *Projection constraints*

First let us consider the transformation between the three-dimensional vertex locations and their corresponding two-dimensional positions in the image plane. The natural transformation that results from a standard imaging system is the *perspective* transformation. However, it is not essential to use this exact relationship in most practical situations. It can be shown that an approximation to perspective, the *affine* transformation, is quite appropriate for most viewing situations [36]. The affine approximation is more realistic than the usual orthographic assumption, but does not exhibit all the properties of the full perspective case. But with more computational difficulty the perspective transformation can also be handled in our approach.

The form of the affine transformation is given by the following matrix relation:

$$p = w[I_2][R]P + p_0 ,$$

where w is an affine scale factor and R represents a rotation matrix for the orientation of the object reference frame relative to the image reference frame. The matrix I_2 indicates the projection from three dimensions into the two-dimensional image plane,

$$I_2 = \begin{bmatrix} 1 & 0 & 0 \\ 0 & 1 & 0 \end{bmatrix} ,$$

p is the location of the projected vertex position vector P in the image plane. The two-dimensional vector p_0 represents a translation in the view plane.

The rotation matrix, R, can be represented as the product of three matrices,

$$R = [R_z][R_y][R_x] ,$$

which represent rotations about each of the view plane coordinate axes. For example,

$$R_x = \begin{bmatrix} 1 & 0 & 0 \\ 0 & \cos \phi & \sin \phi \\ 0 & -\sin \phi & \cos \phi \end{bmatrix} ,$$

where ϕ is the angle of rotation about the x-axis. The complete transformation thus requires six parameters: three rotations, two translation components and a scale factor.

Without loss of generality, we assume that the projection of the object into the first image plane, π, involves no rotation, translation and a unity scale factor. The only unknowns are the depths (z-component) of the three-dimensional object vertices. The x- and y-components of vertex P are just the vertex projection in image coordinates.

The affine viewing projection and the transformation between images are thus combined into a single transformation between corresponding image vertex locations in the two views. That is,

$$p' = w[I_2][R]P + p'_0 ,$$

where p' is the location of the projection of vertex P in the second image. In this case, R represents the rotation between image reference frames. The scale factor w arises from differences in image depths betwen views. p'_0 is the component of the translation vector between viewpoints which lies in the second view plane, π'.

It should be noted that our procedure assumes the location of projected image vertices to be exact. This assumption is not appropriate when dealing with actual intensity image data. Feature locations can be at least several pixels in error for actual images. See a later section about extension of this approach for dealing with errors and imprecise data.

4.2. The cube

We consider a $20 \times 20 \times 20$ cube centered about the origin (this information is not provided to the system) and form two affine projections of it along two diagonals. The resulting images are shown in Fig. 8. The first image corresponds to a rotation of 45 degrees around the x-axis, followed by a rotation of -35.26 degrees around the y-axis, followed by a rotation of -30 degrees about the z-axis. The second image corresponds to a rotation of -45 degrees around the x-axis, followed by a rotation of -35.26 degrees around the y-axis, followed by a rotation of 30 degrees around the z-axis.

From these projections the x- and y-components of the two images are calculated. Since the coordinates are irrational numbers and the Gröbner basis method requires exact coordinates, these numbers must be represented by using polynomial equations. For example, if the x component of a point is $\sqrt{200}$, then it is input as $x^2 = 200$, instead of as $x = 14.142137. \ldots$ Without using inequalities, it is not possible to distinguish between $\sqrt{200}$ and $-\sqrt{200}$. However, if there are two coordinates x_1 and x_2, one whose value is $\sqrt{200}$ and the other whose value is $-\sqrt{200}$, then these can be represented by the two equations, $x_1^2 = 200$, and $x_1 + x_2 = 0$.

Several experiments for this example were performed making different assumptions about available information.

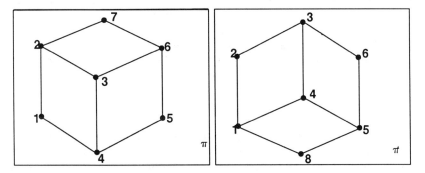

Fig. 8. Two images of a cube.

4.2.1. Coplanarity constraints

The labeling algorithm described earlier is used on the images to identify faces. Derivation about relative positions of the faces from labeling is not used in these experiments since that information can only be expressed using inequalities. Using the labeling algorithm, vertex groups belonging to the same face are identified. This information is translated into algebraic constraints as *coplanarity equations*.

For each vertex (x, y, z) on a face, an equation $ax + by + cz + d = 0$ is generated, where a, b, c, d are parameters of a face. If a face does not pass through the origin, then d is not 0, so a simpler equation can be obtained by dividing the original equation by d.

4.2.2. Projection constraints

The general equation for the points in the second image in terms of the first image is

$$p = w[I_2][R_z][R_y][R_x]P + p_0 \,.$$

Instead of multiplying the three rotation matrices out to get an equation for image coordinates in terms of object coordinates, we take the inverse of the transformation matrix to get an equation for object coordinates in terms of image coordinates. For example, the equation for object coordinate x_0 in terms of image coordinates x, y, and z is

$$x_0 - x \cos \phi \cos \theta - y \sin \phi \cos \theta + z \sin \theta = 0 \,.$$

In these experiments precomputing the inverse transformation improves the efficiency of the Gröbner basis computation considerably. Similar equations for the coordinates of each point in the image were generated.

4.2.3. Trigonometric identities

This set consists of the equations of the form $\cos^2 \psi + \sin^2 \psi = 1$, one for each of the six rotation angles (three per image). The indeterminates are the sine and cosine of the angles; for angle ψ, there are two corresponding variables, *cos-psi* and *sin-psi*.

Experiment 4.1. *Determining depth given the transformation between the two views.* This experiment is the same as stereo matching. We take the face corresponding to vertices $1, 2, 3$, and 4 in Fig. 8 as a vertex group. The transformation from image 1 to image 2 is given by $\psi_2 = -70.53$, $\theta_2 = 0$, and $\phi_2 = 0$. Since $\cos(-70.53) = \frac{1}{3}$, and $\sin(-70.53) = -\sqrt{\frac{8}{9}}$, the equations for ψ_2 are $3 \, cos\text{-}psi\text{-}2 = 1$, and $9 \, sin\text{-}psi\text{-}2^2 = 8$.

We assign vertex 1 in image 1 to vertex 1 in image 2, vertex 2 in image 1 to vertex 2 in image 2, and so on. Using the notation that $v_{i,j}$ is vertex j in image i, the assignment is:

$$v_{1,1} = v_{2,1} \,, \qquad v_{1,2} = v_{2,2} \,, \qquad v_{1,3} = v_{2,3} \,, \qquad v_{1,4} = v_{2,4} \,.$$

In order to assign a vertex in image 1 with object coordinates x, y, and z, with a vertex in image 2 with object coordinates x', y', and z', we would add the three equations:

$$x' - x = 0 \,, \qquad y' - y = 0 \,, \qquad z' - z = 0 \,.$$

The union of all these equations comprises the input to the Gröbner basis algorithm. In all there are over 70 equations in 63 variables. However, many of them are redundant. After 59 seconds and 52 critical pairs, a Gröbner basis is obtained. It consists of over 90 polynomials, including the solution to the vertex depths.

Experiment 4.2. *Determining inconsistency given the transformation between the two views.* This problem is very similar to the first problem. The only difference is in the assignment set. Instead of the consistent assignment given above, the following inconsistent assignment is used:

$$v_{1,1} = v_{2,3} \,, \qquad v_{1,2} = v_{2,1} \,, \qquad v_{1,3} = v_{2,4} \,, \qquad v_{1,4} = v_{2,2} \,.$$

After 48 seconds and 0 critical pairs (just by simplification) the Gröbner basis detects inconsistency. Note that detecting inconsistency is much easier than determining consistency. This is because contradiction might be detected well before all possible pairs are examined. Note that inconsistency has been detected with fewer vertex assignments than are required to actually solve for unknown vertex locations.

Experiment 4.3. *Unknown transformation between views: Matching a face in one image against a face in the other image.* This problem is severely undercon-strained. In fact, with only one face of the cube, any assignment is consistent. Given the same assignment as in Experiment 4.1, the Gröbner basis computation runs for 267 seconds, generating 371 critical pairs. The depths and rotation parameters are still only partially constrained.

For the assignment in Experimental 4.2, the Gröbner basis computation runs for 224 seconds, generating 256 critical pairs.

Experiment 4.4. *Refining the match by matching a second face in the first image to another face in the second image.* To the Gröbner basis generated in

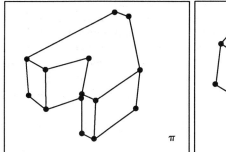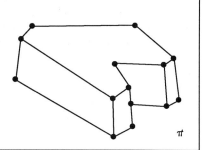

Fig. 9. Two images of a block.

Experiment 4.3, the equations corresponding to the face containing vertices 3, 4, 5, 6 (see Fig. 8) are added. There are 126 equations in 90 variables. With a consistent assignment, the Gröbner basis algorithm terminates after 890 seconds and 706 critical pairs. From the result, the depths of the vertices as well as the transformation parameters can be derived. We can determine that the object under consideration is indeed a cube.

With an inconsistent assignment of vertices, the Gröbner basis detects inconsistency after 113 seconds and 55 critical pairs.

In addition, other experiments on different projections of the cube were successfully performed with different transformation parameters including different scaling factors and translation vectors.

4.3. A polyhedral block

The view consistency approach was also tried on a more complex polyhedral object (Fig. 9). The object has 16 vertices, 24 edges and 10 faces. Different experiments were performed. The results were encouraging for the stereo case (i.e., when the transformation between projections is known). Our implementation could deduce depth parameters in less than a minute. In the case of an incorrect assignment, inconsistency could be determined in a few seconds.

However, when the transformation between the projections is not known, and with a consistent assignment of vertices, the method was able to deduce depth parameters as well as the transformation parameters; but it took considerably longer. The implementation quickly detected inconsistency even when one vertex on the face with 8 vertices was incorrectly assigned.

5. Imprecise Data

Two serious limitations of the use of the Gröbner basis algorithm for the view consistency and other problems are (i) the requirement that all the information should be specified in exact form, and (ii) the inability to deal with inequality constraints that might arise due to viewing constraints, imprecise data, and in parameterized models [6, 14]. Because of these limitations we have so far assumed that the projected image vertices are exact. Further, if a coordinate position in an ideal projection is $\sqrt{20}$, this must be specified implicitly using an equation $x^2 = 20$; it is not possible to rule out the negative value that x could take. Both of these problems can be handled if inequality constraints are also allowed.

Since late 1987, we have been using inequality constraints for model formation and model matching. Since Brooks had reported considerable success in the use of his extension of Bledsoe–Shostak's SUP-INF method for handling nonlinear inequalities in the ACRONYM system, we implemented his method in our geometric reasoning system and integrated it with the Gröbner basis algorithm. The integration is not completely done yet, as some of the steps are currently performed manually.

Unlike Brooks' algorithm where equalities are converted into an equivalent set of inequalities, we first manipulate equality constraints using the Gröbner basis algorithm, possibly deducing additional equality constraints. In the linear case, this results in significant improvement in the performance; in the non-linear case also this seems to help. Equality constraints are then used as rewrite rules to simplify the inequality constraints. All constraints (input as well as deduced) are then transformed into inequalities and the SUP and INF method is invoked. If any new equality constraint is detected (when the satisfiable interval for some variable or term includes only one value, i.e., its upper bound and lower bound are identical), then that equality constraint is further propagated using rewriting and the critical pair computation in the Gröbner basis algorithm.

Another modification made to Brooks' algorithm is to specify a subset of the variables as input variables. When SUP and INF are called on expressions in these variables, no extra computation takes place, rather the user provided bounds are used. This modification is especially useful in our parameterized model matching problems where there are a lot of variables involved.

As reported in [14], Brooks' method does not always give the best possible bounds in a single iteration; instead, many iterations may be required to get the best bounds on variables. Depending upon the order in which bounds for different variables are computed, the parity information about variables which is not available in one iteration may be subsequently propagated. This information is used in later iterations to get better bounds. More than one iteration may also be needed for detecting inconsistency of a set of nonlinear constraints. Examples of nonlinear constraints requiring multiple iterations for checking inconsistency as well as computing bounds are discussed in [14]. Better bounds can also be obtained by the case analysis on variables whose parity cannot be determined [14].

Despite these key changes to Brooks' method which significantly improve its performance, our experience in using the method in view consistency and model matching problems is not positive. For the cube example discussed above, when the transformation is known (the stero case) and vertex positions in images are given within a certain tolerance, the view consistency problem can be adequately solved since we are dealing with linear equalities. In the case where the affine scale parameter is not known the constraints become non-linear, but the SUP-INF method still provides some useful information about the depth. However, when one rotation parameter is not known the equation $\sin^2 \phi + \cos^2 \phi = 1$ has to be linearly approximated in order to obtain any useful information. The general case in which the transformation is unknown cannot be handled using the extended SUP-INF method.

Recently [15], we have developed new heuristics for handling nonlinear inequalities which we are planning to implement and study their effectiveness in dealing with nonlinear inequalities arising in model formation and model matching problems.

6. Future Directions

There are three broad areas in which significant progress needs to be made for this approach to be successful. Firstly, the use of concept hierarchies and higher-level geometric constraints for controlling the search space in reasoning at the algebraic level must be further developed. Interaction between different levels of reasoning and how information is propagated from one level to the other is crucial in making the approach effective. This necessitates the study of heuristics for translating algebraic constraints back to higher-level topological and geometric constraints. We believe that proper organization of geometric and topological knowledge and associated reasoning methods in the form of a concept hierarchy will be useful for this purpose.

Another promising research direction is to structure constraints and control their propagation. One approach in this direction is to associate a *type* with constraints keeping track of the source(s) of each constraint. The type would be determined by geometric and topological relations that define a geometric entity. Interaction between constraints could be limited based on their types and their source. One example of such a type class has already been discussed, the coplanar set of vertices identified through the labeling algorithm; if we had another group, say three mutually perpendicular edges, it is not meaningful to propagate constraints derived from two different groups of such constraint sets. However, with the current general Gröbner basis algorithm there is nothing to prevent the interaction of these two types.

In order for these methods to be used in practical vision problems heuristics must be developed for solving nonlinear inequalities needed to express imprecise data, tolerances for parameters as well as specifying families of models in a parameterized fashion. It is necessary to develop algorithms for inequalities which may not have good worst-case performance but which work well on simple examples. Gröbner basis algorithms are examples of such algorithms for solving nonlinear equality constraints.

Even though our experience in using the Gröbner basis algorithm for solving equations has been quite encouraging, we observe that many unnecessary constraints are generated which are not likely to be useful. Heuristics are also needed to identify what constraints must be made to interact to deduce new constraints. Structuring constraints into groups as discussed above might be helpful for this also. It will also be useful to develop notions of incremental Gröbner bases, combining different Gröbner bases as well as hierarchical Gröbner bases, which exploit the structural information about the constraints as well as their sources.

Appendix A. A Fragment of Concept Hierarchy for Projection

```
concept sequence(x: any);
   functions
      head(sequence): x,
      tail(sequence): sequence,
      cons(x, sequence): sequence,
      null: sequence,
      length(sequence): natural;
   vars
      s: sequence,
      e: x;
   axioms
      head(cons(e, s)) = = e,
      tail(cons(e, s)) = = s,
      length(null) = = 0,
      length(cons(e, s)) = = 1 + length(s);
end;


define sequence(real) into metric-seq;
   functions
      metric(metric-seq): real,
      size(metric-seq): real;
   axioms
      metric(null) = = 0,
      metric(s) = = head(x)² + metric(tail(s)),
      size(s) = = sqrt(metric(s));
end;
```

```
restrict metric-seq into a n-tuple(n: number);
  vars
    s: n-tuple,
    i: natural;
  axioms
    length(s) = = n,
    ith(s,i) = = if i = 1  then  head(s)
                          else ith(tail(s), i − 1);
end;

concept 3d-point;
  functions
    x-coord(3d-point): real,
    y-coord(3d-point): real,
    z-coord(3d-point): real,
    make-point(real,real,real): 3d-point,
    distance(3d-point,3d-point): real;
  vars
    p1, p2: 3d-point,
    x, y, z: real;
  axioms
    x-coord(make-point(x, y, z)) = = x,
    y-coord(make-point(x, y, z)) = = y,
    z-coord(make-point(x, y, z)) = = z,
    distance(p1, p2) = = sqrt((x-coord(p1) − x-coord(p2))² +
                              (y-coord(p1) − y-coord(p2))² +
                              (z-coord(p1) − z-coord(p2))²);
end;

identify 3d-point as n-tuple(3) with
  vars
    p: 3d-point,
    x, y, z: real;
  x-coord(p) = = ith(p, 1),
  y-coord(p) = = ith(p, 2),
  z-coord(p) = = ith(p, 3),
  make-point(x, y, z) = = cons(x, cons(y, cons(z, null)));
end;

concept 2d-point;
  functions
    x-coord(2d-point): real,
    y-coord(2d-point): real,
    make-point(real,real): 2d-point,
```

```
        distance(2d-point,2d-point): real,
        distinct(2d-point,2d-point): bool;
    vars
        p1, p2: 2d-point,
        x, y: real;
    axioms
        x-coord(make-point(x, y)) == x,
        y-coord(make-point(x, y)) == y,
        distance(p1, p2) == sqrt((x-coord(p1) - x-coord(p2))² +
                                 (y-coord(p1) - y-coord(p2))²),
        distinct(p1, p2) == distance(p1, p2) ≠ 0;
end;

identify 2d-point as n-tuple(2) with
    vars
        p: 3d-point,
        x, y: real;
    x-coord(p) == ith(p, 1),
    y-coord(p) == ith(p, 2),
    make-point(x, y) == cons(x, cons(y, null));
end;

concept transformation(object-type: n-tuple(n),
                       transformed-object-type: n-tuple(n - 1));
    functions
        transform(object-type): transformed-object-type;
end;

3d-2d-projection = transformation(3d-point, 2d-point);

restrict 3d-2d-projection into perspective;
    functions
        view-plane: plane,
        eye-point: 3d-point;
    vars
        p: 3d-point;
    axiom
        transform(p) == perspective-trans(p, view-plane,eye-point);
end;

restrict 3d-2d-projection into perspective-projection;
    functions
        focal-length: real,
        rotation: 3d-rotation,
        translation: 3d-translation;
```

```
vars
   p: 3d-point;
axiom
   transform(p) = = perspective-distort(translate(rotate(p, rotation),
                                        translation),focal-length);
end;

restrict perspective-projection into affine-projection;
   functions
      scale: real,
      rotation: 3d-rotation,
      translation: 3d-translation;
   vars
      p: 3d-point;
   axiom
      transform(p) = = scale(translate(rotate(p, rotation),
                                    translation), scale);
end;

restrict affine-projection into orthographic-projection;
   axiom
      scale = = 1;
end;
```

Appendix B. A Fragment of Concept Hierarchy for GEOMETER

```
concept line;
   functions
      point-1(line): 2d-point,
      point-2(line): 2d-point,
      make-line(2d-point, 2d-point): line,
      slope(line): real,
      length(line): real,
      _is on_(2d-point, line): bool,
      parallel(line,line): bool,
      perpendicular(line,line): bool,
      equidistant(line,line): bool;
   vars
      p, p1, p2: 2d-point,
      l: line;
   axioms
      point-1(make-line(p1, p2)) = = p1,
      point-2(make-line(p1, p2)) = = p2,
      distinct(point-1(l), point-2(l)),
```

```
      slope(l) == (y-coord(point-1(l)) − y-coord(point-2(l)))/
                  (x-coord(point-1(l)) − x-coord(point-2(l))),
      length(l) == distance(point-1(l), point-2(l)),
      p is on l == slope(make-line(point-1(l), p)) =
                   slope(make-line(p, point-2(l))),
      parallel(l1, l2) == slope(l1) = slope(l2),
      perpendicular(l1, l2) == slope(l1) = −1/slope(l2),
      equidistant(l1, l2) == length(l1) = length(l2);
   end;


concept circle;
   functions
      center(circle): 2d-point,
      point-on(circle): 2d-point;
      make-circle(2d-point, 2d-point): circle,
      radius(circle): real,
      diameter(circle): real,
      _is on_(2d-point, circle): bool;
   vars
      p, pc: 2d-point,
      c: circle;
   axioms
      center(make-circle(pc,p)) == pc,
      point-on(make-circle(pc,p)) == p,
      radius(c) == distance(point-on(c), center(c)),
      diameter(c) == 2 * radius(c),
      p is on c == distance(p, center(c)) = radius(c);
   end;


restrict 2d-point into origin;
   vars
      p: origin;
   axioms
      x-coord(p) == 0,
      y-coord(p) == 0;
   end;


restrict line into horizontal-line;
   vars
      l: horizontal-line;
   axiom
      y-coord(point-1(l)) = y-coord(point-2(l));
   end;
```

```
restrict line into vertical-line;
  vars
    l: vertical-line;
  axiom
    x-coord(point-1(l)) = x-coord(point-2(l));
end

restrict horizontal-line into x-axis;
  vars
    l:  x-axis,
    o: origin;
  axiom
    o is on l;
end;

restrict vertical-line into y-axis;
  vars
    l:  y-axis,
    o: origin;
  axiom
    o is on l;
end;

concept relation-on-three-points;
  functions
    point-1(relation-on-three-points): 2d-point,
    point-2(relation-on-three-points): 2d-point,
    point-3(relation-on-three-points): 2d-point,
    make-rel-on-three-points(2d-point, 2d-point, 2d-point): relation-on-three-points;
  vars
    p1, p2, p3: 2d-point,
    rel: relation-on-three-points;
  axioms
    point-1(make-rel-on-three-points(p1, p2, p3)) == p1,
    point-2(make-rel-on-three-points(p1, p2, p3)) == p2,
    point-3(make-rel-on-three-points(p1, p2, p3)) == p3;
end;

restrict relation-on-three-points into collinear;
  vars
    rel: relation-on-three-points;
  axiom
    point-1(rel) is on make-line(point-2(rel), point-3(rel));
end;
```

```
restrict relation-on-three-points into not-collinear;
  vars
    rel: relation-on-three-points;
  axiom
    not point-1(rel) is on make-line(point-2(rel), point-3(rel));
end;

restrict relation-on-three-points into mid-point;
  vars
    rel: relation-on-three-points;
  axiom
    point-3(rel) is on make-line(point-1(rel), point-2(rel))
    and equidistant(make-line(point-1(rel), point-3(rel)),
                    make-line(point-2(rel), point-3(rel)));
end;
```

ACKNOWLEDGMENT

The implementation of the Gröbner basis used was developed by Rick Harris. Many ideas reported in this paper were developed during discussions with Chris Connolly, David Musser, Paliath Narendran, Ross Stenstrom, and Alex Stepanov.

REFERENCES

1. Arnon, D.S., Collins, G.E., and McCallum, S., Cylindrical algebraic decomposition I: The basic algorithm, *SIAM J. Comput.* **13** (1984) 865–877.
2. Ayache, N. and Faugeras, O., A new method for the recognition and positioning of 2d objects, in: *Proceedings 7th International Joint Conference on Pattern Recognition*, Montreal, Que. (1984).
3. Ballard, D., Tsuji, S. and Curtiss, M., Parallel polyhedral shape recognition, in: *Proceedings CVPR* (1985).
4. Besl, P. and Jain, R., Three-dimensional object recognition, *Comput. Surv.* **17** (1) (1985).
5. Bledsoe, W.W., A new method for proving certain Pressburger formulas, in: *Advance Papers IJCAI-75*, Tbilisi, U.S.S.R. (1975) 15–21.
6. Brooks, R.A., Symbolic reasoning among 3-D models and 2-D images, *Artificial Intelligence* **17** (1981) 285–348.
7. Buchberger, B., An algorithm for finding a basis for the residue class ring of a zero-dimensional polynomial ideal, Ph.D. Thesis, University of Innsbruck, Austria (1965) (in German).
8. Buchberger, B., An algorithmic criterion for the solvability of an algebraic system of equations, *Aequations Math.* **4** (3) (1970) 374–383.
9. Buchberger, B., Gröbner bases: An algorithmic method in polynomial ideal theory, in: N.K. Bose (Ed.), *Multidimensional Systems Theory* (Reidel, Dordrecht, The Netherlands, 1985) 184–232.
10. Burstall, R.M. and Goguen, J.A., Putting theories together to make specifications, in: *Proceedings IJCAI-77*, Cambridge, MA (1977) 1045.
11. Clowes, M.B., On seeing things, *Artificial Intelligence* **2** (1971) 79–116.

12. Connolly, C.I. and Stenstrom, J.R., Construction of polyhedral models from multiple range views, in: *Proceedings 8th International Conference on Pattern Recognition*, Paris, France (1986).
13. Cyrluk, D., Kapur, D., Mundy, J. and Nguyen, V., Formation of partial 3D models from 2D projections—an application of algebraic reasoning, in: *Proceedings 1987 DARPA Image Understanding Workshop*, Los Angeles, CA (1987).
14. Cyrluk, D., Kapur, D. and Mundy, J., Algebraic reasoning in view consistency and parameterized model matching problems, in: *Proceedings of 1988 DARPA Image Understanding Workshop*, Cambridge, MA (1988).
15. Cyrluk, D., Kapur, D. and Mundy, J., Heuristics for nonlinear inequality constraints, Presented at: *International Workshop on Algorithmic Aspects of Algebra and Geometry*, Ithaca, NY (1988).
16. Fiumicelli, A. and Torre V., On the understanding of line drawings, Internal Rept., University of Genoa (1986).
17. Grimson, E. and Lozano-Pérez, T., Search and sensing strategies for recognition and localization of two- and three-dimensional objects, in: *Proceedings 3rd International Symposium on Robotics Research* (1985).
18. Henle, M., *A Combinatorial Introduction to Topology* (Freeman, San Francisco, CA, 1979).
19. Herman, M., Representation and incremental construction of a three-dimensional scene model, Rept. CMU-CS-85-103, Carnegie-Mellon University, Pittsburgh, PA (1985).
20. Huffman, D.A., Impossible objects as nonsense sentences, in: B. Meltzer and D. Michie (Eds.), *Machine Intelligence 6* (Elsevier, New York, 1971) 295.
21. Kapur, D. and Zhang, H., RRL: A rewrite rule laboratory, in: *Proceedings 9th International Conference on Automated Deduction (CADE-9)*, Argonne, IL, Lecture Notes in Computer Science **230** (Springer, New York, 1988).
22. Kapur, D., Geometry theorem proving using Hilbert's Nullstellensatz, in: *Proceedings Symposium on Symbolic and Algebraic Computation (SYMSAC-86)*, Waterloo, Ont. (1986) 202–208.
23. Kapur, D., Musser, D.R. and Stepanov, A.A., Operators and algebraic structures, in: *Proceedings Conference on Functional Programming Languages and Computer Architecture*, Portsmouth, NH (1981).
24. Kapur, D. and Mundy, J., Wu's method and its application to perspective viewing, *Artificial Intelligence* **37** (1988) 15–36 (this volume).
25. Knuth, D. and Bendix, P., Simple word problems in universal algebras, in: J. Leech (Ed.), *Computational Problems in Abstract Algebras* (Pergamon Press, Oxford, 1970).
26. Lowe, D., *Perceptual Organization and Visual Recognition* (Kluwer Academic Publishers, Boston, MA, 1985).
27. Malik, J., Interpreting line drawings of curved objects, Ph.D. Thesis, Department of Computer Science, Stanford University, Stanford, CA (1985).
28. Nguyen, V., A parallel algorithm for labeling polyhedral images, in: *Proceedings IJCAI-87*, Milan, Italy (1987).
29. Roberts, L.G., *Machine Perception of Three Dimensional Solids* (MIT Press, Cambridge, MA, 1965).
30. Shapira, R. and Freeman, H., Computer description of bodies bounded by quadric surfaces from a set of imperfect projections, *IEEE Trans. Comput.* **27** (9) (1978).
31. Shostak, R., On the SUP-INF method for proving Pressburger formulas, *J. ACM* **24** (1977) 529–543.
32. Silberburg, T., Harwood, D. and Davis, L., Object recognition using oriented model points, *Comput. Vision Image Process.* 35 (1986).
33. Sowa, J., *Conceptual Structures: Information Processing in Mind and Machine* (Addison-Wesley, Reading, MA, 1984).

34. Strat, T., Spatial reasoning from line drawings of polyhedra, in: *Proceedings IEEE Workshop on Computer Vision Representation and Control* (1984).

35. Sugihara, K., An algebraic approach to shape-from-image problems, *Artificial Intelligence* **23** (1984) 59–95.

36. Thompson, D. and Mundy, J., Three-dimensional model matching from an unconstrained viewpoint, in: *Proceedings IEEE Conference on Robotics and Automation*, Raleigh, NC (1987).

37. van der Waerden, B.L., *Modern Algebra*, **I**, **II** (Frederick Ungar, New York, 1966).

38. Walker, E. and Herman, M., Geometric reasoning for constructing 3D scene descriptions from images, *Artificial Intelligence* **37** (1988) 275–290 (this volume).

39. Waltz, D., Generating semantic descriptions from drawings of scenes with shadows, Ph.D. Thesis, MIT, Cambridge, MA (1972).

Received March 1987; revised version received August 1988

On the Geometric Interpretation of Image Contours

Radu Horaud
LIFIA, 46, avenue F. Viallet, 38031 Grenoble, France

Michael Brady
University of Oxford, Department of Engineering Science, Parks Road, Oxford, OX1 3PJ, United Kingdom

ABSTRACT

In this paper we suggest a computational model for the 3D interpretation of a 2D view based on contour classification and contour interpretation. We concentrate on those contours arising from discontinuities in surface orientation. We combine a generic surface description well suited for visual tasks with a model of the image formation process in order to derive image contour configurations that are likely to be interpreted in terms of surface contours. Next we describe a computer algorithm which attempts to interpret image contours on the following grounds. First, an image analysis process produces a description in terms of contours and relationships between them. Second, among these contours, we select those which form a desired configuration. Third, the selected contours are combined with constraints available with the image formation process in order to be interpreted in terms of discontinuities in surface orientation. As a consequence, there is a dramatic reduction in the number of possible orientations of the associated scene surfaces.

1. Introduction

An image is a two-dimensional (2D) projection of a three-dimensional (3D) scene. Many scene characteristics such as discontinuity in surface orientation, changes in surface reflectance, shadows, and textures give rise to image contours. An image contour simply characterizes the variation of image brightness. The analysis of this variation cannot, by itself, provide a correct interpretation in terms of the scene attributes mentioned above.

In spite of this apparent ambiguity, human beings have no difficulty in properly interpreting images. We can easily recognize complex objects, find their spatial orientation, and even more, learn a great deal about objects never seen before. In this paper we suggest a computational model for the 3D interpretation of a 2D view based on contour classification and contour interpretation. We concentrate on those contours arising from discontinuities in surface orientation. We combine a generic surface description well suited for visual tasks with a model of the image formation process in order to derive image contour configurations that are likely to be interpreted in terms of surface contours.

Next we describe a computer algorithm which attempts to interpret image contours on the following grounds. First, an image analysis process produces a description in terms of contours and relationships between them. Second, among these contours, we select those which form a desired configuration. Third, the selected contours are combined with constraints available from the image formation process in order to be interpreted in terms of discontinuities in surface orientation. As a consequence, there is a dramatic reduction in the number of possible orientations of the associated scene surfaces.

1.1. Background and approach

Among many surface description alternatives, generalized cylinders and generalized cones have been introduced by Binford [4] as a convenient object representation within the context of visual recognition. Furthermore, Marr [11] suggested an argument in support of this representation. He argued that under a set of assumptions, there is a one-to-one map between an *occluding contour* and a generalized cylinder. The recognition strategy suggested by Marr is based on the observation that the axis of symmetry of the occluding contour is the image of the generalized cylinder's axis. This result is true only under parallel projection and, more restrictive, when the viewing direction is perpendicular to the cylinder's axis. For a foreshortened view, one of Marr's assumptions is not valid anymore, namely that the *contour generator* of the occluding contour is planar.

This restriction can be partially overcome if an occluding contour is further decomposed into *extremal* and *discontinuity* contours. This distinction has been introduced by Barrow and Tenenbaum [3] and is made clear on Fig. 1. An occluding boundary separates an object from the background. A discontinuity boundary occurs whenever a smooth surface terminates or intersects with another surface. An extremal boundary occurs where a curved surface turns smoothly away from the viewer. Hence, 3D shape recovery from image contours is twofold: interpretation of extremal *and* discontinuity contours. On this line of investigation a certain number of geometric and topological properties have been reported which relate extremal contours to surfaces. See for example Koenderink [9] and Brady et al. [6]. Discontinuity contours are harder to interpret mainly because they correspond to surface intersections whose orientations in space are not constrained by the viewing direction.

A number of researchers have concentrated on the 3D interpretation of an isolated image contour. If this contour is thought of as the projection of a space (scene) contour, the recovery of the space contour shape is not trivial. This is

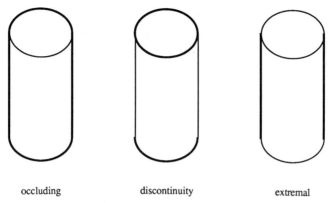

occluding   discontinuity   extremal

Fig. 1. The distinction between *occluding*, *discontinuity*, and *extremal* boundaries.

referred to as "shape from contour". Existing methods generally operate on a closed contour and, with a few exceptions they assume planar space curves. The problem is reduced now to estimating the orientation of this plane with respect to the viewer. Since the problem is underconstrained, additional assumptions about the shape of the space contour are required. Standard approaches make use of the following assumptions: uniform distribution of tangent directions (Witkin [13]), uniformity of curvature (Barrow and Tenenbaum [3]), minimal entropy shape (Barnard [1]), most compact figure assumption (Brady and Yuille [7]), and symmetry (Kanade [8]). In the case of nonplanar interpretations Witkin [13] and Barnard and Pentland [2] offer some suggestions.

Shape from contour methods provide a unique solution, namely the orientation of the plane in which the space curve lies. This solution corresponds to the minimization or maximization of the criterion being used. This standard approach needs to be adapted to the case where the contour in question lies on an object, at the intersection of two surfaces. Rather than producing just one solution, an alternative approach may attempt to represent explicitly a range of possible solutions and to select the one which best matches constraints derived from various sources. Hence, the key idea of our approach is first to interpret separately extremal and discontinuity contours and second to combine their contribution. Instead of producing unique solutions for each contour, we derive constraints in the form of one- or two-parameter loci. These constraints can be combined on the basis of a postulated geometric relationship between the contour interpretations which may lead to a dramatic reduction in the number of solutions, i.e., a small finite set instead of a continuous locus. Moreover, if it turns out that none of these solutions is correct, a different set of solutions can rapidly be hypothesized by applying a different geometric relationship.

2. Relating Image Contours to Surfaces

We analyze the origins of the image intensity changes referred to in this paper as *image contours*. From the physical processes underlying their formation, image contours fall into four classes (see [12]):

(1) discontinuities in distance from the viewer;
(2) discontinuities in surface orientation;
(3) changes in surface reflectance;
(4) illumination effects.

Interestingly, all these classes contribute to the recovery of 3D surfaces. However, we are interested here in those contours that are intrinsically related to the geometry of surfaces being viewed, that is class (2). As has been already mentioned, these contours can be further classified into extremal and discontinuity contours. The former occur wherever a surface turns smoothly away from the viewer while the latter occur where smooth surfaces terminate or intersect. Moreover, reconstruction techniques such as "shape from stereo" and "shape from motion" have difficulties with this class of contours.

2.1. Definition of generalized cylinders

It has been suggested that generalized cylinders are well suited for surface representation. Let's analyze in detail how class (2) image contours may be related to the geometry of a generalized cylinder. A generalized cylinder is a special case of a more general 3D shape, a generalized cone. A generalized cone is defined by:

– a planar cross-section curve $x = f(s)$ and $y = g(s)$, where s denotes the curvilinear abscissa;
– an eccentricity angle ψ;
– a spine function;
– an expansion function h.

A generalized cylinder is a generalized cone with a straight spine (straight axis) and zero eccentricity (the cross-section is perpendicular to the axis). See Fig. 2. Hence, the cross-section and expansion function are sufficient to define a generalized cylinder which can be written as:

$$r(s, z) = h(z)f(s)i + h(z)g(s)j + zk , \qquad (1)$$

Where i, j and k are the unit vectors associated with a cylinder centered reference frame: The cross-section lies in the i-j plane (x-y plane) and k (the z-axis) is parallel to the cylinder's straight axis. It is important to notice that this is simply a generative definition which does not guarantee real surfaces. Also, h, f and g must be analytical.

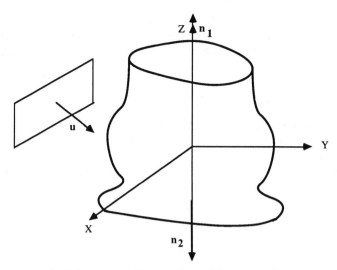

Fig. 2. A generalized cylinder intersected by two planes with normal unit vectors n_1 and n_2 parallel to the z-axis

2.2. Extremal contours

Let n be the unit vector normal to the cylinder's surface at (s, z); this vector is given by [6]:

$$n(s, z) = h(z) \frac{\mathrm{d}g}{\mathrm{d}s} i - h(z) \frac{\mathrm{d}f}{\mathrm{d}s} j + h(z) \frac{\mathrm{d}h}{\mathrm{d}z}\left(g(s) \frac{\mathrm{d}f}{\mathrm{d}s} - f(s) \frac{\mathrm{d}g}{\mathrm{d}s}\right)k . \quad (2)$$

Consider now a unit vector u parallel to the viewing direction and assume orthographic projection. The *contour generator* associated with the viewing direction u is the surface contour defined such as the viewing vector is tangent to the surface:

$$n(s, z) \cdot u = 0 . \quad (3)$$

The projection of the contour generator onto the image plane defines the extremal contour associated with the generalized cylinder and a viewing direction. We now analyze the extent to which an extremal contour constrains the orientation in space of the generalized cylinder.

We restrict the generalized cylinder to be a surface of revolution. Many complex real objects are not *globally* symmetric but nevertheless are composed of parts which have an axis of symmetry. Moreover, flexible objects, such as a hand or a snake preserve this *local* symmetry. This surface of revolution has the same expansion function as the initial cylinder and a circular cross-section; its axis is parallel to the cylinder's axis:

$$r_u(\theta, z) = h(z) \cos \theta \, i + h(z) \sin \theta \, j + zk \,. \tag{4}$$

It is impossible to determine the actual shape of the cross-section by observing an extremal contour. Let's call this surface the "perceived surface of revolution" or PSR. Since we deal with a surface of revolution, its cross-section axes are defined up to a rotation about the z-axis. There is no loss of generality in choosing the y-axis such that the viewing vector lies in the y-z plane, e.g., Fig. 3. The view vector can be written in the PSR's frame as:

$$u = \cos \sigma \, j + \sin \sigma \, k \,, \tag{5}$$

where σ is the usual *slant* angle (the angle between u and k). The vector normal to the PSR can be easily derived from equations (2) and (4):

$$n_u = \cos \theta \, i + \sin \theta \, j - \frac{dh}{dz} \, k \,. \tag{6}$$

A surface point is constrained to belong to the contour generator if it satisfies equation (3) which can be written as:

$$\cos \sigma \sin \theta = \sin \sigma \, \frac{dh}{dz} \,, \tag{7}$$

which gives rise to the following analysis:

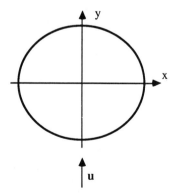

Fig. 3. The x- and y-axes of the perceived surface of revolution are chosen such that the viewing direction lies in the y-z plane.

(1) $\sigma = 0$. This case corresponds to a *side view* and θ may take the values 0 or π. The equation of the contour generator is obtained by replacing θ with either of these two values in the expression of r_u given by equation (4):

$$c_u(z) = \pm h(z)i + zk .$$ (8)

(2) $\sigma = \frac{1}{2}\pi$. This case corresponds to a *top view* in which case equation (7) is reduced to $dh/dz = 0$. The contour generator is the *skeleton* of the PSR.

(3) In the general case, a solution for θ exists only if $|\tan \sigma \, dh/dz| \leq 1$ in which case there are two solutions for θ:

$$\theta_1 = \arcsin\left(\tan \sigma \, \frac{dh}{dz}\right) \quad \text{and} \quad \theta_2 = \pi - \theta_1 .$$

The contour generator can be written as:

$$c_u(z) = \pm h(z) \cos \theta_1 i + h(z) \sin \theta_1 j + zk .$$ (9)

The following conclusions are interesting within the context of image contour interpretation:

(i) A contour generator (and hence an extremal contour) cannot be defined for an arbitrary generalized cylinder and for an arbitrary viewing direction; hence, if an image contour is interpreted as an extremal contour, it constrains both the shape of the viewed surface and its spatial orientation relatively to the viewer.

(ii) For a side view, the contour generator is a planar curve lying in a plane parallel to the image plane and is identical to the expansion function; this situation has been studied by Marr [11].

(iii) In the more general case the contour generator is not planar; however for surfaces whose expansion functions are linear (which are of great practical importance), dh/dz vanishes and hence the contour generator is planar. This is the case for simple man-made object primitives such as cones, cylinders and wedges.

(iv) The contour generator is symmetric about the y-z plane, that is, the plane defined by the viewing direction and the axis of the PSR; it follows that its image projection, i.e., the extremal boundary, is symmetric about the projection of the y-z plane.

(v) The axis of symmetry of the extremal contour is equal to the image of the PSR's axis. Since the PSR is defined such that its axis is parallel to the generalized cylinder's axis, it follows that the axis of symmetry of the extremal contour is parallel to the image of the generalized cylinder's axis.

The last conclusion has practical importance. It means that whenever an image contour has a straight axis of symmetry it can be interpreted as an extremal contour and moreover, the axis of the cylinder which gave rise to this contour is constrained to lie in a plane defined by the contour's axis of symmetry and the viewing direction. This set of conclusions could probably be derived from the more general surface representation envisaged by Koenderink [9]. The reason for which we devised a theory restricted to generalized cylinders is to emphasize the relationship between symmetry detection in an image and a corresponding 3D interpretation. Indeed, it has been recently shown that axes of symmetry are a well-suited two-dimensional shape representation [5]. Relating 2D symmetry to surface representation is therefore an important component of a computational model for image understanding. Under certain assumptions local symmetry is invariant under projection and hence it is an important visual cue.

2.3. Discontinuity contours

We turn now to a more realistic situation: a finite object. Such an object is bounded by piecewise-smoothed surfaces. If the expansion function of a generalized cylinder is defined over a finite domain, the shape vanishes naturally. This is the case with such objects as eggs or fruits. In the more general case the domain of the expansion function is infinite. We bound the object by two planes with normal unit vectors n_1 and n_2. In general these planes may or may not be parallel to the x-y plane. *We restrict our analysis to the case where the two bounding planes are parallel to the x-y plane*, i.e., Fig. 2.

The intersection of a plane with a surface is a planar curve. The projection of this *space contour* onto the image gives rise to a discontinuity contour. Unlike extremal contours, there is no constraint which relates the discontinuity contour to the spatial orientation of an object. It is therefore necessary to provide an additional piece of knowledge about the shape of the space contour.

One way to express knowledge about the global shape of a closed planar curve is to compute the ratio of the enclosed area to the square of the perimeter:

$$M = \frac{\text{Area}}{(\text{Perimeter})^2} \cdot$$

This is a scale-invariant number characterizing the curve. M is maximized by a circle (the most compact shape). This gives the measure an upper bound of $1/4\pi$. Its lower bound is zero and it is achieved by a straight line. The quantity M is commonly used in pattern recognition and industrial vision systems as an attribute that measures the compactness of an object.

Brady and Yuille [7] have used this measure within the shape from contour paradigm. They have developed an extremum principle for determining the orientation of the most symmetric and most compact space contour interpretation. This is achieved for the maximum value of M. For example an ellipse is interpreted as a tilted circle and a parallelogram as a tilted and rotated square. However, apart from psychophysical arguments, there is no reason a priori for selecting this unique interpretation. Instead one may compute M explicitly at each possible orientation and express M as a two-dimensional function with azimuth and elevation as parameters. If a specific shape is expected to occur, the value of the compactness measure determines a one-parameter locus of points on the surface M (see next paragraph for an example).

Let's denote by C the space contour lying in a plane with unit normal vector n and let C_u be its image projection. Let u be the unit normal vector associated with the z-axis of the camera which is also the viewing direction. We want to express M for C as a function of n and C_u. The contour C is described by a set of successive points $V_0, V_1, \ldots, V_m$ where $V_0 = V_m$. Let O' be the intersection of the camera's z-axis with the space plane containing C and let v_i be a vector from O' to V_i. Refer to Fig. 4. The area enclosed by C is:

$$\text{Area} = \left| \sum_{i=1}^{m-1} A_i \right|, \tag{10}$$

where the area element is given by

$$A_i = \tfrac{1}{2} n \cdot (v_i \times v_{i+1}). \tag{11}$$

Similarly, the perimeter is given by:

$$\text{Perimeter} = \sum_{i=1}^{m-1} \| v_i - v_{i+1} \|. \tag{12}$$

A point V on C projects in the image at P on C_u. Let's compute the vector v from O' to V as a function of its image projection, that is the vector p from O to P. We shall first use perspective projection, establish the formula for v and show that M is not defined for any contour and for any spatial orientation. Next, we shall consider orthographic projection as for extremal contours.

Let F be the focal point, f be the focal length (the distance from F to the image plane), d be the distance from O to O', u be the viewing direction and u_p be the unit vector associated with the direction from F to P. See Fig. 4. v is given by the following formula (see Appendix A for details concerning its derivation):

$$v = \frac{d + f}{f} \frac{(n \cdot u_p)p - (n \cdot p)u_p}{n \cdot u_p}. \tag{13}$$

Notice that v is not defined whenever $n \cdot u_p = 0$ which means that for every

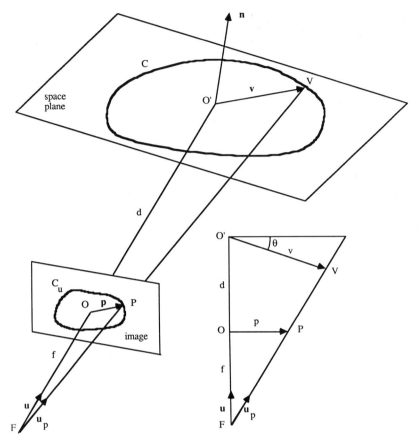

Fig. 4. The geometry of projecting a space contour C onto the image plane. C lies in a plane with normal unit vector n. Equation (13) expresses v ($O'V$) as a function of d, f, n, p (OP) and u_p.

image curve point P_i there exists a locus of orientations for which the space contour is infinitely elongated. Moreover, if n is perpendicular to the plane defined by p and u_p we have: $n \cdot u_p = n \cdot p = 0$; for these orientations the space contour *crosses the image*! Consequently, M has a lot of singularities depending on the shape of the image contour. Although it is worth investigating the behaviour of M within the perspective camera model context, let's consider parallel projection.

In the case of parallel projection f tends to infinity and hence $(d + f)/f$ tends to 1 and u_p tends to u. Therefore equation (13) becomes:

$$v = \frac{(n \cdot u)p - (n \cdot p)u}{n \cdot u}, \qquad (14)$$

which is the formula used in [7]. Notice that v is not defined where $n \cdot u = 0$. Since u is the viewing vector, the locus of spatial orientations for which the space contour is infinitely elongated is a great circle bounding the visible half of the Gaussian sphere. For these orientations M is null. Therefore, the parallel camera model is to be preferred to the perspective model since it involves less singularities.

By combining equations (10), (12) and (14) one can express M as a function of n, u *and the shape of* C_u described by the image points $P_0, P_1, \ldots, P_m$. Notice however that M *does not depend on d*, the distance from the viewer to the space plane.

To summarize, for a fixed camera position, and for a given image closed curve, M can be written as a two-parameter function $M(\alpha, \beta)$ where the two parameters are any suitable Gaussian sphere coordinates of n. The domain of M is the set of surface orientations visible from the camera viewpoint. Assuming opaque objects, this domain is the hemisphere oriented toward the viewer.

2.4. Examples

Let's consider two examples, one of interpreting a pair of symmetric extremal contours and one of interpreting a closed (discontinuity) contour. Figure 5 shows two lines that may be interpreted as extremal contours arising from the projection of a cone. According to the last conclusion of Section 2.2, the axis

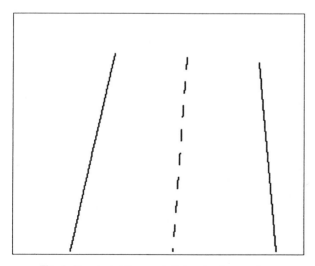

Fig. 5. Two image lines and their axis of symmetry.

of this cone should lie in the plane defined by the viewing direction and the axis of symmetry of the extremal contours. Let u be the viewing direction, s be the unit vector associated with the axis of symmetry and k be the unit vector associated with the cone's axis. The orientation of k is given by the following equation:

$$k \cdot (u \times s) = 0 . \tag{15}$$

That is, the cone's axis lies in the plane defined by u and s. The tip of k lies on a circle given by (15). Figure 6 shows this circle projected on a planar grid as a function of α (azimuth) and β (elevation). α varies from $\frac{1}{2}\pi$ to $\frac{3}{2}\pi$ and β varies from $-\frac{1}{2}\pi$ to $\frac{1}{2}\pi$.

Consider now a closed contour such as that shown in Fig. 7. For this contour M has been computed at every possible orientation. Figure 8 shows a perspective plot of M as a function of azimuth and elevation. This function has two maxima corresponding to two possible orientations of the image contour being interpreted as the most compact shape. Figure 9 shows loci of possible orientations for space contours of a predetermined compactness. Locus 1 corresponds to $M = 0.04$ (an elongated shape), locus 2 corresponds to $M = 0.05$ while locus 3 corresponds to $M = 0.076$. The two maxima correspond in this case to $M = 0.077$. Notice that for a circle $M = 0.079$.

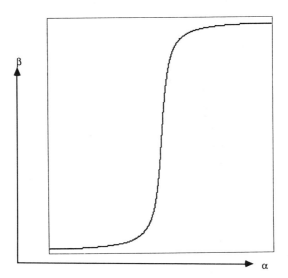

Fig. 6. The locus of possible orientations of the cone's axis lying in the plane defined by the viewing vector and the dotted line of the previous figure.

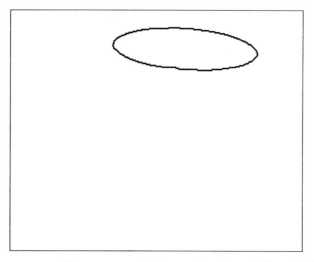

Fig. 7. An image contour. This contour may be interpreted as the projection onto the image of a space contour C lying in a space plane whose associated normal unit vector is n.

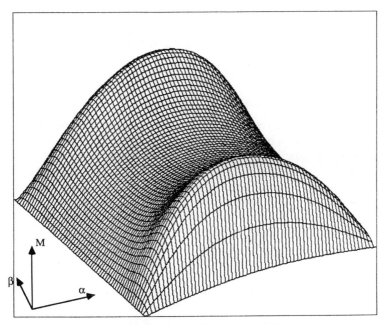

Fig. 8. M (area over the square of the perimeter) for the contour shown in Fig. 7 as a function of the deprojection of the contour. The locations of the maxima of this surface correspond to the orientation of the most compact interpretations of the image contour.

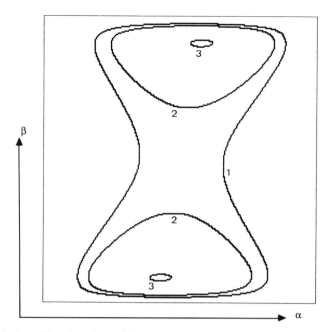

Fig. 9. Loci of possible orientations of the space contours which have the same compactness. 1: $M = 0.04$, 2: $M = 0.05$, 3: $M = 0.076$. Notice that in the case of a circle $M = 0.079$.

3. Interpreting Image Contours

We summarize the main results of the previous section. We have developed a method allowing certain image contours to be interpreted in terms of contours arising from a generalized cylinder. A pair of extremal contours having a straight axis of symmetry constrain both the expansion function of the corresponding generalized cylinder and the spatial orientation of its axis.

A closed discontinuity contour combined with a compactness measure may be interpreted as a closed planar 3D contour. The latter is in fact the cross-section of a generalized cylinder.

Let's consider now an isolated image contour. This contour cannot provide by itself enough information such that it may be classified into extremal, discontinuity, or something else. This section is partially devoted to this problem. First we recall a contour labeling scheme recently suggested by Malik [10]. Next we describe a contour classification algorithm based on this scheme. Finally we suggest a way of combining extremal and discontinuity contours in order to further constrain the shape and orientation of the perceived surface.

3.1. Contour labeling

This section summarizes the labeling scheme developed by Malik [10]. Assume that the boundary of an object is a C^3 piecewise-smooth surface. A generalized cylinder belongs to this class if its cross-section and expansion functions are C^3. Moreover, any object that is a union of such primitives belongs to the class as well. If two C^3 surfaces intersect at a point where the surfaces have distinct tangent planes, then it can be shown that the intersection of the two surfaces is a C^3 arc. Such an arc is called an edge. A point of intersection of three or more edges is called a *vertex*. The projection of edges and vertices onto the image gives rise to *junctions*. The possible geometric configurations of these junctions are given by the following analysis.

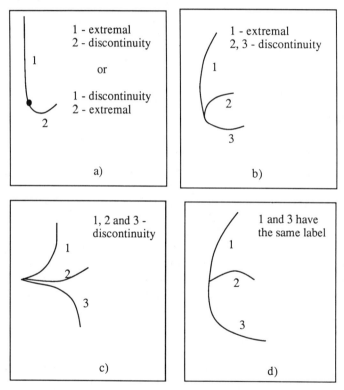

Fig. 10. A catalogue of image junctions. (a) *Curvature-L* may be labeled: 1: extremal and 2: discontinuity, or 1: discontinuity and 2: extremal. (b) *Three-tangent* is labeled: 1: extremal, 2: discontinuity and 3: discontinuity. (c) Projection of a vertex neighborhood: 1, 2 and 3 are all discontinuity boundaries. (d) For a *T-junction* 1 and 3 must have the same label (extremal or discontinuity).

(1) *Projection of an edge neighborhood*. Let S_1, S_2 be the two surfaces meeting at the edge and let P be a point on the edge. Assuming general viewpoint, the viewing direction u defines a contour generator C_u on the first surface. If the contour generator passes through P, the following image junctions may arise:

(a) *Curvature-L*. This is a curvature discontinuity point along a curve. The tangent is continuous because the projection of the intersection curve is tangent to the projection of the contour generator. Figure 10(a) shows the possible labels of such a junction.

(b) *Three-tangent*. Three curves with a common tangent. Two have the same curvature. This junction has a unique labeling as shown on Fig. 10(b).

(2) *Projection of a vertex neighborhood*. The projection of a vertex locally looks like the projection of an equivalent polyhedral vertex formed by replacing each of the surface elements by their tangent planes. If there is no contour generator through the vertex (which would violate the general viewpoint assumption) all the image segments meeting at such a junction are discontinuity contours. An example of such a junction is shown on Fig. 10(c).

To this analysis one may add *T-junctions* where two of the three arcs have the same tangent and curvature and hence they have the same label. See Fig. 10(d). Notice that this junction indicates occlusion.

3.2. A contour classification algorithm

The contour classification algorithm begins with a classical contour detection process: edge detection and edge linking. Next, contours are approximated with straight lines and arcs (segments). This analysis is quickly expanded to include the connecting segments. Each segment has two sets of connecting segments associated with each one of its ends. A junction is defined as a set of at least two segments passing through a common point. Within a junction, colinear lines, arcs with a common tangent, a line tangent to an arc and arcs with the same curvature are detected carefully.

This network of segments and junctions is then mapped into a graph representation. A junction is mapped into a node and a segment is mapped into an arc. Both nodes and arcs are labeled as follows. A node may have a label out of Malik's catalogue: curvature-L, three-tangent, vertex or T-junction. An arc may be labeled discontinuity, extremal, unknown or ambiguous.

Notice that this graph is planar. The planarity is a direct consequence of the fact that two contours never cross each other (a junction is detected whenever contours intersect) and hence, two arcs in the graph never cross. The planarity of the graph implies that the complexity of graph exploration is highly reduced. Contour classification consists of exploring this graph in order to propagate the constraints available with the junction type. The result is a reduction in the number of possible labelings of each arc.

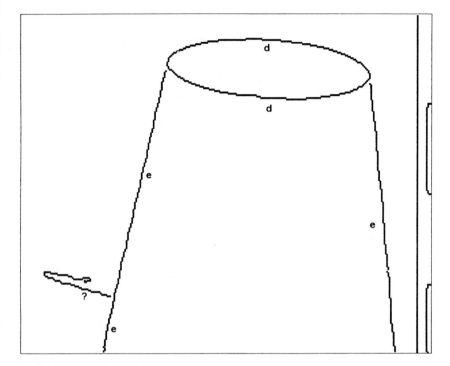

Fig. 11. A line drawing to be interpreted with two three-tangent junctions and one T-junction. The labeling shown on the figure is unique: d, discontinuity, e extremal.

Consider for example the drawing of Fig. 11. The algorithm described above detected two three-tangent junctions and one T-junction. The final contour labeling is shown on Fig. 11.

3.3. Combining contour interpretations

Let's try now to interpret the set of discontinuity and extremal contours of Fig. 11 in terms of a 3D surface, namely a generalized cylinder. Figure 12 shows the constraint (the *S-curve*) derived from the axis of symmetry of the extremal contours *overlapped* onto the constraints derived from the discontinuity contour. The intersections of these constraints provide solutions for the space orientation of the generalized cylinder. If one eliminates exaggeratedly slanted interpretations, it follows that there is no solution for a cross-section with $M = 0.04$, two solutions for a cross-section with $M = 0.05$, four solutions for $M = 0.076$ and two solutions for a circular cross-section.

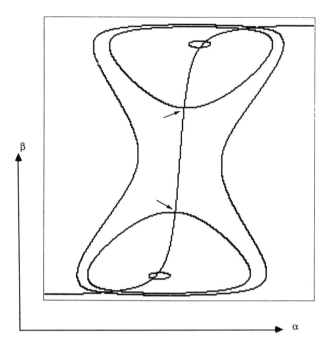

Fig. 12. Combining orientation constraints derived from extremal and discontinuity boundaries. The arrows indicate two distinct solutions corresponding to a generalized cylinder whose cross-section has a compactness of $M = 0.05$.

3.4. Discussion

The Gaussian sphere (the α-β space) provides a common representation for interpreting both extremal and discontinuity contours. This enables to *intersect* constraints derived from various image contours. This common representation provides as well a framework for discussing the relative importance of extremal and discontinuity contours.

Independently of any particular interpretation, a pair of extremal contours provides a one-parameter locus of orientations for the axis of a generalized cylinder. Any selected solution *must* lie along or in the vicinity of this locus. A discontinuity contour provides a two-parameter locus of orientations for the plane containing the deprojected contour. If the compactness of this space contour is known, this locus is reduced to a curve. Moreover, there are only two solutions for the most compact interpretation of a discontinuity contour. These two solutions lie or do not lie along the S-curve. In the first case, the obvious interpretation is an object with a cross-section perpendicular to the axis of the cylinder. The second case may suggest that the cross-section makes an eccentricity angle ψ with the cylinder's axis.

Finally, our approach requires for the discontinuity contours to be closed. In conclusion, extremal contours provide stronger constraints than discontinuity contours.

4. Conclusions

In this paper we have analyzed the extent with which image contours constrain both the shape and orientation of a scene surface. We have focused our attention on those contours arising from a particular surface type, i.e., generalized cylinders. Pairs of extremal contours constrain the axis of the generalized cylinder to one degree of freedom. The shape from contour paradigm may be applied to closed discontinuity contours.

Next we have shown how image contours can be mapped into a graph representation and labeled in terms of surface contours. The labeled contours are backprojected onto the Gaussian sphere where their corresponding constraints are combined.

In the future we plan to extend this approach such that we can deal with generalized cones and with even more complex objects such as a concatenation of generalized cylinders and cones. We also plan to investigate more thoroughly the relationship between two-dimensional symmetry as defined by Brady and Asada [5] and the projection of three-dimensional surfaces. We would also like to devise a method for interpreting nonclosed discontinuity contours and to extend the shape from contour paradigm to nonplanar space curves.

Surface contour interpretation is an important component of computer vision systems since alternative techniques such as stereo and motion have difficulties with interpreting this class of contours.

Appendix A. Derivation of equation (13)

Referring to Fig. 4 we have:

$$v = \|v\| \cdot v' / \|v'\| .$$

We also have:

$$v' = n \times (p \times u_p) = (n \cdot u_p)p - (n \cdot p)u_p$$

and

$$\|v\| = \frac{(d + f)\|e\|}{(d + f) \cos \theta + \|e\| \sin \theta} .$$

The length of e is $\|e\| = \|p\|(d + f)/f$. We also have:

$$\cos \theta = \frac{v' \cdot p}{\|v'\| \|p\|} \quad \text{and} \quad \sin \theta = \frac{\|v' \times p\|}{\|v'\| \|p\|} .$$

We obtain:

$$v = \frac{(d + f)\|p\|^2}{f(v' \cdot p) + \|p\| \|v' \times p\|} \, v' .$$

From the expression of v' we have:

$$v' \cdot p = (n \cdot u_p)\|p\|^2 - (n \cdot p)(p \cdot u_p) ,$$

$$\|v' \times p\| = (n \cdot p)\|p \times u_p\| .$$

The expression of v becomes:

$$v = \frac{(d + f)\|p\|^2}{f(n \cdot u_p)\|p\|^2 - f(n \cdot p)(p \cdot u_p) + (n \cdot p)\|p\| \|p \times u_p\|} \, v' .$$

Let the coordinates of the image point P be x, y and f. Hence, the coordinates of p are x, y and 0 and the coordinates of u_p are x/s, y/s and f/s with $s = (x^2 + y^2 + f^2)^{1/2}$. We easily obtain:

$$p \cdot u_p = \|p\|^2/s \quad \text{and} \quad \|p \times u_p\| = f\|p\|/s .$$

The last two terms of the denominator of v vanish. The expression of v becomes:

$$v = \frac{d + f}{f} \frac{v'}{n \cdot u_p} .$$

By replacing v' by its expression, we finally obtain equation (13).

REFERENCES

1. Barnard, S.T., Interpreting perspective images, *Artificial Intelligence* **21** (1983) 435–462.
2. Barnard, S.T. and Pentland, A., Three-dimensional shape from line drawings, in: *Proceedings Image Understanding Workshop*, Arlington, VA (1983) 282–284.
3. Barrow, H.G. and Tenenbaum, J.M., Interpreting line drawings as three-dimensional surfaces, *Artificial Intelligence* **17** (1981) 75–116.
4. Binford, T.O., Visual perception by computer, in: *Proceedings IEEE Conference on Systems and Control*, Miami, FL (1971).
5. Brady, M. and Asada, H., Smoothed local symmetries and their implementation, *Int. J. Rob. Res.* **3** (3) (1984) 36–61.

6. Brady, M., Ponce, J., Yuille, A. and Asada, H., Describing surfaces, *Comput. Vision Graph. Image Process.* **32** (1985) 1–28.
7. Brady, M. and Yuille, A., An extremum principle for shape from contour, *IEEE Trans. Pattern Anal. Mach. Intell.* **6** (3) (1984) 288–301.
8. Kanade, T., Recovery of the three-dimensional shape of an object from a single view, *Artificial Intelligence* **17** (1981) 409–460.
9. Koenderink, J., The internal representation of solid shape based on the topological properties of the apparent contour, in: W. Richards and S. Ullmann (Eds.), *Image Understanding 1986* (Ablex, Norwood, NJ, 1986).
10. Malik, J., Labeling line drawings of curved objects, in: *Proceedings Image Understanding Workshop*, Miami Beach, FL (1985) 209–218.
11. Marr, D., Analysis of occluding contour, *Proc. Roy. Soc. London B* **197** (1977) 441–475.
12. Marr, D., *Vision* (Freeman, San Francisco, CA, 1982).
13. Witkin, A.P., Recovering surface shape and orientation from texture, *Artificial Intelligence* **17** (1981) 17–45.

Received May 1987; revised version received January 1988

Solid Modeling

The Geometry of Projective Blending Surfaces

Christoph Hoffmann*

Computer Science Department, Purdue University, West Lafayette, IN 47907, U.S.A.

John Hopcroft**

Department of Computer Science, Cornell University, Ithaca, NY 14853, U.S.A.

ABSTRACT

Blending surfaces smoothly join two or more primary surfaces that otherwise would intersect in edges. We outline the potential method for deriving blending surfaces, and explain why the method needs to be considered in projective parameter space, concentrating on the case of blending quadrics. Let W be the quadratic polynomial substituted for the homogenizing variable of parameter space. We show that a blending surface derived in projective parameter space is the projective image of a different blending surface derived in affine parameter space, provided that $W = U^2$ for some linear U. All blending surfaces may therefore by classified on basis of the projective classification of W.

1. Introduction

In computer aided design, geometric models of objects in manufacture are created and manipulated. Virtually all manufactured solid objects contain surfaces meant to round sharp edges or smoothly connect surface areas that otherwise would intersect in creases. These connecting surfaces are known as *blending surfaces* in the literature on solid modeling.

Traditional solid modeling systems have not been successful at incorporating blending surfaces, and only recently successful attempts have been made at identifying surface classes that can be used conveniently as blending surfaces [3–8]. In general, blending surfaces joining curved algebraic surfaces must have

* Supported in part by NSF Grant CCR-86-19817, ONR Contract N0014-86-K-0465, and a grant from AT&T.

** Supported in part by NSF Grants DCR-85-02568, DMC-86-17355, and ONR Contract N0014-86-K-0281.

algebraic degree higher than 2, and extensive classifications of useful blending surface families are not widely available.

In a sequence of papers [3–5], we have identified a class of blending surfaces derived by substitution into base polynomials, and have analyzed some of their geometric properties. Our principal derivation procedure is called the *potential method* and is capable of deriving in a standardized manner blending surfaces for any two intersecting algebraic surfaces. We have explored primarily the properties of blending surfaces when derived from a quadratic base polynomial, due to the practical importance of this case. Higher-degree base polynomials could be used equally well and would permit higher-order continuity between the blending surface and the primary surfaces connected by it.

When we introduced the potential method in [3], we used a quadratic base polynomial in which three free parameters had to be chosen in order to derive a specific surface. These parameters have a very intuitive interpretation: two control the relative distance of the curves at which the blending surface joins the primary surface, i.e., they control the width and centering of the blending surface about the intersection curve of the primary surfaces. The third parameter controls the shape of the blend. In [4] we have investigated the generality of this procedure, for blending quadrics. We found that in order to derive as general a surface class as possible, the quadratic base polynomial must be homogeneous. That is, the underlying parameter space must be projective. However, this introduces additional parameters to be instantiated. The consequences of the additional choices for the resulting surface shapes are not fully understood.

In this paper we summarize and extend our previous work on the properties of blending surfaces derived from homogeneous quadratic base polynomials. Our ultimate goal is to gain a comprehensive and intuitive interpretation of the parameters that must be instantiated in the base polynomial in order to derive specific blending surfaces. To this end, we characterize generic subclasses of our blending surfaces that are invariant under projective transformation.

The paper is structured as follows: After reviewing the necessary background and notation, we summarize in Section 3 the results of [4], leading to a succinct formulation of all quartic surfaces that serve as blending surfaces for two quadrics in general position. Then we review the potential method by considering first the affine formulation, marked by its intuitiveness, and subsequently the projective formulation. We then show the equivalence of the projective formulation for blending quadrics and the surfaces derivable by the methods of Section 3. In Section 6 we investigate how projective transformations map blending surfaces. In Section 7 we finally summarize the other methods proposed, and discuss the prospects for deriving blending surfaces automatically.

We do not explore techniques and configurations for blending corners that require joining more than two blends. From a theoretical perspective, this topic is exceedingly simple, for one could solve it by recursively blending the arising surfaces. There is, however, a practical matter: Proceeding systematically in this way, one quickly arrives at surfaces of very high algebraic degree, thereby seriously complicating the representation and manipulation of such surfaces. In [5] we have considered this problem and proposed practical solutions. See also [11].

2. Notation and Background

Given two surfaces S_1 and S_2, a *blending* surface is any surface S_3 that is tangent to S_1 in a space curve C_1 and tangent to S_2 in a space curve C_2. All surfaces are considered in three-dimensional x-y-z space. For parts of our analysis, we must consider the surfaces in three-dimensional complex projective space. It is our experience, however, that the intuitive content of the results we derive is not distorted by this needed generality. For example, we have never needed surface equations with complex coefficients.

We will consider blending algebraic surfaces of arbitrary degree. Such surfaces always have an implicit equation of the form $F = 0$, where F is a polynomial in x, y, and z. Note that some, but not all such surfaces may possess a parametric representation. For example, all quadratic surfaces have a rational parameterization, but only some quartic surfaces can be so parameterized.

We must distinguish between the surface $S(F)$ with implicit equation $F = 0$, and the polynomial F. The surface $S(F)$ consists of all points (x, y, z) that are zeros of the polynomial F. The distinction is necessary so as to avoid confusing geometric and algebraic arguments.

We will consider algebraic curves and surfaces in other spaces as well. We call these spaces *parameter* spaces and consider mapping them to the x-y-z space by substitution of polynomials in x, y, and z for the principal parameter space coordinates. We use r, s, and t as coordinates of affine parameter space, and r, s, t and u as coordinates of projective parameter space. These coordinates need to take on only real values. Polynomials in parameter spaces are denoted in lower case letters, e.g., f, g, h, . . . , and polynomials in x-y-z space by upper case letters, e.g., F, G, H, ...

2.1. Algebraic geometry

In Section 3, methods from algebraic geometry are needed. This requires that we consider F a polynomial over the ground field $\mathbb{C}$ of complex numbers. Unfortunately, the field $\mathbb{R}$ of reals is not algebraically closed, so most of the results of algebraic geometry no longer hold when only the real roots of F are considered.

The set of all polynomials in x, y, z, and with real or complex coefficients is denoted $\mathbb{C}[x, y, z]$. The complete intersection of two surfaces $S(G)$ and $S(H)$

is denoted by $S(G, H)$, and is in general a space curve. Its algebraic description is provided by an *ideal*. Briefly, a set I of polynomials is an ideal if, for all polynomials G and H of I, and an arbitrary polynomial A in $\mathbb{C}[x, y, z]$, the polynomials AG and $G + H$ are again in I. It is not hard to see that the curve $S(G, H)$ is described by the ideal $I = (G, H)$ generated by G and H, that is, by the set of all polynomials of the form $AG + BH$, where A and B are polynomials in $\mathbb{C}[x, y, z]$.

Given an ideal I, the set of points at which all polynomials in I vanish simultaneously is called the *algebraic set* of I and is denoted $S(I)$. As we have mentioned, the algebraic set $S(G, H)$ of the ideal (G, H) is in general a space curve, whereas the algebraic set $S(G)$ of the ideal (G) generated by G is a surface.

An ideal I may have the property that for all product polynomials AB in I at least one of the factors is also in I. In that case I is called a *prime ideal*. An algebraic set $S(I)$ is *irreducible* if it is not the union of two proper algebraic subsets. One knows that an algebraic set $S(I)$ is irreducible if and only if the ideal I is prime (see, e.g., [2]).

For example, a quadric surface is irreducible if it does not consist of two planes. The space curve $S(G, H)$ is irreducible if the curve does not have separate branches that individually are algebraic sets. Note that the two real branches of the hyperbola are not two separate algebraic sets, so that the hyperbola is irreducible. However, the intersection curve of two parallel circular cylinders has two lines each of which may be described separately as the intersection of a pair of planes, so that this intersection curve is reducible.

If $S(G, H)$ is a space curve and the surface $S(F)$ contains this curve, then there is a connection between the ideal (G, H) and the polynomial F, given by:

Hilbert Nullstellensatz. *If $S(F)$ contains $S(G, H)$, then there is an integer k such that $F^k = AG + BH$. Moreover, if $S(G, H)$ is irreducible, then $k = 1$.*

2.2. Projective space

The reader will be familiar with *affine* three-dimensional space as the set of all points (x, y, z) where x, y and z have values from a ground field, e.g., are real or complex numbers. *Projective* three-dimensional space consists of all lines (rx, ry, rz, rw) where x, y, z and w again have values from a ground field and $r \neq 0$. The case $x = y = z = w = 0$ is excluded. By identifying the affine point (x, y, z) with the projective line (rx, ry, rz, r), $r \neq 0$, three-dimensional affine space is embedded into three-dimensional projective space. Then the only additional "points" in projective space are lines of the form $(rx, ry, rz, 0)$ and are called *points at infinity*. The points at infinity form a plane called the *plane at infinity*.

If F is a polynomial, $S(F)$ its algebraic set in affine space, then the corresponding set in projective space is the algebraic set of the associated *homogeneous form* F_0 of F. This form is obtained by substituting x/w for x, y/w for y, and z/w for z, followed by multiplying with w^k to eliminate the denominator. For example, if $F = x^2 + y^2 + z^2 - 2x - 9$, then its homogeneous form is $F_0 = x^2 + y^2 + z^2 - 2xw - 9w^2$.

In complex projective space a number of algebraic and geometric statements are true without exception. An example is the following standard result.

Theorem 2.1. *If F is a homogeneous polynomial of degree n, then any line L intersects $S(F)$ in n points or is contained in $S(F)$.*

In real affine space, n is only an upper bound on the number of intersection points. The geometric degree of a surface $S(F)$ is the number of intersection points the surface has with a line L in general position. The theorem states that the *geometric* degree of $S(F)$ is equal to the *algebraic* degree of F. The geometric degree of a space curve is the number of intersections with a plane in general position. An important result is the following theorem:

Bezout's Theorem. *A surface $S(G)$ of degree m and a surface $S(H)$ of degree n intersect in a space curve of degree $m \cdot n$ or have a common component.*

A *projective transformation* is a nonsingular linear transformation of projective space. Some projective transformations are familiar from computer graphics where they have been used to change stereographic projection to orthographic projection. Moreover, all nondegenerate conics may be projectively transformed into a circle of unit radius. See also Section 5 below.

When the matrix of the projective transformation is real-valued, then we speak of a *real* projective transformation, otherwise of a *complex* projective transformation. According to [1], the projective classification of all irreducible quadric surfaces under real projective transformation is as follows:

(1) the imaginary sphere $x^2 + y^2 + z^2 + w^2$;
(2) the real sphere $x^2 + y^2 + z^2 - w^2$: this class includes the ellipsoid, the two-sheeted hyperboloid, and the elliptic paraboloid;
(3) the one-sheeted hyperboloid $x^2 + y^2 - z^2 - w^2$: this class includes also the hyperbolic paraboloid;
(4) the imaginary cylinder $x^2 + y^2 + w^2$;
(5) the real cylinder $x^2 + y^2 - w^2$: this class includes all conic cylinders and cones.

Under complex projective transformation the classes (1), (2) and (3) are no longer distinct, as well as the classes (4) and (5).

3. A Completeness Theorem for Blending Quadrics

Approaching the blending problem abstractly, we consider how to determine all degree-4 surfaces $S(F)$ that are tangent to two quadrics $S(G)$ and $S(H)$ at prescribed space curves. This problem was explored in detail in [4], and some preliminary considerations are needed before we can give it an exact formulation. Of course, we will assume that the quadrics $S(G)$ and $S(H)$ are not degenerate. That is, neither splits into a pair of planes.

Recalling Bezout's Theorem, a quartic surface intersects a quadric in a space curve of degree 8. If we require tangency, however, the curve in which the two surfaces are tangent must be counted double as it is the limit of two separate components, infinitesimally apart. In consequence, a quartic surface $S(F)$ is tangent to a quadric $S(G)$ in a curve $S(F, G)$ of degree 4. According to [9], the space curve $S(F, G)$ now must be of one of the following types:

(1) The curve $S(F, G)$ is irreducible but not planar, and so is the intersection of two quadrics.

(2) The curve $S(F, G)$ is irreducible and planar, and so is the intersection of a quartic surface and a plane.

(3) The curve $S(F, G)$ is reducible, and so is one of the following: Four lines, two lines and a conic, two conics, or one line and an irreducible degree-3 space curve.

We study the case when $S(F, G)$ is of type (1). $S(F, G)$ cannot be of type (2), since it then could not lie on $S(G)$ as planar curve of degree 4. When $S(F, G)$ is of type (3), we will need to catalogue a number of special cases, depending on the curve components. This curve type does arise, but neither its practical significance nor its mathematics has been sufficiently explored. With this in mind, we formulate the classification problem for blending quadrics with quartic surfaces as follows:

> Given two irreducible quadric surfaces $S(G)$ and $S(H)$, and given on each an irreducible degree-4 space curve, $S(G, H')$ and $S(H, G')$, as the complete intersection with auxiliary quadric surfaces $S(H')$ and $S(G')$. Characterize the set of all quartic surfaces $S(F)$ where $S(F)$ is tangent to $S(G)$ in the curve $S(G, H')$ and $S(F)$ is tangent to $S(H)$ in the curve $S(H, G')$.

Note that the irreducibility of a space curve $S(G, H)$ in projective space implies that the degree-2 terms of G and of H are coprime polynomials. For if these polynomials are not coprime, then $S(G, H)$ has a planar component at infinity, hence is not irreducible [10].

We solve the above problem under the additional assumption that the two quadrics $S(G)$ and $S(H)$ have an irreducible intersection curve $S(G, H)$. That is, the curve $S(G, H)$ is of type (1) above. Moreover, we assume that the intersection curve $S(G, H)$ is different from $S(G, H')$ and from $S(H, G')$. Clearly this is the case for all blending surfaces considered in practice.

Completeness Theorem. *Let $S(G)$ and $S(H)$ be irreducible quadrics. Let $S(G')$ and $S(H')$ be two quadrics such that $S(G, H')$ and $S(H, G')$ are irreducible, and assume that $S(G, H)$ is irreducible and coincides neither with $S(G, H')$ nor with $S(H, G')$. Then every degree-4 surface $S(F)$ tangent to $S(G)$ in the curve $S(G, H')$ and tangent to $S(H)$ in the curve $S(H, G')$ has the equation.*

$$K^2 - \mu GH = 0 \,,$$

where μ is a constant and $S(K)$ is a quadric containing both $S(G, H')$ and $S(H, G')$.

The proof of this theorem in [4] proceeds as follows: Since $S(G, H')$ and $S(H, G')$ are irreducible and $S(F)$ contains these curves, the polynomial F can be written as $F = AG + B'H'$ and as $F = BH + A'G'$, for some polynomials A, A', B, and B'. These equations follow from Hilbert's Nullstellensatz. By considering the partial derivatives of F, the requirement of tangency to $S(G)$ and $S(H)$ in the curves implies further that $B' = CH'$ and $A' = DG'$, where C and D are some other polynomials. That is, we may write

$$F = AG + CH'^2 = BH + DG'^2 \,.$$

It would be a mistake to make a priori assumptions about the respective degrees of the polynomials A, B, C and D. However, irreducibility of $S(G, H')$ and $S(H, G')$ in projective space has the consequence that A and B must be polynomials of degree 2, and that C and D must be constants. The proof is combinatorial in nature, and makes use of the fact that the degree-2 terms of G and H', as well as the degree-2 terms of H and G' are coprime.

Having so deduced the form of the polynomial F, the difference polynomial $(AG + CH'^2) - (BH + DG'^2)$ is considered modulo the ideal (G, H). Since this polynomial is zero,

$$CH'^2 - DG'^2 \equiv 0 \bmod(G, H) \,.$$

Moreover, since C and D are constants, the polynomial $CH'^2 - DG'^2$ factors over the field of complex numbers. At this point the irreducibility of $S(G, H)$ enters into the proof, for it allows us to conclude, by primality of the ideal (G, H), that one of the factors is in (G, H), i.e., that it can be written $aG + bH$, where a and b are constants. Now it is simple to bring F into the required form $F = K^2 - \mu GH$.

The existence of the quadric K is of considerable interest. For if the two curves of tangency $S(G, H')$ and $S(H, G')$ do not lie on a common quadric surface $S(K)$, then no quartic blending surface $S(F)$ will be found in general. This does not preclude the existence of special cases when one or several of the assumptions of the theorem do not hold. We will demonstrate such an exceptional case:

Example 3.1. In [3, color plate 6], a blending surface is shown that smoothly joins two elliptic cylinders. The two cylinders are given by $G = x^2 + 4y^2 - 4$ and $H = 9x^2 + y^2 - 9$. They intersect in four parallel lines, hence $S(G, H)$ is not irreducible and the Completeness Theorem does not apply. The blending surface has the equation

$$F = (x^2 + 4y^2 - 4)(z - 3)^2 + (9x^2 + y^2 - 9)(z + 3)^2 = 0.$$

We show that F cannot be of the form $K^2 - \mu GH$, for any quadratic polynomial K.

We seek a quadratic polynomial K such that $S(K)$ contains the curves of tangency $S(G, z + 3)$ and $S(H, z - 3)$, two ellipses in parallel planes. Clearly, $K = (z - 3)(z + 3)$ defines the only reducible quadric containing these curves. But $\alpha K^2 + \beta GH$ contains no $x^2 z^2$ term, so that $K = (z - 3)(z + 3)$ does not qualify.

Next, let us assume that an irreducible quadric contains the curves $S(G, z + 3)$ and $S(H, z - 3)$. Since $S(K)$ contains $S(G, z + 3)$, we have $K(x, y, -3) = \alpha G$, for some $\alpha \neq 0$. Without loss of generality we assume $\alpha = 1$ and conclude that $K = x^2 + 4y^2 + zK_1$, where K_1 is linear. Next, the containment of $S(H, z - 3)$ implies $K(x, y, 3) = \beta H$ for $\beta \neq 0$. Comparing the x^2 and y^2 terms on both sides, we have $x^2 = 9\beta x^2$ and $4y^2 = \beta y^2$. Hence there is no irreducible quadric containing both $S(G, z + 3)$ and $S(H, z - 3)$. It follows that F cannot have the form $GH - \mu K^2$.

In principle, the Completeness Theorem provides a constructive procedure for deriving blending surfaces, as follows:

(1) Given the quadrics $S(G)$ and $S(H)$, pick a quadric $S(K)$ intersecting the other two surfaces in the desired curves of tangency.

(2) Pick a parameter μ and set $F = K^2 - \mu GH$. Then $S(F)$ is a blending surface.

After so determining F, only the area between the curves of tangency is of interest as blending surface. Consequently, $S(F)$ must be suitably clipped. We will see later how this is done with the help of $S(K)$.

How should K and μ be selected? Picking $S(K)$ obviously specifies the curves at which we tangentially connect the blending surface to the primary surfaces. The numerical parameter μ then controls the curvature of the resulting blending surface. However, considerable experience is necessary before a designer can skillfully manipulate blending surfaces so derived. Therefore, we explore alternative formulations.

4. Affine Parameter Space Derivations

The blending surfaces characterized above can be derived by substitution from a parametric base curve, as we now explain. The resulting derivation procedure is called the *potential method* [3]. According to whether the base curve is viewed in affine or projective space, we speak of the *affine* or the *projective* potential method, respectively. We now explain the affine potential method.

The potential method derivation has the advantage that a greater intuitive understanding of the resulting shapes is obtained. Moreover, it becomes clear that this formulation can be used to blend arbitrary algebraic surfaces, and that higher-order continuity to the primary surfaces could be achieved should the application require it.

A simple introduction to the parameter space formulation is provided by a two-dimensional example. Consider the circle specified by the polynomial

$$f(s, t) = (s - 1)^2 + (t - 1)^2 - 1$$

in the s-t plane. This circle may be considered a blending curve for the intersecting coordinate axes $t = 0$ and $s = 0$, as shown in Fig. 1. In analogy to the three-dimensional case, denote the circle by $S(f)$, the s-axis by $S(t)$, and the t-axis by $S(s)$. Substitute the polynomial $G(x, y)$ for s, and the polynomial

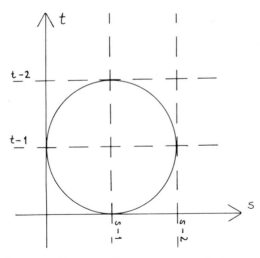

Fig. 1. A circle on rectilinear coordinates; tangency to the lines $s = 0$ and $t = 0$.

$H(x, y)$ for t. Then f becomes the polynomial $F = (G - 1)^2 + (H - 1)^2 - 1$. What is the shape of $S(F)$ in x-y space? The answer is illustrated in Fig. 2 where the circles $S(x^2 + y^2 - 1)$ and $S((x - 1)^2 + y^2 - 1)$ have been used. Intuitively, we have redrawn $S(f)$ in a curvilinear coordinate system. Moreover, we note that $S(F)$ remains tangent to $S(G)$ and $S(H)$. Since G and H have degree 2, F has degree 4.

Consider the point (u, v) on $S(f)$. This point is the intersection of the lines $S(s - u)$ and $S(t - v)$. Corresponding to (u, v) in s-t space are all points of the intersection of $S(G - u)$ with $S(H - v)$, in x-y space. We therefore can think of the substitution for s and t as a deformation of the coordinate system. Note, however, that different points in the curved x-y space may have the same coordinates $(G - u, H - v)$, as is the case in Fig. 2.

We embed s-t space into three-dimensional r-s-t space. Now $S(s)$ and $S(t)$ are planes, and $S(f)$ is a circular cylinder that is tangent to these planes in the lines $S(s, t - 1)$ and $S(s - 1, t)$, respectively. If G and H specify surfaces in x-y-z space and F is obtained from f through substitution as before, then $S(F)$ will be a surface tangent to $S(G)$ and $S(H)$. In particular, $S(F)$ is tangent to $S(G)$ in x-y-z space in the curve $S(G, H - 1)$.

Intuitively, the reason tangency is preserved can be understood as follows: A transformation through substitution maps intersection points to intersection points. Now tangency is a double intersection, hence tangency is preserved. A formal proof is easily found. Briefly, the partial derivatives of F on the curves

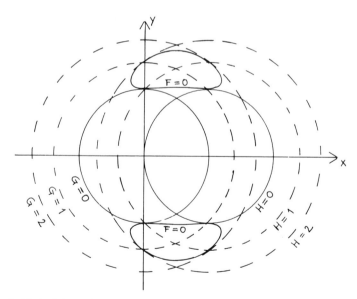

Fig. 2. Circle deformation in curved coordinates; tangency to the lines $G = 0$ and $H = 0$.

$S(G, H - 1)$ and $S(H - 1, G)$ must agree with the corresponding derivatives of G and H. It is then easy to see that the tangent planes must coincide along the curves: see also [3].

We extend the underlying parameter function f to include all conic cylinders tangent to $S(s)$ and $S(t)$. Assuming tangency at $S(s - a, t)$ and $S(s, t - b)$, where a and b are given constants, all such conic cylinders are given by

$$f = b^2(s - a)^2 + a^2(t - b)^2 - a^2b^2 - 2\lambda abst \,.$$

Here λ is a number that should be greater than -1. In the range $-1 < \lambda < 1$ we obtain an elliptic cylinder, for $\lambda = 1$ a parabolic cylinder, and for $\lambda > 1$ a hyperbolic cylinder. See also Fig. 3. For $\lambda = -1$ the cylinder degenerates into the double plane $S((bs + at-ab)^2)$. For $\lambda < -1$ we obtain hyperbolic cylinders that are positioned as shown in Fig. 4. Due to their position, the hyperbolic cylinders for $\lambda < -1$ are not useful for deriving blending surfaces.

Substituting quadric surfaces $S(G)$ and $S(H)$ into this family of cylinders yields quartic blending surfaces. The relationship to the normal form $F = K^2 - \mu GH$ derived previously for blending quadrics is seen directly from the equation for f when it is rewritten as

$$f = (bs + at - ab)^2 - 2(1 + \lambda)abst \,.$$

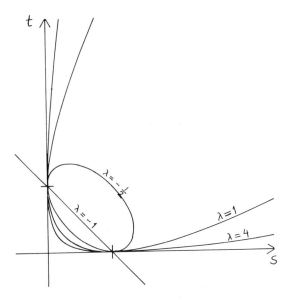

Fig. 3. Conics for selected λ values.

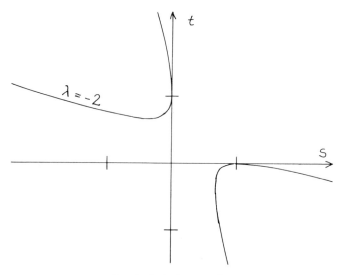

Fig. 4. Conic for $\lambda = -2$.

Hence $S(K)$ is the image of the plane $S(bs + at - ab)$, and $\mu = 2(1 + \lambda)ab$. Referring again to Fig. 3, it is easy to see that the plane $S(bs + at - ab)$ can be used to identify the part of $S(F)$ that is used for blending: Clip those points of $S(f)$ for which $bs + at - ab > 0$, or, equivalently, clip $S(F)$ when $K(x, y, z) > 0$. This will suffice for all elliptic and parabolic base cylinders, but for the hyperbolic cylinders the other branch of the hyperbola must be clipped when $s < 0$ or when $t < 0$, or, equivalently, $S(F)$ is clipped when $G < 0$ or when $H < 0$.

We see now that blending surfaces may be derived by substituting the primary surfaces to be blended in the parametric polynomial f. Intuitively, this is a deformation of the coordinate system in which the coordinate planes $S(s)$ and $S(t)$ are mapped to the primary surfaces $S(G)$ and $S(H)$. The conic cylinder $S(f)$ blending the planes is mapped to the surface $S(F)$ blending $S(G)$ and $S(H)$. Finally, the plane $S(bs + at - ab)$ is mapped to the surface $S(K)$, familiar from the normal form equation for quartic blends. This surface $S(K)$ plays an important role both in defining the curves of tangency, as well as in providing the criterion for clipping $S(F)$.

The blending method described works equally well for blending surfaces of degree higher than 2. No intrinsic property of quadrics is needed to prove tangency of the resulting surfaces $S(F)$, given the primary surfaces $S(G)$ and $S(H)$ [3]. Moreover, one may use other parametric polynomials f. In [5] we have advocated quadratic polynomials for the simple reason that the resulting blending surfaces $S(F)$ have a small degree. If degree is of no concern, or if higher-order continuity to the primary surfaces is needed, higher-degree polynomials f may be used. For example, [7] has used the superellipses as a parametric base polynomial.

It is not necessary to think of a three-dimensional parameter space. In [3], a two-dimensional s-t space is used instead, and an intuitive interpretation of the substitution process given. However, for other purposes such as corner blending the three-dimensional view seems more natural.

Clearly, the substitution paradigm yields a very intuitive derivation method, and for quadratic base polynomials f the quantities a, b, and λ are easily understood. Briefly, the choice of a and b controls the distance the respective curves of tangency on $S(H)$ and $S(G)$ have, from the intersection curve $S(G, H)$. Enlarge a for example, and the curve at which $S(F)$ is tangent to $S(H)$ is further apart from $S(G, H)$. Of course, for a closed quadric surface $S(H)$ a maximum distance cannot be exceeded. Moreover, the choice of λ controls the "sag" of the blending surface, i.e., how closely it follows $S(G) \cup S(H)$. [5] contains a number of pictures illustrating the choice of λ.

The substitution paradigm with a quadratic base polynomial f provides a very intuitive procedure for deriving blending surfaces given G and H. At least in the case of quadrics it is easy to visualize the behavior induced by choosing a, b and λ. Little additional work seems to be needed to automate the method and incorporate it into a solid modeler. Difficulties to be faced for blending higher-degree primary surfaces $S(G)$ all have to do with understanding the shape of the surfaces $S(G - s)$ when $0 < s \leq a$. For quadrics it is easy to see how these surfaces behave, with the cone perhaps exhibiting the most complex behavior. For higher-degree surfaces this relationship may be much more complex, and without a comprehensive surface classification an automated blending surface derivation appears to be difficult.

5. Projective Parameter Space Derivation

The affine potential method described in the previous section is not general enough to derive all quartic blends of the form $K^2 - \mu GH$. The limitation is due to the fact that we formulated the derivation based on affine polynomials f. Only by using a projective base polynomial f and substituting for the homogeneizing variable u as well do we obtain the full generality possible. We now describe the projective potential method.

Consider a projective parameter space with homogeneous coordinates r, s, t, and u. The quadratic base polynomial is then

$$f_1 = b^2(s - au)^2 + a^2(t - bu)^2 - a^2b^2u^2 - 2\lambda abst .$$

As before, we substitute G for s and H for t. However, we now choose a polynomial W to be substituted for u. It is reasonable to limit the degree of W

by the maximum degree of G and H. Thus, when blending quadrics, we substitute a polynomial of degree no higher than 2 thereby obtaining quartic blending surfaces.

This projective method of deriving blending surfaces subsumes the affine method, since by substituting the polynomial $W = 1$ for u the affine method is recovered. This is to be expected, for it corresponds to the usual way of embedding affine space into projective space.

Before exploring the generality of the projective derivation procedure, we seek to simplify the base polynomial. It is well known that in projective space all nondegenerate conics are related by projective transformation. In particular, the base polynomial f_1 above can be transformed into the polynomial

$$f_0 = (s' - u')^2 + (t' - u')^2 - u'^2$$

by the protective transformation

$$r = r', \qquad s = \frac{s'}{bc}, \qquad t = \frac{t'}{ac},$$

$$u = \frac{(1 - c)s'}{abc} + \frac{(1 - c)t'}{abc} + \frac{u'}{ab},$$

where $c = \sqrt{1 + \lambda}$. For $\lambda = -1$ the conic degenerates, and the projective transformation becomes singular. We again assume that $\lambda > -1$, hence $\sqrt{1 + \lambda}$ is real.

We claim that the choice of W already includes the role of a, b, and λ. That is, let F_1 be the result of substituting G, H and W for s, t and u in f_1 above. Then we can find a polynomial W' such that substituting G, H and W' for s', t' and u' in f_0 we obtain F_0 such that $S(F_1) = S(F_0)$. To see this, we rewrite the polynomials as

$$f_1 = (bs + at - abu)^2 - 2(1 + \lambda)abst,$$

$$f_0 = (s + t - u)^2 - 2st.$$

Let

$$W' = (abW - bG - aH)/\sqrt{ab(1 + \lambda)} + G + H.$$

Substituting G, H and W' for s', t' and u' in f_0 we obtain

$$F_0 = (bG + aH - abW)^2/(ab(1 + \lambda)) - 2GH.$$

Since substitution of G, H and W for s, t and u in f_1 yields

$$F_1 = (bG + aH - abW)^2 - 2ab(1 + \lambda)GH ,$$

we have $S(F_1) = S(F_0)$, unless $\lambda = -1$. Hence for nondegenerate conics the projective base polynomial f_0 suffices.

Now consider a quartic blending surface $S(F)$ where $F = K^2 - \mu GH$, $S(G)$ and $S(H)$ are quadrics, and K is of degree 2 or less. Then with $W = G + H - K/\sqrt{\mu}$ we have $S(F) = S(F')$, where F' is obtained from f_0 by substituting G, H, and W. Hence every quartic surface obtained through the methods of Section 3 is also derivable from f_0 using the projective derivation method.

Although based on substitution as in the case of the affine derivation method, the role of W is difficult to visualize. More work is needed to interpret how the form of W influences the shape of the resulting blending surfaces, and automating the projective procedure appears difficult. A specific difficulty arises from the form of polynomials as follows: Given $\alpha \neq 0$, the surfaces $S(G)$ and $S(\alpha G)$ are clearly equal. Yet using αG in place of G when substituting alters the resulting blending surface.

6. Projective Transformation of Blending Surfaces

We investigate the behavior of the blending surface $S(F)$ under projective transformation of the projective x-y-z-w space. In particular, we settle the question when a projectively derived blending surface can be obtained by first deriving an affine blending surface followed by a projective transformation of x-y-z-w space. As in Section 3, we concentrate on quartic blends of quadrics.

Since we embed the blending surfaces into complex projective space, we assume throughout that all polynomials F, G, H, etc., are homogeneous in x, y, z, and w. Because of the results of the previous section, we make the following definition:

Definition 6.1. A blending surface $S(F)$ with $F = K^2 - 2GH$ is *projective* if it is obtained from $f_0 = (s + t - u)^2 - 2st$ by substituting G for s, H for t, and W for u. Moreover, if $W = \alpha w^2$, $\alpha \neq 0$, then $S(F)$ is an *affine* blending surface.

First, let us exclude substituting the zero polynomial for u, for it leads to a degenerate blending surface: If $W = 0$ is substituted into f_0, then $F = G^2 + H^2$, hence $F = (G + iH)(G - iH)$, where $i = \sqrt{-1}$. Since F factors, it is in general a surface that intersects G and H transversally, i.e., it is useless as a blending surface.

Given a projective blend $S(F_0)$ of the quadrics $S(G_0)$ and $S(H_0)$, is there a projective transformation p such that $S(F)$ is the image of an affine blend $S(F)$, i.e., $F_0 = p(F)$? We solve this problem with the following theorem:

Theorem 6.2. *Let $S(F_0)$ be a projective blend where*

$$F_0 = K_0^2 - 2G_0H_0 ,$$

and, G_0, H_0, and K_0 are quadratic. Let p be a projective transformation such that

$$p(F) = F_0 , \qquad p(G) = G_0 , \qquad p(H) = H_0 , \qquad p(K) = K_0 .$$

If F is an affine blending surface, then $W_0 = G_0 + H_0 - K_0 = U^2$, for a linear form U. Conversely, if $W_0 = G_0 + H_0 - K_0 = U^2$, then p may be chosen such that F is an affine blending surface.

Proof. Assume F is an affine blend, so that F is obtained from f_0 via the substitution

$$s = G , \qquad t = H , \qquad u = G + H - K = \alpha w^2 .$$

Let $\beta = \sqrt{\alpha}$. The transformation p effects a substitution

$$w = ax' + by' + cz' + dw' = U .$$

Since p is not singular, U is not the zero polynomial. Then

$$p(G + H - K) = p(G) + p(H) - p(K) = (\beta U)^2 .$$

Moreover, since $F = K^2 - 2GH$, we have $p(F) = F_0 = p(K)^2 - p(G)p(H)$. With

$$G_0 = p(G) , \qquad H_0 = p(H) , \qquad K_0 = p(K) , \qquad W_0(\beta U)^2$$

the projective blend has the required structure.

Conversely, assume that F_0 is a projective blend with $W_0 = G_0 + H_0 - K_0 = U^2$. Let

$$U = ax' + by' + cz' + dw' .$$

If $d \neq 0$, consider the transformation q given by

$$x' = x , \qquad y' = y , \qquad z' = z , \qquad w' = (w - ax - by - cz)/d .$$

Then $q(W_0) = q(U)^2 = w^2$. Since $W_0 = G_0 + H_0 - K_0$, we have

$$q(F_0) = q(G_0 + H_0 - W_0)^2 - 2q(G_0)q(H_0) .$$

Consequently, $q(F_0)$ is an affine blend. If $d = 0$ we may assume without loss of generality that $a \neq 0$. We take as q the transformation

$$x' = (w - cy - bx)/a, \qquad y' = x, \qquad z' = y, \qquad w' = z.$$

Then $q(W_0) = w^2$. The theorem follows with p the inverse transformation of q. $\square$

It is interesting to note that not all projective blending surfaces are the image of affine blending surfaces. Rather, the proof of the theorem suggests classifying the quartic blends $S(K^2 - 2GH)$, based on the form of $W = G + H - K$. This classification is precisely the projective classification of quadrics [1], already mentioned in Section 2:

(1) $W = x^2 + y^2 + z^2 + w^2$, the imaginary sphere;
(2) $W = x^2 + y^2 + z^2 - w^2$, the real sphere;
(3) $W = x^2 + y^2 - z^2 - w^2$, the one-sheeted hyperboloid;
(4) $W = x^2 + y^2 + w^2$, the imaginary cylinder;
(5) $W = x^2 + y^2 - w^2$, the real cylinder;
(6) $W = x^2 + w^2$, two imaginary planes;
(7) $W = x^2 - w^2$, two real planes;
(8) $W = w^2$, the double plane.

The last class consists of all affine blends and the projective blends characterized by the theorem. The other classes can be elaborated similarly.

Note that purely imaginary surfaces are of practical interest as W. For example, we may blend two intersecting cylinders as follows: Let

$$G = 2x^2 + 2y^2 - 2w^2, \qquad H = 2y^2 + 2z^2 - 2w^2,$$

$$W = x^2 + y^2 + z^2 + w^2.$$

The resulting blending surface is tangent at the intersection of the cylinders with $K = x^2 + 3y^2 + z^2 - 3w^2$, and does not have the undesirable "bulge" near the points $(0, 1, 0, 1)$ and $(0, -1, 0, 1)$ seen in the illustration in [6]. This bulge cannot be avoided for affine blending surfaces, i.e., when using $W = w^2$.

7. Other Work and Conclusions

Perhaps the most natural class of blending surfaces are the *canal surfaces* [8]. These surfaces are obtained as envelope of the volume swept by a moving sphere of fixed radius that is kept in contact with both primary surfaces to be blended. There are major difficulties associated with this approach:

(1) Canal surfaces typically are of high algebraic degree. For example, the

canal surface blending two circular cylinders intersecting at right angle has degree 16 in the simplest case.

(2) Generic derivation of canal surface equations is computationally very expensive. Since the surface degree is high and since a generic formulation must make explicit the dependency on shape parameters, very complicated symbolic forms are needed. Expressions with several thousand terms are not uncommon.

(3) As the radius of the moving sphere is increased in an attempt to obtain a broader blending surface, unexpected self intersections may result and a surface with creases may be obtained.

In [8], Rossignac and Requicha give a method to approximate canal surface blends with torus and cylinder segments. By approximating the canal surface, the degree and derivation problems are nicely side stepped. However, while the segments join each other smoothly, the resulting surface is not tangent to curved primary surfaces to be blended. The method is used in a CSG modeler with standard primitives, and much of the charm of the work derives from the fact that the underlying set of primitives needs no extension.

In [6], Middleditch and Sears outline a blending method remarkably similar to the affine potential method. The method is based on conics tangent to coordinate lines in affine s-t parameter space. The conics used are restricted to be tangent at points equidistant from the coordinate lines, i.e., $a = b$ is assumed. Moreover, our parameter λ is expressed as distance of the apex of the conic from the lines. Since Middleditch and Sears seek to derive blending surfaces for which the curves of tangency lie at a fixed Euclidean distance from the other surface, they must substitute complicated offset equations into the underlying conic. In consequence, fairly complex blending surface equations are obtained. For instance, blending a cone and a plane results in a surface of degree 6. Middleditch and Sears observe that substituting the implicit equations of the surfaces to be blended leads to algebraically simpler surfaces. This class of simpler blending surfaces is a subset of the affine blending surfaces. It is a proper subset since $a = b$ is assumed for the underlying conic. The paper also discusses in detail how to integrate the blending method into a CSG modeler with standard primitives.

Rockwood and Owen give a blending method in [7] that is also based on substitution. The basic curve used is the superellipse

$$(1 - s/a)^\lambda + (1 - t/b)^\lambda = 1 \, ,$$

where the parameters a, b, and λ are analogous to the parameters in the affine potential method. The surfaces to be blended are substituted for s and t. The constants a and b can be replaced with functions of the gradients of the primary surfaces. This seems to have the effect of making the curvature distribution more uniform along the length of the blending surface. When $\lambda > 2$, or when gradient functions are used in place of the constants a and b, blending surfaces of fairly high algebraic degree are obtained. Moreover, for large values of λ the order of continuity of the blend with the primary surfaces increases. In both cases numerical difficulties should be expected.

The methods of [6–8] each have been incorporated into some experimental solid modeling systems. This requires some degree of automating the blending process whose prospects we now discuss briefly. Our insights are limited by the fact that so far we have not had the oppurtunity to experiment with these systems.

Two problem types are encountered when incorporating a blending method into a solid modeling systems:

(1) *Local control problems.* The blending surface(s) to be interpolated must be specified in an intuitive and concise manner that delivers predictable results anticipated by the user. This requires an intuitive interpretation of all parameters in the underlying polynomial.

(2) *Blend-blend problems.* When blending edge cycles bounded by different faces, a contiguous blending surface can only be piecewise-algebraic. This not only complicates blending in that smooth transitions between the pieces are required, but also introduces additional complexities for clipping. In particular, in CSG type modelers blending operations must be analyzed for sequence dependency which must be understood fully by the user.

All authors have acknowledged the existence of the two problem types, but concentrate mostly on blend-blend problems. Perhaps this is because these problems must be faced immediately by any implementation.

In the case of [8], it appears reasonable to concentrate on blend-blend problems, since the only parameter that is specified for local shape control is the radius of the moving sphere. Nevertheless, additional results would be desirable that provide information about the precision to be expected when choosing the number of primitive segments with which the canal surface is to be approximated. For instance, when blending two intersecting circular cylinders of radius 10 with a canal surface of radius 1, what precision can be expected from an approximation of, say, 100 segments of tori and cylinders?

The blending method of [6] aims at solving the local control problem by giving the base polynomial a restricted form and explicitly linearizing distance control parameters. However, such a formulation shifts the problem to finding suitable *potential functions* that conform with the shape expectations based on Euclidean distance measures. When the set of underlying primitives is simple and fixed, this appears to be reasonable. However, the potential functions needed to blend blending surfaces recursively, e.g., when blending at corners, quickly complicate the problem, as acknowledged by the authors.

Also in [7] the local control problem remains largely unexplored. One is left with the impression that the user must determine the desired shape parameters interactively, perhaps by inspecting the resulting surfaces visually. However, [7] also suggests a blending method similar to the homotopy technique we have outlined in [3] for which the local control problem seems more tractable.

All blending methods based on substitution face the difficulty that the deformation effected by this substitution has very few intrinsic properties that would allow solving local control problems in general. Therefore, we believe that the geometric properties of blending surfaces for specific surface classes must be explored first, e.g., for the class of all quadrics, or for the class of all CSG primitives. Clearly, these properties must be fully understood and interpreted in the context of the primitive class considered before the method should be automated. Only then is it possible to give to the casual user a clear understanding of the range of specification choices and their results.

REFERENCES

1. Blaschke, W., *Projektive Geometrie* (Birkhäuser, Stuttgart, 1954).
2. Fulton, W., *Algebraic Curves* (Benjamin, New York, 1969).
3. Hoffmann, C. and Hopcroft, J., Automatic surface generation in computer aided design, *Visual Comput.* **1** (2) (1985) 92–100.
4. Hoffman, C. and Hopcroft, J., Quadratic blending surfaces, *Comput. Aided Des.* **18** (1986).
5. Hoffmann, C. and Hopcroft, J., The potential method for blending surfaces and corners, in: G. Farin (Ed.), *Geometric Modeling* (SIAM, Philadelphia, PA, 1986).
6. Middleditch, A. and Sears, K., Blend surfaces for set theoretic volume modeling systems, *SIGGRAPH Comput. Graph.* **19** (3) (1985) 161–170.
7. Rockwood, A. and Owen, J., Blending surfaces in solid geometrics modeling, in: G. Farin (Ed.), *Geometric Modeling* (SIAM, Philadelphia, PA, 1986).
8. Rossignac, J. and Requicha, A., Constant-radius blending in solid modeling, *Comput. Mech. Eng.* **3** (1984) 65–73.
9. Snyder, V. and Sisam, C., *Analytic Geometry of Space* (Holt, New York, 1914).
10. Warren, J., Personal communication (1985).
11. Holmström, L., Piecewise quadric blending of implicitly defined surfaces, *Comput. Aided Geom. Des.* **4** (3) (1987) 171–189.

Received October 1986; revised version received March 1988

Verifiable Implementations of Geometric Algorithms Using Finite Precision Arithmetic*

Victor J. Milenkovic**

*Department of Computer Science, Carnegie-Mellon
University, Pittsburgh, PA 15213, U.S.A.*

ABSTRACT

Two methods are proposed for correct and verifiable geometric reasoning using finite precision arithmetic. The first method, data normalization, transforms the geometric structure into a configuration for which all finite precision calculations yield correct answers. The second method, called the hidden variable method, constructs configurations that belong to objects in an infinite precision domain—without actually representing these infinite precision objects. Data normalization is applied to the problem of modeling polygonal regions in the plane, and the hidden variable method is used to calculate arrangements of lines.

1. Introduction

Geometric reasoning using finite precision arithmetic presents great difficulties because of round-off error. Yet reasoning in a finite precision domain is an area worth investigating because finite precision floating point arithmetic is fast, widely available, and widely used in practice. The common alternative, algebraic systems, are not subject to error, but they can be much less efficient. The goal of this work are verifiably correct finite precision implementations of geometric algorithms.

Implementations based on finite precision arithmetic pose two problems. First, as has been stated, a finite precision implementation of a proven geometric algorithm is not necessarily correct; because of round-off error, it may fail on valid input. Second, finite precision arithmetic does not have the power to allow an implementation to exactly match the behavior of an implementation based on infinite precision arithmetic. At best it can retain

---

*Extensions of the results in this article are described in Tech. Rept. CMU-CS-88-168 with the same title.

**Present address: Harvard University, Center for Research in Computing Technology, Cambridge, MA 02138, U.S.A.

only some of the properties of interest. For example, a polygon modeling
system may maintain planar topology, allow lines to intersect no more than
once, and determine region areas to within a prespecified accuracy, even
though it does not correctly determine the number of vertices of the modeled
polygon. Solving these two problems requires several steps. The implementor
must

- choose a useful set of properties to be retained by the finite precision
  implementation,
- design the implementation,
- prove that the implementation has the chosen properties.

This paper proposes two general methods for the design of correct finite
precision geometric algorithms: *data normalization* and the *hidden variable*
method. It illustrates the use of these methods with concrete examples of
correct implementation designs. The application of the first method, a modeling system for planar polygon regions, has been implemented and is in use as
part of a research tool. The application of the second method seriously
addresses for the first time the problem of round-off error in calculating the
topological arrangement of lines in the plane.

2. Error Resulting from Finite Precision: An Example

This section examines a simple example of the type of error that can occur
when an implementation uses the most naive form of floating point computation. Suppose we have seven line equations and we wish to determine the
topological arrangement of the lines. If, as in Fig. 1, two points of intersection
A and *B* are very close together, round-off error may place them in the wrong
order on line *L*. The result, topologically, is shown in Fig. 2. This arrangement
has the topology of a two-holed doughnut. Any algorithm that depends on
planar topology would fail if presented with such a data structure.

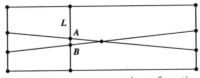

Fig. 1. Error-prone geometric configuration.

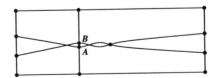

Fig. 2. Topologically incorrect interpretation.

3. Two Approaches to Finite Precision Implementations

Here then is the crux of the problem: Because of round-off error, we cannot depend solely on numerical tests to determine the structure or topology of a particular geometric object. The choice of topology is sometimes arbitrary, given our lack of information. Yet we want to model geometric domains, such as Euclidean or planar projective geometry, with well-defined topological constraints. This paper proposes two approaches to resolving this problem of ambiguity, *data normalization* and the *hidden variable method*.

– *Data normalization.* Alter the structure and parameters of the geometric object slightly so as to arrive at an object for which all numerical tests are provably accurate. After this normalization process there are no arbitrary choices because calculation always gives a definitive and correct answer.

– *Hidden variable method.* Choose a topological structure so that the following holds true: there exist infinite precision parameters for the object, close to the given finite precision parameter values, such that with the infinite precision values, the problem has the chosen structure. This approach is called the hidden variable method because the topology of the infinite precision version is known but not its numerical values.

In Fig. 3 we see how the normalization method might deal with the problem that was shown in Fig. 1. Very close vertices, which can lead to numerical singularities, are either separated, as on the left, or merged, as on the right. With this method we lose the geometric properties of the lines because the lines have been broken up into noncollinear segments, but we retain the properties of planar polygons.

In Fig. 4, we see two possible solutions under the hidden variable method. On the left is one possible topological arrangement: the three interior lines

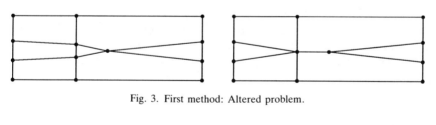

Fig. 3. First method: Altered problem.

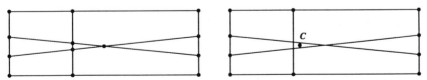

Fig. 4. Second method: Imposed interpretation.

form a triangle. On the right, the three lines pass through a single point C. This choice is possible because one can easily prove that there exists three nearby lines which are indeed concurrent at point C. (The diagram looks awkward because the error has been magnified so as to be visible.) An erroneous interpretation as was seen in Fig. 2 is impossible because no set of "hidden lines" will form that configuration. At least some of the constraints of the domain (Euclidean geometry) are satisfied in that pairs of lines intersect exactly once and the object has planar topology. However we do not have access to the (infinite precision) parameters of the actual lines which satisfy the topology we have chosen. Thus it may be harder to extract information from the model.

The examples given in Sections 2 and 3 are meant to give the reader some idea of the sort of geometric error that can occur and the different means by which the error may be avoided. The following sections contain rigorous definitions of verifiable finite precision implementations. Section 4 contains a model of finite precision arithmetic which can be used as a replacement for the axioms of real arithmetic. The model chosen is perhaps the most pessimistic possible in the sense that nothing is known with greater accuracy than the maximum round-off error. Under this model, the two methods of verifiable geometric computation are demonstrated by means of concrete examples. In Section 5, the normalization method is applied to the problem of modeling polygonal regions in the plane, and in Section 6, the hidden variable method is used to construct the arrangement of lines in the plane. In each case the design is verifiable under the assumptions of the given model of finite precision arithmetic, and the satisfaction of a chosen set of properties is guaranteed.

4. Model of Finite Precision Computation

In order to reason about round-off error, some model of finite precision computation is necessary. The methods of this paper are based on the simplest assumption that round-off is a bounded but random error added to the result of each computation. In evaluating a complicated expression, multiple round-off errors will generally cancel each other, but for purposes of proving correctness, the maximum possible total error must be used.

The implementor must derive an error bound ε. This bound depends on the algorithm being implemented and the type of finite precision arithmetic used to implement it. For every expression evaluated by the implementation, the following must hold true:

– The error may be as large as ε.
– The error is no larger than ε.
– No program can assume an accuracy of a derived result greater than can be verified under the first assumption.

As an example of the last property, suppose an algorithm must calculate the intersection of two lines. The only way to verify an answer under the finite precision model is to evaluate the expressions which determine the distance of the intersection point to each line. This evaluation may differ from the correct value by as much as ε. At best, the calculated intersection point may be any point within ε of the two lines, possibly quite far from the actual intersection point if the lines form a small angle. In Fig. 5, point I is the true intersection, but the calculated intersection may be as far away as C.

The value of ε depends on two factors: the maximum round-off error per arithmetic operation and the number of arithmetic operations per expression. Suppose we use a floating point representation with q bits of accuracy. Evaluating any expression involving quantities of magnitude M can result in errors on the order of $2^{-q}M$. Suppose we bound the magnitude of all real numbers that an implementation uses by some value MAX. Then the smallest guaranteed significant quantity is,

$$\text{SIG} = 2^{-q}\text{MAX}.$$

An expression such as the area of a triangle $p_1 p_2 p_3$,

$$\text{Area} = \tfrac{1}{2}(p_1 \times p_2 + p_2 \times p_3 + p_3 \times p_1),$$

involves six multiplications and five additions (or subtractions). Assuming that the additions can be performed with total error at most $\tfrac{1}{2}\text{SIG}$ and that each multiplication can have round-off error no more that $\tfrac{1}{2}\text{SIG}$, the maximum possible error in the computation of the area is,

$$\tfrac{1}{2}(\tfrac{1}{2}\text{SIG} + 6 \cdot \tfrac{1}{2}\text{SIG}) < 2\text{SIG}.$$

Similarly, most expressions can be evaluated so as to have error no more than a small constant times SIG. To determine the value of ε, the implementor looks at the number of round-offs in the most complex expression evaluated by the system.

Given two quantities calculated under this model of computation, a geometric reasoning system can sometimes show that one is greater than the other or that one is less than the other, but it can never show that the two quantities are

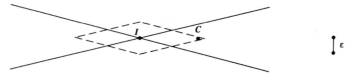

Fig. 5. Error in calculated intersection position.

equal. It is hard to imagine a more pessimistic viewpoint, but it is interesting to see what can be done with these assumptions.

5. Data Normalization

This paper illustrates the method of data normalization by applying it to the problem of modeling polygonal regions in the plane. Central to this approach is a set of rules which a validly normalized object must satisfy. These rules can be correctly tested using finite precision computations. The system provides four types of operations:

- *make*: creation of new normalized objects;
- *move*: translation and rotation operations;
- *combine*: union, complement, and all the other regularized set operations on planar polygonal regions;
- *examine*: a point-in-region predicate, for example.

These operations generate normalized objects so long as they are given normalized objects as input. Since normalization is a precondition and post-condition of all the system operations, the system cannot enter an invalid (unnormalized) state.

The system contains the following types of objects,

- *vertices*: ordered pairs of finite precision values representing points in the plane;
- *edges*: ordered pairs of vertices representing oriented line segments.

As shown in Fig. 6, the interior of a polygonal region is defined to lie to the left of its bounding edges.

To define this system, we must choose a value of ε such that the distance between a point and another point and the distance between a point and a line segment can be calculated with accuracy $\frac{1}{10}\varepsilon$. Given this value of ε, the five normalization rules are:

(1) No two vertices are closer than ε.

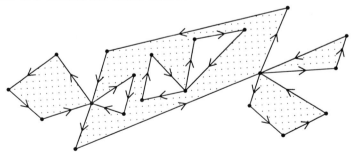

Fig. 6. Example polygonal region.

(2) No vertex is closer than ε to an edge of which it is not an endpoint.

(3) No two edges intersect except at their endpoints.

(4) For each vertex, the angularly sorted list of edges containing that vertex alternates between incoming edges and outgoing edges.

(5) For each point in the plane, the *topological winding number* (defined below) is either 0, 1, or undefined.

The first rule can be checked under all circumstances; the second can be checked so long as the first rule holds; and in general, it is possible to check a rule so long as all the previous rules in the list are satisfied. Once the first two rules are satisfied, the model is no longer subject to topological ambiguities. For example, a set of edges which share a common endpoint can be sorted by angle, and it can be determined whether a vertex lies inside or outside a closed loop of edges. Thus the rules after the first two are basically the same as those of an infinite precision implementation.

5.1. Topological winding number

The *topological winding number* indicates the exterior, interior, and boundary of a polygonal region. This winding number can be defined as follows:

Definition 5.1. The *topological winding number* of a point p with respect to a polygon P: if p lies on some edge of P, the winding number is undefined. Otherwise, let L be the horizontal line (parallel to x-axis) through p, and let R be the ray extending to the right of P. As in Fig. 7, an edge AB *crosses* R positively if A is below L and B is on or above L and AB intersects L to the right of p. Edge AB negatively crosses R if BA positively crosses R. The number of positive crossings minus the number of negative crossings is the winding number of p.

In the finite precision version, the winding number can be calculated accurately if p is no closer than $\frac{1}{4}\varepsilon$ to any vertex or edge of P.

Except on the boundary where it is not defined, the winding number has an integral value. For an arbitrary object satisfying rules (1)–(4), this value may be other than 0 or 1, but rule (5) states that the winding number can take on only these values, and so the polygon has a well-defined exterior and interior. Rules (1)–(4) make assertions about finite sets, and therefore are easily shown to be decidable. Rule (5), on the other hand, makes a statement about all

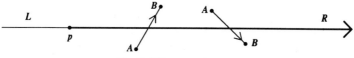

Fig. 7. Edges crossing ray.

points in the plane, including points for which the topological winding number cannot be calculated using finite precision. The following theorem reduces the set of points to be tested to a finite set.

Theorem 5.2. *If rules* (1)–(4) *hold and the topological winding number of every point* $\frac{1}{4}\varepsilon$ *to the left of the midpoint of each edge equals* 1 (*see Fig.* 8), *then rule* (5) *holds.*

Actually, if we partition the edges into connected components, it is sufficient to verify the condition of Theorem 5.2. for just one edge from each component. Thus rule (5) can be tested by only a few applications of the finite precision winding number function.

One final note about the topological winding number: if the polygonal region is unbounded, the value defined by Definition 5.1 will be 0 for points in the exterior of the region and -1 for points in the interior. One can distinguish this case from the bounded case by testing a point as in Fig. 8. The point p should always be inside the region.

Fig. 8. Test point for rule (5).

5.2. Accommodation

Three out of the four basic types of operations on polygonal regions—creation, transformation, or combination—can lead to violations of rules (1) and (2). The polygon(s) being operated on must be altered to accommodate new or transformed vertex locations which may lie within ε of the current vertices and edges of the polygon(s). A basic operation called *accommodation* alters a polygon to accommodate a new vertex, using two more primitive operations *vertex shifting* and *edge cracking*. Normalization of a polygon consists of applying accommodation to the polygon for each vertex which violates rules (1) and (2).

For example, one of the most difficult operations on polygonal regions is the union. In Figs. 9 and 10 we see how vertex shifting and edge cracking allow one polygon to accommodate the vertices of the other. The following pseudo-program defines the operation of accommodation.

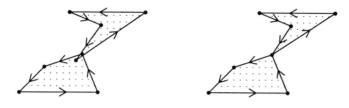

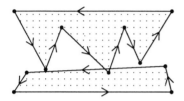 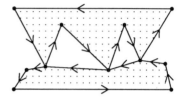

Fig. 9. Vertex shifting.

Fig. 10. Edge cracking.

ACCOMMODATE(polygon *P*, vertex *V*)
    {*P* satisfies rules (1) through (5)}
    SHIFT-VERTEX(*P*, *V*)
    {*P* satisfies rule (1) and normalization invariant}
    While there exists some edge *AB* of *P* within ε of some vertex
        {*P* satisfies rule (1) and normalization invariant}
        CRACK-EDGE(*P*, *AB*)
    {*P* satisfies rule (1) and rule (2) and normalization invariant}
    {*P* satisfies rules (1)–(5)}

The following sections define *vertex shifting, edge cracking* and the *normalization invariant*. Subsequent sections contain proofs that the assertions in this pseudocode are true and that the while-loop terminates.

5.2.1. *Vertex shifting*

Suppose we have a polygon *P* and a new vertex *V* not part of *P*. Shift each vertex of *P* which lies within ε of *V* to coincide with the location of *V*, and eliminate any double edges introduced by this shifting. At this point, the polygon satisfies rule (1). Note that shifting a vertex involves identifying it with the vertex it has been shifted to (otherwise we would have multiple vertices at the same location). The polygon may fail to satisfy rule (2) because

   – the new vertex (and hence the shifted vertices) may be within ε of an edge,
   – edges with a shifted vertex endpoint may have been moved to within ε of a vertex.

These two sources of violations of rule (2) are mutually exclusive for the following reasons. An edge either has a shifted vertex as an endpoint or it does not. If it does not, it has not been changed, and thus only the first type of violation can occur. If the edge does have a shifted vertex as an endpoint, then after shifting it has V as an endpoint. Since every shifted vertex has been shifted to V, any vertex which lies off the edge after shifting must be an unshifted vertex.

5.2.2. Edge cracking

Any edge which passes within ε of a vertex violates rule (2) of the normalization rules. The following steps define a process called *cracking* which eliminates the offending edge.

Step 1. Select all vertices that lie within ε of the edge AB to be cracked.

Step 2. Sort the vertices according to the position of their projections onto AB. Let the sorted list be $V_1, V_2, \ldots, V_k$.

Step 3. Replace AB by edges $AV_1, V_1V_2, \ldots, V_kB$, and eliminate any double edges that result.

The basic idea is to crack edges until no edge is a candidate for cracking. Since edge cracking does not move vertices (although it may eliminate some), it does not introduce violations of rule (1). Cracking an edge may introduce more edges to be cracked, but if the algorithm terminates, the resulting object must satisfy rule (2).

Incidentally, we may not be able to sort the vertices which lie near an edge if two of the vertices project to the same or nearly the same point. In this case, it can be shown that one of the two vertices must lie at least $\frac{1}{2}\varepsilon$ closer to the edge than the other. The more distant vertex can be left out of the list of vertices to be cracked to without resulting in a violation of the normalization invariant defined in the next section.

5.2.3. Normalization invariant

Designing an invariant for the pseudocode above is tricky because the partial results of vertex shifting and edge cracking do not necessarily satisfy rules (1) and (2). Without these, rules (3)–(5) cannot even be checked using finite precision. The solution to this problem is reminiscent of the hidden variable method described in Section 6.

Definition 5.3. A *polygonal approximation* to an edge AB is a sequence of edges, $AC_1, C_1C_2, \ldots, C_kB$, such that each C_i lies within $\frac{1}{2}\varepsilon$ of AB, and the projections of the C_i on AB are in sorted order.

Definition 5.4. The *normalization invariant* for the accommodation algorithm is defined as follows: polygon P satisfies the invariant if there exist polygonal approximations to all the edges of P such that replacing each edge by its approximation results in a polygon which satisfies rules (3)–(5) (in the infinite precision domain).

In order to prove that vertex shifting and edge cracking preserve the normalization invariant, we need the following theorem.

Theorem 5.5. *If AB is an edge and vertices* $V_1, V_2, \ldots, V_k$, *lie farther than* ε *from A and B but closer than* $\frac{1}{2}\varepsilon$ *to AB, then there exists a polygonal approximation to AB which passes to the left of any chosen subset of the* V_i *and passes to the right of the others.*

5.2.4. *Proof of assertions*

Does vertex shifting preserve the invariant? Recall that vertex shifting introduces violations of rule (2) by either moving edges toward vertices or moving vertices toward edges, but not both at the same time. Since the shift distance is less than ε, nothing get moved relative to something else by more than ε. Since the polygon satisfied rule (2) to start with, vertices and edges were separated by at least ε before the shifting. Therefore after shifting, no vertex could have been moved a significant distance to the wrong side of an edge, certainly not as far as $\frac{1}{2}\varepsilon$. Theorem 5.5 implies that there must exist polygonal approximations to the edges that pass by such vertices on the correct side, and thus the normalization invariant can be satisfied.

If we wish to prove that cracking an edge preserves the normalization invariant, we must consider three classes of vertices: those which lie on the wrong side of the edge (in the infinite precision domain), those which lie within ε of the edge (according to finite precision calculation), and those which lie further than ε from the edge. All vertices in the first class must also belong to the second because the normalization invariant tells us that the edge need not be deflected more than $\frac{1}{2}\varepsilon$ to pass on the correct side of the vertices in the first class. Thus the vertices in the first class lie within $\frac{1}{2}\varepsilon$ of the edge, and therefore finite precision calculation will show them to be well within ε of the edge. The cracking process replaces the edge with a chain of edges passing through the vertices in the second class. Since the second class includes the first class, the topological inconsistency caused by the first class will be eliminated by the new chain of edges.

The new edges may pass to wrong side of previously consistent vertices, but those vertices must all belong to the third class because vertices in the first and second class are part of the chain of new edges. The new edges are displaced from the eliminated edge by at most ε. Since the vertices in the third class were ε distant from the eliminated edge, they cannot be more than a small distance to the wrong side of the new edges, certainly not as much as $\frac{1}{2}\varepsilon$. As in the case of vertex shifting, Theorem 5.5 implies that the normalization invariant can be satisfied.

At the termination of accommodation, rule (1), rule (2) and the normalization invariant hold. Rules (1) and (2) imply that vertices and edges are separated by at least ε. The normalization invariant implies that there is some way of replacing each edge with a polygonal path such that the resulting object satisfies rules (3)–(5). But the polygonal path does not stray further than $\frac{1}{2}\varepsilon$ from the edge. Therefore, replacing the paths with the edges themselves should result in an object that satisfies rules (1)–(5).

5.2.5. *Termination of edge cracking*

The only thing remaining to show is that edge cracking does indeed terminate. In the edge cracking stage of the accommodation algorithm, the choice of the next edge to crack is arbitrary. There is a way of ordering the choices so as to assure termination of cracking. We can first perform those crackings which will increase the area of polygonal region. Then, we can perform the crackings which will decrease the area. It can be shown that a cracking that decreases the area cannot create the need for a cracking that increases the area. Since the set of vertices is fixed and finite, there are only a finite number of edge configurations, one of which will have the largest area and one, the smallest area. Thus both the area-increasing stage and the area-decreasing stage will terminate.

While edges are being cracked, the polygonal region may not have an area, even in infinite precision, because the polygon does not necessarily satisfy rules (3)–(5). The polygon whose existence is implied by the normalization invariant does have an area, but it is not unique. The area we seek is the limit of valid approximating polygons whose total edge lengths tend to a minimum. Incidentally, it is the opinion of the author that edge cracking terminates regardless of the order the edges are cracked.

5.3. Error bounds

We have shown that accommodation can be performed correctly, but how much error does it introduce? The measure of error is the area of discrepancy between the original polygonal region and the new normalized region.

Vertex shifting introduces a small amount of error. It can be shown that the region of discrepancy has area at most εp where p is the length of the perimeter.

Edge cracking, on the other hand, can introduce quite a considerable amount of error. In certain pathological cases, the entire region can disappear! The worst-case error is of order $n\varepsilon p$ where n is the number of vertices in the object. The worst case occurs when each vertex is nearly within ε of some other vertex, and thus a single vertex shift can cause a cascade of edge cracking. If the vertices and edges are separated by at least 2ε to start with, the region of discrepancy has area at most εp as in the case of vertex shifting.

5.4. Implementing the union

As an illustration of how accommodation can be used to implement operations on polygonal regions, let us consider the union: given polygonal regions P and Q, we wish to generate the region which represents the set of points lying in either P or Q.

The first step is to accommodate Q to all the vertices of P by repeated calls to the accommodation function. Then P must be accommodated to the vertices of Q.

At this point, the intersection points can be calculated and inserted. If edge AB of P and edge CD of Q intersect at point I, then replace AB by AI and IB and replace CD by CI and ID. Polygons P and Q must be accommodated to the new vertex I.

Finally, by applying the topological winding number function to the midpoints of edges, determine which edges of P lie outside or on the boundary of Q and which edges of Q lie outside or on the boundary of P. These are the edges of the union region.

As presented, this algorithm is rather inefficient. However an optimization similar to the one mentioned at the end of Section 5.1 can be made. If an edge is shown to be part of the boundary of the union polygonal region, then any edge connected to it via unshared vertices (vertices of P or of Q but not of both) is part of the boundary also.

5.5. Advantages, disadvantages, and an implementation

This particular example shows that data normalization is a viable method for correctly implementing geometric algorithms with finite precision. Unfortunately, many properties of the infinite precision domain are lost by normalization. The resulting objects are indeed planar and polygonal, but each normalization introduces a bounded amount of error which can be measured as the area of the discrepancy between the normalized and unnormalized regions. The total error in a sequence of operations grows with the number of normalizations, and it can be quite large in the worst case. The order of application of accommodation and edge cracking is arbitrary, and the result of the algorithm depends on the order in which these operations are applied. Data normalization is also difficult to generalize to more complex domains, such as curved objects. Still, the polygonal region modeling system summarized here is robust and satisfies well defined properties. A version of the implementation is a part of a modeling system for the VLSI manufacturing process designed at IBM Yorktown [4]. To date is has not failed in any way.

6. Hidden Variable Method

We illustrate the hidden variable method by applying it to the problem of determining the topological arrangement of n lines represented by their

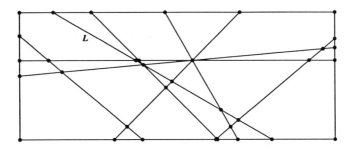

Fig. 11. Arrangement of lines.

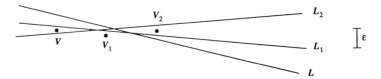

Fig. 12. Difficult case for arrangement algorithms.

equations. The output of the algorithm is a set of (finite precision) vertex locations and a data structure representing the topology of the arrangement (see Fig. 11).

The common methods currently used for calculating arrangements [1, 2] are sensitive to round-off error. Figure 12 shows a configuration that can occur under the model of finite precision arithmetic used by this paper. If the implementation calculates that lines L_1 and L_2 intersect at V and that line L lies above V as shown, then L ought to intersect line L_2 before line L_1. Yet with the value of ε shown, L could intersect L_1 at V_1 and L_2 at V_2, with V_1 appearing well before V_2 on L. The positions of V, V_1 and V_2 are impossible to reconcile with a planar topology.

6.1. Arrangements

Formally, the input of the arrangement algorithm is a set of line equations $\mathcal{L}$ expressed in finite precision. The output of the algorithm contains,

- a set of vertices $\mathcal{V}$,
- a set of edges $\mathcal{E}$,
- some symbolic representation $\mathcal{T}$ of the topological arrangement of the vertices and edges (Guibas and Stolfi [3] have devised a very good representation in their paper about creating Voronoi diagrams).

Each vertex has a numerical location $\langle x, y \rangle$. Each edge in $\mathcal{E}$ is associated with a *bundle* of lines (a subset of $\mathcal{L}$) which represents, by definition, the lines that *contain* that edge. The vertex endpoints of an edge must satisfy the line equations of the lines in that edge's bundle with an error no greater than ε.

The arrangement is limited to a bounding box which represents the maximum allowable magnitudes of the x- and y-coordinates. For every line in $\mathscr{L}$, the set of edges it contains forms a single unbroken chain from one end of the bounding box to the other.

6.2. Ideal case

Ideally we want there to exist a hidden, infinite precision set of lines $\mathscr{L}'$ and vertices $\mathscr{V}'$ which are "close to" the input lines $\mathscr{L}$ and the output vertices $\mathscr{V}$ and which truly satisfy the topological arrangement $\mathscr{T}$. Formally, there must exist mappings from $\mathscr{L}$ to $\mathscr{L}'$ and from $\mathscr{V}$ to $\mathscr{V}'$ which satisfy the following properties

(1) The line mapping is many-to-one and thus partitions $\mathscr{L}$ into equivalence classes—lines which map to the same line in $\mathscr{L}'$—are equivalent.

(2) The vertex mapping is one-to-one.

(3) Each bundle must be an equivalence class of the line mapping. In this way, the mapping from $\mathscr{L}$ to $\mathscr{L}'$ induces a mapping from $\mathscr{E}$ to $\mathscr{L}'$—each edge is mapped to the unique element of $\mathscr{L}'$ to which all the lines in that edge's bundle are mapped.

(4) If a vertex is an endpoint of an edge, the image of that vertex under the vertex mapping must lie on the line to which the induced edge mapping maps the edge.

(5) The elements of $\mathscr{L}'$ and $\mathscr{V}'$ are indeed arranged according the topology $\mathscr{T}$.

The reader can compare this ideal case with the practically realizable approximations of Sections 6.4 and 6.5.

Unfortunately, finite precision computations very probably do not have the power to assure the ideal result. Only an infinite precision algebraic system will always generate arrangements of lines that satisfy every theorem of Euclidean geometry. If it is not possible to model geometric lines using finite precision, we must choose a plane curve to model which has some but not all the properties that lines have. This paper focuses on a defining property of lines called *monotonicity*. The curves modeled by the hidden variable method in this section satisfy weaker properties called *xy-monotonicity* and *approximate monotonicity*.

6.3. Monotonicity

We can generalize the one-dimensional property *monotonicity* to two-dimensional curves and sequences of points.

Definition 6.1. The property v-*monotonicity*, where v is a nonzero direction vector in the plane, is defined for ordered sets of points such as curves and sequences. Let $\gamma(t)$ be a curve in the plane. The curve γ is v-*monotonic* if the inner product of v and $\gamma(t)$ is either nondecreasing or nonincreasing with t. The definition for sequences of points is analogous.

Intuitively, this definition states that v-monotonic curves and sequences tend in only one direction parallel to v and do not backtrack.

A curve or sequence can be monotonic with respect to more than one direction. For example, if a curve or sequence is monotonic with respect to the direction of the x-axis and the direction of the y-axis, then it is said to be *xy-monotonic*. It is decidable using only finite precision calculations whether a sequence is xy-monotonic because xy-monotonicity can be checked using only comparisons of x-coordinates against other x-coordinates and y-coordinates against other y-coordinates. Finite precision comparisons (in particular floating point comparisons) are always accurate.

If a curve or sequence is v-monotonic with respect to all direction vectors v, then it is simply said to be *monotonic*. Lines are the only monotonic curves, and a monotonic sequence of points is always collinear.

Finally, a curve is *approximately monotonic* if it does not backtrack more than ε with respect to any direction.

Definition 6.2. A one-dimensional function f is *approximately nondecreasing* if

$$s > t \quad \text{implies} \quad f(s) > f(t) - \varepsilon.$$

The definition of *approximately nonincreasing* is analogous. A two-dimensional curve is *approximately monotonic* if it is either approximately nonincreasing or approximately nondecreasing with respect to every direction vector.

In Fig. 13 we see an example of an approximate monotonic curve which approximates a line.

In order to implement the hidden variable method, we will proceed from the bottom up. The system design described in the next section models xy-monotonic curves, and the arrangements generated by this lower-level system satisfy only a few geometric properties. The higher-level design described in

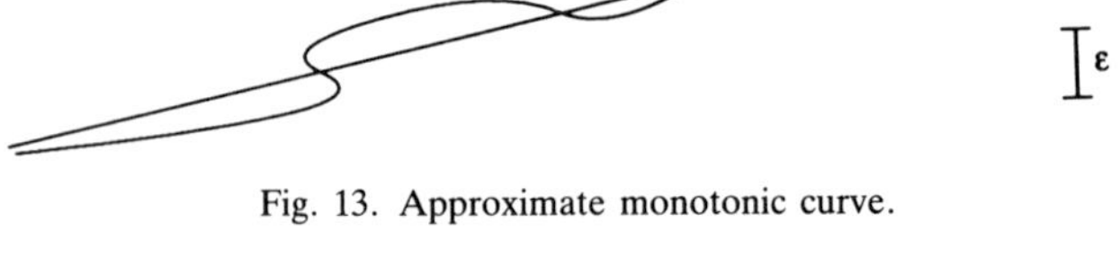

Fig. 13. Approximate monotonic curve.

the subsequent section uses the lower-level system as a subroutine. This higher-level system models approximate monotonic curves, and the arrangements it generates satisfy a larger set of properties included axioms and theorems of Euclidean geometry.

6.4. Lower level: Modeling *xy*-monotonic curves

The system described in this section treats the input lines as *xy*-monotonic curves. The *hidden variables* of the problem are the unrepresented shapes of *xy*-monotonic curves which approximate the input data lines. The system derives vertex locations and a topological structure such that the hidden curves pass through the derived vertices and are arranged according to the derived topology.

6.4.1. *Definition*: *xy-monotonic arrangement*

The following formally describes a valid arrangement of *xy*-monotonic curves. It can be compared with the ideal case in Section 6.2.

(1) As before, the edges contained by a given line form a chain from one boundary of the bounding box to the other. The vertices in each chain must form an *xy*-monotonic sequence of points.

(2) Each edge maps to an *xy*-monotonic curve which has the same endpoints as the edge.

(3) The curve belonging to an edge does not deviate by more than ε from any of the lines in the bundle of that edge, and it does not intersect any other curve except at its endpoints.

Since each line in $\mathscr{L}$ contains an unbroken chain of edges, the curves of these edges can be joined to form one long monotonic curve with the same endpoints on the boundary as the line and which stays within $\varepsilon_{\mathrm{XYM}}$ of the line. The value $\varepsilon_{\mathrm{XYM}}$ (XYM stands for "*xy*-monotonic") can be set to twelve times the maximum error in the calculated distance from a point to a line.

6.4.2. *Some terminology*

For the purposes of describing *xy*-monotonic sequences, let us define the following order relations among points in the plane. Define the relations **n, s, e,** and **w,** pronounced "is north of", "is south of", "is east of", and "is west of", respectively.

$$\langle x_1, y_1 \rangle \mathbf{n} \langle x_2, y_2 \rangle \quad \text{iff} \quad y_1 \geqslant y_2 \,,$$
$$\langle x_1, y_1 \rangle \mathbf{s} \langle x_2, y_2 \rangle \quad \text{iff} \quad y_1 \leqslant y_2 \,,$$
$$\langle x_1, y_1 \rangle \mathbf{e} \langle x_2, y_2 \rangle \quad \text{iff} \quad x_1 \geqslant x_2 \,,$$
$$\langle x_1, y_1 \rangle \mathbf{w} \langle x_2, y_2 \rangle \quad \text{iff} \quad x_1 \leqslant x_2 \,,$$

The relations **nw, ne, sw,** and **se,** pronounced "north-west", "north-east", "south-west", and "south-east", respectively, are formed by combinations of the operations above.

6.4.3. Line resolution

The algorithm for generating models of xy-monotonic curves is called *line resolution*. The following pseudocode works only for lines with positive slope— those which leave the bounding box north-east of the point at which they enter the box. Furthermore, the lines must be oriented so that points north or west of the line lie to the left of the line and points south or east of the line lie to the right of the line.

In the general case, lines can be re-oriented to conform to the orientation condition above. The code for lines with negative slopes is analogous. Not included here is the method for discovering and calculating the intersection of negative slope lines with positive slope lines. This case is very simple to model because a positive slope (x nondecreasing, y nondecreasing) xy-monotonic curve and a negative slope (x nondecreasing, y nonincreasing) xy-monotonic curve can intersect in at most a single vertical or horizontal line segment.

The state of the algorithm is stored in a data structure keyed by a vertex and a line and expressed as SIDE(V, L). For each vertex V and line L, SIDE(V, L) returns a record containing a two-bit field with possible values: *unknown*, *left*, *right*, or *on* (*left* and *right*). The function LEFT(V, L) gives access to the first bit and has value *true* if SIDE(V, L) is *left* or *on*. The function RIGHT(V, L) gives access to the second bit and has value *true* if SIDE(V, L) is *right* or *on*. Finally, the function ON(V, L) accesses the logical *and* of both bits, and it has value *true* if SIDE(V, L) is *on*.

The function EVAL(V, L) evaluates the signed distance between the vertex V and the line L using finite precision arithmetic. In the ideal case LEFT(V, L) would be synonymous with a nonnegative value for EVAL(V, L). However, in the presence of round-off error, we can only manage the following approximation conditions.

- LEFT(V, L) implies that EVAL(V, L) $> -\varepsilon_{\mathrm{XYM}}$,
- RIGHT(V, L) implies that EVAL(V, L) $< \varepsilon_{\mathrm{XYM}}$,
- ON(V, L) implies that $|\mathrm{EVAL}(V, L)| < \varepsilon_{\mathrm{XYM}}$.

To these we add the following *logical conditions*.

- P **nw** Q and LEFT(Q, L) implies that SIDE(P, L) = *left*.
- P' **se** Q' and RIGHT(Q', L) implies that SIDE(P', L) = *right*.

Figure 14 illustrates the rationale for these conditions.

The following three procedures make up the line arrangement algorithm.

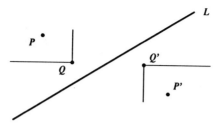

Fig. 14. Logical conditions on SIDE(P, L).

INSERT-VERTEX(vertex V)
    For each line L
        If there exists vertex V_{LEFT} such that
        (V nw V_{LEFT} and LEFT(V_{LEFT}, L))
          LEFT(V, L) ← *true*
        If there exists vertex V_{RIGHT} such that
        (V se V_{RIGHT} and RIGHT(V_{RIGHT}, L))
          RIGHT(V, L) ← *true*
        If SIDE(V, L) = *unknown*
        if EVAL(V, L) ⩾ 0
          LEFT(V, L) ← *true*
        else
          RIGHT(V, L) ← *true*

boolean FIND-INTERSECTION()
    {See Figure 15.}
    If there exists line L_1, L_2 and vertex V_1, V_2 such that
        LEFT(V_1, L_1) and RIGHT(V_2, L_1) and
        RIGHT(V_1, L_2) and LEFT(V_2, L_2)
        {Check if intersection exists already.}
        If there does not exist vertex V_I such that
        V_I ne V_1 and V_I sw V_2 and
        ON(V_I, L_1) and ON(V_I, L_2)
          vertex V_I = CALCULATE-INTERSECTION(L_1, L_2, V_1, V_2)
          ON(V_I, L_1) ← *true*
          ON(V_I, L_2) ← *true*
          INSERT-VERTEX(V_I)
          return *true*
    return *false*

RESOLVE-LINES(set-of line LINES)
    {Bounding box has four lines and four vertices.}
    CREATE-BOUNDING-BOX()
    While FIND-INTERSECTION()

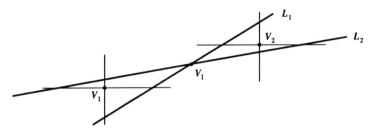

Fig. 15. Intersection condition.

6.4.4. *Discussion and proof*

The intersection condition in FIND-INTERSECTION is illustrated in Fig. 15. Lines L_1 and L_2 must intersect within the rectangle with diagonal points V_1 and V_2. What is more important is that even if L_1 and L_2 were replaced by xy-monotonic curves, the curves would still have to intersect within the rectangle. Incidentally, V_1 or V_2 can lie on one of the lines, but if either vector lies on both lines then it could act as V_I.

We have not seen yet how to implement CALCULATE-INTERSECTION using finite precision arithmetic. In most cases, the straightforward method of solving simultaneous line equations results in valid intersection. In the rare case that this calculated intersection point *IC* lies outside the rectangle, a small vertical (or horizontal) shift will take it to a point *IR* on the boundary of the rectangle, as depicted in Fig. 16. The actual details of this algorithm are somewhat tedious, but in all cases a point *IR* can be found that lies within the rectangle and satisfies,

$$|\text{EVAL}(IR, L_1)|, |\text{EVAL}(IR, L_2)| < \varepsilon_{\text{XYM}} .$$

Figure 17 illustrates another type of problem we may encounter. If RIGHT(V, L_1) and RIGHT(V, L_2) and *IR* se V, then we cannot set SIDE(IR, L_1) and SIDE(IR, L_2) equal to *on*. In this case we simply throw away *IR* and use V as the vertex of intersection.

As in the case of edge cracking, there is the question of whether the

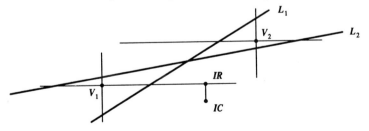

Fig. 16. Calculated intersection lies outside of rectangle.

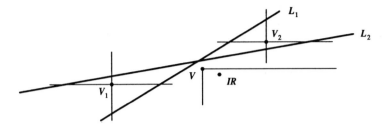

Fig. 17. Vertex *V* invalidates calculated intersection *IR*.

algorithm terminates. Each intersection adds a new vertex, but there are only a finite number of finite precision vertex locations inside the bounding box; thus the process of finding intersections must stop. Of course, one can find much better bounds.

The output of the line resolution algorithm is a set of values for SIDE(V, L) which defines a topology. To convert to the form in Section 6.4.1, we need to introduce edges and bundles. After line resolution, the set of vertices ON a given line can be ordered into a monotonic sequence. By definition, the edges in the topology join consecutive vertices in such sequences. For any given edge *AB* in the topology, the bundle for that edge is the set of lines *L* which satisfy ON(A, L) and ON(B, L).

Theorem 6.3. *After the termination of line resolution on a set of lines, the values of* SIDE(V, L) *define a topology. For this topology, there exist xy-monotonic curves which satisfy the conditions of Section* 6.4.1.

The proof of this theorem involves constructing the *xy*-monotonic curves using infinite precision calculations. The essential step of the proof shows that if two curves intersect, then the condition of function FIND-INTERSECTION can be satisfied. Since the line resolution has terminated, this condition cannot hold.

6.5. Higher level: Approximate monotonic curves

The previous section solves for the arrangement of *xy*-monotonic curves. This result is unsatisfactory for general purposes because the form of such curves varies with orientation. Horizontal or vertical *xy*-monotonic curves are much "flatter" than those with orientation angle closer to 45 degrees. The conditions of the previous section allow "lines" (chains of *xy*-monotonic curves) to intersect more than once or even have sections in common. In these ways, *xy*-monotonic curves differ considerably from the lines they are supposed to model. A second application of the hidden variable method is necessary to arrive at a model which more closely matches the ideal case in Section 6.2.

The result of this higher-level design is the same as the ideal case except that the hidden curves are approximate monotonic curves instead of lines. Thus in the definition in Section 6.2 the set $\mathcal{L}'$ of hidden lines is replaced by a set $\mathcal{A}$ of hidden approximate monotonic curves. The only additional condition is that the elements of $\mathcal{A}$ must not deviate by more than $\varepsilon_{\mathrm{AM}}$ from the lines they represent.

6.5.1. *Tiled highways*

Using the *xy*-monotonic curve modeling system, this design solves a transformed problem. It replaces each line by a pair of parallel lines, each $\varepsilon_{\mathrm{AM}}$ distant from the original. The value $\varepsilon_{\mathrm{AM}}$ is at least four times the error value $\varepsilon_{\mathrm{XYM}}$ of the lower-level system. The higher-level system then solves the $2n$-line problem using the *xy*-monotonic system with its smaller error value $\varepsilon_{\mathrm{XYM}}$. The resulting arrangement is a set of *tiled highways*, a term which is based on the observation that each line has become a strip cut up by intersecting strips. In Fig. 18 the shaded area is the *tiled highway* for line L of Fig. 11, and the polygons within the shaded area are the *tiles* of that highway.

Each tile represents a region within $\varepsilon_{\mathrm{AM}}$ of a certain subset of $\mathcal{L}$, and thus the existence of a common tile to the highways of lines $L_1, L_2, \ldots, L_k$, symbolically answers the numeric question: is there a vertex within $\varepsilon_{\mathrm{AM}}$ of these lines? The difficult numeric work has been done by the first stage.

A partial ordering can be defined among tiles on the same highway.

Definition 6.4. Let A and B be tiles on the highway of some line L. Let v be the unit vector parallel to L. If each vertex of B has a larger v-component than any vector in A, then $B > A$. Define $B \geqslant A$ as the opposite of $A > B$.

The evaluation of the condition $B > A$ involves the finite precision vector inner product. Even so, this partial order is transitive. The relation $A \leqslant B$ is not transitive, however, but it is introduced as a notational convenience.

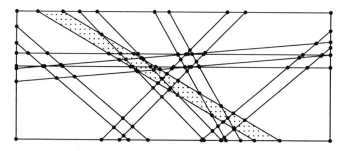

Fig. 18. Tiled highways.

6.5.2. *Paths on the tiled highways*

For each highway, we can create a path that "walks" from one end to the other. This path is purely symbolic (its vertices have no defined numerical location). We can use the following operations to create such paths:

- Split an internal edge of the highway at a new vertex.
- Add an edge joining two such vertices which are on the boundary of a common tile.

Vertices created by the crossing of paths (from different highways) can be reused. At most four edges can meet at any other type of vertex.

The paths on the highways must satisfy the following rules:

(1) A path does not leave its highway, and it crosses tile A before tile B only if $A \leqslant B$.

(2) The path does not cross any edge more than once.

(3) The path does not cross itself.

The second condition assures that there are only a finite number of such paths. Actually, a proof is required that the second condition does not eliminate any meaningful paths; in the case of line modeling it does not because pairs of lines do not cross more than once. The proof is not included here. Figure 19 shows a close-up of four paths and the intersections between them.

6.5.3. *Converting to standard form*

As one would expect, the paths correspond to approximate monotonic curves, and the points at which paths cross are the vertices in the topology. All other vertices of the tiled highway "scaffolding" (to mix a metaphor) are ignored.

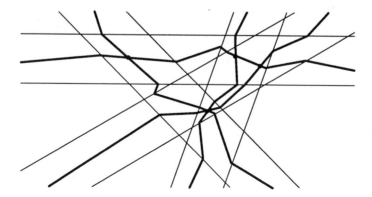

Fig. 19. Constructing paths on the tiled highways.

The finite precision location of each topological vertex is not crucial, but one can always find a point inside the appropriate tile by calculating the mean of the tile's vertex locations. The edges of the topology join consecutive vertices on the paths. One question remains: how can more than one line in $\mathscr{L}$ map to the same path? It turns out that if several lines are close, then it is possible for one path to lie within the highways of all of them. If such a path exists, it can represent all these lines.

Theorem 6.5. *For each set of paths, there exist an set of ideal vertex locations and approximate monotonic curves that satisfy the topology of the paths. For all lines represented by a path, the curve corresponding to that path does not deviate by more than ε_{AM} from any of these lines.*

This result is pretty obvious because we have constrained each path to stay within ε_{AM} of its lines and to pass through tiles in a way that does not violate the partial ordering on tiles.

6.5.4. *Satisfying other properties*

We can enumerate all sets of paths that lead to approximate monotonic curve models. All of these have planar topology, but among these we can choose those which satisfy the condition, two paths cross at once, which is analogous to the axiom of geometry that two lines intersect in at most one point. We can choose to satisfy other results such as Desargue's or Pappus' theorems if we wish.

Even after satisfying various geometric properties of lines, there will still be a number of possible sets of paths to choose from. Among these we can choose the one which minimizes the size of $\mathscr{A}$ first and minimizes the number of vertices second. If more than one set of paths is minimal, we can estimate the "strain", maximum or total deviation from the lines in $\mathscr{L}$, and choose the set of paths that minimizes this deviation measure.

The combination of the two stages of the hidden variable method can thus generate a topological arrangement which satisfies a set of useful geometric properties and minimizes the topological complexity in doing so.

7. Conclusion

The methods of data normalization and the hidden variable method both allow correct finite precision implementations which satisfy a set of useful properties. In Section 5 we saw how a polygonal region could be maintained in a normalized state, with edges and vertices separated by a lower bound distance ε, so that numerical tests would yield correct topological results. The modeling system described in that section generates only valid planar polygonal regions as the result of operations such as union and rotation or translation in the plane. Unfortunately, the normalization step may displace an edge many times the distance ε, and thus normalization can introduce a large deviation from the true infinite precision result.

The hidden variable method described in Section 6 models approximations to geometric lines. These approximations deviate at most ε from the lines they represent. It is a small step, involving only symbolic calculations, from an algorithm for calculating arrangements of lines to a polygonal region modeling system. Such a modeling system would only introduce a small error dependent on the number of lines, not the number of operations. In addition, it would maintain useful properties such as the collinearity of widely separated vertices.

Normalization has the advantage that it is simpler, but it has the potential to introduce more error and it does not retain as many properties of the ideal implementation. The hidden variable method allows more properties to be retained, and it is theoretically interesting in the manner in which it reasons about unspecifiable values. The system in Section 5 is suitable for modeling the growing and shrinking of regions which represent components in the fabrication of VLSI devices. For line-oriented problems, such as the design of buildings and bridges, the methods of Section 6 are more suitable. The normalization method is also very difficult to generalize to more complex domains such as objects with curves or curved surfaces. In the future, I will apply the hidden variable method to the problem of modeling these more complex objects, in particular, planar objects bounded by conic sections and solid objects bounded by quadric surfaces.

ACKNOWLEDGMENT

The research described here was done at AT&T Bell Laboratories, IBM Thomas J. Watson Research Center, and Carnegie-Mellon University. The portion done at CMU was funded by an IBM Manufacturing Research Fellowship. The views and conclusions in this document are those of the author.

I would like to thank Takeo Kanade and Daniel Sleator of Carnegie-Mellon, Michael Wesley of IBM Watson Research Center, and Doug McIlroy of AT&T Bell Laboratories, for their guidance on my research in the area of finite precision geometric reasoning. I am grateful to Takeo Kanade and Mark Stehlik of Carnegie-Mellon for proofreading this paper, and I thank them for their advice on style and presentation.

REFERENCES

1. Edelsbrunner, H. and Guibas, L.J., Topologically sweeping an arrangement, Stanford University Tech. Rept., Stanford, CA 1985).
2. Edelsbrunner, H., O'Rourke, J. and Seidel, R., Constructing arrangements of lines and hyperplanes with applications, in: *Proceedings* 24th Symposium on Foundations of Computer Science (1983) 83–91.
3. Guibas, L.J. and Stolfi, J., Primitives for the manipulation of general subdivisions and the computations of Voronoi diagrams, *ACM Trans. Graph.* **4** (1985) 74–123.
4. Wesley, M. and Koppelman, G., A robot planning system applied to VLSI manufacturing processes, Research Rept. 10510, IBM Thomas J. Watson Research Center, Yorktown Heights, NY (1984).

Received October 1986; revised version received December 1987

Geometric Relationships between Toleranced Features

Alan Fleming*

*Department of Artificial Intelligence, University of
Edinburgh, Edinburgh, Scotland, EH1 2QL,
United Kingdom*

ABSTRACT

*The design for a mechanical part often includes tolerance information. Tolerances can be defined
with tolerance zones and datums. A tolerance zone is a region of space in which a portion of the
surface of a real part must lie. A datum is a point, an infinite line or an infinite plane. This paper
shows how a toleranced part can be represented as a network of tolerance zones and datums
connected by arcs to which inequality constraints are attached. The network can be extended to deal
with assemblies of parts. The work can be applied in computer-aided design where a tolerance
specification needs to be checked.*

1. Introduction

In the design specifications of mechanical parts tolerance information is often
provided. The ultimate goal of providing tolerance information is to show what
variations in the shape of a part are acceptable. Tolerances are chosen so that
it is possible to manufacture the part and so that it can be guaranteed that the
part will function correctly despite its possible variation in shape. It is useful to
analyze a tolerance specification to check that these requirements are met. This
paper describes a representation of parts with geometric tolerances. It shows
how contacts between toleranced parts can be modeled so that assemblies of
toleranced parts can be analyzed. Thus the work has applications in computer-
aided design. The work is described in greater detail in [3].

The standards used by engineers to specify tolerances are contained in [5].
An engineering drawing contains dimensions to indicate the sizes of features,
distances between features and angles between features. Any dimension may
be given a tolerance to indicate an upper and a lower bound for the dimension.

A problem is that dimensions are not always definable on a real part. This is

*Present address: Diagnostic Sonar, Kirkton Campus, Livingston, Scotland, EH54 7BX, United
Kingdom.
This work was funded by a Science and Engineering Research Council Studentship.

because the surface of a manufactured part is not perfectly formed. For example, it is impossible to define a unique distance between two imperfect surfaces.

However, techniques called *geometric tolerancing* enable imperfect form to be taken into account. Use is made of *tolerance zones* which are regions in which a feature of the real part must lie.

During the machining process, a feature may be cut or drilled while the part is being supported by some other feature. Different supports may be used for different cutting operations. Therefore, a feature ends up being positioned with a known accuracy relative to the supporting feature but the accuracy of its position relative to some other feature may not be known directly. These unknown relationships may be important for the satisfactory working of the part and so it is useful to be able to verify that they are within certain bounds.

The work presented in this paper is based upon formalisations of tolerancing techniques made by Requicha [4]. Therefore a brief summary of his paper is made here.

A *datum* is defined as an infinite plane, an infinite straight line or a point embedded in a part. Any nominally symmetric feature of a planar feature can define a datum.

A real imperfect feature has no plane, line or point of symmetry. Despite this, Requicha suggests a technique by which a datum can be located on a real feature but the details are omitted here.

Sometimes systems of datums are ordered. In Fig. 2 datum A is primary and datum B is secondary. This is indicated by quoting A before B in separate partitions of the tolerance specification box. A is positioned as closely as possible to its associated feature and B is positioned as closely as possible to its feature but with the additional constraint that it is correctly positioned relative to A. In this example the datums are constrained to be at right angles to one another.

There are various types of tolerance but for simplicity this paper deals only with tolerances of position, size and form. A tolerance zone for a cylindrical feature is an infinitely long cylindrical shell as shown in Fig. 1. It has three characters, position, size and thickness, which are specified or unspecified depending on the type of tolerance. In the case of a cylindrical zone its "size" is its diameter. The properties of zones of different tolerance types are as follows:

A *form* tolerance zone has fixed thickness but variable size and position.

A *size* tolerance zone has fixed thickness and size but variable position.

A *position* tolerance zone has fixed size and thickness and fixed position relative to a specified system of datums.

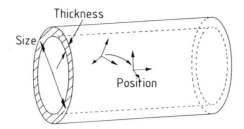

Fig. 1. The three important characters of a tolerance zone: position, size and thickness.

A complication with tolerance specifications is that networks of zones and datums arise. Features can define datums which in turn define the position of other features and so on. A network can be formed with arcs representing relationships and nodes representing features and datums. This paper shows how the network can be represented and analyzed.

2. Types of Relationships

The part shown in Fig. 2 will be explained. It is a plate with two groups of four holes. A dial is to be attached to each group of holes and so the holes within each group must be positioned accurately relative to one another if they are to meet up with holes in the dials. However the relative position of the two dials is not critical and so the relative position of the two hole groups need not be defined so accurately.

There are three small holes round each large hole and a position tolerance of 0.01 is applied to each. The datums used are *C* or *D*, as appropriate, and datum *A*. The holes have a fixed distance from either *C* or *D* and lie at an

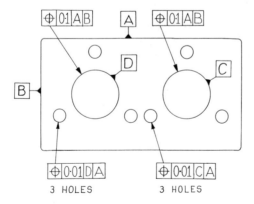

Fig. 2. Datums are shown by letters in square boxes joined to the associated feature. Features have their position tolerance indicated in a box with the symbol ⊕. Adjoining boxes indicate the datums relative to which the tolerance is measured.

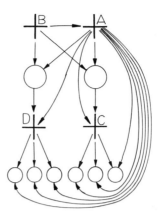

Fig. 3. The network of zones and datums for the part shown in Fig. 2.

angle relative to C or D which is correct relative to datum A. Hence, there is a relationship between the position tolerance zone of each hole and each of the relevant datums.

Figure 3 shows the complete network of zones and datums. Circles represent zones and crosses represent datums. Arcs represent constraints on the relative positions of the items they connect.

There are four ways that relationships occur between zones and datums and these will be discussed in turn. In each case the relationship is a geometric constraint which is converted to an algebraic constraint in terms of variables representing the position components of one zone or datum relative to the other.

2.1. Relationships from datums to zones

A relationship occurs between a zone of position tolerance and the datums relative to which it is correctly positioned. In the example the position tolerance zones of the large holes are defined by datums A and B. Therefore, there are relationships between these zones and each of A and B.

Algebraic constraints are obtained in the form of equalities which partially constrain the position variables of the zone and the datum. The relative position of the zone and datum is not fully constrained because there are redundant degrees of freedom.

2.2. Relationships between datums

In the example datums A and B were constrained to being at right angles to one another. A relationship between them represents this constraint.

As with the previous relationship type equalities are obtained which partly constrain the position variables.

2.3. Relationships between zones

The example in Figs. 2 and 3 includes only position tolerances and each feature has only one tolerance zone. When features have more than one tolerance zone there are relationships between the zones.

The definition of size and form tolerances leaves the positions of their zones completely undefined. However, there is a simple geometric consideration which does put constraints on their positions. This constraint is that there must be room in the intersection of the zones for a real feature. Figure 4 shows examples of zones at extremes of relative inclination and translation with a real feature contained in their intersection.

An assumption is made here that the extent of a real feature is the same as the extent of the corresponding nominal feature. This is a good approximation since tolerances will usually be much smaller than the sizes or extents of the features themselves. Since the extent of a real feature depends on the tolerances applied to other features this assumption allows tolerances on different features to be considered independently of one another.

Algebraic constraints can be associated with relationships between zones by simple consideration of the geometry. The constraints take the form of inequalities.

In a similar way constraints can be found on the *size* of zones of form tolerance. Again these are unconstrained by the formalism but are constrained by the condition that the intersection of zones must be large enough for a real feature.

If a feature has three or more tolerances (Requicha defined position, size, form and other types of tolerance) then each zone makes a relationship with each of the others.

2.4. Relationships from zones to datums

Every datum is defined by a plane feature of a symmetric feature. As a result the position of a datum is constrained relative to the tolerance zones of this feature. The datum will lie within a certain range of the center line or plane of

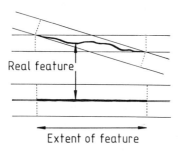

Real feature

Extent of feature

Fig. 4. The most extreme inclination of a datum relative to a tolerance zone where the real feature occupies the "significant portion" of the zone.

Significant portion
of zone

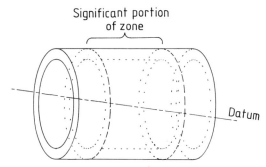

Fig. 5. Extreme relative inclination and extreme translational displacement of two tolerance zones associated with the same feature.

the zone. In the example, line datums C and D are defined by the large holes and so make relationships with their tolerance zones.

Figure 5 shows a real feature, which is nominally cylindrical, lying inside a tolerance zone. The datum corresponding to the center line of the cylinder is shown. It is shown at its maximum inclination relative to the tolerance zone. Part of the zone has been indicated as its "significant portion". This is the part of the zone which is actually occupied by the real feature: although the zone has infinite length only a finite portion of it is actually "occupied" by the real feature.

Simple consideration of the geometry allows constraints to be found that express the possible positions of the datum relative to the zone. The maximum inclination of the datum is determined by the thickness of the zone and the length of the significant portion of the zone. The constraints can be expressed as inequalities involving position variables of the zone and datum.

Different shapes of features constrain their datums in different ways. If the number of different shapes is restricted then a catalogue can be produced of the different forms of constraints that might arise.

The relationship a secondary datum makes with a zone of its associated feature is slightly different. A secondary datum has some of its degrees of freedom fixed by its relationship with a primary datum. Therefore, these degrees of freedom are unaffected by the datum's relationship with its associated feature. Other degrees of freedom are constrained in the same way that they would be if the datum was primary.

3. Analysis of the Network of Relationships

Once equalities or inequalities have been associated with each relationship then the network can be analysed to find the total effect of the constraints. A general method for dealing with the constraints in such a network is described in [2].

The method proceeds by finding all paths between two specified nodes and evaluating the constraints on the two nodes implied by each path. Then the constraints from all paths are combined. The result is a set of constraints describing the total effect of all relationships on the two nodes.

Questions can be answered about the part by analysis of the constraints using the SUP-INF algorithm described in Brooks [1]. For example, we might like to know the minimum separation distance of the closest pair of small holes in Fig. 2. First, the total constraints between the nodes representing zones containing the holes are found. Then, the minimum value of an appropriate variable taken over the constraints is determined

4. Constraints from Contacts

The concept of relationships between tolerance zones and datums can be extended to deal with assemblies of multiple parts. A pair of features which may come into contact are said to have a *potential contact* between them.

Each potential contact converts to a constraint on the relative position of the zones which contain the real features. An assembly is assumed to have been put together from randomly selected parts so that the shapes of the parts are completely independent. Each assembly which is put together from randomly selected parts will be referred to as an *instance of the assembly*.

There are two types of variation in an assembly of toleranced parts. Firstly, there is variation in position of the parts caused by slop and, secondly, there is variation in the shape of parts. The first type of variation occurs within a single production instance of the assembly whereas the second occurs between different instances.

Given an instance of the assembly, each part has a set of possible positions. In a different instance of the assembly the same part will have a different set of possible positions. Hence a set of sets of positions can be associated with each part.

There are two types of variable to represent the two types of variation:

- *Rigid* variables represent variations *between* different instances of the assembly. They include variables defining the relative positions of zones and datums in a single part and variables defining the sizes of zones.
- *Sloppy* variables represent variations in positions of parts in the assembly.

When two real features are in contact the points at which contact takes place is determined by the positions of the features. This is shown in Fig. 6. In two dimensions, with x and y representing the directions indicated in the diagram and θ representing rotation, there is some function, c, such that:

$$x = c(y, \theta) .$$

The potential contact, may be written:

$$x \geq c(y, \theta) , \tag{1}$$

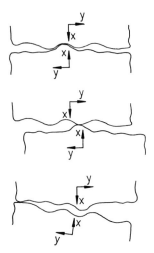

Fig. 6. Two real features in contact—each contained in a tolerance zone. The points of contact
depend on the relative position of the two features.

since x increases as the features are separated. Different shapes of the real
feature give rise to different functions, c. For any pair of features whose shape
is constrained by a tolerance specification there is a set of possible functions c
and certain constraints can be found on this set. The term "c-function" will be
used to mean this category of functions.

Suppose there are two real features contained in tolerance zones and that the
features are in contact. Although a tolerance zone may have infinite extent,
only a finite portion is actually "occupied" because the real feature has only
finite extent. The following can be said about the distribution of air and
material relative to this "significant portion" of the zone:

– Material lies on one side of the zone portion.
– Air lies on the other side of the zone portion.
– The inside of the zone portion is a mixture of air and material.

At contact there are two conditions holding:

– The insides of the zone portions intersect.
– The material sides of the zone portions do not intersect.

These two conditions put lower and upper bounds, respectively, on some
function of the position variables. Denote this function by t so that, at contact
of the real features:

$$L \leq t(x, y, \theta) \leq M ,$$

for some numbers L and M. At contact, x can be replaced by $c(y, \theta)$ so that:

$$L \leq t(c(y, \theta), y, \theta) \leq M . \tag{2}$$

It can be arranged that t increases with x. Then, the following condition is equivalent to (1):

$$t(x, y, \theta) \geq t(c, (y, \theta), y, \theta) . \tag{3}$$

The right-hand side of this inequality is the same as the middle term of (2) and since the latter is bounded above and below by values which are independent of position variables it turns out that the details of this expression can be ignored.

Therefore, taking (2) and (3) together, the complete set of constraints between two zones containing features potentially in contact can be written:

$$t(x, y, \theta) \geq t(c( )) , \tag{4}$$

$$L \leq t(c( )) \leq M ,$$

where the notation $t(c( ))$ reminds us that functions are involved but avoids writing the arguments which are unimportant.

There may be more than one tolerance zone associated with each of the features in contact. If each feature has two zones (of size and position tolerance for example) then there are four possible relationships between the zones of the two features. All four relationships give rise to inequalities of the form (4) above. Each involves a different c-function. But since these c-functions derive from contact between the same real surfaces it follows that they are dependent on one another in some way. It is possible to express this dependence as an equality involving the c-functions.

5. Obtaining Results

The total constraints on any two nodes on the network can be found in the same way as in a network representing a single part. Care has to be taken, however, to distinguish between rigid and sloppy variables. Initially the network is analysed treating rigid variables as though they were constants. The result is a set of inequalities involving only rigid variables. Results can be obtained from these with Brooks' SUP-INF algorithm [1]. Questions that can be asked about the assembly include the following:

– What is the maximum slop?
– Will the parts ever fail to fit together?
– What is the maximum displacement attainable by a part?

6. Conclusion

This paper has briefly discussed a representation of parts which include geometric tolerances. The different types of relationships between tolerance zones and datums were discussed and it was shown how a network of zones and datums is formed. Constraints between contacting parts were expressed as relationships between zones so that they too can be incorporated into the network allowing questions to be answered about assemblies of toleranced parts.

REFERENCES

1. Brooks, R.A., Symbolic reasoning among 3-D models and 2-D images, AIM-343, Department of Computer Science, Stanford University, Stanford, CA (1981).
2. Fleming, A.D., Uncertainties in a structure of parts, AISB85, Warwick, England (1985).
3. Fleming, A.D., Analysis of geometric tolerances and uncertainties in assemblies of parts, Ph.D. Thesis, Department of Artificial Intelligence, University of Edinburgh, Edinburgh, Scotland (1987).
4. Requicha, A.A.G., Toward a theory of geometrical tolerancing, Tech. Memo No. 40, Production Automation Project, University of Rochester, Rochester, NY (1983).
5. British Standards, BS:308, Part 2, Dimensioning and tolerancing of size; and Part 3, Geometric tolerancing.

Received November 1986; revised version received February 1988

Applications of Gröbner Bases in Non-Linear Computational Geometry

Bruno Buchberger[1]

RISC-LINZ, (Research Institute for Symbolic Computation)
Johannes Kepler University, A4040 Linz, Austria

ABSTRACT

Gröbner bases are certain finite sets of multivariate polynomials. Many problems in polynomial ideal theory (algebraic geometry, non-linear computational geometry) can be solved by easy algorithms after transforming the polynomial sets involved in the specification of the problems into Gröbner basis form. In this paper we give some examples of applying the Gröbner bases method to problems in non-linear computational geometry (inverse kinematics in robot programming, collision detection for superellipsoids, implicitization of parametric representations of curves and surfaces, inversion problem for parametric representations, automated geometrical theorem proving, primary decomposition of implicitly defined geometrical objects). The paper starts with a brief summary of the Gröbner bases method.

1. Introduction

Traditionally, computational geometry deals with geometrical and *combinatorial* problems on *linear objects* and simple non-linear objects, see for example [21]. These methods are not appropriate for recent advanced problems arising in geometrical modeling, computer-aided design, and robot programming, which are more *algebraic* in nature and involve *non-linear geometrical objects*. Real and complex algebraic geometry is the natural framework for most of these non-linear problems. Unfortunately, in the past decades, algebraic geometry was very little

---

[1] This research is supported by a grant from VOEST-ALPINE, Linz, (Dipl. Ing. H. Exner), and a grant from SIEMENS, München, (Dr. H. Schwärtzel)

concerned with the algorithmic solution of problems. Rather, *non-constructive* proofs of certain geometrical phenomena and mere existence proofs for certain geometrical objects was, and still is, the main emphasis.

The method of Gröbner bases is an *algorithmic* method that can be used to attack a wide range of problems in commutative algebra (polynomial ideal theory) and (complex) algebraic geometry. It is based on the concept of Gröbner bases and on an algorithm for constructing Gröbner bases introduced in [3,4]. In recent years the method has been refined and analyzed and more applications have been studied. [6] is a tutorial and survey on the Gröbner bases method.

The present paper starts with a brief summary of the *basic concepts and results of Gröbner bases theory* (Section 2). If the reader accepts these basic concepts and results as black boxes, the main part of the paper is self-contained. The internal details of the black boxes together with extensive references to the literature are given in the tutorial [6].

The main part of the paper explains various applications of the Gröbner bases method for problems in non-linear computational geometry as motivated by advanced *applications* in computer-aided design, geometrical modeling and robot programming. The sequence for the presentation of these applications is quite random. Each of them relies on one or several of the basic properties of Gröbner bases summarized in Section 2.

2. Summary of the Gröbner Bases Method

The reader who is interested only in the applications may skip this section and come back in case he needs a specific notation, concept or theorem.

2.1. General notation

N	set of natural numbers including zero
Q	set of rational numbers
R	set of real numbers
C	set of complex numbers
K	typed variable for arbitrary fields
$\overline{K}$	algebraic closure of K
i, j, k, l, m, n	typed variables for natural numbers
$K[x_1, \ldots, x_n]$	ring of n-variate polynomials over the coefficient field K
$K(x_1, \ldots, x_n)$	field of n-variate rational rational expressions over the coefficient field K
a, b, c, d	typed variables for elements in coefficient fields
f, g, h, p, q	typed variables for polynomials

s, t, u	typed variables for power products,
	i. e. polynomials of the form $x_1^{i_1} \ldots x_n^{i_n}$
$\mathrm{C}(f, u)$	the coefficient at power product u in polynomial f
F, G	typed variables for finite sets of polynomials
H	typed variable for finite sequences of polynomials
$\mathrm{Ideal}(F)$	the ideal generated by F,
	i. e. the set $\{\sum_i h_i . f_i \mid h_i \in K[x_1, \ldots, x_n], f_i \in F\}$
$\mathrm{Radical}(F)$	the radical of the ideal generated by F,
	i. e. $\{f \mid f \text{ vanishes on all common zeros of } F\}$
	or, equivalently, $\{f \mid f^k \in \mathrm{Ideal}(F) \text{ for some } k\}$
$f \equiv_F g$	f is congruent to g modulo $\mathrm{Ideal}(F)$
$K[x_1, \ldots, x_n]/\mathrm{Ideal}(F)$	the residue class ring modulo $\mathrm{Ideal}(\mathrm{F})$
$[f]_F$	the residue class of f modulo $\mathrm{Ideal}(F)$

In the definition of $\mathrm{Ideal}(F)$, it is sometimes necessary to explicitly indicate the polynomial ring from which the h_i are taken. If the polynomial ring is not clear from the context, we will use an index:

$$\mathrm{Ideal}_{K[x_1, \ldots, x_n]}(F)$$

In the definition of $\mathrm{Radical}(F)$, by a common zero of the polynomials in F we mean a common zero in the algebraic closure of the coefficient field.

2.2. Polynomial Reduction

The basic notion of Gröbner bases theory is *polynomial reduction*. The notion of polynomial reduction depends on a linear ordering on the set of power products that can be extended to a partial ordering on the set of polynomials. The set of *"admissible orderings"* that can be used for this purpose can be characterized by two easy axioms. The *lexical ordering* and the *total degree ordering* are the two admissible orderings used most often in examples. These two orderings are completely specified by fixing a linear ordering on the set of indeterminates $x_1, \ldots, x_n$ in the polynomial ring. Roughly, f reduces to g modulo F iff g results from f by subtracting a suitable multiple $a.u.h$ of a polynomial $h \in F$ such that g is lower in the admissible ordering than f. Reduction may be conceived as a generalization of the subtraction step that appears in univariate polynomial division. For all details, see [6]. We use the following notation:

$\succ$	typed variable for admissible orderings
$\mathrm{LP}(f)$	leading power product of f (w. r. t. $\succ$)
$\mathrm{LC}(f)$	leading coefficient of f (w. r. t. $\succ$)
$\mathrm{MLP}(F)$	the set of "multiples of leading powerproducts in

$f \to_F g$ F", i. e. $\{u \mid (\exists f \in F)(u$ is a multiple of $LP(f))\}$

$\to_F^*$ f reduces to g modulo F

$\leftrightarrow_F^*$ reflexive-transitive closure of $\to_F$

$\underline{f}_F$ reflexive-symmetric-transitive closure of $\to_F$

             f is in normal form modulo F, i. e.

             there does not exist any g such that $f \to_F g$

A binary relation $\to$ on a set M is called "*noetherian*" iff there does not exist any infinite sequence $x_1 \to x_2 \to x_3 \to \ldots$ of elements x_i in M.

Lemma 2.2.1 (Basic Properties of Reduction)

(Noetherianity)
    For all F: $\to_F$ is noetherian.
(Reduction Closure = Congruence)
    For all F: $\equiv_F = \leftrightarrow_F^*$.
(Normal Form Algorithm)
    There exists an algorithm NF ("Normal Form") such that for all F, g:
    (NF1) $g \to_F^* NF(F, g)$,
    (NF2) $\underline{NF(F, g)}_F$.
(Cofactor Algorithm)
    There exists an algorithm COF ("cofactors") such that for all F, g:
    $COF(F, g)$ is a sequence H of polynomials indexed by F satisfying
    $g = NF(F, g) + \sum_{f \in F} H_f . f$.

Note that, for fixed F, f, there may exist many different g such that $f \to_F^* g$ and $\underline{g}_F$ i. e. , in general, "normal forms for polynomials f are not unique modulo F". A normal form algorithm NF, by successive reduction steps, singles out one of these g for each F and f.

COF proceeds by "collecting" the multiples $a.u.h$ of polynomials $h \in F$ that are subtracted in the reduction steps when applying the normal form algorithm NF to g. Actually, COF can be required to satisfy additional properties, for examples, certain restrictions on the leading power products of the polynomials $H_f . f$.

2.3. Gröbner Bases and the Main Theorem

Definition 2.3.1. [3,4]

F is a Gröbner basis (w. r. t. $\succ$) iff
    "normal forms modulo F are unique", i.e.
    for all f, g_1, g_2:
    if $f \to_F^* g_1, f \to_F^* g_2, \underline{g_1}_F, \underline{g_2}_F$, then $g_1 = g_2$.

Note that $\to_F$ depends on the underlying admissible ordering $\succ$ on the power products. Therefore, also the definition of Gröbner basis depends on the underlying $\succ$. Whenever $\succ$ is clear from the context, we will not explicitly mention $\succ$. Gröbner bases whose polynomials are monic (i. e. have leading coefficient 1) and are in normalform modulo the remaining polynomials in the basis are called "*reduced Gröbner bases*". As we will see, Gröbner bases have a number of useful properties that establish easy algorithms for important problems in polynomial ideal theory. Therefore the main question is how Gröbner bases can be algorithmically constructed. The algorithm needs the concept of "*S-polynomials*". The S- polynomial of two polynomials f and g is the difference of certain multiples $u.f$ and $v.g$. For details see [6]. We use the notation

$$\mathrm{SP}(f,g) \qquad\qquad \text{the S-polynomial of } f \text{ and } g.$$

Theorem 2.3.1. Main Theorem [3,4]

(Algorithmic Characterization of Gröbner Bases)
   F is a Gröbner basis iff
      for all $f,g \in F : \mathrm{NF}(F, \mathrm{SP}(f,g)) = 0.$
(Algorithmic Construction of Gröbner Bases)
   There exists an algorithm GB *such that for all F*
      (GB1) $\mathrm{Ideal}(F) = \mathrm{Ideal}(\mathrm{GB}(F))$
      (GB2) $\mathrm{GB}(F)$ *is a (reduced) Gröbner basis.*

The proof of the (Algorithmic Characterization) is completely combinatorial and quite involved. The whole power of the Gröbner bases method is contained in this proof. The algorithm GB is based on the (Algorithmic Characterization), i. e. it involves successive computation of normal forms of S-polynomials. This algorithm is structurally simple. However, it is complex in terms of time and space consumed. In some sense, this is necessarily so because the problems that can be solved by the Gröbner bases method are intrinsically complex as has been shown by various authors. Still, the algorithm allows to tackle interesting and non-trivial practical problems for which no feasible solutions were known by other methods. Also, various theoretical and practical improvements of the algorithm have enhanced the scope of applicability.

2.4. The Gröbner Bases Algorithm in Software Systems

The Gröbner bases algorithm GB is available in almost all major computer algebra systems, notably in the SAC-2, SCRATCHPAD II, REDUCE, MAPLE,

MACSYMA and muMATH systems. The introduction of [5] contains the addresses of institutions from which these systems can be obtained. In these systems at least the algorithms SP, NF, (COF,) and GB are accessible to the user. In most systems, also a number of other auxiliary routines and variants of these basic algorithms are available and the user can experiment with different coefficient domains, admissible orderings and strategies for tuning the algorithms.

The implementations vary drastically in their efficiency mostly because of the varying amount of theory that has been taken into account. Also, computation time and space depends drastically on the admissible orderings used, on permutations of variables, on treating indeterminates as ring or field variables, on strategies for selecting pairs in the consideration of S-polynomials and on many other factors. Thus if one seriously considers solving problems of the type described in this paper one should try different systems and various orderings, strategies etc.

The rest of the paper is written with the goal in mind that the reader should be able to apply the methods as soon as he has access to an implementation of the basic algorithms NF, COF, SP, and GB viewed as "black boxes".

2.5. Properties of Gröbner bases

In the following theorem we summarize the most important properties of Gröbner bases on which the algorithmic solution of many fundamental problems in polynomial ideal theory (algebraic geometry, non-linear computational geometry) can be based. Actually, not all of these properties are used in the later sections of the paper. However, since the results on Gröbner bases are quite scattered in the literature, the summary may help the reader who perhaps wants to try the Gröbner bases method on new problems. Many of the properties listed in the theorem were already proven in [3,4]. Actually the problems that can be solved with the (Residue Class Ring) properties were the starting point for Gröbner bases theory in [3]. The property (Elimination Ideals) is due to [25]. The property (Inverse Mappings) is a recent contribution by [26] that solves a decision problem that has been open since 1939. (Algebraic Relations) and (Syzygies) seem to have been known already to [23]. However, it is hard to trace were the proofs appeared for the first time. More references are given in [6]. Most of the proofs of the properties below are immediate consequences of the definition of Gröbner bases, the property (Reduction Closure = Congruence), and some well known algebraic lemmas in polynomial ideal theory. The proofs of the properties (Syzygies) and (Inverse Mappings) are more involved. The existence of the algorithm GB based on the above Main Theorem is the crux for the algorithmic character of the properties.

In the following, let $K[x_1, \ldots, x_n]$ be arbitrary but fixed. F and G are used as typed variables for finite subsets of $K[x_1, \ldots, x_n]$. If not otherwise stated, $\succ$ is arbitrary. When we say "y is a new indeterminate" we mean that y is different from $x_1, \ldots, x_n$. By "F is solvable" we mean that there exists an n-tuple $(a_1, \ldots, a_n)$ of elements a_i in the algebraic closure $\overline{K}$ such that $f(a_1, \ldots, a_n) = 0$ for all $f \in F$. Similarly, the expression "F has finitely many solutions" and similar expressions always refer to solutions over the algebraic closure of K.

Theorem 2.5.1. General Properties of Gröbner Bases

(Ideal Equality, Uniqueness of Reduced Gröbner Bases)

For all F, G: $\mathrm{Ideal}(F) = \mathrm{Ideal}(G)$ *iff* $\mathrm{GB}(F) = \mathrm{GB}(G)$.

(Idempotency of GB)

For all reduced Gröbner bases G: $\mathrm{GB}(G) = G$.

(Ideal Membership)

For all F, f: $f \in \mathrm{Ideal}(F)$ *iff* $\mathrm{NF}(\mathrm{GB}(F), f) = 0$.

(Canonical Simplification)

For all F, f, g: $f \equiv_F g$ *iff* $\mathrm{NF}(\mathrm{GB}(F), f) = \mathrm{NF}(\mathrm{GB}(F), g)$.

(Radical Membership)

For all F, f:
$f \in \mathrm{Radical}(F)$ *iff* $1 \in \mathrm{GB}(F \cup \{y.f - 1\})$,
(where y is a new indeterminate).

(Computation in Residue Class Rings)

For all F:

The residue class ring $K[x_1, \ldots, x_n]/\mathrm{Ideal}(F)$ is isomorphic to the algebraic structure whose carrier set is $\{f \mid f_{\underline{F}}\}$ and whose addition and multiplication operations, $\oplus$ and $\otimes$, are defined as follows:

$f \oplus g := \mathrm{NF}(\mathrm{GB}(F), f + g),$
$f \otimes g := \mathrm{NF}(\mathrm{GB}(F), f.g).$

(Note that the carrier set is a decidable set and $\oplus$ and $\otimes$ are computable!).

(Residue Class Ring, Vector Space Basis)

For all F:

The set $\{[u]_F \mid u \notin \mathrm{MLP}(\mathrm{GB}(F))\}$ *is a linearly independent basis for* $K[x_1, \ldots, x_n]/\mathrm{Ideal}(F)$ *considered as a vector space over K.*

(Residue Class Ring, Structure Constants)

For all F, u, v:
if $u, v \notin \mathrm{MLP}(\mathrm{GB}(F))$,
then $[u]_F.[v]_F = \sum_{w \notin \mathrm{MLP}(\mathrm{GB}(F))} a_w.[w]_F$,
where, for all $w, a_w := \mathrm{C}(\mathrm{NF}(\mathrm{GB}(F), u.v), w)$.

(The $a_w \in K$, appearing in these representations of products of the basis elements as linear combinations of the basis elements are the "structure constants" of $K[x_1, \ldots, x_n]/\mathrm{Ideal}(F)$ considered as an associative algebra.)

(Leading Power Products)

For all F: $\mathrm{MLP}(\mathrm{Ideal}(F)) = \mathrm{MLP}(\mathrm{GB}(F))$.

(Principal Ideal)

For all F:
$\mathrm{Ideal}(F)$ is principal *(i. e. has a one-element ideal basis)*
iff $\mathrm{GB}(F)$ has exactly one element.

(Trivial Ideal)

For all F: $\mathrm{Ideal}(F) = K[x_1, \ldots, x_n]$ iff $\mathrm{GB}(F) = \{1\}$.

(Solvability of Polynomial Equations)

For all F: F is solvable iff $1 \notin \mathrm{GB}(F)$.

(Finite Solvability of Polynomial Equations)

For all F:
F has only finitely many solutions iff

for all $1 \leq i \leq n$ there exists an $f \in \mathrm{GB}(F)$ such that
$\mathrm{LP}(f)$ is a power of x_i.

(Number of Solutions of Polynomial Equations)

For all F with finitely many solutions:
the number of solutions of F (with multiplicities and solutions at infinity)
$=$ cardinality of $\{u \mid u \notin \mathrm{MLP}(\mathrm{GB}(F))\}$.

(Minimal Polynomial)

For all F and all finite sets U of power products:
There exists an $f \in \mathrm{Ideal}(F)$ in which only power products from U occur
iff $\{\mathrm{NF}(\mathrm{GB}(F, u)) \mid u \in U\}$ is linearly dependent over K.

(By applying this property successively to the powers $1, x_i, x_i^2, x_i^3, \ldots$ one can algorithmically find, for example, the univariate polynomial in x_i of minimal degree in $\mathrm{Ideal}(F)$ if it exists. On this algorithm a general method for solving arbitrary system of polynomial equations can be based, see [4], which works for arbitrary $\succ$ whereas the elimination method mentioned below works only for lexical orderings.)

(Syzygies)

Let F be a (reduced) Gröbner basis and define for all $f, g \in F$:

$P^{(f,g)} := \mathrm{COF}(F, \mathrm{SP}(f, g))$,
u and v such that $\mathrm{SP}(f, g) = u.f - v.g$,
$S^{(f,g)}$ is a sequence of polynomials indexed by F,
$S_f^{(f,g)} := u - P_f^{(f,g)}$,
$S_g^{(f,g)} := -v - P_g^{(f,g)}$,
$S_h^{(f,g)} := -P_h^{(f,g)}$, for all $h \in F - \{f, g\}$.

Then,

$\{S^{(f,g)} \mid f, g \in F\}$ is a set of generators for the $K[x_1, \ldots, x_n]$-module of all sequences H of polynomials (indexed by F) that are solutions ("syzygies") of the linear diophantine equation

$\sum_{h \in F} H_h.h = 0$.

(This solution method for linear diophantine equations over $K[x_1, \ldots, x_n]$ whose coefficients form a Gröbner basis F can be easily extended to the case of arbitrary F and to systems of linear diophantine equations, see [6], [28].)

Theorem 2.5.2. Properties of Gröbner Bases for Particular Orderings

(Hilbert Function)

> *Let $\succ$ be a total degree ordering.*
> *Then, for all F:*
>
> > *The value $\mathrm{H}(d, F)$ of the Hilbert function for d and F, i. e. the number of modulo $\mathrm{Ideal}(F)$ linearly independent polynomials in $K[x_1, \ldots, x_n]$ of degree $\leq d$, is equal to*
> >
> > $\binom{d+n}{n}$ *- cardinality of $\{u$ of degree $\leq d \mid u \notin \mathrm{MLP}(\mathrm{GB}(F))\}$.*

(Elimination Ideals, Solution of Polynomial Equations)

> *Let $\succ$ be the lexical ordering defined by $x_1 \prec x_2 \prec \ldots \prec x_1$.*
> *Then, for all F, $1 \leq i \leq n$:*
>
> > *The set $\mathrm{GB}(F) \cap K[x_1, \ldots, x_i])$ is a (reduced) Gröbner basis for the "i-th elimination ideal" generated by F, i. e. for $\mathrm{Ideal}_{K[x_1, \ldots, x_n]}(F) \cap K[x_1, \ldots, x_i]$.*
>
> *(This property leads immediately to a general solution method, by "successive substitution", for arbitrary systems of polynomial equations with finitely many solutions, which is formally described in (Buchberger 1985). We will demonstrate this method in the examples in the application section of this paper.)*

(Continuation of Partial Solutions)

> *Let $\succ$ be a lexical ordering.*
> *For all F:*
>
> > *If $F := \{f_1, \ldots, f_k\}$ is a Gröbner basis with respect to $\succ$, $f_1 \prec \cdots \prec f_k$, and $f_1, \ldots, f_l (1 \leq l \leq k)$ are exactly those polynomials in F that depend only on the indeterminates $x_1, \ldots, x_i$, then every common solution $(a_1, \ldots, a_i)$ of $\{f_1, \ldots, f_l\}$ can be continued to a common solution $(a_1, \ldots, a_n)$ of F. (For a correct statement of this property some terminology about solutions at infinity would be necessary.)*

(Independent Variables Modulo an Ideal)

For all F and $1 < i_1 < \ldots < i_m < n$:

The indeterminates $x_{i_1}, \ldots, x_{i_m}$ are independent modulo Ideal(F) *(i. e. there is no polynomial in Ideal(F) that depends only on $x_{i_1}, \ldots, x_{i_m}$) iff GB(F) $\cap K[x_{i_1}, \ldots, x_{i_m}] = \{0\}$, where the $\succ$ used must be a lexical ordering satisfying $x_{i_1} \prec \cdots \prec x_{i_m} \prec$ all other indeterminates. (This property yields immediately an algorithm for determining the dimension of a polynomial ideal (algebraic variety).)*

(Ideal Intersection)

Let $\succ$ be the lexical ordering defined by $x_1 \prec x_2 \prec \ldots \prec x_n \prec y$, y a new variable.
Then, for all F, G:

GB($\{y.f \mid f \in F\} \cup \{(y-1).g \mid g \in G\}) \cap K[x_1, \ldots, x_n]$
is a (reduced) Gröbner basis for Ideal(F) $\cap$ Ideal(G).

(This property yields also an algorithm for quotients of finitely generated ideals because the determination of such quotients can be reduced to the determination of intersections.)

(Algebraic Relations)

For all F:

Let $F = \{f_1, \ldots, f_m\}$, let $y_1, \ldots, y_m$ be new indeterminates and let $\succ$ be the lexical ordering defined by $y_1 \prec \ldots \prec y_m \prec x_1 \prec \ldots \prec x_n$. Then, GB($\{y_1 - f_1, \ldots, y_m - f_m\}) \cap K[y_1, \ldots, y_m]$ is a (reduced) Gröbner basis for the "ideal of algebraic relations" over F, i. e. for the set $\{g \in K[y_1, \ldots, y_m] \mid g(f_1, \ldots, f_m) = 0\}$.

(Inverse Mapping)

For all F:

Let $F = \{f_1, \ldots, f_n\}$, let $y_1, \ldots, y_n$ be new indeterminates and let $\succ$ be the lexical ordering defined by $y_1 \prec \ldots \prec y_n \prec x_1 \prec \ldots \prec x_n$. Then, the mapping from $\overline{K}^n$ into $\overline{K}^n$ defined by F is bijective iff GB($\{y_1 - f_1, \ldots, y_n - f_n\}$) has the form $\{x_1 - g_1, \ldots, x_1 - g_n\}$ for certain $g_j \in K[y_1, \ldots, y_n]$.

The properties stated in the above theorem can be read as the algorithmic solution of certain problems specified by polynomial sets F. Each of these "algorithms" requires that, for solving the problem for an arbitrary F, one first transforms F into the corresponding (reduced) Gröbner basis $GB(F)$ and then performs some algorithmic actions on $GB(F)$. For example, for the decision problem "$f \equiv_F g$?", (Canonical Simplification) requires that one first transforms F into $GB(F)$ and then checks, by applying algorithm NF, whether or not the normal forms of f and g are identical modulo $GB(F)$. Actually, most of the above properties (algorithms) are correct also if, instead of transforming F into a corresponding *reduced* Gröbner basis, one transforms F into an *arbitrary* equivalent Gröbner basis G. (We say "F is equivalent to G" iff $\text{Ideal}(F) = \text{Ideal}(G)$.) In practice, however, this makes very little difference because the computation of Gröbner bases is not significantly easier if one relaxes the requirement that the Gröbner basis must be reduced.

Alternatively, by (Idempotency of GB), the properties stated in the above theorem can also be read as properties of (reduced) Gröbner bases — and algorithms for solving problems for (reduced) Gröbner bases. For example, introducing the additional assumption that F is a (reduced) Gröbner basis, (Canonical Simplification) reads as follows:

For all (reduced) Gröbner bases F, and polynomials f, g:
$f \equiv_F g$ *iff* $\text{NF}(F, f) = \text{NF}(F, g)$.

Some of the properties stated in the above theorem are characteristic for Gröbner bases, i. e. if the property holds for a set F then F is a Gröbner basis. For example, (Leading Power Products) is a characteristic property, i. e. if $\text{MLP}(\text{Ideal}(F)) = \text{MLP}(F)$ then F is a Gröbner basis.

Let us carry through one more exercise for reading the above properties as algorithms. For deciding whether

(Question)
    for all $a_1, \ldots, a_n \in \overline{K}$,
        for which $f_1(a_1, \ldots, a_n) = \cdots = f_m(a_1, \ldots, a_n) = 0$,
        also $g(a_1, \ldots, a_n) = 0$,

i. e. for deciding whether $g \in \text{Radical}(\{f_1, \ldots, f_m\})$, because of (Radical Membership), it suffices to perform the following steps:

1. Compute the (reduced) Gröbner basis G for $\{f_1, \ldots, f_m, y \cdot g - 1\}$,
    where y is a new indeterminate.
2. The (Question) has a positive answer iff $1 \in G$.

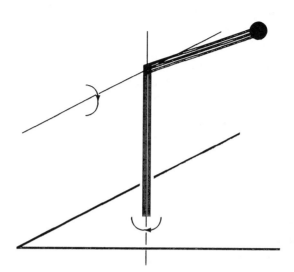

Figure 1: Robot having two "degrees of freedom"

3. Application: Inverse Robot Kinematics

The problem of inverse robot kinematics is the problem of determining, for a given robot, the distances at the prismatic joints and the angles at the revolute joints that will result in a given position and orientation of the end-effector. The mathematical description of this problem leads to a system of multivariate polynomial equations (after representing angles α by their sine and cosine and adding $\sin^2 \alpha + \cos^2 \alpha = 1$ to the set of equations), see [20].

Let us consider, for example, the following robot having two revolute joints (two "degrees of freedom").

We introduce the following variables:

l_1, l_2	lengths of the two robot arms
px, py, pz	x-, y−, and z-coordinate of the position of the end-effector
ϕ, θ, ψ	Euler angles of the orientation of the end effector
	(Euler angles are one way of describing orientation)
δ_1, δ_2	angles describing rotation at the revolute joints

We introduce the sines and cosines of the angles occurring in the above description as separate variables:

s_1, c_1	sine and cosine of δ_1

s_2, c_2	sine and cosine of δ_2
sf, cf	sine and cosine of ϕ
st, ct	sine and cosine of θ
sp, cp	sine and cosine of ψ

The interrelation of the physical entities described by the above variables is expressed in the following system of equations:

$$c_1 \cdot c_2 - cf \cdot ct \cdot cp + sf \cdot sp = 0,$$
$$s_1 \cdot c_2 - sf \cdot ct \cdot cp - cf \cdot sp = 0,$$
$$s_2 + st \cdot cp = 0,$$
$$-c_1 \cdot s_2 - cf \cdot ct \cdot sp + sf \cdot cp = 0,$$
$$-s_1 \cdot s_2 + sf \cdot ct \cdot sp - cf \cdot cp = 0,$$
$$c_2 - st \cdot sp = 0,$$
$$s_1 - cf \cdot st = 0,$$
$$-c_1 - sf \cdot st = 0,$$
$$ct = 0,$$
$$l_2 \cdot c_1 \cdot c_2 - px = 0,$$
$$l_2 \cdot s_1 \cdot c_2 - py = 0,$$
$$l_2 \cdot s_2 + l_1 - pz = 0,$$
$$c_1^2 + s_1^2 - 1 = 0,$$
$$c_2^2 + s_2^2 - 1 = 0,$$
$$cf^2 + sf^2 - 1 = 0,$$
$$ct^2 + st^2 - 1 = 0,$$
$$cp^2 + sp^2 - 1 = 0.$$

Let us call those variables that describe the geometrical realization of the robot "geometrical variables" (for example, the variables l_1, l_2). Let us also call those variables that describe position and orientation of the end-effector shortly "position variables" ($px, \ldots, sf, cf, \ldots$). The other variables ($s_1, c_1, \ldots$) are the "joint variables".

In the case of more complicated robots (with six degrees of freedom), one can specify values for the geometrical variables and the position variables and, with certain restrictions, will always be able to determine appropriate values of the joint variables that yield the given position and orientation of the end-effector. In the above example robot, with only two degrees of freedom however one can only independently choose the value of two position variables, for example px and pz. The value of all the other variables, notably of the other position variables $py, sf, cf, \ldots$, and the joint variables will then be determined by the above system of algebraic equations.

The problem can be considered in three different versions of increasing generality.

(Real Time Version)

- The value of the geometrical variables are numerically given.

- The value of those position variables that can be independently chosen (e. g. px, pz) are numerically given.

- The solution of the problem consists in determining appropriate numerical values for the (remaining position variables and) the joint variables.

(Off-Line Version, Concrete Robot)

- The value of the geometrical variables are numerically given.

- The value of those position variables that can be independently chosen are left open as *parameters*.

- By a "solution of the problem", in this version, one means symbolic expressions involving the position parameters that describe, in "closed form", the dependence of the (remaining position variables and) the joint variables from the position parameters. Of course, a "symbolic closed form solution" of this kind will not always be possible. It is possible for certain classes of robots, see [20], and it is possible in a modified sense also in the general case by using Gröbner bases.

(Off-Line Version, Robot Class)

- The value of the geometrical variables are left open as *parameters*.

- The value of those position variables that can be independently chosen are left open as *parameters*.

- By a "solution of the problem", in this version, one means symbolic expressions involving the geometrical and the position parameters that describe, in "closed form", the dependence of the (remaining position variables and) the joint variables on the geometrical *and* position parameters. A "symbolic closed form solution" in this general sense is even more difficult. Again, it is possible for certain classes of robots and, as we shall see, it is possible in a modified sense also in the general case by using Gröbner bases.

A symbolic solution of the inverse kinematics problem in the (Off-Line Version), can be contrasted to a numerical approach:

(Symbolic Approach)

- Derivation of the symbolic expressions for the solution of the problem in the (Off-Line Version).

- Numerical specification of the parameters.

- Numerical evaluation of the symbolic expressions using the numerical values of the parameters.

(Numerical Approach)

- Numerical specification of the parameters.

- Solution of the problem in the (Real-Time Version) by numerical iteration methods.

It is clear that a symbolic solution of the problem in the (Off-Line Version) can have practical advantages over the purely numerical approach (as long as the resulting symbolic expressions describing the solutions are not too complicated) because the numerical evaluation of the symbolic solution expressions in real-time situations may be faster than a direct iterative numerical solution of the (Real Time Version) of the problem. Also, of course, the symbolic solution may give "insight" into the problem that can not be gained by a numerical solution.

For the above example, we show the solution of the problem in the (Off-Line Version, Roboter Class) by using Gröbner bases. In this version, the geometrical variables l_1, l_2 and the position variables px, pz are considered as symbolic parameters.

The solution method uses property (Elimination Ideals) of Gröbner bases. This property, read as an algorithm, tells us that we first have to compute the Gröbner bases of the set F of input polynomials. Since l_1, l_2, px, pz are to be treated as symbolic parameters, we work over the field $Q(l_1, l_2, px, pz)$ as coefficient field. This is perfectly possible, because the Gröbner bases method works over arbitrary fields (whose arithmetic is algorithmic). Furthermore, we must specify an ordering on the remaining variables, for example $c_1 \prec c_2 \prec s_1 \prec s_2 \prec py \prec cf \prec ct \prec cp \prec sf \prec st \prec sp$. These variables are treated as ring variables, i.e. the Gröbner basis will be computed considering the input polynomials as polynomials in the ring $Q(l_1, l_2, px, pz)[c_1, \ldots, sp]$. The resulting Gröbner basis has the following form:

$$c_1^2 + \frac{px^2}{pz^2 - 2 \cdot l_1 \cdot pz - l_2^2 + l_1^2} = 0,$$

$$c_2 + \frac{pz^2 - 2 \cdot l_1 \cdot pz - l_2^2 + l_1^2}{l_2} \cdot px \cdot c_1 = 0,$$

$$s_1^2 - \frac{pz^2 - 2 \cdot l_1 \cdot pz + px^2 - l_2^2 + l_1^2}{pz^2 - 2 \cdot l_1 \cdot pz - l_2^2 + l_1^2} = 0,$$

$$s_2 - \frac{pz - l_1}{l_2} = 0,$$

$$py + \frac{pz^2 - 2 \cdot l_1 \cdot pz - l_2^2 + l_1^2}{px} \cdot c_1 \cdot s_1 = 0,$$

$$cf^2 - \frac{pz^2 - 2 \cdot l_1 \cdot pz + px^2 - l_2^2 + l_1^2}{pz^2 - 2 \cdot l_1 \cdot pz - l_2^2 + l_1^2} = 0,$$

$$ct = 0,$$

$$cp + \frac{pz^3 - 3 \cdot l_1 \cdot pz^2 - l_2^2 \cdot pz + 3 \cdot l_1^2 \cdot pz + l_1 \cdot l_2^2 - l_1^3}{l_2 \cdot pz^2 - 2 \cdot l_1 \cdot l_2 \cdot pz + l_2 \cdot px^2 - l_2^3 + l_1^2 \cdot l_2} \cdot s_1 \cdot cf = 0,$$

$$sf + \frac{pz^2 - 2 \cdot l_1 \cdot pz - l_2^2 + l_1^2}{pz^2 - 2 \cdot l_1 \cdot pz + px^2 - l_2^2 + l_1^2} \cdot c_1 \cdot s_1 \cdot cf = 0,$$

$$st + \frac{pz^2 - 2 \cdot l_1 \cdot pz - l_2^2 + l_1^2}{pz^2 - 2 \cdot l_1 \cdot pz + px^2 - l_2^2 + l_1^2} \cdot s_1 \cdot cf = 0,$$

$$sp + \frac{pz^4 - 4 \cdot l_1 \cdot pz^3 - 2 \cdot l_2^2 \cdot pz^2 + 6 \cdot l_1^2 \cdot pz^2 + 4 \cdot l_1 \cdot l_2^2 \cdot pz - 4 \cdot l_1^3 \cdot pz + l_2^4 - 2 \cdot l_1^2 \cdot l_2^2 + l_1^4}{l_2 \cdot px \cdot pz^2 - 2 \cdot l_1 \cdot l_2 \cdot px \cdot pz + l_2 \cdot px^3 - l_2^3 \cdot px + l_1^2 \cdot l_2 \cdot px} \cdot c_1 \cdot s_1 \cdot cf = 0.$$

The above Gröbner basis has a remarkable structure:

- The geometrical parameters l_1 and l_2 and the position parameters px and pz are still available as symbolic parameters in the polynomials of the Gröbner basis. Thus, the system is still "general". The Gröbner basis is in "closed form".

- In accordance with property (Elimination Ideals), the system is "triangularized". In this example, this means that the first polynomial of the basis depends only on c_1, the second on $c_1, c2$, the third on c_1, c_2, s_1, ... After substitution of numerical values for the parameters l_1, l_2, px, pz, we can therefore numerically determine the possible values for c_1 from the first equation then, for each of the values of c_1, determine the value of c_2 from the second equation then, for each of the values of c_1, c_2, determine the value of s_1 from the third equation etc.

- Actually, the degrees of the polynomials in this basis are quite low. This is in general not true for the first polynomial in Gröbner bases. The first polynomial, which, in case the solution set is finite, is always univariate, tends to have quite a high degree in general. The degrees of the other polynomials, however, tend to be very low (most times even linear) also in the general case because the polynomial sets describing realistic physical or geometrical situations often define prime ideals, for which linearity in the second, third ... variable can be proven theoretically. This phenomenon needs closer study, however. For numerical practice, low degrees in the second, third ... variable implies that numerical errors from the determination of the value of the first value will not drastically accumulate. In the case where the second, third ... equation is linear, the Gröbner basis has the form $\{p_1(x_1), x_2 - p_2(x_1), \ldots, x_n - p_n(x_1)\}$. In this case, the errors introduced by the numerical solution of p_1 will not accumulate at all.

- The above method of numerical backward substitution based on the Gröbner basis, by property (Elimination Ideals), is guaranteed to yield *all* (real and complex) solutions of the system.

- Again by (Elimination Ideals), *no "extraneous"* solutions of the system are produced. (Other algebraic methods, for example the resultant method, may produce extraneous solutions.)

The above Gröbner basis was produced in 62 sec on an IBM 4341 using an implementation of the Gröbner basis method by R. Gebauer and H. Kredel in the SAC-2 computer algebra system. The computation time is increasing drastically when more complicated robot types are investigated. We are far from being able to treat the most general robot of six degrees of freedom. However, so far, only very little research effort has been dedicated to this possible application of Gröbner bases. Using the special structure of the problem it may well be that more theoretical results can be derived that allow to drastically speed up the general algorithm in this particular application.

4. Application: Intersection of Superellipsoids

Superellipsoids [2] are surfaces in 3D space that have a compact implicit representation as the set of points (x, y, z) such that

$$((\frac{x}{a})^{2/\epsilon_3} + (\frac{y}{b})^{2/\epsilon_2})^{\epsilon_3/\epsilon_1} + (\frac{z}{c})^{2/\epsilon_1} - 1 = 0$$

Superellipsoids are topologically equivalent to spheres. They can be considered as ellipsoids with axes a, b, c whose curvature in the $x-, y-, z-$ directions is distorted by the influence of the exponents $\epsilon_1, \epsilon_2, \epsilon_3$. (The above equation is the implicit equation for the case where the superellipsoid is in standard position with its midpoint at the origin.) The exponents $\epsilon_1, \epsilon_2, \epsilon_3$ open an enormous flexibility for adjusting the shape of superellipsoids in order to approximate real objects. Some basic problems in geometric modeling, for example, the problem of deciding whether a point is inside or outside an object can be easily solved for superellipsoids. Recently, superellipsoids have been proposed for approximating parts of robots and obstacles in order to test for collision. The collision detection problem of robots is thereby reduced to an intersection test for superellipsoids.

Unfortunately, for general superellipsoids, no good intersection tests are known. In this section we report on first attempts to apply Gröbner bases for this question. We restrict our attention to the case of a sphere (with midpoint (A, B, C) and radius R) and a superellipsoid (in standard position) whose exponents satisfy $\epsilon_1 = \epsilon_2 = \epsilon_3 < 2$ (a convex superellipsoid). In this case, the two objects intersect iff the minimal distance between the midpoint of the sphere and the superellipsoid is less or equal to the radius of the sphere. Using Lagrange factors, this approach leads to the following system of equations for the coordinates (x, y, z) of the point on the superellipsoid having minimal distance to (A, B, C):

(Equations for Minimal Distance)

$$\left(\tfrac{x}{a}\right)^{2/\epsilon} + \left(\tfrac{y}{b}\right)^{2/\epsilon} + \left(\tfrac{z}{c}\right)^{2/\epsilon} - 1 = 0$$

$$(x - A) + \lambda . \tfrac{1}{\epsilon.a} . \left(\tfrac{x}{a}\right)^{(2/\epsilon - 1)} = 0$$

$$(y - B) + \lambda . \tfrac{1}{\epsilon.b} . \left(\tfrac{y}{b}\right)^{(2/\epsilon - 1)} = 0$$

$$(z - C) + \lambda . \tfrac{1}{\epsilon.c} . \left(\tfrac{z}{c}\right)^{(2/\epsilon - 1)} = 0$$

If ϵ is of the form $1/k$ (which is sufficiently general for practical purposes), this (System for Minimal Distance) is an algebraic system. We consider a, b, c, A, B, C as parameters, i. e. we work over $K(a, b, c, A, B, C)[x, y, z, \lambda]$. For computing the Gröbner bases, we use the lexical ordering defined by $x \prec y \prec z \prec \lambda$. For $\epsilon = 1$ (which is, actually, the ellipsoid case) we get the Gröbner basis

(Gröbner Basis for Minimal Distance)
$$x^6 - p(x) = 0$$
$$y - q(x) = 0$$
$$z - r(x) = 0$$
$$\lambda - s(x) = 0.$$

Here, $p(x), q(x), r(x), s(x)$ are univariate polynomials in x of degree 5 with coefficients that are rational expressions in the parameters a, b, c, A, B, C. The equation for λ is not interesting for the problem at hand and may be dropped. The printout of these rational expressions consumes approximately 2 pages. (Some simplification by extracting common subexpressions would be possible.) Again, the Gröbner basis has all the advantageous features described in the inverse kinematics application. Note in particular that, in this Gröbner basis, the second, third and fourth equations are linear in the variables y, z, λ, respectively. Therefore the Gröbner basis presents an explicit symbolic solution to the problem as soon as the solution value for x is numerically determined from the first equation, which is univariate in x.

If we change ϵ to $1/2$, the resulting Gröbner basis will again have the structure displayed in (Gröbner Basis for Minimal Distance). The only difference is that the degree of the univariate polynomials $p(x), q(x), r(x), s(x)$ will be 11. We conjecture that the structure of the system will stay unchanged for arbitrary ϵ of the form $1/k$.

The problem with this approach is, again, computation time. While the Gröbner basis computation for $\epsilon = 1$ needs 15 minutes (on an IBM 4341 in the SAC-2 implementation of the Gröbner bases method), the computation already needs 19 hours for $\epsilon = 1/2$. At the moment, this excludes practical applicability of the method. However, one should take into account that the source of complexity seems to be the extraneous extremal solutions that enter through the Lagrange factor method. Actually, the first equation in the Gröbner basis describes the x-coordinate of all relative extremal points on the surface and not only the x-coordinates of the minimal point. This raises the degree of the first polynomial and, hence, also of the other polynomials. More systematic study is necessary. Furthermore, it seems to be possible to guess and subsequently prove the general structure of the polynomials $p(x), q(x), r(x), s(x)$ from the Gröbner bases computations for two or three different ϵ values. This could make the Gröbner basis computation superfluous in the future. As with other symbolic computation methods, Gröbner bases computations can be applied on very different levels including the level of producing and supporting mathematical conjectures.

5. Application: Implicitization of Parametric Objects

As has been pointed out repeatedly, the automatic transition between implicit and parametric representation of curves and surfaces is of fundamental importance in geometric modeling, see for example [22]. The reason for this is that the implicit and the parametric representation are appropriate for different classes of problems. For example, for generating points along curves or surfaces, the parametric representation is most convenient whereas, for deciding whether a given point lies on a specific curve or surface, the implicit representation is most natural. It is also well known that implicitization of parametric surfaces is of importance for deriving a representation of the intersection curve of two surfaces. This problem has a satisfactory solution in case one of the surfaces is expressed parametrically and the other implicitly. In this case, the parameter representation $x(s,t), y(s,t), z(s,t)$ for the first surface can be substituted into the implicit equation $f(x, y, z)$ of the other surface. This results in the implicit representation $f(x(s,t), y(s,t), z(s,t))$ of the intersection curve in parameter space.

Actually, for some time, the problem of implicitization has been deemed unsolvable in the CAD literature. [22], however, presented a solution of the implicitization problem using resultants. The solution is spelled out for surfaces in 3D and curves in 2D. In the general case of $(n-1)$-dimensional hypersurfaces, I guess, the method could yield implicit equations that introduce non-trivial extraneous solutions, see also the remarks in [1]. In [1] it is shown how Gröbner bases can be used for the general implicitization problem of $(n-1)$-dimensional hypersurfaces. The authors sketch a correctness proof for the method that relies on (Algebraic Relations). In this section, we review their method and generalize it to the most general case of hypersurfaces of arbitrary dimension in n-dimensional space. Still, much research will be needed to assess the efficiencies of the methods and to determine their range of practical applicability. Also some theoretical details are not yet completely covered in the literature.

(General Implicitization Problem)
>   Given: $p_1, \ldots, p_m \in K[x_1, \ldots, x_n]$.
>   Find: $f_1, \ldots, f_k \in K[y_1, \ldots, y_m]$,
>   such that for all $a_1, \ldots, a_m$:
> $f_1(a_1, \ldots, a_m) = \cdots = f_k(a_1, \ldots, a_m) = 0$ iff
> $a_1 = p_1(b_1, \ldots, b_n), \ldots, a_m = p_m(b_1, \ldots, b_n)$ for some $b_1, \ldots, b_n$.

The problem requires to construct k polynomials implicitly defining hypersurfaces whose intersection is the hypersurface described by the parameter representation.

(Implicitization Algorithm)
> $\{f_1, \ldots, f_k\} := \mathrm{GB}(\{y_1 - p_1, \ldots, y_m - p_m\}) \cap K[y_1, \ldots, y_m]$,
>   where GB has to be computed using the lexical ordering determined by
> $y_1 \prec \cdots \prec y_m \prec x_1 \prec \cdots \prec x_n$.

Correctness Proof: Let $g_1 \prec \ldots \prec g_l$ be the polynomials in

$$\mathrm{GB}(\{y_1 - p_1, \ldots, y_m - p_m\}) - K[y_1, \ldots, y_m].$$

$\{y_1 - p_1, \ldots, y_m - p_m\}$ and the Gröbner basis $\{f_1, \ldots, f_k, g_1, \ldots, g_l\}$ have the same common zeros. If

$$f_1(a_1, \ldots, a_m) = \cdots = f_k(a_1, \ldots, a_m) = 0$$

then, by (Continuation of Partial Solutions), there exist $(b_1, \ldots, b_n)$ such that

$$g_1(a_1, \ldots, a_m, b_1, \ldots, b_n) = \cdots = g_l(a_1, \ldots, a_m, b_1, \ldots, b_n) = 0.$$

Hence, also

$$a_1 - p_1(b_1, \ldots, b_n) = 0, \ldots, a_1 - p_1(b_1, \ldots, b_n) = 0.$$

The converse is clear.

Example: Let us consider the 3D surface defined by the following parametric representation

(Parametric Representation)
$$x = r.t$$
$$y = r.t^2$$
$$z = r^2$$

Roughly, this surface has the shape of a ship hull whose keel is the y-axis and whose bug is the z-axis. Applying algorithm GB to $\{x - r.t, y - r.t^2, z - r^2\}$ with respect to the ordering $z \prec y \prec x \prec t \prec r$ yields the following Gröbner basis:

(Gröbner Basis)
$$x^4 - y^2.z$$
$$t.x - y$$
$$t.y.z - x^3$$
$$t^2.z - x^2$$
$$r.y - x^2$$
$$r.x - t.z$$
$$r.t - x$$
$$r^2 - z$$

The polynomial depending only on x, y, z is an implicit equation for the surface defined by (Parameter Representation).

By close inspection one will detect that, actually, the implicit equation occurring in the above (Gröbner Basis) does not strictly meet the specification of the (Implicitization Problem). The y-axis is a solution to the implicit equation whereas it does not appear in the surface defined by the (Parameter Representation). This is not a deficiency of the Gröbner basis method but has to do with the particular (Parameter Representation) which, in some sense, is not "general enough" or, stated differently, in the (Continuation of Partial Solutions) property, solutions at infinity have to be taken into account. This question deserves some further detailed study. [24] has already sketched some analysis of this phenomenon. He proposes the following parameter presentation, which includes the y-axis and whose implicit equation is again $x^4 - y^2.z$.

(Parametric Representation)
$$x = u.v$$
$$y = v^2$$
$$z = u^4$$

This example was computed in 4 sec on an IBM AT in the author's research implementation of the Gröbner basis method in the muMATH system. Other examples with more complicated coefficients and similar degree characteristics had computing times in the range of several seconds. I guess that the examples occurring in practice should be well tractible by the method.

Example: The method can also be used for rational parametric representations. We consider the example of a circle in the plane.

(Rational Parametric Representation)

$$x = \frac{1-s^2}{1+s^2}$$
$$y = \frac{2.s}{1+s^2}$$

In the case of rational parametric representations, we first clear denominators. In the example, the input to GB should therefore be $\{x + x.s^2 - 1 + s^2, y + y.s^2 - 2.s\}$. The result is, of course, $x^2 + y^2 - 1$.

6. Application: Inversion of Parametric Representations

The inversion problem for parametric representations is defined as follows:

(Inversion Problem for Parametric Representations)

Given: $p_1, \ldots, p_m \in K[x_1, \ldots, x_n]$ and
          a point $(a_1, \ldots, a_m)$ on the hypersurface
          parametrically defined by $p_1, \ldots, p_m$.

Find: $\{(b_1, \ldots, b_n) \mid a_1 = p_1(b_1, \ldots, b_n), \ldots, a_m = p_m(b_1, \ldots, b_n)\}$.

This problem is closely connected with the (Implicitization Problem). In fact, the (Inversion Problem) is just a special case of the general problem of solving systems of polynomial equations, which is completely solved by the Gröbner basis method based on the (Elimination Ideals) property or based on the (Minimal Polynomial) property. For solving the (Inversion Problem), the general Gröbner bases solution method can be applied to the system $\{y_1 - p_1(x_1, \ldots, x_n), \ldots, y_m - p_m(x_1, \ldots, x_n)\}$, i. e. we have the following algorithm.

(Inversion Algorithm for Parametric Representations)

    $G := \mathrm{GB}(\{y_1 - p_1(x_1, \ldots, x_n), \ldots, y_m - p_m(x_1, \ldots, x_n)\})$,
        where GB has to be computed using the lexical ordering determined by
        $y_1 \prec \cdots \prec y_m \prec x_1 \prec \cdots \prec x_n$.
    $\{f_1, \ldots, f_k\} := G \cap K[y_1, \ldots, y_m]$.
    (If, for some $1 \leq i \leq k$, $f_i(a_1, \ldots, a_m) \neq 0$, then "Input Error".)
    Substitute a_i for y_i in G and solve the system G, which is "triangularized".

In fact, the steps necessary in this algorithm include the steps of the (Implicitization Algorithm). Therefore, when we apply the Gröbner bases method to the (Implicitization Problem), we automatically get also a solution for the (Inversion Problem) and vice versa.

Example: We use again the example of Section 5.

(Parametric Representation)

$x = r.t$
$y = r.t^2$
$z = r^2$

Suppose we want to determine the parameter values defining the point $(2, 2, 4)$ on the surface. Application of GB yields

(Gröbner Basis)

$x^4 - y^2.z$
$t.x - y$
$t.y.z - x^3$
$t^2.z - x^2$
$r.y - x^2$
$r.x - t.z$
$rt - x$
$r^2 - z$

The first polynomial is the implicit equation, which can be used to check whether $(2, 2, 4)$ is, in fact, on the surface: $2^4 - 2^2.4 = 0$. Substituting $(2, 2, 4)$ in the second, third, and fourth polynomial of the Gröbner basis (and making all polynomials monic) yields the system

(Gröbner Basis After First Substitution)

$t - 1$
$t - 1$
$t^2 - 1$

This system of univariate polynomials, by the property (Continuation of Partial Solutions) must always have a common zero that can be determined by forming the greatest common divisor, $g := t - 1$, of the three polynomials and solving for t. This leads to $t = 1$.

Substituting $(2, 2, 4, 1)$ in the fifth, . . .,eights polynomial of the Gröbner basis (and making all polynomials monic) yields the system

$r - 2$
$r - 2$
$r - 2$
$r^2 - 4$

Again, this system of univariate polynomials, by the property (Continuation of Partial Solutions) must have a common zero that can be determined by forming the greatest common divisor, $h := r - 2$, of the four polynomials and solving for r. This leads to $r = 2$.

Actually, it has been shown recently in [12] and, independently, in [8] that the computation of greatest common divisors is not necessary in the above procedure. Rather, as can be verified in the above example, for each of the univariate systems the first non-zero polynomial will always be the greatest common divisor of the system. This is a drastic simplification of the general procedure for solving arbitrary systems of polynomial equations by the Gröbner bases method.

7. Application: Detection of Singularities

In tracing implicitly given planar curves, numerical methods work well except when tracing curves through singular points, see [10]. [11] has pointed out that Gröbner bases yield an immediate approach to detect all singular points of implicitly given planar curves. The singular points of a planar curve given by $f(x, y) = 0$ are exactly the points (a, b) that are common zeros of f, f_x, and f_y. Hence, the problem of determining the set S of singular points of a planar curve f can be treated by the following algorithm.

(Algorithm for Detection of Singularities)

$G := \mathrm{GB}(\{f, f_x, f_y\})$, where f_x, f_y are the partial derivatives of f w. r. t. x and y respectively and GB has to be computed w. r. t. a lexical ordering of x, y.

$S :=$ set of common zeros of G determined by the successive substitution method.

Example: Let us consider the following planar curve in Figure 2. This curve has 9 singular points. We detect them by applying GB to $\{f, f_x, f_y\}$, where

(Four Circle Curve)
$$f := (x^2 + y^2 - 1).((x - 1)^2 + y^2 - 1)((x + 1)^2 + y^2 - 1)(x^2 + (y - 1)^2 - 1).$$

Application of GB, using the lexical ordering determined by $x \succ y$, yields

(Gröbner Basis for Four Circle Curve)
$$y^5.p(y),$$
$$x.y.p(y),$$
$$x^2 - y^4.q(y),$$
$$\text{where} \quad p(y) := y^4 - \tfrac{3}{2}y^3 - \tfrac{1}{4}y^2 - \tfrac{9}{8}y - \tfrac{3}{8},$$

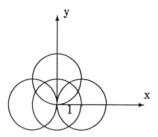

Figure 2: Planar Curve

$$q(y) := \tfrac{2558}{27}y^4 - \tfrac{823}{9}y^3 - \tfrac{3895}{54}y^2 + \tfrac{823}{12}y + \tfrac{5}{4}.$$

One sees that, for any solution y of the first polynomial in the Gröbner basis, the second polynomial vanishes identically whereas the third equation yields at most two different values for x. Proceeding by the general substitution method for Gröbner bases, we obtain the following singular points:

$(-1,1),(1,1),$
$(-1/2,\sqrt{3}/2),(1/2,\sqrt{3}/2),$
$(-\sqrt{3}/2,1/2),(\sqrt{3}/2,1/2),$
$(0,0),$
$(-1/2,-\sqrt{3}/2),(1/2,-\sqrt{3}/2),$

In accordance with the picture, we obtained five different values for y and, altogether, nine singular points. The computation took 78 sec in the author's muMATH Gröbner bases package on an Apollo workstation emulation of an IBM AT.

8. Application: Geometrical Theorem Proving

Automated Geometrical Theorem Proving is intriguing in two ways. First, it is a playground for developing and studying new algorithmic techniques for automated mathematics and, second, it becomes more and more important for advanced geometric modeling, which requires to check plausibility and consistency of inaccurate and numerically distorted geometrical objects and to derive and restore their consistent shape, see for example [14]. Apart from older approaches to geometrical theorem proving based on heuristics, recently there have been developed three systematic approaches based on three different algorithmic methods in computer algebra, namely Collins' cylindrical algebraic decomposition method [7], Wu's method of characteristic sets [20] and the Gröbner basis method. [17] compares the three methods. The use of Gröbner bases for automated geometrical theorem proving has been independently introduced by B. Kutzler and D. Kapur, see for example [18] and [13]. In this section we give an outline of the main idea how Gröbner bases can be used for proving geometrical theorems. We start with an example of a geometrical theorem. For simplicity, we present Kapur's approach, Kutzler's approach is slightly different.

Example: Apollonios' Circle Theorem. *The altitude pedal of the hypotenuse of a right-angled triangle and the midpoints of the three sides of the triangle lie on a circle. See Figure 3.*

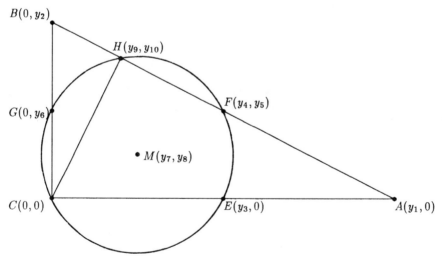

Figure 3: Apollonios' Circle

After introducing coordinates, a possible algebraic formulation of this problem is as follows:

(Hypotheses)

$$h_1 := 2y_3 - y_1 = 0 \qquad (E \text{ is midpoint of } CA),$$
$$h_2 := 2y_4 - y_1 = 0 \qquad (F \text{ is midpoint of } AB, \text{ 1st coordinate}),$$
$$h_3 := 2y_5 - y_2 = 0 \qquad (F \text{ is midpoint of } AB, \text{ 2nd coordinate}),$$
$$h_4 := 2y_6 - y_2 \qquad (G \text{ is midpoint of } BC),$$
$$h_5 := (y_7 - y_3)^2 + y_8^2 - (y_7 - y_4)^2 -$$
$$\qquad -(y_8 - y_5)^2 = 0 \qquad (\text{length } EM = \text{length } FM),$$
$$h_6 := (y_7 - y_3)^2 + y_8^2 - (y_8 - y_6)^2 -$$
$$\qquad -y_7^2 = 0 \qquad (\text{length } EM = \text{length } GM),$$
$$h_7 := (y_9 - y_1)y_2 + y_1y_{10} = 0 \qquad (H \text{ lies on } AB),$$
$$h_8 := -y_1y_9 + y_2y_{10} = 0 \qquad (CH \text{ is perpendicular to } AB).$$

(Conclusion)

$$c := (y_7 - y_3)^2 + y_8^2 - (y_7 - y_9)^2 -$$
$$\qquad -(y_8 - y_{10})^2 = 0 \qquad (\text{length } EM = \text{length } HM).$$

To prove the theorem means to show that

for all $a_1, \ldots, a_{10} \in \mathbf{R}$:
  if $h_1(a_1, \ldots, a_{10}) = 0, \ldots, h_8(a_1, \ldots, a_{10}) = 0$,
  then $c(a_1, \ldots, a_{10}) = 0$.

All expressions h_i and c occurring in this proposition are polynomial expressions. If one replaces $\mathbf{R}$ by $\mathbf{C}$, the proposition, by definition, is just the proposition "$c \in \text{Radical}(\{h_1, \ldots, h_8\})$". However, by (Radical Membership), arbitrary radical membership questions "$c \in \text{Radical}(\{h_1, \ldots, h_m\})$?" can be decided by deciding "$1 \in \text{GB}(\{h_1, \ldots, h_m, z.c-1\})$?", where z must be a new indeterminate.

This method is totally general and automatic for all geometrical theorems whose hypothesis and conclusions are polynomial equations. In fact, it is also efficient. Hundreds of non-trivial theorems have been proven by this approach, most of them in only several seconds of computing time, see [18], [13], and [17] for extensive statistics.

Two remarks are appropriate. First, replacing $\mathbf{R}$ by $\mathbf{C}$ slightly distorts the problem. Of course, if a geometrical theorem holds over $\mathbf{C}$ then it also holds over $\mathbf{R}$. The reverse is not true in general. It turns out, however, that the geometrical theorems occurring in the mathematical literature are generally true over $\mathbf{C}$. Still, one must bear in mind that, if a negative answer is produced by this method for a given proposition, this does not necessarily mean that the proposition is false over $\mathbf{R}$. It is false over $\mathbf{C}$, it could be still true over $\mathbf{R}$.

Second, most geometrical theorems are only true for the "general" case. It may well happen that they are false for "degenerate" situations, for examples, when circles have zero radius, angles become zero, lines become parallel etc. Geometric theorem proving based on the Gröbner bases method can handle degenerate situations automatically in a very strong sense.

1. In situations where the degenerate situations can be described in the form $d(x_1, \ldots, x_n) \neq 0$, d a polynomial, one can again use a new indeterminate to transform the question into an ideal (and, hence, Gröbner basis) membership question. Namely,

$$\forall z((h(z) = 0 \wedge s(z) \neq 0) \implies c(z) = 0)$$

is equivalent to

$$\exists z, u, v((h(z) = 0 \wedge u.s(z) = 1 \wedge v.c(z) = 1)$$

is equivalent to

$$1 \in \mathrm{GB}(h, u.s - 1, v.c - 1).$$

Using this wellknown transformation technique one can actually show that the Gröbner basis method yields a decision algorithm for the following general class of formulae:

(quantifiers)(arbitrary boolean combination of polynomial equations)

where either all the quantifiers must be existential or they must be universal, and the formulae must be closed, i. e. no free variables may occur.

2. The Gröbner bases approach to geometrical theorem proving can also be modified in such a way that, in case a proposition does not hold in general, the method automatically produces a set of polynomials describing the degenerate cases in which the proposition may be false. Roughly, this can be done, for example, by analyzing the denominators of the coefficients that are produced when Gröbner bases are computed over rational function coefficient fields. Quite some research has been devoted to this question, see (Kutzler 1986) and [13].

9. Application: Primary Decomposition

A polynomial ideal is "decomposable" iff it can be represented as the non-trivial intersection of two other polynomial ideals. Geometrically, this corresponds to a representation of the algebraic manifold (set of zeros) of the ideal as the non-trival union of two algebraic manifolds. It is well known in polynomial ideal theory that every polynomial ideal can be decomposed into finitely many ideals that can not be decomposed further ("irreducible components") and that this decomposition is essentially unique. This is the content of the famous Lasker-Noether decomposition theorem, see for example [27]. However, the proof of this theorem is non-constructive, i. e. no general algorithmic method is provided that would find, for a polynomial ideal given by a finite basis F, the finite bases for its irreducible components.

In more detail, the primary decomposition of a polynomial ideal (algebraic manifold) I (algebraic manifold) not only gives its irreducible parts (the corresponding "prime ideals") P_i but also information about the "multiplicity" of these irreducible parts. This information is contained in the "primary ideals" Q_i corresponding to the prime ideals. Each prime ideal and its corresponding primary ideal implicitly describe the same irreducible algebraic manifold. However, the prime ideal and a corresponding primary ideal may be different. In this case, the primary ideal tells us "how often" the irreducible manifold defined by the prime ideal occurs in the algebraic manifold defined by the given ideal I. Summarizing, the algorithmic version of the primary decomposition problem has the following specification (where we use $Z(F)$ for "set of common zeros of F"):

(Primary Decomposition Problem)

> Given: F.
> Find: G_i, H_i such that
>   the Ideal(G_i) are primary,
>   the Ideal(H_i) are the prime ideals corresponding to Ideal(G_i),
>   Ideal(F) = $\bigcap_i$ Ideal(G_i),
>   (i. e. $Z(F) = \bigcup_i Z(G_i)$), and
>   some minimality conditions are satisfied.

Note that the problem depends on the underlying coefficient field. For example, $x^2 + 1$ is irreducible over $\mathbf{R}$ but reducible over $\mathbf{C}$.

Recently the problem of algorithmic primary decomposition has been completely solved using Gröbner bases. Still, the algorithm for the most general case is not yet implemented in a software system. Complete implementations may be expected for the very near future. A number of papers, of different generality and level of detail, contributed to the recent progress in this area: [9, 15, 16, 19].

An exact formulation of the problem and a detailed description of the algorithms, which are quite involved, is beyond the scope of this paper. It should be clear that automatic decomposition of algebraic manifolds (e. g. intersection curves of 3D objects) should be of utmost importance for geometrical modeling where the global analysis of finitely represented objects, as opposed to a mere local numerical evaluation, is more and more desirable in advanced applications.

All the algorithms invented for the solution of the primary decomposition problem heavily rely on the basic properties of Gröbner bases as compiled in Theorem 2.5.1 and Theorem 2.5.2, notably on the properties (Elimination Ideals), (Ideal Membership) and properties derived from these properties as, for example, (Intersection Ideal).

For bringing this important research to the attention of the geometric modeling community we present a simple example showing the kind of information obtainable from a primary decomposition.

Example: Primary Decomposition of Cylinder/Sphere Intersection. Let us consider the intersection of a cylinder with radius r_1 whose axis coincides with the x_3-axis and a sphere with radius r_2 and midpoint at the origin. The intersection curve consists of the common zeros of the following two polynomials:

$$F := \{x_1^2 + x_2^2 - r_1^2, x_1^2 + x_2^2 + x_3^2 - r_2^2\}.$$

Depending on whether $r_1 < r_2$, $r_1 = r_2$, or $r_1 > r_2$, the primary decomposition algorithm, over $\mathbf{R}$, yields the following representation of Ideal(F) as the intersection of primary ideals:

Case $r_1 < r_2$:
$$\text{Ideal}(F) = \text{Ideal}(x_3 + r, x_2^2 + x_1^2 - r_1^2) \cap \text{Ideal}(x_3 - r, x_2^2 + x_1^2 - r_1^2),$$

where $r := \sqrt{r_2^2 - r_1^2}$.
The two primary components are, in fact, prime.

Case $r_1 = r_2$:
$$\text{Ideal}(F) = \text{Ideal}(x_3^2, x_2^2 + x_1^2 - r_1^2).$$
The ideal is already primary with corresponding prime ideal
$$\text{Ideal}(x_3, x_2^2 + x_1^2 - r_1^2).$$

Case $r_1 > r_2$:
$$\text{Ideal}(F) = \text{Ideal}(x_3^2 - r_2^2 + r_1^2, x_2^2 + x_1^2 - r_1^2).$$
The ideal is already primary and identical to the corresponding prime ideal.

In geometrical terms, the above outcome of the primary decomposition algorithm gives us the following information:

Case $r_1 < r_2$: The manifold decomposes in two irreducible components, namely, two horizontal circles of radius r_1 with midpoints $(0, 0, \pm r)$. The multiplicity of these circles is one (the primary ideals are identical to their corresponding prime ideals).

Case $r_1 = r_2$: The manifold does not decompose. It consists of the horizontal circle with radius r_1 with midpoint $(0, 0, 0)$. However, this circle has to be "counted twice" because, in the primary ideal, there appears the term x_3^2 whereas in the prime ideal, which defines the "shape" (i. e. point set) of the manifold, x_3 appears only linearly. This corresponds to the geometrical intuition that the intersection curve results from merging, in the limit, the two horizontal circles of case $r_1 < r_2$.

Case $r_1 > r_2$: The manifold does not decompose (over **R**!). In fact it has no real points. In contrast to the case $r_1 = r_2$, the manifold has multiplicity one because the primary ideal coincides with the prime ideal.

10. Conclusions

The Gröbner bases method provides an algorithmic approach to many problems in polynomial ideal theory. We tried to provide some first evidence that the method could be a valuable tool for the progressing needs of geometrical engineering (geometric modeling, image processing, robotics, CAD etc.).
  Further research should concentrate on two areas:

- The theoretical problems (for example, solutions at infinity in paremtric representations) occurring in the application of the method to geometrical problems must be completely studied.

- The computational behavior of the method must be improved by obtaining new mathematical results that could hold in the special situations (e. g. kinematics of certain robot classes) in which the method is applied.

Research on efficiency aspects and on geometrical applications of the Gröbner basis method is only at the beginning.

ACKNOWLEDGEMENT

I am indebted to C. Hofmann, and B. Sturmfels for personal communications I used in this paper. Thanks also to B. Kutzler, R. Michelic-Birgmayr, and S. Stifter for helping in the preparation of some of the examples.

REFERENCES

1. Arnon, D.S. and Sederberg, T.W., Implicit equation for a parametric surface by Gröbner bases, in: *Proceedings of the 1984 MACSYMA User's Conference* (V. E. Golden ed.), General Electric, Schenectady, New York (1984) 431-436.

2. Barr, A.H., "Superquadrics and angle-preserving transformations" *IEEE Computer Graphics and Applications* 1,1 (1981) 11-23.

3. Buchberger, B., "An algorithm for finding a basis for the residue class ring of a zero-dimensional polynomial ideal" (German), Ph. D. Thesis, Univ. of Innsbruck (Austria), Dept. of Mathematics (1965).

4. Buchberger, B., "An algorithmic criterion for the solvability of algebraic systems of equations" (German), *Aequationes Mathematicae* **4**,3 (1970) 374-383.

5. Buchberger, B., Collins, G.E. and Loos, R., *Computer Algebra: Symbolic and Algebraic Computation* (Springer-Verlag, Vienna - New York, 1982).

6. Buchberger, B., "Gröbner bases: an algorithmic method in polynomial ideal theory, in: *Multidimensional Systems Theory* (N. K. Bose ed.) (D. Reidel Publishing Company, Dordrecht - Boston - Lancaster, 184-232, 1985).

7. Collins, G.E., "Quantifier elimination for real closed fields by cylindrical algebraic decomposition", *2nd GI Conference on Automata Theory and Formal Languages, Lecture Notes in Computer Science* **33** (1975) 134-183.

8. Gianni, P., "Properties of Gröbner bases under specialization", *Proc. of the EUROCAL '87 Conference* Leipzig (June 1987).

9. Gianni, P., Trager, B. and Zacharias, G., "Gröbner bases and primary decomposition of polynomial ideals", submitted to *Journal of Symbolic Computation*. Available as manuscript, IBM T. J. Watson Research Center, Yorktown Heights, New York (1985).

10. Hofmann, C., "Algebraic curves", this volume. Institute for Mathematics and its Applications, Univ. of Minneapolis. (1987).

11. Hofmann, C., Personal Communication. Purdue University, West Lafayette, IN 47907, Computer Science Dept. (1987).

12. Kalkbrener, M., "Solving systems of algebraic equations by using Gröbner bases", *Proceedings of the EUROCAL '87 Conference*, Leipzig (June 1987).

13. Kapur, D., "A refutational approach to geometry theorem proving", *Proceedings of the Workshop on Geometric Reasoning*, Oxford University (June 30 - July 3, 1986), to appear in *Artificial Intelligence.*

14. Kapur, D., "Algebraic reasoning for object construction from ideal images", *Lecture Notes, Summer Program on Robotics: Computational Issues in Geometry*, Institute for Mathematics and its Applications, Univ. of Minneapolis (August 24-28, 1987).

15. Kandri-rody, A., "Effective methods in the theory of polynomial ideals", Ph. D. Thesis, Rensselaer Polytechnic Institute, Troy, New York, Dept. of Computer Science (1984).

16. Kredel, H., "Primary ideal decomposition", *Proceedings of the EUROCAL '87 Conference*, Leipzig (June 1987).

17. Kutzler, B., "Implementation of a geometry proving package in SCRATCHPAD II", *Proceedings of the EUROCAL '87 Conference*, Leipzig (June 1987).

18. Kutzler, B. and Stifter, S., "On the application of Buchberger's algorithm to automated geometry theorem proving", *Journal of Symbolic Computation* **2**,4, (1986) 389-398.

19. Lazard, D., "Ideal bases and primary decomposition: case of two variables", *Journal of Symbolic Computation* **1**,3, (1985) 261-270.

20. Paul, R.P., *Robot Manipulators: Mathematics, Programming, and Control* (The MIT Press, Cambridge (Mass.), London, 1981).

21. Preparata, F.P. and Shamos, M.I., *Computational Geometry* (Springer-Verlag, New York, Berlin, Heidelberg, (1985).

22. Sederberg, T.W. and Anderson, D.C. "Implicit representation of parametric curves and surfaces", *Computer Vision, Graphics, and Image Processing* **28** (1984) 72-84.

23. Spear, D., "A constructive approach to ring theory", *Proceedings of the MAC-SYMA Users' Conference*, Berkeley, July 1977 (R. J. Fateman ed.), (The MIT Press, 369-376, 1977).

24. Sturmfels, B., Private Communication. Institute for Mathematics and its Applications (1987).

25. Trinks, W., "On B. Buchberger's method for solving systems of algebraic equations" (German), *Journal of Number Theory* **10**,4 (1978) 475-488.

26. Van den Essen, A., "A criterion to decide if a polynomial map is invertible and to compute the inverse", Report 8653, Catholic University Nijmegen (The Netherlands), Dept. of Mathematics (1986).

27. Van der Waerden, B.L., *Modern Algebra I, II* (Frederick Ungar Publishing Co., New York, 1953).

28. Winkler, F., "Solution of equations I: polynomial ideals and Gröbner bases", *Proceedings of the Conference on Computers and Mathematics*, Stanford University (July 30 - August 1, 1986).

29. Wu, W.T., "On the decision problem and the mechanization of theorem proving in elementary geometry", *Scientia Sinica* **21** (1978) 150-172.

Uncertain Geometry

Hugh F. Durrant-Whyte
Department of Engineering Science
University of Oxford
Oxford, U.K.

ABSTRACT

Robots must operate in an environment which is inherently uncertain. This uncertainty is important in areas such as modeling, planning and the motion of manipulators and objects; areas where geometric analysis also plays an important part. To operate efficiently, a robot system must be able to represent, account for, and reason about the effects of uncertainty in these geometries in a consistent manner.

Our motivation for this development of uncertain geometry arises from a need to provide a common language by which robot sensors can communicate and integrate information about an environment. We will maintain that uncertainty should be represented as an intrinsic part of all geometric descriptions. We develop a description of uncertain geometric features as families of parameterized functions together with a distribution function defined on the associated parameter vector. We consider uncertain points, curves and surfaces, and show how they can be manipulated and transformed between coordinate frames in an efficient and consistent manner.

1. Introduction

The capabilities of a robot system are strongly dependent on an ability to observe and understand the environment in which it operates. For this reason, an effective and purposeful description of the environment is fundamental to the development of intelligent robotics [2]. There are many different ways in which the problem of description can be approached, resulting in a variety of different environment modeling techniques; solid models, primitive surface models, or functional descriptions, for example. The utility of each description depends on the specific task in which it will be used. Ideally a robot system should provide many different levels of environment description, and be able to move freely and maintain consistency between them.

Our motivating concern is the problem of integrating observations of an environment from many different sensory sources. The ability of a sensor to extract descriptions from the environment is, in part, the dual of the world modeling problem. In the most general sense, a sensor provides a mechanism to extract or reconstruct descriptions of the environment, described by the observed information, in terms of a prior world model. The relation between sensor observations and the robot's description of the world is fundamentally important: The ability to consistently model the environment and manipulate object descriptions provides a mechanism with which to compare and integrate sensor observations. Indeed the representation of an environment maintained by the robot's world model provides a basis for the communication of information between different sensory cues.

We will maintain that geometric primitives, of some form, are a natural environment description for sensor-based robotics: Each sensory cue can be considered as providing the robot system with observations or estimates of a specific type of geometric primitive; edges, surface normals, etc. This information can be communicated to other sensors, observing different types of features, through geometric transforms. These primitive geometric elements can then be compared and aggregated by the robot system, to provide a full and complete environment description, and subsequently used in the planning and execution of tasks.

The geometric elements used for the description and communication of information should consist of object features readily extracted by a single sensory cue; lines, surfaces, depth constraints, etc. Any higher-level description of the environment, in terms of form or function, would require more information than any single sensor could reasonably supply, and as a consequence would force systems to be rigidly organized. Conversely, any lower-level description, in terms of an irradiance image or depth map, provides a plethora of information detail, useful to only single sensor systems. As a consequence, these models inhibit any distributed decision making philosophy and increase the requirement for communication bandwidth.

Using geometric primitives at a sensor system level does not, however, preclude the use of other models at *appropriate* levels within other parts of the robot system; functional models are important when the sensed environment is to be interpreted, irradiance models are required to process and extract geometry from raw sensor data. Indeed, multiple resolutions of model are essential to a complete system, and must be integrated effectively with the geometric primitives used for describing sensor operation. The geometric elements used in sensor processing must take explicit account of the uncertainty inherent to their operation. We must be able to manipulate these descriptions, intersect and aggregate them, and be able to move representations between coordinate systems. Understanding these uncertain geometric descriptions will not only supply an effective environment model but also form a basis for integrating disparate sensory information [4].

We maintain that an effective and consistent description of geometry is fundamental to the efficient operation of sensor systems. It provides a mechanism with which to describe observations, it is the basis for integrating different measurements, and it is the language by which sensors communicate information to each other.

In the following we shall present a probabilistic viewpoint of uncertain geometry. We maintain that uncertainty should be represented as an intrinsic part of all geometric features. The representation of uncertain points, lines, curves and surfaces is developed by considering geometric features as stochastic point processes or random vectors described by a probability distribution on the parameter space of the associated object. The manipulation of uncertainty measures then becomes the transformation and combination of probability distributions. This representation provides a mechanism for the efficient manipulation of geometric uncertainty measures and a methodology for providing a consistent interpretation of geometric objects in terms of an invariant stochastic topology. This topology describes the relationships between geometric objects that do not change when the environment is uncertain. We develop the idea of an invariant measure over the group of transforms appropriate to Euclidean space (descriptions of geometric uncertainty that do not change when transformed in Euclidean space) and show that the Gaussian distribution is a reasonable approximation to this. Using a Gaussian-feature assumption it is shown how uncertain geometry can be manipulated in an efficient and consistent manner. We show that invariant relations between geometric objects can be considered as invariant elements of a stochastic topological network. This allows the consistent composition or propagation of geometric uncertainty, providing a mechanism with which to reason about the effects of uncertain geometric descriptions.

Section 2 outlines the development of geometric environment models in robotics. Section 3 develops a representation for uncertain geometry in terms of constrained, parameterized functions. Each function describes a particular type of geometric feature, and each specific parameter value represents an instance of this feature type. Uncertainty is described by placing a probability distribution function on the parameter vector of a given feature type. The properties of these descriptions are discussed, and techniques for building consistent representations of geometric objects and relations are discussed. Section 4 describes how these uncertain representations can be manipulated and transformed between coordinate systems. Section 5 develops techniques to describe changes in feature location and description when the probability distribution on parameter vectors is assumed to be Gaussian. Section 6 demonstrates how constraints between descriptions can be used to maintain consistency amongst uncertain geometric features.

2. Geometric Environment Models

The problem of building a geometric model of the robot environment has received considerable attention (see for example Brady [5], Pentland [20], Requicha [21]). There are essentially two classes of geometric representations, the functional model and the image model.

Functional models derive from the need to solve problems in planning, assembly, computer aided design (CAD), and other high-level robot operations. There is a great variety of functional models in use, usually specialized for a particular task or to solve a specific representation problem (generalized cylinders, or solid geometry, for example). In general the CAD approach to environment and object modeling is to utilize some subset of constructive solid geometry (CSG) [21]. It is rare that these models provide any mechanism for the representation of uncertainty in their descriptions. This consideration often precludes their use in sensory driven robot operations where uncertainty is intrinsic to problem solution., and where elemental descriptions are too global to allow single-sensor decision making.

Conversely, models of geometry as images; relations between small elemental image parts, and stochastic or Markovian random field models (MRF), provide a view of geometry as an array of simple scaler components, with no attempt to provide a functional description. These image models provide a great deal of statistical micro-structure from which uncertain descriptions of the environment can be reconstructed (Marroquin [17]). However they do not provide the functional representation or level of abstraction that we require to develop a multi-sensor paradigm, nor do they allow task level descriptions of the environment.

There is clearly a need for some compromise between these two extremes: We require a level of representation which can generally allow the development of geometric models for specific tasks but which takes explicit account of the intrinsic uncertainty introduced by sensor driven recognition and task execution. Ambler [2] has suggested that the representation of objects in a robot system's world model should be sympathetic to the nature of the sensor systems observations of the environment. Such a "representation for sensing" results in a surface and feature based description of objects. Within a system consisting of many diverse sensor agents, different models of the environment will be appropriate for different types of sensory information. We maintain that the overall representation of the world model should encourage a homogeneous description of all types of geometric features observed by sensors. This representation should provide for the description of uncertainty and partial information, and be capable of supporting, manipulating and comparing a variety of geometric sensor primitives including their intersections, relations and extents.

3. Uncertain Geometry

We maintain that the key to both environment and sensor modeling is to find an efficient representation of uncertain geometry and to develop effective methods for manipulating, comparing and combining uncertain geometric structures. The need for a representation of geometric uncertainty has been recognized in the literature. Some notable examples occur in planning (Brooks [6], Taylor [25]), object recognition (Grimson [14]) and navigation (Brooks [7], Smith [23]).

The general policy in all these representations is to assume error bounds on geometrical parameters, resulting in "error manifolds" and "uncertainty cones", over which the error is implicitly assumed to be uniform. The problem with such measures of uncertainty is that they are difficult to manipulate and reason with in a consistent manner. It is generally not sufficient to consider uncertainty in a single coordinate system, we must also be able to reason about the effects of error in coordinate frames other than those in which the uncertainty measure was initially defined. In this case, simple geometric objects describing uncertainty in one coordinate system may no longer be simple in another frame of reference. This problem is further compounded when any sequence of uncertainty measures must be aggregated to study their cumulative effect. Problems also arise when two or more different features must be compared, how for example, should an uncertainty cone be combined with an error manifold, and how does the result affect objects described in other coordinate systems? In a statistical sense there are complications resulting from the combination of two or more uncertainty measures; are the initial measures independent, is the assumption of uniform distributions appropriate, what is the combined distribution of the uncertainty measures and how should partial information (infinite uncertainty in one or more degrees of information) be represented?

To answer these questions we require a method which can represent uncertain geometric features in a consistent, homogeneous manner, which allows these uncertainties to be manipulated easily, and which provides an ability to reason about the effects of uncertainty in the planning and execution of tasks.

In section 3.1 we introduce a probabilistic description of uncertain geometry described in terms of implicit parameterized functions together with a probability distribution defined on the parameter vector. This provides a homogeneous framework for describing all the elements of classical geometry. We note the relation between this framework and the theory of random sets. Section 3.2 identifies certain desirable properties of these parameterizations, outlining a procedure for verifying that a specific representation of a geometric element is statistically well-behaved. This leads directly to the development of general mechanisms for transforming geometric elements between coordinate systems and for aggregating or intersecting different geometric objects. Section 3.3 develops the idea of stochastic invariance, in which geometric properties or relations remain unchanged when they are made uncertain. These invariants are closely related to classical topological invariants, so that we shall call the study of stochastic invariance, stochastic topology. The importance of stochastic topology lies in its ability to provide a consistent interpretation for uncertain geometric objects, and as a consequence, to act as a constraint system through which geometric information can be propagated.

3.1. Stochastic Geometry

All geometric objects (features, locations and relations), can be described by a parameter vector $\mathbf{p}$ and a vector function

$$\mathbf{g}(\mathbf{x}, \mathbf{p}) = 0; \qquad \mathbf{x} \subseteq \Re^n, \quad \mathbf{p} \in \Re^m \tag{1}$$

This function can be interpreted as a model of the physical geometric object, that maps a (compact) *region* $\mathbf{x} \subseteq \Re^n$ in Euclidean n-space to a *point* $\mathbf{p} \in \Re^m$ in the parameter space. Each function $\mathbf{g}$ describes a particular type of geometric object; all straight lines, or the family of quadratic surfaces, for example. Each value of $\mathbf{p}$ specifies a particular instance of a geometric object modeled by $\mathbf{g}$. For example, *all* plane surfaces can be represented by the equation;

$$g(\mathbf{x}, \mathbf{p}) = p_x x + p_y y + p_z z + 1 = 0 \tag{2}$$

with $\mathbf{x} = [x, y, z]^T$ and $\mathbf{p} = [p_x, p_y, p_z]^T$. A specific plane can be represented as a point $\mathbf{p} \in \Re^3$ in the parameter space.

Consider a sensor observing a particular type of geometric object in the environment. The sensor can be considered as observing values of $\mathbf{p}$. The uncertain *event* that the sensor "sees" a specific instance of this geometric object can be described by taking the parameter vector $\mathbf{p}$ to be a random variable. The likelyhood that a particular instance of a geometric feature is observed can now be described by a probability density function (p.d.f.); $f_g(\mathbf{p})$. For a specific type of feature represented by Equation 1, this p.d.f. describes the probability or likelyhood of observing a particular instance of the associated geometric object. It should be noted that this is *not* a noise model.

In this context, the analysis of uncertain geometry can, in theory, be reduced to a problem in the transformation and manipulation of random variables. The study of random geometry (stochastic geometry, geometric probability, and integral geometry [22]) has a long and illustrious history. It differs from conventional probability in requiring a physical interpretation to be placed on random variables, resulting in physical (geometric) constraints on functions and relations. It is this difference which makes stochastic geometry a more difficult problem than just the manipulation of random variables. The classic example of this situation is the ubiquitous Bertrand's Paradox, in which the probability of a random line intersecting a circle is shown to depend on the definition of 'line' and 'circle'. Such problems have resulted in random geometry being largely neglected as a sub-discipline of random variable theory. There have, however, been some important contributions to the subject in recent years.

In their book, Kendall and Moran [16], describe a method of choosing distributions on geometric elements which provide a consistent interpretation of physical geometric elements. Although they concentrate on the distributions of points in Euclidean space (geometric probability), some important properties of stochastic lines and planes are also described.

In his thesis, Davidson [8] made the important observation that arbitrary random geometric objects can be described by a point process (random point) in a parameter space. These point processes are in general restricted to lie on a manifold in parameter space. For example, consider a line on the plane described by the equation

$$g(\mathbf{x}, \mathbf{p}) = r - x \cos \theta - y \sin \theta = 0 \qquad (3)$$

with $\mathbf{x} = [x, y]^T$ and $\mathbf{p} = [r, \theta]^T$ (Figure 1). We can describe any 'randomness' of this line as a random point $\mathbf{p}$ in the corresponding parameter space. In general, if the space in which this point is defined is of greater dimension than $\mathbf{p}$ itself, then the process generating this parameter vector will be restricted to a subspace of this defined space. In the case of a line parameterized by $[r, \theta]^T$, we can consider the point process as unconstrained on a plane, or restricted to the surface of an infinite right cylinder (θ orientation and r height) in three dimensions (Figure 2), for example. We will generally restrict our interest to spaces in which the point process $\mathbf{p}$ is unconstrained, although the description in higher dimensional spaces may be useful when two or more *different* geometric objects must be considered simultaneously.

The advantage of describing uncertain geometry by a point in parameter space together with an associated p.d.f., is that to transform uncertain geometries to other coordinate systems, we need only transform their probability distribution functions. The representation of all geometric locations and features by point processes lends a homogeneity to the description of stochastic geometries. This considerably simplifies the transformation and manipulation of geometric elements, and provides a powerful framework in which to describe all uncertain geometric features and relations.[1]

---

[1]More recently, Harding [15] has extended these ideas toward a theory of random sets. In this case $\mathbf{x} \subseteq \Re^n$ is the set, and $\mathbf{p} \in \Re^m$ a point characterizing this set such that there exists a Borel-measurable function $\Omega(\mathbf{x}) \mapsto \mathbf{p}$ with the usual closure and uniqueness properties. The point $\mathbf{p}$ is considered as a characteristic or indicator of the set $\mathbf{x}$. As such, the theory of random sets is directly applicable to problems in stochastic geometry.

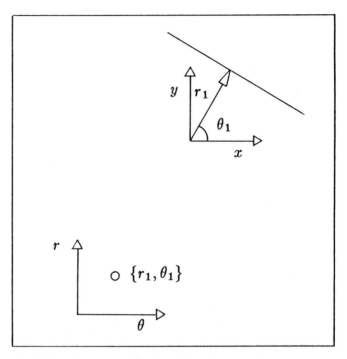

Figure 1: A random line on a plane and its corresponding point process in parameter space

3.2. Well-Condition Stochastic Geometries

There are many different functions of the form of Equation 1 which can be used to describe a single type of geometric feature. In choosing which representation is most appropriate for a particular feature, we should be concerned with the stability of the parameterization to perturbations or uncertainties. A statistically well-conditioned representation can be of major benefit when features must be manipulated or transformed between coordinate systems. For example, a straight line on a plane could be described by any of the following forms:

$$g(\mathbf{x}, \mathbf{p}) = r - x\cos\theta - y\sin\theta = 0, \qquad \mathbf{p} = [r, \theta]^T$$
$$g(\mathbf{x}, \mathbf{p}) = ax + by + c = 0, \qquad \mathbf{p} = [a, b, c]^T$$
$$g(\mathbf{x}, \mathbf{p}) = y - mx + l = 0, \qquad \mathbf{p} = [m, l]^T$$

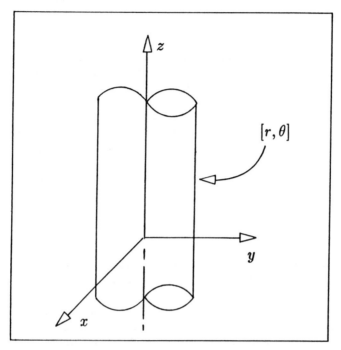

Figure 2: The point process of a line restricted to a cylinder.

The first representation is well defined for all parameter values, although its periodic form can cause confusion. The second representation has the undesirable property that a given feature does not have a unique parameter vector. The third representation cannot parameterize lines parallel to the x-axis.

There are three basic criteria which every representation should satisfy if they are to be considered statistically well-conditioned:

1. Every feature instance must have a unique parameterization. This excludes any representation for which a parameter vector does not exist for all possible feature instances, and it excludes representations where there is a symmetric ambiguity.

2. Every parameterization must be associated with a unique feature. This excludes homogeneous tensor representations or any other parameterization in which the parameter vector is of greater degree than the geometric variety that it describes.

3. The parameter vector must change "smoothly" with physical feature motion. This ensures that small changes in feature do not result in abrupt changes in the describing parameter.

Conditions 1 and 2 require a representation to be a one-to-one (bijective) relation between feature and parameter. Condition 3 is a stability condition (in which it is possible to subsume the first two conditions) which ensures that changes of coordinate system in which the feature is described does not result in rapid changes of the parameter vector.

To analyze this stability condition, we need to consider what happens to the parameter vector $\mathbf{p}$ and it's associated p.d.f $f_g(\mathbf{p})$ when they are moved between coordinate systems. Suppose we start with a representation described by Equation 1 and parameterized by the vector $\mathbf{p}$. In general if we transform the point set $\mathbf{x}$ to $\mathbf{x}'$ as $\mathbf{x}' = \mathbf{T}(\mathbf{x})$, the parameter vector describing the set is also changed as $\mathbf{p}' = \mathbf{h}_g(\mathbf{p})$ (say), so that:

$$\begin{aligned} \mathbf{g}(\mathbf{x}, \mathbf{p}) &= 0 \\ \text{and} \quad \mathbf{g}(\mathbf{T}(\mathbf{x}), \mathbf{h}_g(\mathbf{p})) &= 0 \end{aligned} \tag{4}$$

It is important to note that the function $\mathbf{g}$ is the same in any coordinate system, and the transformation $\mathbf{T}(\mathbf{x})$ has the same form for any set $\mathbf{x}$. It follows that when $\mathbf{T}$ is fixed, $\mathbf{h}_g(\mathbf{p})$ is completely defined by the function $\mathbf{g}$.

We want to ensure that for all transformations $\mathbf{T}$ the parameter vector $\mathbf{p}$ and hence the representation $\mathbf{g}$ is well defined. In particular, $\mathbf{p}$ should be well behaved for *differential changes* in coordinate system. Consider the transformation of a parameter vector

$$\mathbf{p}' = \mathbf{h}_g(\mathbf{p}) \tag{5}$$

from a coordinate system c to c'. Keeping $\mathbf{T}$ fixed, suppose we perturb the vector $\mathbf{p}$ (due to error or noise) by an amount $\delta\mathbf{p}$, so that:

$$\mathbf{p}' + \delta\mathbf{p}' = \mathbf{h}_g(\mathbf{p} + \delta\mathbf{p}) \tag{6}$$

Using a Taylor series expansion, results in:

$$\delta\mathbf{p}' \approx \nabla_p \mathbf{h}|_p \delta\mathbf{p} \tag{7}$$

The Jacobian $\nabla_p \mathbf{h}$ can be interpreted as a change *magnifier*, describing the change in parameter $\delta\mathbf{p}$ viewed from different coordinate systems. It follows that if $\nabla_p \mathbf{h}$ is well defined as a function of $\mathbf{p}$ then the transformation of a feature representation between arbitrary coordinate systems must also be well behaved.

In statistical terms, $\mathbf{p}$ and $\mathbf{p}'$ are random vectors to which we associate the p.d.f.'s $f_g(\cdot)$ and $f_g'(\cdot)$. We are concerned that these distributions are well behaved when the parameter vectors are transformed between coordinate systems.

Consider a differential volume $d\mathbf{p} = dp_1 \cdots dp_m$ of a parameter space. If we interpret a change of coordinate system as a change of variables, and if this transform is bijective, then we can write;

$$dp'_1 dp'_2 \cdots dp'_m = |\nabla_p \mathbf{h}| dp_1 dp_2 \cdots dp_m \tag{8}$$

where $|\nabla_p \mathbf{h}|$ is the determinant of the transform Jacobian. The probability mass associated with a given differential volume must remain constant regardless of the coordinate system in which it is defined, so that:

$$f'_g(\mathbf{p}') dp'_1 dp'_2 \cdots dp'_m = f_g(\mathbf{p}) dp_1 dp_2 \cdots dp_m \tag{9}$$

Substituting Equation 8 into this relation gives

$$f'_g(\mathbf{p}') |\nabla_p \mathbf{h}| dp_1 dp_2 \cdots dp_m = f_g(\mathbf{p}) dp_1 dp_2 \cdots dp_m \tag{10}$$

which results in the usual equation for the transformation of probability distributions:

$$f'_g(\mathbf{p}') = \frac{1}{|\nabla_p \mathbf{h}|} f(\mathbf{h}^{-1}[\mathbf{p}']) \tag{11}$$

A detailed development of this equation and its properties can be found in [18]

Consideration of Equation 11 shows that if $|\nabla_p \mathbf{h}|$ is well behaved as this vector is transformed between coordinate systems, then the distribution on a parameter vector will be statistically well conditioned. This agrees with the result obtained in Equation 7. The analysis of $\nabla_p \mathbf{h}$ can provide an important insight into the effectiveness of a particular geometric representation. Recall that the parameter transform $\mathbf{h}$ can be found uniquely from g by considering arbitrary transforms on the set $\mathbf{x} \subseteq \Re^n$. When $\mathbf{h}$ has been found, the stability of the representation provided by $\mathbf{g}$ can be analyzed by considering the Jacobian $\nabla_p \mathbf{h}$ as a function of $\mathbf{p}$.

To illustrate this, we will take the example [16] of a straight line on a plane described by either of:

$$\begin{aligned} g(\mathbf{x}, \mathbf{p}) &= \quad ux + vy + 1 = 0, & \mathbf{p} &= [u, v]^T \\ g(\mathbf{x}, \mathbf{p}) &= \quad r - x\cos\theta - y\sin\theta = 0, & \mathbf{p} &= [r, \theta]^T \end{aligned}$$

We consider arbitrary transforms of the form

$$\begin{bmatrix} x' \\ y' \end{bmatrix} = \begin{bmatrix} \cos\phi & -\sin\phi \\ \sin\phi & \cos\phi \end{bmatrix} \begin{bmatrix} x \\ y \end{bmatrix} + \begin{bmatrix} T_x \\ T_y \end{bmatrix} \tag{12}$$

So that the parameter transforms are:

$$\begin{bmatrix} u' \\ v' \end{bmatrix} = \frac{\begin{bmatrix} u\sin\phi + v\cos\phi \\ u\cos\phi - v\sin\phi \end{bmatrix}}{[1 + T_x(u\cos\phi + v\sin\phi) + T_y(u\sin\phi + v\cos\phi)]} \tag{13}$$

and

$$\begin{bmatrix} r' \\ \theta' \end{bmatrix} = \begin{bmatrix} r + T_x \cos(\theta + \phi) + T_y \sin(\theta + \phi) \\ \theta + \phi \end{bmatrix} \tag{14}$$

These parameter transforms describe the relocation of lines. To find out how stable these transforms are, we need only consider the determinant of the transform Jacobians. Differentiating Equations 13 and 14 we obtain

$$|\nabla_{u,v}\mathbf{h}| = \left(u^2 + v^2\right)^{\frac{3}{2}}$$
$$|\nabla_{r,\theta}\mathbf{h}| = 1$$

Using these in Equation 8 interpreted in the form of Equation 11 results in the differential measures $(u^2 + v^2)^{-3/2}dudv$ and $drd\theta$ These quantities are known as the invariant measure of a representation; the differential probability mass that remains invariant under all rotations and translations appropriate to the Euclidean group. From this example, it is clear that $[r, \theta]^T$ is a natural representation for the line on a plane. (In this example, $drd\theta$ is the *only* measure invariant representation for this geometry.)

The importance of finding well behaved representations for uncertain geometric objects is that it allows observed features to be manipulated and transformed between coordinate systems in a well defined, robust manner. We have demonstrated a verification procedure for analyzing the statistical properties of a specific representation. Ideally it would be useful to find an algorithm to determine which representation is best for every given feature type. Although we do not know how this can be done, Kendall and Moran [16] suggest a more general verification principle which may lead to a solution of this problem.

3.3. Stochastic Topology

We are primarily interested in geometric objects embedded in the usual Euclidean space. These objects are conceptually linked together by virtue of the geometric relations resulting from this embedding. It is therefore impossible to consider operations on a geometric object in isolation from other objects in this space. We can describe these links between different objects as a set of relations - a topology - which can be characterized by some simple rules of invariance. These rules can be interpreted as constraints on the set of relations between uncertain geometric objects. For example, consider two uncertain objects related to each other by virtue of their embedding in real space; if the information we have about one object changes, what effect will this have on the second object to which it is related, if we change the relation between these objects, what can be said about the resulting change in object description? This same argument applies to the relations between many different objects, linked together by a network of general relations resulting from their embedding in Euclidean space.

We will call the set of relations on probabilistic geometries a *stochastic topology*. The invariants of this topology will be termed *stochastic invariants*. The invariants of the topology associated with uncertain geometric objects are those properties of the relations between objects that remain unchanged when the parameters **p** that describe the features are "distorted" or perturbed about their nominal values. If we consider the probability distribution function $f_g(\mathbf{p})$ associated with the representation $g(\mathbf{x}, \mathbf{p}) = 0$ as some likelyhood of distortions, then it follows that the stochastic invariants of relations between uncertain geometric objects are exactly those topological invariants associated with the Euclidean set.

The invariant properties of relations between objects provides a very powerful tool with which to maintain consistency between feature descriptions and propagate geometric observations through the robots world model. The reason for this is that the relations between features can be used to provide constraints on possible descriptions. These constraints can be interpreted as information and used, whenever feature descriptions are changed, to apply corresponding changes to related features.

The simplest case of an invariant relation occurs in the loop created by the relations between three geometric objects. In this instance, the vector sum of the relations between objects is zero, regardless of the absolute location of these objects. Consider for example the *random* placement of three points on a plane (Figure 3);

$$\mathbf{p}_1 = [x_1, y_1]^T, \quad \mathbf{p}_2 = [x_2, y_2]^T, \quad \mathbf{p}_3 = [x_3, y_3]^T \tag{15}$$

and the (random) relations created between them:

$$e_1 = \mathbf{p}_2 - \mathbf{p}_1, \quad e_2 = \mathbf{p}_3 - \mathbf{p}_2, \quad e_3 = \mathbf{p}_1 - \mathbf{p}_3, \tag{16}$$

There are three important observations that can be made about this simple case:

1. Regardless of the initial distribution on the placement of points, the sum of the relations between these points will be zero with probability 1, so that $e_1 + e_2 + e_3 = 0$. Note that providing the distribution on points is not degenerate, the event that the points are co-linear has measure zero. However this is *not* the impossible event.

2. Although the location of points $\mathbf{p}_i$ can be chosen arbitrarily, the line vectors e_i cannot. For example, if e_1 is fixed, then any choice of e_2 and e_3 is constrained by $-e_1 = e_2 + e_3$. Further, any two independent line segments completely specify the relative relations between three points.

3. The joint distribution on relations $f(e_1, e_2, e_3)$ is guaranteed to be degenerate, even if the joint distribution on the points $f(\mathbf{p}_1, \mathbf{p}_2, \mathbf{p}_3)$ is well defined.

The importance of these results to the problem of maintaining consistent geometric descriptions can best be appreciated by reference to a simple example.

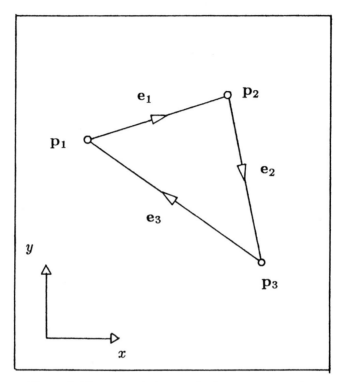

Figure 3: The general three-node three-arc network.

Consider three surfaces, intersecting to form a corner and three edges, each edge
with two surfaces in common (Figure 4). Let each plane be described by a parameter vector $\mathbf{p}_i = [\alpha_i, \beta_i, r_i]^T$ and defined by the function

$$g(\mathbf{x}, \mathbf{p}_i) = x \sin \alpha_i \cos \beta_i + y \sin \alpha_i \sin \beta_i + z \cos \alpha_i - r_i = 0 \qquad (17)$$

with $\mathbf{x} = [x, y, z]^T$. These three planes can be represented as points $\mathbf{p}_1$, $\mathbf{p}_2$, $\mathbf{p}_3$
in the parameter space $[\alpha, \beta, r]^T$ (Figure 5). The location of these points can
be chosen arbitrarily and still be interpreted as a consistent geometric objects
with three edges meeting at a common corner. The location of the corner can
be uniquely determined by solving the three simultaneous equations (Equation
17) for $\mathbf{x} = [x, y, z]^T$. A corner in Euclidean space corresponds to the surface
generated by three points in parameter space. Any one edge can be found by
solving for x and y in terms of z between any two corresponding equations of

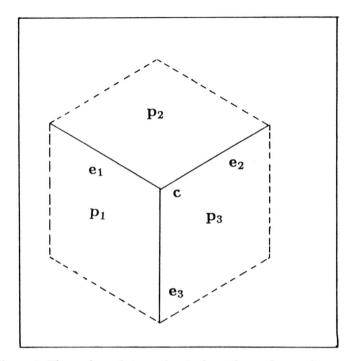

Figure 4: Three planes intersecting to form three edges and a corner.

the planes. An edge in Euclidean space corresponds to a line generated by two points in parameter space.

The network of points in parameter space is equivalent to the network in Euclidean space and consequently shares the same properties: If any one plane description p_i is changed to some new value p'_i, a consistent geometric object, with edges and a corner, is maintained without the need to change any other plane description. Conversely, if any one edge description e_i is changed, both of the other edge descriptions must also be changed if consistency is to be maintained. Figure 5 illuminates this, showing that the change in edge descriptions must be constrained to satisfy, in some form, a relation $e'_2 + e'_3 = -e'_1$.

As before we can consider these changes as a measure of the uncertainty in the description of geometric features. In this case any change in feature estimate or distribution of uncertainty is constrained by it's relation to other descriptions. Consider again the example of three surfaces forming three edges and a corner.

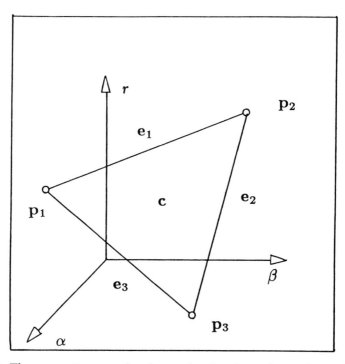

Figure 5: The parameter space for planes, showing three planes, three edges and a corner.

Suppose we initially have an estimate of the object parameters with some measure of uncertainty, and suppose we now make a new observation of an edge; e_i. Combining prior and observed estimates of the edge parameters results in some new estimate e_i'. To maintain geometric consistency of the object, this new information must be propagated through the constraining relations to provide new consistent estimates for the other edges of the object. This idea of consistency, constraint and propagation is fundamental to the representation of uncertain geometry and the interpretation of sensory data.

   We can generalize these simple principles to any number of different features and relations: Consider a connected, directed network consisting of n nodes representing features or object locations and m arcs $(n \leq m)$ representing geometric relations between nodes, together forming r loops. Index the nodes (features) by p_i $(i = 1, \cdots, n)$ and label the arcs with random variables e_j, $(j = 1, \cdots, m)$ representing the *uncertain* relations between features. This network can be described by either a path matrix $\mathbf{C}$ $(r \times m)$ or an incidence matrix $\mathbf{M}$ $(n \times m)$. The path matrix describes the arcs contained in each network loop. The elements of $\mathbf{C}$ can only take the values 0 or 1 describing if an arc is in a loop. The path matrix need only contain a basis set of independent loops to completely define the network. The incidence matrix describes which nodes are connected by each arc. The elements of $\mathbf{M}$ can only take on the values 0, 1 or -1 denoting incidence of an arc out of or into a node. For example the three node three arc network of Figure 3 has:

$$
\mathbf{M} = \begin{bmatrix} 1 & 0 & -1 \\ -1 & 1 & 0 \\ 0 & -1 & 1 \end{bmatrix} \quad \text{and} \quad C = \begin{bmatrix} 1 & 1 & 1 \end{bmatrix} \tag{18}
$$

It can be shown [Chartrand 68] that for all directed connected networks:

$$
\mathbf{CM}^T = \mathbf{0} \quad \text{or} \quad \mathbf{MC}^T = \mathbf{0} \tag{19}
$$

This means that for every node contained in a loop, there are two arcs, one into and one out of the node, which are part of this loop.

Let $\mathbf{e} = [e_1, \cdots, e_m]^T$ be the random vector of arc labelings and define $\gamma = [\gamma_1, \cdots, \gamma_r]^T$ to be the random vector of "distances" around a loop, so that

$$
\mathbf{Ce} = \gamma \tag{20}
$$

describes the structure of the network. A connected directed network is such that if we introduce another node $n + 1$ to the network and connect it to all other nodes with n new arcs labeled with random variables x_i, $(i = 1, \cdots, n)$, then $\mathbf{x} = [x_1, \cdots, x_n]^T$ must satisfy

$$
\mathbf{e} = \mathbf{M}^T \mathbf{x} \tag{21}
$$

The following results are true for arbitrary probability distributions on arc labels $\mathbf{e}$:

Result 1: If $\mathbf{e}$ is the vector of random variables labeling a constrained network then $\mathbf{e}$ is in the null-space of $\mathbf{C}$ with probability 1:

$$
\mathbf{Ce} = \mathbf{0} \tag{22}
$$

Proof: We have $\mathbf{Ce} = \gamma$ and $\mathbf{e} = \mathbf{M}^T \mathbf{x}$ with $\mathbf{x}$ an arbitrary n dimensional random vector. Then $\mathbf{CM}^T \mathbf{x} = \gamma$, but $\mathbf{CM}^T = \mathbf{0}$ so $\gamma = 0$ with probability 1.

Result 2: The variance-covariance matrix $\mathbf{\Lambda}_e$ of the vector $\mathbf{e}$ is singular.
Proof: $\mathbf{Ce} = \mathbf{0}$ so with $\hat{\mathbf{e}} = E[\mathbf{e}]$, ($E$ is the expectation operator; $E[x] = \int_X x f(x) dx$):

$$
CE\left[(\mathbf{e} - \hat{\mathbf{e}})(\mathbf{e} - \hat{\mathbf{e}})^T\right] \mathbf{C}^T = \mathbf{C}\mathbf{\Lambda}_e \mathbf{C}^T = \mathbf{0} \tag{23}
$$

and as Λ_e is symmetric, it must also be singular.

Result 3: For any symmetric matrix Λ_x, the matrix $M^T\Lambda_x M$ is singular.
Proof: $e = M^T x$ so $\Lambda_e = M^T\Lambda_x M$ is singular. As x is arbitrary, so is Λ_x.

These results can be applied to relations between all types of locations and geometric features. They provide a mechanism with which consistency between descriptions can be maintained and by which relations between objects can be described. This consistency requirement also results in geometric constraints through which changes in description or new information can be propagated.

4. Manipulating Geometric Uncertainty

It is important to consider how information about geometric objects and features change when they are described in different coordinate systems. This becomes especially apparent when we have mobile sensor systems that change their perspective of the environment. In addition, it is often important to be able to represent information about one geometric object in terms of another type of object. This occurs for example if we wish to find the contribution of an edge or curvature to a surface description or when integrating information from sensors that provide disparate geometric observations. We shall generally consider the case of a geometric feature described by Equation 1 with $x \in \Re^6$ and $p \in \Re^m$. To each uncertain geometric object defined by g and parameterized by p we associate a distribution function $f_g(p)$ which describes the likelyhood of a particular feature instance. We will require that $f_g(p)$ is not degenerate; where the probability mass is concentrated on a hypersurface in the parameter space, or where perfect information exists on one or more degrees of freedom. We do not preclude the case where the distribution function is improper, where there is infinite uncertainty or no information in one or more degrees of freedom. In all cases, the density $f_g(p)$ will be assumed to have finite moments of all orders.

There are two basic operations that we will want to perform on uncertain geometric descriptions: Changing the coordinate system in which the object is described; corresponding to transforming the feature parameter vector. Changing the description of the object itself; corresponding to both a transformation of parameter vector and a change of representing function. Both of these operations require that the parameter density function be changed in addition to any purely geometric change. This is equivalent to a transformation of probability distributions.

4.1. Transforming Probability

The key to manipulating geometric uncertainty is to be able to transform the information or probability density function on a feature available in one form in to another form of interest. This is the case when comparing surfaces (for planning and mating operations) or viewing objects from different locations. Consider first the transformation of a feature between coordinate systems. Suppose the random vector $\mathbf{p}_i$ describes a geometric feature with respect to a coordinate system i. In this frame $\mathbf{p}_i$ has probability density function $f^i(\cdot)$. If we describe this feature with respect to another coordinate frame j as $\mathbf{p}_j$ then in general the relation between the two density functions $f^j(\cdot)$ and $f^i(\cdot)$ will be described by Equation 11. In general if the transformation $\mathbf{p}_j = {}^j\mathbf{h}_i(\mathbf{p}_i)$ is non-linear, the calculation of the transformed distribution functions using Equation 11 can be very complex. Changing between feature descriptions increases this complexity: In this case $\mathbf{p}_i \in \Re^m$ and $\mathbf{p}_j \in \Re^l$ are usually of different dimension so that the transform ${}^j\mathbf{h}_i\colon \Re^m \to \Re^l$ is not always well defined in a deterministic sense. If $m > l$, when features are aggregated for example, then $f^j(\cdot)$ will be degenerate (over-constrained). Conversely if $m < l$, when higher order descriptions are calculated, then $f^j(\cdot)$ will be improper (under-constrained). However, even if the transform is not well defined in a deterministic sense, it can always be properly represented in a stochastic sense. Where ${}^j\mathbf{h}_i$ is over-constrained, the dimension of $\mathbf{p}_j$ can be reduced to satisfy the topological properties of the feature space. If ${}^j\mathbf{h}_i$ is under-constrained, indeterminacy can be accounted for by providing no information (infinite uncertainty) in one or more degrees of freedom.

The geometric complexity of the transform ${}^j\mathbf{h}_i$ can make the solution of Equation 11 very difficult. This situation is further aggravated when sequences of transformations $\mathbf{p}_i \to \mathbf{p}_j \to {}^k\mathbf{p}$ are considered. This problem arises in even very simple situations: Brooks [7] has described a method of constructing uncertainty manifolds generated by the motion of a mobile robot in a plane. The robot moves with uniformly distributed uncertainty in location and heading. After each (stochastic) motion the robot arrives at a location bounded by a closed manifold in $\Re^3$. This has two main problems, firstly the continuing assumption of uniformity in the location distribution after each step is invalidated by Equation 11, (although the exact density is not hard to calculate). Secondly after each motion the manifold gets increasingly difficult to describe as a geometric surface, indeed after several motions, Brooks (justifiably) approximates the manifold by a cylinder.

There are two parts to this complexity issue: the geometry associated with the transformations and the underlying process described by the distribution functions f. There is unfortunately little that we can do to alleviate the geometric complexity of the environment. Even in the simplest case, where a change in feature description is linear with respect to Euclidean transformations, we may often have to choose another description to satisfy the requirements of representation stability. The transformation of probability distributions faces many of the same problems as do geometric transforms. Ideally we should find a distribution function f_g which has invariant measure over all objects and transforms of the Euclidean group; so that $f_g(\cdot)$ is the same function in all coordinate systems. In general such a distribution function does not exist, however it can often be found for particular objects or motions. We can relax the invariance requirement and just look for a density which is *conjugate* over all possible translations and rotations. That is, after transforming the random variable by $\mathbf{p}_j = {}^j\mathbf{h}_i(\mathbf{p}_i)$, the two distributions f^j and f^i on $\mathbf{p}_j$ and $\mathbf{p}_i$ come from the same family $\mathcal{F}$ of distributions: $f^j, f^i \in \mathcal{F}$, which can be parameterized by some simple transformation ($\mathcal{F}$ is conjugate over all transforms ${}^j\mathbf{h}_i$). Given the possible generality of the transforms ${}^j\mathbf{h}_i$ it is clear that such a family would be difficult to find.

In general, the only way around these complexity problems is to use an approximation to the exact transformation of information.

4.2. Approximate Transforms

An alternative to calculating and propagating exact probability distributions is to expand the transformation equation in to its corresponding moments and truncate this series at some appropriate point. Consider the transformation

$$\mathbf{p}_j = {}^j\mathbf{h}_i(\mathbf{p}_i) \tag{24}$$

As expectation is a linear operator, we have:

$$\hat{\mathbf{p}}_j = E[\mathbf{p}_j] = E[{}^j\mathbf{h}_i(\mathbf{p}_i)] = {}^j\mathbf{h}_i(E[\mathbf{p}_i]) = {}^j\mathbf{h}_i(\hat{\mathbf{p}}_i) \tag{25}$$

Taking perturbations about the distribution mean;

$$\hat{\mathbf{p}}_j + \delta\mathbf{p}_j = {}^j\mathbf{h}_i(\hat{\mathbf{p}}_i + \delta\mathbf{p}_i) \tag{26}$$

and expanding using a Taylor series,

$$\hat{\mathbf{p}}_j + \delta\mathbf{p}_j = {}^j\mathbf{h}_i(\hat{\mathbf{p}}_i) + \left(\frac{\partial^j\mathbf{h}_i}{\partial\mathbf{p}_i}\right)\bigg|_{p=\hat{p}} \delta^i\mathbf{p} + O(\mathbf{h}^2) \tag{27}$$

results in the first order relation:

$$\delta\mathbf{p}_j \approx \left(\frac{\partial^j\mathbf{h}_i}{\partial\mathbf{p}_i}\right)\bigg|_{p=\hat{p}} \delta\mathbf{p}_i \tag{28}$$

Squaring Equation 28 and taking expectations

$$
\begin{aligned}
{}^{j}\Lambda_p &= E\left[\delta\mathbf{p}_j\delta\mathbf{p}_j^T\right] \\
&\approx E\left[\left(\frac{\partial^j\mathbf{h}_i}{\partial\mathbf{p}_i}\right)\delta\mathbf{p}_i\delta\mathbf{p}_i^T\left(\frac{\partial^j\mathbf{h}_i}{\partial\mathbf{p}_i}\right)^T\right] \\
&= \left(\frac{\partial^j\mathbf{h}_i}{\partial\mathbf{p}_i}\right)E\left[\delta\mathbf{p}_i\delta\mathbf{p}_i^T\right]\left(\frac{\partial^j\mathbf{h}_i}{\partial\mathbf{p}_i}\right)^T \\
&= \left(\frac{\partial^j\mathbf{h}_i}{\partial\mathbf{p}_i}\right){}^{i}\Lambda_p\left(\frac{\partial^j\mathbf{h}_i}{\partial\mathbf{p}_i}\right)^T
\end{aligned}
\tag{29}
$$

Approximating Equation 11 by Equations 25 and 29 is equivalent to a linearization of Equation 11. The mean values of the transformation follow the usual laws of geometry (Equation 25), and the distribution variances are transformed as differential changes (Equation 29). Providing the density function $f^i(\cdot)$ has finite moments of all orders, we could, in theory, calculate the transformed density by an infinite expansion of transformed moments. These successive moments can be found by equating higher order terms from Equation 27. In practice, using higher order terms is neither viable nor desirable, as any computational simplicity will be lost. However, if this linear approximation is to be used, we should first attempt to justify its validity.

4.3. Properties of Transformations

The mean values of the parameter distribution function are transformed in exactly the same manner as in the case of a purely deterministic environment model (Equation 25). The first moment (variance) of this distribution is transformed by pre and post multiplying by the transform Jacobian (Equation 29). If the matrix $\frac{\partial\mathbf{h}}{\partial\mathbf{p}}$ becomes singular or ill-conditioned at some value of $\mathbf{p}$ then this first order approximation will be invalidated. However, in our development of conditions for the stability of uncertain feature representations, we required that the transform Jacobian be well-behaved under all transformations in order that the feature description be statistically well-conditioned. Thus the fact that a geometric representation is stochastically well conditioned ensures that the linearized transformation is a good approximation to the true distribution.

In linearizing the transformation of a probability distribution we must make an implicit assumption that both the initial density $f(\cdot)$ and the transformed density $f'(\cdot)$ are symmetric, unimodal and have finite moments of all orders. Specifically, if $f(\cdot)$ satisfies these conditions, we must be able to guarantee that the same applies to $f'(\cdot)$ under all possible transformations of $\mathbf{p}$. In the case where the transformation corresponds to a change in coordinate system, this can easily be satisfied. However, in the case corresponding to a change in representation, care must be taken to check that the resulting distribution meets these conditions. For example, consider the line formed by the intersection of two infinite planes in three dimensions (The correspondence problem in a line-based stereo algorithm [1]). If the distribution function defined on the parameter vector of each plane is symmetric and unimodal, what can be said about the distribution on the parameter vector of the resulting line? In theory, each such case must be considered individually; by checking that the transformed distribution is unimodal and symmetric, with density tails enclosed by a Gaussian. In practice however, the stability requirement ensures that any valid parameter transformation is locally smooth, so that these conditions are usually satisfied.

The linear approximation to a transformed density and its resulting conditions on the feature representation, lead inexorably to an assumption of Gaussianity. We shall make a case for considering the probability distribution on the parameter vector describing a feature to be jointly Gaussian. A detailed technical development of these arguments may be found in [3], [11]. It is well known that a jointly normal distribution is conjugate with respect to addition of random vectors. This results in very simple algorithms for the aggregation of information. The central limit theorem states that the continued aggregation of any independent identically distributed random variables will converge to a Gaussian density. Aggregation of information in this way results in convergence to a Gaussian decision rule regardless of initial distribution. This effect is called the principle of stable estimation. Initial robustness can be obtained by forcing variances to be large enough to enclose all possible distributions. This process can result in information loss, and care must be taken to ensure suitable distribution-tail behavior is obtained. If we assume Gaussianity, then the mean $\hat{p}$ and variance Λ_p are sufficient information to completely define the feature density function. This means that Equations 25 and 29 are all we need to transform information amongst coordinate systems.

The ease with which Gaussian distributions can be manipulated allows the development of fast and efficient algorithms for the manipulation of uncertain geometry.

5. Gaussian Geometry

We maintain that a reasonable policy for modeling and propagating geometric uncertainty will always tend to Gaussianity and in case, can be approximated by such. We will present some elements of a theory of Gaussian geometry, where all geometric objects and features are parameterized by a jointly Gaussian random vector. We shall show how information and uncertainty can be manipulated in an efficient manner, providing a mechanism for reasoning about the effects of geometric uncertainty. We will first consider the problem of changing coordinate systems, and then apply these ideas to a change in feature description.

5.1. Changing Locations

It is important to consider how information about geometric objects and features change when they are described in different coordinate systems. This becomes especially apparent when we have mobile sensor systems that change their perspective of the environment information. Our motivating example will be the case of a six dimensional location vector composed of a position and a roll-pitch-yaw orientation. The case for specific features can often be reduced to a problem of locating coordinate systems by attaching a reference frame to the feature of interest. Considering a feature transform as a coordinate transform usually results in an underconstrained change in representation due to the ambiguity involved in attaching frame to feature. The direct manipulation of feature representations follows a similar but usually simpler formulation.

Consider the transformation of a random vector

$$\mathbf{p} = [x, y, z, \phi, \theta, \psi]^T$$

that parameterizes an oriented point in $\Re^3$. The transformation of the parameter mean $\hat{\mathbf{p}}$ follows the usual laws of geometry (Equation 25). Of more interest is the information content of representations in different coordinate frames as described by the transformation of variance-covariance matrix Λ_p or the information matrix Λ_p^{-1}. Suppose the function ${}^j\mathbf{h}_i$ that transforms a description vector $\mathbf{p}_i$ to $\mathbf{p}_j$ can be described by a homogeneous transform ${}^j\mathbf{T}_i$ that transforms a coordinate frame i to a frame j. The mean $\hat{\mathbf{p}}_i$ in frame i is transformed to $\hat{\mathbf{p}}_j$ in frame j by Equation 25, the variance-covariance matrix ${}^i\Lambda_p$ in frame i is transformed to ${}^j\Lambda_p$ in frame j by the transformation Jacobian ${}^j\mathbf{J}_i = \frac{\partial \mathbf{h}}{\partial \mathbf{p}}$:

$$
{}^j\Lambda_p = {}^j\mathbf{J}_i\, {}^i\Lambda_p\, {}^j\mathbf{J}_i^T \tag{30}
$$

If

$$
{}^j\mathbf{T}_i = \begin{bmatrix} \mathbf{n} & \mathbf{o} & \mathbf{a} & \mathbf{q} \\ 0 & 0 & 0 & 1 \end{bmatrix}
$$

then the Jacobian ${}^j\mathbf{J}_i$ can be found from the transformation [19] as:

$$
\mathbf{J} = \begin{bmatrix} \mathbf{r} & \mathbf{m} \\ 0 & \mathbf{r} \end{bmatrix}, \quad
\mathbf{r} = \begin{bmatrix} \mathbf{n}^T \\ \mathbf{o}^T \\ \mathbf{a}^T \end{bmatrix}, \quad
\mathbf{m} = \begin{bmatrix} (\mathbf{q} \times \mathbf{n})^T \\ (\mathbf{q} \times \mathbf{o})^T \\ (\mathbf{q} \times \mathbf{a})^T \end{bmatrix} \tag{31}
$$

where $\mathbf{r}$ is the 3×3 rotation matrix and $\mathbf{m}$ the 3×3 magnification matrix.

We state some results without proof:

Result 5:

1. $\mathbf{rr}^T = \mathbf{I}$: $\mathbf{r}$ is Hermatian.

2. $\mathbf{mr}^T$ is skew symmetric;

$$\mathbf{mr}^T = \begin{bmatrix} 0 & \mathbf{q} \cdot \mathbf{a} & -\mathbf{q} \cdot \mathbf{o} \\ -\mathbf{q} \cdot \mathbf{a} & 0 & \mathbf{q} \cdot \mathbf{n} \\ \mathbf{q} \cdot \mathbf{o} & -\mathbf{q} \cdot \mathbf{n} & 0 \end{bmatrix} \tag{32}$$

hence $\mathbf{rm}^T = -\mathbf{mr}^T$, or; $\mathbf{m}^T = -\mathbf{r}^T \mathbf{mr}^T$

3. $\mathbf{mm}^T$ is symmetric

4. $\mathbf{mm}^T = \mathbf{rmm}^T \mathbf{r}^T = \mathbf{qq}^T + \mathbf{rqq}^T \mathbf{r}^T$; $\mathbf{mm}^T$ is rotation invariant.

Using these results, the Jacobian, it's transpose and inverse can be found from **T**:

$$\mathbf{J}_T = \begin{bmatrix} \mathbf{r} & \mathbf{m} \\ \mathbf{0} & \mathbf{r} \end{bmatrix} \qquad \mathbf{J}_T^T = \begin{bmatrix} \mathbf{r}^T & \mathbf{0} \\ \mathbf{m}^T & \mathbf{r}^T \end{bmatrix} \tag{33}$$

As $\mathbf{J}_T^{-1} = \mathbf{J}_{T^{-1}}$, we have:

$$\mathbf{J}_T^{-1} = \mathbf{J}_{T^{-1}} = \begin{bmatrix} \mathbf{r}^T & \mathbf{m}^T \\ \mathbf{0} & \mathbf{r}^T \end{bmatrix}, \quad \mathbf{J}_T^{-T} = \mathbf{J}_{T^{-1}}^T = \begin{bmatrix} \mathbf{r} & \mathbf{0} \\ \mathbf{m} & \mathbf{r} \end{bmatrix} \tag{34}$$

With **T** the transform between coordinate frames i and j, from Equation 31 and Equations 33 and 34, we have the following relations:
Variance:

$$^j\mathbf{\Lambda}_p = \mathbf{J}_T{}^i\mathbf{\Lambda}_p \mathbf{J}_T^T, \qquad {}^i\mathbf{\Lambda}_p = \mathbf{J}_{T^{-1}}{}^j\mathbf{\Lambda}_p \mathbf{J}_{T^{-1}}^T = \mathbf{J}_T^{-1}{}^j\mathbf{\Lambda}_p \mathbf{J}_T^{-T} \tag{35}$$

Information:

$$^j\mathbf{\Lambda}_p^{-1} = \mathbf{J}_T^{-T}{}^i\mathbf{\Lambda}_p^{-1} \mathbf{J}_T^{-1} \qquad {}^i\mathbf{\Lambda}_p^{-1} = \mathbf{J}_T^T{}^j\mathbf{\Lambda}_p^{-1} \mathbf{J}_T \tag{36}$$

We will now consider the effect of moving information among coordinate frames by the transformation of the covariance and information matrices by the appropriate Jacobian. Let

$$^i\mathbf{\Lambda}_p = \begin{bmatrix} {}^i\mathbf{\Lambda}_{11} & {}^i\mathbf{\Lambda}_{12} \\ {}^i\mathbf{\Lambda}_{12}^T & {}^i\mathbf{\Lambda}_{22} \end{bmatrix}$$

be the variance-covariance of **p** described by appropriate 3×3 variance matrices for position, orientation and their cross correlation. Neglecting cross correlations ($^i\mathbf{\Lambda}_{12} = 0$), we obtain:

$$^j\mathbf{\Lambda}_p = \mathbf{J}_T{}^i\mathbf{\Lambda}_p \mathbf{J}_T^T = \begin{bmatrix} \mathbf{r}^i\mathbf{\Lambda}_{11}\mathbf{r}^T + \mathbf{m}^i\mathbf{\Lambda}_{22}\mathbf{m}^T & \mathbf{m}^i\mathbf{\Lambda}_{22}\mathbf{r}^T \\ \mathbf{r}^i\mathbf{\Lambda}_{22}\mathbf{m}^T & \mathbf{r}^i\mathbf{\Lambda}_{22}\mathbf{r}^T \end{bmatrix} \tag{37}$$

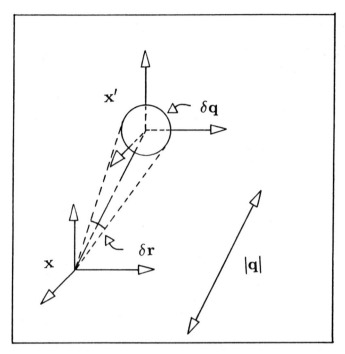

Figure 6: Schematic diagram of the magnification of position errors due to orientation errors following a change in location

The transformed position variance $^{j}\Lambda_{11} = \mathbf{r}^{i}\Lambda_{11}\mathbf{r}^{T}+\mathbf{m}^{i}\Lambda_{22}\mathbf{m}^{T}$ has an interesting interpretation. Clearly $\mathbf{r}^{i}\Lambda_{11}\mathbf{r}^{T}$ is just the position variance rotated to the new perspective, the additional term $\mathbf{m}^{i}\Lambda_{22}\mathbf{m}^{T}$ is the magnification of orientation uncertainties due to the distance between coordinate frames. Figure 6 shows that as $|\mathbf{q}|$ increases in size, so does position uncertainty, much in the same way that small changes in a cameras pan-tilt angle results in large changes of viewpoint. The terms $\mathbf{r}^{i}\Lambda_{22}\mathbf{m}^{T}$ reflect this correlation (relation) between the uncertainty in position and orientation.

Often we only have partial information on the vectors $\mathbf{p}$ (infinite uncertainty in one or more degrees of freedom), whence the distribution function $f_p(\cdot)$ is improper and Λ is not strictly defined. In this case (and in general) it is easier and safer to work with the information matrix $\Sigma = \Lambda^{-1}$, where the diagonal zero elements of Σ imply that no information is available in the associated degree of freedom (infinite uncertainty). Following similar arguments to those above, let:

$$^i\Sigma_p = \begin{bmatrix} ^i\Sigma_{11} & ^i\Sigma_{12} \\ ^i\Sigma_{12}^T & ^i\Sigma_{22} \end{bmatrix}$$

Neglecting cross information ($^i\Sigma_{12} = 0$), (in this case we will also obtain $\Sigma_{11} = \Lambda_{11}^{-1}, \Sigma_{22} = \Lambda_{22}^{-1}$) we have:

$$^j\Sigma_p = \mathbf{J}_{T-1}^T \, ^i\Sigma_p \mathbf{J}^{T-1} = \begin{bmatrix} \mathbf{r}^i\Sigma_{11}\mathbf{r}^T & \mathbf{r}^i\Sigma_{11}\mathbf{m}^T \\ \mathbf{m}^i\Sigma_{11}\mathbf{r}^T & \mathbf{m}^i\Sigma_{11}\mathbf{m}^T + \mathbf{r}^i\Sigma_{22}\mathbf{r}^T \end{bmatrix} \quad (38)$$

The term $^j\Sigma_{22} = \mathbf{m}^i\Sigma_{11}\mathbf{m}^T + \mathbf{r}^i\Sigma_{22}\mathbf{r}^T$ is the dual of the term $^j\Lambda_{11}$ of Equation 37 and has an important but less obvious interpretation. Again $\mathbf{r}^i\Sigma_{22}\mathbf{r}^T$ is just the rotated orientation information, the additional component $\mathbf{m}^i\Sigma_{11}\mathbf{m}^T$ is the *extra* information gained from the position information. Intuitively, the more information we have about position (the larger the elements of Σ_{11}), or the further our new perspective is away from the original coordinate frame, the better the orientation information we obtain. As before, the terms $\mathbf{m}^i\Sigma_{11}\mathbf{r}^T$ reflect this correlation between orientation and position information.

Equation 38 has a number of important consequences: It enables information in one coordinate system to be described in another frame of reference which in turn provides an ability to reason about the effects of uncertainty on geometric descriptions of a robot environment. The effect of partial information, or conversely very accurate information, about geometric observations becomes clear by noting the transformation of the elements of the matrices Σ_{11} and Σ_{22}.

This ability to transform uncertainty between coordinate systems also allows sensor observations obtained in one coordinate system to be transformed to another sensor's coordinate system so that information may be integrated. Correspondingly, if a sensor is mobile, then these transformations can be used to develop sensor strategies, making decisions as to where a sensor should be placed to best observe a given feature [10].

5.2. Changing Feature Descriptions

It is often important to be able to change the way in which a feature is described; to provide other levels of geometric representation or to allow disparate descriptions to be compared. This occurs, for example, if we wish to make inferences about one type of geometric feature when we only have information about another different feature, or if we wish to combine sensor observations made of many different types of geometric features. Transforming information from one description to another involves not only a transformation of information, but also supplying an interpretation that accounts for a change in constraints.

Let $\mathbf{g}_i(\mathbf{x}, \mathbf{p}_i) = 0$ and $\mathbf{g}_j(\mathbf{x}, \mathbf{p}_j) = 0$ describe two physically disparate geometric features with $\mathbf{p}_i \in \Re^l$ and $\mathbf{p}_j \in \Re^m$ defined on $\mathbf{x} \in \Re^n$. Suppose these two features are related so that the (geometric) function $^j\mathbf{h}_i : \Re^l \to \Re^m$ maps the parameter vector of one feature to that of the other $\mathbf{p}_j = {}^j\mathbf{h}_i(\mathbf{p}_i)$. In general the functions $^j\mathbf{h}_i$ are not well defined in a *deterministic* sense. This is because the two related features may have differing degrees of freedom as described by the different dimension of their associated parameter vectors. For example, the observation of an edge by a sensor implies the existence of two intersecting surfaces. Given the equations describing these surfaces, we could, in theory, derive the equation representing the resulting edge. Conversely, given the equation of the observed edge, the equation of either surface can not be derived without using some other constraining information. However, if the functions $^j\mathbf{h}_i$ are considered in a *stochastic* sense then this lack of constraint can be represented as partial information and described by placing zero elements in the information matrix corresponding to the indeterminate degrees of freedom of the transformation. In the edge to surface example, the equations of the edge and some *arbitrary* surface can be used to calculate a resultant second surface. The parameters of this arbitrary surface can then be assigned zero information, thus providing a stochastic description of possible surfaces, resulting from a single edge equation, in terms of a set of free parameters.

Suppose we initially have a feature $\mathbf{g}_i$ parameterized by $\mathbf{p}_i$ which we wish to convert to a new feature description $\mathbf{g}_j$ parameterized by $\mathbf{p}_j = {}^j\mathbf{h}_i(\mathbf{p}_i)$. If our information about the feature parameter vector $\mathbf{p}_i$ is described by a Gaussian probability distribution as $\mathbf{p}_i \sim \mathrm{N}(\hat{\mathbf{p}}_i, \Lambda_i)$, then we can approximate the information available to describe this new parameter vector by another Gaussian distribution;

$$\mathbf{p}_j \sim \mathrm{N}(\hat{\mathbf{p}}_j, \Lambda_j) \tag{39}$$

with

$$\hat{\mathbf{p}}_j = {}^j\mathbf{h}_i(\hat{\mathbf{p}}_i) \tag{40}$$

and

$$\Lambda_j = \left(\frac{\partial^j\mathbf{h}_i}{\partial \mathbf{p}_i}\right) \Lambda_i \left(\frac{\partial^j\mathbf{h}_i}{\partial \mathbf{p}_i}\right)^T \tag{41}$$

or

$$\Lambda_j^{-1} = \left(\frac{\partial^j\mathbf{h}_i^{-1}}{\partial \mathbf{p}_i}\right) \Lambda_i^{-1} \left(\frac{\partial^j\mathbf{h}_i^{-1}}{\partial \mathbf{p}_i}\right)^T \tag{42}$$

The fact that $\mathbf{p}_j$ and $\mathbf{p}_i$ are of different dimension is accounted for by the dimension of the Jacobian. If the transformation is over-constrained, then the resulting Λ_j will be singular (Result 4). If the transformation is under-constrained then Λ_j^{-1} must be calculated, to provide for infinite uncertainty in the unconstrained degrees of freedom.

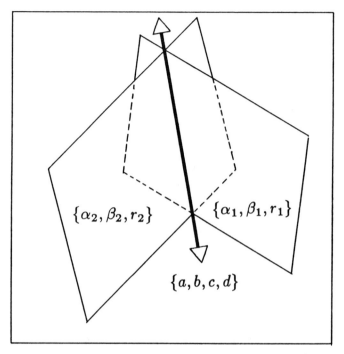

Figure 7: A three-dimensional line segment found by projecting two infinite planes.

This result can easily be extended to consider the aggregation of feature descriptions by defining $\mathbf{p}_i = [\mathbf{p}_{i,1}^T, \cdots, \mathbf{p}_{i,k}^T]^T$ with $\mathbf{p}_{i,l} \sim N(\hat{\mathbf{p}}_{i,l}, \boldsymbol{\Lambda}_{i,l})$ and letting $\mathbf{p}_j = {}^j\mathbf{h}_i(\mathbf{p}_{i,1}, \cdots, \mathbf{p}_{i,k})$. If the $\mathbf{p}_{i,l}$ are statistically independent, this results in an information transformation of the form

$$\hat{\mathbf{p}}_j = {}^j\mathbf{h}_i(\hat{\mathbf{p}}_{i,1}, \cdots, \hat{\mathbf{p}}_{i,k})$$

$$\boldsymbol{\Lambda}_j = \sum_{l=1}^{k} \left(\frac{\partial^j \mathbf{h}_i}{\partial \mathbf{p}_{i,l}}\right) \boldsymbol{\Lambda}_{i,l} \left(\frac{\partial^j \mathbf{h}_i}{\partial \mathbf{p}_{i,l}}\right)^T$$

To illustrate this transformation process we will consider the simple example of matching infinite planes in a line-based stereo correspondence problem, (this example was suggested by Faugeras [13]). Suppose we have two cameras (a stereo pair) each observing two-dimensional line segments in image space (Figure 7). From these two sets of line observations, we wish to construct a single three-dimensional line. This problem can be approached in two ways, either by assuming each observed two-dimensional line segment is already a three dimensional edge with infinite uncertainty perpendicular to the image plane, or by representing the line segments in each image as infinite planes whose intersection will form an edge. The former case has the advantage that the line segments in one image can be used to generate line-hypotheses in the other image plane by applying the transformations developed in the previous Section. The latter case is a more illustrative example of the techniques described in this section.

Consider an infinite plane corresponding to an observed line segment in an image described by

$$g(\mathbf{x}, \mathbf{p}_i) = x \sin \alpha_i \cos \beta_i + y \sin \alpha_i \sin \beta_i + z \cos \beta_i - r_i = 0$$

parameterized by $\mathbf{p}_i = [\alpha_i, \beta_i, r_i]^T$ with $\mathbf{x} = [x, y, z]^T$ defined in some global coordinate system. A three-dimensional line segment is described by;

$$\mathbf{g}(\mathbf{x}, \mathbf{q}) = \begin{bmatrix} x + az - c \\ y + bz - d \end{bmatrix} = 0$$

with $\mathbf{q} = [a, b, c, d]^T$. The equation for this edge can be calculated from two observed plane equations $\mathbf{p}_1$ and $\mathbf{p}_2$ by elimination, to obtain the parameter transform $\mathbf{q} = {}^q\mathbf{h}_p(\mathbf{p}_1, \mathbf{p}_2)$. If each plane parameter vector is independent and Gaussian $\mathbf{p}_i \sim N(\hat{\mathbf{p}}_i, \Lambda_i)$, then the mean value of the resulting edge can be found from

$$\hat{\mathbf{q}} = {}^q\mathbf{h}_p(\hat{\mathbf{p}}_1, \hat{\mathbf{p}}_2)$$

and it's variance from

$$\Lambda_q = \left(\frac{\partial^q \mathbf{h}_p}{\partial \mathbf{p}_1}\right) \Lambda_1 \left(\frac{\partial^q \mathbf{h}_p}{\partial \mathbf{p}_1}\right)^T + \left(\frac{\partial^q \mathbf{h}_p}{\partial \mathbf{p}_2}\right) \Lambda_2 \left(\frac{\partial^q \mathbf{h}_p}{\partial \mathbf{p}_2}\right)^T$$

This provides an estimate of edge location from two line segments in image space. The dimension of each Jacobian in this case is 4×3, so each single line segment contribution is underconstrained.

The important steps in this transformation of geometric information are to describe the change in parameter vector by the function $\mathbf{h}$, calculate the Jacobian $\mathbf{J}$ and ensure it is well behaved, and to account for the resulting constraints in the new representation. This technique applies to all geometric information described by Equation 1.

6. Gaussian Topology

The representation and transformation of geometric information must also be coupled with a mechanism to maintain constraints between Gaussian feature

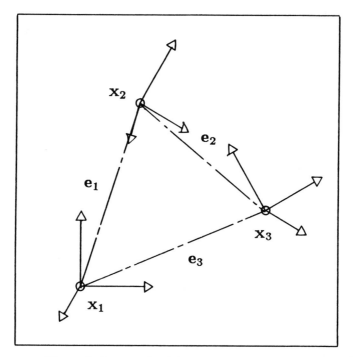

Figure 8: A network of three geometric features.

descriptions. In this section, we will develop stochastic topology in a Gaussian framework, providing a means to propagate changes in description and maintain consistency between Gaussian features.

In section 3.3 we described how constraints between geometric features could be represented by a directed network with arcs labeled by random variables. The three results presented, applied to all possible probability distributions on arc labels e_i. In the Gaussian approximation, we will only be interested in constraints on the mean and variance of these distributions. Clearly, the relations on mean values will be the same as those previously developed, therefore our interest in this section is to derive similar constraints on the arc-label variance under the Gaussian assumption.

Consider first the three feature network in Figure 8, described by the vector of relations $e = [e_1^T, e_2^T, e_3^T]^T$. To apply the results of Section 3.3 we must first describe each relation in a *common*, but otherwise *arbitrary*, coordinate frame;

c^0 for example. This transforms each relation as $^0e_i = {^0h_i}(e_i)$. Using the path matrix C, Result 1 shows that we must have;

$$
\begin{aligned}
C[{^0h_1}(e_1), {^0h_2}(e_2), {^0h_3}(e_3)] &= {^0h_1}(e_1) + {^0h_2}(e_2) + {^0h_3}(e_3) \\
&= {^0e_1} + {^0e_2} + {^0e_3} \\
&= 0
\end{aligned}
$$

with probability 1. Taking expectations, we obtain:

$$
{^0\hat{e}_1} + {^0\hat{e}_2} + {^0\hat{e}_3} = 0 \tag{43}
$$

If $^0J_i = \frac{\partial {^0h_i}}{\partial e_i}\big|_{e_i = \hat{e}}$, then the variance matrix on each arc label will be transformed to the new coordinate system c^0 by:

$$
{^0\Lambda_i} = {^0J_i}\Lambda_i {^0J_i^T} \tag{44}
$$

In this common coordinate system, Result 2 requires that:

$$
C^0\Lambda C^T = C \begin{bmatrix} {^0\Lambda_1} & {^0\Lambda_{12}} & {^0\Lambda_{13}} \\ {^0\Lambda_{12}^T} & {^0\Lambda_2} & {^0\Lambda_{23}} \\ {^0\Lambda_{13}^T} & {^0\Lambda_{23}^T} & {^0\Lambda_3} \end{bmatrix} C^T = 0 \tag{45}
$$

Without loss of generality we can assume the cross correlations are symmetric whence:

$$
{^0\Lambda_1} + {^0\Lambda_2} + {^0\Lambda_3} + 2{^0\Lambda_{12}} - 2{^0\Lambda_{13}} - 2{^0\Lambda_{23}} = 0 \tag{46}
$$

Result 3 states that for an arbitrary set of vectors $x = [x_1, x_2, x_3]^T$ we must have $^0e = M^T x$. As x can be arbitrary, we will choose it so that its joint variance matrix Γ is block diagonal,

$$
\Gamma = \begin{bmatrix} \Gamma_1 & 0 & 0 \\ 0 & \Gamma_2 & 0 \\ 0 & 0 & \Gamma_3 \end{bmatrix}
$$

We then have:

$$
{^0\Lambda} = M^T \Gamma M = \begin{bmatrix} \Gamma_1 + \Gamma_3 & -\Gamma_1 & -\Gamma_3 \\ -\Gamma_1 & \Gamma_1 + \Gamma_2 & -\Gamma_2 \\ -\Gamma_3 & -\Gamma_2 & \Gamma_2 + \Gamma_3 \end{bmatrix}
$$

Together with Equation 45 this implies that the following relations must be satisfied:

$$
\begin{aligned}
{^0\Lambda_1} &= -{^0\Lambda_{12}} - {^0\Lambda_1} \\
{^0\Lambda_2} &= -{^0\Lambda_{12}} - {^0\Lambda_{23}} \\
{^0\Lambda_3} &= -{^0\Lambda_{13}} - {^0\Lambda_{23}}
\end{aligned} \tag{47}
$$

If we now wish to infer $^0e_3$ from $^0e_2$ and $^0e_1$, or equivalently to propagate information through $^0e_1$ and $^0e_2$, then we assume independence of these vectors $(^0\Lambda_{12} = 0$) and obtain from Equations 46 and 47:

$$^0\Lambda_3 = {}^0\Lambda_1 + {}^0\Lambda_2$$

Reverting to our initial coordinate system, we have:

$$^0J_3\Lambda_3{}^0J_3^T = {}^0J_1\Lambda_1{}^0J_1^T + {}^0J_2\Lambda_2{}^0J_2^T \tag{48}$$

Equation 48 describes how geometric uncertainty measures can be propagated or combined between different coordinate systems. For example if c^0 were defined with $^0h_1(e_1) = e_1$ and hence $^0h_3(e_3) = -e_3$, then Equation 48 becomes

$$\Lambda_3 = \Lambda_1 + J_1\Lambda_2 J_1^T \tag{49}$$

The corresponding relation for information is given by:

$$\Sigma_3 = J_1^{-T}\Sigma_2 J_1^{-1}\left[J_1^{-T}\Sigma_2 J_1^{-1} + \Sigma_1\right]^{-1}\Sigma_1 \tag{50}$$

These three-relation results find an important application in maintaining consistency between features observed in different locations. A good example of this is given by Smith and Cheesman [23], who have considered the problem of a robot observing a beacon and using the resulting over-constraint to reduce the uncertainty in the robots new location (Figure 9). This same propagation and constraint mechanism can also be applied to other types of features, used as beacons or landmarks.

The general Gaussian constraint-network follows the same principles as this three-feature development. However, if there is no change in the vectors e_i during propagation, then all that need be considered is a sequence of these triangular relations (in a similar manner to reducing an electric circuit using Kirchoff's voltage law). If however the vectors do change, then larger networks must be considered. This problem will be encountered when sensor observations must be integrated into an existing prior constraint network.

This propagation mechanism provides an efficient means to reason about the cumulative effects of geometric uncertainty. When combined with the ability to transform uncertain geometric objects between coordinate systems and different feature representations, this allows a consistent interpretation to be made of the state of the environment.

7. Discussion and Summary

We have presented an outline of a theory of uncertain geometry. The key elements of this theory are to provide a homogeneous description of uncertain geometric

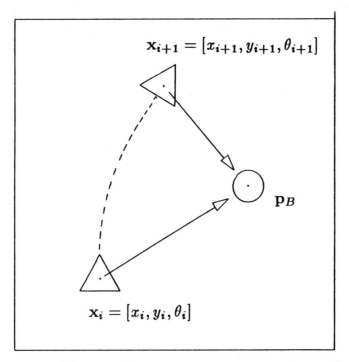

Figure 9: A mobile robot observing a beacon from two different locations.

features, to develop procedures to transform and manipulate these descriptions, and to supply a mechanism for the consistent interpretation of relations between uncertain features.

Given a unique and stable representation for a geometric object, the assignment of a probability distribution and the manipulation of families of these objects can easily be accomplished using the techniques described. However, the problem of choosing a representation for a given geometric object should not be underestimated. Indeed, this difficulty has so far limited the application of the ideas presented to planar geometries.

The reason why good representations for more complex geometric objects are difficult to obtain derives from the conditions for representation stability. For example, the usual polynomial representation for surfaces can not be used because they violate the one-to-one mapping condition, thus making the assignment of a p.d.f an impossibility. This problem has so far restricted interest to those representations that are naturally described in a stable form. There are two ways out of this impasse; either to analytically derive stable representations for more complex geometric objects, or to find some way of describing and manipulating non-minimal representations. It is not clear which of these methods would be most productive.

REFERENCES

1. Ayache, N. and Faugeras, O., "Building, registrating, and fusing noisy visual maps", *Proceedings of International Conference on Computer Vision*, London, U.K. (June 1987) 73.

2. Ambler, A.P., "Robotics and solid modeling", *Third International Symposium on Robotics Research* (MIT Press, 361, 1986).

3. Berger, J.O., *Statistical Decisions* (Springer Verlag, 2nd ed., 1985).

4. Bolle, R.M. and Cooper D.B., "On optimaly combining pieces of information, with application to estimating 3-D complex-object position from range data", *IEEE Transactions on Pattern Analysis and Machine Intelligence*, 8,5 (September 1986) 619.

5. Brady, J.M., "Computational approaches to image understanding", *Computer Surveys* 14 (1982) 3.

6. Brooks, R.A., "Symbolic error analysis and robot planning", *International Journal of Robotics Research*, 1 (1982) 29.

7. Brooks, R.A., "Aspects of mobile robot visual map making", *Second International Symposium on Robotics Research* (MIT Press, 287, 1984).

8. Davidson, R., "Some arithmetic and geometry in probability theory", Ph.D thesis, University of Cambridge, U.K. (1968).

9. Durrant-Whyte, H.F., "Integration of disparate sensor observations", *Proceedings IEEE International Conference on Robotics and Automation* (1986) 1464.

10. Durrant-Whyte, H.F., *Integration, Coordination and Control of Multi-sensor Robot Systems* (Kluwer Academic Publishers, Boston MA, 1987).

11. Durrant-Whyte, H.F., "Consistent integration and propagation of distributed sensor observations", *International Journal of Robotics Research* 6,3 (1987).

12. Erdman, M.A., "On motion planning with uncertainty", MIT M.Sc. thesis (1984).

13. Faugeras, O. and Ayache, N., "Building visual maps by combining noisy stereo measurements", Proc. IEEE Conf. Robotics and Automation, 1986.

14. Grimson, W.E.L., and Lozano-Perez, T., "Model based recognition and localization from sparse range or tactile data", *International Journal of Robotics Research* 3 (Fall 1984) 3.

15. Harding, E.F. and Kendall, D.G., *Stochastic Geometry* (John Wiley, 1974).

16. Kendall, M.G. and Moran, P.A.P., *Geometric Probability* (Griffin Academic Press, 1963).

17. Marroquin, J.L., "Probabilistic solution of inverse problems", MIT AI Tech Report 860 and MIT Ph.D Thesis (1985).

18. Papoulis, A., *Probability, Random Variables and Stochastic Processes* (McGraw Hill, 1965).

19. Paul, R., *Robot Manipulators* (MIT Press, 1981).

20. Pentland, A.P., "Perceptual organization and the representation of natural form", SRI Tech Note 357 (1985).

21. Requicha, A.A.G., "Representations for rigid solids: theory, methods and systems", *Computing Surveys* **12** (1980).

22. Santalo, L.A., *Integral Geometry and Geometric Probability* (Addison Wesley, 1976).

23. Smith, R.C. and Cheesman, P., "On the representation of spatial uncertainty", *International Journal of Robotics Research* **5,4** (1987) 56.

24. Takase, K., Paul, R. and Berg, E., "A structured approach to robot programming and teaching", *IEEE Trans. Systems Man and Cybernetics* **12** (1981) 274.

25. Taylor, R., "A synthesis of manipulator control programs from task level specifications", Stanford University Ph.D. Dissertation, AIM-282 (1976).

Some Speculations on Feature Recognition

J.R. Woodwark
IBM UK Scientific Centre
St. Clement Street
Winchester SO23 9DR

ABSTRACT

It is a paradox that today's automated systems for geometry-based engineering activities such as process planning are not able to use geometric information directly. While geometric models have been available for some time, it is not proving easy to link them to decision-making systems. The main hope for building this bridge is feature recognition, in which the geometry of an object is interpreted in terms of geometric elements of engineering significance. In this speculative paper, some of the problems of applying such a process to shape models are outlined, and some lines of advance are suggested. In particular, the possible use of the set-theoretic (CSG) solid model for feature recognition is discussed.

1. Introduction

"Probably the most challenging research problem in the field is automation of mechanical design. We believe that large portions of the functional (non-aesthetic) design activity can be automated, but decades of research may be needed to reach this goal." Voelcker and Requicha, 1977 [39].

"I do not believe we have yet found the optimum form of representation for solid components and assemblies. The implicit descriptions have drawbacks in efficiency for interactive working, and make the attachment of non-geometric data awkward. With explicit descriptions, one has the feeling that they are too low a level, and take insufficient account of the features of a shape, such as holes, slots, and patterns of different kinds." Braid, 1979 [8].

Reviewing progress in solid modelling over the last five to ten years, one cannot help feeling that Voelcker and Requicha got it just about right. It is true that we have seen considerable improvements in the domain of solid modelling systems, in the ease with which models can be created, and in the speed and range of rendering algorithms. However, the number of different *processes,* other than graphics, which can be performed on solid models is still small. Here is a list of most of the significant ones:

a) Mass property calculations [21].

b) Determining stable orientations [40].

c) Interference detection [6].

d) Finite element mesh generation (meshes not yet fully acceptable) [49].

e) Some limited calculations for casting and forging [11].

Two problems can be identified which make it difficult to get computers to help us with the design of solid objects. The first is the *automation of design and analysis* processes *per se,* and the second is *formulating object representations* suitable for such processes. In the long term, the first problem is doubtless the more challenging (and far beyond the scope of this paper). In the short term, however, there is enthusiasm that "expert system" techniques may be able to help us to automate some of the more repetitive processes. (Such tasks are in any case the least attractive to people and therefore the better candidates for responsible automation.) A number of systems have been written which have shown an ability to operate on geometry-based engineering problems. For example:

a) Process planning [14].

b) Crankcase design [31].

However, and perhaps remarkably, these programs rely on human interpretation of component geometry. They are not able to act directly on a shape model.

That brings us to the second problem mentioned above, that of formulating, or reforming, our present shape descriptions to suit such processes, and this is where the quotation from Braid is relevant. Today's wisdom on this subject is that *feature recognition* is the most promising approach. By feature recognition, we mean the recognition of expected patterns of geometry, corresponding to particular engineering functionality, in parts of objects. (This approach is echoed by a more cautious and more immediately application-inclined desire simply to be able to record, and then to use, "feature" information supplied by the creator of a model [2,22]. It will not be mentioned further here, as being essentially a half-way house.)

Feature recognition is a positive, but inchoate, development. One concern is its technological applicability. While "features of engineering interest" is a phrase that trips off the tongue, there is little existing experience with formal schemes of this sort, with the exception of parts classification. (It was natural for parts classification to form the subject of one of the first essays at feature recognition based on shape models [19].) It is not obvious whether a particular problem may or may not be susceptible to a feature recognition approach, irrespective of practical difficulties.

Another concern, which is the subject of this paper, is the technical feasibility of feature recognition by computer. When we look at the problems that have occurred with computerizing shape representation when a reasonably formal medium (the engineering drawing) existed already, there is no cause for optimism for an early resolution of the problems of feature recognition. In particular, as presently conceived, it implies a unique interpretation of a component as a particular set of features, derived in a single process. In fact, shapes should "look different" when being considered for different processes. This is not a fatal objection to feature recognition as such, merely to some present-day techniques. More pressing are limitations in feature recognition techniques which largely stem from the nature of object representations. This highly speculative paper outlines some ways in which solid models might perhaps be made more suitable for feature recognition. For a *review* of feature recognition techniques, the reader would be well advised to consult one of Pratt's papers on the subject [28, 29].

2. Current Feature Recognition Techniques

Although many different computer-based representations of shape are in use [30,45], solid modelling systems are currently understood to be those relying on one or both of two structures. The *set-theoretic* (or CSG) model is a description of an object as a set-theoretic combination of primitive solids (possibly half-spaces), while the *boundary* model (B-rep) consists of elements of the surface of the object, linked together so as to be consistent topologically. To date, the boundary model has been the one favoured for feature recognition [10,15,16,17,18,33]. Essentially, the current approach is to create groups of faces – "face sets" – which have certain relationships between them, and these are labelled as features. The set-theoretic model, on the other hand, has not been widely used to support feature recognition, with the exception of the pioneering work of Woo [41,42] and, more recently, that of Lee and Fu [20]. (While Woo's work has been widely interpreted as being concerned with set-theoretic models, there have been severe restrictions in the types of model that his program could handle, and to an extent set-theoretic to boundary model conversion has been embedded in his recognition processes.)

While there is no doubt that feature recognition based on boundary models will make a considerable contribution to developing an interface between "intelligent" programs and computer-based shape models, it is possible to suggest two fundamental difficulties with this approach.

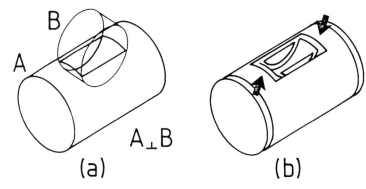

Figure 1: Diagrammatic representations of (a) a set-theoretic model and (b) a boundary model of a Woodruff keyway. The arrows in (b) point to edges which are cylinder-cylinder intersection curves.

The first is a philosophical one, and is really a reservation about boundary models in general. If we wished to identify models representing, say, shafts with Woodruff keyways, then the set-theoretic model of figure 1(a) would intuitively seem to encapsulate that information very nicely. On the other hand the boundary representation of the same shape, shown diagrammatically in figure 1(b), is equally easy to recognize. But in creating it, we have had to do a lot of processing, and in particular to identify and create representations of two cylinder-cylinder intersection curves (arrowed in the figure). These may be necessary for some purpose, for instance producing a line drawing; but many recent and efficient techniques for creating pictures do not require edge information: either the set-theoretic representation is rendered directly, or a faceted boundary model is prepared. (Additionally, it is interesting to note that, in this particular case, approximating the curves as circular arcs would be adequate on most engineering drawings.) One way or another, these complicated curve equations *may never be used,* and it would seem logical to try to do without them. (This contradiction has been noticed by the designers of some boundary modellers, such as ROMU-LUS, who sensibly delay evaluating curve equations until they are needed, as far as this is possible. However, the need for the topology of a boundary model to be made explicit restricts the scope of this approach.)

My second reservation is more practical. While essentially topological features can readily be obtained from a boundary model, many features of engineering interest require *spatial* constraints to be met which, while not unobtainable from the boundary model, are expensive to compute from it. For instance, the compo-nent in figure 2(a) is a keyed shaft that has been cut into two using a slitting saw. The keyway is still both intuitively recognizable and practically usable. But, in the boundary model, there is no topological connection at all between the two sets of faces of which it is comprised. Figure 2(b) shows the reverse example. The slot in that shaft would be recognized topologically as a Woodruff keyway, but technologically it is useless because a key cannot be inserted. (The keyway cannot be machined either, but that is another matter.) Again, the interfering material could be topologically distant or disjoint from the feature itself.

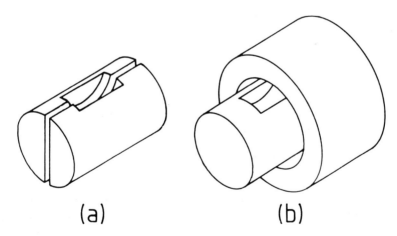

(a)   (b)

Figure 2: Two Woodruff keyways which pose problems for feature recognition. The keyway (a) is made in two parts, that the faces which comprise it are topo-logically disconnected. The faces of (b) are recognizable as a keyway, but the feature is technologically useless.

3. Problems With the Set-Theoretic Model

There is always a lot of head-shaking when the set-theoretic model is mentioned in the context of feature recognition, but what are the problems? One set of difficulties spring from the non-uniqueness of the set-theoretic model, another from its global nature.

The *non-uniqueness* of the set-theoretic model is well known. If we consider the simple model of figure 1(a), which is "obviously" represented as the difference of primitives A and B, that is A $\perp$ B, then it is easy to show that the alternative set-theoretic expressions (A $\perp$ B) $\cup$ (A $\perp$ B) and A $\cap$ (A $\perp$ B) are equivalent. Furthermore their equivalence is purely set-theoretic, and not dependent on the geometry of A and B. A rather different type of non-uniqueness occurs in the case of figure 3. The primitive C is irrelevant to this model, but that fact can only be determined geometrically. (Recent work [32,48] has started to show reasonably efficient ways to eliminate such redundant primitives.)

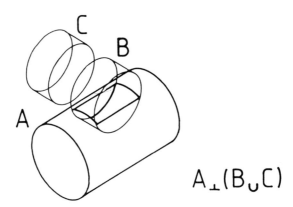

$$A \perp (B \cup C)$$

Figure 3: In this set-theoretic model of a Woodruff keyway the primitive C is redundant.

Considering the purely set-theoretic problems, one place to search for a solution is in the techniques used by electrical engineers for simplifying Boolean logic [23]. But algorithms appear only to be available for small numbers of variables (< 13). The problems which involve geometry would be even more difficult to solve. Firstly, we would need Boolean simplification techniques capable of accepting conditions such as A $\subset$ B, or A $\cap$ B=0. Even if such simplification techniques existed, we would need to have some way to determine which primitives and subsets to test for inclusion, disjointedness, or whatever. (The representation of relevant conditions is also a topic of interest in logic design. Recently, methods for coping with it in a modelling context have also made an appearance [37].)

Finally, we would have to face up to the fact that, even after all possible simplifications, there is generally no minimal canonical form of a set-theoretic expression. For instance:

$$(A \cap (B \cup C)) \cup (B \cap C)$$
$$= (B \cap (C \cup A)) \cup (C \cap A)$$
$$= (C \cap (A \cup B)) \cup (B \cap A).$$

The best that we could try to achieve would be some selection between such alternative forms based on, perhaps, an arbitrary ordering of the primitives.

This all seems so hopeless that it has been suggested that the best approach to set-theoretic model simplification is via conversion to a boundary model! While set-theoretic to boundary model conversion is indeed well understood, there is still no generally-available three-dimensional algorithm for the reverse process (although at least one algorithm has been published [12]). The recursive decomposition into convex hulls proposed by Woo [42] can (and for most complicated shapes does) terminate before decomposition is complete. (Although the same approach has been effective in two dimensions [26,38,44].)

Having seen the difficulties arising from non-uniqueness, let us move on to those caused by the *global* nature of the set-theoretic model. Even were a set-theoretic representation of a model made unique in some way, or our feature recognizer tolerated different representations, the problem of *localization* remains. What this means in practice is that we are rarely concerned with identifying a model as simple as that in figure 1(a). As the word "feature" implies, such a shape usually occurs as part of a much larger model. It will contain many primitives which are very distant from the region of interest, or which are excluded from it by their relation with other primitives in the set-theoretic expression. (A recent paper [20] has demonstrated simple feature recognition by means of the rearrangement of a set-theoretic model. This involved considerable complexity, despite the simple geometric domain involved. The extendibility of the approach must be judged to be in doubt at present.)

One approach to this problem is to *prune* the model to a sub-space. That is to say, to choose a subset of the space occupied by the model, and to simplify the set-theoretic expression by replacing references to primitives the surfaces of which do not pass through that sub-space, by codes for solid or empty. The set-theoretic expression is then simplified using DeMorgan's rules. Sub-spaces may be generated from a space-filling segmentation [43], or be based on the primitives themselves [35].

An immediate problem with this process in the present context is to choose appropriate sub-spaces. If we wanted to identify sub-models of the form of figure 1(a), we could prune the expression to the volume of each positive (see [35] for an explanation of this) cylindrical primitive in the model, and then again to the volume of each negative one remaining in the corresponding pruned expressions. Ignoring both regularization and expression simplification problems, each resulting model of the form A ⊥ B would correspond to an appropriate empty region.

Recollect that, with the boundary model, we could not easily detect topologically distant parts of the model that in fact interfered with the region of interest. In one way we have done a little better this time; the intersection volume A ∩ B is at least known to be empty. However, we have lost the information supplied by the boundary model, confirming the existence of surface of the form shown in figure 4(a). We could actually have the situation shown in figure 4(b), a configuration intuitively very different to the feature for which we were searching.

All this looks a terrible mess, compared with the idealistic identification of figure 1(a) as A ⊥ B! Rather than give up, we will go on to look at three possible ways around these problems, still avoiding the creation of an entire boundary model.

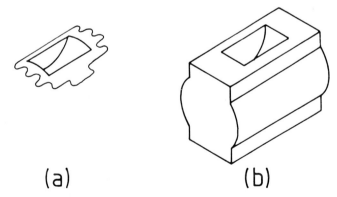

(a)   (b)

Figure 4: a) the surface elements corresponding to a Woodruff keyway. b) A cavity corresponding to a Woodruff keyway rendered technologically useless by the addition of extra material.

4. Ways to Attack the Problems

The most difficult problems outlined in the foregoing section were almost certainly those involving the building or rearrangement of large set-theoretic expressions. It seems likely that many of these problems are provably hard [23] and thus computationally intractable, and they will be avoided in the following three proposals.

The first idea, which has already been used to construct a number of systems, is to restrict the scope of the set-theoretic definition in some way. We would certainly expect any increase in regularity to make the recognition process easier. The second concept is to accept that features cannot be recognized directly from a set-theoretic expression, but to use the information in the expression to trigger "canned" templates, which we then try to match to the model. This could be regarded as a typical engineer's "numerical" solution. The third approach is essentially to give up on the set-theoretic model *per se,* but to see whether the boundary model could be modified to be more spatially oriented, and to eliminate some of the calculations presently involved in its construction.

Simplified Set-Theoretic Models

Three ways to simplify set-theoretic solid models are apparent:

a) To restrict the domain of the model, that is the range of primitives and/or of orientations that they may assume.

b) To restrict the ways in which primitives may interact spatially.

c) To restrict the allowable forms of the set-theoretic expression defining the model.

The first of these alternatives, *restricting the domain of the model,* has been important in the history of modelling, in permitting early systems to get off the ground. It might well be a way to make expression simplification slightly less daunting, by making it easier to determine whether primitives and sub-models intersect. The drastic measure of eliminating curved surfaces would appear to make geometry-based simplifications of set-theoretic expressions rather easier, by excluding some difficult cases. (For instance, see figure 5, in which primitive C cannot be eliminated but hampers recognition because a number of different geometries are equally valid.) However, elimination of curved surfaces offers no assistance with the simplifications of set-theoretic expressions which can be made without reference to geometry, and this ability is a prerequisite.

The second suggestion, *restricting the allowable spatial interactions between primitives,* was used by Woo [41] to simplify his earlier feature recognition technique. In his program, primitives can only be joined at coincident faces, and

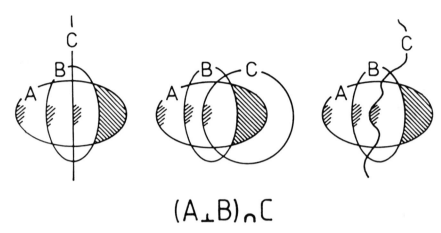

$$(A \perp B) \cap C$$

Figure 5: The primitive C is essential to the two-dimensional model shown, but may exhibit many different valid geometries.

cannot be allowed to overlap. "Negative" primitives, forming holes, must be similarly joined, and entirely included in the primitive from which they are being subtracted. A number of early boundary modellers, such as the original version of BUILD [7], had a similar, but less onerous, restriction that *sub-models* had to be "glued" together in the same way. In Woo's implementation, the maintenance of this condition devolves on the user. It would make creating many shapes very tedious, but such a condition could be maintained by the system, rather than the user, as in a more recent system with the same limitation [50].

The third possibility, *restricting the set-theoretic expression*, has also been tried before. Both the TIPS-1 system [25], and the more recent UNIBLOCK system [24], effectively allow only "positive" and "negative" copies of the basic "block" primitives. Thus, the set-theoretic expression is of the form

$$(P_1 \cup P_2 \cup \cdots \cup P_n) \perp (Q_1 \cup Q_2 \cup \cdots \cup Q_n).$$

(The presentation of this section of the paper is considerably simplified by ignoring the possibility of complementation.)

At a stroke this makes the expression *set-theoretically* unique, but a given object still does not have a unique model; more than one geometric arrangements of primitives can still be used to make up a given shape. However, the main problem with this representation is that shapes containing "objects in holes" (such as figure 6(a)), become impossible to describe. Nevertheless, the existence of TIPS-1 and UNIBLOCK would indicate that there is still a reasonable range of shapes that can be modelled, especially single machined components, in which such "objects in hole" constructs arise infrequently, because of technological limitations. It would certainly be a reasonable representation to explore, providing that some hope could be offered of eventually extending the techniques developed to cover a more general range of shapes.

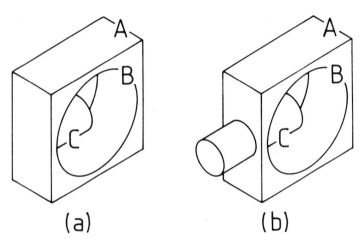

Figure 6: Shapes containing "objects in holes" which are difficult to represent using restricted set-theoretic expressions.

One intermediate regime, with rather promising properties, is that of models of the form

$$((P_1 \cup P_2 \cup \cdots \cup P_n) \perp (Q_1 \cup Q_2 \cup \cdots \cup Q_n))$$
$$\cup ((R_1 \cup R_2 \cup \cdots \cup R_n) \perp (S_1 \cup S_2 \cup \cdots \cup S_n))$$
$$\cup ((T_1 \cup \cdots$$
$$\cdots))$$

where the idea is that the terms R_i represent "objects in holes", T_i represent "objects in objects in holes", and so on. There are, however, problems with shapes such as that in figure 6(b). The "positive" cylindrical primitive C must appear as one of the terms R_i, because it contributes solid with the "hole" formed by the "negative" cylinder B. But this means that any further primitives to be differenced from C *outside* A must be, counter-intuitively, one of the terms S_i, rather than a term Q_i. The logical answer is to split C into two pieces. In fact the form of the model could be redefined as

$$((P_1 \cup P_2 \cup \cdots \cup P_n) \bot (Q_1 \cup Q_2 \cup \cdots \cup Q_n))$$
$$\cup ((P_1 \cup P_2 \cup \cdots \cup P_n) \cap (((R_1 \cup R_2 \cup \cdots \cup R_n) \bot (S_1 \cup S_2 \cup \cdots \cup S_n))$$
$$\cup ((R_1 \cup R_2 \cup \cdots \cup R_n) \cap (((T_1 \cup T_2 \cup \cdots \cup T_n) \bot (U_1 \cup U_2 \cup \cdots \cup U_n))$$
$$\cup ((T_1 \cup T_2 \cup \cdots$$
$$\cdots))))))$$

so that the effect of positive primitives in "holes" is automatically limited to cavities ("cavities" being identified as empty regions created by difference operations). There would be no need to generate set-theoretic expressions of the above form explicitly; a more compact notation could be used. Note that objects involving intersection, like that in figure 7, still could not be constructed. Intuitively, such shapes seem less useful in engineering. Is there, perhaps, an identifiable relationship between set-theoretic and engineering complexity?

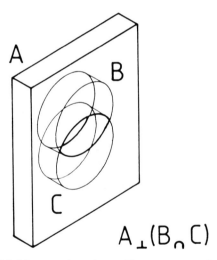

Figure 7: A shape of dubious engineering utility constructed using the intersection operator.

Matching to Shape Templates

If we abandon the struggle to deduce the relationship between primitives from a set-theoretic expression, the geometry of the individual primitives still gives hints as to what features may be present in a model. As a simple example, if there are no tori in a particular model, then there will be no fillets on circular shafts. There is a little more information obtainable from the "signs" (again, as used by Tilove [35]) attached to the primitives. We can discover, for instance, whether a particular cylinder is capable of contributing part of a shaft or of a drilled hole.

Returning to the example in figure 1(a), one simple method of discovering all shafts with Woodruff keyways in a model would be to find all pairs of cylindrical primitives that *might* produce such a situation, and then to instantiate a master version of the expected model, together with a volume in which it is expected to be valid. We then prune the original model to this volume, and perform a *null-object detection* test on the symmetric difference between the two models: the real and the ideal. If the two models match, then the feature has been identified.

Note that this approach gets around the difficulties experienced with "pure" recognition, from either a boundary or a set-theoretic model, because the subspace that is associated with an instance of a feature can be designed to encompass a region which is *technologically* associated with the feature, not merely with the nature of a particular representation. Figure 8(a) shows the pruning volume that might be associated with a Woodruff keyway. Of course, there *is* some rigidity in the method. For instance, someone might decide (for whatever reason) to create two Woodruff keyways diametrically opposed in the same shaft. The existence of the second would stop the first being identified, and *vice versa*. In general such situations would be common, but a reasonable solution is to have a sequence of patterns of decreasing scope which are fired by a particular geometric arrangement. In this case, for instance, matching to a secondary pattern as shown in figure 8(b) could be attempted, following the failure to match with the more specific, larger pattern.

This approach assumes the existence of a reliable null-object detection process. Cameron [9] and Tilove [36] both report algorithms. However, while the use of null-object detection to determine the identity of two models via a symmetric difference is obviously valid, reasonable performance will only be achieved by null-object detection algorithms which are good at dealing with coincident primitives, as this will be the case most commonly encountered. If the pattern does correspond to the model, then both Cameron's and Tilove's algorithms require us to create tentative boundary over the entire object, and then to discard it. Both algorithms would be improved in practice by being able to recognize certain common simple expressions, such as $(A \cup B) \perp (B \cup A)$ for instance, as null. Note that this does not return us to the impasse associated with recognition from the set-theoretic algebra, because we are not *relying* on such simplifications: they are merely quick ways to deal with common cases (and can be undermined by an inefficiently created model).

A glaring problem with the approach outlined above is that the matching process is fired by the existence of geometric combinations of primitives, without reference to the set-theoretic expression. That means that $O(n^2)$ combinations

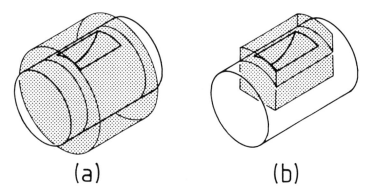

(a)   (b)

Figure 8: A pattern (a) invoked to recognize a Woodruff keyway and (b) a pattern of reduced scope which may be invoked if the first pattern fails to match the feature.

must be examined for matches involving only two primitives, but the identification of more complex situations involving three and more will require $O(n^m)$ combinations to be examined, where m is the number of primitives required to be matched. In practice, patterns will contain information about the geometric types of primitive to be matched and their signs (surface orientations), and this will reduce the work involved. However, a more fundamental attack on this problem can be made by pruning the model to sub-spaces in a more or less arbitrary way. For each feature pattern, certain primitives will be known to intersect. Only pairs of features which occur together in a sub-model can interact in this way. Therefore, a limited number of such pairs needs to be examined, and this limits the potential features to be considered. (This is effectively a search for *edges*, for which the author has already used a similar technique [46].) Looking for features by matching templates does not prevent primitives (or faces) from contributing to two features. On the other hand, there is no guarantee that all of the surface of the model will be involved in the features identified. Further, even if we show that all the *primitives* are involved in constructing the features, this is not equivalent to showing that all the *faces* are accounted for.

Modifying the Boundary Model

A third possible way to avoid algebraic work in preparing a model suitable for feature recognition is to retain an essentially graph-based boundary structure, but to avoid explicit computations as far as possible. In the object in figure 1(a), we would aim to recognize the keyway as a particular combination of primitive and edge *types*, without actually calculating faces or bounded edges, as already mentioned. Representing complicated edge types implicitly has long been recognized as a possible way to store such curves, although most boundary modellers do create explicit representations.

If we segment a set-theoretic model spatially, and prune it to the sub-space created, then in general we obtain simpler sub-models. If a sub-model is found of the form A*B, where "*" is any set-theoretic operator, then we know that, if the two surfaces of the two primitives intersect within the corresponding sub-space, there is an edge between them. Similarly, an expression of the form A*B*C indicates that any mutual intersection of the three primitives within the sub-space is a vertex. With a plane-faced model, these sub-models define edges and vertices uniquely, and the ability to re-create edges from such sub-models has been demonstrated, as mentioned above [46]. With curved primitives, however, there is ambiguity; to take a simple example, a cylinder and two planes may have two mutual intersections. It is possible that, with a small range of primitives, such as the "natural" quadrics and torus, such situations could be tagged by a similar technique to the "near" and "far" keywords used in two dimensions for labelling geometry in systems like GNC [13]. If we could in that way identify all the vertices and all the edges in the model, we would know:

a) Which edges created faces from which primitives.

b) Where each edge met with others at a vertex.

From this, we could create something like a classical winged-edge data structure [3], except that single faces and edge segments are not explicit defined, but merely implied as limits to the unbounded elements.

Of course, we have been assuming that division and pruning always create easily identifiable sub-models of the form A*B or A*B*C at edges and vertices. As we have discussed in some detail above, they do not. In these cases, we must create a boundary model locally, and from it re-create the set-theoretic description. At an edge, this is relatively easy, as the reconstruction is essentially one-dimensional. The resulting set-theoretic model is always either of the form

$$(P_1 \cap P_2) \cup (P_3 \cap P_4) \cup \cdots \cup (P_{n-1} \cap P_n)$$

or the form

$$P \cup Q \cup (R_1 \cap R_2) \cup (R_3 \cap R_4) \cup \cdots \cup (R_{n-1} \cap R_n).$$

At a vertex, however, the process is two-dimensional. It could be solved on the basis of recent work in two-dimensional boundary to set-theoretic model conversion, especially that by Peterson [26], but it is actually only necessary to identify the edges which meet at the vertex, and the author has shown (for the plane-faced case) [46] that this can be done without simplifying the vertex model. In any case, re-created set-theoretic vertex models would still not be unique.

So, we now have a boundary model of the usual topologically-linked structure, but with all the numerical data available only implicitly. This seems worth creating only if we can generate most of it without deriving explicit boundary data and then throwing it away, and if we can recast processes acting on the model so that they do not constantly calculate explicit edges. Even if this could be done, the basic algorithms acting on the structure would be those associated with boundary models, which, as we have already mentioned, are less satisfactory for spatially-oriented processes. For instance, with this new sort of model, membership tests would have to be performed by ray-casting, rather than by the numerically more stable methods [34] available with true set-theoretic models.

A better approach might be to construct a secondary structure more suitable for representing spatial, rather than topological, relationships. Here are three possibilities:

a) Retain the spatially-segmented set-theoretic model we have already constructed.

b) Create a digital Dirichlet tesselation (Voronoi diagram) of the faces of the model.

c) Create an approximate Delaunay triangulation of the faces of the model.

The *Dirichlet tesselation* of a set of points in space [4] consists of a number of convex polyhedral "tiles", each corresponding to a point in the set. Anywhere in a tile is nearer to the point that "owns" the tile than to any other point. More complex geometric entities than points can be tessellated, but tile boundaries are in general both of higher order than the structure being tiled, and with derivatives that are only piecewise continuous [5]. This creates greater problems with complicated edge equations than those experienced with the original model.

However, recently a number of people [1,27] have come up with the idea of the *digital* Dirichlet tessellation, in which each cell in a discretization of the space of interest is marked with the tile or tiles to which it belongs. Creating such a structure involves only computing distances from the cells to the geometric elements being tessellated, and no boundary curves or surfaces are explicitly generated. A discretized tiling allows us to perform membership tests, for instance, by determining the tile in which a candidate point lies, and then comparing it with the face "owning" that tile. However, this approach shares with option (a) the necessity of imposing an arbitrary tiling on to the object. While the author has made good use of such structures in the past [47], they do not seem natural in this case, where the relationship between parts of the model should be unobstructed by boundaries unrelated to the object's geometry.

An interesting way to obtain some spatial indexing without an externally imposed structure would be to construct a discrete tiling, but to use the information gleaned to generate the *Delaunay triangulation* of the faces, and then to discard the segmentation. The Delaunay triangulation of a set of points is a set of line segments connecting adjacent tiles. Here, we propose a set of *links* between geometric elements whose tiles share boundaries in the Dirichlet tessellation. In practice, we would construct this approximately by connecting faces whose tiles both appeared in any leaf sub-space of the regular tiling. Doing it this way, we would obtain extra, unnecessary linking, but that need not be too significant. This approximate pseudo-Delaunay triangulation of the faces of an object would allow us to detect situations such as that in figure 2(a) much more easily.

5. Conclusions

This paper is intended to be a catalogue of *ideas* on the subject of feature recognition, and does not try to prove anything, or to report on experiments.

It is possible to discern a trend in the history of modelling, that the boundary model has often arrived first, but the set-theoretic model has followed it into most applications. The algorithms associated with the set-theoretic model are often as fast, or faster, than those using the boundary model, almost always theoretically easier to justify, and numerically more robust. Graphics is perhaps the classic example. In early systems, pictures were obtained from a solid model first by conversion to a boundary model (if necessary), and then by (further) conversion to a face model, to which pre-existing hidden-line and hidden-surface techniques were applied. Now, techniques of recursive division and their application to rendering, especially ray-casting, make it both simple and efficient to generate pictures directly from set-theoretic models. This process is so far advanced that these techniques are now the most common in computer graphics work itself, and the algorithms originally devised for set-theoretic models are being applied (albeit less neatly) to boundary and face models.

In this paper some of the problems in feature recognition which relate to shape representations have been outlined. After noting that the boundary model currently occupies the limelight, it has been suggested that, while this model has enabled early progress in feature recognition, it does not necessarily offer a smooth route to systems suited to engineering applications. The more obvious problems with the set-theoretic model have also been outlined. Finally, ways in which solid models might be changed to make them more suitable for feature recognition have been suggested.

Since this paper was originally presented, there have been one or two contri-

butions to the literature (to which references have now been included) which
suggest that progress in these directions, however slow and painful, is already
being made.

ACKNOWLEDGEMENTS

I would like to thank Adrian Bowyer, Graham Jared, Ralph Martin and Tom Heywood
for their most helpful comments on the draft version of this paper.

REFERENCES

1. Angell, I.O., Graphics on the IBM PC for teaching and research, in: *The Research and Academic Users Guide to the IBM PC*, IBM (1985) 94-103.

2. Arbab, F., Cantor, D.G., Lichten, L. and Melkanoff, M.A., The MARS CAM-oriented modeling system, Proceedings of an MIT Conference on CAD/CAM Technology in Mechanical Engineering (1982) 181-288.

3. Baumgart, B.G., A polyhedron representation for computer vision, Proceedings of the (US) National Computer Conference (1975) 589-596.

4. Bowyer, A., Computing Dirichlet tessellations, *Computer Journal* 24,2 (1981) 162-166.

5. Bowyer, A., Personal communication, 1986.

6. Boyse, J.W., Interference detection among solids and surfaces, *Communications of the ACM* 22,1 (1979) 3-9.

7. Braid, I.C., The synthesis of solids bounded by many faces, *Communications of the ACM* 18,4 (1975) 209-216.

8. Braid, I.C., Geometric modelling - ten years on, Proceedings of a CAM-I Geometric Modeling Seminar, Bournemouth (1979) 105-124.

9. Cameron, S.A., Modelling solids in motion, PhD Thesis, University of Edinburgh (1984).

10. CAM-I, Requirements for support of form features in a solid modeling system, CAM-I Report R-85-ASPP-01 (1985).

11. Chan, Y.K. and Knight, W.A., MODCON: a system for the CAM of dies and moulds, Proceedings of the CAD-80 Conference, Brighton (1980) 370-381.

12. Christensen, N.C., Emery, J.D. and Smith, M.C., System for the conversion between the boundary model and a constructive geometry model of an object, US Patent A6728367 (1986).

13. Davies, K.J., GNC – a graphical NC processor, in *Computer Languages for Numerical Control*, North-Holland (Proceedings of the PROLAMAT-73 Conference, Budapest) (1973) 51-61.

14. Descotte, Y. and Latombe, J.-C., GARI: A problem solver that plans how to machine mechanical parts, Proceedings of the IJCAI-81 Conference (1981) 766-771.

15. Henderson, M.P. and Anderson, D.C., Computer recognition and extraction of form features, *Computers in Industry* 5 (1984) 329-339.

16. Jakubowski, R., Syntactic characterization of machine part shapes, *Cybernetics and Systems* 13 (1982) 1-21.

17. Jared, G.E.M., Shape features in geometric modelling, in *Solid Modeling – from Theory to Applications* (Proceedings of a General Motors Research Laboratories Symposium, Detroit, September 1983) Plenum (1984) 121-133.

18. Jared, G.E.M., Feature recognition in geometric modelling, Proceedings of the 4th Anglo-Hungarian Conference on Computer-Aided Geometric Design (1985).

19. Kyprianou, L., Shape classification in computer-aided design, PhD Thesis, University of Cambridge (1980).

20. Lee, Y.C. and Fu, K.S., Machine understanding of CSG: extraction and unification of manufacturing features, *IEEE Computer Graphics and Applications* 7,1 (1987) 20-32.

21. Lee, Y.T. and Requicha, A.A.G., Algorithms for computing the volume and other integral properties of solids, *Communications of the ACM* 25,9 (1982) Part 1: 635-641 Part 2: 642-650.

22. Luby, S.C., Dixon, J.R. and Simmons, M.K., Creating and using a feature data base, *Computers in Mechanical Engineering* (November 1986) 25-33.

23. Martin, R.R., Personal communication, 1986.

24. Nykanen, M., Nyström, M. and Katainen, A., Uniblock modelling system, Proceedings of the 2nd CAM-I Geometric Modeling Seminar (CAM-I Report P-83-GM-01) (1983) 432-439.

25. Okino, N., Kakazu, Y. and Kubo, H., TIPS-1: Technical information processing system, for computer-aided design, drawing and manufacturing, in *Computer Languages for Numerical Control*, North-Holland (Proceedings of the PROLAMAT-73 Conference, Budapest) (1973) 141-150.

26. Peterson, D.P., Boundary to constructive solid geometry mappings: a focus on 2D issues, *Computer-Aided Design* 18,1 (1986) 3-14.

27. Phillips, T. and Matsuyama, T., The labeled discrete Voronoi diagram, University of Maryland Center for Automation Research Report TR-CAR-4 (1983).

28. Pratt, M.J., Solid modeling and the interface between design and manufacture, *IEEE Computer Graphics and Applications* (July 1984) 52-59.

29. Pratt, M.J., Current status of form features research in solid modelling, *in preparation*.

30. Requicha, A.A.G., Representations of rigid solids: theory methods and systems, *ACM Computing Surveys* 12,4 (1980) 437-464.

31. Reynier, M. and Fouet, J.-M., Automated design of crankcases: the Carter system, *Computer-Aided Design* **16**,6 (1984) 308-313.

32. Rossignac, J.R. and Voelcker, H.B., Active zones in constructive solid geometry for redundancy and interference detection, IBM Yorktown Heights Research Report RC 11991 (June 1986).

33. Staley, S.M., Henderson, M.R. and Anderson, D.C., Using syntactic pattern recognition to extract feature information from a stored geometric data base, *Computers in Mechanical Engineering* (September 1983) 61-66.

34. Tilove, R.B., A study of geometric set-membership classification, University of Rochester Production Automation Project Technical Memorandum TM-30 (1977).

35. Tilove, R.B., Exploiting spatial and structural locality in geometric modeling, University of Rochester Production Automation Project Technical Memorandum TM-38 (October 1981).

36. Tilove, R.B., A null-object detection algorithm for constructive solid geometry, *Communications of the ACM* **27**,7 (1984) 684-694.

37. Todd, S.J.P. and Halbert, A.R., Fast redundant primitive removal in CSG processing, IBM UK Scientific Centre Report 175, *in preparation.*

38. Tor, S.B. and Middleditch, A.E., Convex decompositions of simple polygons, *ACM Transactions on Graphics* (October 1984) 244-265.

39. Voelcker, H.B. and Requicha, A.A.G., Geometric modeling of mechanical parts and processes, *IEEE Computer Magazine* (December 1977) 48-57.

40. Wesley, M.A., Lozano-Perez, T., Lieberman, L.I., Lavin, M.A. and Grossman, D.D., A geometric modeling system for automated mechanical assembly, *IBM Journal of Research and Development* **24**,1 (1980) 64-74.

41. Woo, T.C.-H., Computer understanding of design, PhD Thesis, University of Illinois (1975).

42. Woo, T.C.-H., Feature extraction by volume decomposition, Proceedings of an MIT Conference on CAD/CAM Technology in Mechanical Engineering (1982) 76-94.

43. Woodwark, J.R. and Quinlan, K.M., The derivation of graphics from volume models by recursive subdivision of the object space, Proceedings of the CG-80 Conference, Brighton (1980) 335-343.

44. Woodwark, J.R. and Wallis, A.F., Graphical input to a Boolean solid modeller, Proceedings of the CAD-82 Conference, Brighton (1982) 681-688.

45. Woodwark, J.R., *Computing Shape*, Butterworths (1986).

46. Woodwark, J.R., Generating wireframes from set-theoretic models by spatial division, *Computer-Aided Design* **18**,6 (1986) 307-315.

47. Woodwark, J.R. and Bowyer, A., Better and faster pictures from solid models, *Computer-Aided Engineering Journal* **3**,1 (1986) 17-24.

48. Woodwark, J.R., Eliminating redundant primitives from set-theoretic solid models by a consideration of constituents, *IEEE Computer Graphics and Applications* **8**,3 (1988) 38-47.

49. Wordenweber, B., Finite element mesh generation, *Computer-Aided Design* **14**,2 (1984) 285-291.

50. Wyvill, G. and Kunii, T.L., A functional model for constructive solid geometry, *The Visual Computer* **1**,3 (1985) 3-14.

(This paper was first published in *Computer-Aided Design* **20**,4, May 1988.)

Index